ELIZABETH I
& HER PEOPLE

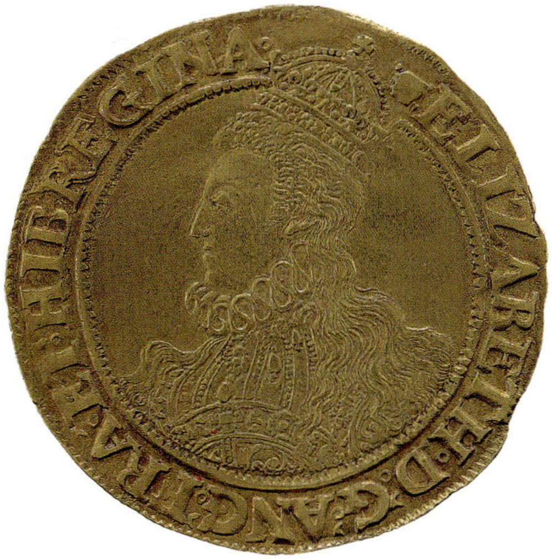

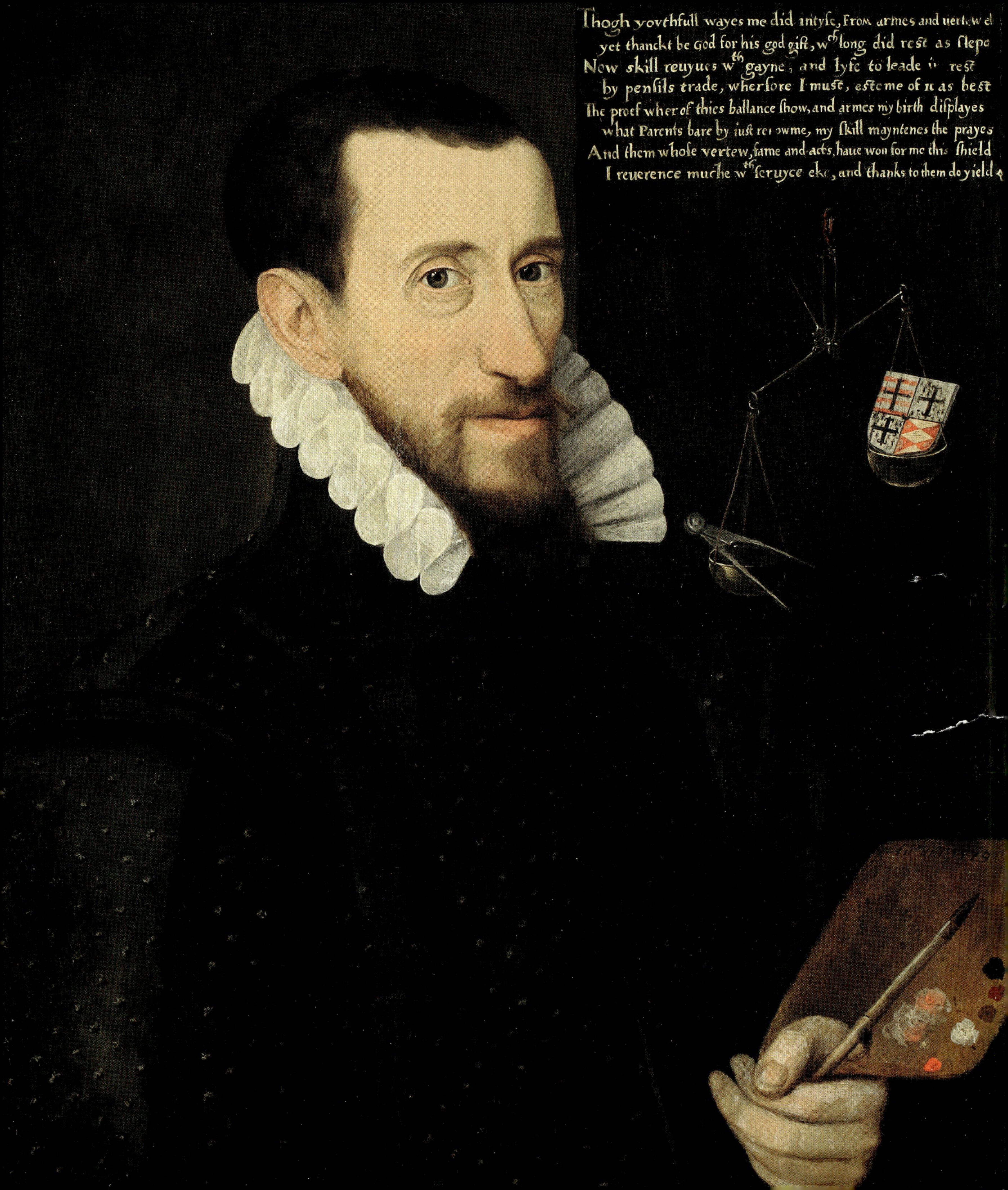
Thogh yovthfull wayes me did intyſe, From armes and uertew el
yet thanckt be God for his god gift, wch long did reſt as ſlepe
Now skill reuyues wth gayne, and lyfe to leade in reſt
by penſils trade, wherfore I muſt, eſteme of it as beſt
The proef wher of thies ballance ſhow, and armes my birth diſplayes
what Parents bare by iuſt renowme, my ſkill mayntenes the prayes
And them whoſe vertew, fame and acts, haue won for me this ſhield
I reuerence muche wth ſeruyce eke, and thanks to them do yield

ELIZABETH I & HER PEOPLE

Tarnya Cooper

WITH

Jane Eade

WITH ESSAYS BY

Ian W. Archer, Lena Cowen Orlin
and Susan North

NATIONAL PORTRAIT GALLERY, LONDON

Published in Great Britain by
National Portrait Gallery Publications,
St Martin's Place, London WC2H OHE

Published to accompany the exhibition
Elizabeth I & Her People
10 October 2013–5 January 2014

Exhibition supported by The Weiss Gallery

This exhibition has been made possible by the provision of insurance through the Government Indemnity Scheme. The National Portrait Gallery, London, would like to thank HM Government for providing Government Indemnity and the Department for Culture, Media and Sport and Arts Council England for arranging the indemnity.

For a complete catalogue of current publications, please write to the National Portrait Gallery at the address above, or visit our website at www.npg.org.uk/publications

ISBN 978 1 85514 465 1

A catalogue record for this book is available from the British Library.

10 9 8 7 6 5 4 3 2 1

Printed in Italy

MANAGING EDITOR Christopher Tinker
EDITOR Sarah Ruddick
PICTURE RESEARCH Zuzu Dowd
PRODUCTION MANAGER Ruth Müller-Wirth
DESIGN Philip Lewis
ORIGINATION DL Imaging Ltd
PRINTING Printer Trento Srl

PAGE 1 Gold sovereign (cat. 15c)
FRONTISPIECE George Gower, self-portrait, dated 1579 (cat. 67)

Contents

Director's Foreword

ELIZABETH I ESTABLISHED, through the many portraits made of her during a reign of around forty-five years, an image of a strong and powerful female monarch. The creation of these portraits – with artful poses, costume and jewellery – has done much to reinforce the sense of her dominating authority within a complex historical period. Whatever the challenges to her sovereignty, this is a period in which England emerged with greater economic power, in large part due to increased trade built on growth in European and international exchanges, the expansion of the city of London, a nascent national and local political infrastructure, a more stable religious order and a flourishing literary culture, much of this being driven by a burgeoning middle class. It is also a period during which personal appearance became more self-conscious, with calls for the enforcement of sumptuary laws that attempted to determine what was appropriate dress for people of different stations.

This exhibition brings together the images of these people – adventurers and merchants, physicians and artists, bankers and writers, courtiers and a queen – in order to better understand this multi-layered society. More than ever before, they appear in painted portraits, but are also represented in the fascinating objects they commissioned or made, through their clothing and ornaments, and the maps and documents of this newly self-aware country.

Such an exhibition would not be possible without the support of many private and public collections, and I am very grateful to all those who have generously lent precious works. In particular, we have had very welcome support from National Trust properties, and from other great houses around the country.

The exhibition has been devised and energetically curated by Tarnya Cooper, Chief Curator and Curator of Sixteenth-Century Portraits, with the able assistance of Jane Eade, Associate Curator. I am very grateful to both of them and also to Rosie Wilson for exhibition management and Jude Simmons for leading the design work. I should also like to warmly acknowledge Pim Baxter, Charlotte Bolland, Nick Budden, Naomi Conway, Andrea Easey, Neil Evans, Richard Hallas, Susie Holden, John Leslie, Ruth Müller-Wirth, Vivienne Reiss, Sarah Ruddick, Polly Saltmarsh, David Saywell, Christopher Tinker, Sarah Tinsley, Edward Town, Denise Vogelsang, Ulrike Wachsmann, Helen Whiteoak and Cathy Yexley, the art handling team, and all the other National Portrait Gallery staff who have contributed to the exhibition and publication. Particular thanks should also go to Dr Ian W. Archer, Susan North and Professor Lena Cowen Orlin, who have contributed such excellent essays to this publication.

I am also very grateful to the members of the exhibition advisory board: Dr Ian W. Archer, Dr Susan Doran, Professor Andrew Hadfield, Professor Lena Cowen Orlin, Sir Roy Strong, Dr David Taylor and Professor Robert Tittler. The exhibition has been generously supported by The Weiss Gallery, and I am very grateful to Mark Weiss for this help.

SANDY NAIRNE, DIRECTOR
National Portrait Gallery, London

The Procession Portrait of Queen Elizabeth I
Unknown Netherlandish artist, c.1600–3
(detail of cat. 1)

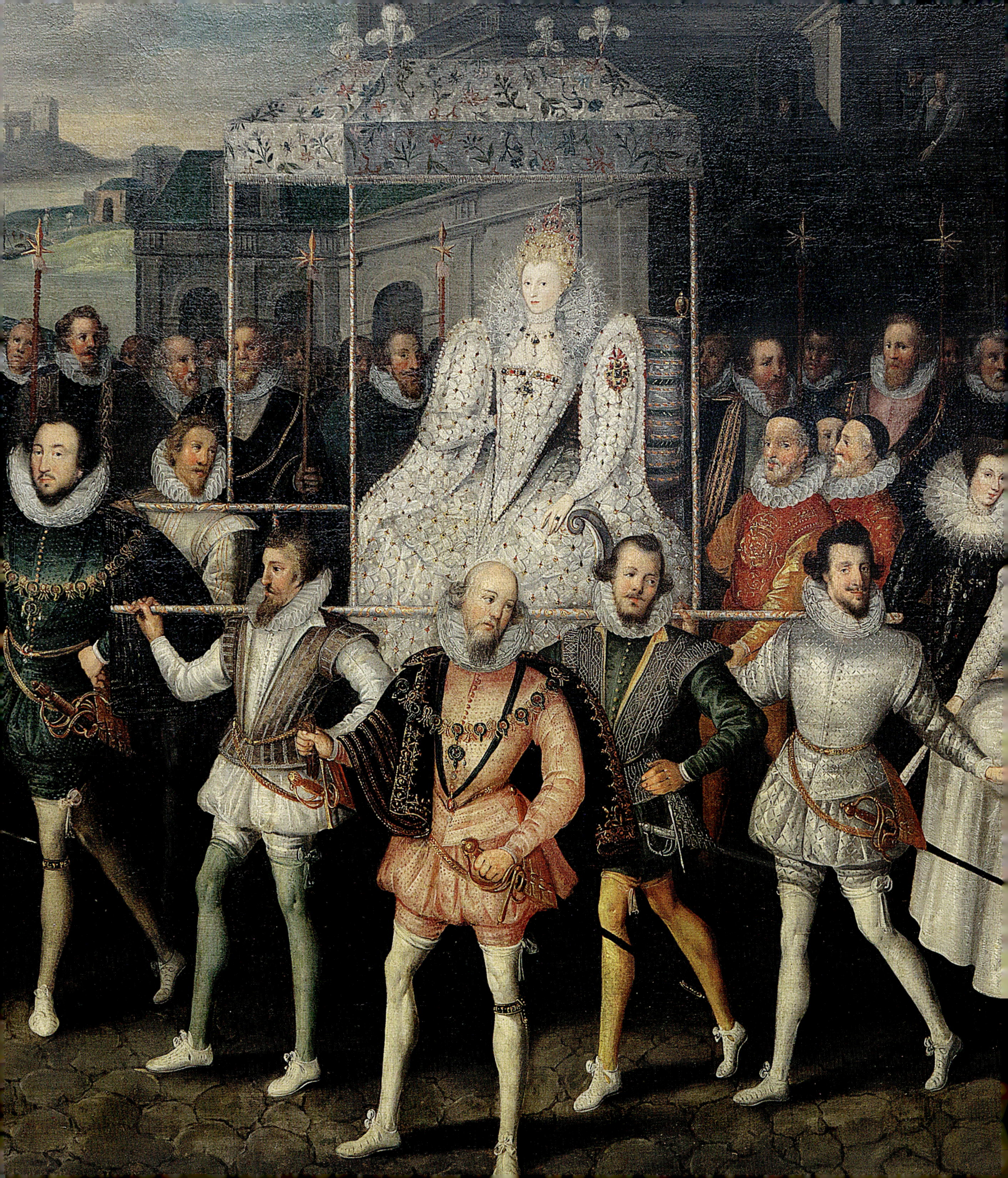

Acknowledgements

THIS EXHIBITION WOULD not have been possible without the generosity of the many lenders who have enabled so many remarkable objects to be displayed to the public together, some of them for the first time. We have also benefited from the help of an excellent advisory team who have offered their support and expertise over the last two years, overseeing aspects of the selection and the resulting interpretation as well as writing some of the catalogue entries. I am especially grateful to Ian W. Archer, Lena Cowen Orlin and Susan North for their clear and enlightening essays and to Roy Strong, David Taylor, Robert Tittler, Susan Doran and Andrew Hadfield for their advice and support. All the contributors to this catalogue (listed on p.43) have been extremely helpful, and I am grateful to them for sharing their expertise in this way. However, my largest debt of gratitude is to Jane Eade, who has worked tirelessly alongside me on this exhibition, helping to locate and research objects while brilliantly supporting the organisation of the material with dedication and enthusiasm.

Many other people have helped with the production of this exhibition and this catalogue: I am particularly grateful to our Editor, Sarah Ruddick; Head of Exhibitions, Rosie Wilson; Exhibitions Manager, Michelle Greaves; and Exhibitions Assistant, Ulrike Wachsmann. Richard Hallas, Sophie Plender and Polly Saltmarsh have been extremely helpful in supporting the conservation and assessment of paintings and objects. I am also grateful to all members of National Portrait Gallery staff for their support and dedication in the making of this exhibition, especially Sarah Tinsley, Denise Vogelsang, Neil Evans, Catharine MacLeod, Edward Town, Charlotte Bolland, David Saywell, Helen Whiteoak, Catherine Daunt and our art handling team, led by Karl Lydon. I would also like to thank our interns, Orla Cullen, Oliver McCall and Adam Sammut, for their help on various aspects of research, and Philip Lewis at Lewis Hallam for designing this catalogue. Laura Popoviciu has kindly helped with Latin translations.

Numerous other people have helped us with enquiries and research over the past three years, and we are especially grateful to:

David Adshead (National Trust), Beatrice Behlen (Museum of London), Nicholas Bell (British Library), Rachel Church (V&A), Andrea Clarke (British Library), Glyn Davies (V&A), Nick Davis (University of Liverpool), Richard Edgcumbe (V&A), Hazel Forsyth (Museum of London), Gareth Fitzpatrick (Boughton House), Julie Gardham (Glasgow University Library), Moira Goff (British Library), Nickos Gogolos (Museum of London), Sir John and Lady Guinness, James Hamilton (University of Birmingham), Edward Harley (private collection), Jim Harris (Ashmolean Museum), Maria Hayward (University of Southampton), Karen Hearn (UCL), Clive Hurst (Bodleian Library, Oxford), Pat Jackson (National Portrait Gallery), Susan Jenkins (English Heritage), Dana Josephson (Bodleian Library), Jackie Kelly (Museum of London), Vasant Kumar (Trinity Hall, Cambridge), Phil Manning (St Olave's Church), Tessa Murdoch (V&A), Susan North (V&A), Helen Parkin (British Museum), Angus Patterson (V&A), Nicole Ryder (independent conservator), Emma Shepley (Royal College of Physicians), Dora Thornton (British Museum), Paul Tod (St John's College, Oxford), Madeline Slaven (Bodleian Library, Oxford), David Spence (Museum of London), Stefanie De Sterck (private collection), Elaine Uttley (Fashion Museum), Helen Williams Ellis (private collection) and Jon Whiteley (Ashmolean Museum).

I am grateful to the Henry Moore Foundation and the Trustees of the Portrait Trust Fund for grants that enabled us to move and conserve the remarkable sculpture of Piero Capponi (cat. 49) in order for it to be seen in this exhibition.

Finally, I am also extremely grateful to our exhibition supporter, Mark Weiss, for his generosity.

TARNYA COOPER

Curator's Preface

WHEN WE THINK of the Elizabethan period, we perhaps think of the glittering Queen herself in an elaborate costume, surrounded by a group of adoring courtiers. This image is not simply the product of films and costume dramas, but can be seen in a painting made in her lifetime. The 'procession portrait' (detail seen overleaf; cat. 1) depicting Elizabeth dressed in white, carried in a chariot and accompanied by many of her courtiers and guards, was made towards the end of her life; it shows her as ever-youthful and universally admired. However, the one portrait with which the Queen herself would probably have been most pleased and that has survived for posterity is the so-called 'Darnley' portrait (cat. 8), one of the few pictures of Elizabeth that we think was painted directly from life. This portrait was painted by an exceptionally talented Continental artist, and in it we see the Queen vividly present before us. Holding our stare, she appears as an attractive, confident and evidently powerful woman.

However, there is much about the Elizabethan period that cannot be told by looking at portraits of the Queen alone, or indeed of her courtiers. This exhibition explores different spheres of Elizabethan life, from the Queen herself to the nobility and gentry, retailers and merchants, professionals, writers and artists and, where evidence survives, the working poor. Occasionally, remarkable examples of social permeability existed between these groups, and some fortunate individuals found opportunities to excel and to rise up the social ladder, creating an increase in the numbers of what historians call the 'middling sort'.

The Elizabethan period was a time of extraordinary enterprise. The known world was expanding through maritime exploration and trade, the widespread publication of the Bible in English encouraged literacy, and actors performed in public theatres for the first time, creating opportunities for writers to shape public discourse. It was also a time when cities, particularly London, expanded and a significant middle class developed. Among those who succeeded at court and in other areas of public life were individuals from relatively modest backgrounds, such as the great maritime explorer Sir Francis Drake (the son of a West Country shearman), or the property magnate Bess of Hardwick (the daughter of a Derbyshire gentleman), who rose to become the Countess of Shrewsbury; while among those working in the City of London were many sharp-witted merchants who achieved considerable financial success through their own labour, ingenuity and appetite for risk, allowing them in turn to lend money to members of the nobility and the gentry. Others, such as the self-promoting craftswoman Esther Inglis (cat. 70) or the English artist George Gower (cat. 67), contributed through their work to a dialogue about the importance and value of skill, wit and imagination over and above hereditary social status.

In essence, this exhibition uses surviving portraits to explore the lives of a wide range of men and women and asks if this period might be understood as an early meritocracy. Some of these issues are skilfully explored in the essays in this catalogue: in examining the social structure of society at this period, the historian Ian W. Archer considers the phenomenon of social mobility; the literary scholar Lena Cowen Orlin looks at how a new self-consciousness developed at this time linked to the changes brought about by the Reformation in religion; and the dress historian Susan North sheds new light on the types of clothes worn by the middling sort using evidence from surviving inventories.

As the curator of an exhibition of this sort, conceived and researched over several years, I owe many debts of gratitude: first and foremost to the many generous lenders who have made this exhibition possible. In the acknowledgements opposite I have listed the many people who have so kindly given their support. Considerable research on the world of the Elizabethan court has already been produced, and I am grateful to those scholars who have published on English portraiture and costume in this period over many years – particularly the late Janet Arnold, and Sir Roy Strong and Karen Hearn – for their insightful research, without which a catalogue like this could not have been written.

TARNYA COOPER

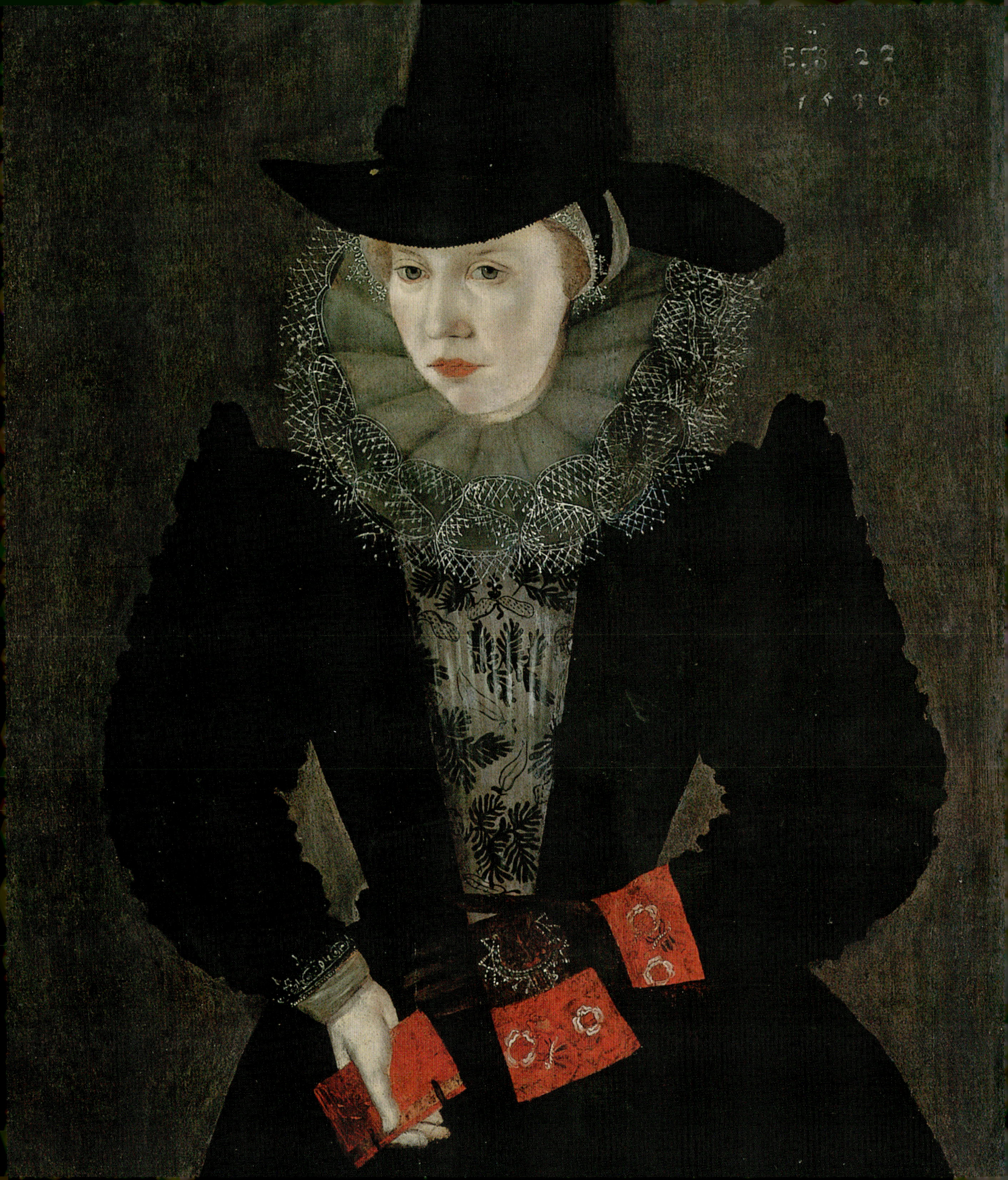
1596

Elizabethan Portraiture: Taste, Style and Patronage

TARNYA COOPER

'nowe every citizens wife that weares
a taffeta kirtle [skirt] *and a velvet hatt …*
must have her picture in the parlour'[1]

THESE WORDS FORM PART of a playful scene within a royal entertainment about a poet, a painter and a musician, performed at Mitcham in Surrey towards the end of Elizabeth I's reign in 1598. The entertainment is attributed to John Lyly (1554–1606) and the author's comments refer to the increased interest in portrait painting that developed throughout the Elizabethan period. While he may have been exaggerating slightly for effect, his remarks reflect the pretensions of the newly enriched citizenry. An example of the type of portrait of a 'citizens wife' that the writer may have had in mind is perhaps that of Joan Alleyn, wife of the theatre owner and actor Edward Alleyn, dated 1596 (fig. 1). Like several of the portraits of London citizens shown in this exhibition, Joan Alleyn appears smartly dressed in clothes typical of the so-called 'middling sort'.[2] She is wearing a tall black hat (perhaps of velvet) and a blackwork embroidered bodice, and holds gloves and a prayer book. She seems both contemplative and self-assured at the same time, and we might expect her portrait to have hung comfortably in her own parlour.

In the reigns of Elizabeth's father Henry VIII, her half-brother Edward VI and half-sister Mary I, surviving evidence indicates that it was principally royalty, members of the court and the nobility who commissioned portraits. Yet in the first few decades of Elizabeth's reign we find an expanding range of sitters who chose to be portrayed, not only increasing numbers of the country gentry but also London merchants and bankers, drapers, goldsmiths, cloth and wool merchants, wealthy wholesalers, clergymen, preachers, lawyers, writers, musicians and their wives and families.[3] What prompted this new interest in visual representation? And what was it about the Elizabethan period that popularised portrait production? Over the course of the sixteenth century the growth of urban populations, the increase in university entrance, the expansion of London as an international trading centre and the rise of the professions all certainly played a part, and some of these changes are explored later by Ian W. Archer (pp.20–5). But there was also a shift throughout Europe in the understanding of individuality, a factor long debated by historians and examined in greater detail by Lena Cowen Orlin (pp.26–33). Another part of the answer lies in the influence of Continental travel, the import of printed imagery, the presence of foreign artists in England and, of course, the emulation of peers. Portraits of the citizenry and the 'middling sort' had certainly been popular in Europe, particularly in the Low Countries, for several decades and would have been seen by travellers and merchants abroad, who sometimes brought newly commissioned portraits home, as for example did Thomas Gresham, Richard Clough and Katheryn of Berain (cats 45, 47 and 48).

With the Reformation and the re-establishment of the Church of England in 1559, which marked the conversion in official religion from Roman Catholicism to the Protestant faith, the production of religious images for worship rapidly declined in the form of independent easel paintings. However, religious images did frequently appear in a decorative context. The Elizabethan period also saw an increased interest in the presentation of family lineage and an awareness of the importance of historical narratives (see for example cat. 36). In short, the Elizabethans gained a taste for history. In London, as well as provincial cities and towns,

FIG. 1
Joan Alleyn
Unknown English artist, 1596

history plays were performed at public theatres to an audience of gentry, citizenry and ordinary town dwellers, who could attend for as little as a penny. Historians such as William Camden (1551–1623) and John Stow (1524/5–1605) published widely read surveys, chronicling the history of Britain in general and the city of London in particular.[4] After more than sixty years of Tudor monarchy, the Elizabethans could afford to look back on the period of internal strife that preceded the reign of Elizabeth's grandfather Henry VII with antiquarian interest, rather than anxiety. In turn, throughout the Elizabethan period external threats from Roman Catholic Europe, particularly Spain, helped to unite the nation against a common enemy. The break with Roman Catholic traditions perhaps made narratives of both national and familial identity, based on historical precedents, more necessary. Portraiture played a part in these national, regional and personal narratives as newly recreated images of past monarchs and heroes were popular decorative features in wealthy houses. One example among several is a set of sixteen portraits of monarchs from William the Conqueror to Mary I (fig. 2), painted *c.*1600, which would have made a colourful, amusing and educational display in a domestic or institutional context.[5] Such groups would probably have concluded with a portrait of the current queen (perhaps one commissioned outside the set) to create a sense of continuity and rightful natural order.

Portraiture had been an effective tool in the service of the monarchy and the state under previous Tudor monarchs, but it was in the Elizabethan period that it developed in order to serve individual agendas on a wider scale. Portraits of Elizabeth I (1533–1603) employed symbolism to reflect her virtues of virginity, wisdom, charity and learning, while portraits of the nobility, gentry and private citizenry presented a range of different roles and virtues including military endeavour, statesmanship, mercantile ingenuity, civic office, scholarship, beauty, piety, humility and charity. As access to portraiture increased, sitters and patrons customised portraits for their own ends – either to endorse existing assumptions or to re-situate personal identities and reputations. A significant quantity of painted imagery from the period has been lost over time, and what survives in museums, galleries, country houses and private collections does not reflect the considerable breadth or the varied quality of work produced by Elizabethan painters. Paintings by the most talented foreign artists, and those depicting portraits of high-profile court sitters, inevitably have survived more successfully than portraits of lesser-known sitters by anonymous native artists. I explore here some of the characteristics of Elizabethan portraiture and reflect on the relationships between visual imagery, social change and our reading of the past, and consider the possible causes for the rather idiosyncratic appearance of Elizabethan paintings, in comparison with continental art, and the relative isolation of the Elizabethan style.

English contexts for the making and display of paintings

The reform in religion that took place in much of northern Europe over the course of the sixteenth century – known as the Reformation – re-focused attention on the Bible as the sole guide for religious instruction. In England and Wales the second Commandment, which forbade the use and reverence of images for religious purposes, was largely taken at its word and painted icons – the source of idolatry – were considered unlawful.[6] This change in religious practice had a significant impact on the appearance of churches, where images were removed and interiors were whitewashed. It also had an effect on the general public's confidence in the proper purpose of visual representation and the value of depicting – or, as some sixteenth-century audiences saw it, literally counterfeiting through paint – God's natural world. Thus, image making could be seen as potentially presumptuous.[7] However, there were many different interpretations of religious reform and not all of Protestant Europe took the same attitude to the proper purpose and usage of visual imagery. In Germany and the Low Countries, artists readily found new audiences for the emerging genres of painting, including landscapes, townscapes, still-lifes, scenes of merry-making, historical

FIG. 2
The Hornby Castle Set of early Kings and Queens
First row, left to right: King William I ('The Conqueror'); King Henry I; King Stephen; King Henry II.
Second row: King John; King Edward II; King Edward III; King Richard II.
Third row: King Henry IV; King Edward IV; King Edward V; King Richard III.
Fourth row: King Henry VII; King Henry VIII; Anne Boleyn; Queen Mary I.
Unknown artists, late sixteenth century – *c.*1620

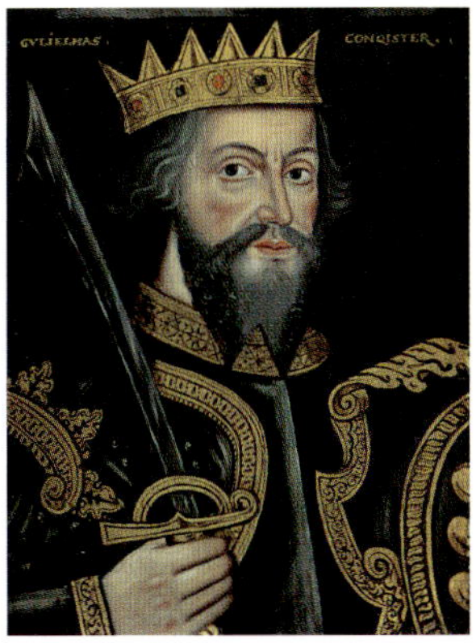

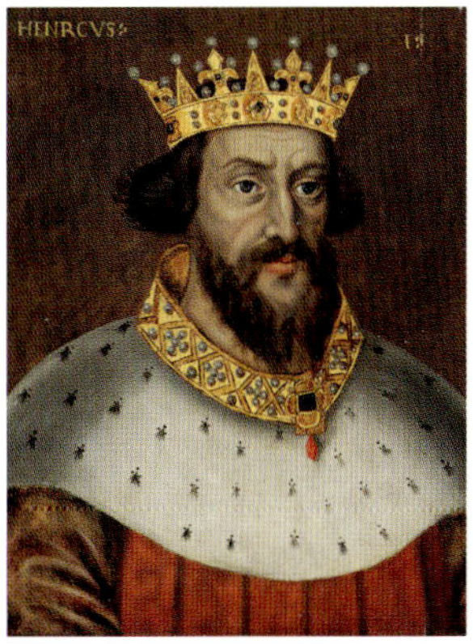

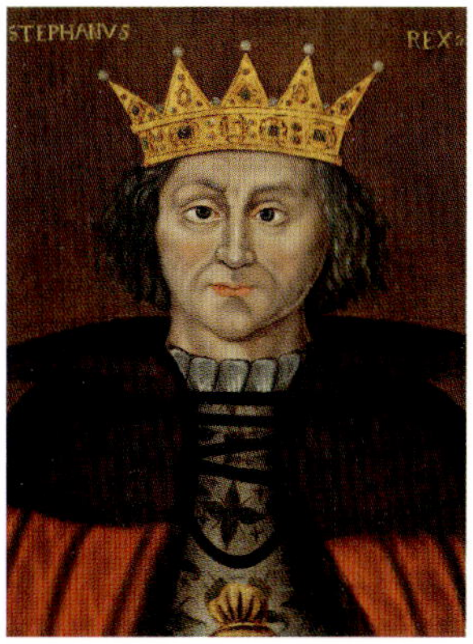
STEPHANVS REX

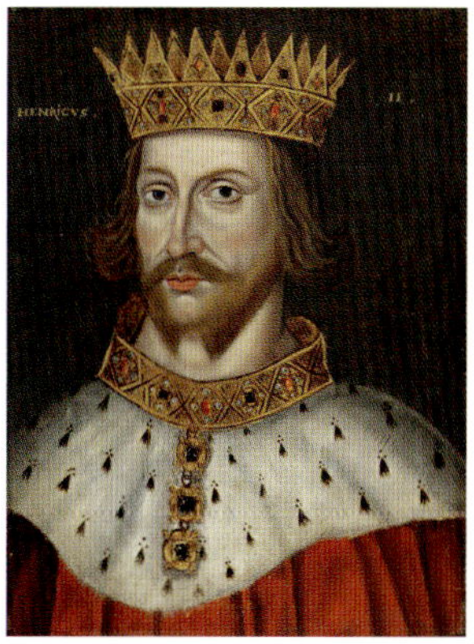

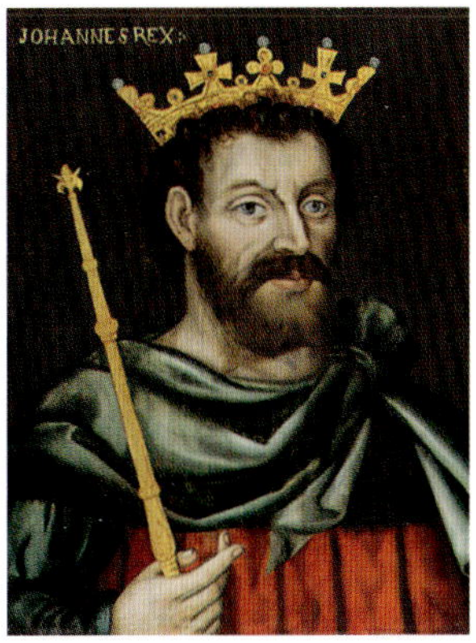
JOHANNES REX

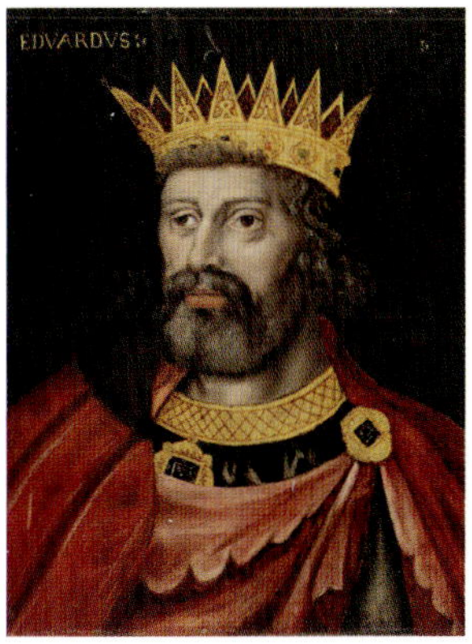

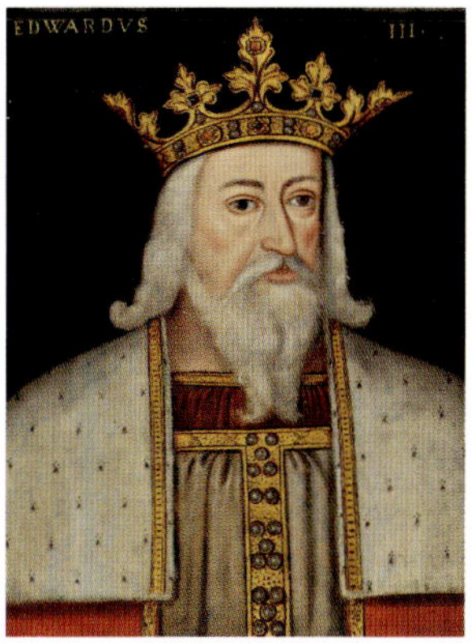
EDWARDVS III

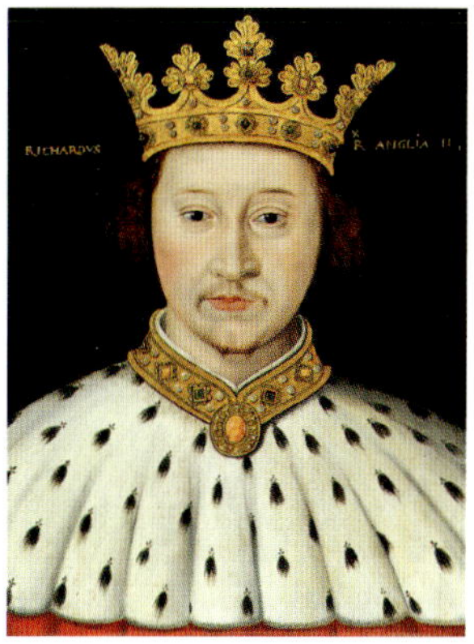

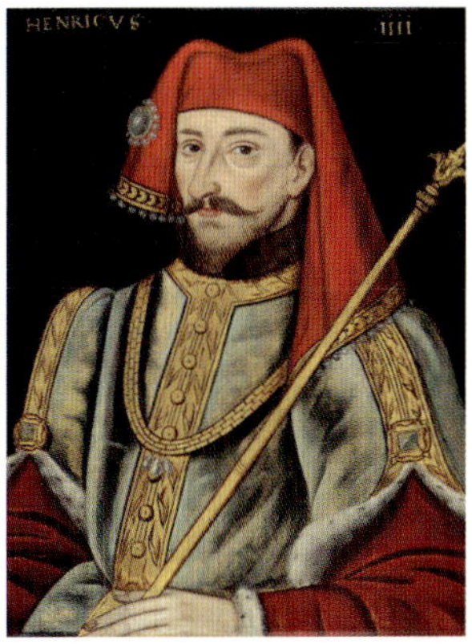
HENRICVS IIII

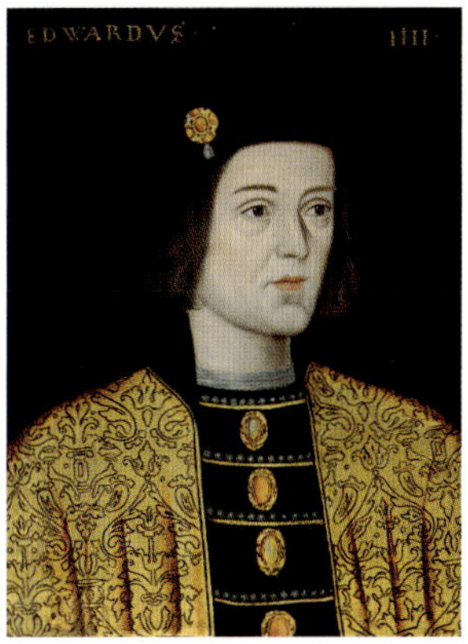
EDWARDVS IIII

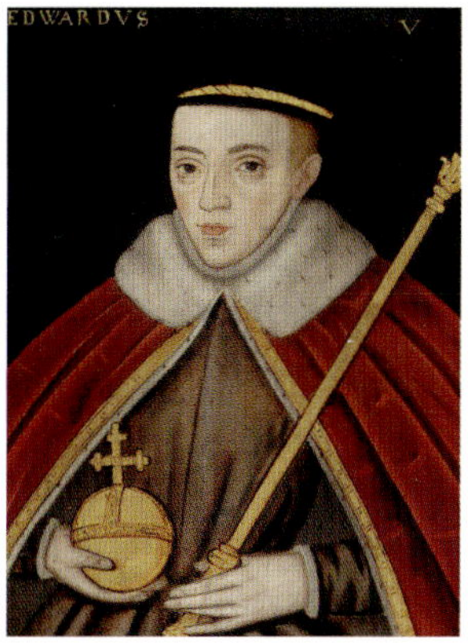
EDWARDVS V

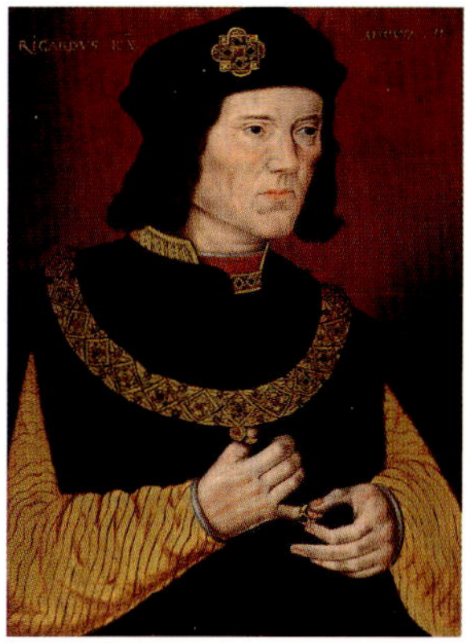

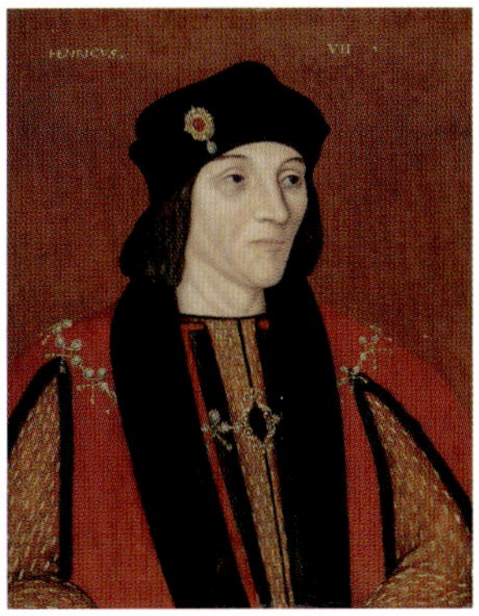

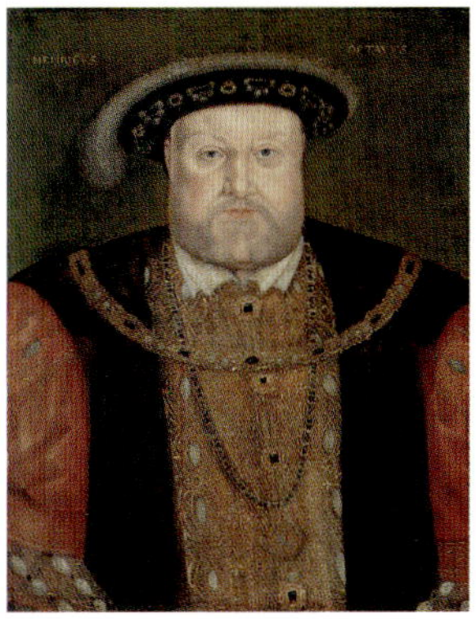

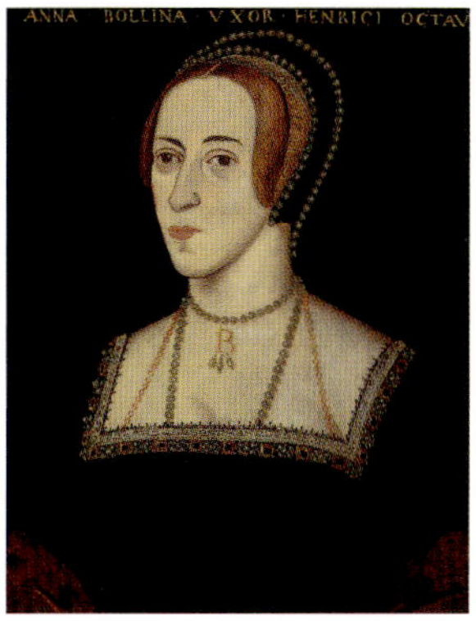
ANNA BOLLINA VXOR HENRICI OCTAV

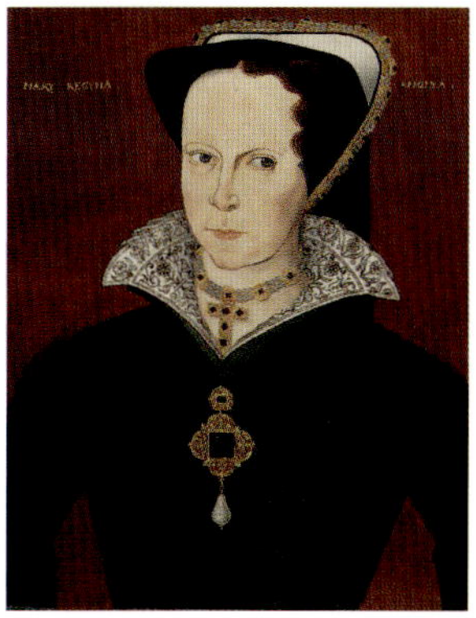

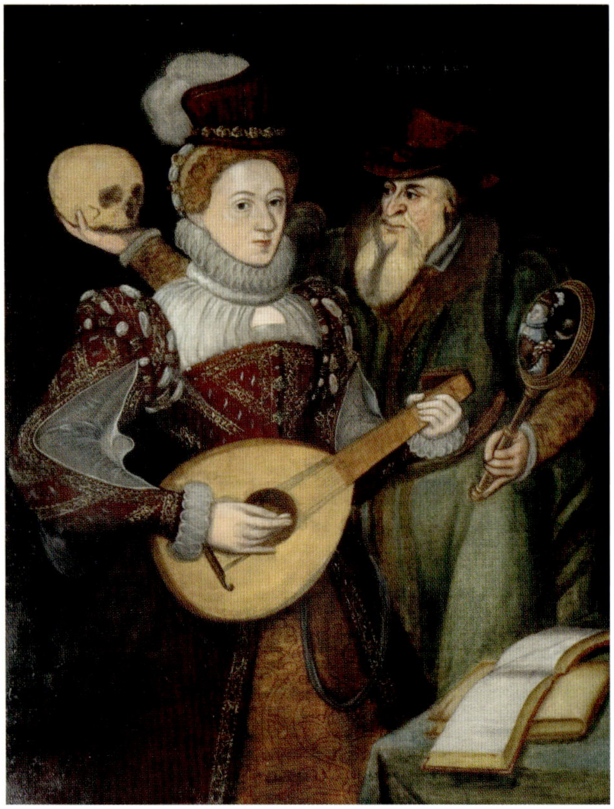

FIG. 3
Death and the Maiden
English School, dated 1570

and allegorical subjects, all of which flourished alongside portraiture. Patrons in England appear to have had less interest in such works in the form of independent easel paintings, as very few examples survive from this date.[8] One important surviving example depicts a young woman being confronted by an older man holding a mirror, which can be read as an allegory of youth and age (fig. 3). The picture is competently painted by a native artist and may be the work of a painter who also took on decorative work. Indeed, such subject pictures do occasionally appear in domestic inventories, and this picture provides an indication of the type of paintings that may once have been more common in the sixteenth century. Most middle-class homes, shops, inns and chambers within institutions would also have hung painted cloths as decorative wall hangings, as is evident from significant numbers of surviving inventories.[9] In addition, the contents of Elizabethan houses would have included wall paintings, plasterwork and carvings depicting both narrative religious and allegorical scenes, often based on European print sources, all of which have been well documented by Anthony Wells-Cole, Tara Hamling, Michael Bath and Kathryn Davies.[10] Unfortunately, most of this painted decoration was discarded in the seventeenth and eighteenth centuries by later generations, whose taste followed the Continental trends of plainer panelling or wallpapered rooms, decorated with framed European pictures alongside British family portraits. Although it is true that patronage of the arts in England was more limited than in many other parts of Western Europe, Elizabethan patrons were not, as described by some historians, image 'phobic'. Instead, they were often cautious of overt (that is, visually deceptive) forms of realism.[11] The loss of painted hangings and interiors, and conversely the large-scale survival of portraiture, has in turn created a false impression that Elizabethan visual culture was exclusively concerned with royal propaganda, and the promotion of rank, fame and personal virtue through the medium of portraiture.

The style of Elizabethan painting

In the centuries that followed the reign of Elizabeth I, it was the general consensus that she had not been well served by her painters.[12] In the eighteenth century, Elizabethan style apparently looked feeble and misconceived, its portraits stiff and awkward, compared with the styles that followed. In 1760, when Horace Walpole recorded his views of the appearance of Hardwick Hall, Derbyshire (which had retained the original Elizabethan furnishings and pictures owned by Elizabeth Talbot, Countess of Shrewsbury; cat. 28), he described it as having 'vast rooms, [and] no taste' containing 'bad tapestry and worse pictures' (fig. 4).[13] It is clear that what we might think of as a native Elizabethan aesthetic was distinct from the prevailing trends in continental Europe. Portraits of the Queen, her courtiers and those of the 'middling sort' by native artists, illustrated throughout this catalogue, are characteristically linear and flat in style, and regularly employ heraldic and other emblems as markers of social status or categories of virtue. Inscriptions recording the date and age of the sitter were also routinely applied and so portraits also served as a marker of time, ensuring that the person represented could be securely documented for posterity as of a particular age at a specific date, as seen in the portrait of Walter Ralegh (1552–1618; cat. 22). This allowed the sitters themselves to look back over their lives and see how time had altered their features, which in itself provided opportunities for reflection and remembrance of the fragility of life. The use of inscribed dates and ages is not by any means unique to Elizabethan works of art, but does appear more frequently in England and Wales than virtually anywhere else in Europe, perhaps indicating the importance attached to the documentary characteristics of portraiture.[14] Some patrons found it expedient to include verses or mottos reflecting family associations or personal narratives, as can be seen in the portraits of the Welsh merchant Gawen Goodman (cat. 51), the courtier and statesman Christopher Hatton (cat. 20) and the artist George Gower (cat. 67), so turning a portrait into a personal puzzle or a visual polemic.

FIG. 4
The Long Gallery at Hardwick Hall, Derbyshire

The style adopted by English artists was also distinctive for its boldly conceived outlines and doll-like presentation of the body. Bodily form appears as if contained by cloth rather than naturalistically covered by it. This was partly due to a lack of training in proportion and perspective; few English apprentices would have learnt either of these skills as part of their seven or more years' training under masters of the Painter-Stainers Company at this date.[15]
A good example is the extraordinary portrait of Elizabeth I, *c.*1598–9, in a dress decorated with land and sea creatures (fig. 5, cat. 10). The English artist seems unaware how to represent a three-dimensional object on a two-dimensional surface and even though the work was perhaps originally based on a design for a miniature, the composition and execution seem almost purposely archaic. It is important to note that this picture was displayed at Hardwick Hall around

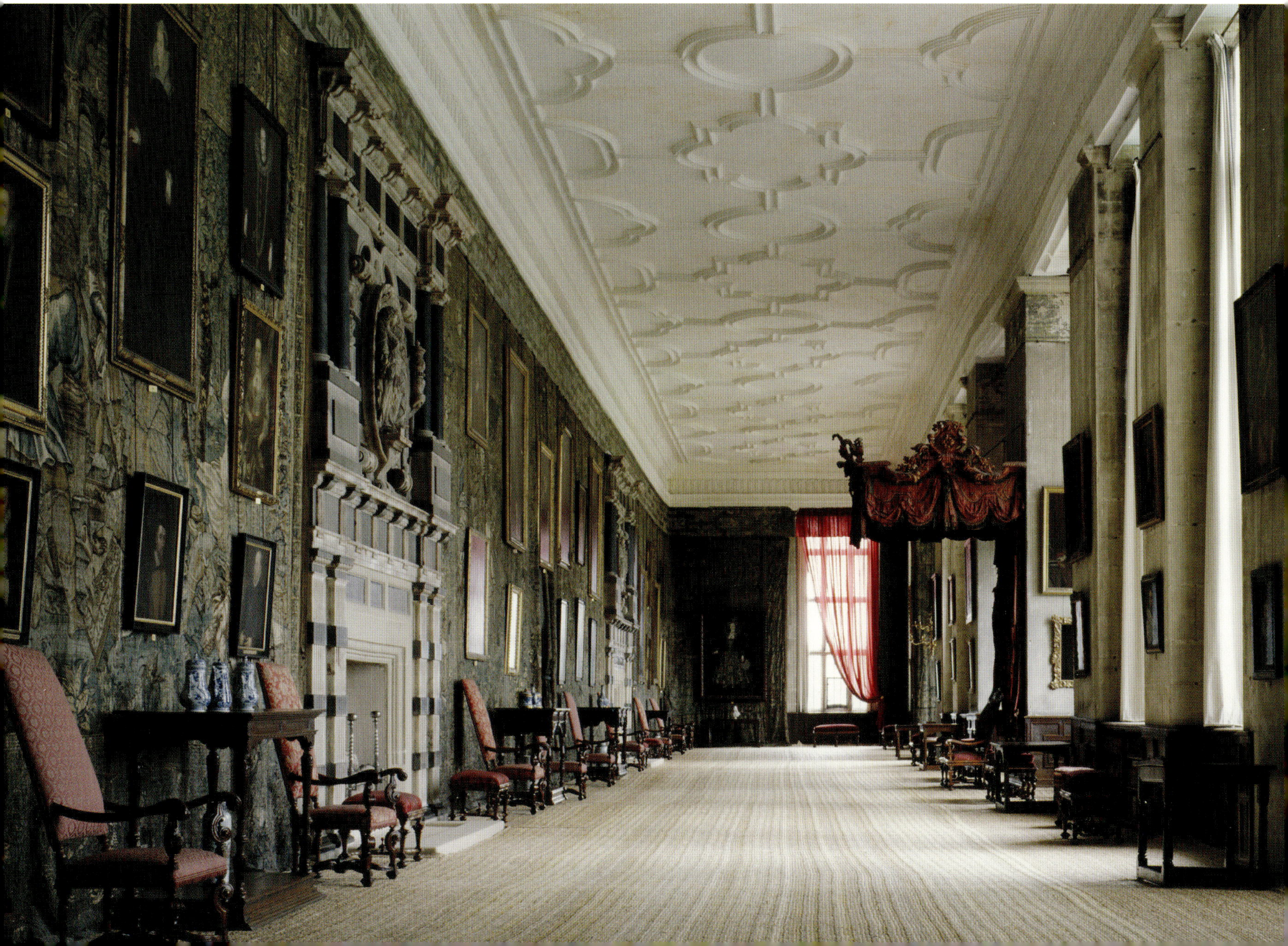

1601; it was probably commissioned by the Countess of Shrewsbury herself (and thus must have gained her approval) and would have been seen and appreciated by countless peers and contemporaries.

Elizabethan portraits also show a marked interest in accurately capturing the detail of pattern and design of costume and jewellery, occasionally at the expense of the overall harmony and coherence of the image. A portrait of the courtier Elizabeth Knollys, dated 1577 (fig. 6), is a characteristic example. She is depicted with a fashionable high-brimmed hat and wears a lace ruff and an unusual doublet, fastened with decorative ties and slashed to reveal a coral-coloured (probably once red) tunic and sleeves. A jewelled parrot or dove, hanging from an artfully twisted braid, and a string of pearls and gold beads are slung diagonally across her body. The complexity of her costume and the wealth of different layers, slashes and bows, jewelled embellishments and emblems create the effect of an over-decorated Christmas tree to the modern eye. Yet to courtiers of the 1570s, this look was exceptionally stylish.

The confidence and bravado with which Elizabeth Knollys presents herself also betrays a lifetime surrounded by decorative accessories as she served as one of the Mistresses of the Queen's Wardrobe. The excesses of Elizabethan fashion reached a high point in the 1580s and 1590s, and with so much evident labour, ingenuity and actual wealth invested in dressing and decorating the body, it is entirely understandable that life-sized portraiture became such a popular medium in which to represent personal appearance.

Simply put, in terms of aesthetics, the Elizabethan period stood at the polar opposite of the 'less is more' principle. The use of emblems and allegorical imagery was popular across Europe at this date but it took a particular hold in England, where anxieties created by the Church of England's interpretation of the second Commandment (not to worship images) may have led to a reliance on known meanings, and the predominance of the textural over the visual. The viewer had to unravel such devices and symbols in order to decode the intentions behind the work. In this way, the visual arts became a 'text' to be read, with labels

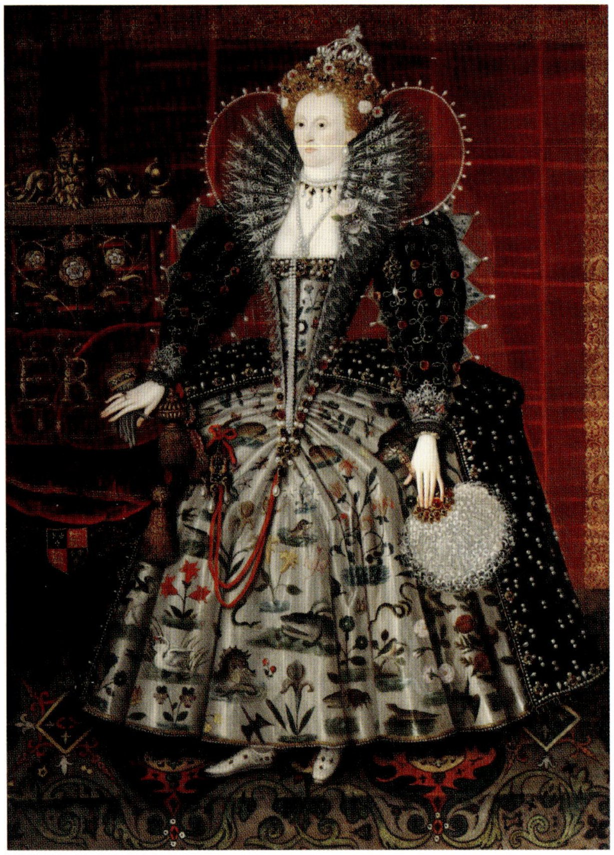

FIG. 5
Elizabeth I (cat. 10) and detail
Unknown artist, *c.*1598–9

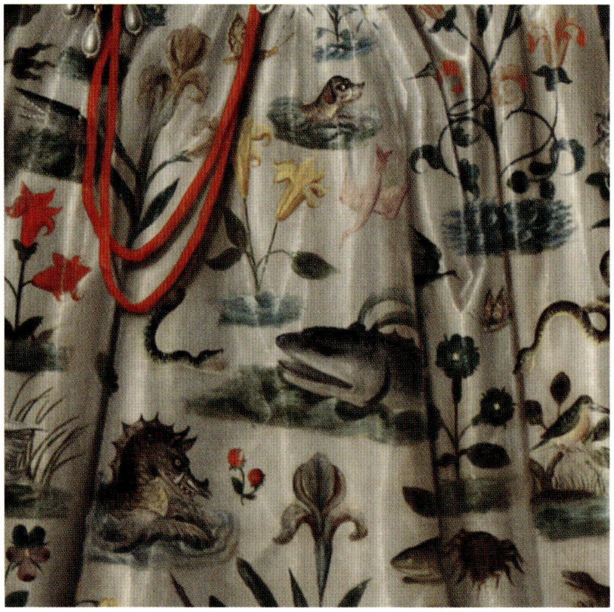

in Latin or English used to verify or explain further.[16] Although there were significant numbers of foreign artists and craftsmen working in England during this period, it was two English painters, Nicholas Hilliard (1547–1618) (see cat. 16) and George Gower, who dominated portrait production of the Queen for several decades and their work was characteristic of a native style that was employed by many other nameless native painters. It was a style that was perhaps popular in England because, in its language and execution, it acknowledged that painting was representative rather than mimetic (or purposely deceptive), allowing the representation of artifice to be clearly evident. Such portraits, while recognisable as depictions of specific people, were not realistic likenesses. As such they were never going to be confused with the pre-Reformation concept of images embodying the essence of the person – the original cause of concern among ardent Protestants regarding religious icons.

As the portraits presented in this exhibition and catalogue reveal, a wide range of different styles were in use simultaneously. Not all patrons valued the native style and throughout the Elizabethan period there are numerous instances when courtiers, wealthy merchants and professionals commissioned foreign artists (as well as English painters trained or influenced by Dutch or Flemish artists) to paint startlingly life-like portraits. For example, Sir Henry Lee's impressive portrait, painted by Anthonis Mor (1516–75/6) in 1568 (fig. 7), was probably commissioned when Lee was in Antwerp and is one of the most powerfully subtle portraits to be found in sixteenth-century Europe. Mor's skills as an insightful and supremely accomplished portraitist were on a par with those of Hans Holbein the Younger (1497/8–1543), who had captured the likeness of the court of Henry VIII thirty years previously. In turn, the portrait of Katheryn of Berain (cat. 48), the wife of a Welsh merchant resident in Antwerp, also dated 1568, by an unknown but talented Netherlandish painter, presents an eerily vivid image of a woman in sombre contemplation of mortality. The illusion of physical presence that these portraits conjure is palpable and must have impressed, or shocked, their first audiences in England. By the 1590s, the influence of numerous foreign artists, and naturalised émigrés who worked with English artists, was apparent; the native style of Elizabethan England was slowly becoming less distinct and patrons were gaining a greater appreciation of artists who exercised skills associated with realism. Isaac Oliver (*c.*1565–1617), for example, trained with Nicholas Hilliard and while his portrait miniatures (see cat. 68) look formally similar, his style combined fluency of expression with an illusionist rendering of features and a more comprehensive understanding of the arts of proportion and perspective.

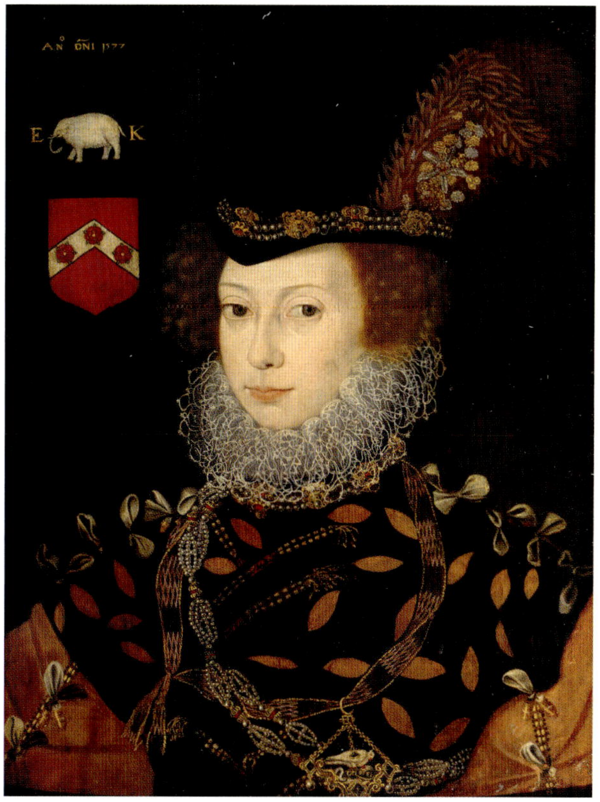

FIG. 6
Elizabeth Knollys, Lady Layton
Attributed to George Gower, 1577

Portrait formats, ownership and display

There is only limited evidence of the process of commissioning a portrait in sixteenth-century England. In London, which had a population of around 200,000 in 1600, there must have been many hundreds of painters producing painted images of all kinds, including decorative house painting, subject pictures and hangings, heraldic work and portraiture at a wide range of prices.[17] In general, paintings were far cheaper to commission than a new suit of clothes, decorative silver, gilt plate or a tomb monument, all of which arguably performed similar roles in terms of enhancing the status of the sitter.

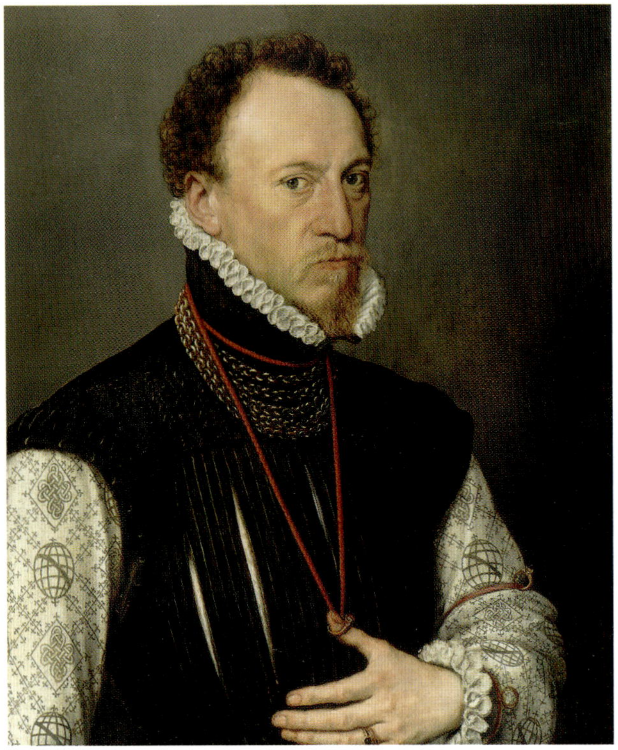

FIG. 7
Sir Henry Lee
Anthonis Mor, 1568

The composition and format of portraits was determined largely by the patron, as was the size, which helped to establish the price. Potential purchasers would commission portraits and other pictures directly from the painter, perhaps being guided in the choice of composition by what was on the walls of the artist's studio, either as templates or uncollected work.[18] Alternatively, some pictures – including portraits of the Queen – could be purchased ready-made, direct from the stock of a retailer, stationer or master painter who would sell the work of several artists.[19] Prices varied enormously but it was possible to purchase a portrait from around 5 shillings up to several pounds depending on size, materials, the complexity of the composition and level of detailed decorative work, and the prominence or reputation of the artist.[20] Elizabethan easel paintings were most commonly painted on wooden panels (using Baltic, or less often English oak), but canvas was in use throughout the period and for practical reasons it became more popular in the 1590s, often for use in large-scale pictures. The length of time required for a sitting is open to conjecture, and different artists must have worked in different ways depending on the complexity and price of the work. In the seventeenth century, the artist Edward Norgate recommended that at least three sittings would be needed to gain a good likeness from the life, and this may have been the practice established from an earlier period.[21] Modern technology in the form of infrared reflectograms gives us an insight into the artist's working method by detecting the initial underdrawing, which was made on the surface of the panel before painting began. This indicates that artists sometimes worked up sketches freehand, but more often transferred carefully worked-out drawings as a pattern on to the surface of the picture, which then served as a close guide for the painted composition. The use of such patterns seems to have occurred even where no further copies or versions were required, and it is likely this was part of artistic practice in developing an accurate likeness.[22] It appears highly probable that separate underdrawings would have been made for the head, and perhaps also for the whole composition, to agree the pose; however, as these were simply workshop tools, very few such drawings survive.[23]

Portraiture certainly expanded in the Elizabethan period for a myriad of different reasons, the increase in personal opportunities, the range of available artists and a patron's interest in emulation all being major factors. Although it is clear that portraiture did not extend to the Elizabethan working poor, it is now evident that it was accessible to many men and women among the Elizabethan 'middling sort'. Perhaps the most interesting fact to emerge is that these new sitters did *not* try to emulate the nobility or the gentry. In contrast to the diarist Samuel Pepys, who a hundred years later hired a special gown in which to have his portrait painted, these middle-class Elizabethans appear to be depicted wearing their own, albeit respectable clothes, presenting the virtues suitable to their own position in life.[24] A vast amount of this new category of portraiture has been lost over time, perhaps because rather than being harboured in the estates of the landed classes, it was produced to be hung in leased houses and rented rooms, and thus could not easily be cared for by the sitters' later descendants, when family fortunes changed. We are thus unlikely ever to know the full extent of portrait types produced at this time, or those who were depicted. However, after the death of Elizabeth I, under the rule of James I, portraiture became yet more popular and surviving Jacobean portraits, such as those of actors and master carpenters, depict an ever more diverse range of sitters whose likenesses were captured for posterity.

1 Possibly John Lyly, *Queen Elizabeth's Entertainment at Mitcham: Poet, Painter, and Musician* (Yale University Press, New Haven CT, 1953) p.27, v236–49. The writer uses this passage to agree with his fellow musician and poet as to how the art of painting has become devalued by over use. 'Our arts grows stale; for where in elder ages, none were coloured [i.e. painted] but memorable for their vertues to paynt out imitation to posterity, nowe every Citizens wife that weares a taffeta kirtle and a velvet hatt, and every gentlewoman that can board a paire of borders [embroidered accessories worn at the neck] must have her picture in the parlour. And if one hereafter aske, who was this? It was one of the companies of such a trade, or a Justice of peace his wife, of such a shire. But it is not on vs only, but in mocking of auncyent monuments; for now if one dye riche, he must have a toumbe and an eptaphe, where nothing remayneth for memory, but that he dyed so much worth; so that heretofore virtue was interred in toumbes of gold; now gold is buryed with the vertues of ensigns'.

2 For the term 'middling sort' see Jonathan Barry and Christopher Brooks, 'Introduction', *The Middling Sort of People: Culture, Society and Politics in England 1550–1800* (Macmillan, London, 1994); Keith Wrightson, 'Sorts of People in Tudor and Stuart England' in Barry and Brooks (eds),*The Middling Sort of People*, pp.28–51; Michael Mascuch, 'Social Mobility and Middling Self-Identity: the ethos of British Autobiographers 1600–1700', *Past and Present*, vol. 33, 1966, pp.16–55.

3 For a fuller explanation of the types of sitters depicted in portraits, and further illustrations, see Tarnya Cooper, *Citizen Portrait: Portrait Painting and the Urban Elite of Tudor and Jacobean England and Wales* (Yale University Press, London and New Haven, CT, 2012).

4 John Stow, *A Summarie of Englyshe Chronicles*, first published in 1565 and repeatedly updated throughout the Elizabethan period; John Stow, *The Annales of England*, first published in 1598, and then again in 1601 and 1631; John Stow, *Survey of London*, published in 1598 and 1603; William Camden, *Britannia*, edited and with an introduction by Robert Mayhew, first published 1586 (Thoemmes Press, Bristol, 2003).

5 Robin Gibson, 'The National Portrait Gallery's Set of Kings and Queens at Montacute House', *The National Trust Yearbook*, 1975, pp.81–7; Robin Gibson, 'A Jacobean Gallery of the Kings and Queens of England', *Folio*, Spring 1995. For NPG 4680 (1–16) see www.npg.org.uk/research/programmes/making-art-in-tudor-britain/case-studies/picturing-history-a-portrait-set-of-early-english-kings-and-queens.php (accessed April 2013).

6 Margaret Aston, 'Gods, Saints and Reformers: Portraiture and Protestant England', *Albion's Classicism: The Visual Arts in Britain 1550–1660*, ed. Lucy Gent (Yale University Press, New Haven CT and London, 1995), pp.181–220. The wording of the Commandment in fact appears to make a case for a blanket ban on images, as it states 'thou shalt make no graven image, neither any similitude of things / that are in heaven above, neither that are in the earth beneath, nor that are in the water under the earth / Thou shalt not bow downe to them, neither serue them for I am the Lord thy God'. Exodus 20: 4–5. However, as Richard Williams has shown, many Protestants interpreted the Commandment not as a ban on all images but as a prohibition on their use in religious worship. Richard Lindsey Williams, *Religious Pictures and Sculpture in Elizabethan England*, University of London, 2003 (unpublished PhD thesis).

7 The fact that the Homilies (p.28) also had to mention specifically that 'the arts of painting and image making' were not 'wicked of themselves' is indicative that there was an element of confusion regarding the proper use of visual imagery, both secular and religious. 'An Homily Against Peril of Idolatry', *Sermons or Homilies*, 1811, p.200.

8 Evidence from inventories indicates that popular subject pictures were occasionally on display in the houses of the nobility, gentry, merchants and artisans and even in inns, and depicted subjects as various as personifications of Pride and Death, images of St Jerome, Mary Magdalene and various emperors, and painted tables of the 'kings of the realme', the seasons or the months of the year. See, for example, inventories of Ralph Warren, London, 1554 (TNA Prob 2 256): 'a table of St. Jerome', 'a table of Soloman [*sic*] sitting'; John Pope of Mountressing, Essex, 1557 (TNA Prob 2/280): 'a picture of mary Magdalyn', 'a picture of st. John'; William Lovelace, Serjeant at Law, Canterbury (TNA Prob 2 404B): 'a table with a frame of the kings of this realm written', 'one other of death and pride', 'diverse emperors and kings'; John Savell, Gent of the Royal Chapel, 1579–80 (TNA C239/46/115 and C239/46/123): 'a little table of the monthes of the year valued at 11 pence'. See also Susan Foister, 'Paintings and other Works of Art in Sixteenth-Century English Inventories', *Burlington Magazine*, vol. 123, 1981, pp.273–82 and Robert Tittler, *Portraits, Painters and Publics in Provincial England 1540–1640* (Oxford University Press, Oxford, 2012), ch. 3, pp.46–59.

9 In the inventory of John Pope of Mountressing, Essex, 1557 (TNA Prob 2/280): 'a painted cloth with the supper of Christ with his apostles, valued at 2 shillings', 'a cloth of the heding of St. John valued at 12 shillings'. In the inventory of Chris Woode, Innholder, 1567–8 (TNA C239/33/91), each room has painted hangings typically described as 'the olde paynted clothes counteying by estimation xii yards at 8 he yard'. Narrative subjects were also common in tapestries and carpets at this period, and were also owned by the 'middling sort', for example, the inventory of William Lovelace, Serjeant-at-Law, 1577, lists a tapestry with 'the Storie of Solomon' (TNA Prob 2 404B).

10 Anthony Wells-Cole, *The Art of Decoration in Elizabethan and Jacobean England: The Influence of Continental Prints, 1558–1625* (Yale University Press, New Haven CT and London, 1997); Tara Hamling, *Decorating the 'Godly' Household: religious art in post-Reformation Britain* (Yale University Press, New Haven CT and London, 2010); Kathryn Davies, *Artisan Art: Vernacular Wall Paintings in the Welsh Marches, 1550–1650* (Logaston Press, Almeley, Herefordshire, 2008); Michael Bath, *Renaissance Decorative Painting in Scotland* (National Museum of Scotland, Edinburgh, 2003).

11 Patrick Collinson, *From Iconoclasm to Iconophobia: The Cultural Impact of the Second English Reformation* (University of Reading, 1986). See Cooper 2012, 'Categories and Contexts, Visual Description and the English Reformation', ch. 1, pp.19–39.

12 For example, in 1662 John Evelyn recorded that many portraits of Elizabeth I had been destroyed in the later seventeenth century by being used as pastry baking boards (known as 'peels'). He notes that 'Had Queen Elizabeth been thus circumspect, there had not been so many vile copies multiplied from an ill Painting; as being calle'd in, and brought to Essex-house, did for several years, furnish the Pastry-men with Peels for the use of their Ovens'. John Evelyn, *Sculptura: or the Art of Chalcography* (J.C., London, 1662), p.25.

13 Horace Walpole 'Visits to Country Seats', *Walpole Society*, XVI, 1928, 29–30.

14 Inscriptions concerning the relationships of the sitter to other family members, for example, 'wife of . . .' or 'father of . . .', are almost always applied at a later date to provide a context for more recent images of the same family.

15 Cooper 2012, pp.45–52; W.A.D. Englefield, *History of the Painter Stainers' Company of London* (Chapman & Dodd, London, 1923).

16 See also Mary E. Hazard, *Elizabethan Silent Language* (University of Nebraska Press, Lincoln NE and London, 2000).

17 Recent research by Robert Tittler has identified over 2,300 painters working in England and Wales in the period 1500 to 1640. Separate research by Edward Town focusing on painters in London has identified numerous other painters working in the period 1547 to 1625. See Edward Town, 'A Biographical Dictionary of London Painters 1547–1625', Walpole Society, forthcoming, 2014.

18 The autobiography of the Elizabethan composer Thomas Whithorne states that when he visited a painter in 1562, in order to have his portrait made, the artist's house or studio contained portraits of people of all ages, described as 'many pictures, as well of those that were much elder than I, as of some such that were of my years, yea, and much younger than I was'. James M. Osborn (ed.), *The Autobiography of Thomas Whythorne* (Modern Spelling Edition, Oxford University Press, 1962), p.115.

19 Cooper 2012, pp.55–63. The inventory of Nicholas Lentall, a Gentleman, lists 'An Image of Queen Elizabeth xii shillings', November 1558. As this gentleman owned no other portraits, the picture most likely represents Elizabeth I (rather than Elizabeth I's grandmother, Elizabeth of York). The inventory of Nicholas Lentall (TNA Prob 2 346 B). For wider evidence of ownership, see the inventories of John Cumberland (artisan): 'an ould picture' valued at 6 pence in 1590, p.38; Richard Cornelis (joiner): 'fowre small pictures' valued at 3 shillings in 1610, p.75. Michael Reed (ed.), 'The Ipswich Probate Inventories 1583–1631', Suffolk Record Society, vol. 12, 1981. See also the inventories of Richard Mascoll (butcher): 'a picture of the queen [perhaps Elizabeth I or Anne of Denmark?] & ii brass candlesticks' valued at 3 shillings in 1609, p.8. Edwin George, Stella George and Peter Fleming, 'Bristol Probate Inventories', Bristol Records Society, 2002.

20 I am grateful to Edward Town for further information on evidence for the wide range of prices at which pictures were valued or sold in the Elizabethan period. See also Susan Foister, 'Paintings and other Works of Art in Sixteenth-Century English Inventories', *Burlington Magazine*, vol. 123, 1981, pp.273–82 and Tittler, *Portraits, Painters and Publics*, ch. 3, pp.46–59.

21 In the 1620s the artist and connoisseur Edward Norgate (1581–1650) advised that three sittings of several hours' length were needed to gain a likeness. The first (of 2–4 hours) for 'colouring the face with red lake and white', the second (of 4–6 hours) to 'goe over the face, very curiously observing what soever may condue to the likenes . . . in close sharp and neat workmanship'. The third sitting (of around 2–3 hours 'according to the patience of the sitter') was for adding finishing details and 'giveing to every deepe shadow their strong touches', but this was 'never to be done, til all the apparel, haire and ground be finished.' Norgate 1997, pp.71–80.

22 See www.npg.org.uk/research/programmes/making-art-in-tudor-britain/workshops/workshop-3-abstract-3.php (accessed April 2013).

23 A small group of important surviving English portrait drawings dating from the sixteenth century appear to be the remnants of an artist's studio and are held in the National Portrait Gallery collection. They include coloured face patterns (some of which are silhouetted) depicting St John Fisher after Holbein (NPG 2821), George Talbot, 6th Earl of Shrewsbury (NPG 2822), Sir Henry Sidney (NPG 2823), 'An unknown divine' (NPG 2824) and 'An unknown woman, possibly Elizabeth I' (NPG 2825). The random nature of this selection of sitters, and the fact they are by different artists, indicates that this may be a chance survival of a larger set of drawings used for the production of copies or versions of portraits within an Elizabethan artist's workshop. For the provenance see Roy Strong, *Tudor and Jacobean Portraits* (National Portrait Gallery, London, 1969), vol. 1, p.120.

24 Robert Latham (ed.), *The Diary of Samuel Pepys: A Selection* (Penguin Classics, London, 2003), p.602.

Up and Down the Social Ladder in Elizabethan England

IAN W. ARCHER

ELIZABETHAN SOCIETY WAS dominated by its land-owning elite. They owned two-thirds of the land; they dominated the court, council and parliament, and held the levers of power in the localities, where they often served as Justices of the Peace. At the pinnacle of the landed hierarchy were the fifty-five hereditary peers; beneath them came knights, esquires and mere gentlemen, whose status distinctions correlated roughly with their wealth. Gentlemen probably had average incomes of £200–250 per annum, esquires £500 per annum, and knights £800 upwards. There was, of course, a world of difference between the mighty magnate, such as the 4th Duke of Norfolk (cat. 17a), with an income of £6,000 per annum, who in 'his tennis court at Norwich ... thought himself in a manner equal with some kings', and the struggling mere gentleman at the bottom of the heap, perhaps with an income as low as £80 per annum and distinguishable from his yeomen neighbours only by his coat of arms and sense of lineage.[1] But the landed elite was bound together by a powerful sense of honour. One of the means by which claims to membership of this community were asserted was through portraiture, which might incorporate heraldry-embedding lineage, and which referenced the various virtues through which honour was articulated. There was disagreement about the balance between conventional martial prowess and the virtues based on learning that became more prominent under humanist influences: Thomas Churchyard claimed that 'the pen and the sword can never agree', and in the 1590s these tensions added fuel to the conflict between the military followers of the Earl of Essex (cat. 26) and the bureaucrats allegedly surrounding the Cecils.[2] But the conflict should not be exaggerated: Essex was extremely well educated and attracted leading intellectuals to his orbit. The sociability of hunting, local government institutions like quarter sessions and assizes, and, for the fortunate, the Queen's court, emphasised their solidarity. Claims to gentility were jealously guarded and gentlemen expected deference from their inferiors. Social commentators often resorted to binary divisions – there were gentlemen and there were commoners, them and us.

But the boundary was a permeable one. Gentility, for all that the officers of the Elizabethan College of Arms (or heralds) sought to police it, lacked juridical definition in England. As the cleric William Harrison put it, 'who soever studieth the laws of the realm, who so studieth in the university or professeth physic and the liberal sciences, or ... can live idly and without manual labour, and thereto is able and will bear the port, charge, and countenance of a gentleman, he shall be called master, which is the title that men give to esquires and gentlemen, and reputed for a gentleman'.[3] Being a gentleman was essentially about being accepted as such by other gentlemen, and that meant mastery of the unwritten codes of honour. The number of gentlemen in Elizabeth I's reign proliferated, the heralds making 4,000 grants of arms between 1560 and 1640. Thomas Wilson, Robert Cecil's man of business, estimated that there were 16,500 knights, esquires and gentlemen in 1600, about 2 per cent of the population; he was probably not far off.[4]

This expansion in numbers was, as we shall see, in part a result of the ways in which younger sons were able to reinsert themselves in the ranks of the gentry through the fortunes made in trade and the law. But it also reflected the upward mobility of prospering yeomen able, over the course of a couple of generations, to acquire the trappings of gentility and gain acceptance as gentlemen by others. The key to that rural prosperity was the rising price of agricultural produce. Over the course of Elizabeth's reign the population increased from 2.98 million to 4.1 million, and although agricultural output was rising, it was not rising fast enough to meet this demand, so prices rose. The cost of living for Londoners was about 50 per cent higher by the end of Elizabeth's reign than at her accession. For those who were on the right side of the equation, that is those who were producing a surplus of foodstuffs for sale in the marketplace, this meant rising profits, especially when rents lagged behind.[5] Those dependent on the market, particularly wage labourers, suffered, real wages in London falling by nearly 30 per cent over the reign. Within rural society the key dividing line in terms of economic fortunes was not between gentry and commoners but between yeomen and husbandmen. Yeomen were defined by their superior wealth, by their form of tenure (they were usually freeholders), and by local office-holding, whereas husbandmen tended to be less wealthy and held their land by more restrictive tenures such as copyhold. But another way of expressing this is to say that the yeomanry were commercially market-orientated farmers and the husbandmen were subsistence farmers. It would appear that small farmers, particularly in the sheep-corn districts, were being squeezed out, the harvest failures of the 1590s accelerating the process as husbandmen fell into debt, unable to produce enough grain even to feed their own households. The beneficiaries were, as often as not, the yeomen, whose holdings tended to increase in size. William Harrison, an acute observer, noted their rising living standards, claiming that they 'have for the most part learned ... to garnish their cupboards with plate, their joint beds with tapestry and silk hangings, and their tables with carpets and fine napery'.[6] This is borne out by the evidence of probate inventories: the average number of goods per household increased by 68 per cent in Lincolnshire and 120 per cent in Chesterfield between 1520 and 1600.[7] Although very few yeomen would have owned portraits, they were probably among the consumers of the woodcuts of monarchs that circulated in increasing numbers (although few survive to the present day; see fig. 8). To sum up, rural society was becoming more polarised; the rich got richer and the poor got poorer. And as the yeomen prospered, so they might become assimilated to the gentry.

Rural prosperity, at least for some, assisted the recovery of the urban sector, though its scale should not be exaggerated. The 800 or so market towns benefited from the growth in the agrarian economy and from rising demand for consumer goods. Some regional centres continued to suffer from the competition of industries in the countryside where costs were lower, though some, such as Norwich, were revitalised by the skills brought by immigrants, who fostered the production of new draperies, while others were developing their roles as regional centres for the gentry. All were dwarfed, however, by the monstrous growth of London from about 70,000 people in 1550 to 200,000 in 1600; the next largest city – Norwich – had a population of 15,000 in 1600.[8] London's phenomenal growth was due to two main factors: as a capital city it benefited from the gradual centralisation of government and the increasing propensity of the elites to litigate there, and as a port it benefited from the expansion in cloth exports in the early sixteenth century and in Elizabeth's reign from import-led growth, especially in luxury goods such as silks and wine.

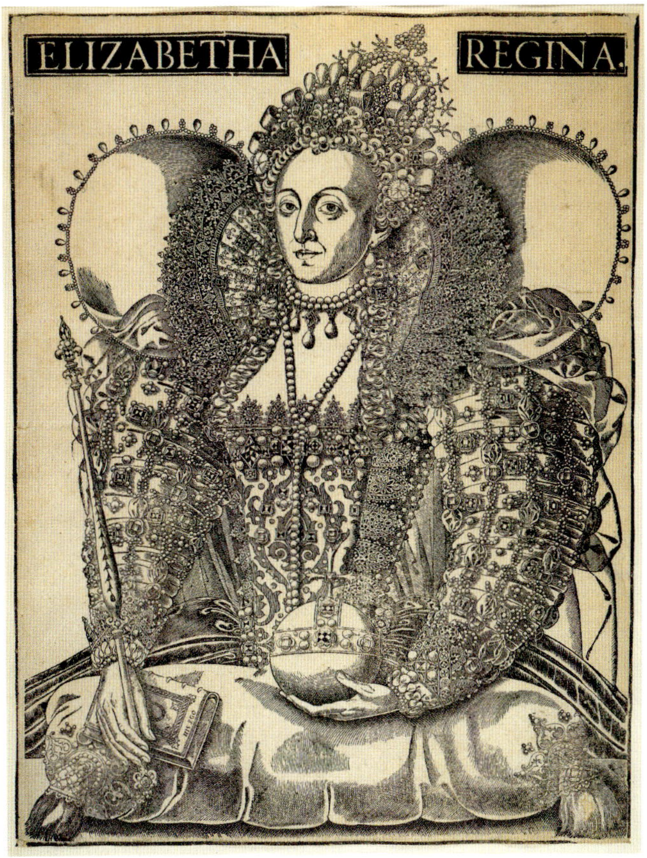

FIG. 8
Woodcut of Elizabeth I
Unknown artist, late sixteenth century

Sir Thomas Gresham (cat. 45), in part because of his capacity for relentless self-promotion, stands out among the merchant princes. The prosperity of the House of Gresham came from the combination of a varied business portfolio, close court connections and kin solidarity. Thomas's father Richard had built up the fortune through the mercery trade, but he also speculated in monastic lands, and he was an intimate of Thomas Cromwell. After an apprenticeship to his uncle John, Thomas Gresham combined overseas trade with service to the Crown as its financial agent in the Netherlands. That Gresham is so well commemorated owes a lot to his foundation of the Royal Exchange (cat. 46) and of Gresham College, but things would have been very different had it not been for the death of his son and heir in 1564, which caused him to re-orientate his goals. More typical among Elizabethan merchants, perhaps, was John Isham (fig. 9), who hailed from a modest gentry background in Northamptonshire; along with two of his brothers, he was apprenticed in the Mercers' Company and traded as a merchant adventurer on the London–Antwerp axis; another brother pursued a legal career and became steward to the Earl of Bedford, a fourth entered the Church. John Isham's working capital, like that of so many, was boosted by his marriage to the widow of a fellow merchant adventurer, and his credit rating was increased by the support of his brothers. But in the 1560s he began to downsize his commercial activities, and in 1572 retreated to the manor of Lamport in his native county, enjoying an income of about £500 per annum, lower than he had enjoyed as a merchant, but perhaps with a lower anxiety level.

Purchases of land by the merchant elite may have been as much a form of risk-spreading as an expression of social aspiration. Commercial fortunes were notoriously fragile, vulnerable to the misfortunes of shipwreck, unreliable business agents and the unravelling of the networks of personal trust on which credit depended. Because of the liability of the guarantors of a loan in the event of its non-payment, the 'breaking' of one merchant could have unexpected knock-on effects through the system. In his portrait medal of 1562 the London goldsmith Richard Martin (cat. 69) looks most self-assured; it was perhaps a slightly pretentious statement (but one presumably arising from his direct associations with the artist) for a young man only a few years out of his apprenticeship, who did not secure the key office of Warden of the Mint until ten years later. Martin enjoyed a glittering civic career, serving twice as Lord Mayor, but in 1602 he went bankrupt and lost his civic office; by the time he died in 1617 he was dependent on a pension supplied by his former colleagues on the aldermanic bench.[9] For many businessmen it was the insecurity bred of the fear of indebtedness (the debtors' prisons, Counters and Ludgate, loomed as large as the Exchange in civic consciousness) rather than a driving sense of upward mobility through accumulated profit that provided the wellsprings of action.

It is clear that a career in trade would not have been attractive to all, not least because of the sneering attitude of social conservatives who claimed that it was incompatible with gentility. As we have seen in the case of the Isham brothers, there were alternative career paths open to younger sons in either the legal profession or the Church. Of these the law was the most lucrative (see cat. 74), and it is noteworthy that elder sons were as prominent among barristers as their younger brothers. Elizabeth's reign witnessed an extraordinary explosion in litigation. We have telling data for the central courts: there were 781 cases at an advanced stage in King's Bench at the beginning of the reign, 6,639 by its end; in Common Pleas the case load grew from 4,497 to 23,147.

At the level of borough courts, which handled small debts among tradesmen, it would appear that virtually all adult males had recourse to litigation. Unsurprisingly, the number of lawyers grew too. Whereas there were 85 calls to the bar in the 1560s, by the 1590s there were 411; there were

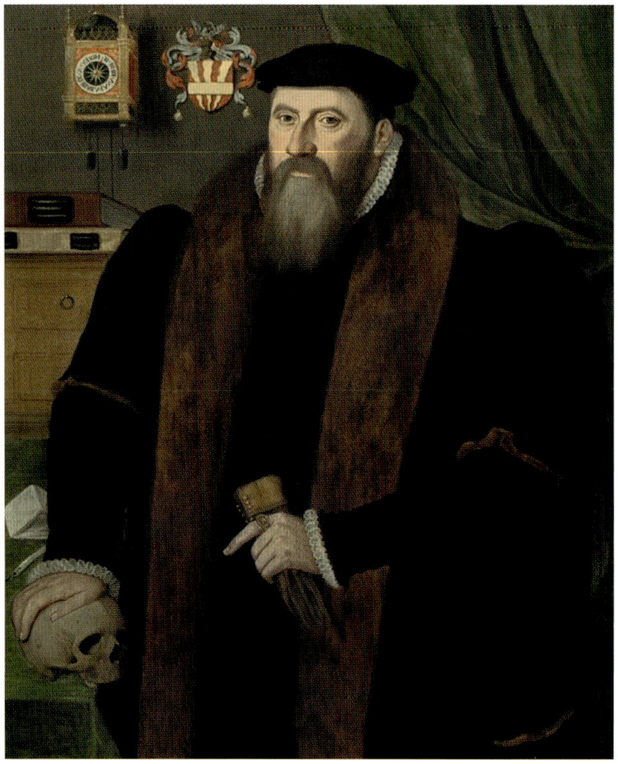

FIG. 9
John Isham, Warden of the Mercers' Company
Unknown English artist, *c.*1567

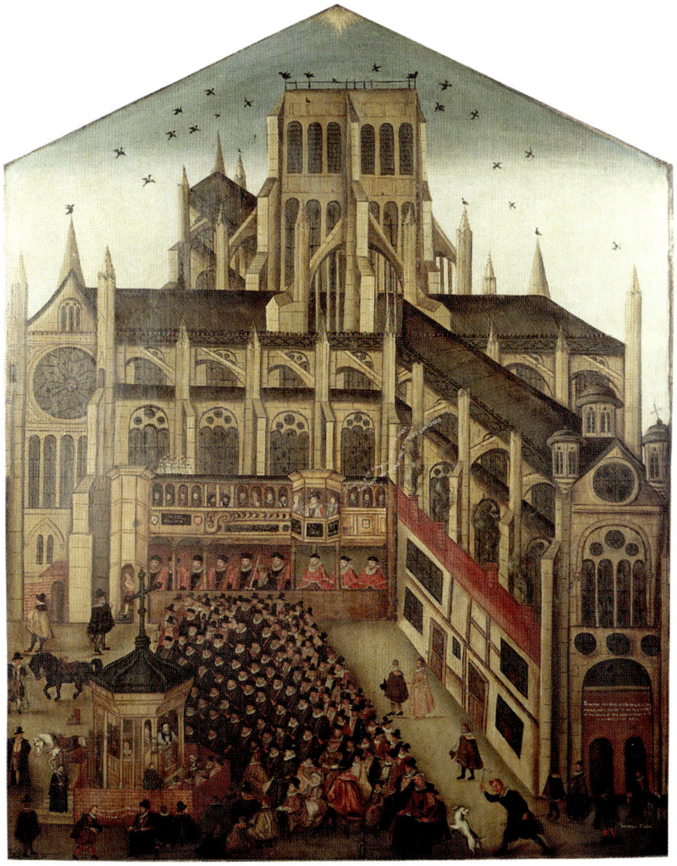

FIG. 10
Dr King preaching at Old St Paul's before James I
John Gipkyn, 1616

Public preaching became increasingly important in the Elizabethan period, and attracted large crowds in urban areas.

probably nearly 500 practising barristers in 1600, a ten-fold increase since 1500 and, according to Wilfred Prest, as many per head of population as in the 1970s. The number of attorneys also grew rapidly. In 1560 there were about 200 attorneys attached to the central courts; by 1606 there were 1,050.[10] The growth of litigation was accompanied by a great deal of criticism about their profiteering which has a rather familiar ring, though in fact in real terms the costs of litigation were falling. It also needs to be emphasised that while there were some fabulously rich lawyers such as Henry Yelverton and Edward Coke, there were others whose fortunes were very modest. Of Richard Langley, town clerk of London, it was noted that although he 'bore a high sail, yet he died a poor man and in debt' in 1612.[11]

The clergy were radically downsized in the course of the Reformation, their numbers being reduced from 35,000 to 15,000, and there remained a strong strain of anti-clericalism marked by scepticism about 'proud prelates', but over the course of the reign the clergy became more like a profession. There were huge problems, not least of which was the inadequacy of many livings for the needs of a preaching ministry: at the beginning of the reign there were complaints about mass ordinations of poorly qualified individuals of lowly status. But there was an enormous drive to evangelise the populace and by 1600 there were many more graduates. Model pastors, such as Henry Birde of Norwich (cat. 75), who were committed to energetic preaching routines, engaged with their communities in charitable and educational provision, and closely allied with the magistracy, were a particular feature of the urban scene (fig. 10). The clerical profession was less obviously a vehicle for upward social mobility. Many clergy were recruited from middling rather than gentle backgrounds, their incomes and lifestyles – their book-lined studies apart – being very similar to those of the yeomanry. But for those at the top of the ecclesiastical hierarchy, the rewards could still be very considerable. For all the asset stripping perpetrated by the Tudor state (Elizabeth was notorious for her unfavourable 'exchanges' of property with her senior clergy), some bishoprics remained choice plums. By favouring his family in the allocation of leases, prebends and church offices, Archbishop Edwin Sandys of York (cat. 73) was somehow able to launch seven sons into county society as well as providing for his two daughters, though the price he paid was a reputation for rapacity, not assisted by his irascible nature. Sandys' case reminds us that another change in the position of the clergy was the fact that after the Reformation they could marry. Some have suggested that this softened the force of the moralists' patriarchal discourse, their experience of marriage producing a stronger emphasis on companionship and mutuality. The practice may in any case have been far more permissive than the rhetoric suggests.

Within elite families, women might share in the running of the estate. Although their property rights were limited at common law, the use of settlements enforceable in the equity courts could give greater financial security. Likewise, the notion that a woman could not trade independently (because under couverture her debts were her husband's) was evaded in some urban jurisdictions. Although most women's work was casual and low paid, and poorer widows would find themselves vulnerable to destitution, widows in the upper echelons could wield considerable power. Joyce Frankland (cat. 53), the daughter of a London goldsmith who had been twice widowed by London clothworker husbands, endowed charities with a value of nearly £5,000, although as with Gresham the impulse was focused by the tragic death of her son. Bess of Hardwick (cat. 28) came from a modest gentry background, but through a series of four advantageous marriages culminating in that with George Talbot, 6th Earl of Shrewsbury, she became a seriously wealthy woman. Once Shrewsbury died in 1590, her income was about £8,000 per annum, about one-third of which came from the Talbot dower lands.

An exhibition looking at Elizabeth's people through the lens of portraiture is bound to focus on the landowners, merchants, artisans and professional elites. There are few visual images of men and women among the group that the leading intellectual Sir Thomas Smith called 'the fourth sort of men which do not rule' and who have 'no voice nor authority in our commonwealth, and no account is to be made of them but only to be ruled'.[12] Their lack of visibility runs the risk of reinforcing contemporary prejudices. Yet evidence of their lives can be found in documentary sources in abundance, including inventories, court records and wills, such as that of one Susan Baker (cat. 87), the dying wife of a poor seaman, or even in material survivals like the remarkable fisherman's outfit (cat. 84). These people were the victims of that process of social polarisation we described earlier: the poor husbandmen forced off the land by indebtedness or the aggressive estate policies of an 'improving' landlord, or the labouring poor who saw their living standards collapsing in the face of rising prices and stagnant wages. The spectre of vagrancy and criminality haunted the Elizabethans, who read with fascinated horror the stories of the criminal underworld popularised by contemporary writers such as Edmund Harman in the so-called cony-catching pamphlets, which offered salutary warnings to the gullible about a host of conmen and petty criminals (fig. 11).[13]

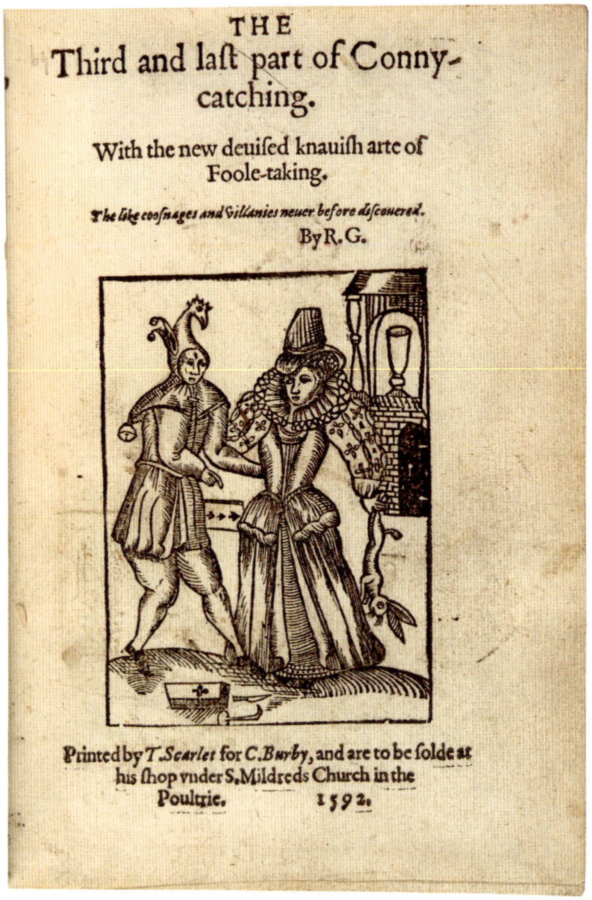

THE
Third and laſt part of Conny-catching.

With the new deuiſed knauiſh arte of Foole-taking.

The like coosnages and villanies neuer before diſcouered.

By R. G.

Printed by T. Scarlet for C. Burby, and are to be ſolde at his ſhop vnder S. Mildreds Church in the Poultrie. 1592.

FIG. 11
Frontispiece to *The Third and last part of Conny-catching. With the new deuised knauish arte of Foole-taking. The like coosnages and villanies never before discouered.*
Robert Greene, 1592

One painting where some people of the so-called 'meaner sort' appear is the *Fête at Bermondsey* (cat. 4), where we do see a cross-section of society. Working people here include the cook and his servants (fig. 12); a maid preparing and serving the feast; and in the background a carter driving his goods to market, a porter carrying goods on his head, watermen on the river, and a group of carpenters cutting wood in the distance. Beside the cookshop is a pair of stocks with one of the victims of Tudor justice (fig. 13): is he a tradesman convicted of selling goods by fraudulent measures, an obstreperous neighbour who has crossed the threshold of local tolerance, or a vagrant or conman like those described by Harman? We do not know. The social status of others shown here was sometimes contested. Where did the group of musicians, figured on the right (see fig. 26 on p.40), fit into the social hierarchy? Towns maintained groups of approved musicians called 'waits', and many gentlemen paid fees to musicians, but wandering minstrels were labelled as vagrants. Where, for that matter, did the artist fit in? If the figure looking out at us by the tree is, as is commonly believed, a self-portrait of the artist Joris Hoefnagel, are we looking at just another guildsman, a working craftsman painting to demand, or are we looking at an artist whose creativity and originality might enable him to be accepted among his gentle and noble patrons? His appearance in the painting, perhaps commissioned by William Cecil (cat. 19), might suggest the latter. Or was the

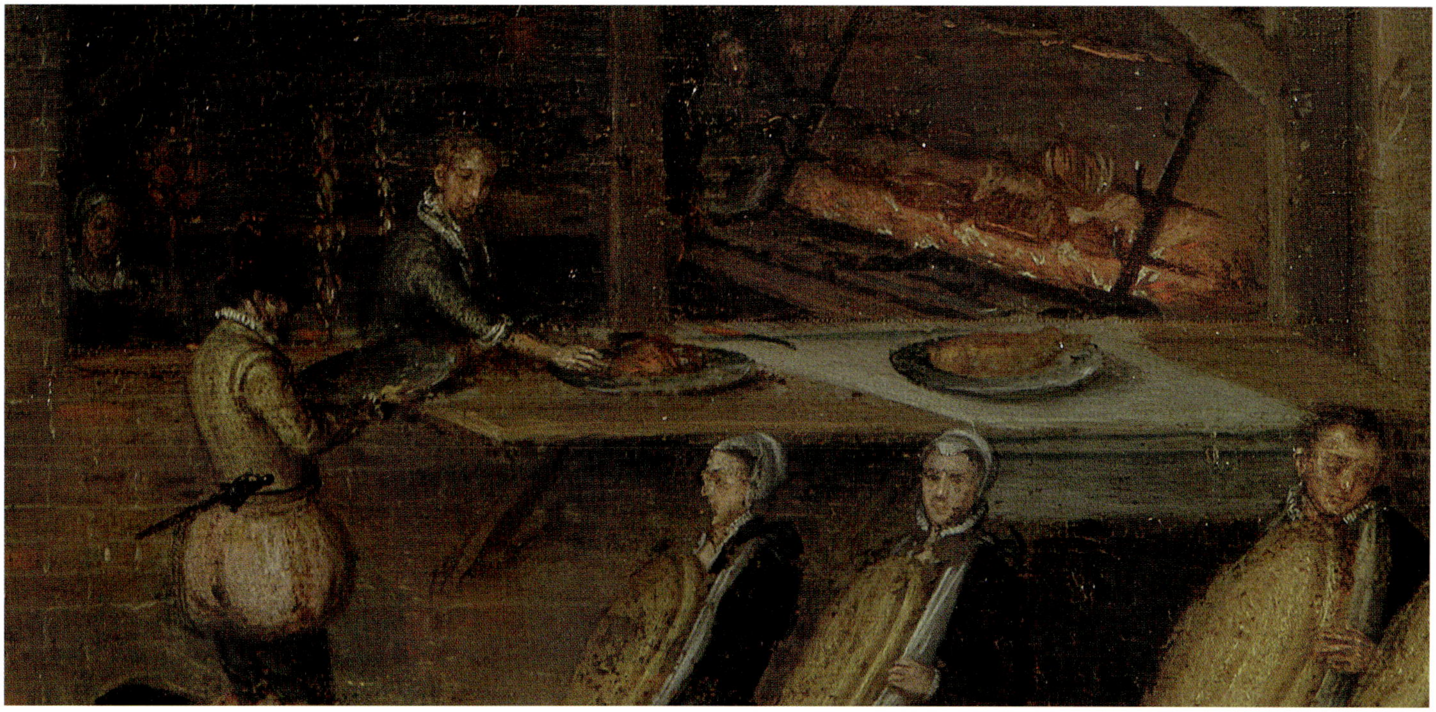

salient element of his identity the fact that he was an alien, subject to a raft of discriminatory legislation and abused in the London streets by apprentices? There are many puzzles, but rare genre paintings such as this give us fascinating glimpses of the wider social world of Elizabethan England.

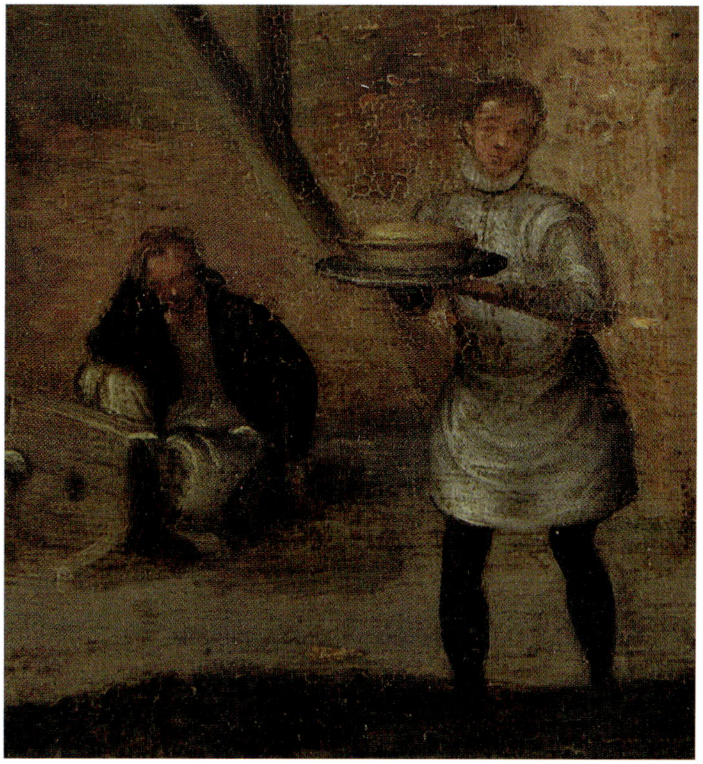

FIGS 12 and 13
Details from *A Fête at Bermondsey* (cat. 4)
Joris Hoefnagel, *c.*1568–70

1 W. Camden, *The historie of the most renowned and victorious princesse Elizabeth*, trans. R.N. [R. Norton] (London, 1630), p.130.
2 T. Churchyard, *A general rehearsall of warres* ... (London, 1579), sigs. Miiiv–Ni.
3 W Harrison, *The Description of England*, ed. Georges Edelen (Washington DC, 1968), pp.113–14.
4 *English Historical Documents V(A), 1558–1603*, ed. Ian W. Archer and F. Douglas Price (2011), p.470.
5 Keith Wrightson, *English Society 1580–1680* (1982), ch. 5.
6 Harrison, *Description*, p.200.
7 Craig Muldrew, *The Economy of Obligation: The Culture of Credit and Social Relations in Early Modern England* (1998), pp.24–9.
8 David M. Palliser, *The Age of Elizabeth: England under the Later Tudors, 1547–1603* (London, 1992), p.203.
9 ODNB; LMA, COL/CA/01/01/034, f. 63.
10 C.W. Brooks, *Pettyfoggers and Vipers of the Commonwealth: the 'Lower Branch' of the Legal Profession in Early Modern England* (Cambridge, 1986), pp.50–4; Wilfred Prest, *The Rise of the Barristers: A Social History of the English Bar 1590–1640* (Oxford, 1986), pp.6–7.
11 *The Letters of John Chamberlain*, ed. N.M. McClure (2 vols., Philadelphia, 1939), i. 440.
12 T. Smith, *De Republica Anglorum*, ed. Mary Dewar (Cambridge, 1982), p.76.
13 Thomas Harman, *A caveat for commen cursetors vulgarely called vagabones* (1567).

Personhood in the Age of Reformation

LENA COWEN ORLIN

IF YOU WANT TO KNOW where privacy was born, it was England. So says the premier historian of private life in the Western world, Philippe Ariès. Of the many sorts of privacy, that most often associated with the Renaissance is what might also be called subjectivity. Ariès refers to the personal diaries and memoirs that appeared earlier among the English than other Europeans, beginning at about the time Elizabeth I came to the throne.[1]

If you want to know when privacy was born, however, you might look back to the reign of her father, Henry VIII. In 1532 Henry made his last-ditch attempts to persuade Pope Clement VII that the Vatican had erred in authorising Henry's marriage to his brother's widow, Catherine of Aragon. The King wrote that to continue to obey the Pope would 'offend God and our conscience'. Papal legate Lorenzo Campeggio had warned Clement that 'if an angel was to descend from heaven, he would not be able to persuade' Henry that the marriage was legitimate, so certain was the King in his heart.[2]

Henry personally assured Clement that, failing mitigation, he would disobey 'with charity, not intending to spread it abroad'. It is hard to think of anything that was less private in early modern England, and the public consequences of the King's domestic crisis were vast. He broke with Rome, divorced Catherine, married Anne Boleyn, fathered Elizabeth, and in 1534 was declared by Parliament to be Supreme Head of the Church of England (fig. 14). All of Elizabeth I's people were heirs to the years of turbulence that followed from what was called Henry's 'Great Matter'.

The first effects of the schism were not religious, as Henry had few doctrinal differences with Rome. Indeed, about a decade earlier, the Vatican had declared him 'Defender of the Faith' for writing a polemic maintaining the supremacy of the Pope and condemning the reforms of Martin Luther. England's 1534 Act of Supremacy, which was devised for parliamentary endorsement by Thomas Cromwell, was about power rather than religion. Associating the papacy with 'foreign laws' and 'foreign authority', it introduced a view of English exceptionalism that intersected with a rising interest in national self-identity. This was to play out in published chronicles such as Edward Hall's *Union of the Two Noble and Illustre Families of Lancaster and York* (1548), Richard Grafton's *Abridgement of the Chronicles of England* (1562), Raphael Holinshed's *Chronicles of England, Scotland, and Ireland* (1577) and also the stage histories written by Shakespeare and others in the 1590s. Cromwell further mandated, in 1538, that parish clerks should maintain registers of all baptisms, marriages and burials, and in 1560 Elizabeth I would issue a proclamation warning Protestant iconoclasts not to destroy tombstones and monuments. To do so would 'darken' the 'true understanding of divers families in this realm'.[3] Narratives of the past encouraged all individuals to have a sense of ownership in a national story, while the new habits of recording and memorialising created a place for every individual in history.

Henry's consolidation of political and religious power had extensive economic repercussions as well. Taking command of the Church, he also commandeered its holdings. These included monasteries, abbeys, nunneries, chantries and lands that had been donated by the faithful – as much as a third of all property in England. At first Henry thought of his acquisitions in the old way, as part of the royal patrimony, some portions of which he might selectively bestow on those he wished to reward. Dominion had otherwise seemed inalienable, mostly descending within established families via inheritance. It may not have been profit alone that inspired Henry to begin to see things differently; the administrative burden of his vast and sudden acquisitions was crushing. But the end result was profit, as he decided to make seized Church properties available for sale. The process of commodification was another epochal change. Thinking about land had been almost magical, but now it was within reach, at a price, to individuals who would once have had no chance of ownership. In an expanding, proto-capitalist economy, with unprecedented opportunities in the professions and in trade, there was a corresponding broadening of access to the privilege of proprietorship. The sell-off continued across the reigns of all Henry's children. For those above the poverty line, these were heady new horizons of expectation.

The break with Rome had another important consequence for private life. A subtext of the Act of Supremacy was the notion that the king derived his authority from God. It was generally presumed that he did not require the consent of his people to govern, but, given that this was a power grab of unprecedented proportions, there developed an extensive ideological apparatus to promulgate the king's rights and, in effect, secure popular consent. Tudor philosophy held that the entire cosmos was an interlocking system of hierarchies: the universe was ruled by God, the kingdom by the king, the family by the father, the body by the head.[4] As perhaps the least mystical of the hierarchies, the household structure thus served to ground royal prerogative in common experience. Further, since the fifth Commandment dictated obedience to mother and father, so, too, the Bible, otherwise inconveniently silent on this subject, could by analogy be understood to enjoin obedience to the monarch. The household had a mixed identity in that it was conceived not only this way, as a counterpart to the kingdom, but also, at the same time, as a component part of it. Both notions elevated and empowered the household in new ways; every householder was like a king in his own 'petty commonwealth', 'his house was his castle', and he held a share of responsibility for the larger social order.[5] Another arm of the nascent publishing industry was devoted to domestic advice, such as Miles Coverdale's translation of *The Christen State of Matrimony* (1541), Henry Smith's *Preparative for Marriage* (1591), John Dod and Robert Cleaver's *Godly Form of Household Government* (1598) and many more.

As the titles of these guidebooks suggest, the amalgamation of Church and State meant that there was a religious cast to social and political thought. Almost in spite of himself, Henry had also set the country on a path to religious reform. The Bible was first translated into English in 1537, and in 1538 Thomas Cromwell instructed that every church

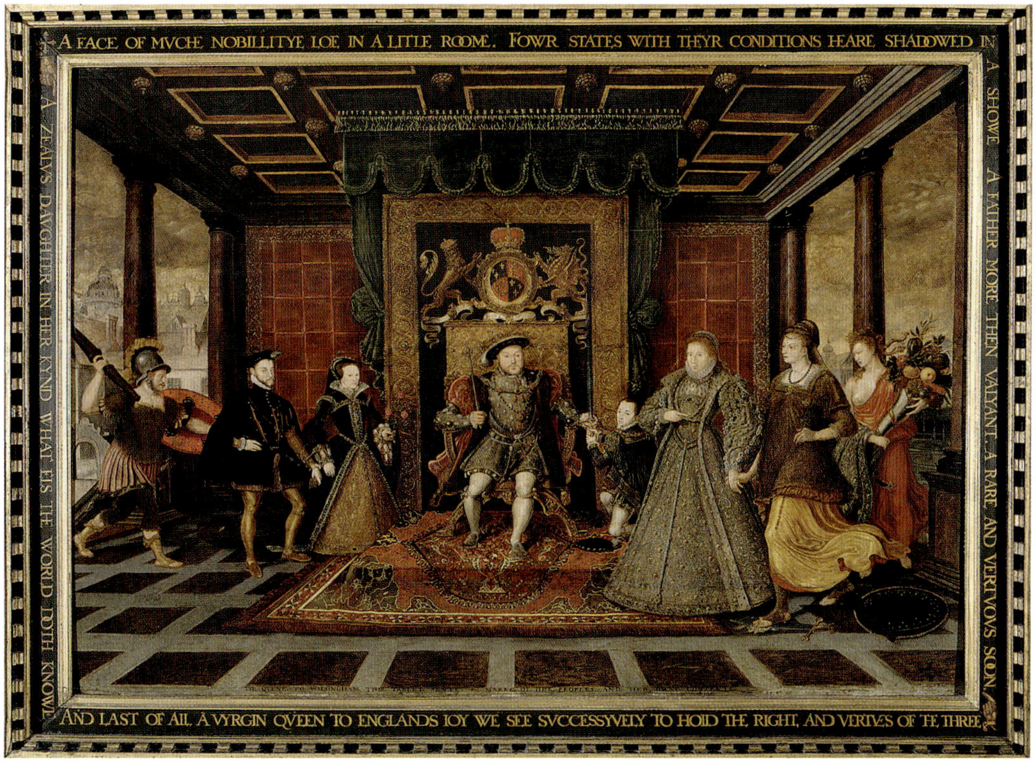

FIG. 14
The Family of Henry VIII: An Allegory of the Tudor Succession
Lucas de Heere, *c.*1570–5

In this dynastic portrait, Henry VIII is shown with all his children. At the centre, he hands the sword of justice to his kneeling son, Edward. To the left, Mary and her husband, Philip of Spain, are accompanied by the war god, Mars. To the right, Elizabeth stands with Peace clasping her hand and Plenty nearby.

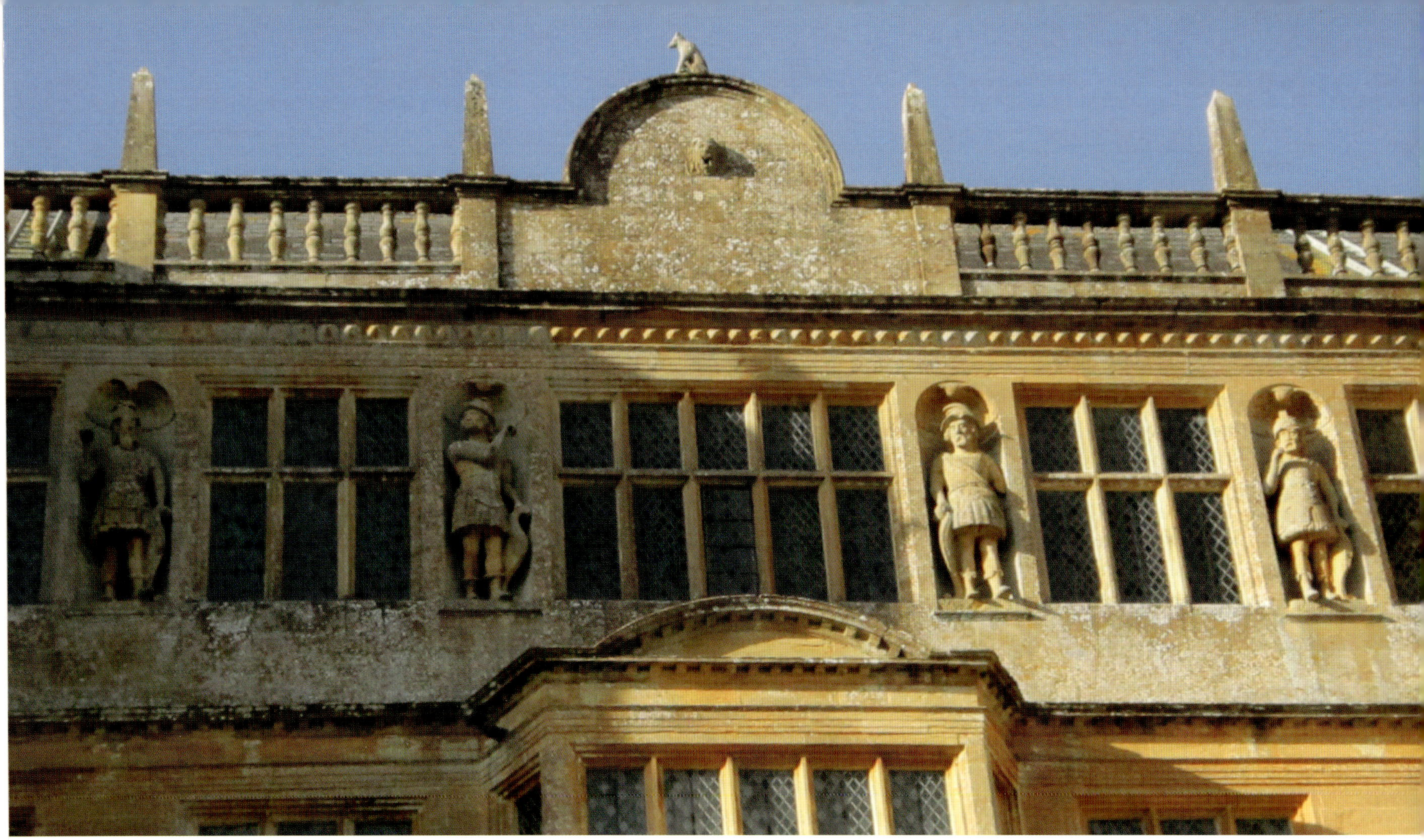

FIG. 20
Four of the Nine Worthies that embellish the East Front of Montacute House, Somerset. All the figures are depicted as classical Roman soldiers.

unobjectionable distinction from the discarded saints. Individuals could also compose their own pantheons of inspiration from among their contemporaries. In Thomas Heywood's 1605 play *If You Know Not Me, You Know Nobody*, the purported dean of St Paul's shows visitors his portrait gallery, with a collection of charitable Londoners, both men and women, from whom to 'learn to refresh your souls'.[14] This was another aspect of fame, that the viewer of a portrait could measure himself against the subject depicted.

To commission a portrait was a measuring act, too. Thomas Whithorne (fig. 15), who left what many regard as the first full-length autobiography, sat for one painting to learn how a period of illness had affected him as well as to judge the effects of age. For Whithorne a mirror image was treacherous in its temporality. It showed 'the disposition of the face for the time present, and not as it was in time past'. A portrait did not vary with time; it marked a moment in time, and became a lasting standard of reference, a memento for absent friends, and a memorial for survivors. It was also superior to a mirror, Whithorne wrote, because the glass 'showeth the face the contrary way, that is to say, that which seemeth to be the right side of the face is the left side in deed; and so likewise that which seemeth to be the left side is the right'.[15] In a portrait, in other words, Whithorne could be sure that he was seeing himself as others saw him. This sort of concern for one's fame made the individualism of the Renaissance a layered thing, a composition of reception and projection as well as expression.

Whithorne had yet another use for portraiture, adding a woodcut to his 1590 volume, *Cantus and Bassus of Duos, or Songs for two voices* (cat. 81b). He was a musician in unsettled circumstances, endlessly in search of a patron, and he knew that his reputation was not in his sole control. In the post-Reformation church-court culture, fame was community property. Whithorne suggested that the portrait was educational, demonstrating the dress, ornaments and arms associated with gentility. But it was declarative, too, an attempt to create his own fame and show what he called 'the outward marks as in the inward man'.[16] An important way to look at Tudor paintings is to consider the artistry of the sitters as well as the painters, for what these subjects chose to communicate, through their poses, costumes and accessories, about their standing and their subjecthood. Portraiture was one place where the ideas of inwardness and self-performance met.

1 Philippe Ariès, 'Introduction' to Roger Chartier (ed.), *A History of Private Life, iii: Passions of the Renaissance*, trans. Arthur Goldhammer (Harvard University Press, Cambridge MA, 1989), p.5.

2 Henry's letter (BL MS Harleian Vitellius B.13:168) has been transcribed by Gilbert Burnet, *The History of the Reformation of the Church of England* (London, 1681), pp.108–10. Campeggio's report can be found in *The Letters of King Henry VIII*, ed. M. St Clare Byrne (Cassell, London, 1936), p.86.

3 From *A Proclamation against Breakinge or Defacing of Monumentes of Antiquitie, beyng set up in Churches or other Publique Places for Memory and not for Superstición* (London, 1560).

4 The classic account of such analogical thinking is in E.M.W. Tillyard, *The Elizabethan World Picture* (Vintage, New York, 1959).

5 Both quoted phrases were proverbial during Elizabeth's reign. Among many who described the household as a 'petty' or 'little' commonwealth were John Dod and Robert Cleaver in *A Godly Form of Household Government* (London, 1598), sig. B1^{r}. The great jurist Edward Coke famously declared that 'the house of every one is to him his castle and fortress, as well for defense against injury and violence as for his repose' in his Report on Semayne's Case of 1605 (*Reports of Sir Edward Coke* [1658], sig. Pp3^{r}), but legal precedents can be traced back to 1505.

6 James M. Osborne (ed.) *The Autobiography of Thomas Whythorne* (Modern Spelling Edition, Oxford University Press, 1962), p.116.

7 Henry VIII's Lord Chancellor Sir Thomas More refused to take the oath of Royal Supremacy and was beheaded in 1535; in 1553, during the different political climate of Mary I's reign, More's son-in-law William Roper was able to describe this as a Catholic martyrdom in his *Life of Sir Thomas More*. Anne Askew was also executed by Henry VIII, but for being too zealous a Protestant. She was burnt at the stake in 1546; in 1547 John Bale published a transcript of her trial in *The First Examination of the Worthy Servant of God, Mistress Anne Askew, Lately Martyred in Smithfield by the Romish Pope's Upholders*. John Foxe compiled a massive history of religious persecution that began with the early Christians but is most famous for documenting Protestant suffering under Mary, including that of her half-sister, Elizabeth. The first edition of the *Acts and Monuments of Martyrs, with a General Discourse of these Latter Persecutions, Horrible Troubles, and Tumults Stirred Up by Romish Prelates in the Church*, published in 1563, had 1,800 pages. In 1571 it was ordered that every cathedral and collegiate church should make publicly available a copy of 'Foxe's Book of Martyrs'.

8 Francis Bacon, 'A Discourse in Praise of Queen Elizabeth', *The Works of Francis Bacon*, 10 vols, vol. 3 (W. Baynes, London, 1824), p.73.

9 For Jacob Burckhardt, *The Civilization of the Renaissance in Italy* (published as *Kultur der Renaissance in Italien* in 1905) was inextricable from 'The Development of the Individual' (the title of a section of this influential book). The idea was picked up by, among others, Erving Goffman in *The Presentation of the Self in Everyday Life* (Doubleday, New York, 1969), and was applied to English history by Stephen Greenblatt in *Renaissance Self-Fashioning: From More to Shakespeare* (University of Chicago Press, Chicago, 1980) and Michael Mascuch in *Origins of the Individualist Self: Autobiography and Self-Identity in England, 1591–1791* (Stanford University Press, Stanford, 1996). Christopher Hill also discusses a 'rise of the spirit of individualism' in *Society and Puritanism in Pre-Revolutionary England* (Secker and Warburg, London, 1964), p.469.

10 Ernst Cassirer, *Mythical Thought*, vol. 2 of *The Philosophy of Symbolic Forms*, trans. Ralph Manheim (Yale University Press, New Haven CT, 1955), p.137.

11 See especially Natalie Zemon Davis, 'Women on Top', in *Society and Culture in Early Modern France* (Stanford University Press, Stanford, 1975), p.140. Despite the title, she describes rough ridings in England and Scotland, speculating that the name 'skimmington' came from 'the big skimming ladle sometimes used by women in beating their husbands'.

12 For the language and prosecution of sexual slander see Laura Gowing, *Domestic Dangers: Women, Words, and Sex in Early Modern London* (Oxford University Press, Oxford, 1996).

13 See Lena Cowen Orlin, *Locating Privacy in Tudor London* (Oxford University Press, Oxford, 2007), ch. 1.

14 Thomas Heywood, *If You Know Not Me, You Know Nobody, Part II*, ed. Madeleine Doran (Malone Society Reprints, Oxford, 1935), II, 759–63.

15 *The Autobiography of Thomas Whythorne*, p.115. For more on Whithorne, see the Introduction in James M. Osborne's 'Old Spelling' edition of *The Autobiography* (Oxford University Press, Oxford, 1961).

16 Whithorne explains: 'And because that the users of those books should see that, as in the beginning of them I do add unto my name the title of a gentleman, so I mean to show myself to be one, as well in the outward marks as in the inward man' (p.175).

What the Elizabethans Wore: Evidence from Wills and Inventories of the 'Middling Sort'

SUSAN NORTH

THE EXTRAORDINARY RICHNESS of the dress of Elizabethan royalty and aristocracy is well documented in both visual and manuscript sources, and forms the focus of dress histories of this period.[1] In terms of surviving examples of English dress, the Elizabethan period is much more sparsely represented than the seventeenth century.[2] Assessing the dress of the non-elite classes of Elizabethan society is particularly difficult. While portraits of members of the middling sort, particularly those connected to the Church and local government, exist in considerable numbers, they have been photographed and published only recently, allowing analysis of the clothing depicted.[3] In turn, very few sixteenth-century English genre scenes survive that illustrate the dress of ordinary Elizabethans, *A Fête at Bermondsey* being a rare example (cat. 4).

However, wills and probate inventories provide some idea of what those of the labouring, trade and professional classes wore in sixteenth-century England.[4] Social historians have used such records for information on the material life of the non-elite, despite certain exclusions of class (the very poor), gender (married women) and types of wealth (land and buildings).[5] Wills and inventories provide a fascinating window, however imperfect, into the domestic comforts of ordinary Elizabethans. Dress historians have shown the value of using wills to illustrate non-elite English dress in the sixteenth century.[6] Although most probate inventories simply lump clothing and cash together as 'his apparel and his purse', a few do offer detailed lists of dress. Between one and two million probate inventories exist in English archives – far too many for a single study. This short essay relies mainly on those that have been published, some 600 inventories, which provide a sample of locale, occupation and social status.[7] In the analysis of men's dress, the wills and inventories have been roughly categorised according to occupation, taking into account the considerable overlaps in wealth and flexibility in class definitions, discussed by Ian W. Archer on pp.20–5.

These records demonstrate the complexity of the relationship between dress and social status. Increased wealth in any class could be expressed sartorially in a number of ways: by acquiring a greater number of garments of the same type, by purchasing clothing made of more expensive materials, by acquiring garments in more fashionable styles, or by buying a wider variety of accessories. The documents reveal the workings of all these strategies, and each played its role in the intricate process of dressing one's part in Elizabethan England. Clothing was subject to sumptuary law – statutes continuing from the reign of Henry VIII and those passed by Elizabeth I – restricting textiles worked with precious metals and imported fabrics to particular levels of society associated with either rank, property or income.[8]

Elizabethan men and dress

For all men of this period, the doublet and hose/breeches were the main items of dress, along with gowns and cassocks for certain classes and professions. Men wore a variety of outer garments: cloaks, jerkins, jackets and coats, all of which can be seen on many of the figures depicted in *A Fête at Bermondsey*, although precise definitions of these are unclear.[9] The terminology for both men's and women's dress of this period is often confusing, and the precise shapes and styles of the garments listed in inventories are rarely described. Although portraits illustrate a variety of dress, they do not identify the names of the garments depicted. Nor are there any sixteenth-century English tailoring manuals that would connect a particular style with a contemporary name. Although terms such as 'jacket' and 'gown' are still in use today, they do not necessarily refer to the same style as they did in the Elizabethan period. The distinctions between men's jackets, coats and jerkins appear to be based on how long they were, the presence of sleeves and how fitted each was; however, the many references in wills and inventories to 'sleeveless coats' and 'jerkins with sleeves' only complicate these definitions. Headwear – in the form of knitted caps or felted beaver hats – and shoes or boots were also essential, while linen shirts formed the basic underwear; girdles (belts) and purses were regularly worn.

Husbandmen and labourers

Labourers and husbandmen are the most humble members of society represented in inventories and wills. The inventory of Nicholas Bacon exemplifies the minimum: 'A Jakyt [jacket], a dublett [doublet], a payre of hoose [hose], shert [shirt], a cappe, a payre of shoes, a gyrdle and a kniffe'.[10] Yorkshire dalesman Galfryde Calvert had a more extensive wardrobe, with one old red jacket, one old frieze (a thick hairy wool) jacket, two pairs of old white hose, a camlet (silk/wool) doublet, a leather doublet, two pairs of old frieze slops (loose breeches), a pair of boots, a belt and a dagger, two swords and a sword belt, two old shirts, a pair of spurs, one old hat and a night cap, an old jerkin, and two cloaks.[11] Swords were the accessories of gentlemen, as well as those aspiring to be, and the two in Calvert's inventory are intriguing; did he actually wear these or were they a gift or inheritance that he intended to sell on?[12]

Calvert's inventory mentions colours and materials, and such details occasionally emerge from other examples: warm, sturdy wools such as frieze, worsted and russet, and heavy hempen fabrics like canvas and sackcloth.[13] Buckskin was likely to have been more highly valued than leather from sheep or cows and possibly demonstrated the wearer's hunting prowess. Colours are rarely mentioned; 'white' was probably undyed and blue was usually associated with livery or servant's dress.[14] Two Surrey inventories cite coats, hose and jerkins of 'rycot' – a patchwork or variegated pattern.[15]

Yeomen

The yeoman 'lifestyle' of rural farming was the same as that of a husbandman, the former, however, being a land-holder and usually (but not always) wealthier in material possessions.[16] The apparel of one Surrey yeoman comprised two coats, a cloak, three pairs of breeches, a leather jerkin, two doublets, two pairs of stockings, a hat, cap, girdle and pouch, two pairs of shoes and a pair of boots.[17] A number of inventories list two of each garment, and wills distinguish 'workaday' from 'Sunday best'. Roland Nell of Derbyshire had roughly the same types of garments, but more of each and a wider range of accessories, including 'A paire of blewe frenche hose', '7 shirtes with bandes [collars] and ruffes', as well as a sword and dagger.[18] Like the husbandmen, yeomen wore not only canvas, leather, worsted, russet and frieze, but also the better quality fustian (linen/cotton), kersey and stammel (wools), camlet and rash (wool/silk).[19] Gowns – garments associated with leisure and/or the professions

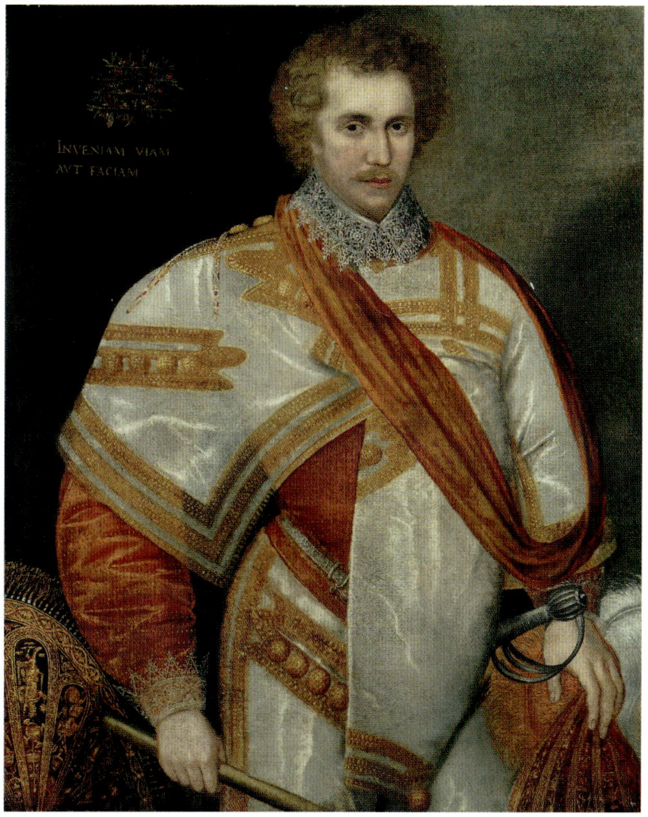

FIG. 21
Robert Sidney, 1st Earl of Leicester, showing a 'mandillion' jacket.
Unknown artist, *c.*1588

conducted sitting down – appear in a few yeomen inventories, some lined with fur.[20] Richard Bynks of Yorkshire bequeathed his 'best furred gowne lyned with conie [rabbit]' and Humphrey Carr of Newcastle his 'foxefurred gowne' and a 'blake gowne furred with lambe'.[21] According to sumptuary laws passed in 1533, yeomen were only allowed lamb or rabbit; strictly speaking, Carr's fox fur was illegal.[22]

A few examples of more fashionable dress appear in some yeoman inventories: the ruffs that accompanied Roland Nell's shirts and his 'frenche hose'; William Kytchiner's 'mandilion' – a fashionable jacket with hanging sleeves, as can be seen in fig. 21; the holland band (a very fine linen shirt collar) and a velvet purse that belonged to another yeoman.[23] References to 'riding geare and all the raiment that I did ride withal, that is to saye, dublett, hoose, jacket and jerkine, one hatt, with one brooche sworde and dagger' represented the wealth required to own a horse, in addition to the practice of yeomen wearing swords.[24]

Craftsmen

Wills and inventories also provide information about a range of craftsmen and artisans and their dress. These include those involved with textiles and clothing – tailors, glovers, shoemakers, weavers, fullers (who finished wool fabrics after weaving) and shear men; those employed in the smithing and woodworking crafts – blacksmiths, loriners (who made iron parts of saddles and bridles for horses), armourers, bell-founders, joiners, carpenters and shipwrights; together with a brewer, barber, butcher, cooper, miller and saddler. In terms of dress and domestic comfort, most were on par with husbandmen. For example, the inventory of shoemaker John Wilshire lists two each of cloaks, coats, doublets, hose and stockings, three shirts, a hat and shoes.[25] Those working in the textile and clothing crafts occasionally reveal an awareness of fashion; a Yorkshire fuller owned 'a pair pincke [pinked] hose' – breeches embellished with a pattern of decorative holes.[26] The will of a Newcastle tailor included a taffeta doublet, a hat lined with velvet, a Spanish leather jerkin, violet breeches and stockings.[27] On the other hand, every item of apparel – doublet, hose, stockings, shoes, hat, sword and daggers – in the 1598 inventory of a deceased, indebted London tailor was described as 'ould'.[28]

A few well-off craftsmen had clothes of silk, coloured with expensive dyestuffs and trimmed with lace; anyone earning over £200 per annum was allowed the same clothing as sons of barons and knights.[29] Income is never explicitly indicated in probate inventories, so it is not clear if 'a violet greyne gowne' (a gown dyed violet with an expensive dyestuff), satin doublet and damask jerkin belonging to a Worcester pewterer and bell-founder were within sumptuary law.[30]

Tradesmen and merchants

The wills and inventories of clothiers, grocers, ironmongers, undefined 'small tradesmen' and others providing services, such as innkeepers, show that their wardrobes were equivalent to those of yeomen. A few, with more extensive inventories, have more clothes, made of more expensive materials and in fashionable styles. The inventory of a Stratford-upon-Avon innkeeper featured '10 shirtes, 13 ruff bandes, a greene jerkyn, a coate of medley [multi-coloured] clothe, a tufte[d] taffita cloke', ' Spanishe lether jerkin', 'a cloke, French tawny', 'a gowne furred with fox', 'a gowne of browne blew, lyned with lambe and faced with foynes (marten fur)'.[31]

The inventories of merchants living in Newcastle-upon-Tyne and Southampton, two major trading ports, demonstrate the extent of their accumulated wealth. Southampton merchant Richard Goddard had the most impressive wardrobe with eleven doublets, four pairs of breeches and thirteen of hose, seven gowns, two cassocks, three jerkins, three cloaks, five jackets and three coats, along with numerous accessories including four girdles, eighteen night caps, two felt hats, two 'Scottish' caps and nine pairs of gloves. Materials used included the practical worsteds, canvas, fustians and broadcloths as well as silk weaves of damask, satin, taffeta and grosgrain. The trimmings of these garments – such as fringing, woven laces, facings (borders) of silk and velvet, silver buttons and clasps – also indicate a degree of luxury.[32] From the values of their estates, these very wealthy merchants were probably earning more than £200 per annum and were therefore entitled to wear velvet, leopard fur and gold embroidery.[33] However, very few textiles worked with precious metal appear in their wardrobes, which were ample and varied, but modest in fabric and embellishment.

Professionals

Forming another group of similar status were those involved with the Church, law and medicine; most were country vicars, rectors or parsons (see cats 73–6 and 79). Richard Whitworthe of Derbyshire was among the poorest, but his wardrobe included six wool gowns, one cloak, two hoods, two coats, two doublets, three pairs of hose, two caps, two surplices, three shirts, two pairs of shoes and a velvet night cap.[34] Gowns, cassocks and hoods distinguish this group, particularly those who had attended university (cats 73–6). George Nevill was Doctor of Divinity and Master of the Hospital at Well in Yorkshire, and his inventory listed a scarlet gown (indicative of his status as Doctor of Divinity), five cassocks – one of velvet, one grosgrain, one worsted and two 'old' – and his 'Devinitie hood'.[35] The inventory of a Lincoln's Inn lawyer included 'his best barister gowne', 'a tufted velvet jerken, his best saten dublet, his worste saten dublet', 'hose and dublett new of silk rashe', 'velvet breaches plain', and 'Barister gownes, two'.[36] A Lancashire schoolmaster had a much more modest wardrobe, with only two gowns but 'handruffs' and a satin doublet and breeches.[37] Another example of a satin doublet can be seen in Isaac Oliver's portrait of the Browne brothers (fig. 22, cat. 30)

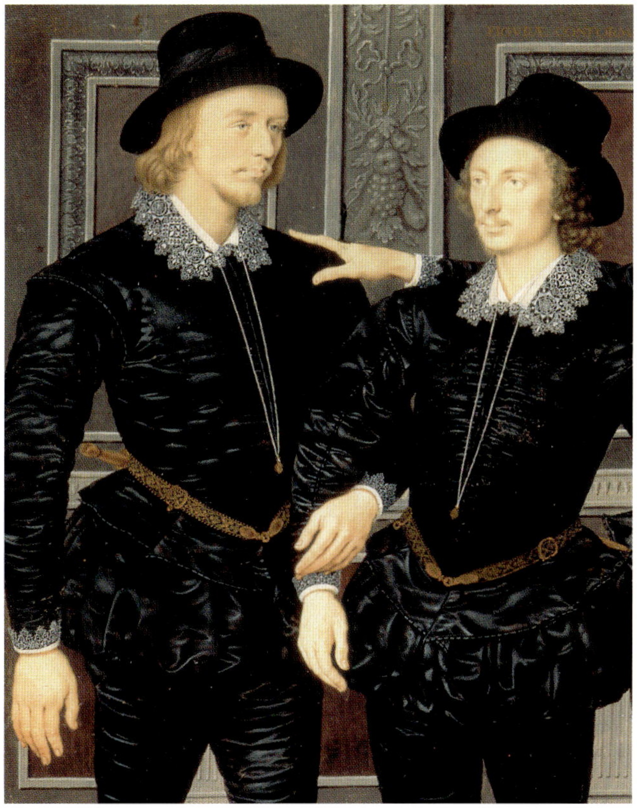

FIG. 22
Detail from *Anthony, John and William Browne with an Unidentified Man* (cat. 30), showing satin doublets.
Isaac Oliver, dated 1598

The gentry

As Ian W. Archer has discussed, the category of 'gentlemen' is difficult to define. In wills, such a term might be applied by the testator himself, but not necessarily by those compiling his inventory. Some of the 'gentlemen' appear no better off than the poorer yeomen and none of the inventories examined listed as much clothing as that of Southampton merchant Richard Goddard. Nevertheless, there are subtle indications of higher status in the materials used, especially furs, as well as the colours and decoration of their clothing. The inventory of Thomas Myddelton of Yorkshire, 'gentleman', included 'cremysene velvet bryches', and 'a cremysene velvet cotte of clothe of gold'.[38] Velvet was one of the most expensive types of silk, 'cremysene' was silk dyed with a costly red dyestuff, 'cloth of gold' was silk woven with threads wrapped in thin layers of gold-plated silver – all materials that were restricted by sumptuary law to dukes and marquesses.[39] Myddelton clearly owned garments well above his station, but he may have received them as gifts or payment while in service to the Marquess of Northampton, and as long as he did not *wear* them, he was not violating sumptuary law.[40]

The clothing of gentlemen was often more decorative, with silk fringes, woven laces and slashing, as seen in the miniature of Francis Drake (cat. 24) and listed in Sir Roger Woodhouse's inventory as a 'blacke Satten Dublet cutt' (see also fig. 22).[41] Scarlet gowns, like that of Serjeant William Lovelace (cat. 73) were the official robes of such civic offices and they appear in the 1599 inventory of Sir Thomas Ramsey, who was Lord Mayor of London in 1577. He owned three – one lined with marten fur, another faced with black velvet, and an 'olde' one – as well as three violet gowns and five black gowns, all lined or faced with fur or silk. Also listed was an 'olde dublet of purple satten', but his new doublets were of modest fustian or wool.[42]

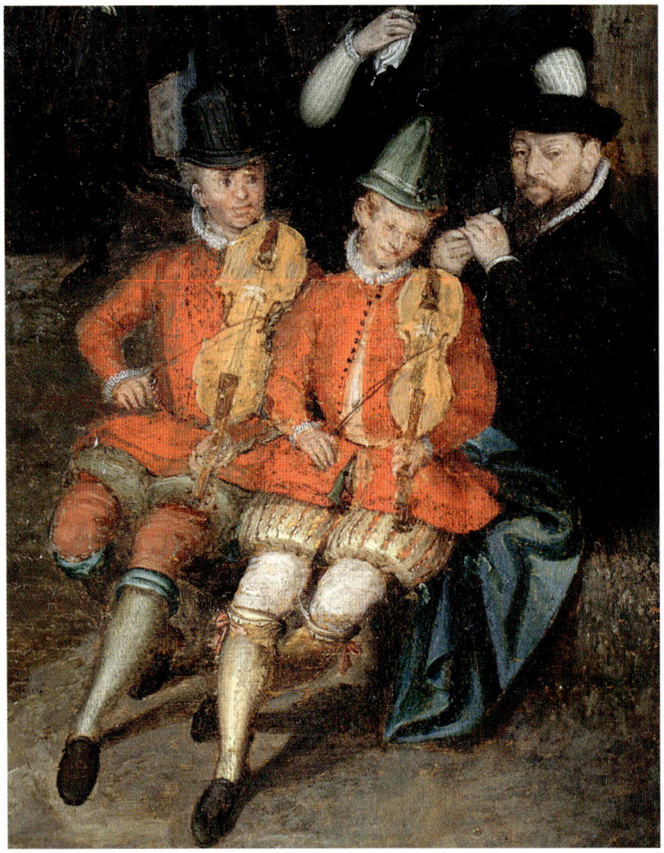

FIG. 23
Detail of musicians from *A Fête at Bermondsey* (cat. 4)
Joris Hoefnagel, *c.*1568–70

was perhaps in the service of the Arundels, for his inventory included a velvet coat trimmed with satin, 'which was my Lord of Arundells livery'.[46]

Masculine fashion

The inventories document a particular vogue for the 'Spanish leather' jerkin, often with silver buttons. Jerkins are ubiquitous in the inventories and leather examples appear frequently.[47] Figure 24 shows a rare surviving sixteenth-century example. The Earl of Pembroke owned eleven Spanish leather jerkins with buttons of gold, jet or silver.[48] Worcester gentleman William Gower had '1 jyrkin of Spanishe lether' and those of two Southampton merchants were adorned with silver buttons (for examples of silver buttons, see cat. 65).[49] An Oxfordshire ironmonger possessed a variation of this fashion – 'a French greene jerkin with 2 dossen of silver buttens'.[50]

Unusual occupations and livery

The inventories also record some distinctive occupations. A Southwark waterman had a black cloak with silk braid and a wide velvet collar.[43] The modest wardrobe of a Southampton tennis-court keeper included an 'olde fured gowne'.[44] Two inventories that list musical instruments may be those of professional musicians. Henry Goddard owned a gown lined with black damask, and a jacket and tippet of velvet, along with his lute and case, while Edward Hadshead's sartorial luxuries extended only to an 'ould velvet hatte' and silk girdle, which are recorded together with his pipes and reed.[45] Such garments may correspond to the clothing worn by the musicians seen at the right in *A Fête at Bermondsey* (fig. 23). On the other hand, the Bermondsey musicians may be wearing livery, that is, a particular ensemble of specific design and colours, provided by their patron or employer. Livery was widely worn by the many men of all social classes who served in royal and aristocratic households, but few specific references appear in the inventories. Southampton gentleman Thomas Mill

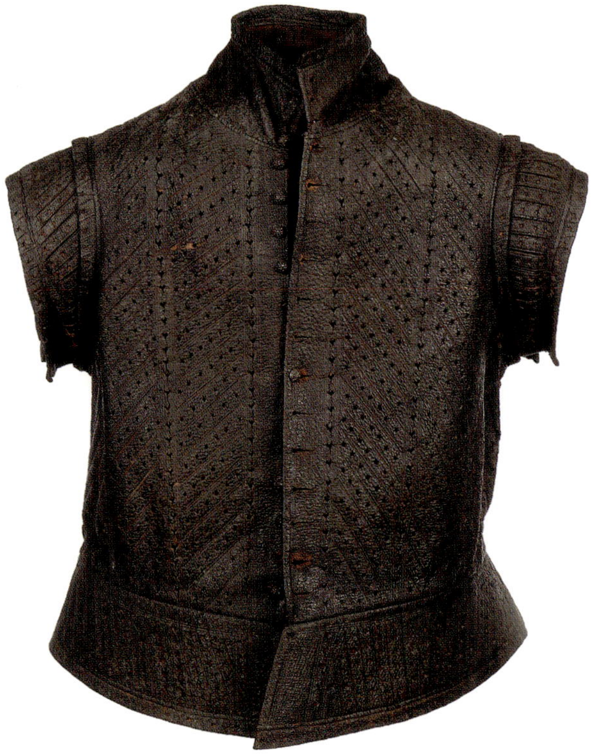

FIG. 24
Youth's jerkin of pinked leather with pewter buttons, *c.*1560

Elizabethan women and dress

There are far fewer wills and inventories for women because the property of married women automatically belonged to their husbands. Such documents do exist for both widows and spinsters but surviving examples are identified by marital status rather than social rank, so assessing information about women's clothing is much more difficult. The basic items of Elizabethan women's dress were gowns, frocks, cassocks, kirtles, petticoats (or coats) and waistcoats, inventoried in various combinations. Margaret Pyd of Southampton owned five gowns, two kirtles, three cassocks and a petticoat, while Elizabeth Gibbs had 'a frock, a kyrtell, 3 petycotes'.[51]

Originally the gown and kirtle comprised what we would now call a bodice and skirt, sewn together. The gown was an outer garment and the kirtle worn underneath.[52] By the start of Elizabeth's reign, the kirtle was evolving into two distinct parts: an upper garment known as 'bodies' (later to become the modern word 'bodice') and the kirtle (skirt), which was also known as a petticoat.[53] This latter word was sometimes contracted to 'coat', clearly a quite different garment from a man's coat. The word 'frock' appears in women's inventories and probably refers to an unfitted style, similar to the man's loose gown.[54] Women also wore cassocks, and these may have resembled a man's cassock.[55] The inventories give some clues about garments meant to go together: the 'new worsted frock and kirtle' of Jane Rigges; Jane Fullthropp's 'kirtle of tawnye velvet and a pair of sleves of the same'; and Eleanor Cook's 'one gown lyned with unwattered chamlet and a kyrttell of the same, belonginge to the same gowne'.[56] Outer wear for women included cloaks and mantles – the distinctions between the two are not clear – which were also worn when riding, along with a safeguard (protective petticoat), all listed in wills and inventories.[57]

Women's dress featured a variety of headwear. Jane Rigges's inventory listed six caps of 'lettice' (snow-weasel fur) as well as a velvet bonnet, and another Southampton widow had 'a Frenche houde of velvet', like that of Cecily Sandys (cat. 73).[58] Elizabethan portraits depict non-elite women with their heads completely covered, while those of the aristocracy show that they commonly revealed their hair. The nurse in the portrait of John Dunch (cat. 32) and Esther Kello in her portrait (cat. 70a) wear masculine-style hats over linen coifs; wills and inventories frequently list hats, sometimes qualified as of silk or beaver, or lined with

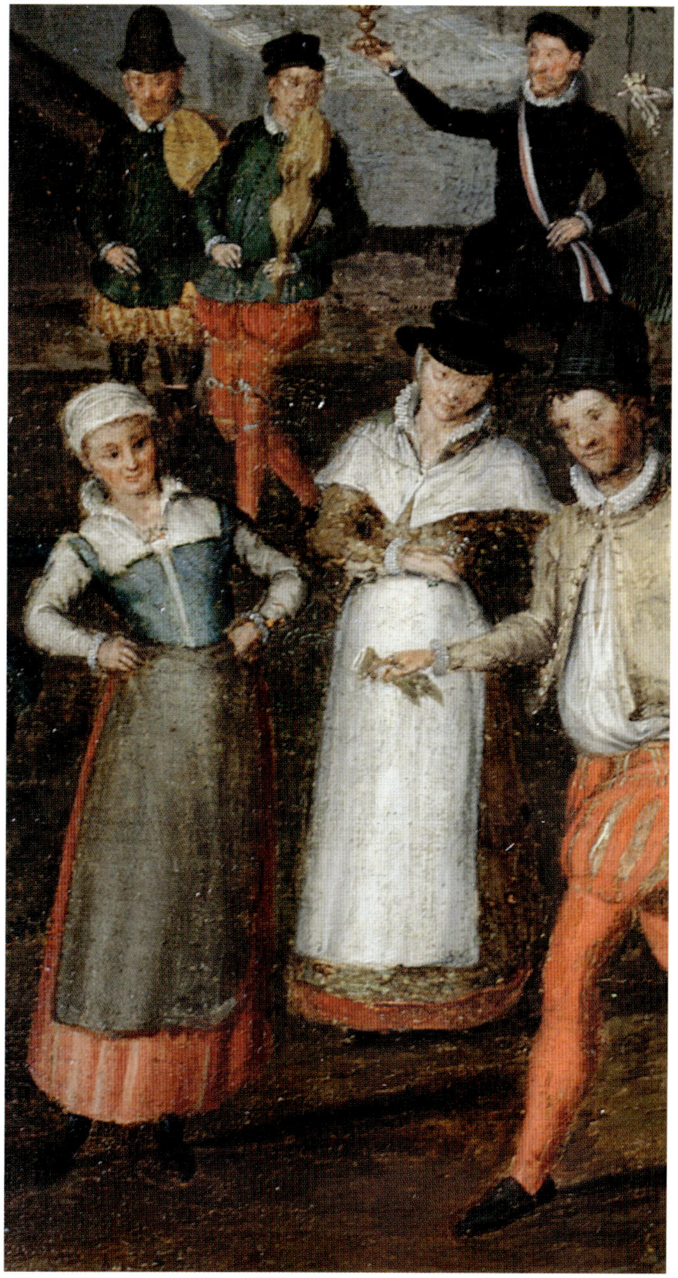

FIG. 25
Detail of women wearing aprons from *A Fête at Bermondsey* (cat. 4)
Joris Hoefnagel, *c*.1568–70

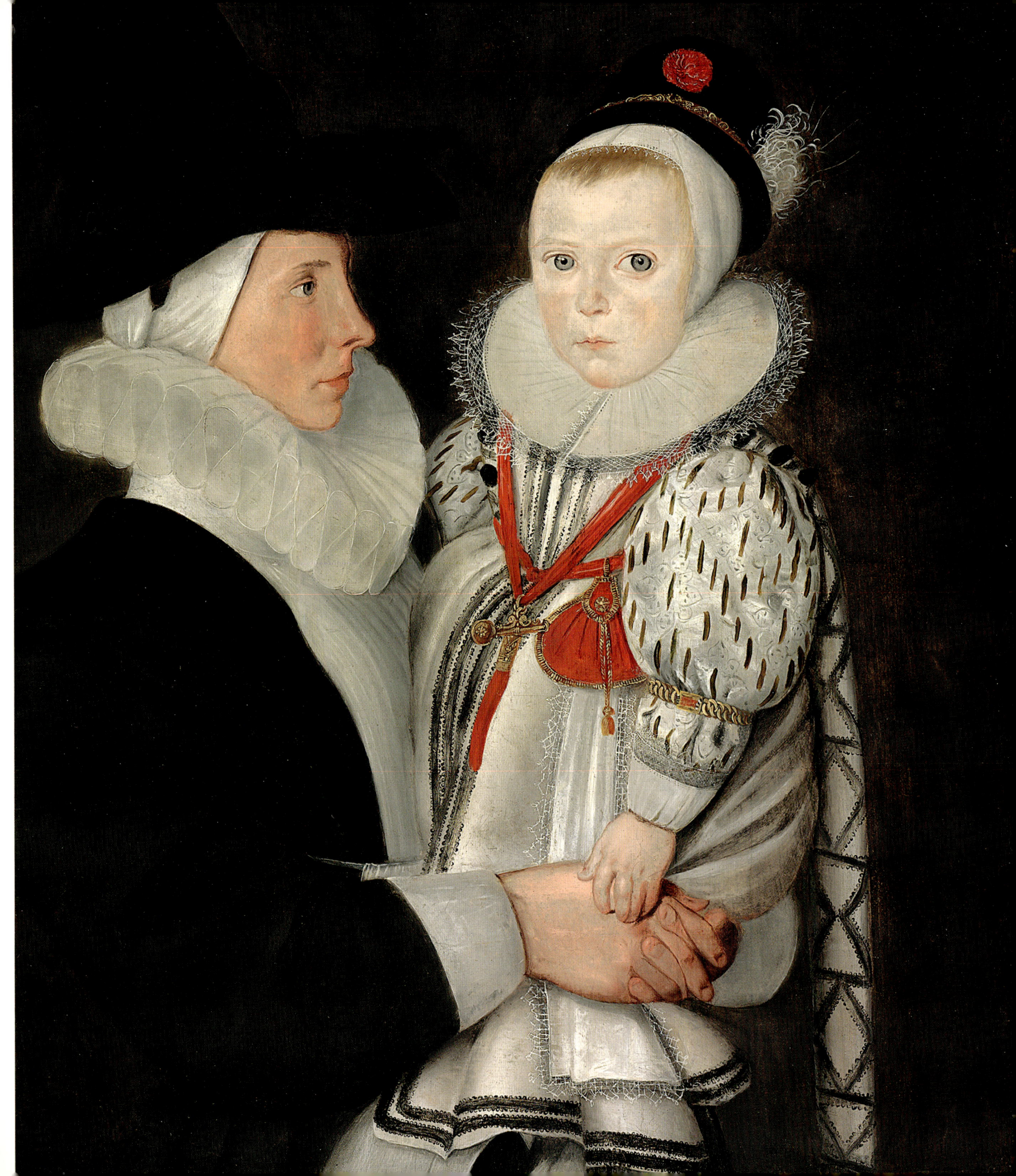

Catalogue

KEY TO CONTRIBUTORS

NAD Dr Natasha Awais-Dean
Independent scholar

CB Dr Charlotte Bolland
Project Curator, Making Art in Tudor Britain, National Portrait Gallery, London

BC Barrie Cook
Curator of Medieval and Early Modern Coinage, British Museum

TC Dr Tarnya Cooper FSA
Chief Curator and Curator of Sixteenth-Century Portraits, National Portrait Gallery, London

JE Dr Jane Eade
Associate Curator, Sixteenth-Century Collections, National Portrait Gallery, London

HF Hazel Forsyth FSA
Senior Curator, Medieval and Post-Medieval, Museum of London

AH Professor Andrew Hadfield
Professor of English (Centre for Early Modern Studies), University of Sussex

SJ Dr Susan Jenkins
Senior Curator, London and East, English Heritage

SN Dr Susan North
Curator, Fashion, Textiles and Furniture Department, Victoria and Albert Museum

AO Dr Amy Orrack
Independent scholar

AP Angus Patterson
Senior Curator, Department of Sculpture, Metalwork, Ceramics and Glass, Victoria and Albert Museum

ET Dr Edward Town
Postdoctoral Research Assistant, National Portrait Gallery, London

CATALOGUE NOTES

Measurements
These are given unframed. It has not always been possible to measure paintings, and so some measurements are approximate. Illustrations are not to scale.

Provenance
Not all pictures have a full provenance history, and gaps are indicated by an ellipsis (...).

Literature and exhibition information
Only select literature and previous exhibition references are provided.

Dates
The source for biographical dates is the *Oxford Dictionary of National Biography* (*ODNB*). All dates quoted have been modernised following the calendar beginning on 1 January (i.e. the Gregorian 'New Style' calendar). Where a date is unknown for a sitter or artist, a question mark (?) signifies that the date is likely to be that year. Where *c.* (circa) is used, the date is approximately that year but could be before or after.

Spellings
These have usually been modernised, except in quotations and original titles of publications. *ODNB* is the source used for names.

Inscriptions
All inscriptions have been recorded as they appear on the object. For clarification, missing contractions have been expanded and are shown in square brackets ([ ]).

Abbreviations

BL	British Library
KHLC	Kent History and Library Centre
LMA	London Metropolitan Archives
NRO	Norfolk Record Office
TNA	The National Archives

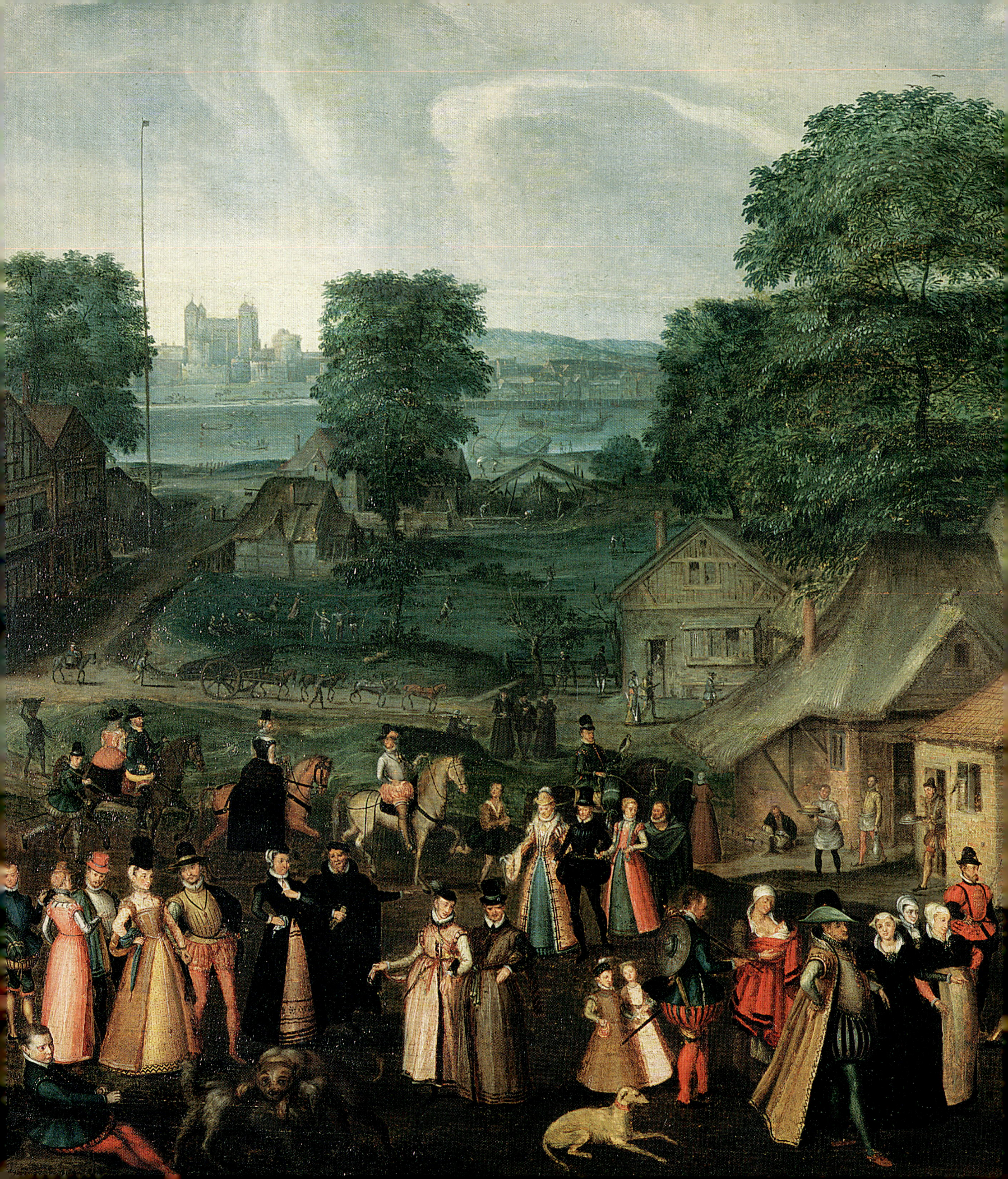

1 ELIZABETHAN ENGLAND AND WALES

The changes that took place during the reign of Elizabeth I, from 1558 to 1603, dramatically shaped the future of England and Wales. Following the death of the Roman Catholic monarch Mary I, the secure re-establishment of the Church of England under Elizabeth meant that by the end of her long reign much of the population was broadly accepting of the Protestant faith. This was partly the result of the passage of time. It was also due to a carefully orchestrated religious settlement, which was acceptable to the conservative silent majority, while comprising just enough reformed ideology to retain the loyalty of moderate puritans. Subjected to persecution, Roman Catholicism may have lost its influence over the masses, but for the authorities it continued to retain a significant and troubling hold over the landed elite.

The dominions that Elizabeth I claimed to rule included England, Wales, Ireland and a part of France. However, in reality Calais had recently been lost and long-term unrest in Ireland was worsened by inconsistent government policies, culminating in the Nine Years' War at the end of her reign.
The country also faced the threat of invasion. The division of Europe into Protestant and Roman Catholic faiths earlier in the century set the stage for conflict. The execution of Mary, Queen of Scots (the Catholic heir to the throne), preceded the attack by the Spanish Armada, launched in 1588. Its subsequent failure was seen as an act of divine providence.

As the population at large grew, and the capital city of London more than doubled in size, trade prospered, literature flourished and the professional and merchant classes expanded. The opportunities for exploration around the globe were readily exploited by the sea-faring nation, and new trade routes to Asia and Africa, and to fledgling colonies in North America, were established. Immigration into the country by skilled craftsmen and merchants also increased, particularly following the persecution of Protestants in the Netherlands. All these changes were favourable to the rise of educated men (and sometimes women) with wit and ingenuity, and the Elizabethan period saw new opportunities for social mobility.

1

The Procession Portrait of Queen Elizabeth I (1533–1603)

Unknown Anglo-Netherlandish artist, *c.*1600–3

Oil on canvas, 1327 × 1905mm
John Wingfield Digby, Sherborne Castle Estates

A rare painting of Elizabeth I surrounded by her subjects, this unusual portrait group provides a window into the ceremony and artifice of the late Elizabethan court. Many of the sitters are readily identifiable, but the precise subject or occasion of the painting has been closely debated; it is likely that rather than accurately documenting a specific event, the painting functions as an image about royal power and the influence of the Queen's closest courtiers. Throughout her reign the Queen certainly travelled in processions similar to the one depicted here. For example, a description given by the French diplomat Monsieur de Maisse in 1597 records that:

> When the Queen goes abroad in public the Lord Chamberlain walks first, being followed by all the nobility who are at Court, and the Knights of the Order that are present walk after, near the Queen's person, such as the Earl of Essex, the Admiral and others. After comes the six heralds who bear maces before the Queen. After her march fifty gentlemen of the Guard, each carrying a halberd, and sumptuously attired; and after that the Maids and Ladies who accompany them, very well attired.[1]

The Queen would have been about seventy years old when this picture was painted, but she is presented as a much younger woman; her portrait is a prettified version of the 'Ditchley Portrait' (*c.*1592; NPG 2561), by Marcus Gheeraerts the Younger (1562–1636). Elizabeth appears to be seated on a wheeled car, pushed along by three grooms in red, and she is sheltered by an embroidered canopy, held above her head by four young gentlemen. The route is lined with the Queen's personal bodyguards, known as Gentleman Pensioners, of which in 1600 there were almost fifty in her service. Beyond this group, more heads and figures at the windows of the building suggest a crowd of citizen onlookers. Many of those in Elizabeth's retinue can be identified from other contemporary portraits, although some of the identifications remain conjectural. Immediately before the Queen walk six Knights of the Garter, five of whom can be identified as follows: Edmund Sheffield, 3rd Baron Sheffield (far left, in red); Charles Howard, Baron Howard of Effingham, the Lord Admiral (in silvery white); George Clifford, 3rd Earl of Cumberland (in red, behind); George Carey, 2nd Baron Hunsdon (carrying his white rod of office) and Gilbert

PROVENANCE

Kildare Digby, 2nd Lord Digby of Coleshill, Warwickshire (d.1661); by descent to William, 5th Lord Digby; seen by Vertue at Coleshill in 1737 and by Horace Walpole at Sherborne in 1762.

EXHIBITIONS

Art Treasures, Manchester, 1857 (64); *First Special Exhibition of National Portraits ending with the Reign of James II*, South Kensington Museum, London, 1866 (256); *Exhibition of the House of Tudor*, New Gallery, London, 1890 (368); *Exhibition of Late Elizabethan Art*, Burlington Fine Art Club, London, 1926 (19); *Kings and Queens of England*, Walker Art Gallery, Liverpool, 1953 (100); *The Elizabethan Image*, Tate Gallery London, 1969–70 (80); *Artists of the Tudor Court – The Portrait Miniature Rediscovered 1520–1620*, Victoria and Albert Museum, London, 1983 (204), pp.127–8; *Armada: An International Exhibition to Commemorate the Spanish Armada*, National Maritime Museum and Ulster Museum, London and Belfast, 1988 (3.21); *In Celebration – The Art of the Country House*, Tate Gallery, London, 1998–9

Talbot, 7th Earl of Shrewsbury (bearing the sword of state in a crimson scabbard).

A seventh Knight of the Garter stands in the foreground directly below the Queen; he is balding and holds his gloves in his right hand. This figure has been identified as Edward Somerset, 4th Earl of Worcester, who replaced Essex as Master of the Horse in 1601, a role that required him to be master of ceremonies at court and to accompany Elizabeth on her progresses. Sir Roy Strong was the first to argue that Worcester's prominence in the painting may suggest that he commissioned it in celebration of his appointment as Master of the Horse.[2] Worcester's son, Henry Somerset, Lord Herbert of Chepstow – the canopy bearer in silvery white seen at the extreme right looking out at the viewer – gestures with his left arm towards the train of ladies following the Queen.

These include his bride, Lady Anne Russell, who is also in white. It does seem probable that the painting refers in part to the wedding of Somerset and Anne Russell, which took place at Blackfriars in June 1600.[3] The Queen is known to have attended the event and to have travelled in a litter. However, the artist has employed some artistic licence as not all of the details recorded at the occasion match the painting; for example, Elizabeth attended on a litter borne by six, rather than four, gentlemen, and of the Garter-Knights portrayed here only one, Lord Cumberland, was present at the wedding.

Large-scale narrative pictures are rare in English art at this date. However, the few other examples that exist, such as the Somerset House Conference (NPG 665), indicate that it may have been workshop practice to utilise pre-existing portraits to create complex compositions. The background architecture seen here is Netherlandish in appearance, and it was recently discovered that the large building on the right and the more distant castle have been copied directly from the landscape of an engraving by Hieronymus Wierix (1553–1619) after Maarten de Vos (1532–1603) depicting the Sermon on the Mount.[4] TC & AO

LITERATURE

Ilchester 1920–1, pp.1–19; Strong 1963, pp.86–7; Strong 1977, pp.30–46; Strong 1983a, p.127; Armitage 1990, pp.301–7; Wells-Cole 1997, p.208; Leahy 2005, pp.143–52; Wells-Cole 2012.

NOTES

1 *A journal of all that was accomplished by M. de Maisse*, 1597, ed. G.B. Harrison and R.A. Jones (Nonesuch Press, London, 1931), p.93, cited in Strong 1963, p.87.
2 Strong 1977, pp.30–46.
3 Ilchester 1920–1, pp.1–19.
4 Wells-Cole 2012, p.835.

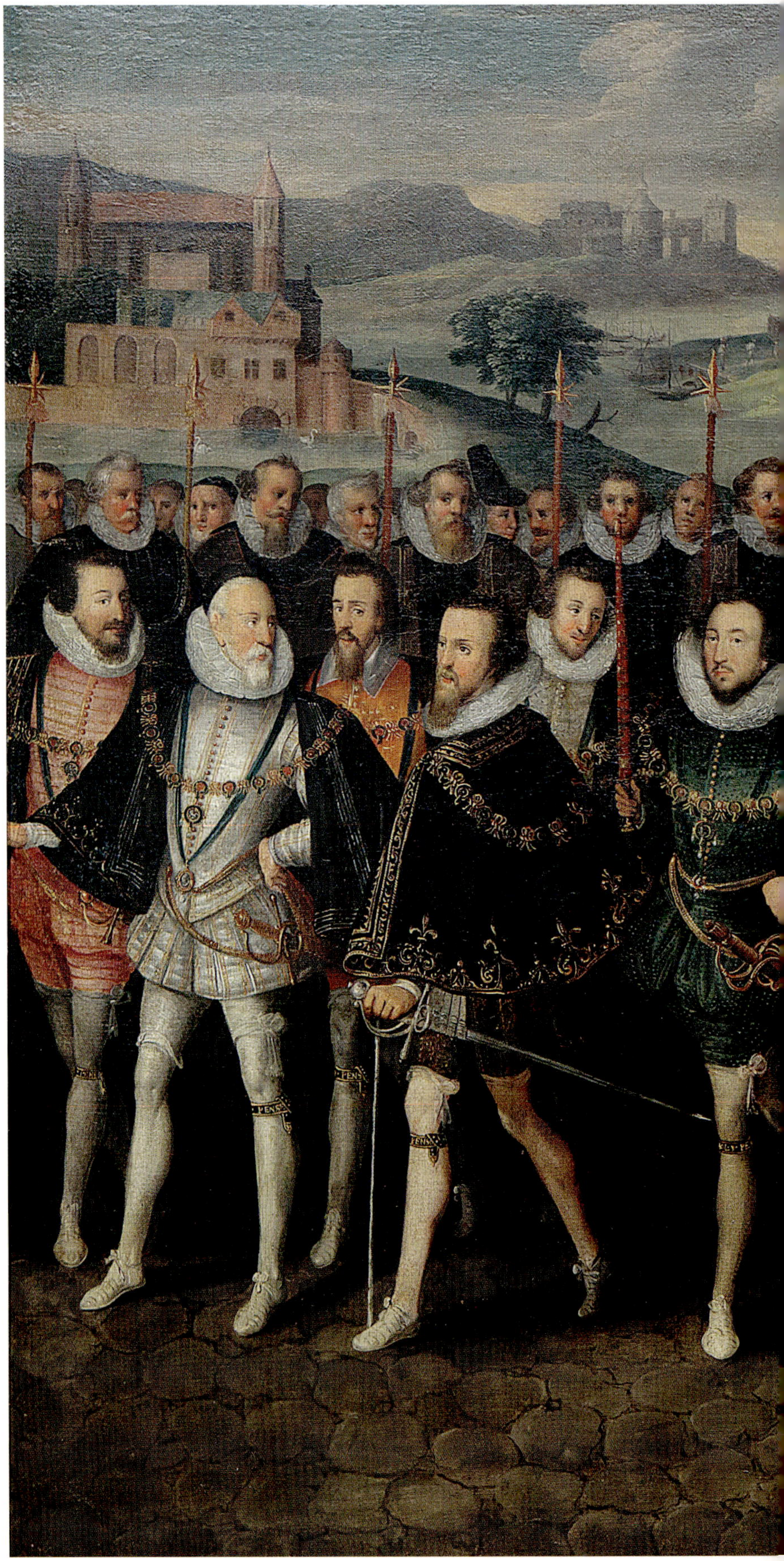

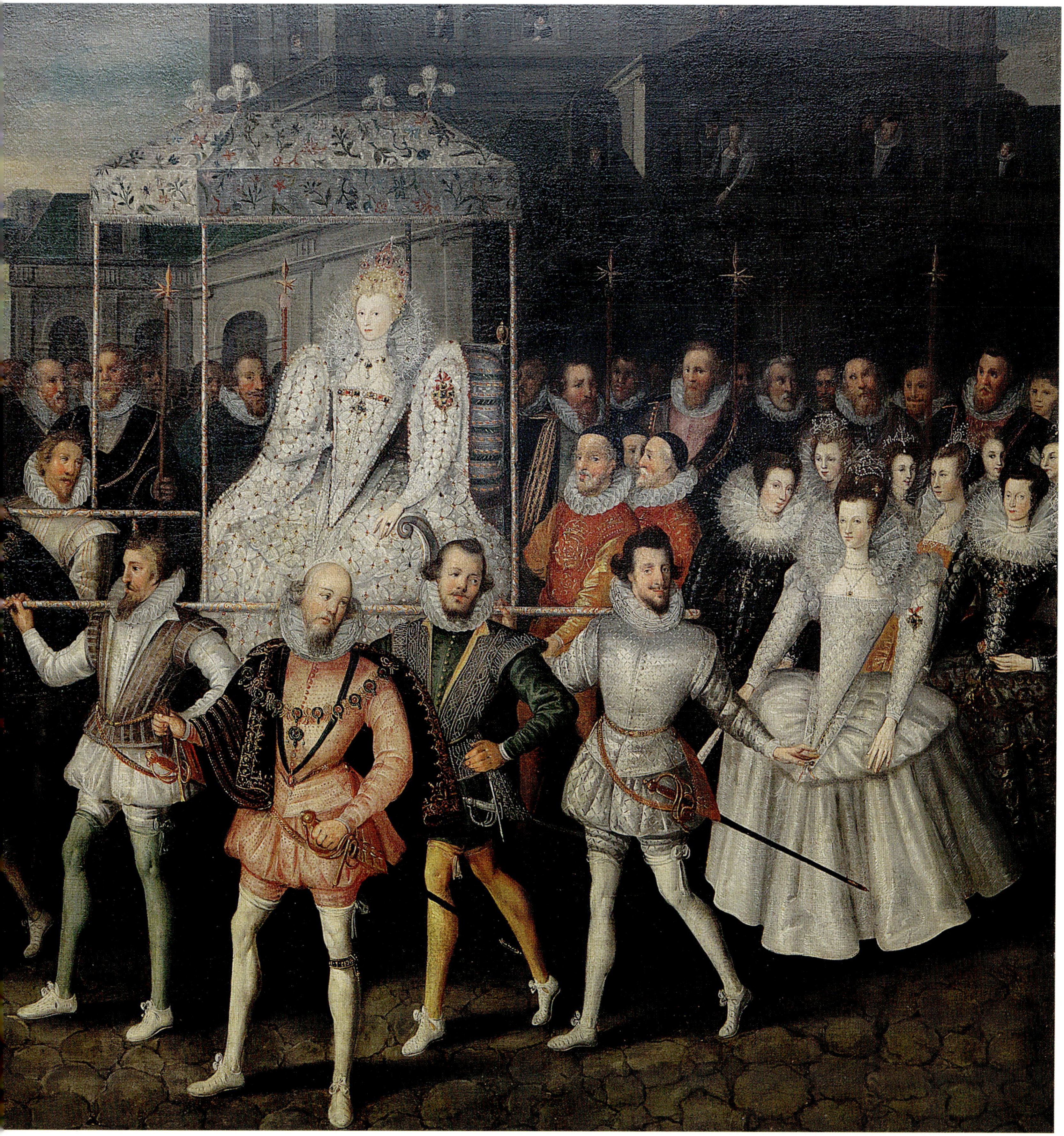

2

Map of Britain and Ireland (or *Angliae Et Hiberniae Nova Descriptio Veretibus Et recentioribus nominibus distincta ad doctissimi viri Guiliel*[*mi*]. *Camdeni Britanniam topographice illustrandam accommodata. Anno Domini 1592*)

Jodocus Hondius [Joost de Hondt], London, 1592

Engraving, 550 × 785mm
Llyfrgell Genedlaethol Cymru/The National Library of Wales, Aberystwyth (MAP 05391)

This exceptionally rare and important large hand-coloured map of England, Wales and Ireland was made by the Flemish engraver and cartographer Joost de Hondt, better known as Jodocus Hondius (1563–1612; fig. 27). Hondius had fled to England in 1583 with his master Hendrick van der Keere following the capture of Ghent by the Spanish forces led by the Duke of Parma. Judging by the title of the engraving (superimposed over Scotland), the map seems to have been prepared to accompany an edition of William Camden's great topographical and historic survey *Britannia*, the first edition of which appeared in 1586. The map mirrors the format of Camden's *Britannia* by delineating each of the country's counties and alludes to some of its content by including the names of the ancient tribes associated with particular regions. It also depicts the country's main geographic features, along with the major towns and settlements, with a particular focus on the great houses of the ruling elite.

Hondius's conception of the nation played up to the political vanities of Elizabeth I and her government, presenting a unified nation, a subjugated Ireland, and the nominal but persistent claim to territories in France. In reality, discontent in Ireland was soon to break out into a disastrous and costly war that would continue into the following reign. Within the map, the legitimacy of Elizabeth's rule was further reinforced with the inclusion of a genealogical table tracing the progeny of England from the Norman Conquest to the present sovereign. This genealogy was supplied by the sometime letter-writer to the Queen, household steward and aspiring herald Morgan Colman (d.*c*.1625).

Colman's involvement in the production of this map gives weight to the idea that it was made in London rather than elsewhere. In 1593 Hondius left London for Amsterdam where he spent the rest of his career. ET

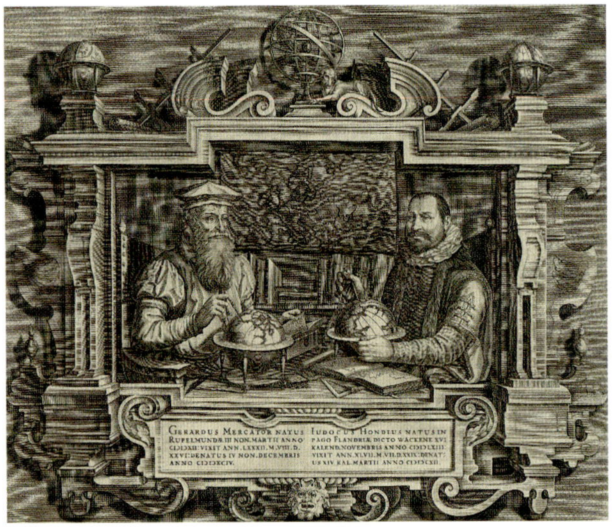

FIG. 27
Gerardus Mercator and Jodocus Hondius
Unknown artist, mid-seventeenth century

PROVENANCE
Discovered in 1940, folded in one of the Library's Ortelius atlases, and thought to have been part of the Mervyn Pritchard Collection, which was acquired that year.

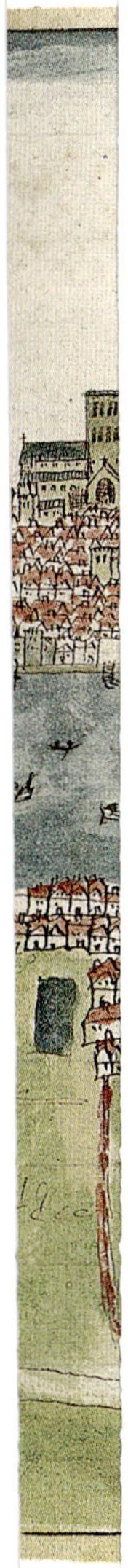

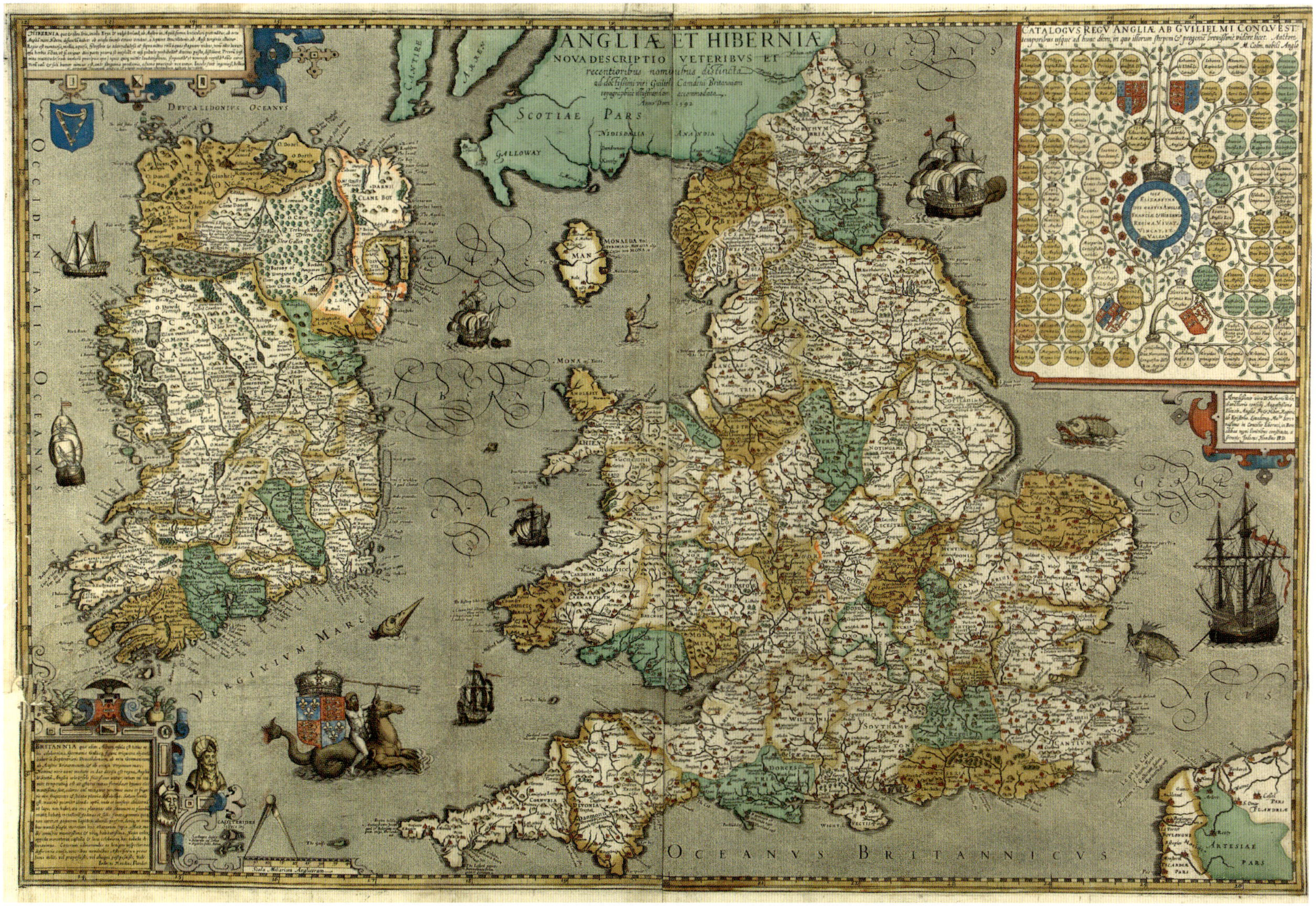
ANGLIÆ ET HIBERNIÆ
NOVA DESCRIPTIO VETERIBUS ET
recentioribus nominibus distincta
SCOTIAE PARS
GALLOWAY
MAN
CATALOGUS REGU ANGLIÆ AB GUILIELMI CONQUEST.
DEUCALIDONIUS OCEANUS
OCCIDENTALIS OCEANUS
VERGIVIUM MARE
OCEANUS BRITANNICUS
ARTESIAE PARS

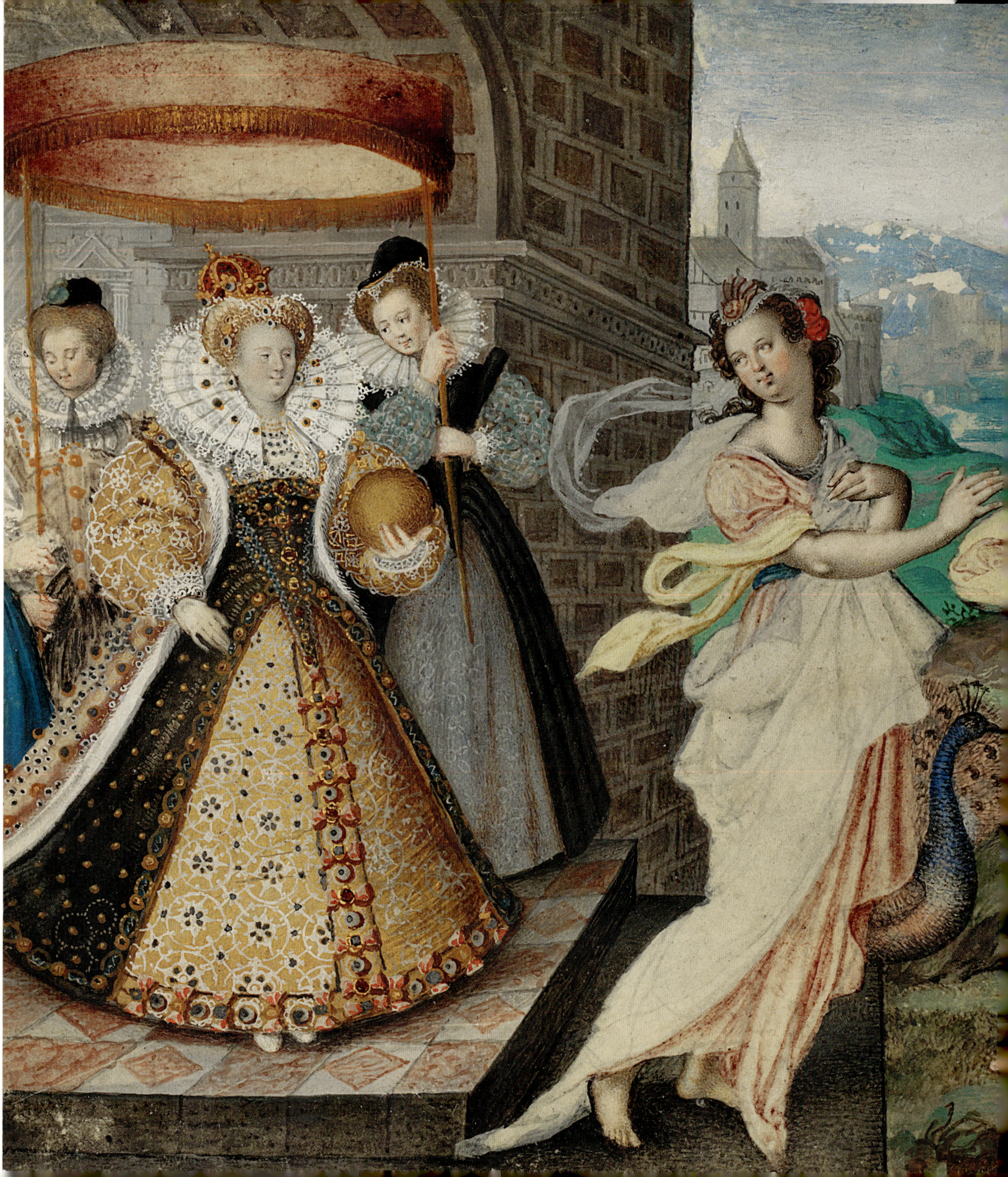

2 ENCOUNTERING THE QUEEN

In the first few decades of her reign, the Queen's royal coat of arms was newly installed in many parish churches. This emblem would have reminded churchgoers of Elizabeth I's presence as monarch and her authority over the re-established Church of England. Although few of her subjects would have met the Queen, most would have known her face through her portrait on the newly minted coins, first circulated in 1561 (cat. 16). Elizabeth was probably the most widely recognised of all Tudor monarchs as a result of the extensive circulation of her portrait. The Queen's portrait could be bought readymade in the form of prints and painted images, and from early in her reign ownership of her likeness can be found in the inventories of households of the clergy and merchant classes as well as the nobility and gentry. The portraits of Elizabeth included here would originally have been owned and displayed by a range of different patrons, from the Queen herself to members of the nobility, gentry, universities, guildhalls and others.

Surviving early painted portraits of Elizabeth show her simply presented, without a crown or other attributes of monarchy. The Queen's striking appearance, with her red hair and dark eyes, and her liking for elaborate clothes gave her portraits a distinctive look, which then came to be copied by her female courtiers. From the 1570s onwards new commissions (usually financed and orchestrated by her courtiers) became more complex and began to include sophisticated emblems and clever allegorical devices celebrating her specific virtues. For example, emblems such as the ermine (representing purity), pelican (representing charity), phoenix (referring to her unique nature) and numerous other emblems indicating chastity appear in several portraits from the mid-1570s until the end of her reign.

As the Queen rarely sat for artists to take her likeness, most portraits were produced from existing compositions, or from patterns kept by artists' workshops (see cats 8 and 12). Attempts to control the appearance and circulation of the Queen's portraits, although considered, were never enacted. Unfortunately, many portraits of Elizabeth I have been lost and what survives today is certainly only a small part of what was produced in her lifetime.

5

Elizabeth I and the Three Goddesses

Hans Eworth, dated 1569

Oil on panel, 629 × 844mm
Inscribed lower right: *1569 / HE*; on frame: *IVNO POTENS SCEPTRIS ET MENTIS ACVMINE PALLAS / ET ROSEO VENERIS FVLGET IN ORE DECVS / ADFVIT ELIZABETH IVNO PERCVLSA REFVGIT / OBSTVPVIT PALLAS ERVBVITQ Q[UE] VENVS* (Juno was the queen of might, Pallas had the sharpness of mind / And the rosy face of Venus was shining bright / Then Elizabeth came and Juno, disheartened, took flight / Pallas was astounded and Venus blushed for shame)
Royal Collection Trust/HM The Queen (RCIN403446)

This unusual allegorical portrait of Elizabeth I is one of only a handful of works known to have been displayed at the Palace of Whitehall during the Queen's reign, where it was seen in 1600 by a visiting nobleman, Baron Waldstein.[1]

The painting restages the classical narrative of the Judgement of Paris, with Elizabeth cast as the main protagonist. In the legend Paris, a Trojan mortal, must award a golden apple to the goddess he considers the fairest; Juno (Queen of Heaven), Pallas Athena (Goddess of War) or Venus (Goddess of Love). Paris chooses Venus, and is rewarded with Helen of Sparta, an outcome that initiates the Trojan War. Here Elizabeth, in the role of Paris, is shown on the left, elevated on three steps, holding a golden orb in place of an apple. Rather than repeat Paris's folly by selecting one of the goddesses, the Queen instead retains the golden orb for herself because she alone combines the three qualities that they embody separately. The use of this narrative within a portrait flatters the Queen and implies that the outcome of her reign will be peace, not war. This favourable comparison was also applied to other female rulers and consorts, including Elizabeth's mother, Anne Boleyn, in the form of a pageant held during her coronation as Queen Anne in 1533.[2]

Elizabeth is shown emerging from beneath an archway decorated with her initials, roses and fleurs-de-lis, accompanied by two ladies-in-waiting. Against Elizabeth's steadfast composure, the three classical goddesses are shown discomposed or unclothed. With her back to the Queen, Juno has dropped her sceptre and lost a slipper, while Pallas Athena, despite her armour, holds up her hand in surprise or submission. Venus reclines, unashamed of her nudity, and casts a protective arm around her son, Cupid. It would seem likely that the picture was presented to the Queen rather than having been commissioned by her, and the fact that it was displayed prominently at Whitehall alongside state portraits of other rulers suggests that Elizabeth approved of this likeness of herself as 'goddess supreme'.[3]

The 'HE' monogram, found in cursive script on a rock in the foreground, has led to the proposal of three different Netherlandish artists, all of whom were known to be working in England in the late 1560s: Hans Eworth (d.1574), Lucas de Heere and Joris Hoefnagel. Recent analysis shows that the painting can convincingly be accepted as being by Hans Eworth. The 'HE' monogram is original and not unlike other authentic examples, while the paint handling is very similar to that seen in his signed works *Allegory of the Wise and Foolish Virgins* (1570; Statens Museum for Kunst, Copenhagen) and *Mary Nevill, Lady Dacre and Gregory Fiennes, 10th Baron Dacre* (NPG 6855).[4]

TC & AO

PROVENANCE

Valued at £2 among the pictures out of the Galleries at Greenwich [sic] by the Trustees for Sale (15 August 1649–1 February 1653); sold to Hunt and Bass 1 March 1653. Recovered at the Restoration.

EXHIBITIONS

First Special Exhibition of National Portraits ending with the Reign of James II, London, South Kensington Museum, 1866 (219); *The King's Pictures*, London, Royal Academy, 1946–7 (13); *British Portraits*, London, Royal Academy, 1956–7 (22); *Hans Eworth*, London, National Portrait Gallery, 1965–6 (37); *Kings and Queens*, London, Queen's Gallery, 1982–3 (16); *The Queen's Pictures*, London, National Gallery, 1991 (62); *Dynasties: Painting in Tudor and Jacobean England 1530–1630*, London, Tate Gallery, 1995–6 (29), p.73–4; *Elizabeth*, London, National Maritime Museum, 2003 (192), pp.190–2; *In Fine Style: The Art of Tudor and Stuart Fashion*, London, Queen's Gallery, 2013.

LITERATURE

Millar 1963, pp.36 and 69 (cat. 58); Strong 1987; Pomeroy 1989, pp.30–8; Evett 1990, pp.117–19; Hearn 1995, no. 29; Doran 2003, pp.190–2; Sharpe 2009, pp.366–8.

NOTES

1 *The Diary of Baron Waldstein, A Traveller in Elizabethan England*, translated and annotated by G.W. Groos (Thames & Hudson, London, 1981), pp.46–7. The picture was recorded again at Whitehall in 1611 by Otto, Prince of Hesse.

2 John D. Reeves, 'The Judgement of Paris as a device of Tudor Flattery', *Notes and Queries* (1954), pp.7–11; Louis Adrian Montrose, 'Gifts and Reasons: The Contexts of Peele's Araygnement of Paris', *ELH*, 47, 1980, pp.433–61.

3 Waldstein described the picture as being hung in 'one very fine gallery or dining-hall', alongside state portraits of William of Orange, Elizabeth of Valois, Mary of Hungary, the Duke and Duchess of Savoy, Emperor Charles V and Holbein's likeness of Edward VI as a child (*The Diary of Baron Waldstein*, pp.46–7).

4 Lionel Cust, 'The Painter HE: Hans Eworth', Walpole Society, II, 1912–13.

We are grateful to Helen Hackett for her advice on this entry and cat. 6.

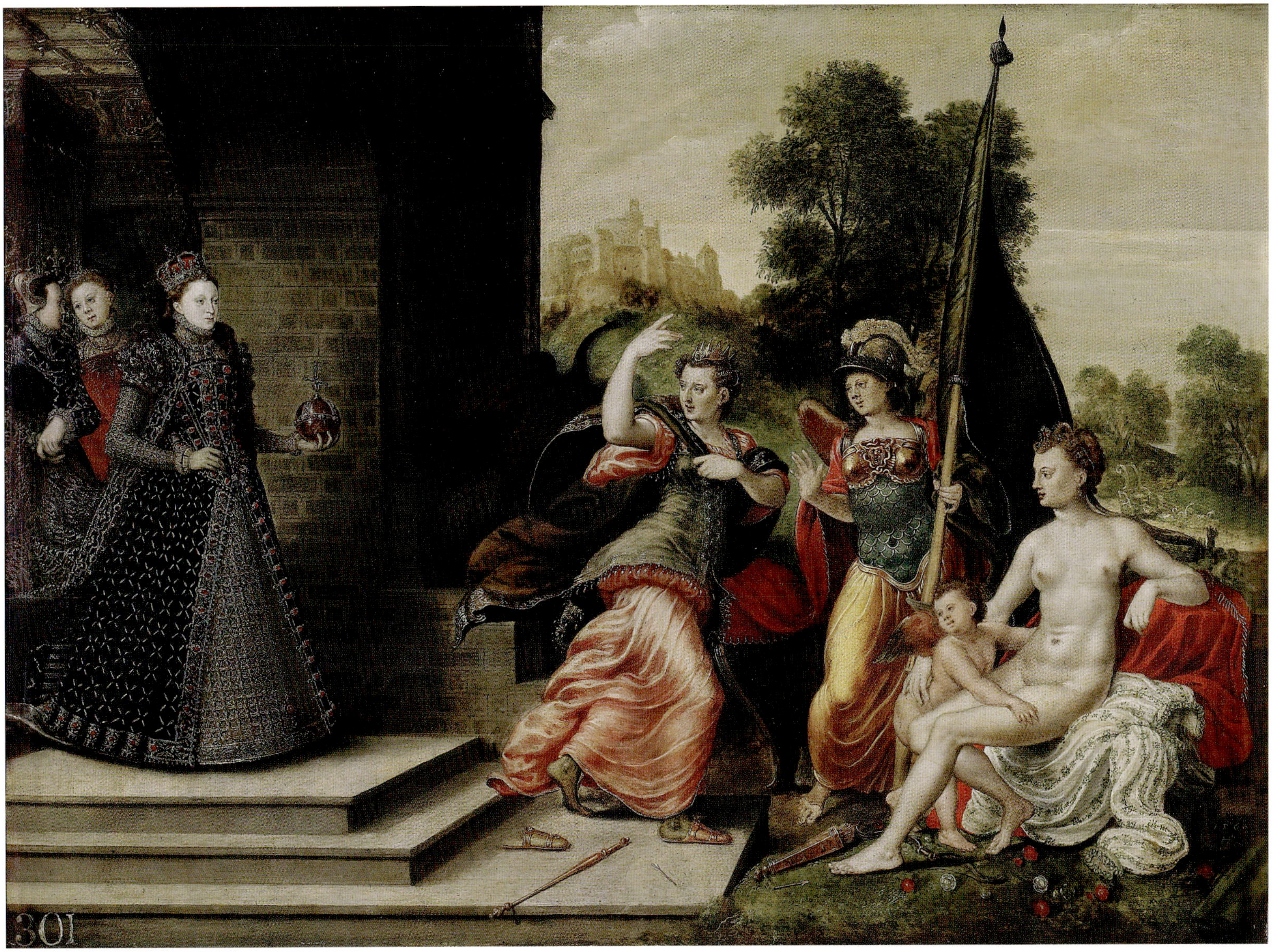
301

6

Elizabeth I and the Three Goddesses

Attributed to Isaac Oliver, *c.*1590

Watercolour and body colour, heightened with gold, on vellum stuck to card,
115 × 157mm
National Portrait Gallery, London (NPG 6947)

This previously unknown miniature reinterprets the theme of *Elizabeth I and the Three Goddesses*, found in the Royal Collection painting of the same title (cat. 5). Although the artist certainly appears to borrow some of the essential formal elements of the composition from the earlier painting, it is markedly different in terms of the Queen's appearance, the background landscape and the costumes of the goddesses, and so the miniature can be considered an original reworking of the subject. Comparing Elizabeth to the Goddesses had become a standard form of courtly flattery by the closing decades of the century, with notable literary examples being George Peele's *Araygnement of Paris* of 1584 and Richard Barnfield's *Cynthia* of 1595.[1]

Elizabeth is shown in a remarkable dress of cloth-of-gold, wearing a diamond necklace and a golden crown, and her wide ruff and jewelled headpiece suggest the fashions of the later 1580s or early 1590s, as seen in works such as the 'Armada Portrait' (*c.*1588; Woburn Abbey, Bedfordshire). Her rounded face and small features are unusual, but they also appear in the portrait made by Nicholas Hilliard in *c.*1585 for the Great Seal, and there is no doubt that this is meant to be a flattering portrait that shows the Queen as perpetually youthful.

It is difficult to speculate about who this unknown cabinet miniature might have been produced for – the provenance provides us with no further clues – but the small scale and remarkably high quality of this work indicate that it would have been painted for a patron close to the court. The picture is not signed, but the highly accomplished technique and Continental influence – particularly in the mannerist, twisted figure of Juno – suggest an attribution to Isaac Oliver (*c.*1565–1617; see cat. 68) or another, as yet unknown, Continental follower of Nicholas Hilliard. French-born Oliver may have visited the Low Countries in the late 1580s, and he certainly visited Italy in the 1590s.[2] The figures of the goddesses here have parallels with figures in signed drawings by Oliver such as *The Lamentation over the Dead Christ* (1586; Fitzwilliam Museum, Cambridge). Oliver produced large-scale multi-figured cabinet miniatures throughout his career, but the combination here of portrait 'types' confronting allegorical figures before a panoramic Netherlandish landscape most closely resembles his complex miniature *An Allegorical Scene: Virtue Confronting Vice* (*c.*1590–5; Statens Museum for Kunst, Copenhagen).
TC & AO

PROVENANCE

Private collection; Christie's, London, lot 43, Old Master and Early British Drawings and Watercolours, 3 July 2012; Mark Weiss Gallery, London; acquired by the National Portrait Gallery, 2012, with support from Mark Weiss.

NOTES

1 John D. Reeves, 'The Judgement of Paris as a device of Tudor Flattery', *Notes and Queries*, 1954, pp.7–11; Louis Adrian Montrose, 'Gifts and Reasons: The Contexts of Peele's Araygnement of Paris', *ELH*, 47, 1980, pp.433–61.
2 Strong 1983b, pp.142–85.

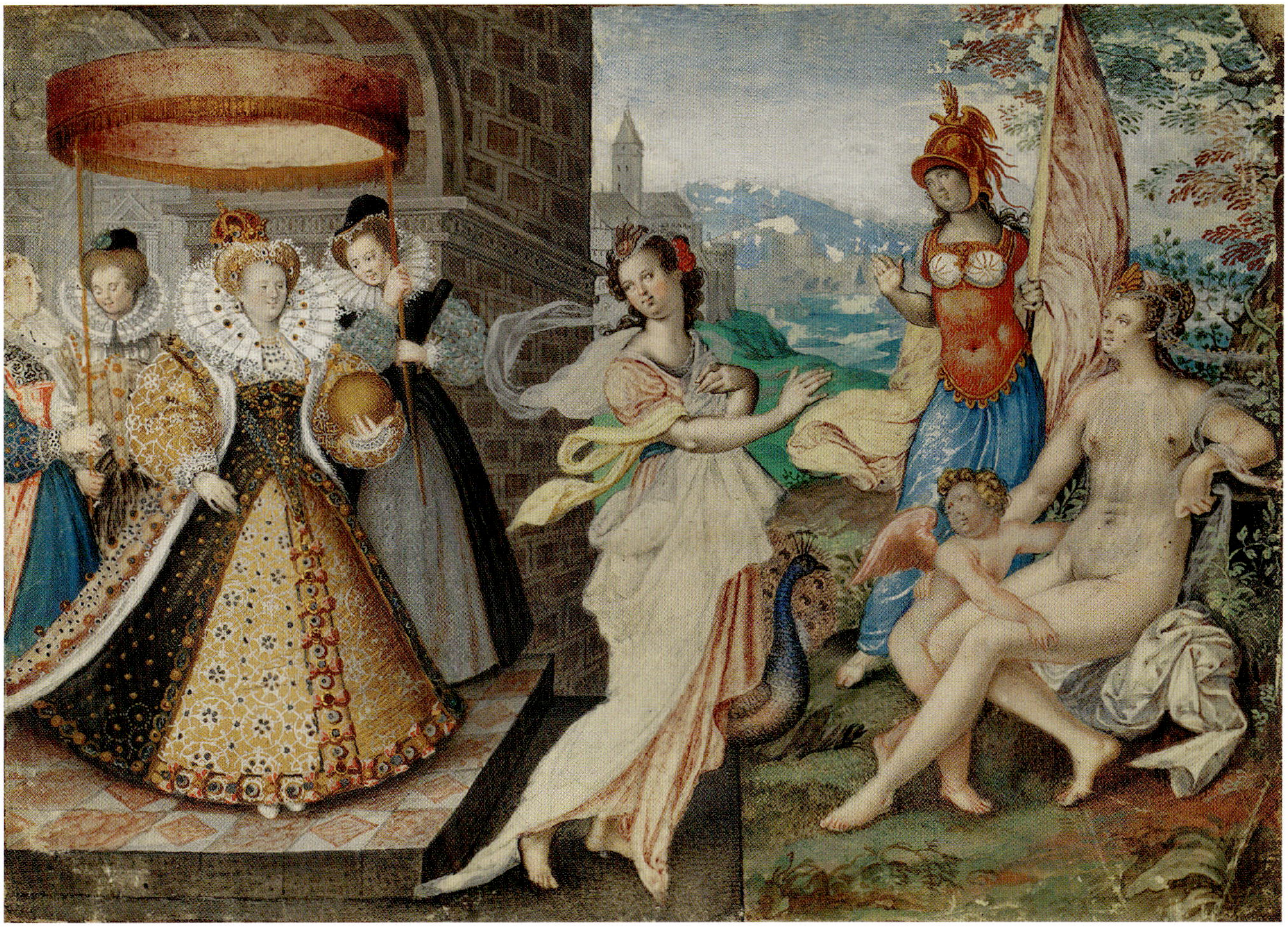

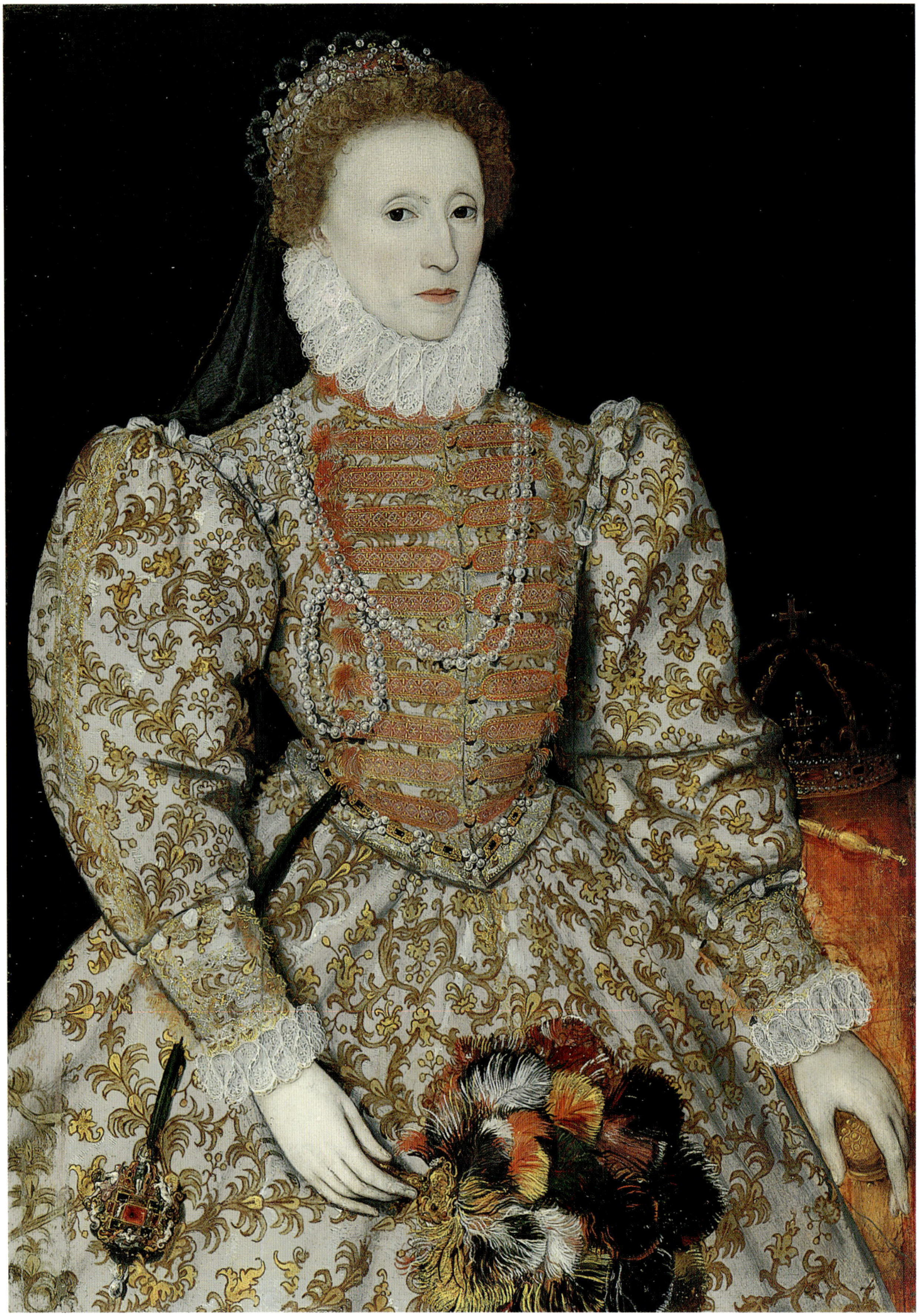

8

Elizabeth I

Unknown Continental artist, c.1575

Oil on panel, 1130 × 787mm
National Portrait Gallery, London (NPG 2082)

This important portrait of Elizabeth I, dating from the mid-1570s, is one of the most remarkable of the Queen and shows her as a confident ruler, aged around forty. Most surviving portraits of Elizabeth were painted from existing patterns, but this example, in which the artist records the Queen's distinctive high-boned face and hooded dark brown eyes, must have been painted following a direct sitting from life. The work in turn provided a pattern that was to be reused in a large number of later portraits (see cat. 12).[1] The repetition of this 'face mask' in portraits of the Queen for around another twenty years of her reign indicates that it must have gained her approval. The persistent use of this likeness also ensured that she continued to appear youthful, even in advancing age.

Elizabeth wears a rather masculine dress consisting of a skirt and matching bodice with scarlet frogging that fastens down the front like a doublet. Compared to later portraits, the composition is relatively simple. Wearing a looped string of pearls about her neck and a caul, or hairnet, of pearls upon her head, she stands against a plain background. Pigment analysis has revealed that the colours in the painting have faded considerably over time. Her gold and white dress would originally have been crimson and white, and her complexion would have been much rosier. Although it is clear that the Queen – along with many female courtiers – wore make-up to lighten the skin in later life, it is probable that at this date her complexion was more natural.[2]

The artist remains unknown, but close examination of the sophisticated and swiftly rendered paint handling suggests that he was a highly talented Continental painter (see fig. 28). As the work cannot be linked with other surviving portraits, the artist may have been in England for just a short period, perhaps specifically for this commission. Recent technical analysis has revealed lively underdrawing, indicating that the composition of the portrait was evolving as the artist worked. Analysis has also shown that the crown and sceptre, visible on the table behind, are late additions by another less competent hand, and thus may have been included at the request of the patron, or the Queen herself. The portrait is likely to have been commissioned by a courtier close to Elizabeth; the colourful ostrich feather fan and jewelled pendant hanging from a green ribbon at her waist may indeed have been gifts from the same person. The pendant consists of a large ruby surrounded by diamonds and the figures of Minerva and Mercury, perhaps symbolic of Elizabeth's desire for peace and her maritime prowess. The portrait was at Cobham Hall, Kent, for many years and may have been owned originally by William Brooke, Lord Cobham, although it is known as the 'Darnley Portrait' after its eighteenth-century owner. TC & AO

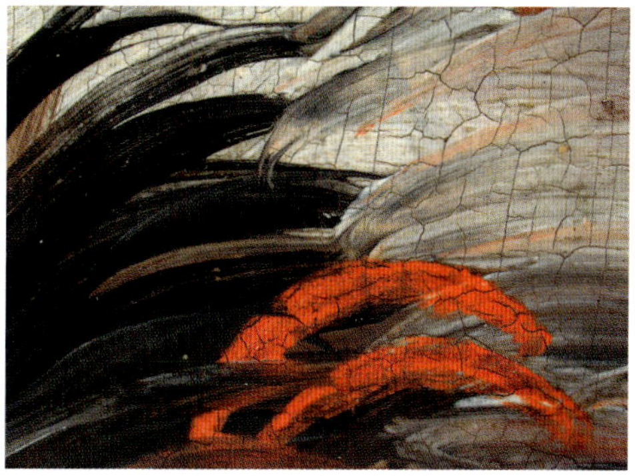

FIG. 28
Detail showing the painting technique used for the feathers of the fan, where the various colours are worked up together 'wet-in-wet'.

PROVENANCE

Possibly always at Cobham Hall and painted for William Brooke, Lord Cobham (1527–97), Lord Warden of the Cinque Ports; his son forfeited his estates for his part in the Maine Plot (1603) and Cobham passed to the Dukes of Richmond and Lennox, descending via the Baronesses Clifton to John Bligh, 1st Earl of Darnley (1687–1728); purchased by the National Portrait Gallery, 1925.

EXHIBITIONS

Art Treasures, Manchester, 1857 (65), p.115; *The Monarchs of Great Britain and Ireland*, London, New Gallery, 1902 (78).

LITERATURE

Strong 1963, pp.60–8; Strong 1969b, pp.102–3; Ribeiro 2000, p.42; Cooper 2008, p.34.

NOTES

1 In this portrait the 'Darnley' face pattern is reversed. Strong 1963, pp.60–8.
2 Ribeiro 2000, p.42; Farah Karim-Cooper, *Cosmetics in Shakespearean and Renaissance Drama* (Edinburgh University Press, Edinburgh, 2006), p.62.

9

Elizabeth I, the 'Ermine' Portrait

Attributed to Nicholas Hilliard, dated 1585

Oil on panel, 1054 × 864mm
Dated on sword hilt: *1585*; inscribed on sword: *Justitia*
The Marquess of Salisbury, Hatfield House

It is likely that this painting was owned by Elizabeth I's chief advisor, Sir William Cecil, Lord Burghley (1520/1–98), and as such it would almost certainly have hung within the grand surroundings of one of his two major country estates (Burghley House, Lincolnshire, or Theobalds, Hertfordshire). Inventories record that by the seventeenth century the Cecil family owned four portraits of Elizabeth I. However, the first conclusive reference to this painting being at Hatfield (a property in Hertfordshire, built by Burghley's son, Robert Cecil) dates from the early eighteenth century.[1]

A small white ermine on the Queen's arm gives the portrait its traditional title. The creature, a stoat in its winter coat, had long been seen as a symbol of purity as, according to legend, the ermine died if the whiteness of its fur became soiled. The fourteenth-century writer Petrarch had used an ermine to adorn the banner carried before Laura in his *Trionfo della Castità* ('Triumph of Chastity'), a work that was widely referenced in the second half of the sixteenth century and provides the basis for the symbolism found in this painting. Such symbolism would have been readily understood by the original audience for this painting, which probably consisted of Elizabeth's inner circle of courtiers.

Ambitious and bright, Burghley had served Elizabeth since she was a princess and was promoted to Lord Treasurer in 1572. He hosted a number of royal visits at his country home, Theobalds, which became a favoured venue in which to lodge for Queen and court during their summer progresses. Elizabeth is known to have visited Theobalds in June 1585, the year that this work is dated, and it is conceivable that this royal event provided the occasion for the painting's commission.

Elizabeth wears a black dress richly studded with gold daisy-like rosettes. Among her necklaces is a collar seen in portraits of Henry VIII, from which hangs one of the most celebrated of the royal jewels: a pendant consisting of three pearls, three oblong rubies and a pointed diamond set in a triangle known as the 'The Three Brothers', which had once belonged to the Dukes of Burgundy.[2] In her right hand she holds an olive sprig, a reference to peace, while on the table beside her left hand rests the sword inscribed Justitia ('Justice').

The portrait is painted in a flat, highly decorative manner typical of English art of this period. The artist is not certainly known; once attributed to William Segar (b. in or before 1564–1633), the painting has also been attributed to the limner and goldsmith Nicholas Hilliard (1547?–1619). Burghley was an active patron of Hilliard, and the artist was certainly responsible for designing an official portrait likeness of the Queen for the Second Great Seal in 1584, the year before this picture was painted.[3] However, Hilliard may have supervised rather than painted works in oil. The position of the Queen's head is similar to that found in his miniatures and it is probable that he was closely associated with this outstanding portrait. TC & AO

PROVENANCE

First recorded at Hatfield by Vertue, 1731.

EXHIBITIONS

Nicholas Hilliard and Isaac Oliver: An Exhibition to Commemorate the 400th Anniversary of the Birth of Nicholas Hilliard, London, Victoria and Albert Museum, 1947 (110)

LITERATURE

Auerbach 1957, p.205; Strong 1963, no. 86; Auerbach and Kingsley Adams 1971, pp.56–9; Strong 1977, pp.146–51; Strong 1987, pp.113–15; King 1990, pp.30–74; Doran 2003, p.185.

NOTES

1 The family collection moved to Hatfield House in 1607, when James I offered to exchange Theobalds for the Old Palace and manor of Hatfield. Household inventories dating from 1611, 1612 and 1620/1 mention several portraits of Queen Elizabeth, but it is not until Vertue's report of 12 July 1731 that this painting can be identified precisely: 'Queen Elizabeth on board (half len.) a small creature an Ermine on her left arm in her right hand a branch of green flower. The sword lying on the Table.'

2 In 1587 it is recorded as: '… a faier flower with three great ballaces and in the middes a great pointed diamond and three great pearles sett with a fair great pendaunt pearle. Called the Brethren' (British Museum, Royal MS Appendix 68, f.2).

3 Erna Auerbach, *Nicholas Hilliard* (Routledge and Kegan Paul, London, 1961), pp.20–7. In an undated letter to Lord Burghley or his son Sir Robert Cecil, Hilliard asks his patron to intervene in his favour when he is threatened with arrest; in 1587 Burghley wrote to an Exchequer official declaring himself willing to act as surety for the painter; in 1593 two painter-stainers petitioned Burghley for a monopoly in heraldic decoration for funerals under Clarenceux, and again imply that Hilliard was one of Sir Robert's favourites.

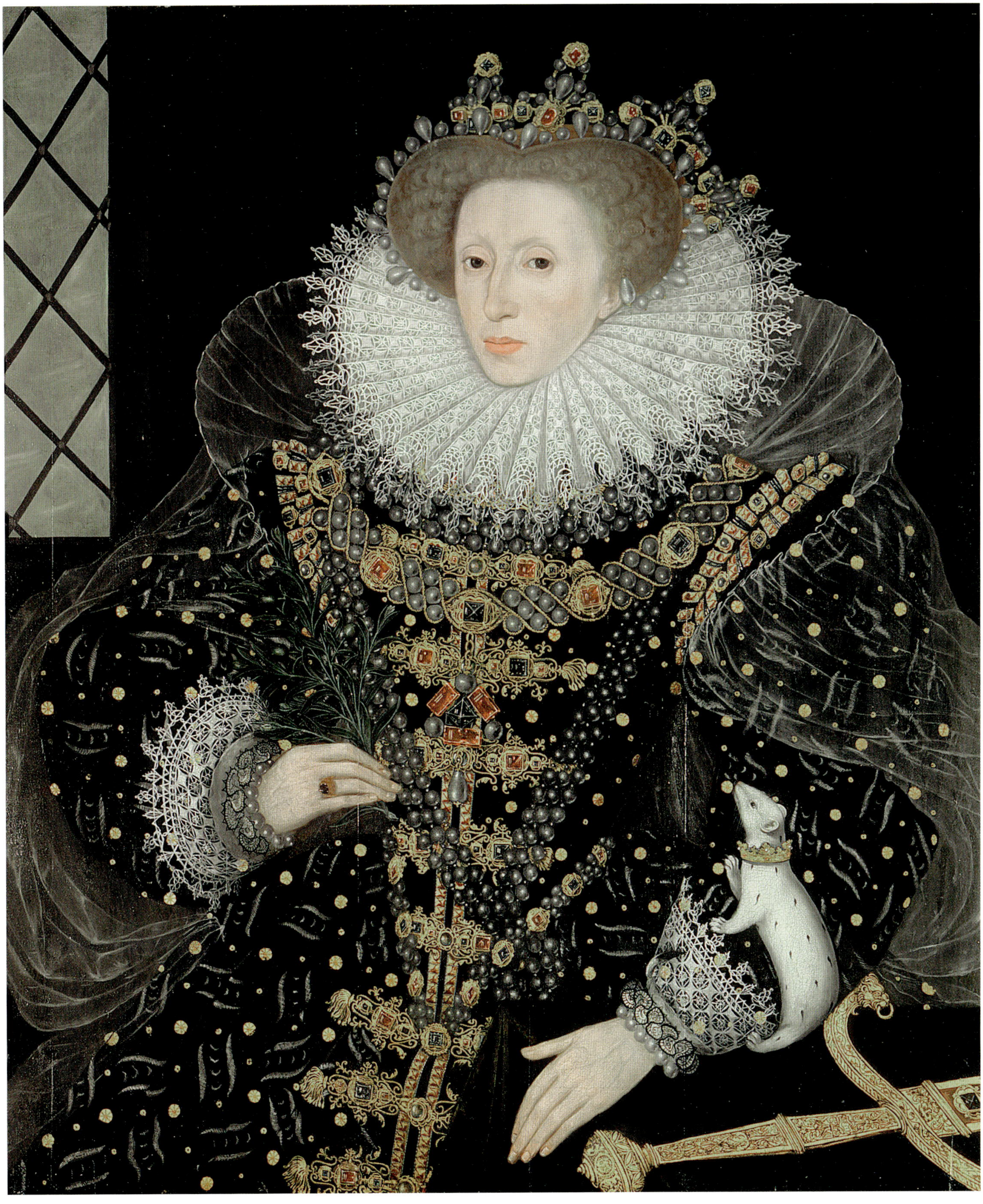

10

Elizabeth I

Unknown artist, previously attributed to the studio of Nicholas Hilliard, c.1598–9

Oil on canvas, 2235 × 1689mm
Hardwick Hall, The Devonshire Collection
(acquired through the National Land Fund and transferred to the National Trust in 1959)
National Trust inventory number 1129128

This remarkable portrait of Elizabeth I wearing a dress decorated with land and sea creatures appears to have been acquired by Elizabeth Talbot, Countess of Shrewsbury ('Bess of Hardwick', *c.*1527?–1608), and was almost certainly on display during the Queen's lifetime. The grand scale and imposing presence of this portrait would have made it a suitable centrepiece for one of the public rooms at the Countess's newly refurbished manor house – Hardwick Hall, Derbyshire. An inventory of Hardwick, made in 1601, records several pictures of the Queen ('one in the high great Chamber, two in the Gallerie, and other "pictures" in the low great Chamber').[1] In 1760, the antiquarian Horace Walpole (1717–97) recorded this portrait hanging in the 'Gallerie' at Hardwick, where it was described as 'Queen Elizabeth, whole length, in a gown embroidered with animals & Sea monsters ...'.[2] The portrait can be dated on the basis of style and costume to the late 1590s and the Countess's accounts mention payment for the carriage of a portrait of the Queen brought to Hardwick from London in 1599, which plausibly might record the acquisition of this painting.[3]

The composition presents the Queen as a rigid, regal icon and the curious style and handling indicate that it must be the product of an English artist's studio. It would seem probable that the composition was copied or adapted from another source, possibly from a drawing or miniature now lost. The portrait type is also similar to that found in woodcuts of the Queen produced in 1589 and 1592.[4] The artist does not appear confident with the creation of three-dimensional space; Elizabeth seems to stand almost weightless on the tipped-up carpet, while her grasp of the grey gloves and white feather fan is unconvincing.

The picture has previously been attributed to the studio of the Queen's official limner (or miniature painter), Nicholas Hilliard (1547–1619), and while there are some broad similarities in the rather flat, diagrammatic approach, it is less competently painted than any of Hilliard's works in miniature. Although Hilliard may have been responsible for larger portraits in oil paint, none can be conclusively identified as by his hand. Our current understanding of workshop practice suggests that Hilliard may have passed finished drawings and designs to an accomplished painter working in oils in his style. One suggestion for the authorship of this picture, among several, is Hilliard's former apprentice Rowland Lockey (*c.*1566–1616), who had already painted pictures for Bess of Hardwick in 1592 and continued to work for her son from 1608 to 1613.[5]

Although nothing has certainly survived of Elizabeth's wardrobe, we have no reason to think that this incredible costume is not accurate; the headdress and girdle resemble items described in the 1587 inventory of the Queen's jewels, and Thomas Platter described seeing the Queen in 1599, finding her 'most lavishly attired in a gown of pure white satin, gold-embroidered ... in short she was most gorgeously apparelled.'[6] Like many other portraits of the Queen, Elizabeth's lavish outfit is ornamented with hundreds of pearls, including a prominent pearl positioned to emphasise her virginity. These adorn every part of her costume from her crown to her gloves, shoes, dress and hems, showing that even late in her reign the symbols of virginity and purity remained as potent an aspect of her public persona as thirty years previously.[7] TC & AO

PROVENANCE

Apparently always at Hardwick Hall, first certainly recorded there in 1760 by Horace Walpole (see 'Visits to Country Houses', *Walpole Society*, XVI, 1927, p.30).

EXHIBITIONS

First Special Exhibition of National Portraits ending with the Reign of James II, London, South Kensington Museum, 1866 (229); *The Royal House of Tudor*, London, New Gallery, 1890 (418); *The Royal House of Tudor*, Manchester Art Gallery, 1897 (148); *The Monarchs of Great Britain and Ireland*, London, New Gallery, 1902 (77), p.72; *Princely Magnificence: Court Jewels of the Renaissance*, 1500–1630, London, Victoria and Albert Museum, 1980 (pl.14), pp.104–5; *Artists of the Tudor Court: The Portrait Miniature Rediscovered 1520–1620*, London, Victoria and Albert Museum, 1983 (206), pp.128–9.

LITERATURE

Princely Magnificence, 1980–1, pp.14, 104–5; Girouard 1999, p.65; Levey and Thornton 2001.

NOTES

1. Santina M. Levey and Peter Thornton, *Household Stuff: The 1601 inventories of Bess of Hardwick* (National Trust, London, 2002), pp.48–52.
2. 'Horace Walpole's Journals of Visits to Country Seats', *Walpole Society*, vol. XVI, 1927–8, p.30.
3. Chatsworth Archive: Hardwick accounts (MS 8 f.56 v.19 July 1599).
4. For the woodcuts see Strong 1963, p.111, no. 17 and p.113, no. 21.
5. Erna Auerbach, *Nicholas Hilliard* (Routledge and Kegan Paul, London, 1961), pp.254–6.
6. Jane Ashelford, *The Art of Dress: Clothes and Society 1500–1914* (National Trust, London, 1996), p.41.
7. Andrew and Catherine Belsey, 'Icons of Divinity: Portraits of Elizabeth I', *Renaissance Bodies: The Human Figure in English Culture, c.1540–1660*, ed. Lucy Gent and Nigel Llewellyn (Reaktion Books, London, 1990), pp.11–35.

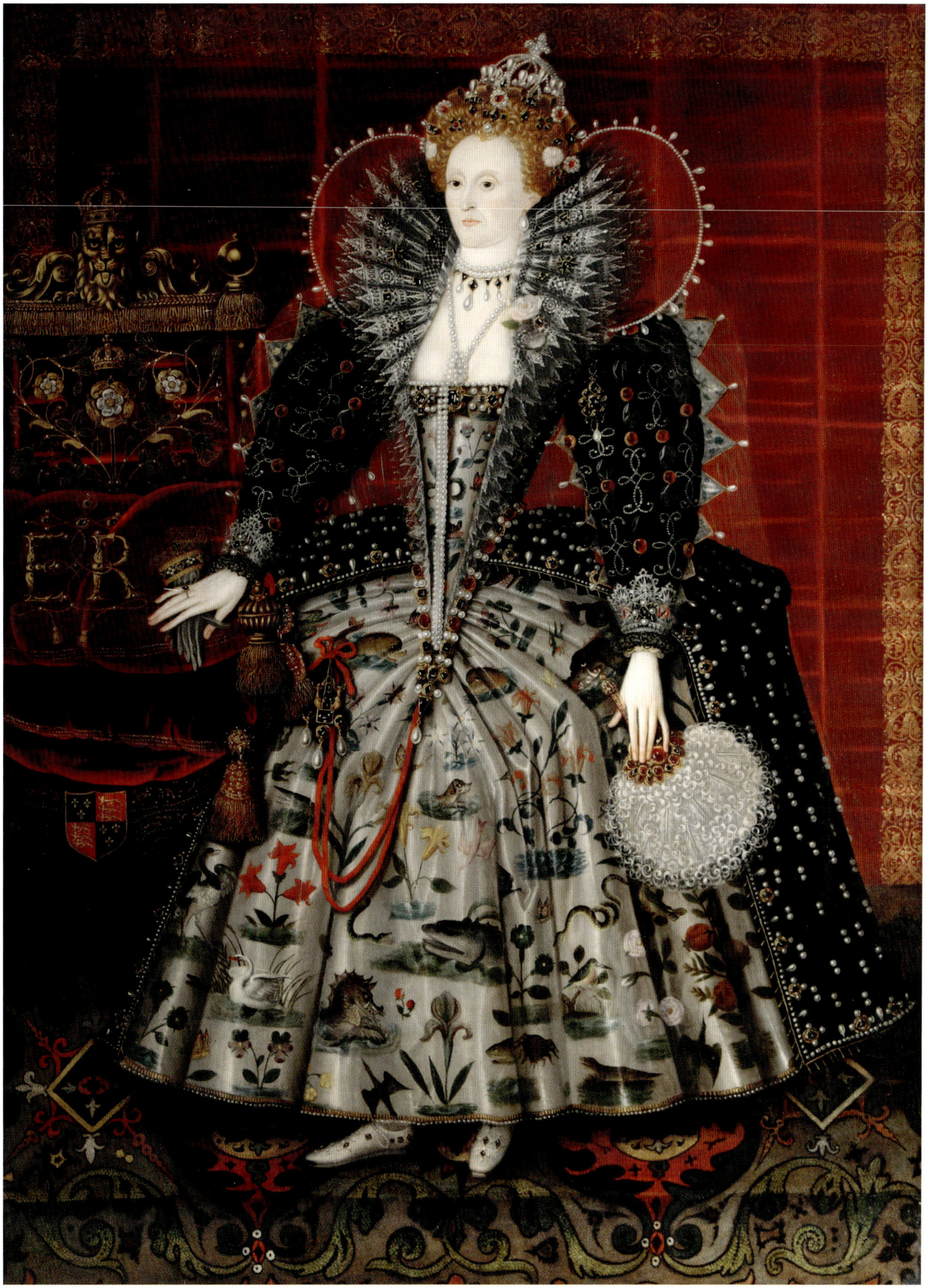

11

Elizabeth I

Remigius Hogenberg, c.1572

Etching and engraving, 306 × 197mm
Inscribed in margin underneath: ELISABETH DEI GRATIA ANGLIAE, FRANCIAE ET HIBERNIAE REGINA, FIDEI DEFENSOR. ETC. (Elizabeth, Queen of England, France and Scotland, by the Grace of God, Defender of Faith, etc.) *Corporis effigies tua pulchra est, Elizabetha: / Pulchrior, ast animi forma decorq* [*ue*]. *Tui, / Tu rigidos froeno cohibes, Regina, Britannos. / Justitiae custos lux pietate nitens, / Flos es labe carens, sanctae virtutis amatrix. / Anglorum foelix, quae diadema tenes* (Your portrait, Elizabeth, is beautiful, and more so your soul. With firmness you hold together the Britains, oh Queen! You direct the guardians of justice towards the light through piety. You are a flower without blemish, lover of holy virtue, good fortune of the English people, you who have the crown); in margin at bottom right: *Remigius Hoge*[*n*]*bergius fecit* (Made by Remigius Hoge[n]berg); in pen and ink, in an old hand, below: *Nata 1533. Obijit 1603. 24. Martij. / 7.7bris. / Memoriae aeternum / Elisabethae Angliae, Franciae & Hiberniae* … (Born 1533. Died 1603. 24 March./ 7 September / Eternal Memory to Elizabeth, Queen of England, France and Scotland …)
The British Museum, London (1862-1213.1)

This portrait engraving was produced when Elizabeth I was in her late thirties and may have been created either as an independent portrait print, or perhaps for inclusion in a printed book. It bears the signature of Remigius Hogenberg (*c*.1540–90), a talented engraver from Mechelen who established himself in England between 1572 and 1587. It is unclear whether Remigius left the Netherlands for professional reasons or as a religious refugee, but once in England he entered the services of the Archbishop of Canterbury, Matthew Parker. Resident at Lambeth Palace, Archbishop Parker was a keen patron of the arts, writing in a letter of 9 May 1573 to Lord Burghley: 'I have within my house in wagis, drawers and cutters, paynters, lymmers, wryters, and boke-bynders..'[1]

Only a small number of portrait prints produced in the Queen's lifetime survive. Most engraved examples were produced as part of published volumes within, for example, books of Christian prayers, Bible frontispieces (such as that for the 1568 Bishop's Bible by Remigius's brother, Franciscus Hogenberg), histories, or maps (such as Christopher Saxton's *Atlas of the counties of England and Wales* of 1579).[2] The Queen is shown in the costume of the early 1570s wearing jewels appropriate to her rank, and the Latin couplets refer to her beauty and piety, her just rule over the 'Britains', and her strength in upholding a Protestant nation. TC & AO

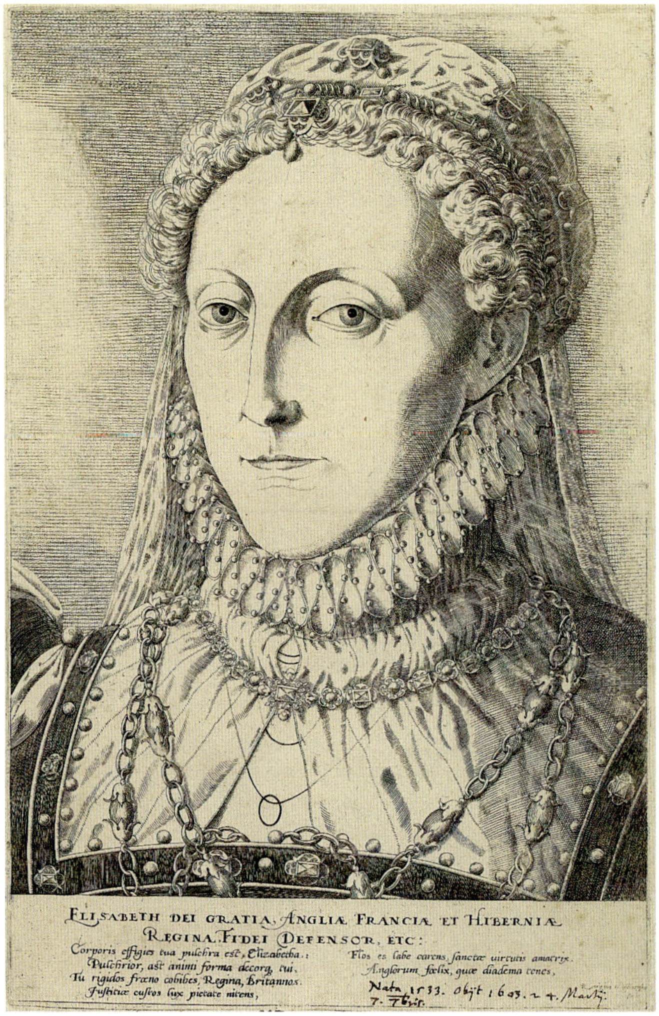

PROVENANCE

Acquired in 1862.

LITERATURE

O'Donoghue 1908–25, vol. II, p.150; Mayger Hind 1952, vol. I, p.72; *New Hollstein* 2009, no. 28.

NOTES

1 Mayger Hind 1952, pp.13–14.
2 *New Hollstein* 2009, nos 16 and 120.

12

Elizabeth I

Unknown artist, c.1575–80

Oil on canvas
(no sign of being transferred from wood),
647 × 508mm
The University of Cambridge

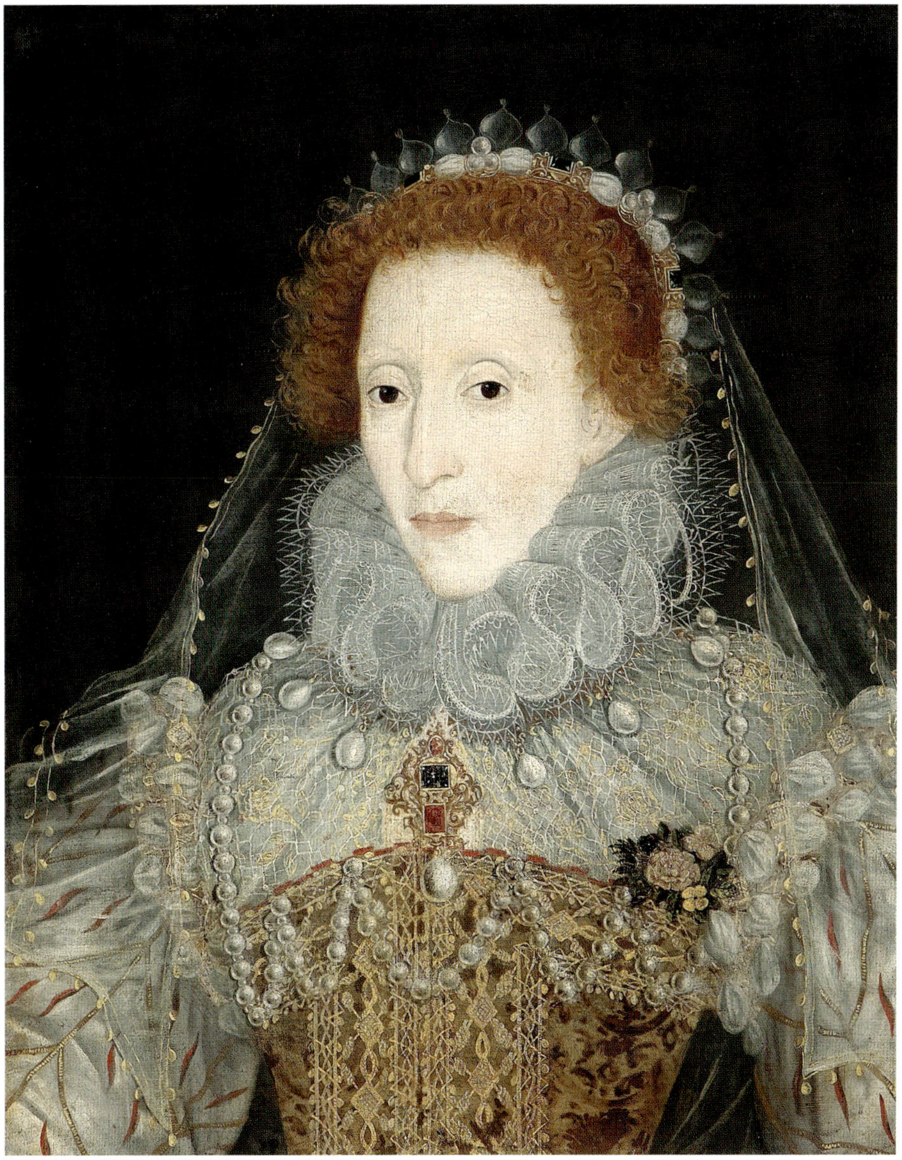

This portrait of the Queen was probably displayed at the University of Cambridge in Elizabeth's lifetime, and it is possibly the portrait given by a 'Mr Sckinner' in 1588/9. It depicts Elizabeth in her late forties or early fifties and shows her elaborately dressed, wearing a distinctive necklace consisting of a gold collar, from which hang six large pearls and a jewelled central pendant. The composition derives from a portrait type common in the late 1570s and early 1580s, and would have been made from an established pattern (derived from the Darnley Portrait, cat. 8) that circulated between workshops, rather than painted directly from the life. Portraits of Elizabeth I were certainly produced in far larger numbers than survive today and were probably available ready-made for an expanding market.

This painting can be linked with a picture that is recorded in the University archives, where payments are recorded for the carriage of a painting in 1588 as follows: 'Item for bringinge of the Queenes picture which Mr Sckinner gave Vnto the Universitye ijs [2 shillings]'.[1] 'Mr Sckinner' is perhaps Vincent Skinner (d.1616), who is mentioned in other places in the University accounts in association with William Cecil, Lord Burghley (cat. 19), Chancellor of the University 1559–98, and his younger son, Robert Cecil (High Steward 1591–1601 and then Chancellor 1601–12). He is known to have served as secretary to Lord Burghley between 1578 and 1593, and was MP for various seats that fell under Burghley's influence (Truro, 1571; Barnstaple, 1572; Boston, 1584, 1586, 1589; Boroughbridge, 1593; St Ives, 1597 and Preston, 1604).[2] He also served as auditor of the receipts of the Exchequer between 1593 and 1609, and was knighted in May 1603, although he died intestate in a debtors' prison.[3] TC & AO

PROVENANCE

Probably the portrait recorded in the Vice-Chancellor's accounts for the year 1588/9 as being given to the university by (Sir) Vincent Skinner.

LITERATURE

Venn 1927, p.85; Kelly 1944, p.78; Auerbach 1953, p.202; Goodison 1955; Strong 1963, p.63; Hasler 1981, vol. III, pp.390–1.

NOTES

1 Account of Thomas Neville, Vice-Chancellor, 1588, in Vice-Chancellor's and Proctors' accounts, 1575–1600 (VCV 2: 10, 10a).
2 Hasler, p.390–1.
3 Hasler, p.391.

13

Elizabeth I with the Cardinal and Theological Virtues

Unknown English artist, c.1598

Oil on panel, 1190 × 960mm
Dover Museum and Bronze Age Boat Gallery

This striking portrait is one of the few surviving paintings of Elizabeth I known to have been displayed in a civic context during her lifetime. While the Queen's image would have been familiar to her subjects through official reproductions on coins, and in prints and woodcuts, we can imagine that this painting, purchased by the Corporation of Dover for display in the town hall, would have provided a far more engaging likeness for the townspeople. Elizabeth had visited Dover for five days while on a progress through Kent in August 1573, although this painting is not connected to this visit. The picture was paid for in 1598 and cost 25 shillings, while its wooden frame carved with the heraldic supporters of a dragon and a lion cost an additional 6 shillings and 9 pence.[1] Elizabeth is depicted wearing her Parliament robes, which were made of crimson velvet lined with ermine. This type of portrait, painted in a naive style, would not have been made from the life, but would have relied on numerous existing sources. The Queen's face, with its small mouth and slightly hooked nose, is distinctive and may have been adapted from patterns available to artist's workshops.

The pillar to the left of the composition depicts personifications symbolic of Fortitude, Chastity and Imperial Destiny. Pillars were regularly incorporated into the Queen's personal iconography; for example, a crowned pillar rising from the sea decorates the reverse of a cameo dating from the 1580s, two pillars topped with a phoenix and a pelican flank the Queen in an engraving of 1596, and in the 'Sieve Portrait' (*c.*1580; Pinacoteca, Siena) an elaborate pillar is inset with medallions depicting the story of Dido and Aeneas.[2] The medallions decorating the Dover Corporation portrait contain female personifications of the three theological virtues of Faith, Hope and Charity at the top, with the four cardinal virtues of Justice, Prudence, Temperance and Fortitude shown below. Personifications of the virtues were a common form of Renaissance symbolism, found in literature, plays and prints, and would have been readily understood by many of the educated, middling sort who originally viewed this painting. TC & AO

PROVENANCE

Purchased by the Corporation of Dover, 1598.

EXHIBITIONS

Elizabeth, London, National Maritime Museum, 2003 (200), pp.196–8.

LITERATURE

Wollaston Knocker 1898;
Strong 1987, pp.101–7; Doran 2003, no. 200, pp.196–8.

NOTES

1 Wollaston Knocker 1898.
2 Strong 1987, pp.101–7.

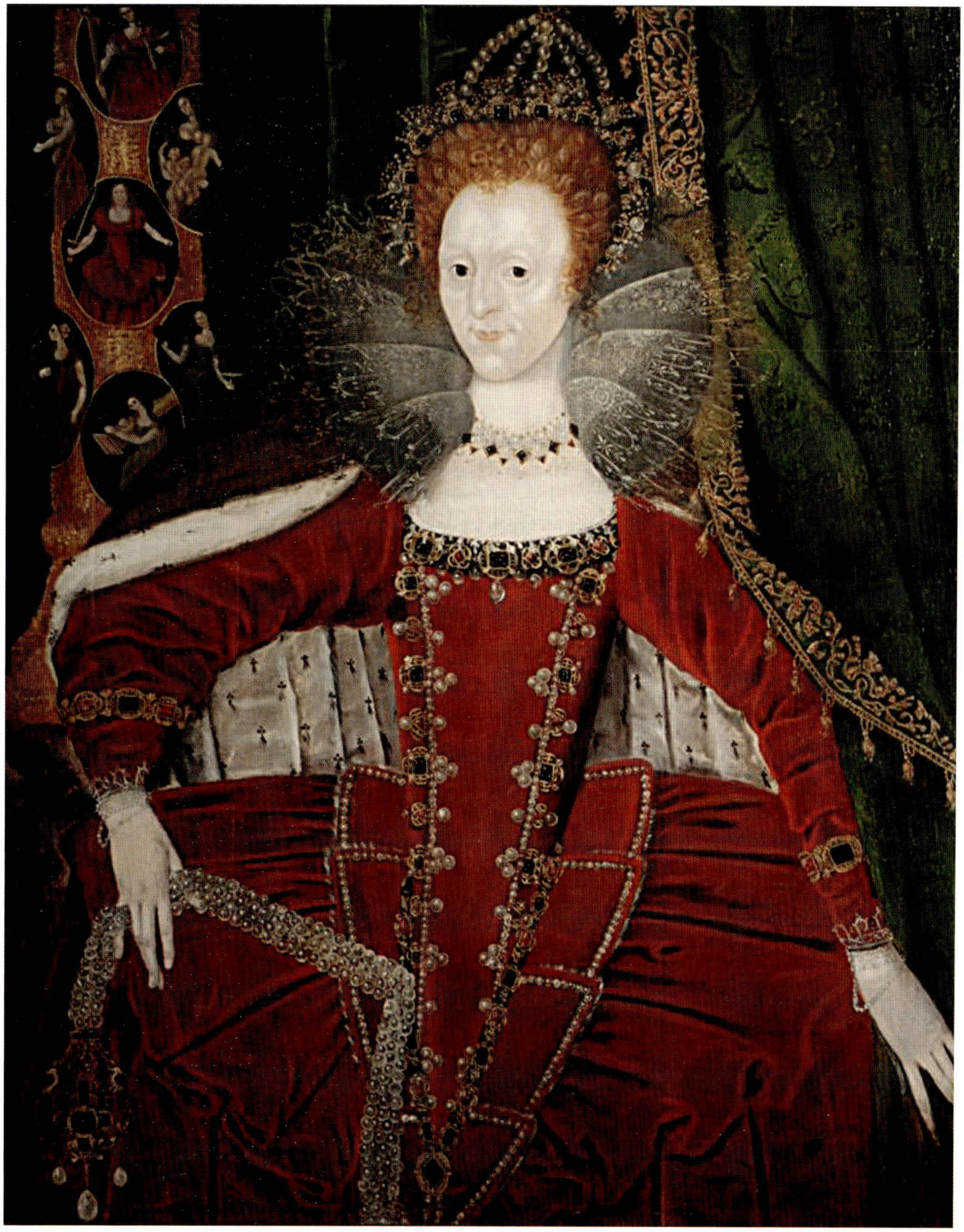

16

Queen Elizabeth I

Nicholas Hilliard, dated 1572

Watercolour on vellum, 51 × 48mm
Inscribed: *An[n]o D[omi]ni 1572 / Aetatis Suae 38*
National Portrait Gallery, London (NPG 108)

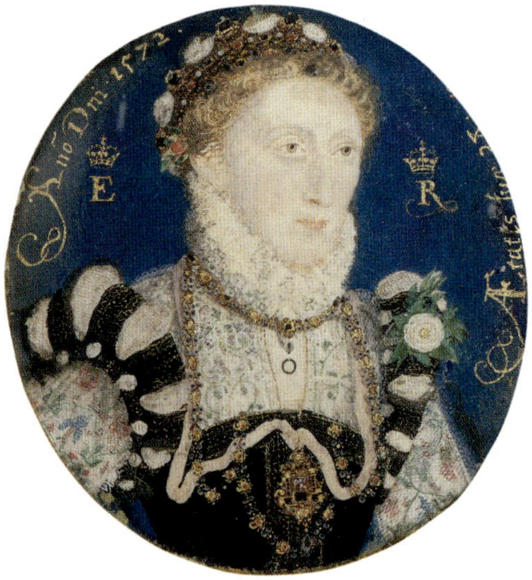

This remarkable portrait is Hilliard's earliest known miniature of the Queen, painted when she was thirty-eight years old and the artist was just twenty-five. Elizabeth was to appoint Hilliard as her official limner, a service to the monarch that he would continue to perform after the accession of James I in 1603.

This may be the portrait that the artist describes painting in his treatise *The Arte of Limning* (*c*.1598–1603). Here, he relates a discussion with the Queen in which she remarks on an absence of shadow in the works of the best Italian draughtsmen. Hilliard explains his view that 'the line without shadow showeth all to a good judgement', especially for small pictures, which are to be 'viewed of necessity in hand near unto the eye'. As a consequence of this conversation, the Queen chose to sit in 'the open alley of a goodly garden, where no tree was near, nor any shadow at all'. The likeness may have been taken in one of the gardens of one of the royal palaces, for example, Whitehall, Hampton Court or Greenwich. Hilliard tactfully concludes his account of this sitting by stating how the Queen's curiosity about the art of painting greatly bettered his judgement.[1] The pattern for the Queen's face, as created here by Hilliard, was closely followed in two later, large-scale oil paintings: the so-called 'Phoenix' and 'Pelican' portraits (*c*.1575; National Portrait Gallery, London and Walker Art Gallery Liverpool, respectively), which are associated with Hilliard's studio.[2]

Thin strokes of orange, painted directly on to the vellum, describe the curls of the hair, on which sits a diamond and emerald jewelled band (detail a). The costume is equally detailed; the light, transparent material of the undershirt and sleeves indicated by fine diagonal strokes of white paint (detail c). The skilful economy of Hilliard's painting technique can be seen in the ribbon of the Queen's pendant, which is deliberately left unpainted to reveal the pale pink priming ground beneath (detail c). JE

PROVENANCE

National Portrait Gallery, purchased 1860.

EXHIBITIONS

Hilliard and Oliver, London, Victoria and Albert Museum, 1947 (6).

LITERATURE

Auerbach 1961, pp.63–4; Strong 1963, pp.90–1; Strong 1969b, p.108 and pl.90; Reynolds 1971; Thornton and Cain 1981, pp.84–7; Strong 1987, p.79.

NOTES

1 All quotations from Hilliard's *Treatise* are from Thornton and Cain 1981, pp.85–7.
2 For further information see: www.npg.org.uk/research/programmes/making-art-in-tudor-britain/the-phoenix-and-the-pelican-two-portraits-of-elizabeth-i-c.1575.php

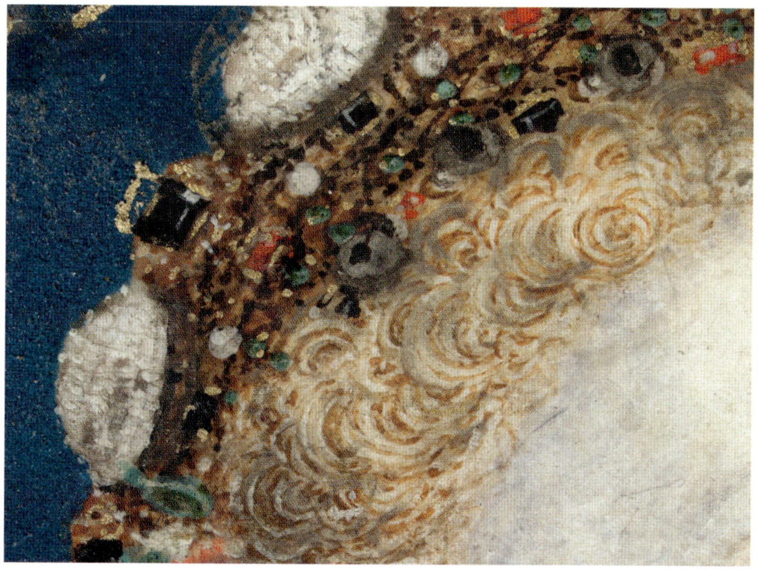
a

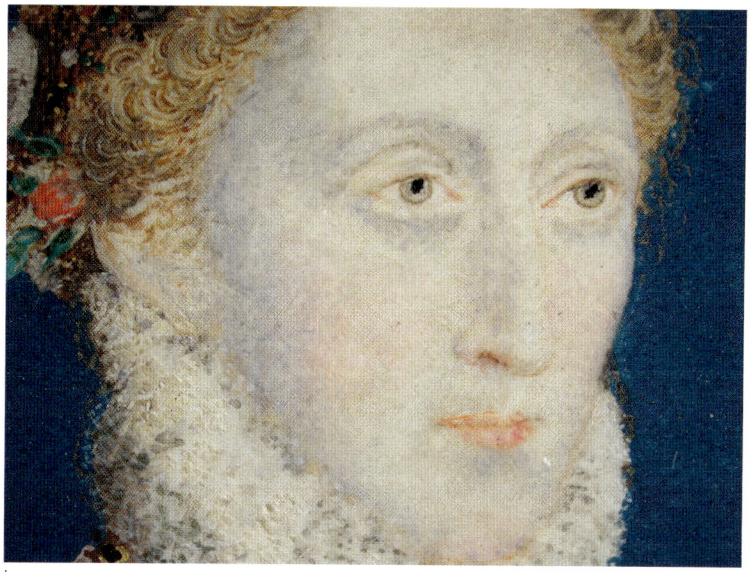
b

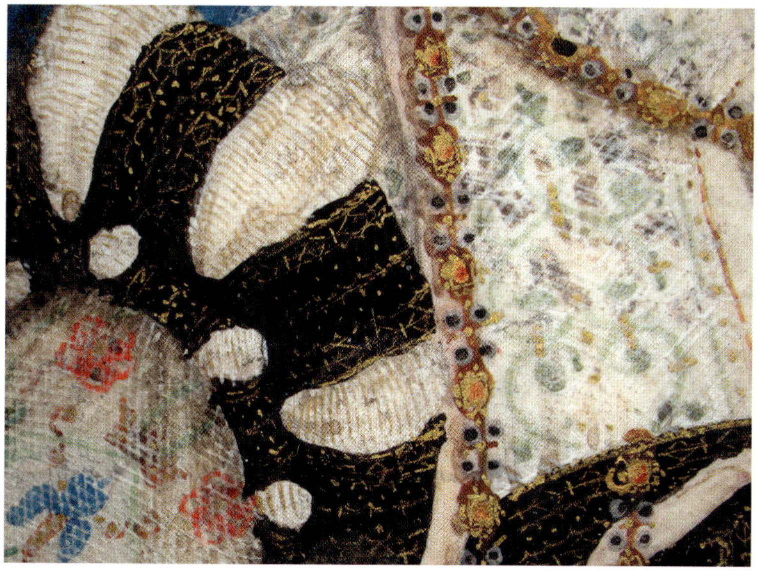
c

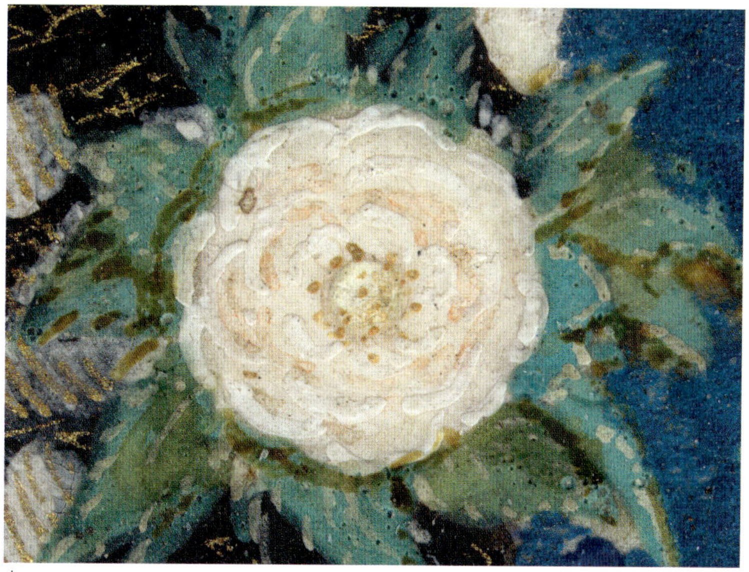
d

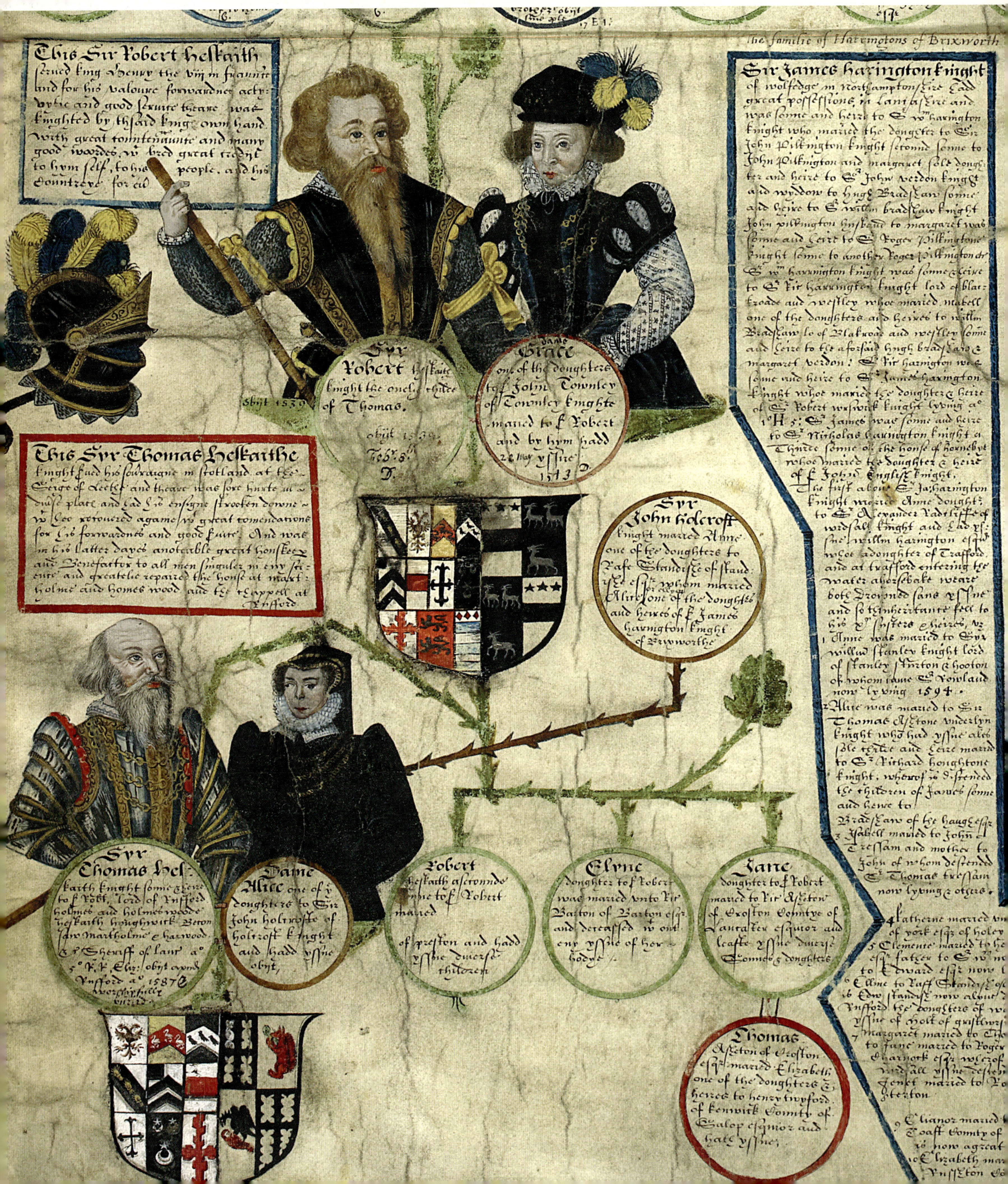
the familie of Haringtons of Brixworth
This Sir Robert Heskaith
Sir James Harington knight
This Syr Thomas Heskaithe
Syr Robert
Dame Grace
Syr John Holcroft
Syr Thomas Hes-
Dame Alice
Robert
Elyne
Jane
Thomas

3 NOBILITY, GENTRY AND THE COURT

The Elizabethan nobility derived their power from the ownership of land and hereditary titles. Their rank and honour were accorded to them by the monarch for services to the realm, which then passed to their descendants. The monarch, in turn, was considered to have been put in place by God and thus the right of the nobility to rule their estates was not only a result of inheritance, but also divine sanction.

The nobility and the gentry demonstrated their rank and wealth by building country houses, maintaining large estates and households, and by commissioning luxury goods, tomb monuments and portraits. They also had representation in Parliament in the House of Lords. In person, the nobility wore elaborate clothes (often made from expensive imported fabrics and rare furs) and were adorned with jewels. The wearing of particular fabrics and types of clothing was restricted and regulated by legislation known as sumptuary laws. In theory, this meant a man's rank and wealth could be estimated by his clothes alone. Portraits of members of the nobility reflect this heavy investment in sumptuous clothes, as seen in portraits of Thomas Howard, 4th Duke of Norfolk, and his wife, and Sir Walter Ralegh (cats 17 and 22).

The gentry owned land but did not enjoy hereditary titles. With rising agricultural prosperity, entry into their ranks became gradually more fluid, and increasingly gentility became associated with a leisured lifestyle. Younger sons of gentry families often went into the professions or sometimes trade, while daughters of particularly wealthy merchants might marry into the gentry or nobility. By the end of the Elizabethan period, both professional men and those with the right credentials often presented themselves as gentlemen, whether or not land was the primary source of their income.

Both the nobility and the gentry were awarded heraldic badges of honour, (coats of arms), which were overseen by the heralds at the College of Arms, as displayed in many of the portraits illustrated in this chapter.

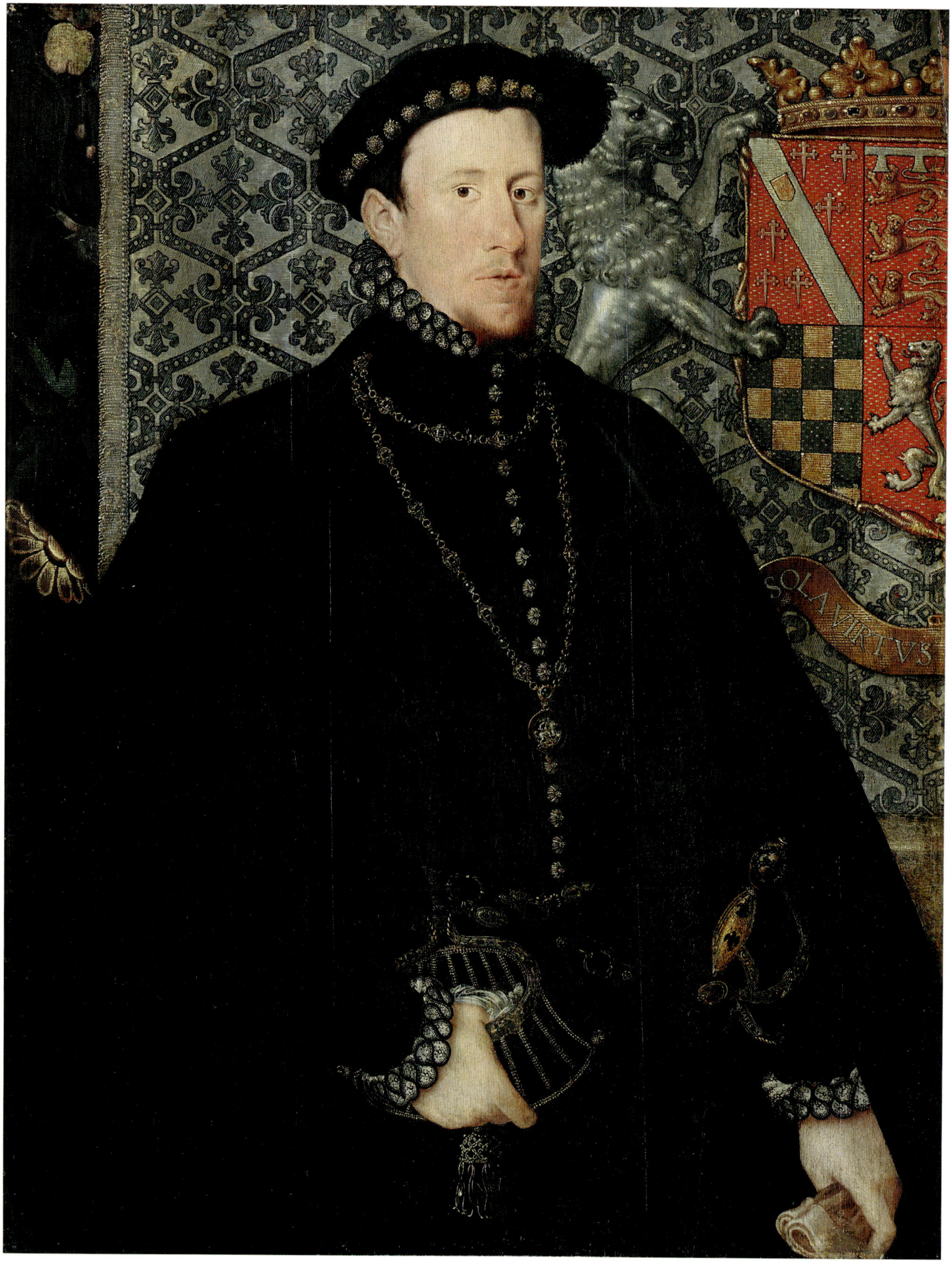

17a

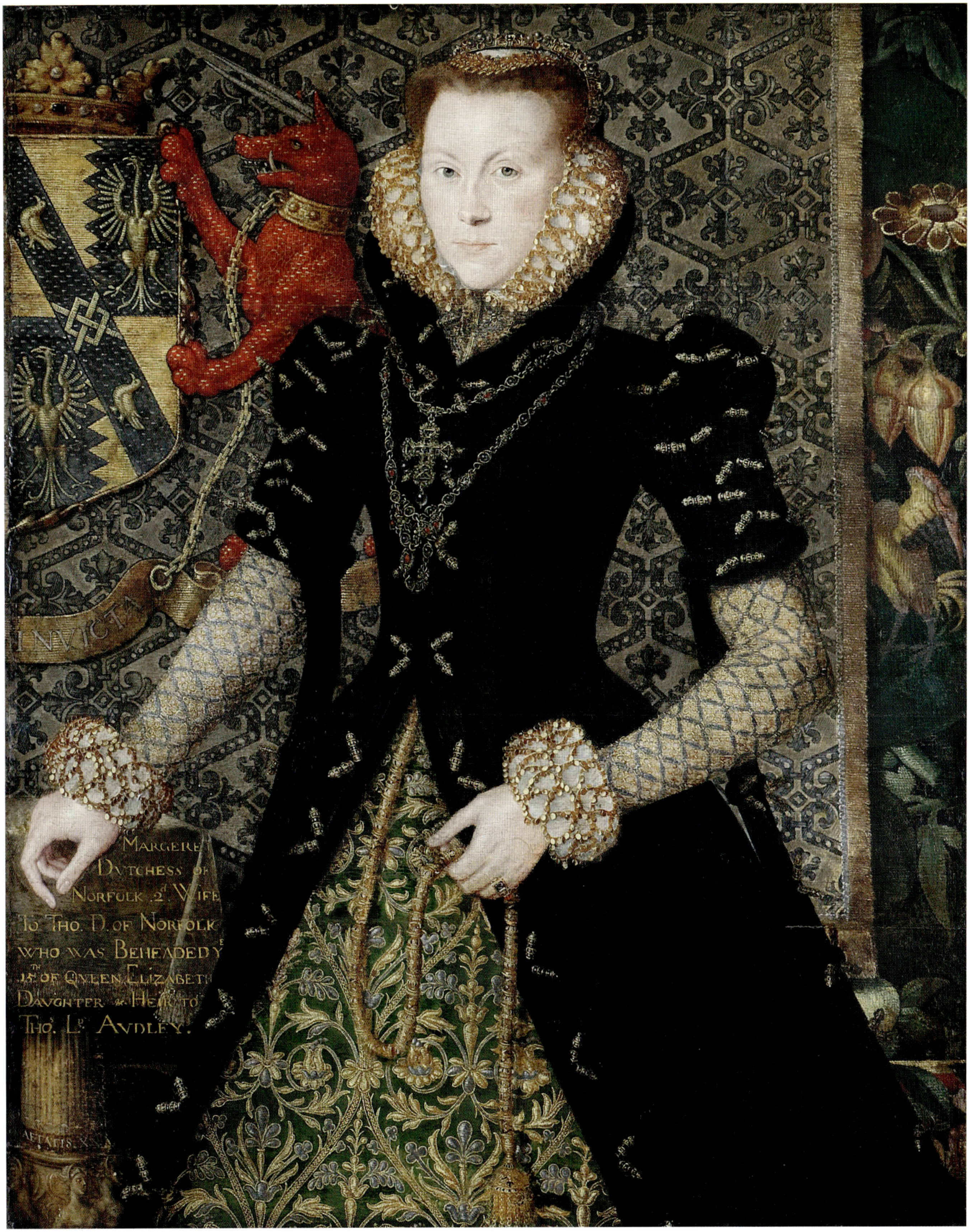
INVICTA
MARGERE
DVTCHESS OF
NORFOLK 2d WIFE
TO THO. D. OF NORFOLK
WHO WAS BEHEADED YE
15TH OF QVEEN ELIZABETH
DAVGHTER & HEIR TO
THO. LD AVDLEY.

17b

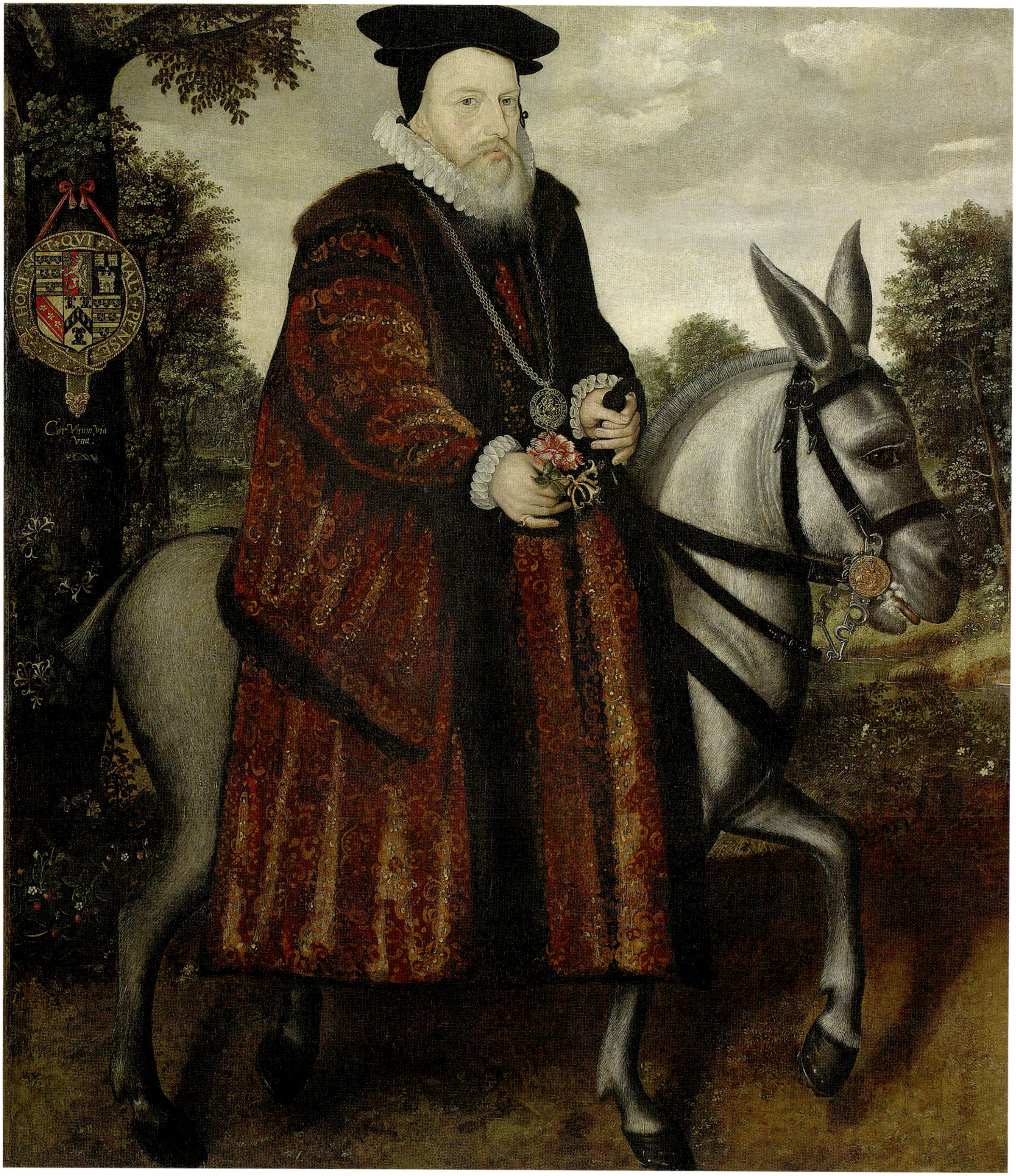
HONI·SOIT·QVI·MAL·Y·PENSE
Cor Vnum via
Vna.

19

William Cecil, 1st Baron Burghley (1520/1–98)

Unknown Anglo-Netherlandish artist, *c.*1580s

Oil on canvas (transferred from panel), 1302 × 1105mm
Inscribed: *Cor Unum, Via/Una* (One Heart, One Way)
The Bodleian Libraries, University of Oxford (LP 38)

Numerous contemporary portraits of Burghley attest to his great political influence and importance as a patron. This image of the Lord Treasurer upon a mule in a landscape setting is exceptional, however, and does not appear to have been copied in his lifetime. Burghley is known to have enjoyed riding a mule in his gardens at Theobalds. His biographer maintained that, with so little time for relaxation, 'riding in his garden walks, upon his little mule' was 'his greatest disport'.[1] He was given his first animal by the French ambassador to Elizabeth I's court, Mauvissière, in *c.*1575; it was replaced in 1586 courtesy of Sir Edward Stafford, then English ambassador in Paris.

The bucolic setting and association of Christian humility are combined in the portrait of Burghley with references to his dependence upon Elizabeth. In 1571 the Queen created him Baron Burghley and the following year he was admitted to the Noble Order of the Garter. Burghley is depicted wearing the lesser George (or smaller badge of the order) on a heavy gold chain around his neck and his coat of arms appears within a Garter badge affixed to the tree. Visually balancing the emblems of the Garter is the bridle bit of Burghley's mule. This shows a club-wielding man between two horses, perhaps riding a chariot or trampling a figure beneath, and may represent Hercules taming the horses of Diomedes.[2]

The portrait probably dates from the 1580s, like other paintings of the Lord Treasurer with the Garter badge on a pillar, although the face pattern belongs to an earlier period. Although the artist is unknown, the picture is painted with considerable skill and economy. The exceptional attention to detail – as seen in the beautifully rendered landscapes and strawberry flowers, the coat and eyelashes of the mule and the scene within the gold medallion of the mule's bridle – indicates that the artist is likely to be a Netherlandish émigré, or a native painter influenced by a Netherlander. The picture was cut down when it was transferred from panel to canvas.

The portrait is replete with symbols of loyalty (and possibly Herculean labour and penance), reinforced by the inscription 'One Heart, One Way'. It has been suggested that the commission may have been a response to the political turmoil occasioned by the trial and execution of Mary, Queen of Scots, in 1587, when Burghley was shunned by the Queen for several months.[3] JE

PROVENANCE

The portrait is probably that recorded as a gift from William Fletcher, Mayor of Oxford, to the Bodleian Libraries, 1797.

EXHIBITIONS

National Portraits, London, South Kensington, 1866 (245); *Armada*, London, National Maritime Museum, 1988 (33.3); *Sir Thomas Bodley and his Library*, Oxford, Bodleian Library, 2002 (11).

LITERATURE

Cor 1904, pp.93–4; Poole 1912, vol. I, pp.15–16; Strong 1969b, vol. 1, p.32, vol. 2, pl. 56; Auerbach and Kingsley Adams 1972, pp.51–2; Poole 2004, p.57; Croft 2007, pp.61–75.

NOTES

1 A.G.R. Smith, 'Lord Burghley and his Household Biographers: John Clapham and Sir Michael Hickes', in *Patronage, Culture and Power: the Early Cecils 1558–1612*, ed. Pauline Croft, Yale Studies in British Art 8 (Yale University Press, New Haven and London, 2002), p.253. Smith identifies Burghley's anonymous biographer as Sir Michael Hickes, one of his secretaries.

2 If correct, the use of this symbol on the mule's bridle may be a punning reference to the fact that Hercules was said to have tamed the 'unbridled jaws' of the steeds of Diomedes 'with the bit' (Euripides, *Hercules*, 380).

3 Croft 2007, pp.61–75.

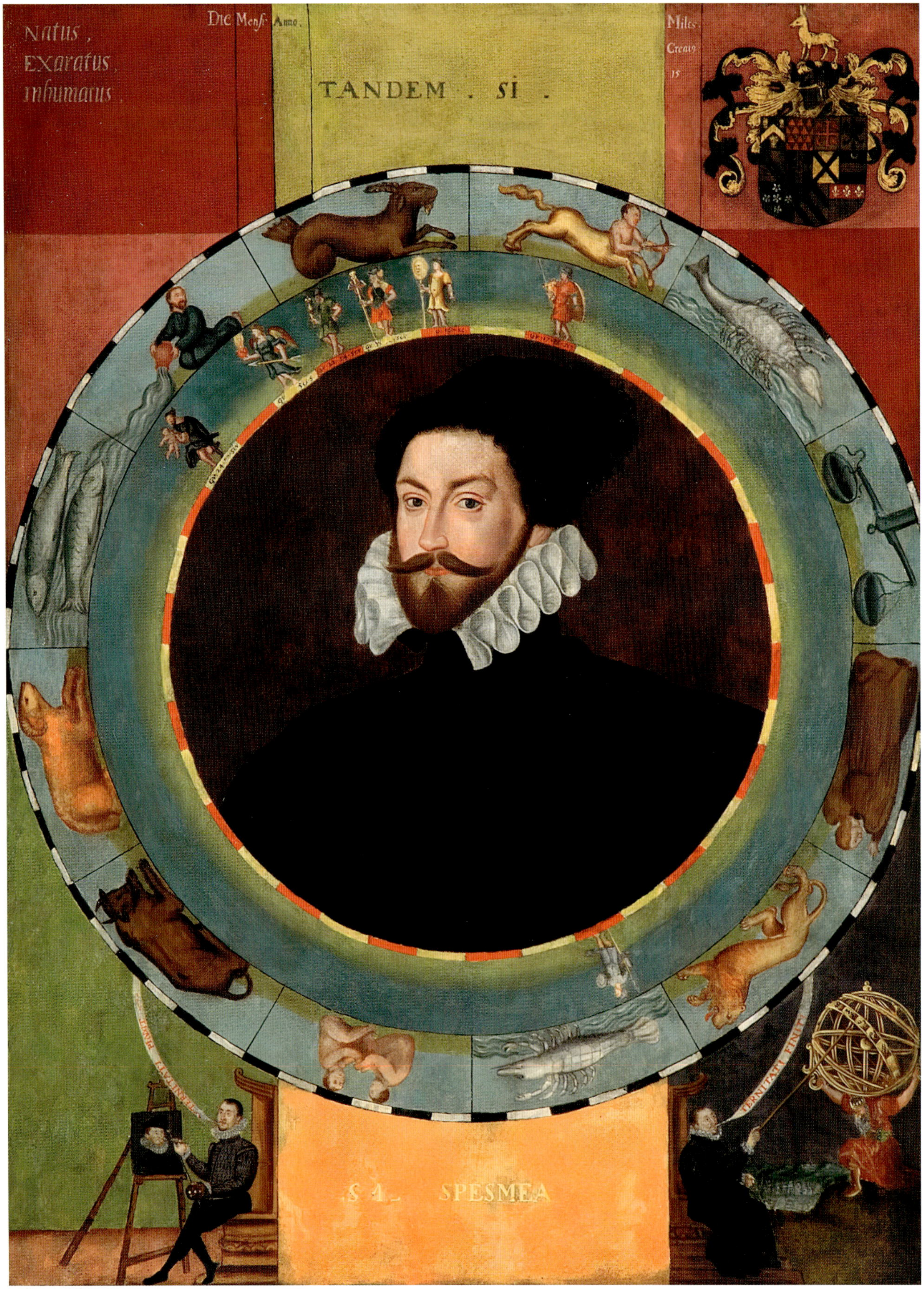
Natus ,
Exaratus ,
inhumatus .
Die Mens: Anno.
Miles
TANDEM . SI .
SPESMEA

20 recto

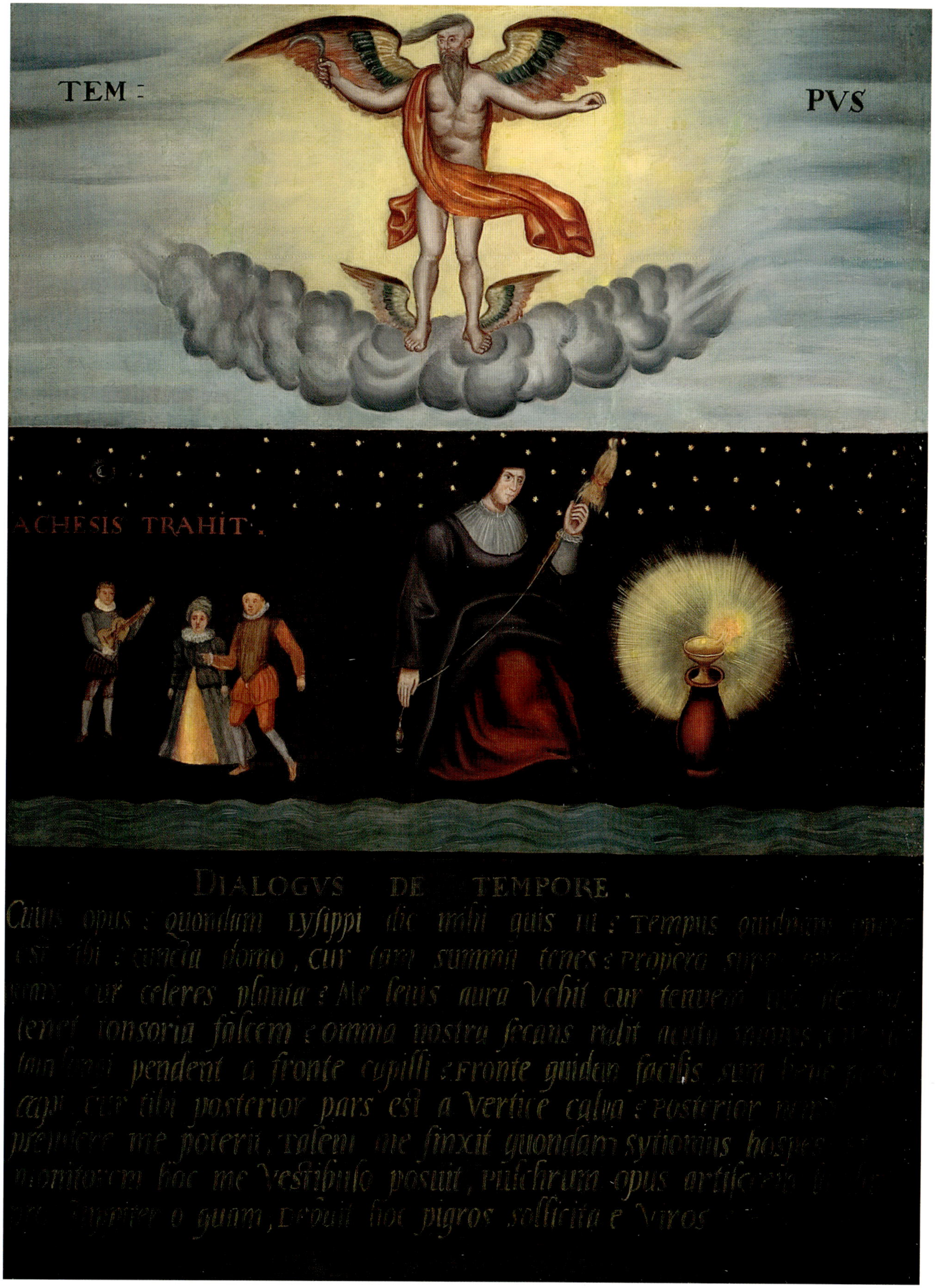

20 verso

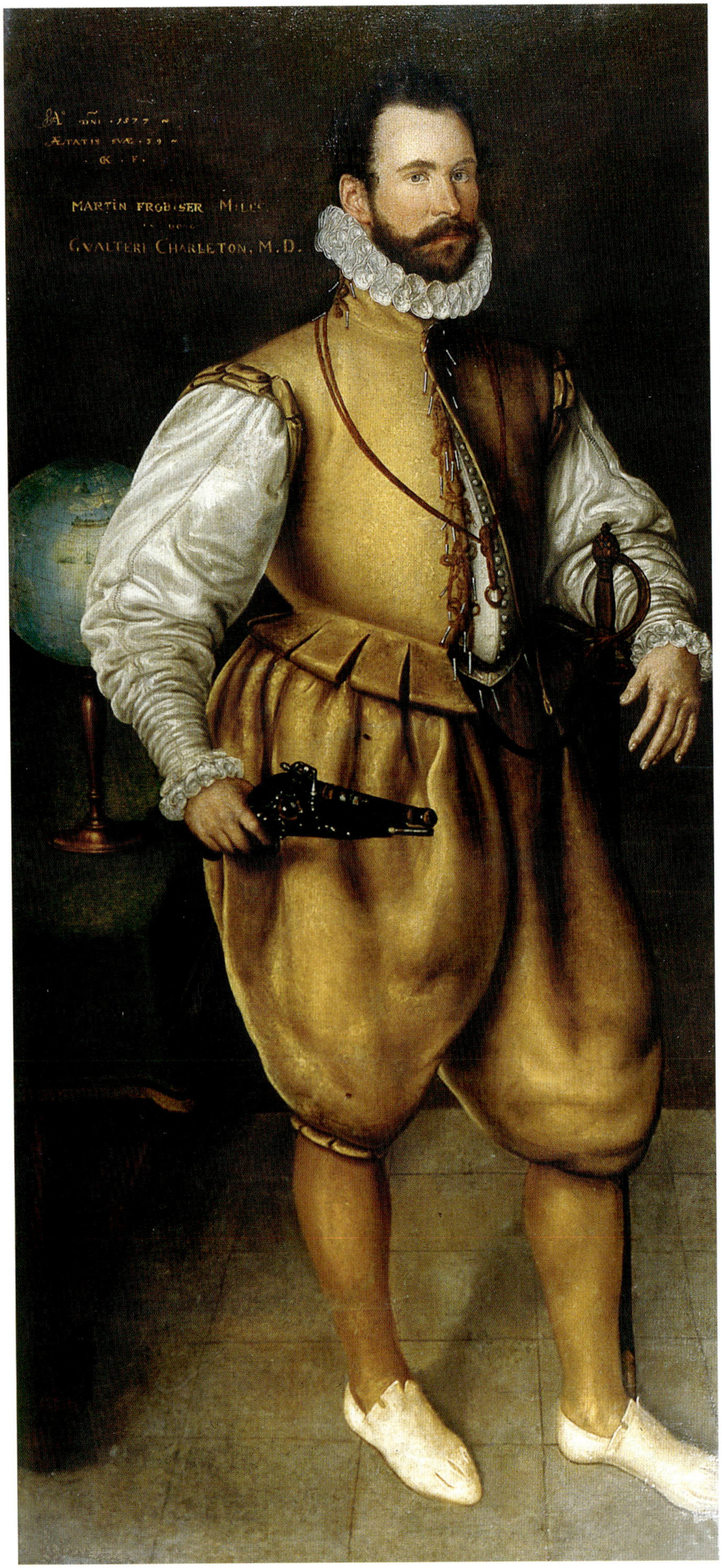
MARTIN FROBISER
GVALTERI CHARLETON, M.D.

21

Sir Martin Frobisher (1535?–94)

Cornelis Ketel, dated 1577

Oil on canvas, 2070 × 940mm
Inscribed: *A[NN]° D[OMI]NI 1577 / AETATIS SVAE 39; CK. F* and in a later hand: *MARTIN FROBISHER MILES. EX DONO GVALTERI CHARLETON, M[EDICINAE].D[OCTOR]* (MARTIN FROBISHER, KNIGHT, DONATED BY WALTER CHARLETON, DOCTOR OF MEDICINE)
The Bodleian Libraries, University of Oxford (LP 50)

Martin Frobisher was a privateer, explorer and naval commander, best known for his three Arctic voyages to discover a north-west passage to the fabled Cathay (China) and for the Inuit captives he returned with from what is now called Frobisher Bay in Canada. This arresting portrait of a man characterised as 'uncultured and semi-literate' with 'an acutely violent temperament' was painted in 1577 to commemorate Frobisher's return from his second voyage, in which the Queen herself had invested by supplying a ship.[1]

The portrait is one of a series commissioned from the Dutch artist Cornelis Ketel (1548–1616) by the Cathay Company, of which only this 'great picture of Captayne furbusher', for which Ketel was paid £5, survives.[2] Others in the series included a painting of Frobisher's ship, the *Gabriel*, and a set of portraits – in 'great' and 'smalle' – of an Inuk male captive 'whose like was never seen, read, nor heard of before, and whose language was neither known nor understood ...'.[3] One of these portraits was specially cased to be sent to the Queen.[4]

Full-length portraits of non-royal sitters were rare in England at this date, making the format of this portrait particularly commanding. Frobisher is presented as the man of action he was, attired in a plain doublet and the voluminous hose known as 'Venetians'. He wears the honoured badge of a 'bosun's whistle' around his neck, used for passing orders at sea.[5] The globe on the table signifies the extent of his travels, while the fine examples of a wheel-lock pistol, rapier and dagger, all carefully rendered, are not only status symbols but allude to the nature and potential danger of his activities.[6]

Frobisher's final expedition collapsed in debt when the ore he had mined proved worthless. His reputation suffered, but was rehabilitated during the 1588 Armada campaign when he commanded the *Triumph* and was knighted by the Lord Admiral aboard the flagship. JE

PROVENANCE

Painted for the Cathay Company; given to the University of Oxford by Walter Charleton, 1674.

EXHIBITIONS SINCE 1900

Tudor Exhibition, London, New Gallery, 1900 (327); *Historical Portraits*, Oxford, Examination Schools, 1904 (68); *16th Century Portraits of Famous Early Elizabethans*, Manchester City Art Gallery, 1953 (38); *Between Renaissance and Baroque*, Manchester, Manchester City Art Gallery, 1965 (141); *A Pageant of Canada*, Ottawa, National Gallery of Canada, 1967 (6); *Armada*, Greenwich, National Maritime Museum, 1988 (33.27); *Inuit and Englishmen*, Hull (Quebec), Canadian Museum of Civilization, 1999.

LITERATURE

Poole 1912, vol. I, pp.20–1; Strong 1969, p.154; McDermott 2001; Poole 2004, p.143.

NOTES

1 James McDermott, 'Frobisher, Sir Martin (1535?–94)', *ODNB*, 2004, p.55.
2 TNA E 164/35 f.63v. Many thanks to Edward Town for providing both a copy and a transcript of this document.
3 George Best, *A true discourse of the late voyages of discoverie ...* (Henry Bynnyman, London, 1578).
4 TNA E 164/35 f.15v.
5 I would like to thank Hazel Forsyth (Museum of London) and Barbara Tomlinson (National Maritime Museum) for corresponding with me about this object and providing many useful references.
6 I am grateful to Angus Patterson (V&A) for confirming the presence of an ornamented hilt of a dagger, matching the sword, in the crook of Frobisher's left arm, and for pointing out that these have been blued and gilded.

22

Sir Walter Ralegh (1554–1618)

Unknown English artist, dated 1588

Oil on panel, 914 × 746mm
Inscribed upper left: *AMOR ET VIRTUTE* and upper left:
AETATIS SVAE 34 /AN [NO DOMINI] 1588
National Portrait Gallery, London (NPG 7)

This portrait, shown here before restoration, is one of only a few contemporary portraits of the court explorer Sir Walter Ralegh in his prime. Famously handsome, he rose quickly in Elizabeth I's favour. Made an Esquire of the Body in 1581, he secured a patent to colonise North America in 1584 and was knighted in 1585. This portrait was painted in the year of the attack by the Spanish Armada in 1588, when Ralegh's reputation and influence soared. The previous year he had been involved in surveying England's coastal defences, and was nominated to succeed Christopher Hatton as Captain of the Guard.

The painting would have been widely understood as a visual statement of Ralegh's devotion to the Queen. He wears the Queen's colours of black and white and his costume is covered with pearls, which were associated with Elizabeth as symbols of virginity. Recent research and subsequent restoration have shown that below the emblem of a crescent moon at the top left there is a small patch of wavy blue water to represent the sea. Elizabeth had been compared to the moon goddess Cynthia, and here the water must refer to Ralegh himself (using the pun Walter/water). The symbolism indicates Ralegh's willingness to be controlled by the Queen as the moon controls the tides, and is also found in the 'Cynthia' cycle of poems that Ralegh wrote for Elizabeth (cat. 23). The pearls on Ralegh's sable-trimmed cloak form the rays of a 'sun in splendour', a heraldic device also found in portraits of the Queen, possibly reinterpreted here as a 'moon in splendour'. Ralegh's cycle of poems was referred to in Edmund Spenser's *Fairie Queen* of 1590, and Spenser probably saw it in manuscript form in 1589 while both were in Ireland. The discovery of this symbolism suggests that Ralegh employed the representation of the moon goddess in a variety of ways during his relationship with the Queen in the late 1580s.

It seems possible that this painting belonged to Ralegh's elder brother, Sir Carew Ralegh, as it was recorded in the seventeenth century as being built into the panelling of his family home in Salisbury, where it remained until the nineteenth century.[1] The portrait has previously been attributed to the monogrammist 'H' (*fl.* 1580s), about whom we know very little, on the basis of the calligraphy of a lost inscription, which was similar to that of a monogrammed portrait of Sir John Shirley dated the same year (Metropolitan Museum, New York). Although there are some similarities in handling, Ralegh's portrait has suffered over time and its current condition hinders a secure attribution. Recent restoration indicates that the picture is subtly and skilfully painted by a native English artist. Technical analysis has also shown that the artist originally intended to show Ralegh with his right hand on his hip, instead of on the table. This evidence indicates that the picture was certainly devised as an original composition rather than from an existing portrait. TC & AO

PROVENANCE

First recorded at Downton House, Salisbury, c.1669–96, by John Aubrey; by descent with the house; removed by John Gibbs Bailey when he gave up the lease c.1825; purchased by the National Portrait Gallery, 1857.

EXHIBITIONS

Elizabeth, London, National Maritime Museum, 2003 (181), pp.165–6; *A New World: England's First View of America*, London, British Museum, 2006 (17), p.25.

LITERATURE

Cust 1920, VIII, pp.1–15; Strong 1969b, pp.254–9; Cooper 2012, p.172.

NOTE

1 Strong 1969b (quoting John Aubrey's *Lives*), p.256.

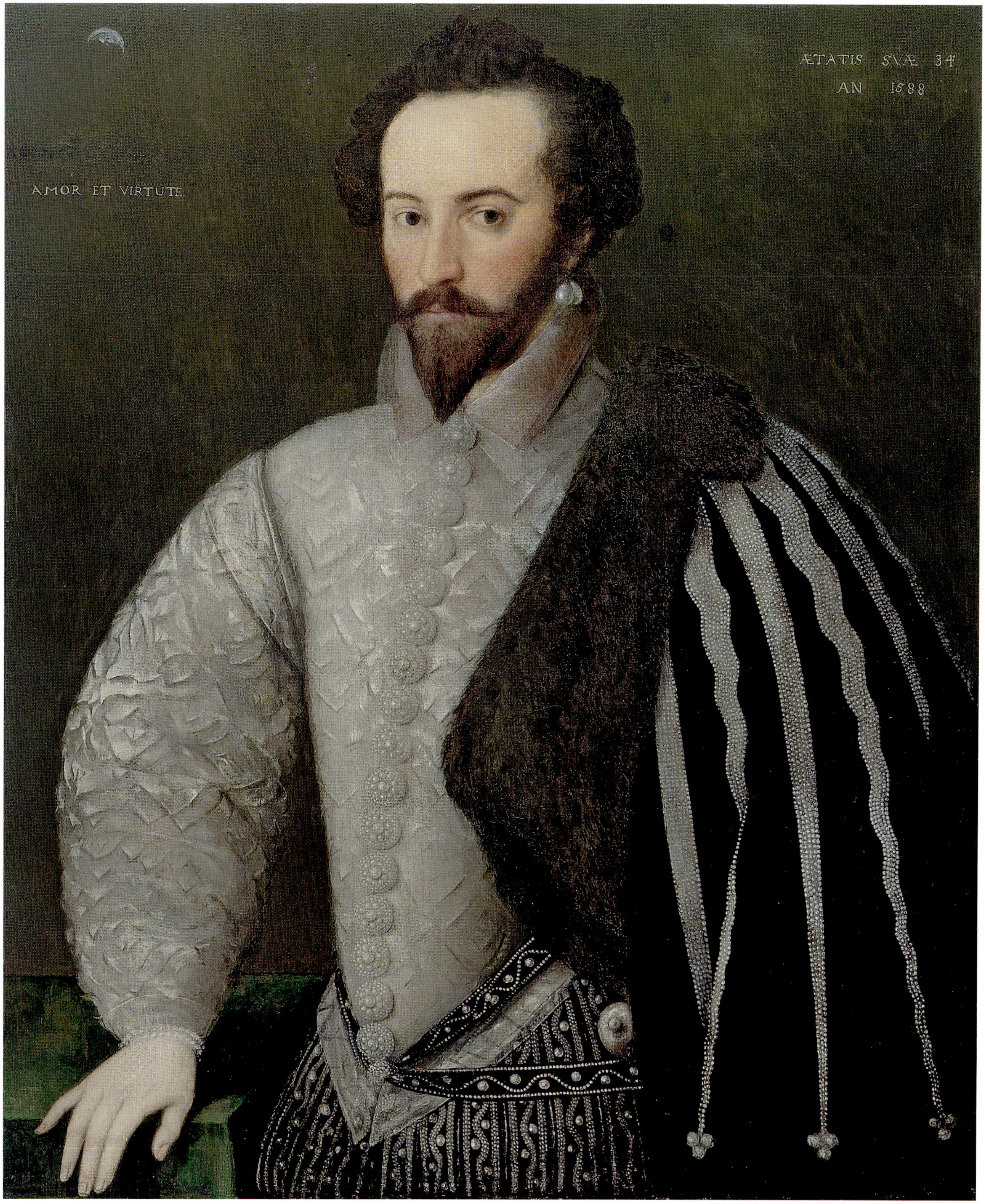
ÆTATIS SVÆ 34
AN 1588
AMOR ET VIRTUTE

23

Poem to Cynthia

Sir Walter Ralegh, c.1588–92

Manuscript, 290 × 200mm
The Marquess of Salisbury, Hatfield House
(Cecil Papers 144/238)

This poem is one of four in Sir Walter Ralegh's italic handwriting preserved in a composite manuscript among papers belonging to Lord Burghley (cat. 19). It was previously thought to have been written after Ralegh's secret marriage to Elizabeth Throckmorton, one of Elizabeth's ladies-in-waiting in 1591. Both were imprisoned when the Queen discovered what she considered a subterfuge that was a serious affront to her dignity, and Ralegh's fall from grace was spectacular. The cycle, of which this poem forms a part, seems very much like a series of extravagant supplications for a return to favour, a combination of exaggerated praise for a poetry-loving Queen and an earnest confession of guilt. We cannot be sure that Elizabeth ever saw it.

In this poem Ralegh represents Elizabeth I as Cynthia, the moon goddess, a powerful, benevolent virgin, who was also known to be capricious and difficult when affronted. Ralegh's use of such symbolism flatters the Queen, while recognising his own difficult position and Elizabeth's complicated relationship with her male courtiers.

The Cynthia fragments are original and fascinating works that reveal the extent of Ralegh's considerable literary talent. Ralegh makes a series of extravagant comparisons to illustrate the extent of his plight; having been rejected by the Queen, he refers to himself as 'unblest' and 'ill borne', one who was once happy to 'inebrase [embrace] the dust her boddy bearinge'. He emphasises the nature of his devotion to the monarch in ways that are surely at least partially humorous, suggesting that his love for Elizabeth is a 'burden to my beinge'. The page reproduced here explores the image of Ralegh as a pastoral figure serving the Queen at sea: he is the shepherd of the ocean, pining for his distant mistress, and despairing of ever finding his way back home.

Ralegh's poetry is written with the knowledge of Edmund Spenser's *Faerie Queene*, the first edition of which was published in 1590. Spenser and Ralegh had known each other in Ireland and then travelled to court together in 1591 (Spenser would later defend Ralegh in the second edition of his own great poem). In a prefatory sonnet to the 1590 *Faerie Queene*, Spenser described a work by Ralegh that addressed the Queen as 'Cynthia', which, along with the use of this motif in his portrait of 1588 (cat. 22), would suggest that Ralegh had started his poems before his disgrace and perhaps revised them later. Whether what we have is part of a longer sequence that has now been lost is disputed. AH

wch now to others do ther sweetnes send
th'incarnat, snow driven white, and purest asure.
who from high heaven doth on their feilds dissend
fillinge their barns with grayne, & towres with treasure,
erringe or never erringe, such is Love
as while it lasteth scornes th'accompt of thos
seekinge but sealf contentment to improve
and hydes if any bee, his inward woes,
and will not know while hee knowes his own passion
the often and uniust perseverance
in deeds of love, and state, and every action
from yt first day and yeare of their ioyes entrance,

But I unblessed, and ill borne creature
that did enbrace the dust her boddy bearinge
that loved her both, by fancy, and by nature
that drew even with the milke in my first suckinge
affection from the parents brest yt bare mee
have found her as a stranger so severe.
improvinge my mishapp in each degree
But love was gone, So would I, my life weare.
a Queen shee was to mee, no more Belphebe
a Lion then, no more a milke white Dove,
a prissoner in her brest I could not bee
~~but~~ shee did untye the gentell chaynes of love
~~[illegible]~~
~~[illegible]~~
~~[illegible]~~,
Love was no more the love of hydinge
all ~~trespase~~ trespase, and mischance, for her own glorye
It had byn such, it was still for th'elect
but I must bee th'exampell in loves storye
this was of all forpast the sadd effect...
But thow my weery sowle and heavy thought
made by her love a burden to my beinge
dust know my error never was forthought
or ever could proceed from ~~sight~~ sence of Lovinge
of other cause if then it had proceedinge

24

Sir Francis Drake (1540–96)

Nicholas Hilliard, dated 1581

Watercolour on vellum, diameter 28mm
Inscribed: *Aetatis Suae. 42. An[n]o D[omi]ni: 1581:*
On the reverse of the playing card, written in ink:
Franciscus Drake Miles
National Portrait Gallery, London (NPG 4851)

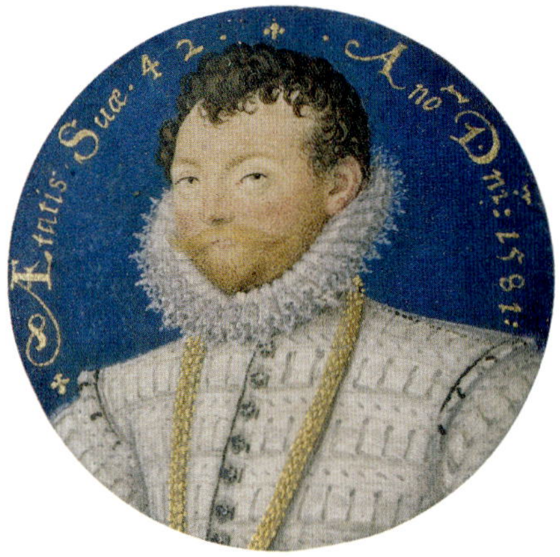

Francis Drake, pirate, explorer, sea captain and naval commander, was born in Devon, the eldest son of a shearman (of woollen cloth) and curate. Drake appears to have lived since boyhood in Plymouth with his kinsman William Hawkins, going to sea at an early age with Hawkins' sons William and John. Drake was to serve for several years under John Hawkins (1532–95), taking command of his first ship, *The Judith*, in 1567. From then on, his raids on the coast of the Spanish Indies made him a rich and feared man.

In 1577, Drake set off on what would become an astonishing three-year voyage around the world. Investors included Sir Christopher Hatton (cat. 20) and the Queen herself. He returned in September 1580 loaded with treasures, the full extent of which was disclosed in a lengthy private audience with Elizabeth. Knighted by the Queen in 1581, this miniature (painted on an ace of hearts playing card) celebrates his achievement.[1] Granted arms the same year, the sitter is presented as a gentleman and courtier, with a splendid gold chain (detail b) that may have been a gift, or perhaps booty from a raid as when a wealthy trader off the coast of Mexico 'surrendered a large gold chain and 7000 pesos in silver and goods'.[2] His appearance accords well with the description of him as 'broade Breasted, round headed, browne hayre, full Bearded, his eyes rounde, Large and Cleare, well-favoured, fayre and of a cheerefull countenance'.[3] In the miniature, the red pigment Hilliard has used for the nose and cheeks gives Drake's flesh a pronounced ruddy tone (detail a). Stow also records that Drake's enemies as well as his friends 'in his life time desired his Picture', making it all the more extraordinary that so few authentic portraits of him appear to have survived.[4] JE

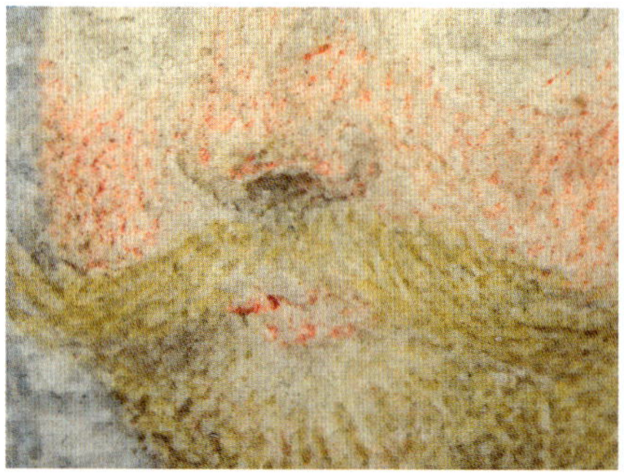

a

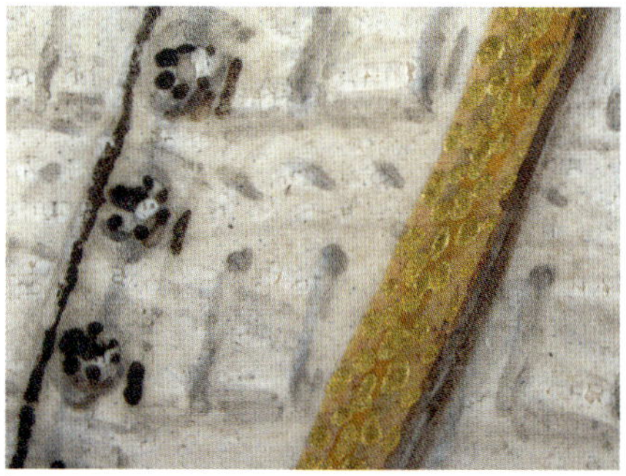

b

PROVENANCE

Horace Walpole, Strawberry Hill sale, 17 May 1842, lot 5, bought by the Earl of Derby; sold Christie's, 8 June 1971, and purchased by the National Portrait Gallery with help from the Wolfson Foundation and HM Government.

EXHIBITIONS

Sir Francis Drake, London, British Library, 1977 (107); *The Famous Voyage of Sir Francis Drake*, Exeter, Royal Albert Memorial Museum, 1980; *Armada 1588–1988*, London, National Maritime Museum, 1988 (13.22).

LITERATURE

Auerbach 1961, pl.48; Strong 1969b, pp.70–1.

NOTES

1 A similar miniature in the Kunsthistorisches Museum, Vienna, has an elaborate contemporary frame that records Drake's explorations. A copy of this miniature, painted in oils, was made for the collection of the Archduke Ferdinand of Tyrol, now also in the Kunsthistorisches Museum.

2 BL, Harley MS 280, fol.86v, quoted in Harry Kelsey, 'Drake, Sir Francis (1540–1596), *Oxford Dictionary of National Biography* (Oxford University Press, Oxford, 2004), pp.862–3.

3 John Stow, *The Annals, or, General chronicle of England/ begun first by maister Iohn Stow; and after him continued and augmented with matters forreyne and domestique, auncient and modern, unto the end of this present yeere 1614 by Edmond Howes . . .*, Londini: Impensis Thomae Adams, 1615, p.808.

4 Stow, The *Annals*, op. cit.

25

Mary Herbert, Countess of Pembroke (1561–1621)

Nicholas Hilliard, c.1590

Watercolour on vellum, diameter 54mm
National Portrait Gallery, London (NPG 5994)

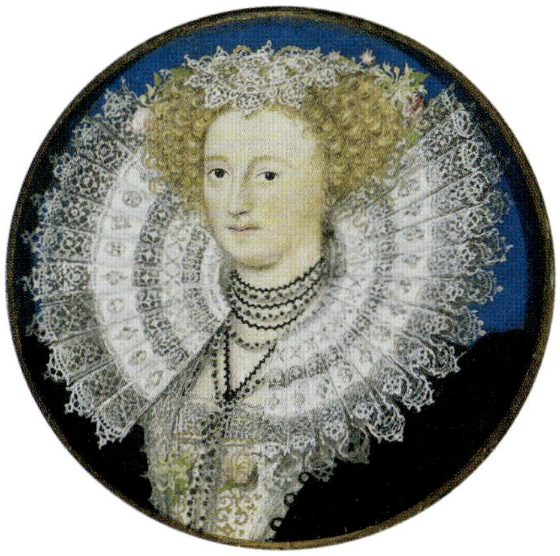

This miniature is one of the few portraits identified as a credible authentic likeness of the literary patron Mary Herbert, Countess of Pembroke. Mary's marriage to the widowed Henry Herbert in 1577 was arranged by her uncle, and the Queen's favourite, Robert Dudley, Earl of Leicester (cat. 18). The Pembroke family home was at Wilton, near Salisbury, where Mary engaged in literary pursuits in collaboration with her eldest brother, Sir Philip Sidney. Following his early death in 1586 she became a noted patron of his former supporters and was the first non-royal Englishwoman to be rewarded with numerous literary dedications.[1] She was celebrated by the writers Samuel Daniel, John Donne, Michael Drayton, George Herbert, William Shakespeare and Edmund Spenser among others. Pembroke would eventually oversee the publication of the manuscripts of Philip's poems, including *The Countess of Pembroke's Arcadia* (1593 and 1598), which her brother had dedicated to her, and would complete his paraphrasing of the Psalms. The latter shows the extent of her scholarship in English, French and Latin as well as knowledge of Hebrew.

The identification of this portrait with Mary Herbert is probable rather than certain, but the portrait shows some similarity to a later engraved likeness by Simon van de Passe, dated 1618. This miniature dates from the 1590s, when Mary's literary activity was at its height. The sitter wears an elaborate cartwheel ruff that was fashionable in this period (detail a), and the roses and honeysuckle depicted in her hair and on her bodice are suggestive of early summer (detail b). JE

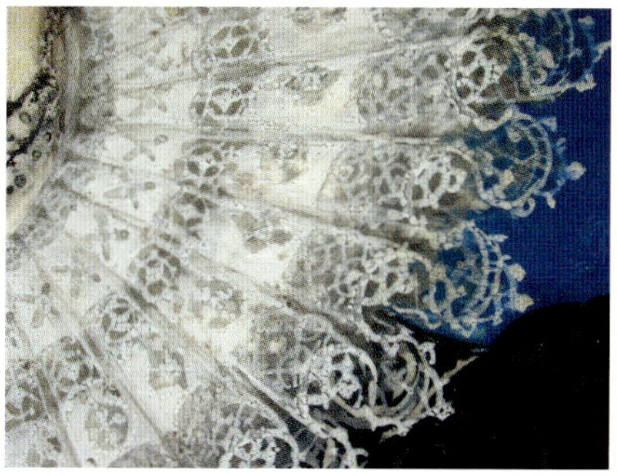

a

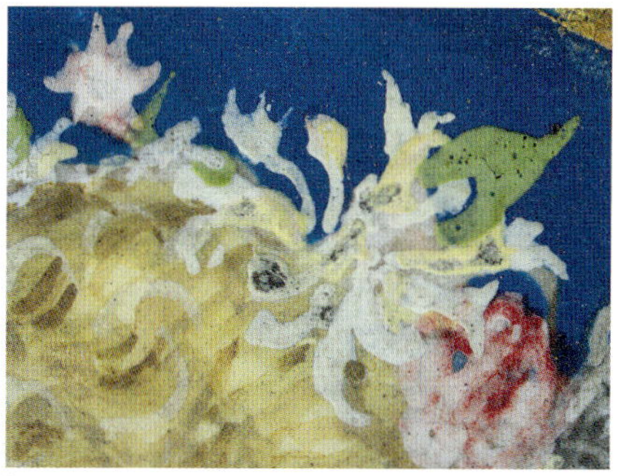

b

PROVENANCE

Lady Yonge; bequeathed to her niece Lady Anson; given by Lady Anson to the Harcourt family; Rev. William Vernon Harcourt; accepted in lieu of tax by H.M. Government and allocated to the National Portait Gallery, 1988.

EXHIBITIONS

Portrait Miniatures, London, South Kensington Museum, 1865; *Holbein to Hockney: 500 years of British Art*, Madrid, Fundacion Juan, 2012–13.

LITERATURE

Strong 1985, pp.694–9.

NOTE

1 F. Williams, 'The Literary Patronesses of Renaissance England', *Notes and Queries*, 207, 1962, pp.364–6.

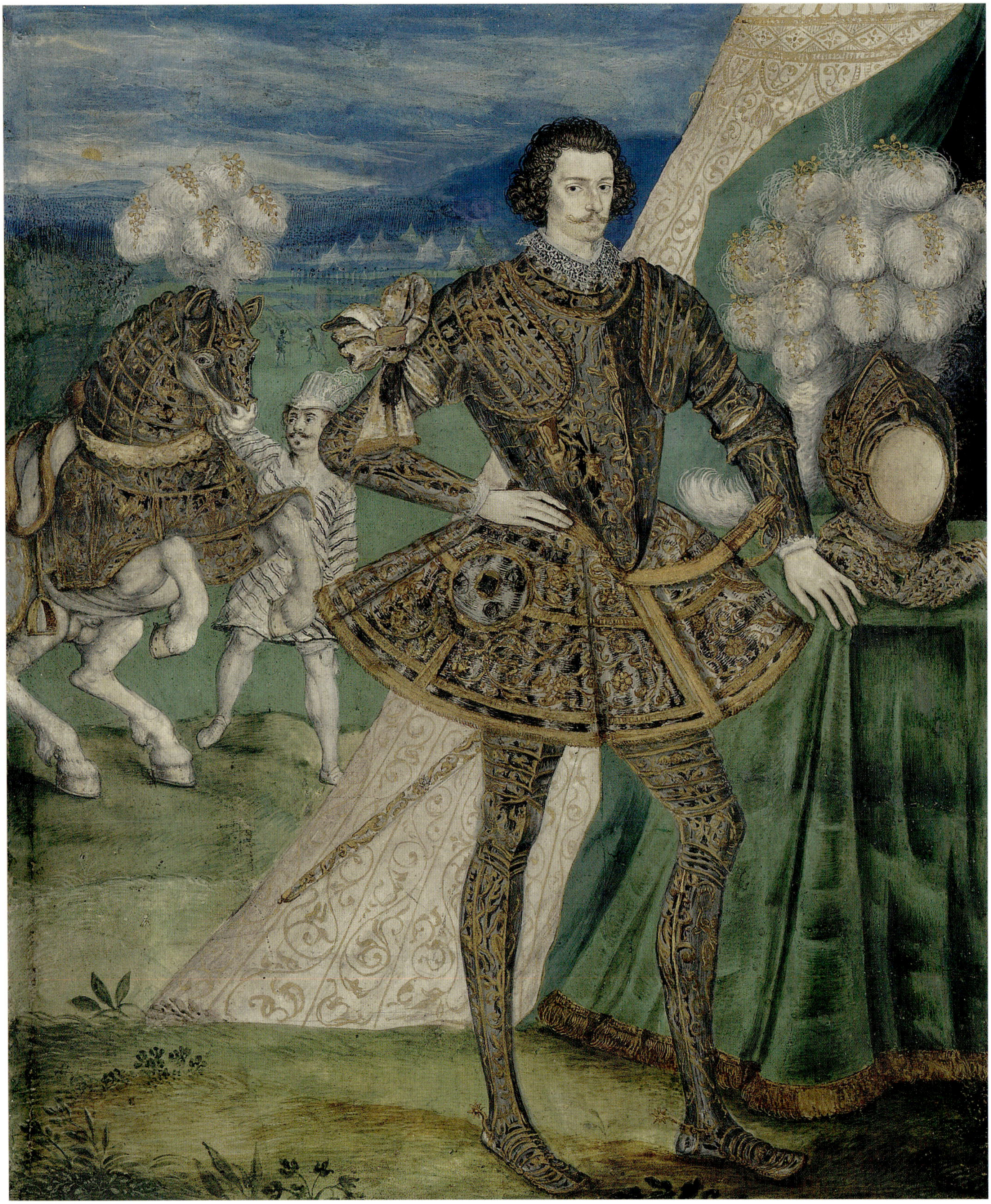

26

Robert Devereux, 2nd Earl of Essex (1565–1601)

Attributed to the studio of Nicholas Hilliard, c.1595

Watercolour and bodycolour on vellum, 248 × 203mm
National Portrait Gallery, London (NPG 6241)

Politician and soldier Robert Devereux, 2nd Earl of Essex, was Elizabeth I's last favourite. This portrait is related to a series of full-length cabinet miniatures produced by Nicholas Hilliard and his followers in the late 1580s and 1590s. It probably celebrates Essex's role in the Accession Day tilt of 1595, for which he staged an ambitious entertainment.[1] The miniature depicts the Earl in elaborate armour with what is probably the Queen's glove tied with a bow around his right arm. The youthful Essex rapidly became a rival to Sir Walter Ralegh for the Queen's affections, and was said to spend so much time with her 'at cardes or one game or another ... that he commeth not to his owne lodging till the birdes singe in the morninge'.[2]

The portrait is richly evocative of what would become the leitmotif of Essex's career: the belief that martial endeavour was the noblest form of royal service and deserved the greatest reward. In 1585, Essex had accompanied his stepfather, Robert Dudley, Earl of Leicester (cat. 18), to the Netherlands, where English forces were aiding the United Provinces against the Spanish, and had been knighted by Leicester for his bravery at the Battle of Zutphen. The finely painted battle scene in the distance may refer to Essex's experiences in the Netherlands , or to his expedition to join the forces of Henry IV of France in 1591, and highlights the abilities that lay behind his prowess in the tournaments.[3] The figure holding the horse is likely to have been copied from a print, and technical analysis reveals that the positions of the horse's hooves and the tent have been altered, the latter originally planned to extend further towards the front of the composition.

On the skirt (tonlet) of Essex's armour can be found an *impresa*, or combination of picture and motto, combining the device of a circle filled with uncut diamonds along with the letters 'DUM FORMAS, MINUIS' ('While you form me, you deform me').[4] Described by his friend Francis Bacon as having 'a nature not to be ruled',[5] the device is a bold allusion to the fact that, while wholly dependent on the favour of the Queen, Essex could not be fashioned without an element of his nature being lost.

Despite being confirmed as a public hero after the taking of Cadiz in 1596, Essex's military and political ambitions, and tendency to contravene orders, led to increasingly acrimonious differences with the Queen and her counsel over policy and appointments. During an infamous dispute over Ireland, Essex is said to have turned his back on Elizabeth, who struck him across the head.[6] The Earl was nevertheless sent as Lord Lieutenant to Ireland in 1599 to crush the rebellion of the Earl of Tyrone. Unable to effect this, Essex disobeyed orders by agreeing a truce and abandoning his post to return to England, where he was stripped of all public office and placed under house arrest to await trial. Ruined, he led his supporters on a march to rouse the support of the City. The revolt failed, and Essex was found guilty of treason and executed at the Tower of London. JE

PROVENANCE

Private collection; accepted in lieu of tax by H.M. Government and allocated to the Gallery, 1994.

EXHIBITIONS

This Popular Traitor: The Execution of the Earl of Essex, The Tower of London, 2001–2.

LITERATURE

Auerbach 1961, pp.125–6, pl.98; Hammer 1999, pp.206–8, pl.4; Piper 1957, pp.302–3; Strong 1969b, pp.115–17 (vol. 1) and pl. 229 (vol. 2); Strong 1983a, pp.136–7; Strong 1983b, pp.104–6, pl.IV; Strong 1999, pp.156–9; Young 1987, p.140.

NOTES

1 Paul E.J. Hammer, 'Upstaging the Queen: The Earl of Essex, Francis Bacon and the Accession Day celebrations of 1595' in D. Bevington and P. Holbrook (eds), *The Politics of the Stuart Court Masque* (Cambridge, Cambridge University Press, 1998) pp.41–66.

2 Folger Shakespeare Library, Bagot papers, L.a.39.

3 I am grateful to Angus Patterson (V&A) for pointing out that Essex's armour, and that on his horse, is fitted for foot combat in the tournaments, or lists.

4 This *impresa* was seen in the Shield Gallery at Whitehall by John Manningham in 1602 (*The Diary of John Manningham of the Middle Temple, 1602–1603*, New Hampshire, USA: The University Press of New England, 1976, p.33) and was recorded as belonging to Essex by William Camden in his *Remaines of a greater Worke, Concerning Britaine*, London (printed by G[eorge] E[ld] for Simon Waterson, 1605, p.174). 'While you form me, you deform me' is the translation given in Alan R. Young, *English Tournament Imprese*, New York, AMS Press, Inc., 1988, p.58.

5 J. Spedding (ed.), *The Letters and Life of Francis Bacon, including all his Occasional Works*, 7 vols (London, Longman, vol. 2, 1890, p.41).

6 'Devereux, Robert, Second Earl of Essex (1565–1601)', by Paul E.J. Hammer, ODNB, 2004, p.956.

27

Elizabeth Vernon, Countess of Southampton (1573–c.1655)

Unknown English artist, c.1598

Oil on panel, 1422 × 890mm
The Buccleuch Collection, Boughton House, Northamptonshire

One of Elizabeth I's chief maids of honour, Elizabeth Vernon was the daughter of John Vernon of Hodnet and the first cousin of Robert Devereux, 2nd Earl of Essex. In 1595 she became involved in a scandalous union with the flamboyant courtier Henry Wriothesley, 3rd Earl of Southampton (1573–1624) and in 1598 they were married in secret, after Elizabeth Vernon discovered that she was pregnant. The marriage was a happy and enduring one, but their actions incurred significant royal displeasure; the Queen had both Elizabeth and her husband locked in Fleet prison. The pair were soon released, but they never recovered the Queen's favour.

This remarkable portrait of Elizabeth Vernon shows her in the process of dressing, while combing out her long hair and staring directly out at the viewer. The pose is exceptional in English portraiture of the period and the scene creates a powerful sense of private intimacy, suggesting it may have been painted for Southampton. Details of the costume suggest that it probably dates from around the time of Elizabeth's marriage, which took place before August 1598. The ermine-lined red mantle, which is draped over the cushions below, refers to the sitter's status as a Countess, a title she acquired on her marriage. Attached to a curtain to the right is Elizabeth's ruff and an elaborate set of wired jewels, designed to cover her chest and bodice. The display of her long hair may refer back to her virgin state and the words 'Menez moi doucement' ('Lead me gently') on her comb could be taken as referring to their recently contracted union. Unusually, the sitter is partially undressed; her jacket, which would usually have been worn tightly laced and then fastened with ribbons or pins, has here been left undone.

Elizabeth is depicted in a private chamber with a little white dog at her side and her dressing table provides an interesting opportunity for a visual inventory of her worldly wealth and status. The table displays an open jewellery casket showing coiled ropes of pearls, two jewelled carcanets (necklaces or collars) with red ribbon fastenings, and three large pendants set with diamonds, rubies and pendant pearls. The artist cannot be currently identified but is particularly competent in depicting detail. However, in common with many English artists at this date, he has less understanding of proportion and perspective. The wooden panel, which may derive from English oak (rather than Baltic oak, which was more common at this period), is unusually constructed from both horizontal and vertical sections. This could indicate either that the panel was once part of a domestic interior or that it was created by a painter and/or craftsmen less familiar with working on this scale. At a time when most portraits present the public face of their sitters, the self-consciously private likeness seen here marks out this portrait as one of the most extraordinary of the late Elizabethan period. TC & AO

PROVENANCE

By descent from the sitter to Elizabeth Wriothesley, daughter of the 4th Earl of Southampton, who married as her second husband, Ralph, later the 1st Duke of Montagu.

EXHIBITIONS

Princely Magnificence: Court Jewels of the Renaissance, 1500–1630, London, Victoria and Albert Museum, 1980–1 (P18), pp.106–7; *The Treasure Houses of Britain*, Washington, National Gallery of Art, 1985–6 (52), p.129.

LITERATURE

Goulding 1919–20, pp.17–94; *Princely Magnificence*, V&A, London, 1980–1, no. 18, pp.106–7; Ashelford 1983, no. 143, p.130; *Treasure Houses*, National Gallery of Art, Washington DC, 1985, no. 52; Ribeiro 2003, pp.64–6; *English Embroidery*, Metropolitan Museum, New York, 2008.

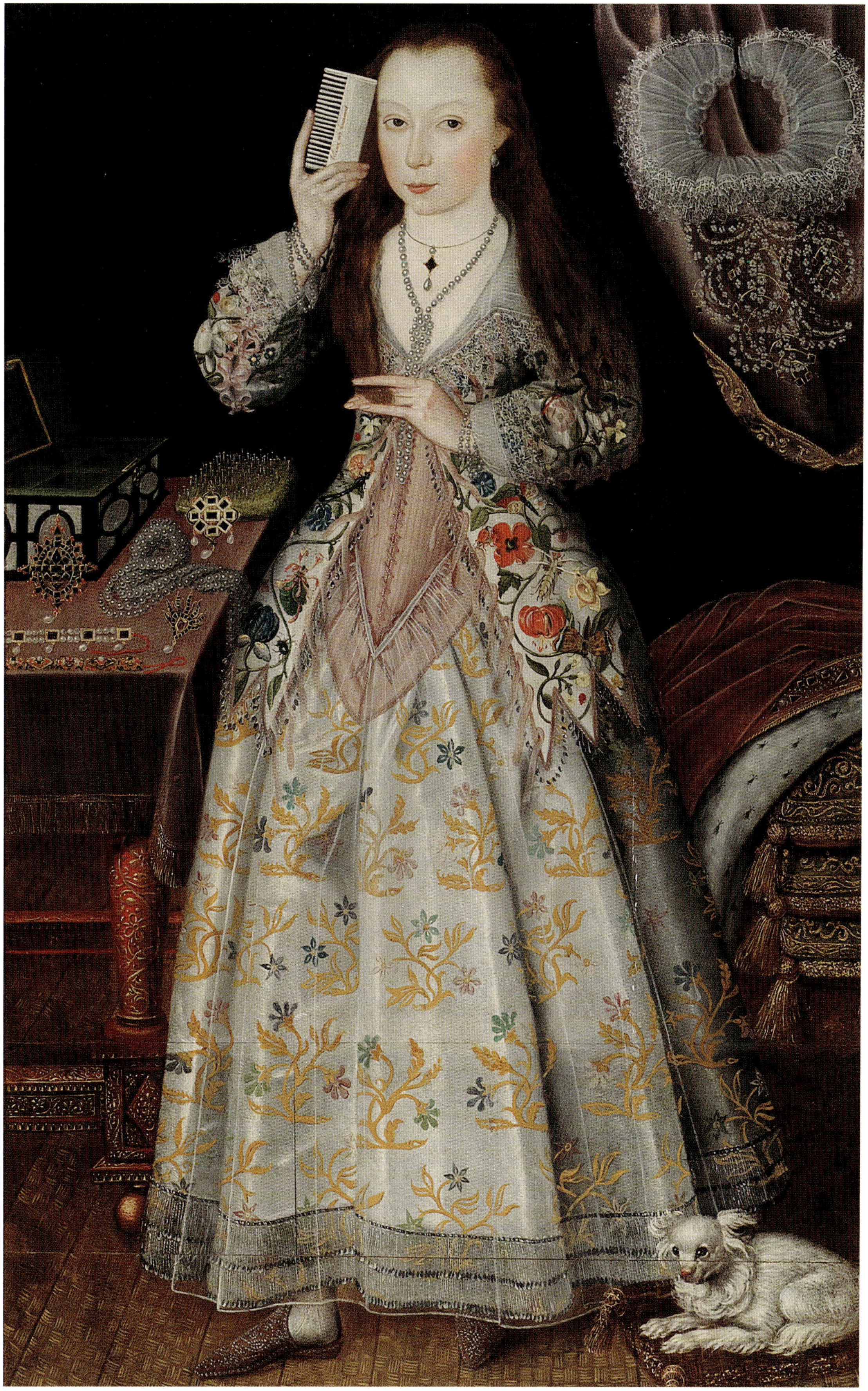

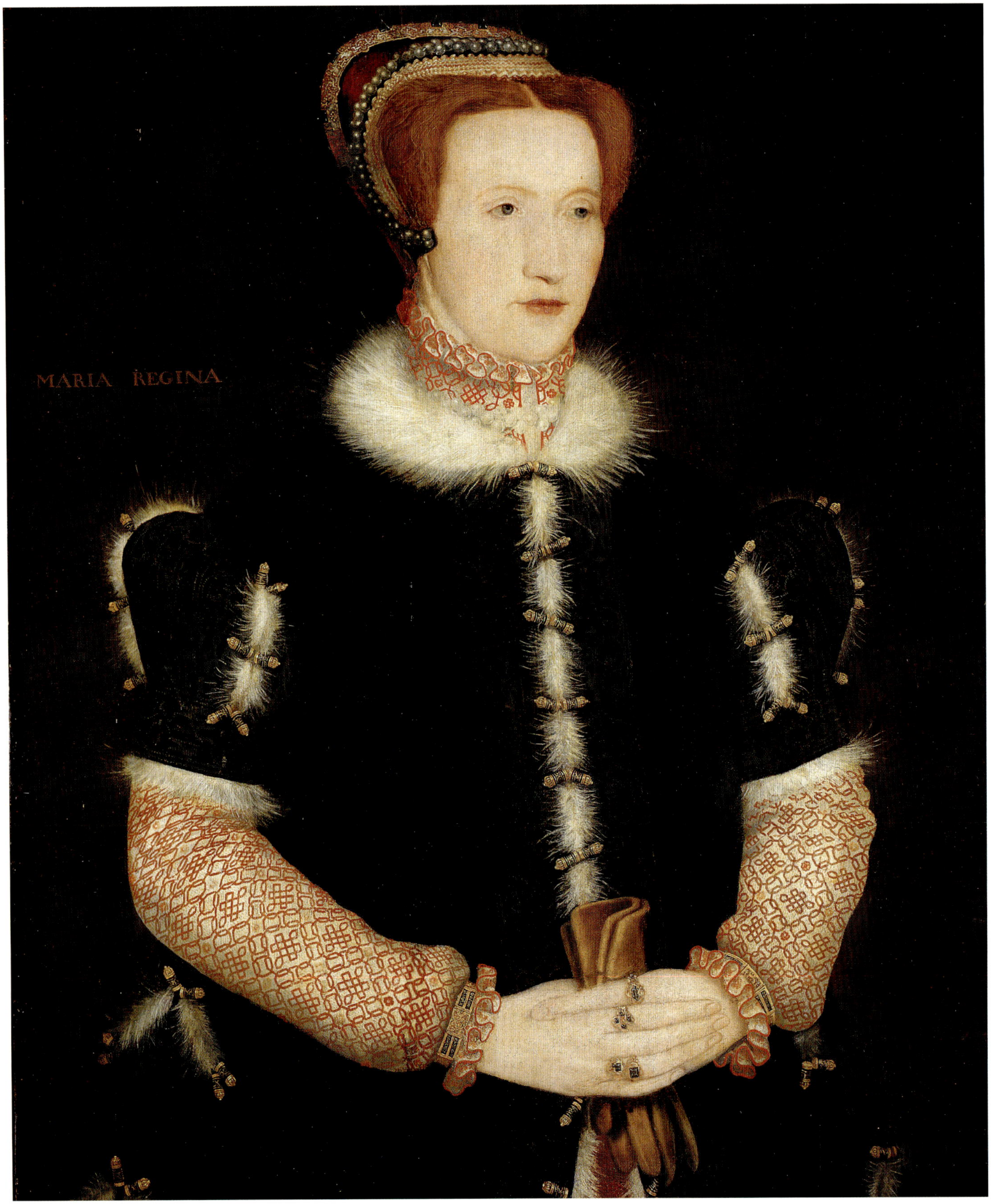
MARIA REGINA

28

Elizabeth Talbot ('Bess of Hardwick'), Countess of Shrewsbury (1527?–1608)

Follower of Hans Eworth, c.1560

Oil on panel, 850 × 705mm
Inscribed above shoulder at left (a false later addition): *MARIA REGINA*
Hardwick Hall, The Devonshire Collection (acquired through the National Land Fund and transferred to the National Trust in 1959)
National Trust Inventory Number 1129165

This portrait depicting 'Bess of Hardwick' in her thirties was formerly identified as Mary I and then as Margaret Douglas, Countess of Lennox. With her distinctive red hair and determined expression, the painting corresponds to later portraits of Bess, now at Hardwick Hall, and to her funeral effigy in All Saints Church, Derby. Ambitious, intelligent and well connected, Bess had the misfortune of being widowed four times in her life, but it was also a position that gave her an unusual degree of autonomy and wealth. She is shown expensively dressed, wearing a fur-lined gown and several gemstone rings. An inventory of goods at the Hall, taken in 1601, lists three portraits of 'My ladie': one in the 'Gallerie', one in the 'lowe great Chamber' and one in the 'with drawing Chamber', and this portrait may have been among them.[1] The picture was painted by a Netherlandish émigré working in the style of Hans Eworth.

The death of her second husband, William Cavendish, in 1557 had left the 30-year-old Bess a widow for the second time, responsible for six young children and with debts to the Crown exceeding £5,000. By the end of the decade, Bess's fortunes had reversed. Her loyalty to Princess Elizabeth was rewarded on the Queen's accession to the throne with an appointment as a Gentlewoman of the Queen's Privy Chamber. Her third husband, William St Loe, was Captain of the Queen's Guard and later Chief Butler, and left her a considerable fortune on his death in 1565. She went on to marry once more; an unhappy union with George Talbot, 6th Earl of Shrewsbury. Her life was marked by a passion for building and renovating houses – at Chatsworth, Oldcotes and Hardwick, the last mentioned being one of the finest surviving Elizabethan houses. She died in 1608 in her eighties, one of the richest people in England. TC & AO

PROVENANCE

First certain recording at Hardwick Hall by Edward Swift, 1811: 'Picture Gallery: A 3/4 Portrait of Queen Mary'.

EXHIBITIONS

The Royal House of Tudor, Manchester Art Gallery, 1897 (111); *Holbein and Other Masters*, London, Royal Academy, 1933 (65); Royal Academy Winter Exhibition, London, 1950.

LITERATURE

Strong 1969b, pp.287–8; Ashelford 1996, pp.24–5; Durant 1999; Girouard 1999, p.68; Levey and Thornton 2001.

NOTE

1 Levey and Thornton 2001, pp.52–3.

29

Edward, 3rd Lord Windsor (c.1532–75), his wife Katherine de Vere (1538–1600) and family

Unknown British artist, dated 1568

Oil on panel, 940 × 1238mm
Inscribed: *ANNO DOMINI 1568/ AETATIS SVAE. 35. / AETATIS SVAE 25. / AETATIS SVAE 61 / AETATIS SVAE. 8. / AE[TATIS]. S[VAE]. 6½ / AE[TATIS]. S[VAE] 3½ / AE[TATIS]. S[VAE]. 2.* And in a later hand: *Edward Lord Windsor, his Lady, / Daughter to the Earl of Oxford. / their Children: Lord Fredrick Windsor, Lord Harry Windsor / & two Younger Brothers*
The Bute Collection at Mount Stuart

This is an early example of the family group, a genre of portraiture that would reach the height of its popularity in England in the eighteenth century. It depicts the family of Edward, 3rd Lord Windsor, who succeeded to his father's title in 1558, the year of Elizabeth I's accession. He later married Katherine de Vere, the daughter of the 16th Earl of Oxford. Two years before this portrait was painted, the Queen visited the family at Bradenham, their seat in Buckinghamshire. The painting shows Windsor and his wife with their four sons and an unidentified woman, and is inscribed with the age of each sitter.[1] The composition is rather unbalanced as the unidentified woman faces in the opposite direction to the other sitters, perhaps to indicate that she is not a member of the family.

All four sons (the couple went on to have four daughters) are dressed in matching doublets and wear identical circular pendants suspended from a ribbon around the neck. The unusually detailed bequests of jewels in Lord Windsor's will suggest their importance to the family.[2] To his 'Soveaigne Ladye and mystris Quene Elizabeth' he bequeathed 'my crosse of diamoundes in demonstraconn the in my life tyme I lyved to dye with demonstraconn to fighte under the same banner nexte to offer my Bodye to be ymployed in any her Maiesties service'. To his 'beloved wife Katherine' he also gave 'a little crosse of goulde . . . sett with aleven diamoundes', which may be that shown at the base of her throat in this portrait, above the elaborate pendant she presents to the viewer.[3]

The children are depicted at the 'royal' or 'philosopher's' game of chess and at cards, both pastimes that may have been particularly associated with the festivities of Christmas. Elizabeth herself was a noted player of chess, as were several of her favourites including Sir Walter Ralegh (cat. 22) and Robert Dudley, Earl of Leicester (cat. 18) to whom a number of chess manuals were dedicated. Thomas Elyot's treatise on princely education (1531), which continued to be reprinted throughout Elizabeth's reign, recommended the game for sharpening both wit and memory.[4] In this portrait the eldest son, Frederick, appears to be holding the chess piece of the queen, and his brother Henry (Harry) holds the king.[5] JE

PROVENANCE

The Bute Collection at Mount Stuart, by descent from Charlotte Windsor (1746–1800), who married John Stuart, 4th Earl of Bute (1744–1814) in 1766.

LITERATURE

Cust 1913, p.36; Strong 1969a, pl. 60.

NOTES

1 The inscribed ages may not be wholly accurate, perhaps because unknown or approximate. Katherine de Vere, for example, was aged thirty in 1568.
2 TNA/PROB 11/57/332. I am indebted to Edward Town for his transcription of this document.
3 Katherine's portrait appears to have been drawn from an identical head and shoulders dated 1567, sold at Christie's, 19 July 1985, lot 70, in which the cross of diamonds is particularly clear. The Renaissance pendant below it is similar to jewellery designs by Hans Collaert of Antwerp, for which information I would like to thank Diana Scarisbrick.
4 *The boke named the Gouernour, dueysed by s[ir] Thomas Elyot knight* (Thomas Bertheleti, London, 1531), fol.97–8.
5 I am grateful to Nigel Short for corresponding with me about the chess pieces in this portrait, which appear to have been placed more for contrast with the squares than for accuracy, and to David Parlett for discussing the playing cards.

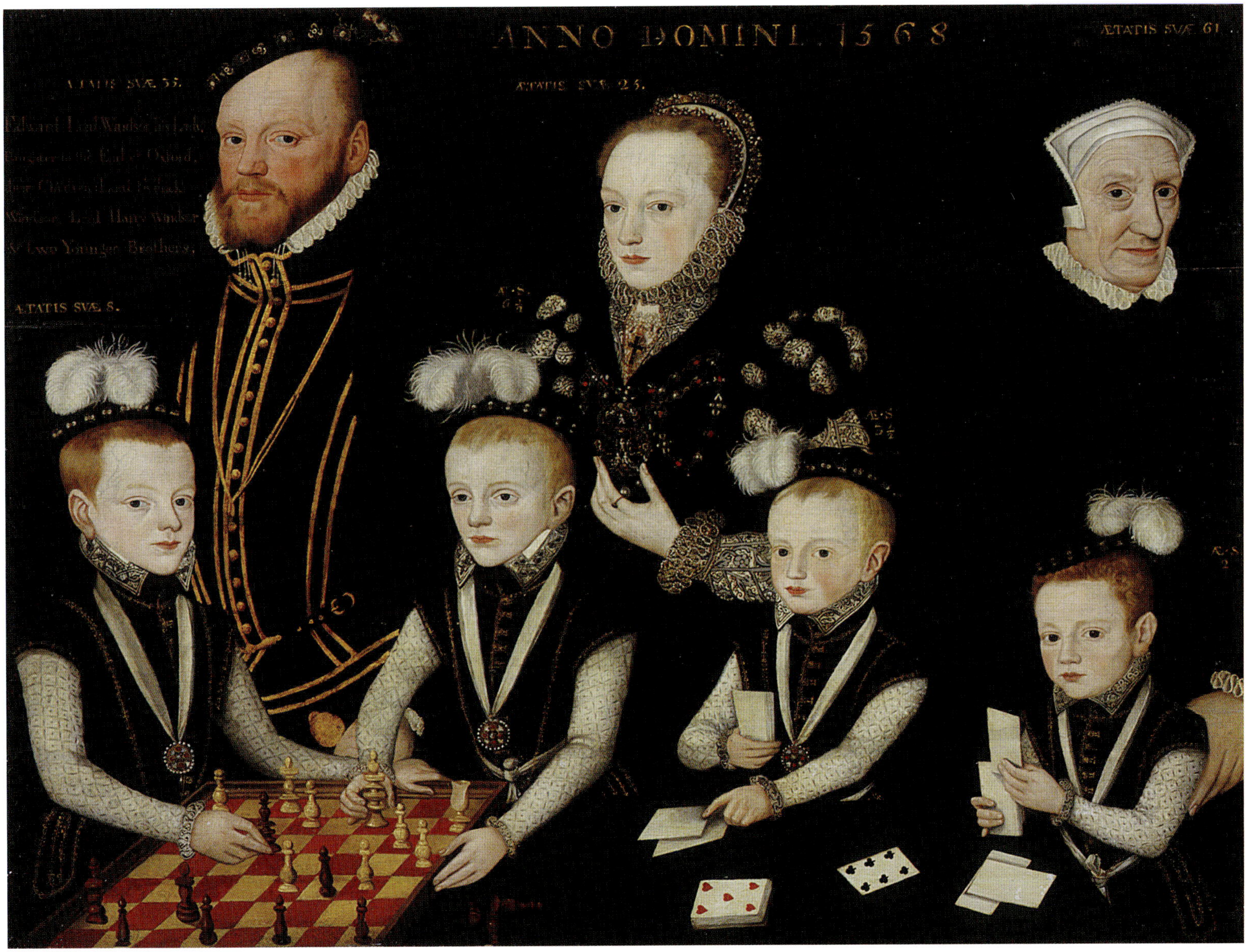
ANNO DOMINI. 1568
ÆTATIS SVÆ 61
ÆTATIS SVÆ 25

30

Anthony, John and William Browne with an unidentified man

Isaac Oliver, dated 1598

Gouache and watercolour on vellum mounted on card, 240 × 260mm
Inscribed top left: *A*[*n*]*no Dom*[*ini*].*1598*; below, left to right, the ages of the sitters: *AEtatis.21.*, *AEtatis 24*, *AEtatis.18.*, *AEtatis 21*; top centre: *FIGVRAE CONFORMIS AFFECTVS* (in the figures conforms the character); on a pilaster signed in monogram: *IO*
The Burghley House Collection, Stamford

This outstanding and accomplished small-scale watercolour painting by Isaac Oliver depicts the three brothers Anthony, John and William Browne with their arms interlinked in a pose of fraternal devotion.[1] The brothers were born into a prominent Catholic family that had prospered under the reign of Mary I; their grandfather, Sir Anthony Browne (*c.*1528–92) had been elevated to the peerage as 1st Viscount Montagu on the occasion of Mary's marriage to Philip II. Despite speaking publicly against the religious policies of Elizabeth I, Viscount Montagu retained a good relationship with the Queen. Following the death of his grandfather, and then his father in 1592, the eighteen-year-old Anthony Maria (1574–1629) became the 2nd Viscount Montagu and heir to a vast fortune.

Anthony (aged twenty-four) is shown in the middle, flanked by John (aged twenty-one) on the left and William (aged eighteen) on the right. Oliver has carefully recorded the date at the top left and inscribed the sitters' ages beside their heads, suggesting that the year 1598 might hold some particular significance for the family. The identity and role of the man (aged twenty-one) in the striped costume, carrying a sword and holding a fur-lined cloak across his body, is unresolved. It is possible that he is a close friend or an extended family member, but he has also been described as a servant. He has removed his hat, and as gentlemen's retainers were criticised for being indistinguishable from their masters in the fineness of their clothes, this identification remains possible.[2] The men may be standing in one of the two long galleries at Cowdray, the family seat, which was substantially destroyed by fire in 1793.

Born in France but brought to London by his goldsmith father to study limning, Isaac Oliver trained under Nicholas Hilliard but retained a resolutely Continental outlook. His miniatures were prized for their Italianate qualities, and he travelled to Venice in 1596.[3] This miniature contains several allusions to Continental art and the engraving by Marc Duval of *Les Frères Coligny* (1579) may be one of the sources referenced by Oliver, as it also shows three Catholic brothers linking arms. The illusionistic recession of the floor and the virtuoso manner in which the contours of the young men's bodies are modelled in their shiny satin outfits is quite unlike the English style of Hilliard. With its lifelike clarity, this miniature seems to anticipate the art of the next century. TC & AO

PROVENANCE

By descent in the family of Browne, Viscounts of Montagu, Cowdray; first recorded by Vertue on a visit to Cowdray, c.1730 (*Notebooks*, LL, p.82); by the marriage of Isabella, daughter of William Stephen Poyntz of Cowdray House, to Brownlow, 2nd Marquess of Exeter, 1825; thence by descent.

EXHIBITIONS

Artists of the Tudor Court: The Portrait Miniature Rediscovered, 1520–1620, London, Victoria and Albert Museum, 1983 (272), p.164; *The Treasure Houses of Britain*, Washington, National Gallery of Art, 1985–6 (43), p.119; *Dynasties: Painting in Tudor and Jacobean England 1530–1630*, London, Tate Gallery, 1995–6 (81), p.134.

LITERATURE

Strong 1983a, no. 272; Jackson Stops 1985, p.119; Reynolds 1988, p.23; Hearn 1995, p.134.

NOTES

1 Two copies after the miniature, made on copper, have been recorded: one in the collection of Earl Spencer and one auctioned at Sotheby's on 17 February 1988; see Graham Reynolds, *Nicholas Hilliard & Isaac Oliver* (V&A, London, 1971), no. 155.
2 Protestant preachers frequently argued against excess in elaborate apparel, particularly for those whose dress was not merited by their rank. The popular preacher William Perkins commented that 'for every common man now a – daies must be a gentleman, and it is hard sometimes for a stranger to discerne the master from the servant, and there is such excess in all degrees, that now for daily attire, the noblest are the plainest'. William Perkins, *A Treatise of the Vocations, or Callings of men, with the sorts and kings of them, and the right use therof* (John Legat, Cambridge, 1603) p.19.
3 John Murdoch, Jim Murrell, Patrick J. Noon and Roy Strong, *The English Miniature* (Yale University Press, New Haven & London, 1981), p.63. CT

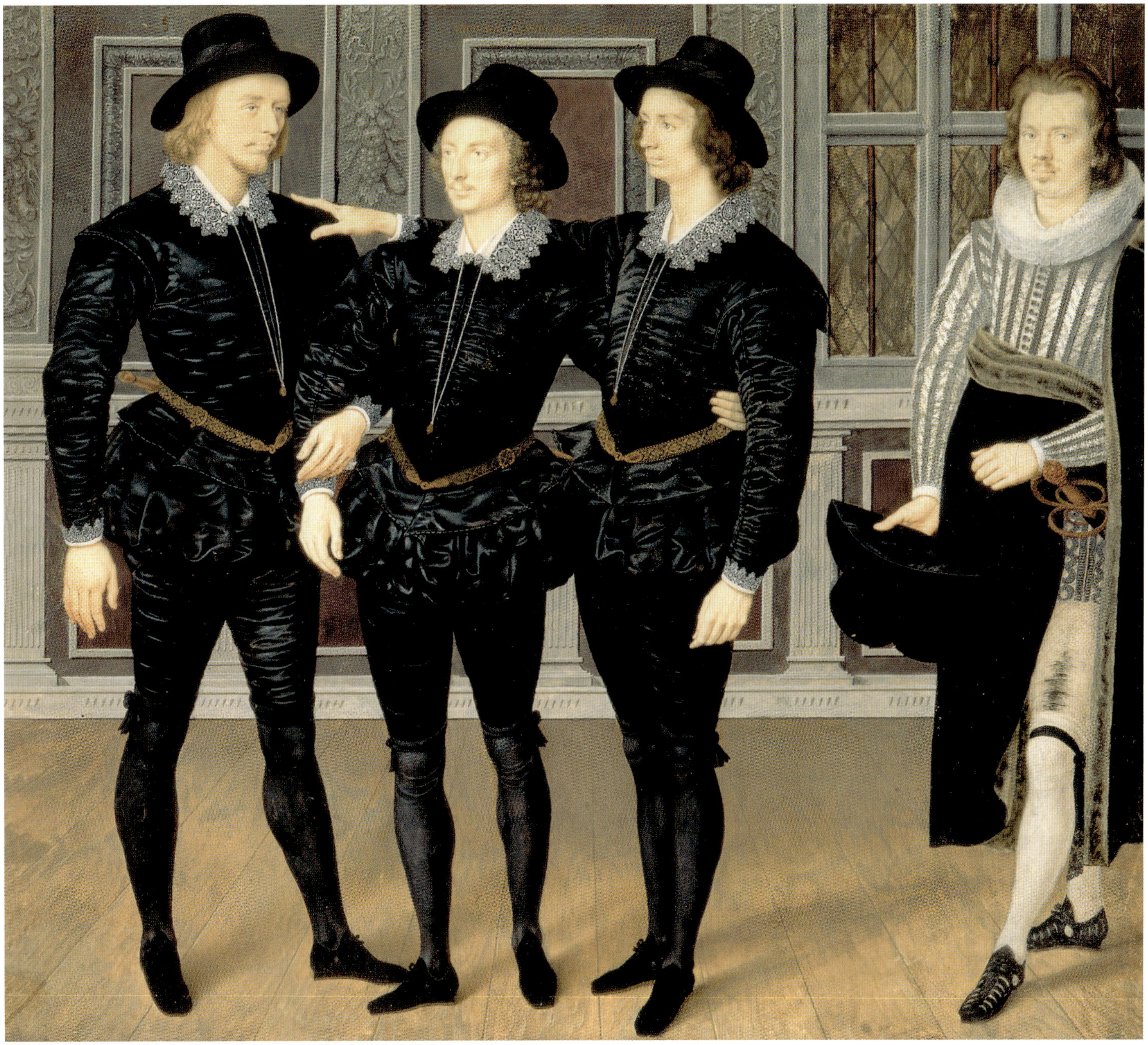

31

Three unknown Elizabethan children

Unknown Anglo-Netherlandish artist, c.1580

Oil on panel, 730 × 570mm
Inscribed left to right: *AETATIS SV[A]E:6: / AETATIS [SVAE]:7: / AETATIS:SV[A]E:5:*
Privately owned

This charming portrait depicts three children aged six, seven and five. The family resemblance is striking, although their identities remain unknown. Siblings are typically shown, as here, with their arms touching or interlinked and their ages recorded. The sitters almost certainly belong to a wealthy family of the nobility or gentry as they are expensively and fashionably dressed: the boys in slashed doublets of yellow satin with the feathers of their hats just visible at the edge of the panel, and their sister in a highly decorated gown and elaborate lace ruff with matching wrist cuffs. The coloured floral embroidery of the boys' collars, or falling bands, appears to have been an exclusively English fashion, and like the shirt cuffs the collars are edged with gold braid.[1] Similar jewelled pendants, one with a cameo head, hang from ribbons around their necks and are threaded through the slashes of the doublet to anchor them on the left breast.

Two of the children hold pets: the youngest boy a small bird, probably a finch, and his sister a multi-coloured guinea pig. The finch was a particularly popular pet with children because of its striking plumage. Its representation in children's portraiture may be intended to symbolise the Christian soul by association with depictions of the infant Christ with a goldfinch. The guinea pig, cradled by the boy's sister, may be the earliest known depiction of this animal in a portrait.[2] Popular in Europe as exotic pets, guinea pigs were introduced from South America by Spanish traders. Recent research suggests that they may have been popular pets among the middle classes as well as the elite.[3]

The skilful painting of this portrait suggests that it is the work of an artist familiar with Netherlandish techniques. Portraits of children became popular among the nobility and gentry in the sixteenth century across Europe, enabling families to document lineage and fertility, and to capture individual likeness, at a time when child mortality was high. JE

PROVENANCE

Christie's, 20 May 1938, lot 41 (property of the first Earl Beatty); privately owned.

LITERATURE

Ashelford 1983, p.90.

NOTES

1 With thanks to Susan North (V&A) for her comments on the costume in this portrait.
2 The first accurate depiction of a guinea pig in the West appeared in 1544 in *Historium Animalium*, the work of Swiss naturalist Conrad Gesner.
3 See Fabienne Pigière, 'New archaeozoological evidence for the introduction of the guinea pig to Europe', *Journal of Archaeological Science*, April 2012, vol. 39, issue 4, pp.1020–4.

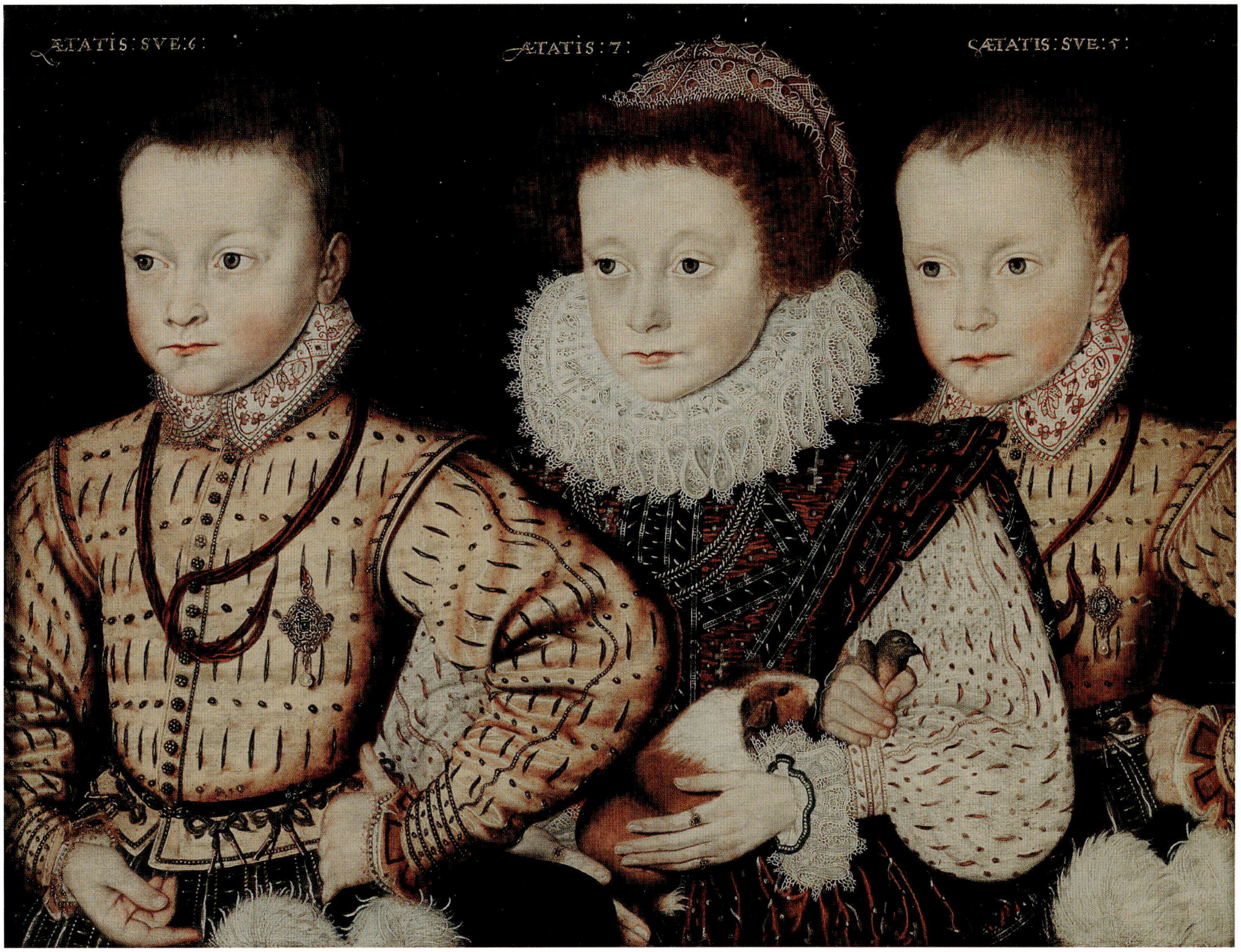
ÆTATIS: SVE: 6:
ÆTATIS: 7:
ÆTATIS: SVE: 5:

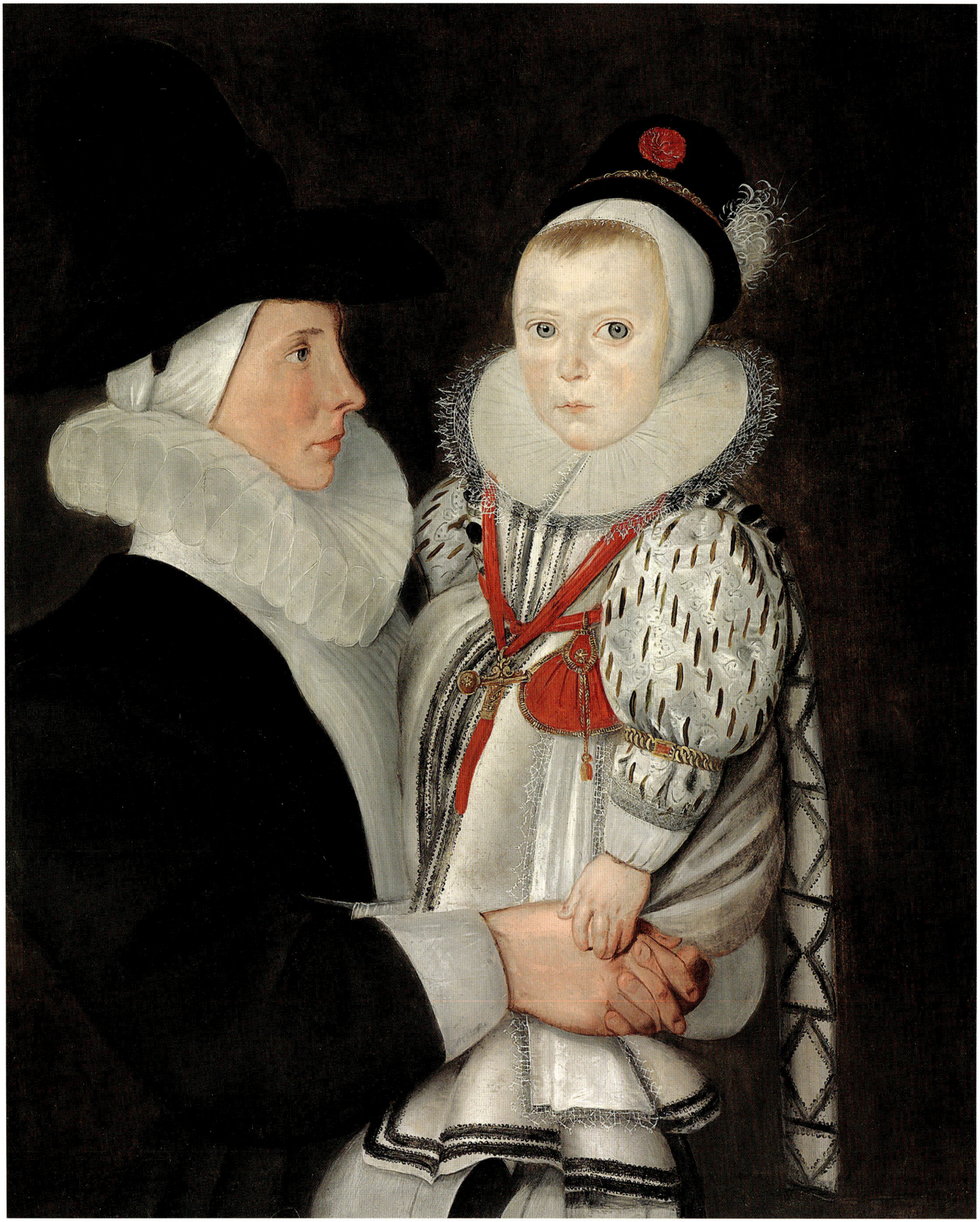

32

A child, possibly John Dunch (d.1589), and his nurse

Unknown English artist, c.1580s–early 1590s

Oil on panel, 780 × 620mm
Private collection

By historic tradition this tender double portrait has been identified as 'John Dunch and his Nurse'. An old label, written in an eighteenth- or nineteenth-century hand, now lost, read: 'Supposed to be the portraits of John Dunch and his nurse./ John Dunch sone of Edmund Dunch and Anne his wife. This chile being of the age of one year deceased the 12th May 1589 and is buried in the chancel in Little Wittenham / Berks.' The costume in the portrait dates from the late 1580s or early 1590s, and the sitter may indeed be the child 'John Dunch sone of Edmund Dunch', whose burial is recorded in the parish records of the Church of St Peter, Little Wittenham, Oxfordshire, on 20 May 1589.[1] The child is depicted with particularised features including piercing blue eyes and pale skin, and may have been painted just before his death.

The Dunches were a prominent Berkshire family who received a grant of arms under Edward VI.[2] The Church of St Peter contains a number of monuments to them, including a brass plate depicting the founder of the family, William Dunch (1508–97), which states that he was appointed 'sworn Esquire extraordinary of the body of Queen Elizabeth', and a large funeral effigy dedicated to his grandson (John's brother), also called William Dunch (1578–1612). The infant John was one of seven children born to Edmund Dunch and Anne Fettiplace, but little else is known about him.[3]

The handling of this painting and the clothes of the sitters indicate that the picture is English; it is painted in a highly competent but relatively simple linear style by an unidentified native painter. The painting may have been one of several family portraits; Elizabethan society witnessed an increased interest in children and their welfare, and it was not uncommon for parents to commission individual portraits of their children, or to include them in their own portrait sittings. The child's outfit, the gold bracelet and the gold and coral teething soother all show that he belonged to a wealthy family. It is certainly plausible that he is aged one, or perhaps slightly older; he is no longer swaddled.[4] The plain clothes and ruddy cheeks of his nurse suggest that she is a servant rather than his mother; she was perhaps included in the portrait because of her importance in her family and because the child was unable to stand unaided, or unwell. If this is a portrait of John Dunch, then the nurse may be Elizabeth Field, a servant who was held in high regard by the family.[5] TC & AO

PROVENANCE

Bought by Harriette Morrell (née Winter) of Black Hall, Oxford, pre-1900: Mrs Frederick P. Morrell, of Black Hall, Oxford; thence by descent to Frederica Peel (née Morrell) of Stonesfield Manor, near Oxford; sold in 2008 by John Beazor and Sons Ltd, Cambridge; Weiss Gallery, London; thereafter private collection.

EXHIBITIONS

The Oxford Exhibition of Historical Portraits, Oxford, 1904 (79)

LITERATURE

Blakiston 1904, pp.211–19.

NOTES

1 Burial register for Little Wittenham, St Peter, ref. D/P152/1/2, Berkshire Record Office, Reading.
2 Recorded in *The Visitation of Berkshire* (1623). See *The Four Visitations of Berkshire* (Harleian Society, London, 1907), vol. 56, pp.87–8.
3 *The Four Visitations* (as cited in note 2), pp.87–8. John Dunch's age is not listed in his burial record and there is no record of his baptism.
4 Swaddling bands were normally abandoned after the first year. Boys were normally breeched at the age of six or seven years old. See Ashelford 1983, pp.71, 127 and 131.
5 Elizabeth Field was left £10 in the will of Anne Dunch (John's mother). Berkshire Record Office: D/A1 /62 /89, cited by Pete Annells, *The Berkshire Dunches* (privately printed, 2006), p.92.

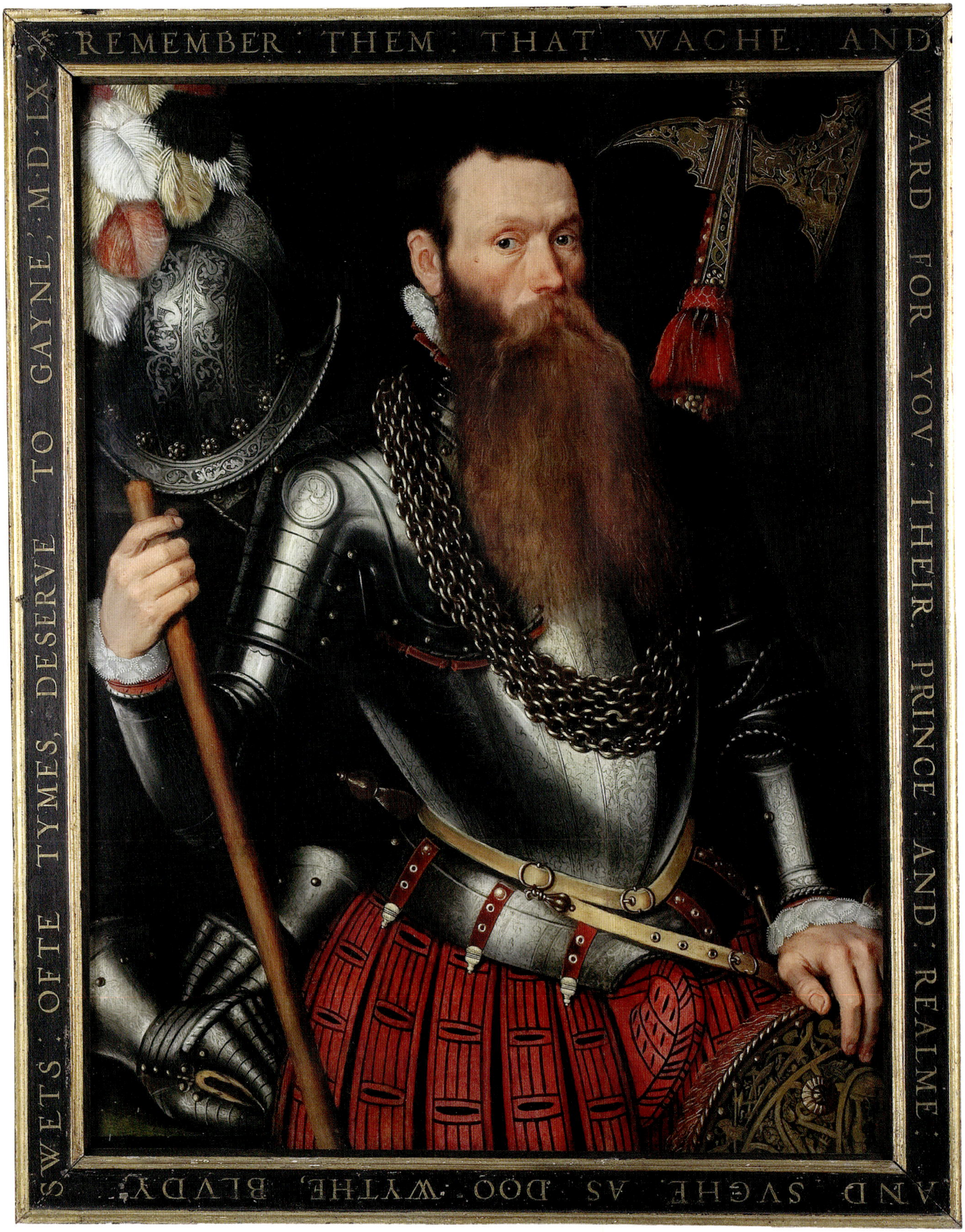
REMEMBER: THEM: THAT WACHE. AND
WARD FOR YOV: THEIR: PRINCE: AND: REALME:
AND SVGHE AS DOO WYTHE BLVDY
SWETS. OFTE TYMES, DESERVE TO GAYNE. M·D·LX

33

An unknown soldier, possibly Cuthbert Vaughan (c.1519–63)

Unknown artist, dated 1560

Oil on panel, 984 × 724mm
Inscribed around the frame: *REMEMBER : THEM THAT WACHE AND WARD FOR YOV : THEIR. PRINCE : AND : REALME : AND SVCHE AS DOO WYTHE BLVDY SWETS : OFTE TYMES, DESERVE TO GAYNE : M.D.LX.*
Edward Harley Esq.

This striking portrait of a man in armour shows him holding a rod of office in one hand, with the other resting upon a round target or small shield. The sitter may be Cuthbert Vaughan, thought to be of the Hergest branch of the Vaughan family.[1] A distinguished soldier, Vaughan was involved in the siege of Leith in April 1560, the year this portrait was painted, for which he was commended for his bravery.[2] He was described by William Cecil, Lord Burghley (cat. 19), as a man 'who orders his soldiers well, and of "rude men" makes good soldiers in short time'.[3] Vaughan had complained to Cecil that, while he spent most of his time at war, he was seldom rewarded; a grievance that accords well with the reproachful motto around the frame of the portrait, which asks the viewer to remember those who deserve to gain for their service to the monarch and country. Following Vaughan's service in Scotland, however, he was granted land in Kent and Sussex.[4]

The exceptional quality of the portrait indicates an artist of Netherlandish origin or training. The armour on display in the portrait appears to derive from several different suits and, along with the heavy gold chain, may have been acquired as gifts.[5] The helmet is a fine example of a north Italian comb morion, and the gilded shield is similar to Milanese parade armour of this period.[6] The halberd (a weapon consisting of an axe head and pick on a pole) displays images of deer hunting and the elaborate gilded *pointillé*, or punched, decoration is common to the type of Italian armour purchased by Henry VIII for his personal guard.[7] A visitor to England in 1586 described seeing Elizabeth I and her retinue at Hampton Court, with her bodyguard marching before her bearing 'gilt halberds'.[8] The continuation of this tradition is probably what gave rise to this portrait being thought, at one time, to represent a member of Elizabeth's bodyguard, the Gentleman Pensioners, though no one of the name of Vaughan appears on the list for 1560. JE

PROVENANCE

Probably by descent from Gwyn Vaughan of Trebarried, whose daughter married John Harley, Bishop of Hereford (d.1788), the son of Edward Harley, 3rd Earl of Oxford and Earl Mortimer; by descent to Edward Harley Esq.

EXHIBITIONS

The First Special Exhibition of Portraits ending with the Reign of James II, London, South Kensington Museum, 1866 (306); *An Exhibition of Treasures from Midland Homes*, Birmingham, City Museum and Art Gallery, 1938 (49); *British Portraits*, London, Royal Academy, 1956–7 (16); *Between Renaissance and Baroque*, Manchester, City Art Gallery, 1965 (8); *Dynasties: Painting in Tudor and Jacobean England 1530–1630*, London, Tate Gallery, October 1995–January 1996 (46); *Painting the Dragon*, Cardiff, National Museum of Wales, 2002 (32).

LITERATURE

Hearn 1995.

NOTES

1 This identity was first suggested by Karen Hearn (*Dynasties*, Tate Gallery, London, 1995–6, p.93). A nineteenth-century stipple engraving of the same man, after an unknown artist, is in the National Portrait Gallery, London (Macdonnell Collection, NPG D38820). A handwritten note on the reverse of the engraving identifies the sitter as Cuthbert Vaughan, from an original portrait at Roydon Hall, and later Charts Edge, Kent. Unfortunately, it has not been possible to trace this painting.
2 Lords Grey, Scrope & company to the Duke of Norfolk, urging him to commend Vaughan to the privy council. Joseph Bain (ed.), *Calendar of the State Papers Relating to Scotland, Volume 1: 1547–1563* (1898), p.387. The Duke of Norfolk later wrote to Cecil that 'Captain Reede and Captain Vaughan, as he is informed, showed themselves very stout and valiant at the skirmish', 'Cecil Papers: April 1560', *Calendar of the Cecil Papers in Hatfield House, Volume 1: 1306–1571* (1883), p.211.
3 Bain (ed.), op. cit., p.435.
4 C.P. Croly, 'Vaughan, Cuthbert (c.1519–1563)', ODNB 2004, p.163.
5 See Hearn 1995, p.92.
6 I am grateful to Angus Patterson (V&A) for this information.
7 G. Rimer, T. Richardson and J. Cooper (eds), *Henry VIII: Arms and the Man* (Royal Armouries, Leeds, 2009), pp.264–71.
8 V. von Klarwill, *Queen Elizabeth and Some Foreigners* (Bodley Head, London, 1928), p.322.

34

Abd el-Ouahed ben Messaoud ben Mohammed Anoun, Moorish Ambassador to Elizabeth I

Unknown artist, dated 1600

Oil on panel, 1130 × 880mm
Inscribed: *1600 ABDVLGVAHID. LEGATUS REGIS BARBARIAE IN ANGLIAM. AETATIS: 42* (1600 Abd el-Ouahed. Ambassador of the king of Barbary in England. Aged: 42)
University of Birmingham Research and Cultural Collections (A0427)

This unique portrait commemorates the embassy to London of the King of Barbary, a colossal state in northern Africa that included modern-day Morocco. The sitter was the principal secretary to the King, 'Muley Hamet' (Mulai Ahmad al-Mansur), who landed with his embassy at Dover in August 1600. The English Barbary Company had been established in 1585 and the portrait marks a dynamic period in Anglo-Islamic trade. The main purpose of the embassy, however, was to request aid for a Moorish re-conquest of Catholic Spain, following the English successes against the Spanish Armada in 1588 and the capture of Cadiz by the Earl of Essex in 1596. Discussions with the Queen about a military alliance were inconclusive, and both rulers died within two years of the embassy.

London was a cosmopolitan capital in the Elizabethan period. North Africans and Ottoman Turks were to be seen on the streets and had a stage presence as undifferentiated 'Moors' in plays such as Shakespeare's *Titus Andronicus* and *The Merchant of Venice*. The pose and inscriptions – with the sitter's title, date and age – are typical of English portraiture in this period, though the contrast between the portrait format and the Ambassador's bold gaze, turbaned dress and exotic scimitar (curved sword) is striking. Nothing is known about the circumstances of the commission but as it remained in England it is likely to have been requested by a member of Elizabeth's court as a record of the Barbary king's deputation. The painting is on three oak boards and it has recently been discovered that one of these is from the same tree as a board in a panel portrait of Thomas Nevile, Master of Trinity College, in Cambridge.[1] This may indicate that both portraits were painted in the same London workshop at around the same time. JE

PROVENANCE

Purchased by George Higgins from Christie's, 11 November 1955, lot 65; acquired by the Ruskin Gallery, Stratford on Avon, 1956; Shakespeare Institute, University of Birmingham Research and Cultural Collections, 1956.

EXHIBITIONS

East–West: Objects between Cultures, London, Tate Britain, September 2006–February 2007; *The Image of the Other: England and North Africa in 1607* (Cycle III of a four-part exhibition), Virginia (USA), Jamestown-Yorktown Foundation, October 2007–January 2008; *Shakespeare: Staging the World*, London, British Museum, July–November 2012.

LITERATURE

Harris 1958, pp.89–97; Bate and Thornton 2012, pp.34–7.

NOTE

1 I am grateful to Ian Tyers, dendrochronologist, for this information.

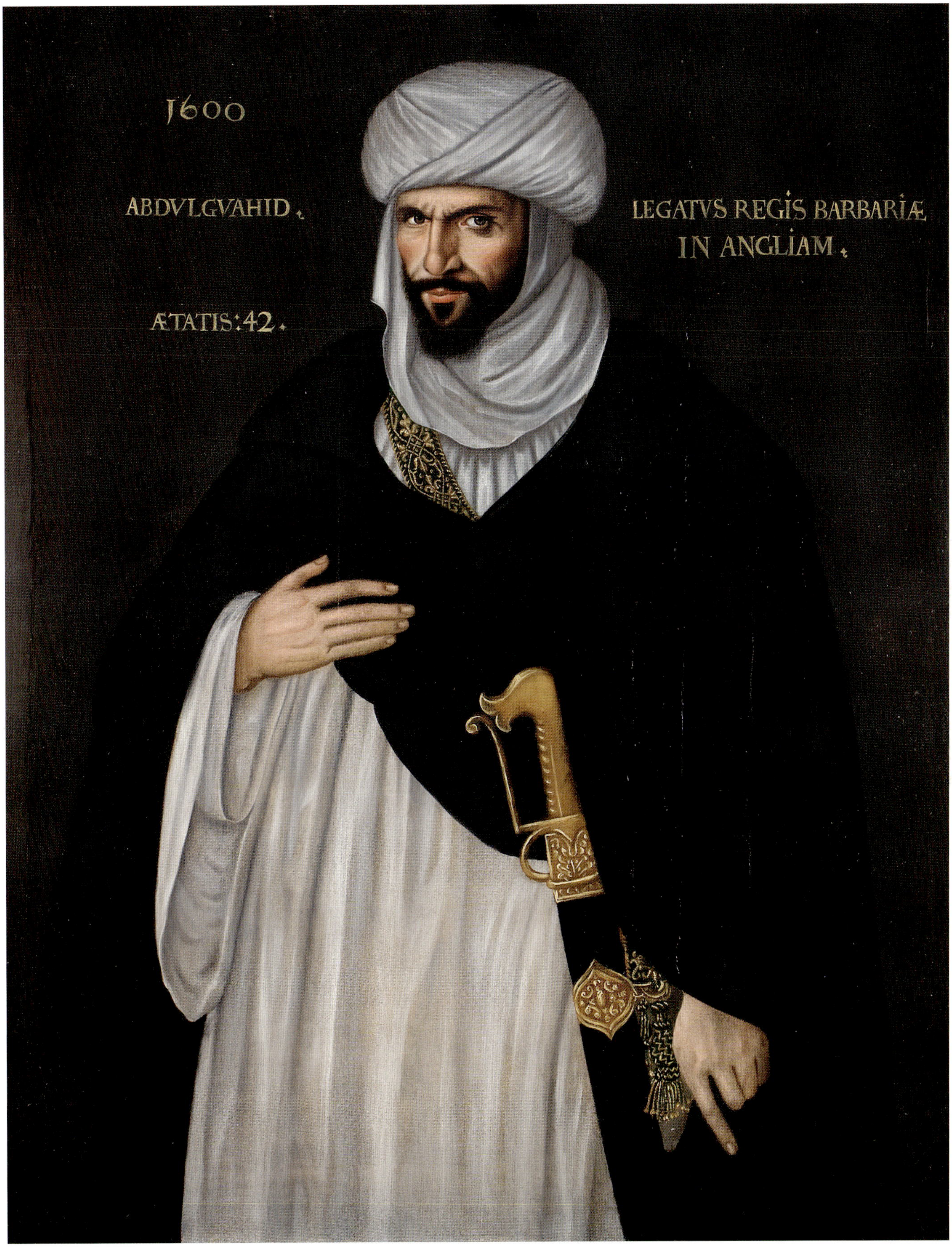
1600
ABDVLGVAHID.
ÆTATIS:42.
LEGATVS REGIS BARBARIÆ
IN ANGLIAM.

35

Mr Symonds of Norfolk

Unknown English artist, c.1595–1600

Oil on panel, 760 × 965mm
Inscribed bottom left: *SYMONDS of / C° Norfolk*
Ancient House, Thetford – Norfolk Museums & Archaeology Service

This unusual, naively painted portrait depicts a member of the English country gentry on horseback, out hawking with his dogs. An early view of Norwich is visible in the distance. While the inscription identifying the sitter is later, the gentleman represented is probably John Symonds (d.1609), a freeman of Norwich, who is buried in the Church of St George's, Tombland. The kneeling figure of his wall tomb, where he is commemorated with his wife, Olive, depicts a man with a similar beard.[1]

The portrait is by a provincial artist, presumably local to Norfolk. It is remarkable both for the large-scale presentation of a landscape and its portrayal of a member of the gentry on horseback, a format usually reserved for monarchs and military heroes. This landscape is likely to record fields owned or farmed by the sitter. A coloured plan from a Norfolk parish of a 'Mr Symonds, his lands' of *c.*1583 shows a similar pattern of strip cultivation.[2] Hawking was a gentleman's pursuit and the choice of such a portrait format is indicative of the sitter's status. The proportions of the horse and the figure are at odds, and the equestrian format may have been copied from Continental engravings, or from illustrations in hunting manuals. Mr Symonds is shown in a black doublet with a 'falling band' collar, delicately edged with lace and painted to suggest its translucency, and a broad-brimmed Spanish felt hat. JE

PROVENANCE

Bought in Norfolk by Walter Rye from a member of the Symonds family, 1898; bought Prince Duleep Singh, by whom bequeathed to the Mayor and Corporation, Thetford, 1926.

EXHIBITIONS

Family and Friends, Norwich Castle Museum, 1992 (15); *Dynasties: Painting in Tudor and Jacobean England 1530–1630*, London, Tate Gallery, October 1995–January 1996 (123).

LITERATURE

Rye 1916, p.105; Farrer 1927, no. 63; 'Norfolk Archaeological Society Excursion' 1929, p.15; Hearn 1995, p.181.

NOTES

1 Hearn 1995, p.181.
2 Rental document of the Toftrees parish of c.1583. NRO 'Toftrees rental' ref: BL/SY 1. Extant records show that members of the numerous Symonds family were established in the county as farmers from the 1540s.

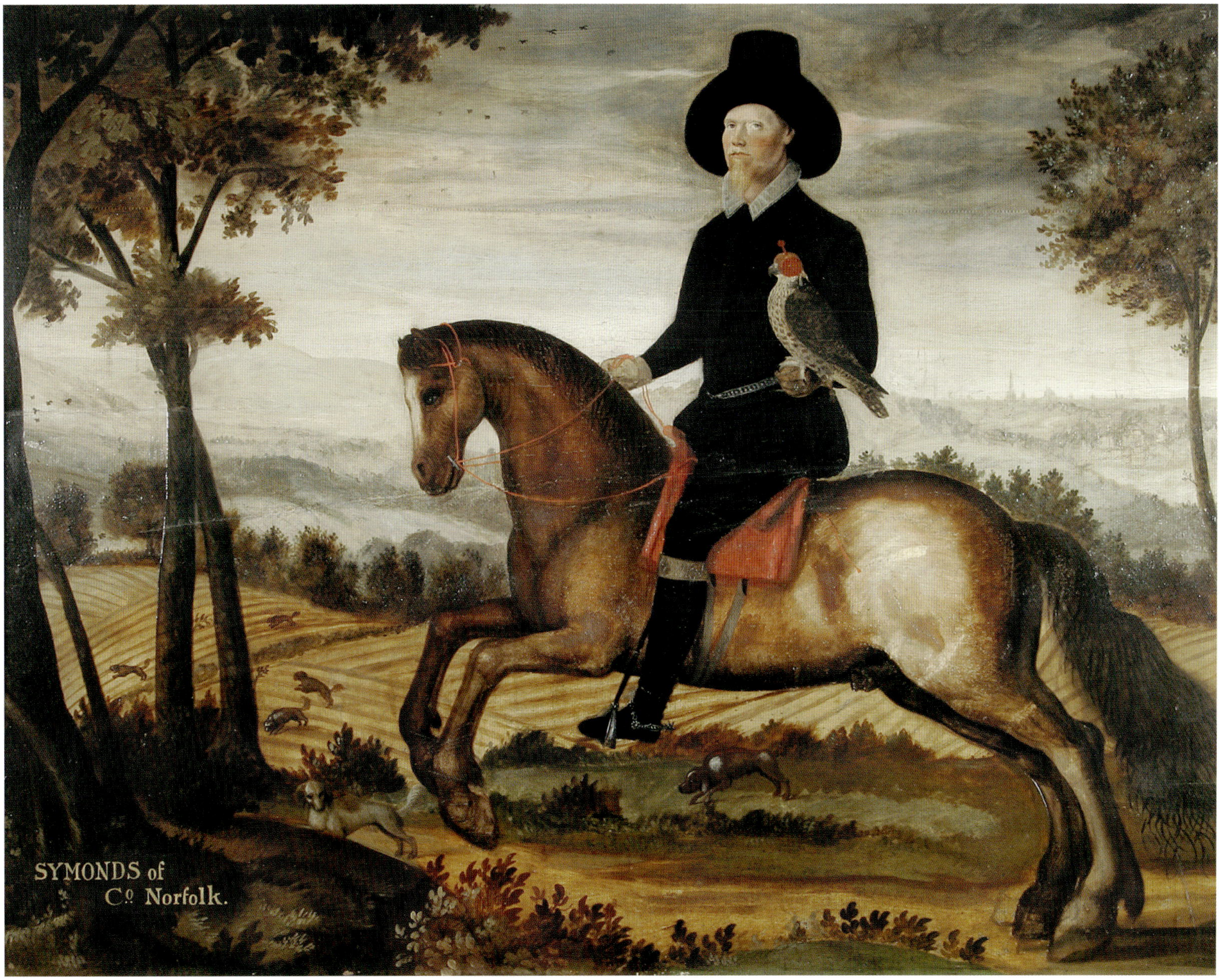
SYMONDS of
Cº Norfolk.

36

The Hesketh Genealogy

Unknown English artist, c.1594

Watercolour on vellum (formerly rolled but now bound and mounted in a large quarto volume), 1000 × 550mm
The British Library, London (Additional MS 44026)

This pedigree of the ancient family of Hesketh of Rufford, Martholme and Great Harwood in Lancashire is a fine example of the genealogical tables that were once common in the houses of the gentry and nobility.[1] Although it is now bound and mounted, the pedigree would originally have been rolled and displayed on a stand in a prominent area of the family home. In the age of the 'new man', tracing your descent back to the Norman Conquest or beyond did much to validate your credentials as a member of the ruling elite. The combination of the anxieties of the established order, coupled with the pretensions of the rising middle class (who had few qualms about presenting their own family history in the most advantageous light), meant that the demand for these 'tables', as they were then called, increased steadily during the second half of the sixteenth century.

What makes this genealogy remarkable is the inclusion alongside the text of a series of miniature portraits, which depict the family line from Sir William Hesketh in 1275 to Robert Hesketh (1560–1620).[2] The likenesses of the immediate family appear to have been based upon existing prototypes, but the earlier portraits are imaginary generic depictions of figures whose costume is at best a loose approximation of the dress of the period. It is possible that this genealogy, and the portraits contained within it, were the work of the London Painter-Stainer Richard Scarlett (d.1607), who is known to have produced tables of this kind and whose extant work is closely comparable in style.[3] The genealogy was probably commissioned by Robert Hesketh, who was head of the Hesketh family in 1594, the date in which the pedigree appears to have been made. Early in his life, Robert had to refute claims from his own sisters that he was illegitimate and presumably he saw the creation of this genealogy as a means by which to legitimise his role, not only within his own family but also as one of the leading figures in county affairs. ET

PROVENANCE

Presented to the British Museum by Thomas Fermor-Hesketh, 1st Baron Hesketh, 1935.

LITERATURE

The Genealogye of the Heskaythes 1869; Proctor 1911, pp.58–66.

NOTES

1 N.M. Sutherland, 'Hesketh, Robert (1560–1620), of Rufford and Martholme, Lancs.', ed. P.W. Hasler, *The History of Parliament: The House of Commons 1558–1603, II Members D–L*, London, 1581, pp.304–5.

2 Although the inclusion of portraits in this genealogy is unusual, it is not without precedent. For example, the 'Salisbury Roll' in the collection of the Duke of Buccleuch contains fifty pairs of figures linked by a cord or a chain. See Anthony Richard Wagner, *A Catalogue of English Medieval Rolls of Arms* (Oxford University Press, Oxford, 1950), p.103. The Sackville Pedigree of 1599 (V&A, MSL.41-1981) at the Victoria and Albert Museum also incorporates portraits into its composition.

3 British Library, Harleian MS 1354 contains a series of portraits depicting the ceremonial attire suitable to the ranks of a duke, a marquis and an earl by Richard Scarlett. There is also a depiction of an earl in an older form of the same type of clothing, and an unfinished image of a nobleman in his robes. The careful and linear handling has much in common with the figures in the Hesketh genealogy.

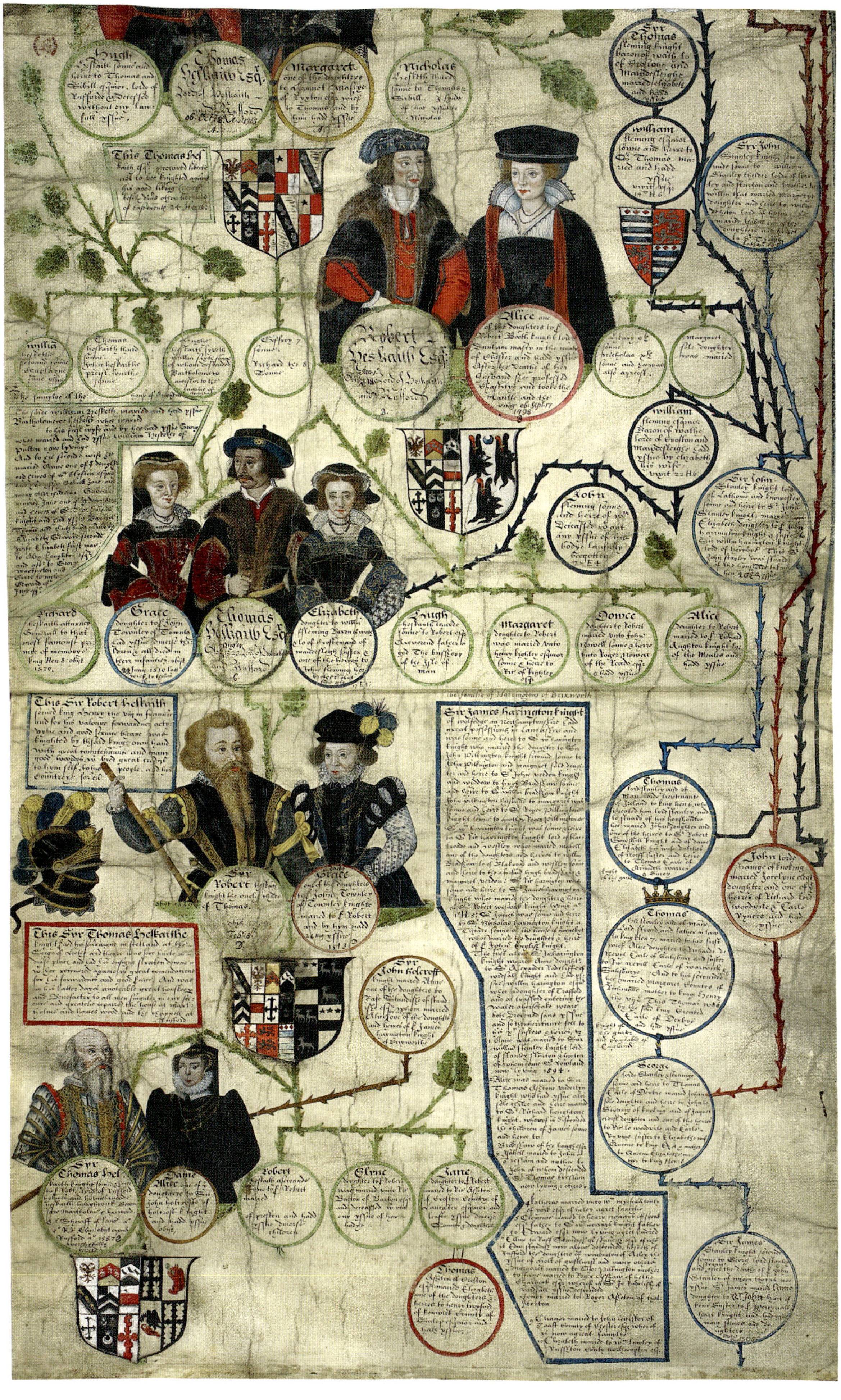

Hugh
Thomas Heskaith Esq.
Margaret
Nicholas
Syr Thomas
William
Syr John
Robert Heskaith Esq.
Alice
William
John
Richard
Grace
Thomas Heskaith Esq.
Elizabeth
Hugh
Margaret
Dowce
Alice
Sir James Harington knight
Thomas
John
Syr Robert
Grace
This Syr Thomas Heskaithe
Syr John Holcroft
George
Syr Thomas Hesketh
Dame Alice
Robert
Thomas
Sir James

37

Wheel-lock Pistol

England (probably London), c.1580

Steel barrel and lock damascened with gold and silver, wooden stock inlaid with engraved antler
Pistol: length 580mm; barrel: length 373mm, calibre 50mm
Victoria and Albert Museum, London, purchased with the assistance of the National Heritage Memorial Fund (Museum No. M.949-1983)

This pistol is the only known complete English wheel-lock pistol of the sixteenth century. It originally belonged to Sir William Harris of Shenfield House, Essex, along with a powder flask and a snaphaunce musket, dated 1588.

The pistol is elaborately decorated in a style influenced by Italian and Spanish metalwork and is similar to one depicted in the portrait of Sir Martin Frobisher (cat. 21). It is likely that the maker was an immigrant German craftsman working in London. The decoration, which survives in remarkable condition, depicts hunting scenes including men on horseback with dogs chasing wild boar, foxes and hares. The steel barrel is damascened (overlaid) with gold and silver, and its wooden stock is inlaid with engraved antler. Although this example may have been made primarily for display, the growing use of pistols for hunting was contentious among some writers who felt that valuable sets of skills, and a noble tradition of stalking with sword and spear, were being abandoned.

The pistol is fitted with a wheel-lock firing mechanism that enabled it to be carried loaded and ready to fire. A sprung wheel inside the gun was wound to high tension. When the trigger was pulled, a clamp holding a block of iron pyrites against the spinning wheel created sparks that ignited the priming pan, causing the gun to fire. Wheel-lock pistols came equipped with a set of tools including measured charges, powder flasks, priming flasks and cartridge cases that were decorated in a similar style. As sophisticated technical devices, such pistols attracted wealthy patrons. However, they also struck fear into Elizabethan lawmakers. Edicts in 1575, 1579 and 1597 restricted their ownership to 'noblemen and such known gentlemen which be without spot or doubt of evil behaviour.'[1] AP

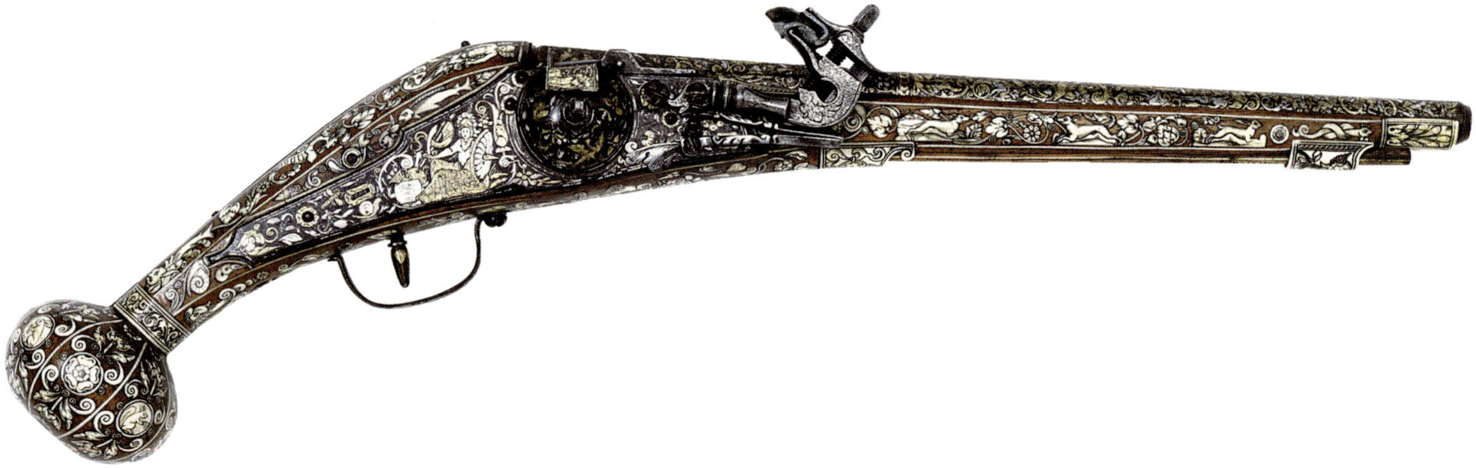

PROVENANCE

Sir William Harris of Essex, descended through the Raymond family of Belchamp Hall, Suffolk.

LITERATURE

Hayward 1965, pp.121–3; Jardine 2005, pp.96–7, cover ill. (detail); Patterson 2009, pp.99–100, ill. pl. 95.

NOTE

1 Frederick Wilkinson, *Those Entrusted with Arms: A History of the Police, Post, Customs and Private Use of Weapons in Britain* (Royal Armouries and Greenhill Books, London, 2002), p.49.

38

Rapier

England, c.1600

Steel, the hilt damascened in gold and encrusted with chiselled silver; length 1248mm, width 225mm, depth 124mm
Stamped: *CAINO* and *TO* in a shield
Victoria and Albert Museum, London (Museum No. M.51-1947)

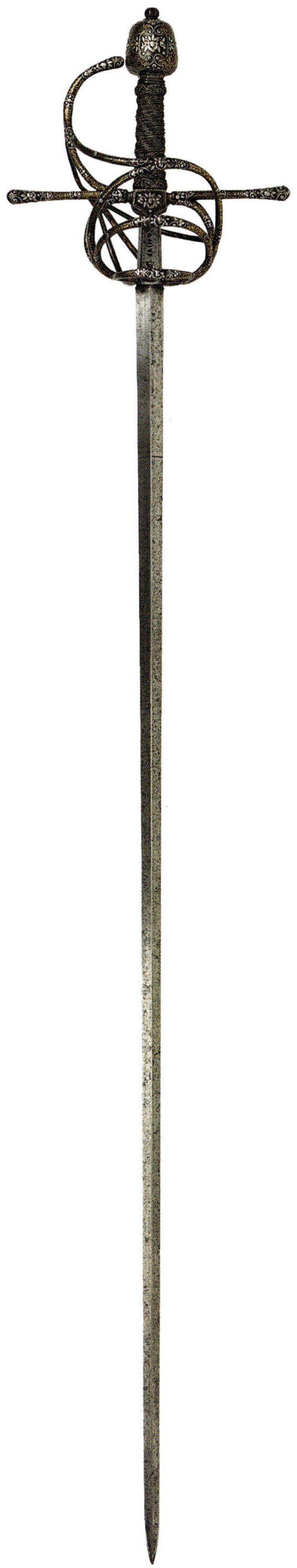

This is one of the finest known Elizabethan rapiers. Its graceful 'swept' hilt of twisting bars and rings is overlaid with gold and silver flowers and vines, a technique known as damascening.

Rapiers were the expensive accessories of the Renaissance nobleman. They were worn in a scabbard at the left hip, suspended at 45 degrees from a sling (hanger) and were often accompanied by a matching dagger. In England the decoration of swords was regulated by sumptuary laws. A 1574 law stated, 'None shall wear spurs, swords, rapiers, daggers, … or hangers, buckles or girdles, gilt, silvered or damasked: except knights and barons' sons, and others of higher degree or place, and gentlemen in ordinary office attendant upon the Queen's majesty's person.'[1]

Although the blade is of fine quality, the crowned 'TO' mark is a contemporary fake of the town mark of Toledo in Spain. Toledo blades were prized internationally and this mimicry speaks of brand identity. The satirist Robert Greene rebuked swordsmiths who exploited the yearnings of the fashionable: 'to a poore man that cannot skill of it you sell him a sword or rapier new over glased, and sweare, the blade came either from Turky or Toledo.'[2] Even so, the 1070mm blade marks this rapier as a high-status sword. An earlier law of 1562 forbade anyone below the rank of the son of a baron to 'wear any sword, rapier, or any weapon in their stead, passing the length of one yard and half a quarter of blade at the uttermost.'[3]

The rapier was not only a fashion item. If its facade failed to elicit due respect, it could also be drawn from its scabbard as a lethal weapon of self-defence. As a specialist civilian weapon, its long, rigid and sharply pointed blade was designed to pierce clothing rather than armour. George Silver, in *Paradoxes of Defence*, scorned the rapier's 'inconvenient length and unwieldinesse' and ridiculed those who have 'lusted like men sicke of a strange ague, after the strange vices and devices of Italian French and Spanish Fencers'.[4] AP

PROVENANCE

Francis Mallett Bequest.

LITERATURE

Hayward 1963, cat. 16; Patterson 2009, p.62, ill. pl.56; Dmitrieva and Murdoch 2013, fig. 144, pp.20–1.

NOTES

1 Sumptuary Law: 'The Excess of Apparel…', Westminster, 15 June 1574, 16 Elizabeth I (transcribed at elizabethan.org/sumptuary/who-wears-what.html, accessed 28 Jan. 2013).
2 Robert Greene, *A Quip for an Upstart Courtier: or, A quaint dispute betweene velvet breeches and cloth breeches Wherein is plainely set downe the disorders in all estates and trades* (G.P. [George Purslowe], London, first printed 1583, reprinted 1620), p.12.
3 Sumptuary Law: 'The Excess of Apparel…', Westminster, 7 May 1562, 16 Elizabeth I (transcribed at elizabethan.org/sumptuary/ruffs-hose-swords.html, accessed 28 Jan. 2013).
4 George Silver, *Paradozes of Defence* (Edward Blount, London, 1599) in Cyril G.R. Matthey, *The Works of George Silver* (George Bell & Sons, Covent Garden, 1898), the Epistle Dedicatorie and p.9.

39

Renaissance Rings set with Gemstones

a **Emerald-set ring, sixteenth century**

England?
Gold, emerald
The British Museum, London (AF.1943)

b **Diamond-set ring, sixteenth century**

England?
Gold, diamond, enamel
The Ashmolean Museum, University of Oxford (WA1897.CDEF.F468)

c **Sapphire-set ring, c.1525–75**

Western Europe
Gold, sapphire, enamel
Victoria and Albert Museum, London (201-1906)

d **Signet ring with crystal intaglio and initials 'TS', sixteenth century**

England
Gold, crystal, foil
The Ashmolean Museum, University of Oxford (WA1897.CDEF.F596)

e **Cabochon ruby ring, c.1575–99**

Venice, Italy
Gold, ruby, enamel
The Ashmolean Museum, University of Oxford (WA1897.CDEF.F475)

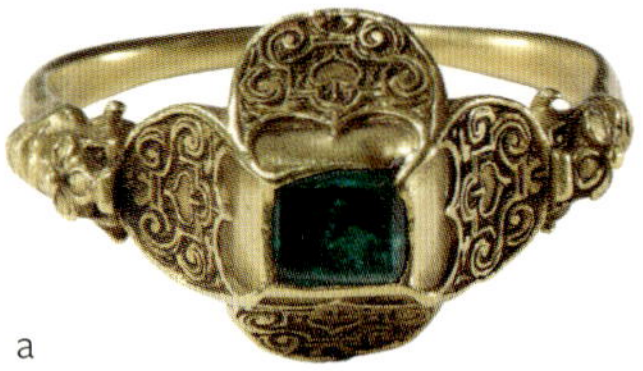
a

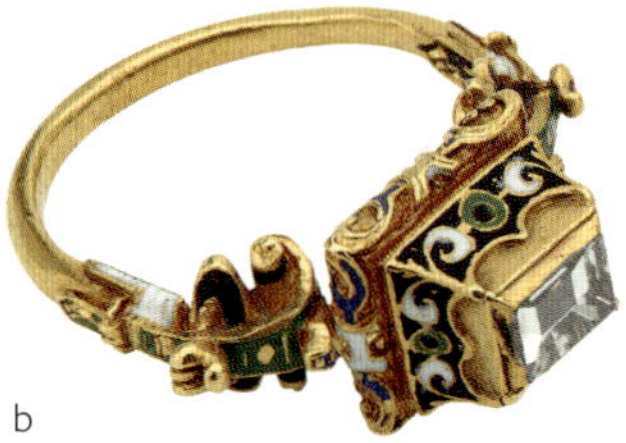
b

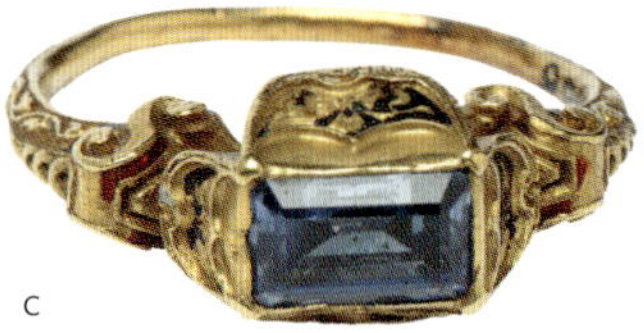
c

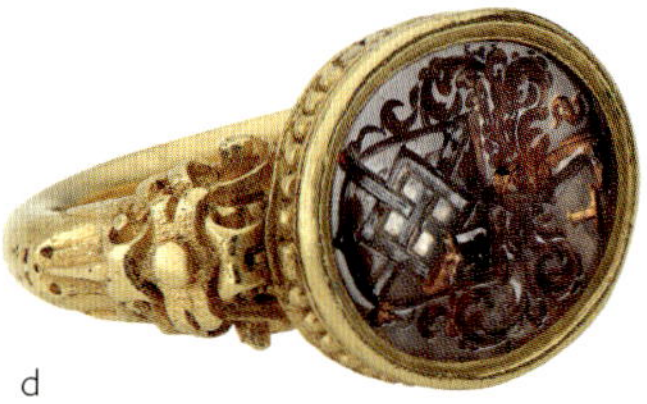
d

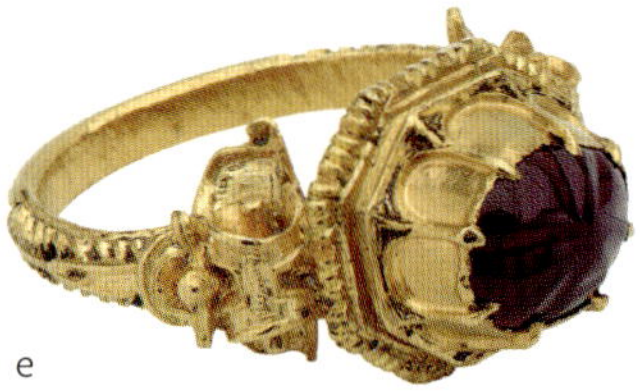
e

Finger rings were a particularly popular form of jewellery across Renaissance Europe, worn by both men and women from a range of social groups. Many portraits of both men and women of the English nobility and gentry depict their sitters with fine gem-set rings adorning their hands. These gold rings often featured engraved scrollwork decoration, as seen in some of the examples here, which was often also enamelled as in the case of the exquisite diamond ring (cat. 39b). The gemstones set within these rings mostly came from the East. India dominated the diamond trade and the stones would enter Europe in an unfinished state to be cut in centres such as Antwerp, Lisbon, or Paris. Rubies from Burma were particularly highly regarded, though stones of a lesser quality could be sourced from Thailand, Ceylon and India. These gemstones were traded by means of an international network of well-connected merchants, who sold their goods at fairs and directly to goldsmiths for setting.

Evidence from post-mortem inventories shows that some members of the nobility were in possession of loose gemstones, providing a powerful indication of an individual's ability to commission jewellery to his precise specifications. At the time of his death, the courtier Henry Howard (1540–1614), Earl of Northampton, owned eighty-two loose gemstones, including fifteen small rubies, ten uncut rock emeralds and thirty-eight small diamonds.[1]

The crystal signet ring (cat. 39d), showing a family coat of arms, is of a type that was popular among the nobility and gentry as it remained distinct from gold signets that sometimes displayed non-heraldic devices. The coat of arms (possibly of the Stoke family) is engraved in reverse on the surface of the stone, on which the heraldic colours may have been originally reverse-tinted, gilded or silvered. NAD

PROVENANCE (a)

Bequeathed by Sir Augustus Wollaston Franks, 1897.

PROVENANCE (b)

Presented by Dr C.D.E. Fortnum in honour of Queen Victoria's Diamond Jubilee, 1897.

PROVENANCE (c)

Purchased from Mr R.C. Howes, 1906.

PROVENANCE (d)

Presented by Dr C.D.E. Fortnum in honour of Queen Victoria's Diamond Jubilee, 1897.

PROVENANCE (e)

Presented by Dr C.D.E. Fortnum in honour of Queen Victoria's Diamond Jubilee, 1897.

LITERATURE

Dalton 1912; Oman 1930; Scarisbrick 1994; Scarisbrick 1995; Scarisbrick and Henig 2003; Scarisbrick 2007; Awais-Dean 2012.

NOTES

1 Evelyn Philip Shirley, 'An Inventory of the Effects of Henry Howard', *Archaeologia* 42, no. II, 1869, p.349.

We are grateful to Rachel Church (V&A) and Dora Thornton (British Museum) for their help in making this selection.

40

a **The Gatacre Jewel, c.1550–60**

Probably England
Gold, amethyst, enamel, pearl, 70 × 40 × 12mm
Victoria and Albert Museum, London (M.7-1982)

b **Plaquette, sixteenth century**

Italy
Gilt bronze, 47.5mm
The British Museum, London (1915,1216.134)

In the sixteenth century, the wearing of jewelled goods was common among men and women across all social classes. Wealthier individuals could afford items of gold and had access to precious and semi-precious gemstones. By comparison with the artisanal or merchant classes, they also owned a far greater quantity of jewellery, such as pendants, necklaces, brooches and hat ornaments. The Gatacre Jewel represents a type of jewel that would have been owned by members of the nobility and gentry in Elizabethan England, while the plaquette, identified as a hat ornament, reflects the way in which elite fashions filtered down to all levels of society.

This pendant jewel is also known as 'The Fair Maid of Gatacre' after Mary (b.1509), only daughter of Sir Robert Gatacre of Shropshire. It is formed of an amethyst cameo of Medusa placed in an enamelled gold scrollwork frame, from which hang three drop pearls which may be later replacements. The reverse of the gold frame and setting is also enamelled. Pendants such as these were popular among women and one can be seen clearly in the portrait of Elizabeth Vernon, Countess of Southampton (cat. 27), at her toilet. Vernon's pendant is set with an abundance of table-cut diamonds and at its base hangs a drop pearl. The frequent inclusion of drop pearls on jewellery of this period may be attributed to the fact that the pearl had come to signify both Queen Elizabeth's purity and England's expanding network of global connections towards the end of the sixteenth century.

It is probable that the circular plaquette was originally enamelled, and its wreathed border has been pierced with holes to allow it to be sewn onto a hat. A fashion for these hat ornaments, which were also produced in enamelled gold and set with precious gemstones, spread across Europe during the sixteenth century. Subjects depicted included biblical tales, classical themes and common folklore, and the ornaments were worn to show political, religious or personal allegiances. This piece shows Laocoon and his sons being overcome by serpents, a popular theme in sixteenth-century Italy following the discovery in Rome in 1506 of an ancient marble of the same subject. The plaquette was cast in one piece and represents an early form of mass production, allowing for dissemination to wider audiences. NAD

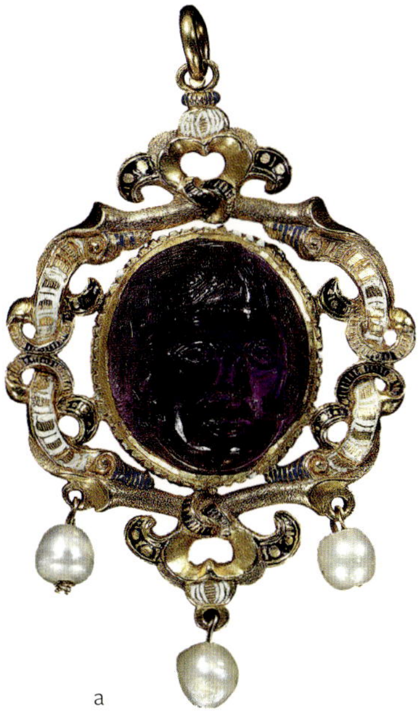

a

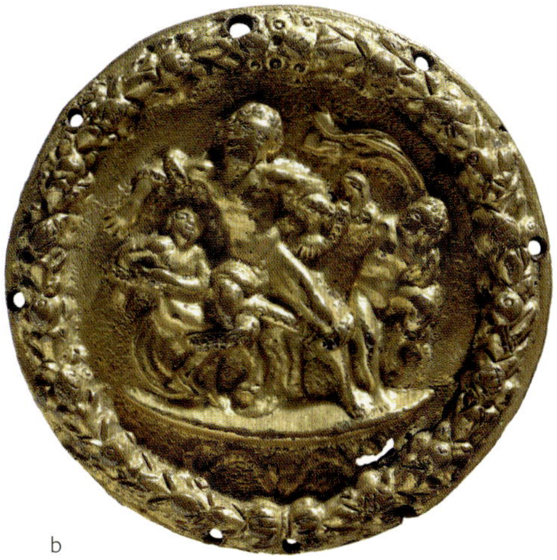

b

PROVENANCE (a)
Purchased with the assistance of the Art Fund, 1982.

PROVENANCE (b)
Donated by Thomas Whitcombe Greene, 1915.

LITERATURE (a)
Awais-Dean 2012.

LITERATURE (b)
Leino 2004.

41

Sweet Box and Pomander

a **Pomander for carrying scent**

England, c.1600–10
Silver-gilt and niello; height 70mm, diameter 40mm, depth 65mm
The Rosalinde and Arthur Gilbert Collection on loan to the Victoria and Albert Museum, London
(GILBERT.578:1, 2-2008)

b **Sweet box**

England, 1579
Iron, damascened with gold and silver; height 40mm, width 95mm, depth 60mm
Victoria and Albert Museum, London
(M.665-1910)

The value of functional, yet highly decorative, objects such as this damascened box and niello pomander lay in the quality of the craftsmanship that they displayed. Such decorative techniques could be used on a wide variety of objects. The box bears the heraldic device of Robert Dudley, Earl of Leicester (cat. 18)– the bear and ragged staff – on the underside of the lid and was probably intended to contain sweetmeats, or comfits. These were preserved fruits that were often given as gifts at New Year, and, as the date 1579 is recorded on the box, it is likely that it formed part of such an exchange. Evidence of Dudley's engagement in gift exchanges of this type can be found in his household accounts, which include a payment of 6 shillings and 2 pence for 'ij boxis of cumsetts which your lordship gave to my Lord of Darbye'.[1] The iron box is intricately decorated using the technique of damascening. This involved darkening the iron using heat or chemicals, and then pushing gold and silver ribbon into the surface over a cross-hatched design.

The pomander is a personal item of jewellery that usually hung from a suspension ring on the end of a long chain secured at the waist, as can be seen in the portrait of Katheryn of Berain (1534/5–91, cat. 48), or worn around the neck. This example consists of six numbered compartments engraved with floral decoration; each compartment is hinged in order to open, and could contain a different scent. CB

PROVENANCE (a)
Baron Wharton; purchased from Asprey and Company, London, 1984.

PROVENANCE (b)
Bequeathed by George Salting in 1909.

LITERATURE (a)
Schroder 2009, p.30, pl.14.

LITERATURE (b)
Patterson 2009, pp.96–7, ill. pl.92.

NOTE

1 Simon Adams (ed.), *Household Accounts and Disbursement Books of Robert Dudley, Earl of Leicester* (Cambridge University Press, Cambridge, 1995), p.93.

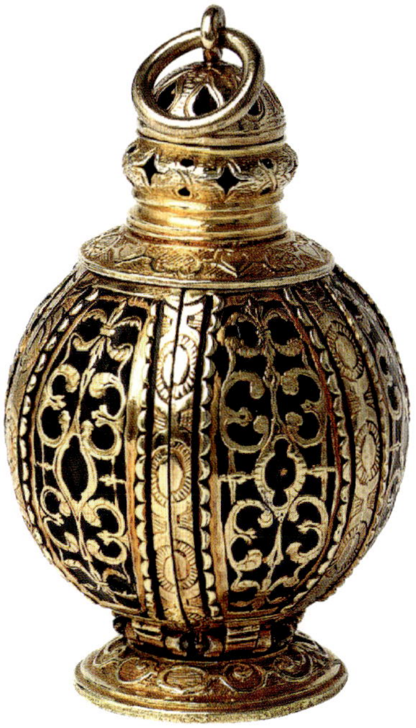

a (closed)

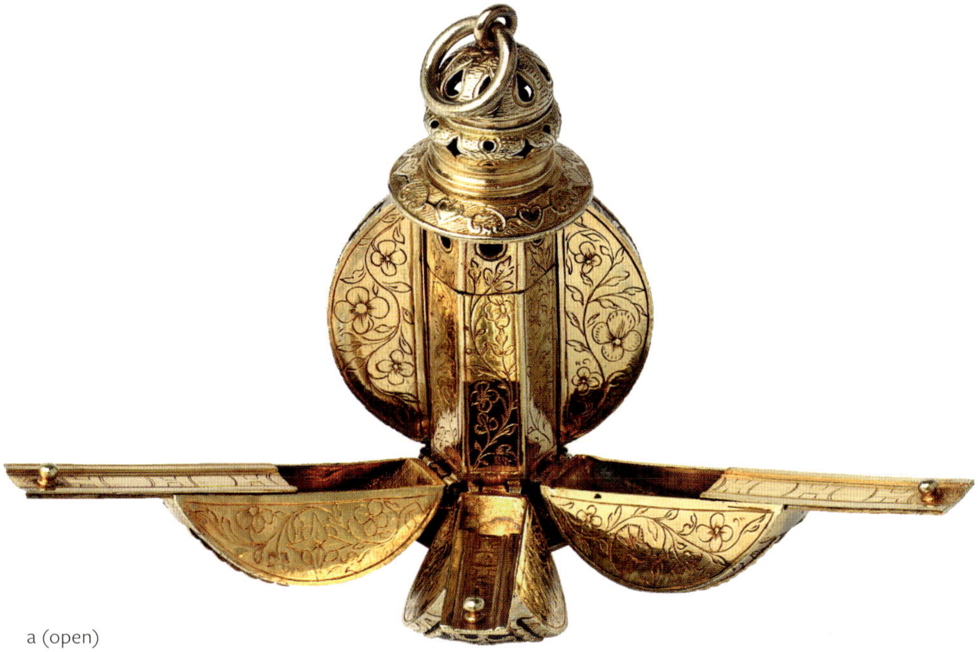

a (open)

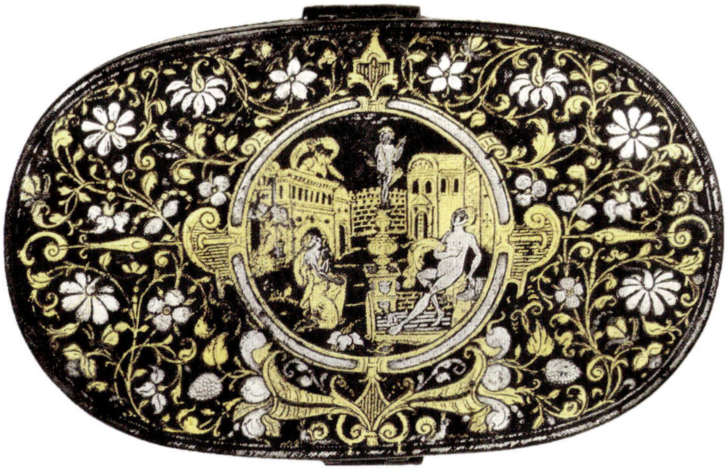

b (closed)

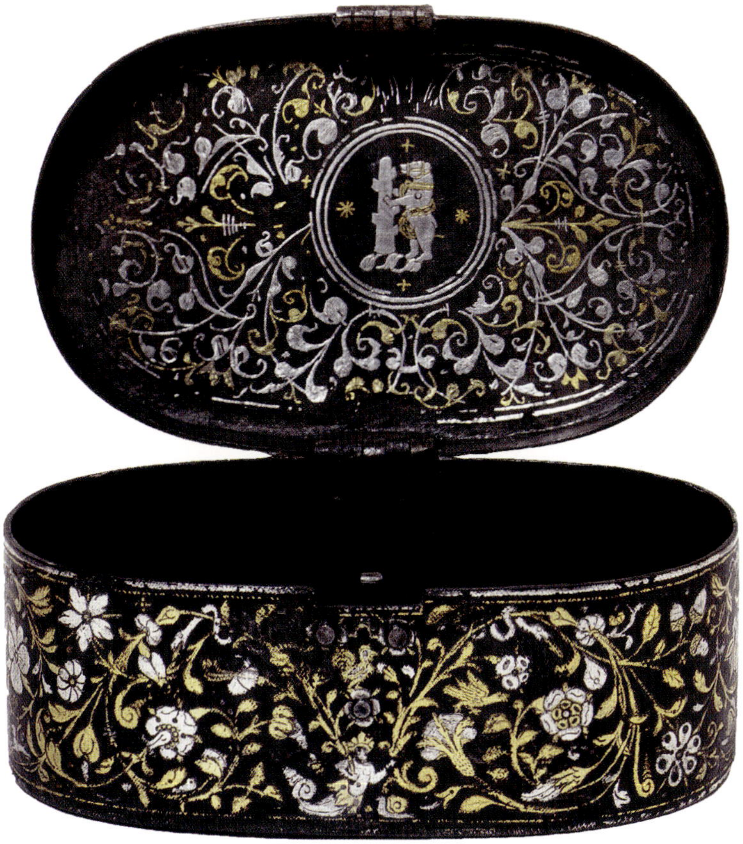

b (open)

Personal Accessories

a Comb

Probably French or Netherlandish, c.1520–30
Carved ivory, depicting on one side the Judgement of Paris and on the other, David's message to Bathsheba, 133 × 148mm
Victoria and Albert Museum, London
(Accession no. 2143-1855)

b Sweet bag

England, 1600–30
Linen embroidered with coloured silks, silver and silver-gilt threads, lined with silk, 330 × 170mm
The Burrell Collection, Glasgow Museums
(Accession no. 29.310)

c Purse

England, 1600–20
Leather, silk, silver-gilt thread and wire and glass beads, 60 × 80 × 20mm
The Ashmolean Museum, Oxford
(Accession no. WA1947.191.324)

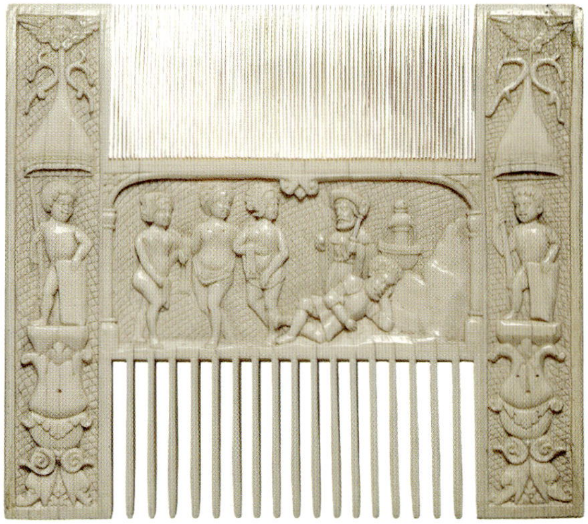

a

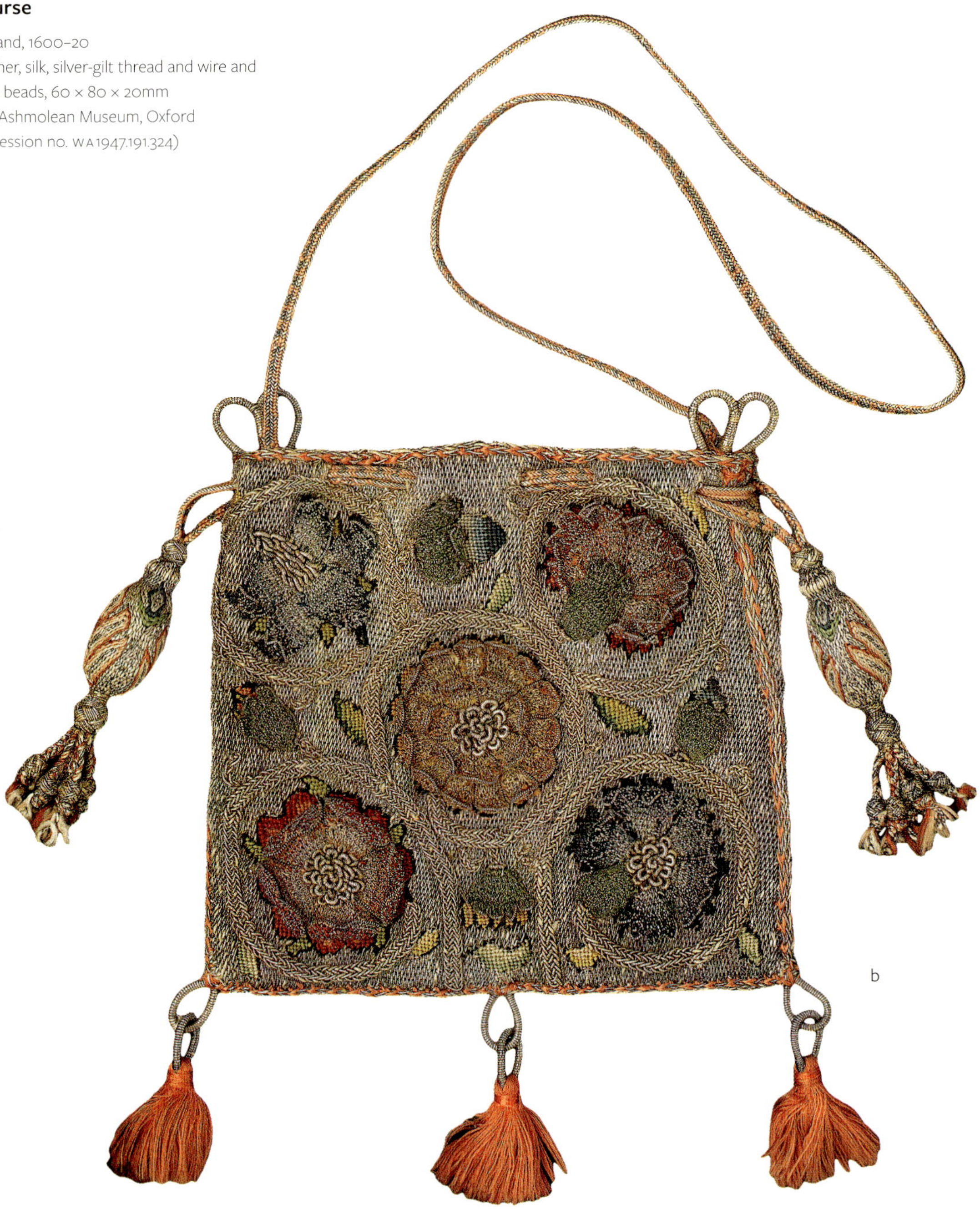

b

NOTES

1 Janet Arnold, *Queen Elizabeth's Wardrobe Unlock'd* (W.S. Maney & Son, Leeds, 1988), p.194.
2 John Partridge, *The Treasurie of commodious Conceits* (Richarde Jones, London, 1573), f. D3verso.
3 Arnold, op. cit., p.194.
4 Edward Roberts and Karen Parker (eds), *Southampton Probate Inventories 1447–1575, I*, Southampton Record Society, vol. 34, 1992, pp.371–83.

Personal appearance was important in Elizabethan England. Advice on social conduct circulated throughout England and Europe in manuscript form during the medieval period and, by the 1500s, it began to appear in printed versions. Such manuals were often addressed to young boys of all social classes, serving as pages, yeomen, grooms and servants in Tudor aristocratic households. A neat and clean appearance with spotless tidy apparel, combed hair, scrubbed hands and faces, was essential.

Many items of dress in the aristocratic Elizabethan wardrobe were perfumed. Sweet bags held perfumed powders or dried flowers and were stored with clothing, to impart an agreeable scent as well as to protect wool and fur from moths.[1] A 1573 recipe for a sweet powder typically used dried rose leaves, cloves, lavender and musk.[2] Sweet bags were often ornately decorated with floral motifs, such as the borage, gillyflower and rose, as shown here. Queen Elizabeth often received them as New Year gifts and her skinner, Adam Bland, also provided them directly, as in 1562 when she received: 'one gross of Crimsen Sarsent swete Bagges and viii lb of swete powder'.[3] Small decorative purses also served to convey a gift of coin or to hold implements for sewing (scissors, threads) or grooming (small mirrors and combs). Naturalistic shapes were popular and purses were worked in the form of bunches of grapes, or the frog, as here.

The inventories of rural grocers and mercers feature a variety of grooming items for the rest of England's populace. Materials and styles are rarely described, but they were clearly less luxurious versions of the objects illustrated here. Southampton merchant John Lughting's 1564 inventory included over 600 combs, numerous purses of silk and satin, as well as the essential looking glasses – to ensure the effectiveness of one's toilette – valued at a halfpenny each.[4] SN

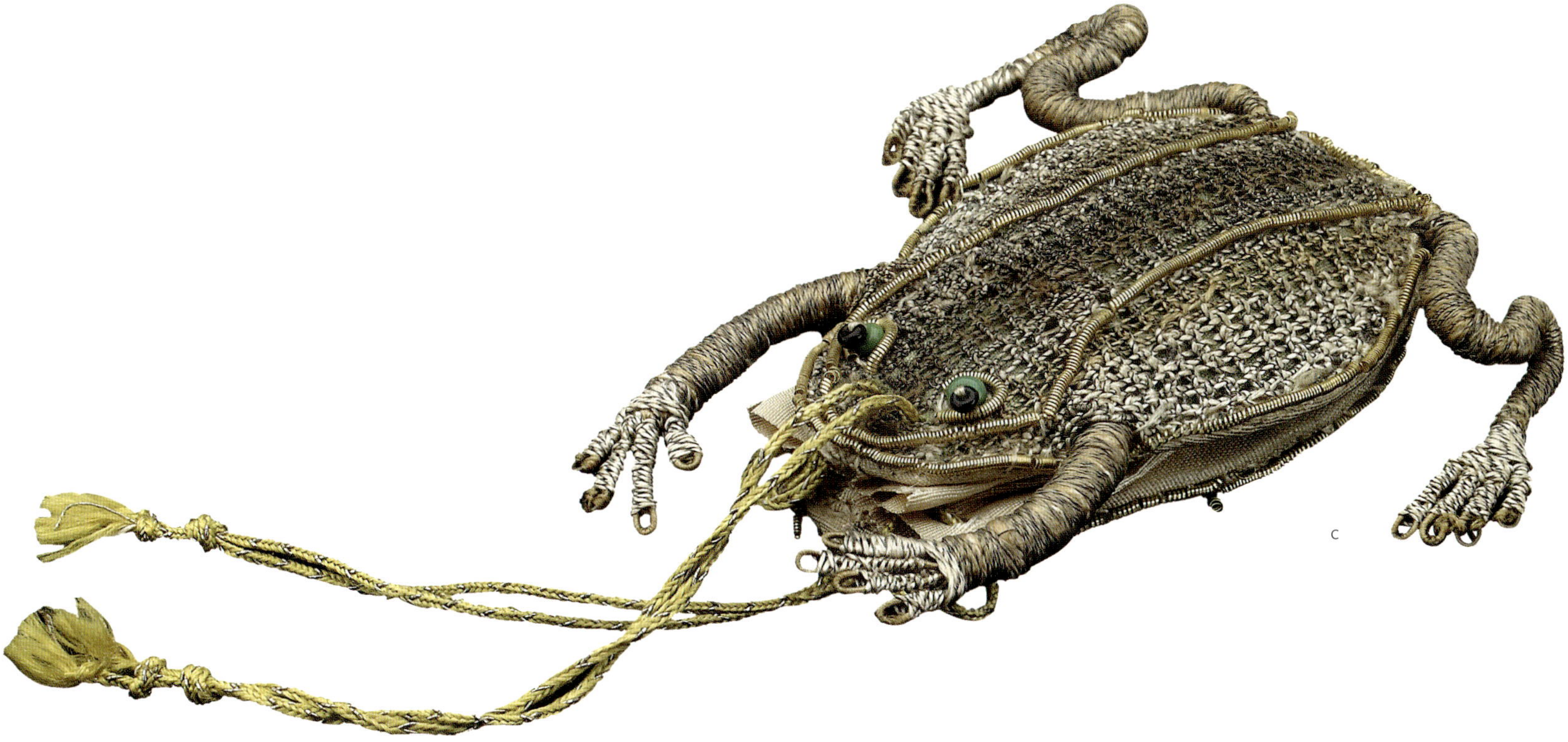

C

43

Lord Burghley's Tankard

London, probably factory of Jacopo Verzelini, c.1575

Silver-gilt, enamel and glass, height 213mm
The British Museum, London (AF.3134)

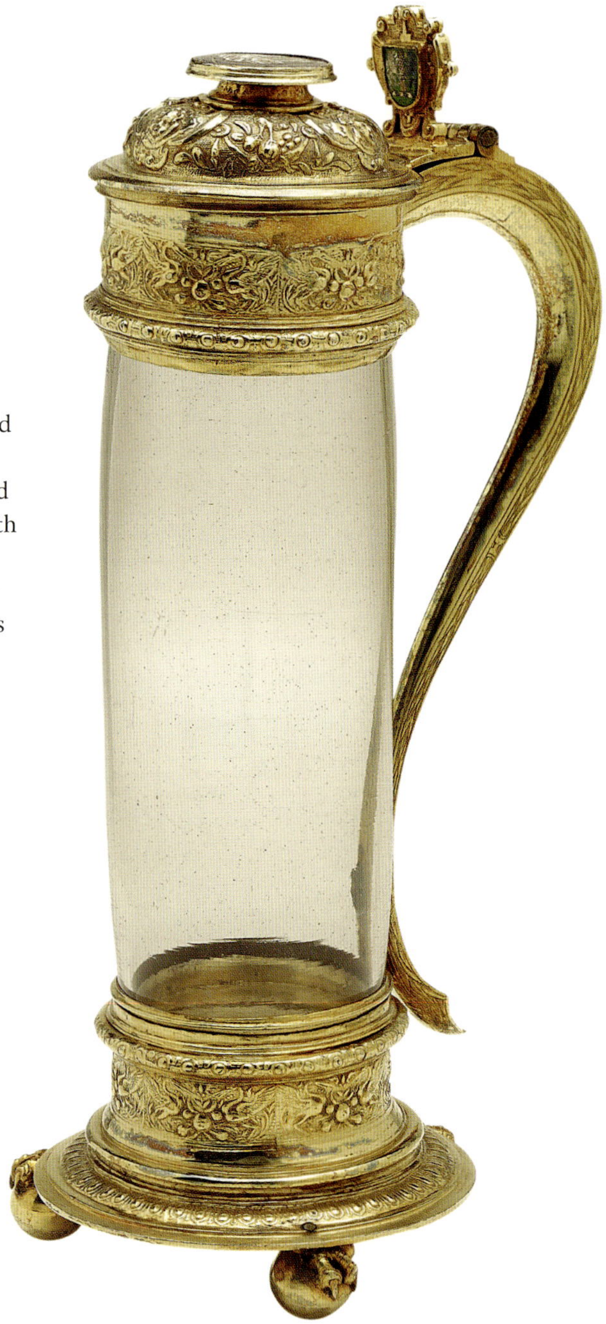

This unusual tankard is formed from an open-ended tube of thin *cristallo* glass with silver-gilt mounts. It belonged to William Cecil, Lord Burghley (cat. 19), whose arms are enamelled on the embossed lid. It is likely to have been produced in London by the Venetian glassmaker Jacopo Verzelini (1522–1607). Burghley sought to encourage the development of new manufacturing techniques in England, and Verzelini may have presented the tankard to him in order to secure the patent to produce *cristallo* glass in England. On 15 December 1574 Verzelini obtained a patent that granted a monopoly 'to make drinking and other glasses like those made at Morano near Venice'. The patent also included a ban on imports, which was 'to the commodity of the common weal, since great sums of money have passed beyond seas for that manner of ware'.[1]

Clear *cristallo* glass, made by Venetian craftsmen, was prized across Europe. The Elizabethan author William Harrison noted that the nobility and gentry preferred to drink from 'Venice glasses' rather than gold or silver vessels because man 'most coveteth things difficult to be attained'.[2] Those who could afford to do so were prepared to pay high prices; the 1582 English Book of Rates records that a dozen 'Drinking glasses of Venice' were valued at 4 shillings, while 'Drinking glasses of French' came in at 8 pence.[3] CB

PROVENANCE

Previously in the collection of Arthur Maitland Wilson; bequeathed by Sir Augustus Wollaston Franks, 1897.

LITERATURE

Tait 1979, p.56; Tait 1991, p.169; Schroder 2004, pp.3–12.

NOTES

1 *Calendar of Patent Rolls*, 1572–75, 3209.
2 Raphael Holinshed, *Chronicles of England, Scotland and Ireland*, 6 vols (printed for J. Johnson et al., London, 1807), I, pp.230–1.
3 Thomas Stuart Willan, *A Tudor Book of Rates* (Manchester University Press, Manchester, 1962), p.23.

44

Embroidered Textiles

a **Embroidered panel with stag**

England, 1559–64/5

The Hardwick Crest (a stag) with the initials 'ES'
Silk velvet embroidered with silver, silver-gilt thread and coloured silk threads, 297 × 295mm
National Trust inventory number 1129780

b **Textile figures of a 'Falconer' and 'Gentleman'**

England, 1580–1600
Coloured silks tent-stitched on linen canvas ground, with additional embroidery in chain and stem stitches, Falconer height 490mm; gentleman height 495mm

Hardwick Hall, Devonshire Collection (acquired through the National Land Fund and transferred to the National Trust in 1988)

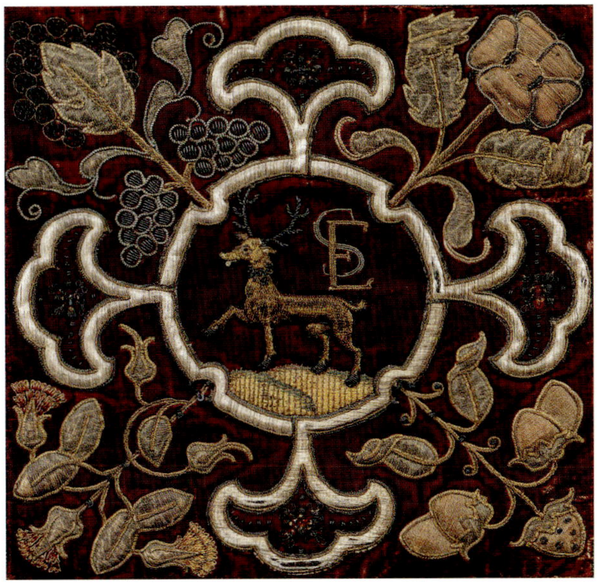

The velvet embroidered panel is one of a series and was probably intended for use on a wall or as a bed hanging at Hardwick Hall, commissioned by Bess of Hardwick during her marriage to Sir William St Loe. It is typical of the type of embroidery that was also used extensively on the clothing of royalty and the aristocracy during this period, which was made using similar techniques. The naturalistically rendered rose, strawberry, grapes and lungwort were inspired by the illustrations from contemporary herbals and are also found in the embroidery embellishing items of clothing such as shirts, smocks, night caps, coifs and bags. Spangles and a variety of textured threads of silver and silver-gilt feature in the needlework embellishing furnishing textiles and fashionable dress in the sixteenth century.

The two figures depicting a falconer and a gentleman are part of a large number of separate motifs in needlework, used and reused in the decorative textiles that adorned Sheffield Castle, Chatsworth and Hardwick Hall between 1580 and 1640. The silhouette of the figures and the style of the garments worn suggest that they were probably worked in the 1590s. Both figures wear the full-sleeved doublets with curved peascod belly and the high-crowned hats fashionable in this period.

It is difficult to attribute any specific social class to either figure. Although the 'falconer' has a falcon on his wrist, his falling band 'collar' is worked with blue spots to suggest some sort of expensive cutwork or needle lace, and he also wears a sword – supposedly the attribute of a gentleman, but one prone to appropriation by aspiring young men.[1] The so-called 'gentleman' wears a ruff and cuffs, but carries a shepherd's staff instead of a sword. Research into the Hardwick textiles did not reveal any iconographic sources for these figures, and they appear to be 'fanciful' pieces executed for the variety of embroidery they employ rather than faithful representations of a known narrative.[2] SN

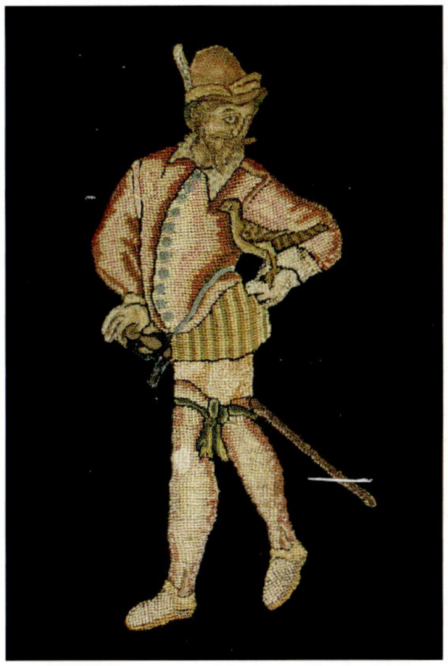

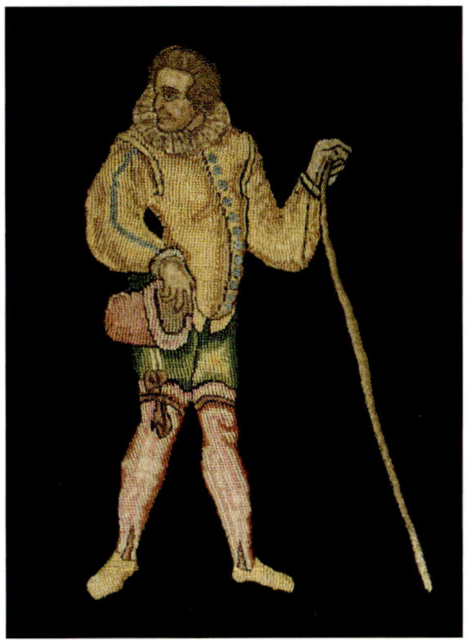

PROVENANCE

Presumably always at Hardwick Hall.

LITERATURE

Levey 2007, pp.207, 352.

NOTES

1 Angus Patterson, *Fashion and Armour in Renaissance Europe* (V&A Publishing, London, 2009), pp.18, 58–60.
2 Santina Levey, *The Embroideries at Hardwick Hall* (National Trust Books, London, 2007), p.354.

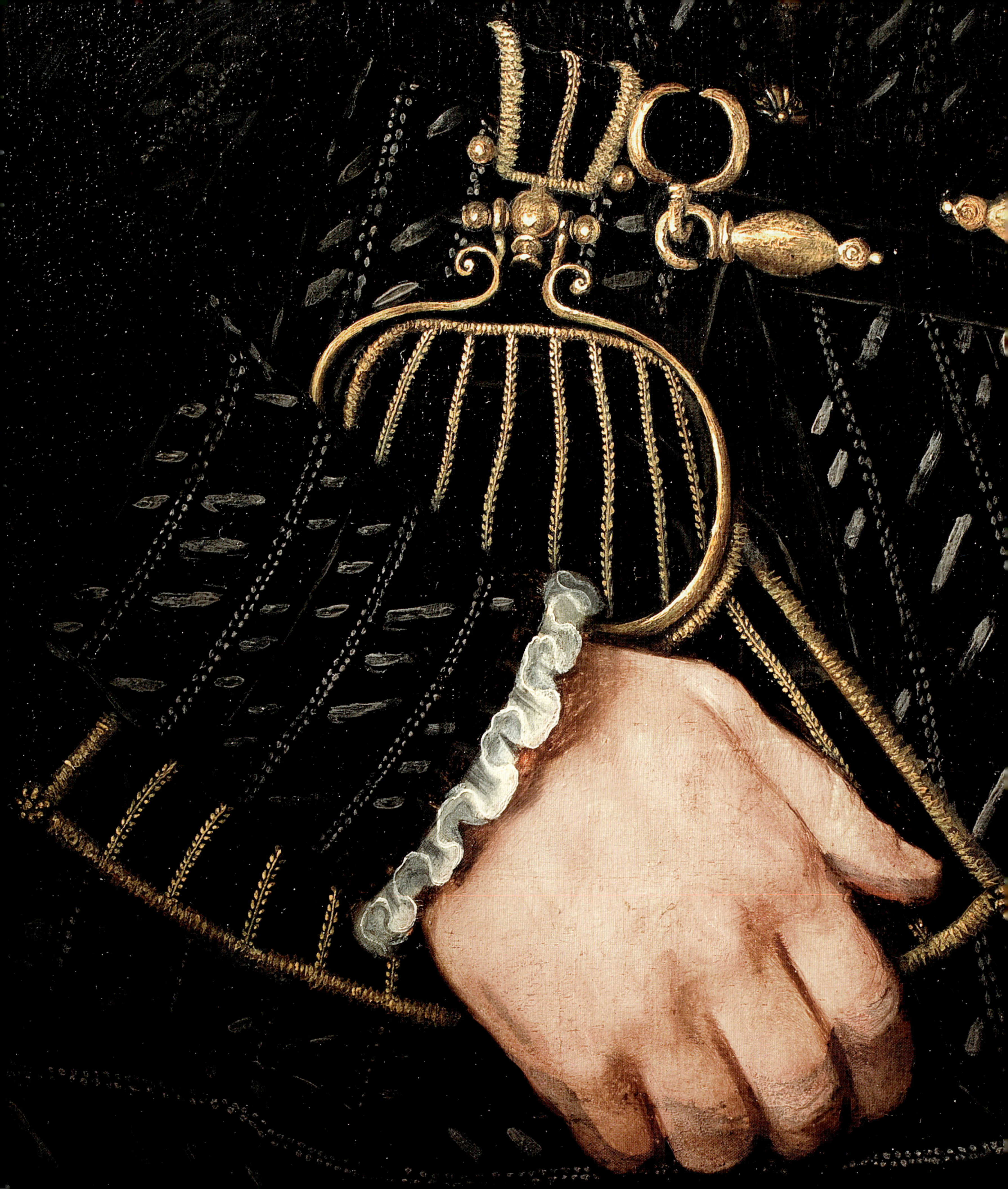

4 MERCHANTS AND TRADERS

The economic stability of the Elizabethan period encouraged new opportunities for wealth creation. The programme of restoring the debased coinage from 1560–1 and the impact of customs reforms helped to ensure economic viability and more favourable conditions for foreign trade. Although cloth exports were sluggish, imports (particularly of luxury goods such as wine, spices and sugar) grew rapidly, and London's merchants responded to difficulties in their traditional north-west European markets by opening new trade routes to the Levant and, at the end of Elizabeth's reign, the East Indies.

Emblematic of the increasing prominence of merchants in the country's politics and their close association with the royal court was Sir Thomas Gresham. He was responsible not only for securing loans to the Crown but also for financing the Royal Exchange, London's first purpose-built international trading market, which also had shops on the upper floors. In a world that depended upon credit, the reputation of a merchant for fair and scrupulous dealing was essential, but the risks could be high if ships were lost, stock damaged or credit was called in. Merchants were criticised by clergymen not only for their own greed, but also for selling luxury goods that encouraged a consumer culture, creating a cycle of envy, avarice and debt, particularly among city dwellers.

By the end of Elizabeth I's reign, many Londoners, and others in cities such as Portsmouth and Norwich, had benefited from the increase in trade and growth in retail opportunities, underpinned by growing rural prosperity and elite demand. Many of those whose fortunes had flourished chose to commission portraits, including mercers, brewers, goldsmiths, butchers and wool merchants. Religion remained a central part of life for all levels of society. Perhaps wisely, many of these men and women often appear in their portraits not with attributes of their wealth and new found confidence, but instead with emblems such as skulls and timepieces, which demonstrate their awareness of death, piety and hope for eternal Christian salvation.

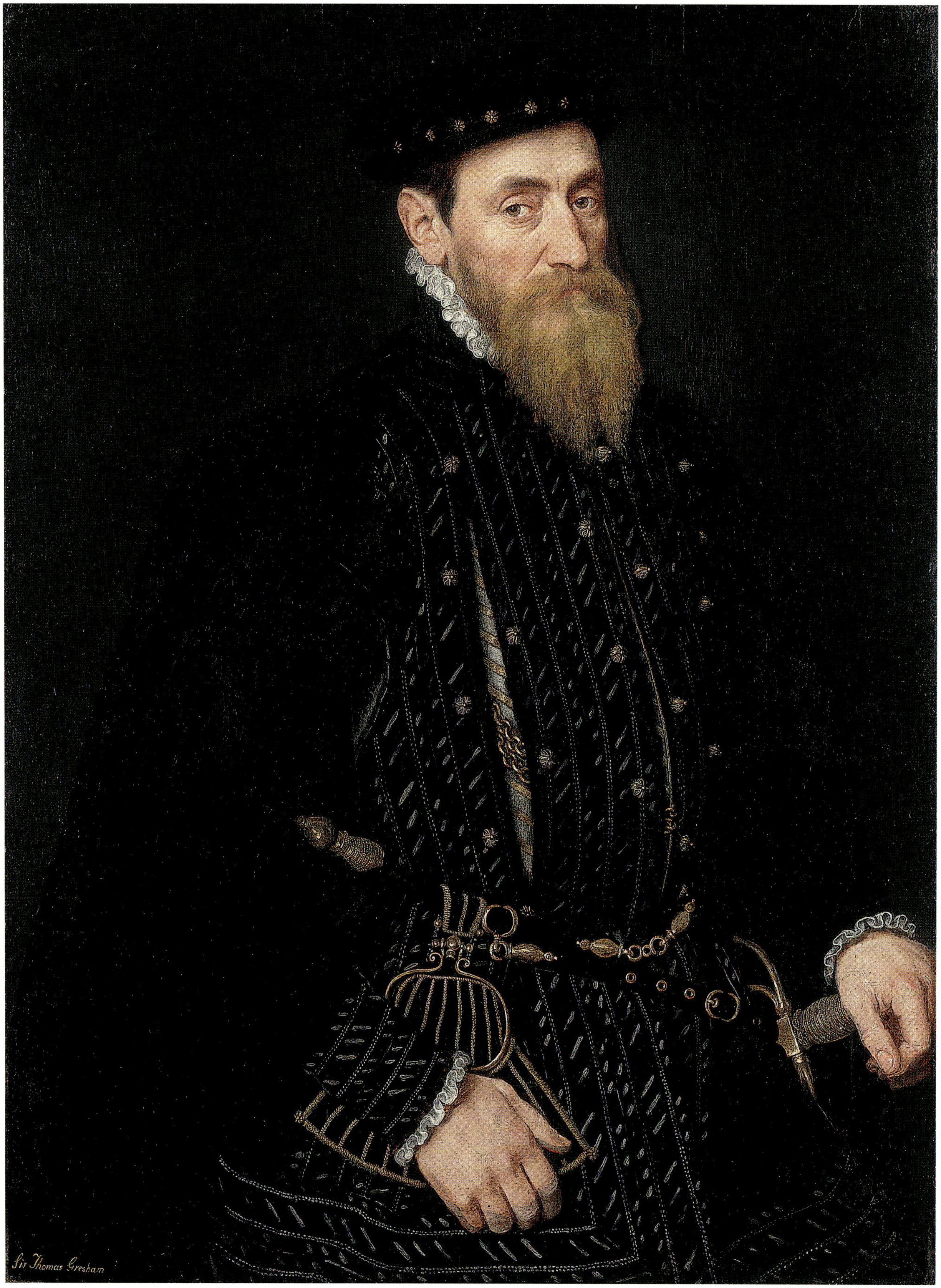
Sir Thomas Gresham

45

Sir Thomas Gresham (c.1518–79)

Unknown Netherlandish artist, *c.*1565

Oil on panel, 1003 × 724mm
National Portrait Gallery, London (NPG 352)

Present at the Queen's first council, the financier, mercer and diplomat Thomas Gresham was to play an essential role in securing the economic stability of Elizabeth I's long reign. Moving between the worlds of city and court and dividing his time between London and Antwerp, where he acted as Royal Agent, Gresham successfully managed the Crown's debt and was involved in schemes such as the re-coinage of 1560 (see cat. 55). Professionally, he achieved great wealth and high status (he was knighted in 1559), but the loss of his only son in 1564 left Gresham without an heir. This event almost certainly led him to seek out the grand projects for which he is best remembered, including the founding of the Royal Exchange, a scheme that began in 1565 (see cat. 46), at around the time this portrait was painted.

The portrait was almost certainly painted while Gresham was living in Antwerp, where the practice of merchant portraiture was well established.[1] The small slashes in his long-sleeved jerkin reveal a gold and silver doublet beneath and provide a glimpse of a heavy gold chain, a fashion that was particularly popular in Germany and the Netherlands. Standing with his left hand on his sword hilt, Gresham appears powerful and dynamic. His right hand grasps the large purse that hangs at his waist, the gesture providing a metaphor for the sitter's hold on England's purse strings. Recent scientific examination of the portrait has revealed that the fingers on Gresham's right hand were lengthened during the painting process so that his grip appeared more relaxed – the financier was perhaps wary of seeming overly avaricious.

Given Gresham's personal and institutional connections, there may well have been contemporary demand for several portraits, and this portrait is known in three versions. The similarity in both the pattern and the final changes to the composition (or *pentimenti*) between this work and a version owned by the Mercer's Company suggests that Gresham commissioned several portraits from the same workshop at the same time.[2]

Towards the end of his life, Gresham became increasingly concerned with his legacy. In addition to commissioning portraits and funding the building of the Royal Exchange he erected eight almshouses for the poor behind his mansion – Gresham House in Bishopsgate – and arranged for the building itself to house Gresham College following the death of his widow. TC & AO

PROVENANCE

Sir Henry Bedingfield of Oxborough, Norfolk; recorded by Vertue, 1739 (*Notebooks*, IV, p.162); by Britton in the early nineteenth century (*Beauties of England*); purchased by the National Portrait Gallery from Henry Graves, 1872.

LITERATURE

Strong 1969b, pp.129–31; Ribeiro 2000, p.39; Blanchard, 'Gresham, Sir Thomas (c.1518–1579)', ODNB 2004 (accessed online Dec. 2012).

NOTES

1 Cooper 2012, pp.90–1. The wooden panel employed here (identified by dendrochronology as Eastern Baltic oak and likely to have been felled in the period 1546–78) has recently been linked to another Netherlandish portrait of an unknown Flemish man (private collection), which included wood from the same tree but was almost certainly painted by a different artist. This technical evidence indicates that this portrait was painted in the Netherlands and that wood from the same trees may have been used in different artists' studios.

2 A third version of the portrait was recorded at Titsey Place, Oxted, Surrey, in 1883 (purchased from Dr Crompton of Manchester) (Strong, *Tudor and Jacobean Portraits*, 1969, p.130). Sir John Gresham of Titsey (d.1556) was Gresham's uncle.

46

The Royal Exchange, London

Frans Hogenberg, c.1569

Engraving, 386 × 522mm
The British Museum, London (1863, 1114.692)

This print depicts the internal courtyard of the Royal Exchange, which opened for business in 1568 as a purpose-built commercial centre. Financed and orchestrated by the supremely wealthy merchant Thomas Gresham (cat. 45), the Royal Exchange, as it was renamed after Elizabeth I's visit of 1571, was completely destroyed during the Great Fire of 1666, but the south facade and the interior court were recorded in two engravings by the émigré artist Frans Hogenberg (*c.*1540–90). This print shows the arcaded walkways where business was negotiated. Elsewhere within the complex there were shops and stalls for retail trade and various warehouses and storage spaces for goods.

Gresham's experience of the European money markets had highlighted the need for a financial exchange in London to serve as a commercial centre for the capital. He began negotiations with the City of London in 1565, and together they identified and purchased land for the building on the north side of Cornhill.[1] In building his Exchange, Gresham not only imported the idea but also the necessary skilled foreign craftsmen from Continental Europe. Work began in 1566 under the supervision of the mason and architect Henryck van Paesschen (*c.*1510–82) of Antwerp, one of the leading craftsmen of that city, and it has been suggested that he may have worked to designs made by Cornelius Floris (1514–75).[2] The resulting building was closely modelled on the Antwerp Bourse of 1531 and introduced a form of northern-European classicism that was entirely new in London. The use of classical orders and an internal arcade was quickly picked up on by English patrons, and Van Paesschen was later employed by Sir William Cecil, Lord Burghley (cat. 19).

It seems likely that Hogenberg's views show Gresham's Exchange as envisaged, rather than as built. Maurice Howard has noted that the enormous Corinthian column surmounted by Gresham's grasshopper crest is a fantasy, and was never built.[3] An additional view of the internal courtyard gives the impression of a rather less elaborate structure, indicating that the Exchange was still incomplete at the time of Gresham's death in 1579. As late as 1610, the series of sculptures depicting English monarchs, as seen in the print, was still being completed. These 'pictures' were to be carved in wood, covered in lead, and then gilded and painted in oil.[4] ET

PROVENANCE

Acquired by the Museum in 1863.

LITERATURE

Hollstein 1993, Part II, vol. 31; Hind 1952, vol. 1, pp.70–1.

NOTES

1 Anne Saunders, *The Royal Exchange* (London Topographical Society, London, 1997).
2 Mark Girouard, *Elizabethan Architecture: Its Rise and Fall, 1540–1640* (Paul Mellon Centre for British Art, Yale University Press, New Haven CT and London, 2009), p.167.
3 Susan Doran (ed.), *Elizabeth: The Exhibition at the National Maritime Museum*, exh. cat. (National Maritime Museum, London, 2003), pp.53–4.
4 Walter Thornbury, *Old and New London*, vol. 1 (Cassell, Petter & Galpin, London, 1878), pp.494–513.

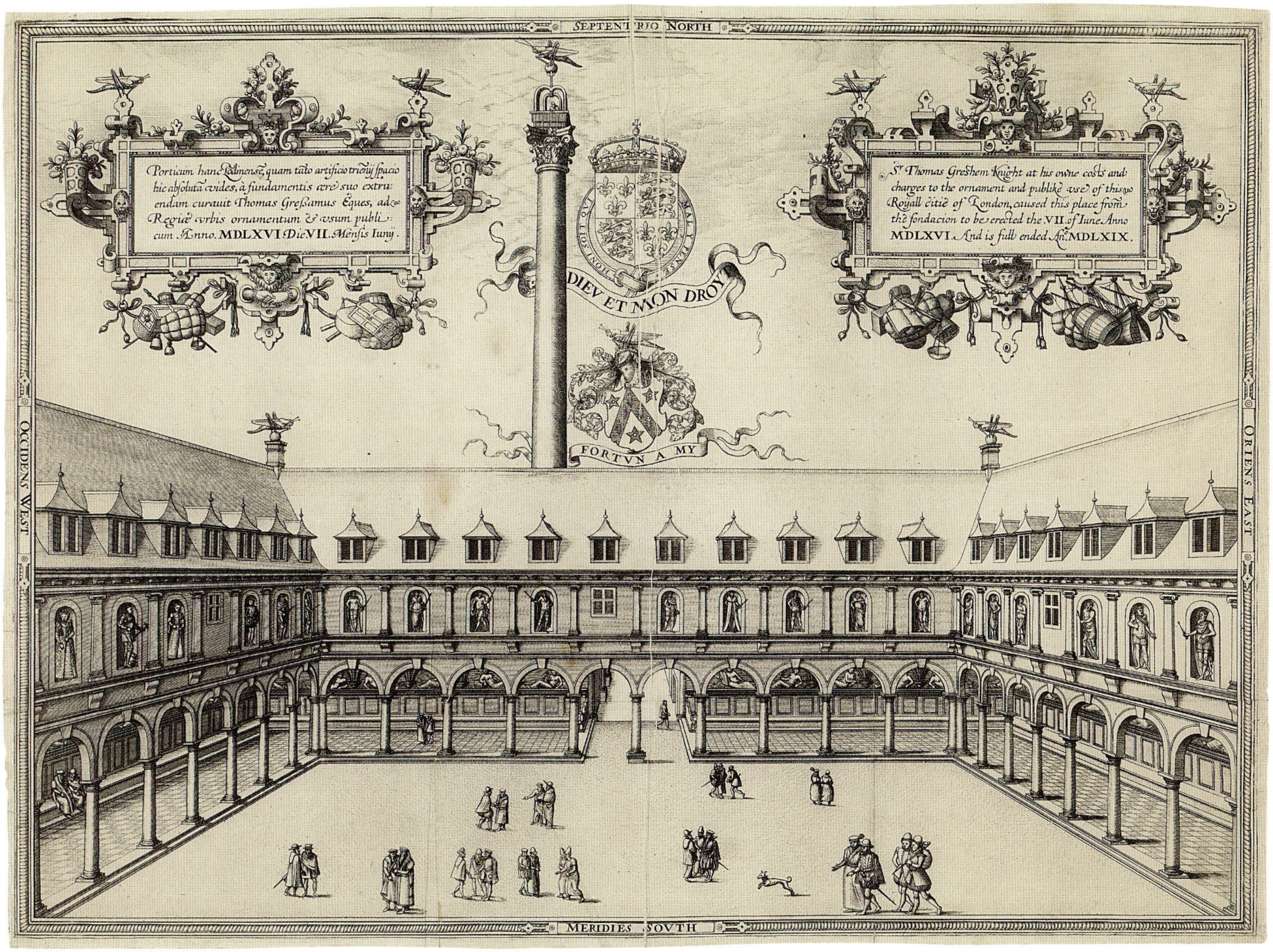
SEPTENTRIO NORTH
Porticum hanc Londinensem, quam tanto artificio triennij spacio hic absolutam vides, à fundamentis ære suo extruendam curauit Thomas Gressamus Eques, ad Regiæ vrbis ornamentum & vsum publicum. Anno. MDLXVI Die VII. Mensis Iunij.
DIEV ET MON DROY
FORTVN A MY
Sr Thomas Greshem Knight at his owne costs and charges to the ornament and publike use of this Royall citie of London, caused this place from the fondacion to be erected the VII. of Iune Anno MDLXVI. And is full ended An.o MDLXIX.
OCCIDENS WEST
ORIENS EAST
MERIDIES SOUTH

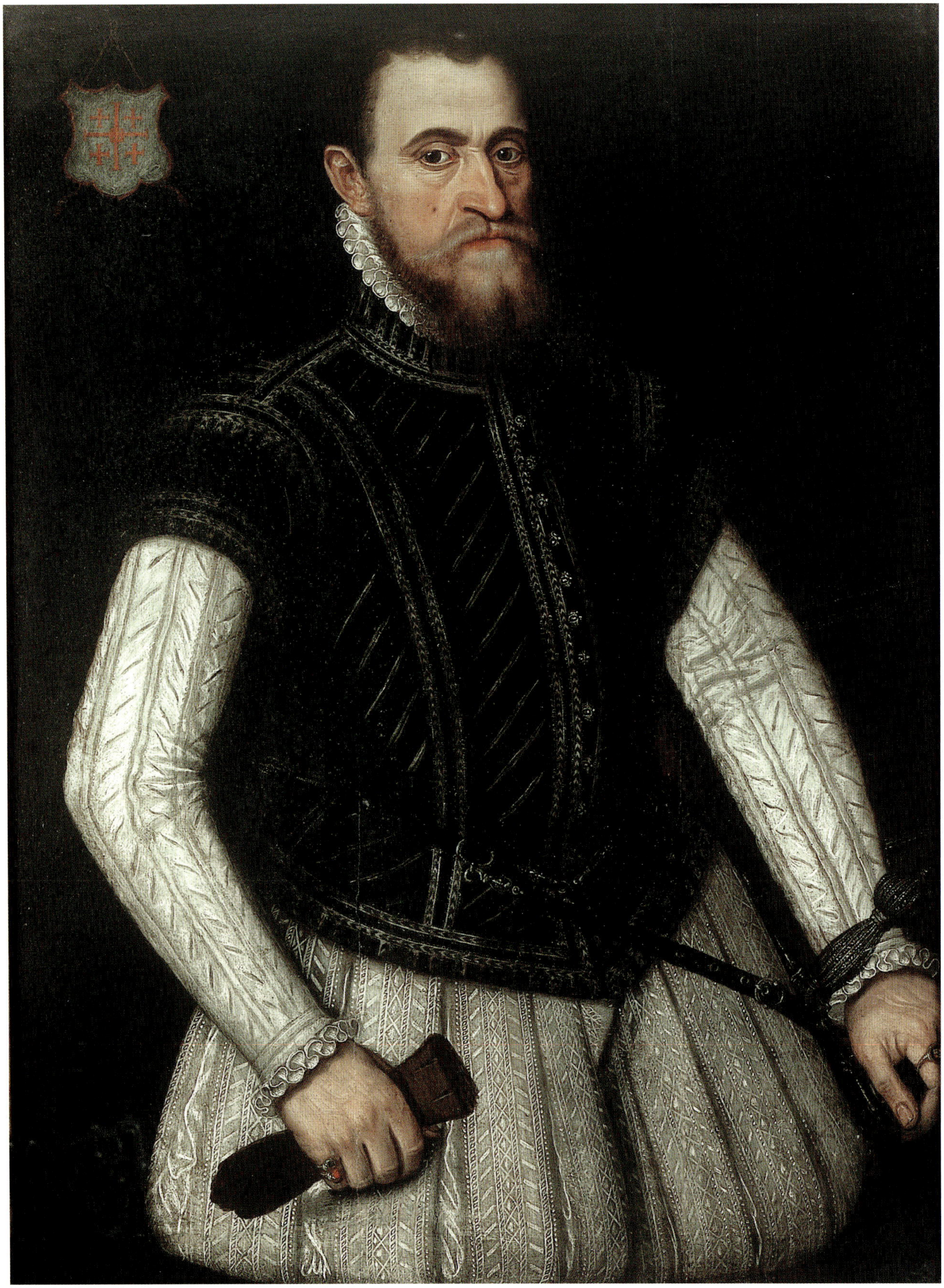

47

Richard Clough (d.1570)

Unknown Netherlandish artist, *c.*1565

Oil on panel, 965 × 702mm
Private collection

The life of Richard Clough is illustrative of the increasing social mobility during the sixteenth century that enabled men of the middling sort to prosper. The fifth son of a glover from Denbigh, Wales, Clough was apprenticed as a mercer in London and at the time of his death owned numerous estates in Wales. Following his apprenticeship, he began work with Thomas Gresham (cat. 45), the newly appointed Crown Agent in the Netherlands. Clough was resident in Antwerp periodically from 1552, and by 1558 had been promoted to head 'factor' of Gresham's business operations in the Netherlands, negotiating loans and providing critical commercial and political intelligence to Gresham and to Sir William Cecil, Lord Burghley (cat. 19). In 1567 he married the widow Katheryn of Berain (cat. 48) after a short romance of three weeks. Soon after their wedding, Clough took Katheryn to live in Antwerp, where she gave birth to two daughters.

Antwerp in the middle of the sixteenth century was at Europe's financial heart. A mecca for wealthy merchants and artists alike, the city had an unparalleled luxury goods market, in which Clough would have been well immersed. Alongside his negotiations on behalf of the Crown and for the house of Gresham, he was also directly involved in commissioning works of art from Netherlandish artists (including pictures and jewellery) for patrons among the English court.[1]

Clough's portrait was most likely painted in Antwerp in the late 1560s and it is one of two portraits painted around the same time; the other (location unknown) shows the sitter wearing a dark suit. Here Clough wears pale-coloured hose and a dark, short-sleeved slashed doublet. His identity is confirmed by one of his three rings, which records his coat of arms, also found at the upper left of the composition. The current condition of this portrait makes assessment of authorship difficult, but it bears some formal similarities to Gresham's portrait of around the same date, which was probably also painted in Antwerp (cat. 45).

Clough's fortunes allowed him to improve his Denbigh properties with the Dutch-style mansions of Bachegraig and Clough Hall (Plas Clough), both of which were completed in 1567. In a letter to Cecil of September 1568, Clough declared himself 'in right good health and merry', but this was short-lived as his health deteriorated and, in March 1570, he died in Hamburg.[2] Clough had proved extremely loyal to Gresham and towards the end of his life he changed a previous will, which had favoured his new family, so as to leave all his goods to his master. Gresham, however, showed decency and compassion, renouncing the last hastily made will and allowing Clough's family to benefit instead.
TC & AO

PROVENANCE

Private collection.

LITERATURE

Blanchard, 'Clough, Richard (d.1570)', *ODNB* 2008; Cooper 2012, p.92.

NOTES

1 A letter from Clough to Gresham, 17 August 1567, states that he has 'received the pictures he writes of, whereof [he] will cause the Queen's to be made and will send [him] the rest.' Crosby (ed.), *Calendar of State Papers, Foreign Series, of the Reign of Elizabeth, 1566–8* (London, 1871), cited in Cooper 2012, p.92.

2 Blanchard, 'Clough, Richard (d.1570)', *ODNB*, 2008.

48

Katheryn of Berain, 'The Mother of Wales' (c.1540–91)

Netherlandish artist, dated 1568

Oil on panel, 972 × 686mm
Inscribed upper left: *AN[NO] D[OMI]NI 1568*
National Museum of Wales, Cardiff (NMW A 19)

The life of Katheryn of Berain has become one of the most famous romances of North Wales. The daughter of Tudur ap Robert Vychan of Berain, Denbighshire, and granddaughter of an illegitimate son of Henry VII, she married four times to wealthy, well-connected Welshmen. Katheryn had six children and over thirty grandchildren, gaining the nickname 'Mam Cymru' ('Mother of Wales') because so many families could claim ancestry to her. Katheryn's first husband, John, son and heir of Sir John Salusbury of Llewenni, died in 1566, and the following year she married Sir Richard Clough, a wealthy merchant also from Denbighshire (cat. 47). Clough had properties in Denbighshire but lived in Antwerp, where he worked for Thomas Gresham (cat. 45). Following her marriage in spring 1567, Katheryn returned with Clough to Antwerp, where this portrait was painted.

Katheryn would have been thirty-four when this portrait was painted in 1568, and may have been pregnant with the couple's first daughter, Anne, who was born the same year. Katheryn's choice of outfit for such an important commission is appropriately sober, yet luxurious and elegant enough to befit the wife of a wealthy merchant. Perhaps the most striking elements of the picture are the skull that Katheryn holds at an angle on the green tablecloth, and the prayer book worn on a long chain around her waist. Taken together, these objects draw attention to both the brevity of life and the importance of Christian piety: in addition to demonstrating her pious nature, the juxtaposition of Katheryn's translucent, life-like skin with the cool bone of the skull highlights the contrast between her youthful, fertile body, which will die and decay, and the eternal life that is possible through Christian salvation.

Following the collapse of the Antwerp markets the couple left for Hamburg, where Clough died in 1570. Katheryn returned to Berain, via London, probably with this portrait. She married twice more, first to Maurice Wynn of Gwydir, who died in 1580, and then, in 1584, to Edward Thelwall of Plas y Ward. She died in 1591 and is buried next to her first husband in Llanefydd Church.

The portrait has previously been attributed to the Friesian artist Adriaen van Cronenburgh (*c.*1520/25–*c.*1604), although this remains speculative.[1] It is possible that this work was commissioned as one of a pair with another portrait of Clough; Katheryn's pose suggests that her portrait could have been a pendant, although neither of the surviving portraits of Clough makes an obvious partner and are clearly by different Netherlandish artists.[2] TC & AO

PROVENANCE

Denbighshire for almost 400 years; sold 1939 by M.F.L. Tringham (via Marshall Spink Ltd, London) to D.A. Hoogendijk & Co. of Amsterdam. Taken to Germany, apparently for Goering's collection, and returned to the Netherlands in 1945. James Hamilton, sold via Marshall Spink and purchased by the Friends of the National Museum of Wales, 1957.

LITERATURE

Ballinger 1929; Hoogewerff 1941–2, vol. IV, pp.400–13; Cooper 2012, pp.101–5.

NOTES

1 A similar outfit and set of attributes appear in his portrait *A Young Mother and her Daughter* (1567; Prado, Madrid).
2 Cooper 2012, p.101.

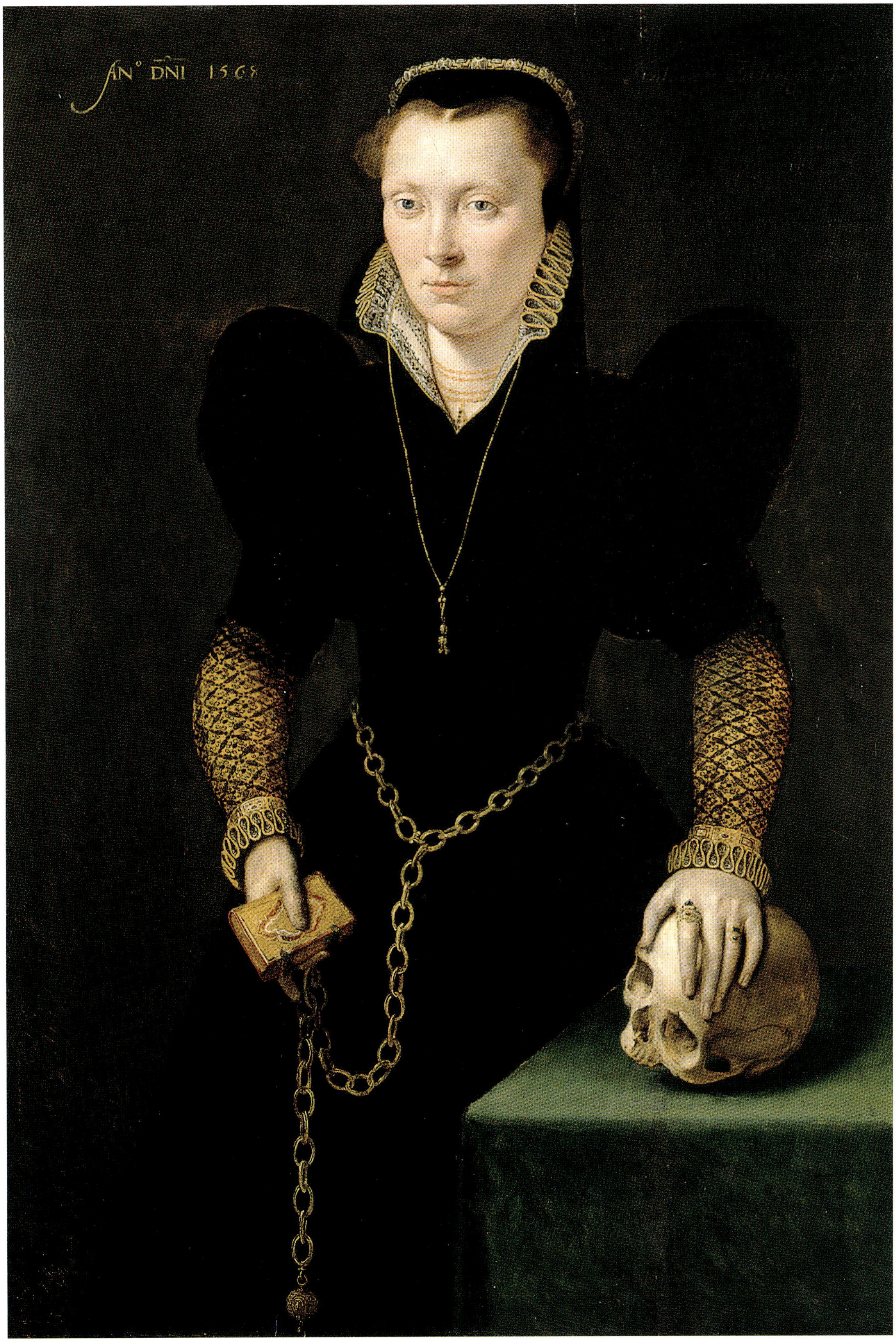
AN° DNI 1568

49

Tomb Sculpture of Piero Capponi (1550–82)

London workshop, c.1582

Alabaster, 1480 × 580 × 540mm
St Olave's Church, Hart Street, London

The alabaster figure that forms the central part of this funerary monument represents Piero Capponi, a Florentine exile resident in London. He was buried in 1582 at St Olave's in Hart Street, one of few medieval churches to survive the Great Fire of 1666. Capponi is depicted kneeling in the act of prayer and the quality of craftsmanship – in terms of the refined composition and the skilful handling of the materials – suggests that the monument was the product of one of the most accomplished London workshops.

Although the church was badly damaged during the Second World War, Capponi's monument remained in situ following bombing raids in 1941. It was later restored and re-erected after the church was rebuilt in 1951–4, and is a rare survival of an Elizabethan London tomb monument.

The story of Capponi's short life is equally as remarkable as his funerary monument. He was born in Florence in 1550 into an exceptionally wealthy banking dynasty, but was forced to flee the city in 1574 following the discovery of his part in a plot to oust the Medici. Declared as a rebel of Florence and with his assets confiscated, Capponi travelled in exile to Poland and France before finding refuge in England under the protection of Elizabeth I. Capponi joined a circle of Italian merchants and financiers resident in London who supplied information to Elizabeth I's spymaster and Secretary of State, Francis Walsingham. Given the nature of this work, it is not surprising to find that Capponi was accused of betraying state secrets; it was alleged that he was on close terms with Catherine de' Medici (1519–89) and that gifts were frequently exchanged between the two.[1] Intrigue and suspicion were part and parcel of the business of espionage, and there is no evidence to support the allegations that Capponi compromised the interests of his English patrons.

There has also been some debate regarding the circumstances and cause of Capponi's death. It has been suggested that he was murdered in Paris by an agent of the Duke of Florence in retribution for his part

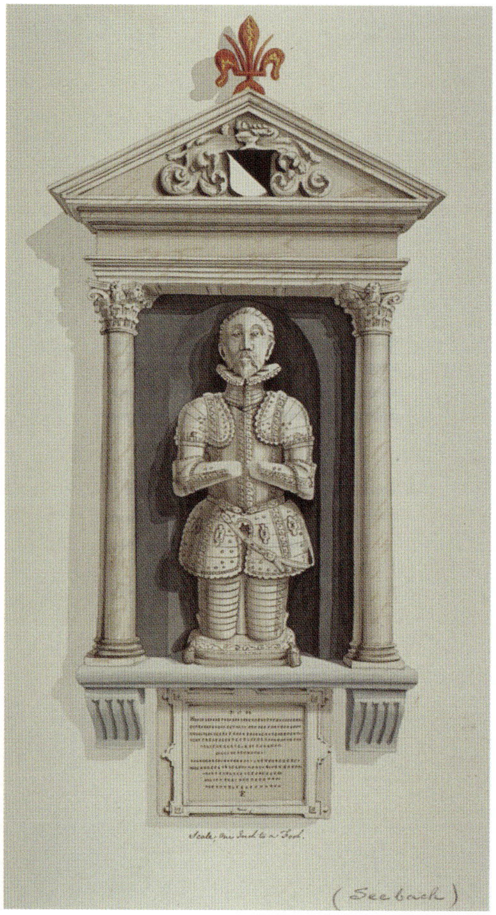

FIG. 30
This anonymous early nineteenth-century watercolour shows Capponi within his tomb setting, with the Latin inscription below, on the south wall of the north chancel in St Olave's Church.

PROVENANCE

South wall of the north chancel of St Olave's Church, Hart Street, London.

NOTES

1 Arthur John Butler (ed.), *Calendar of State Papers Foreign, Elizabeth May–December 1582*, vol. 16, May–December 1582, London, 1909, p.2.
2 Caroline P. Murphy, *Murder of a Medici Princess* (Oxford University Press, Oxford, 2008), p.292.
3 Will of Piero Capponi. TNA/PROB 11/64/531.
4 London Metropolitan Archives, St Olave Hart Street, Composite register: P69/OLA1/A001/MS28867.

in a plot known as the Pucci conspiracy.[2] However, a letter written by Capponi from London, in the final throws of 'suddayne syckenes', to his friend Peter Landi (also an exile of Florence) described the delirium suffered by those who had contracted the plague.[3] This is confirmed by the parish registers of St Olave's, which on 27 October 1582 recorded the burial of 'Mr Peter Capony gent.' and noted that he was one of the many thousands of victims that died of the plague that year.[4] His letter also served as his will and made generous bequests to the Italian merchants Nicholas di Gozzi (d.1595) and Jacopo Manucii (d.1594), and also to the Spanish Ambassador Bernardino de Mendoza (*c.*1540–1604). The Latin inscription beneath the figure relates that the monument had been erected at the request of Landi, and attests both to Capponi's lineage and his constancy in the face of adversity. ET

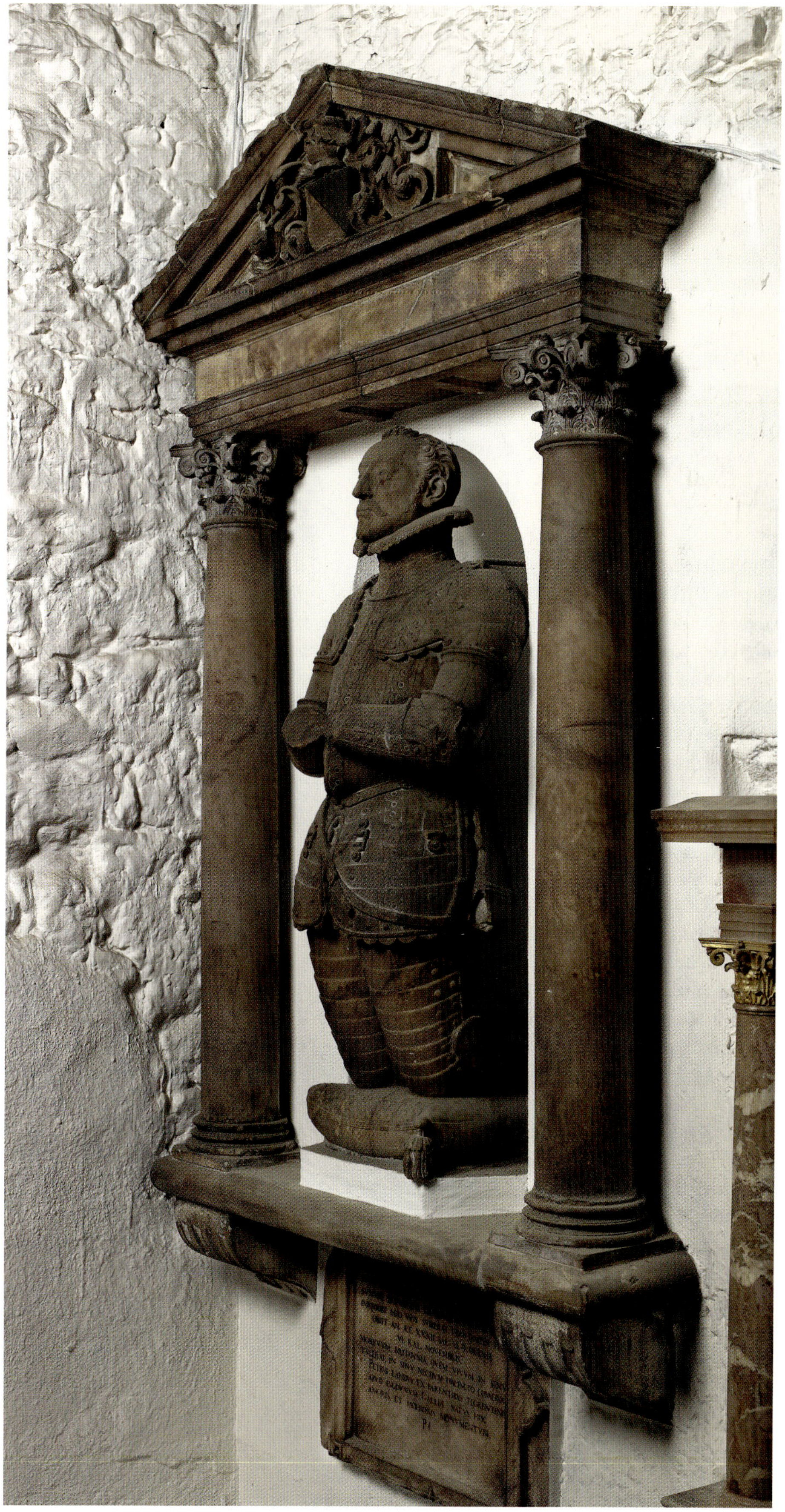

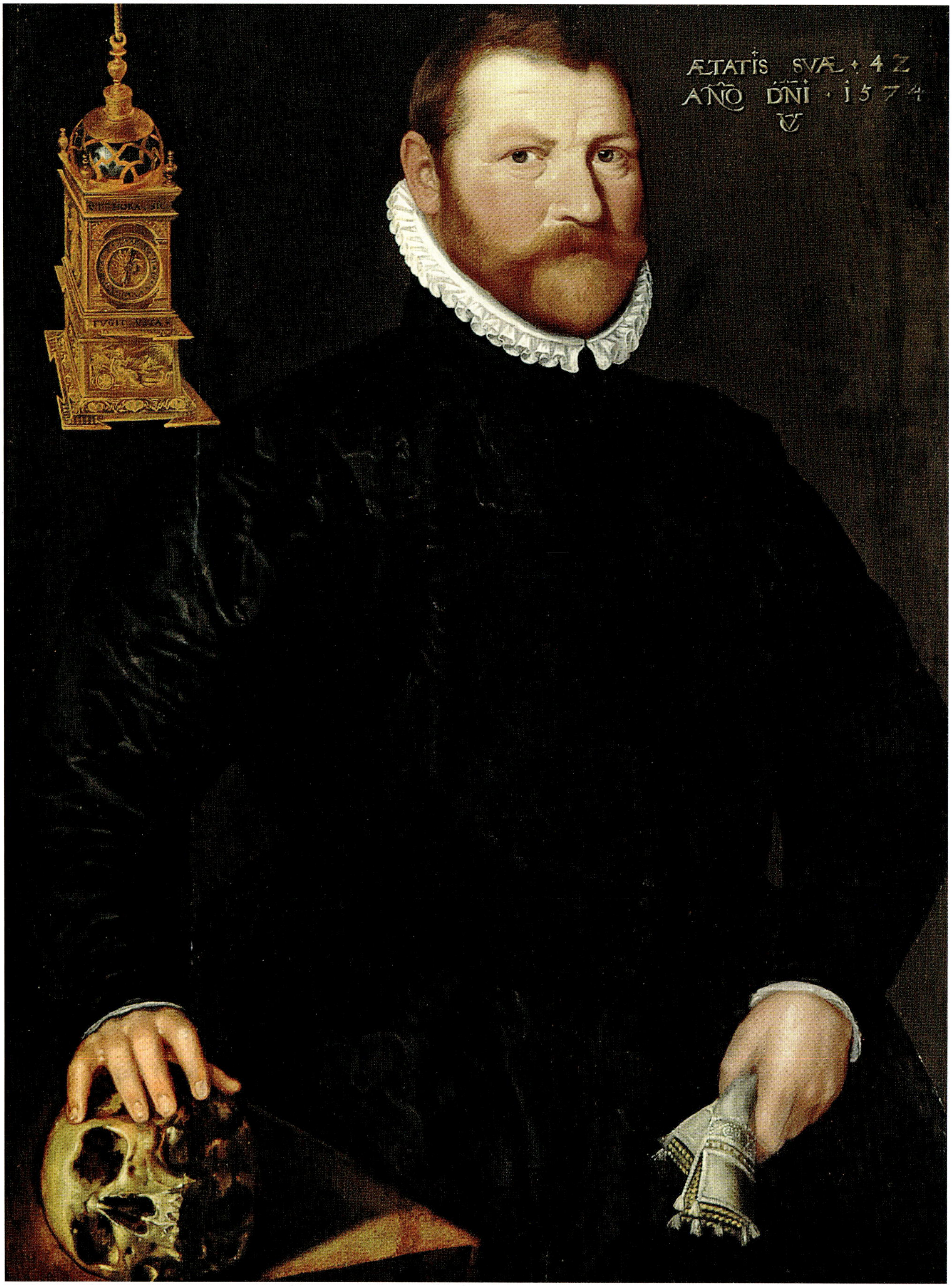

50b

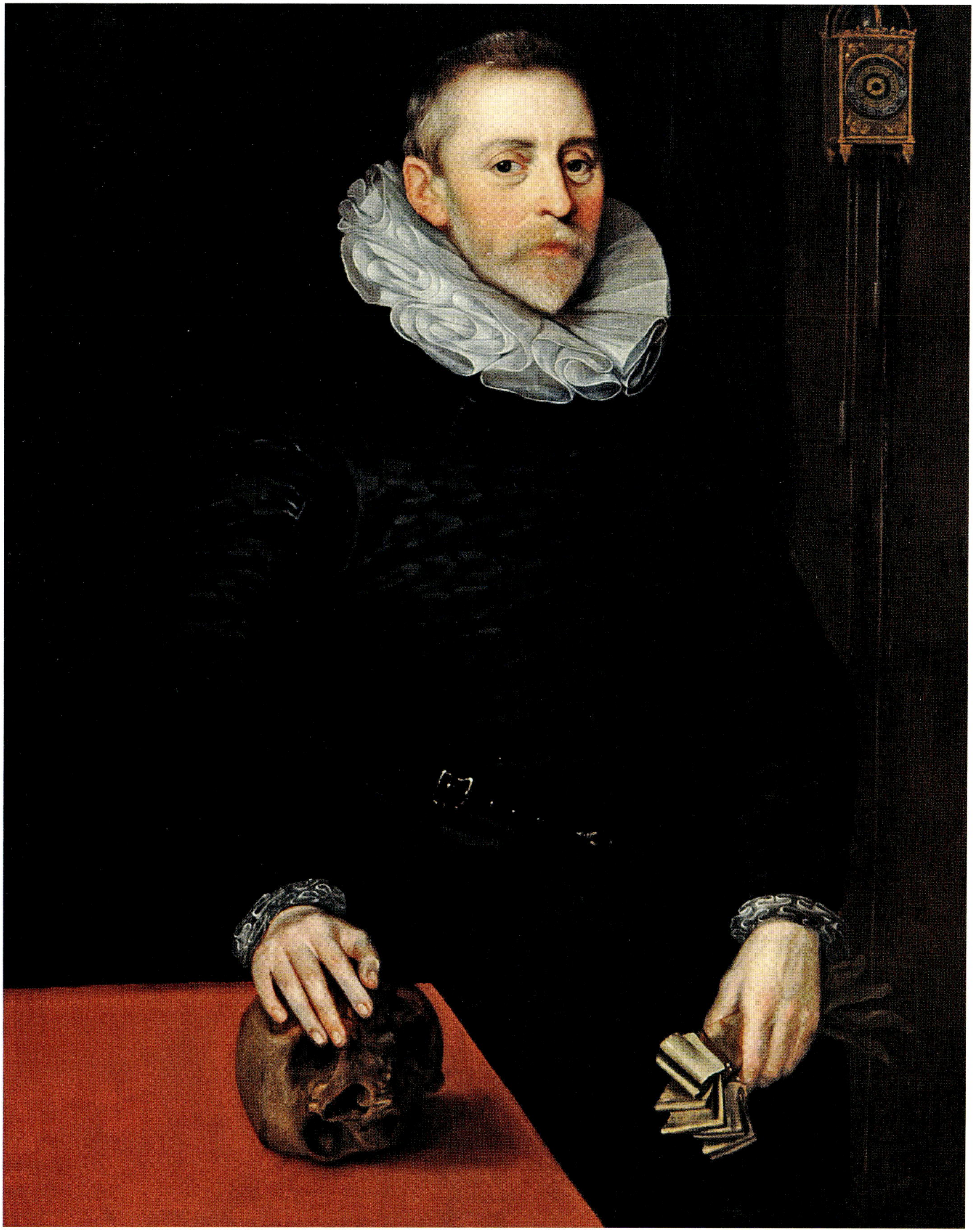

50c

51

Gawen Goodman of Ruthin (1526–1604)

Unknown British artist, dated 1582

Oil on panel, 495 × 420mm
Inscribed top right: A[NN]O NATVI XPI [CHRISTI] *1582*; top left: *Denue timete* (Fear God); *Sobry iuste vita* (A sober just life); top left and right: *Jesus est amor meus* (Jesus is my love); right: ANNO [A]ETATIS. /SV[A]E *56*; below the skull: COGITA *Mori* (Remember that you will die); either side of sitter: *Laurea desidie prebetur nulla* (Let him not be estimated by laurelled or literary sloth)
National Museum of Wales, Cardiff (NMWA 3453)

This portrait of Gawen Goodman of Ruthin in Denbighshire, North Wales is a rare surviving example of regional portraiture from the Elizabethan period. It is one of several surviving portraits of members of the Goodman family, including Gawen's father, the mercer Edward Goodman (1476–1560), and Edward's son, Gabriel Goodman (1528–1601), who became Dean of Westminster. Although this portrait depicts a sitter who lived away from the major artistic centres of court and capital, it is no more or less naive in quality than many London portraits of sitters of similar status produced at around the same date. It may have been painted by a journeyman, or perhaps when Goodman visited London.

Gawen appears to have followed his father's profession, becoming a mercer or merchant, based in Ruthin. He wears a plain black doublet and ropes of thick gold beneath a fur-lined gown, and two gold rings; the one on his index finger may be the same death's-head ring worn in a portrait of his father, Edward (National Museum of Wales, Cardiff), as rings were regularly passed down through the generations (see cat. 57g for a similar surviving example). The background of this portrait includes several inscriptions in Latin that promote the Christian understanding of salvation with such phrases as 'Fear God', 'Jesus is my love' and 'A sober just life'. Gawen's pious nature is further indicated by the prayer book, or psalter, that he holds in his right hand and by the skull in the niche – attributes that are often found in portraits of merchants from the second half of the sixteenth century.[1] Despite these outward signs of piety, one contemporary anecdote records a different side of Gawen Goodman's character, that of a man who liked to drink and be merry, who could be 'a generous and godly man … when in his cups'.[2]

Gawen's will of 1603 records that this painting hung in the parlour of the family home, Exmewe House in Ruthin, beside the portrait of his father and a portrait of the Lord Mayor of London, Thomas Exmewe (1454–1529), also from Ruthin, who was the original owner of the house.[3] As such, these portraits would have made a powerful statement about the family's commercial networks and status. TC & AO

PROVENANCE

Bequeathed to the National Museum of Wales by the Hon. Mrs Lawrence Brodrick, 1930.

LITERATURE

Cooper 2012, pp.100–1.

NOTES

1 For other examples, see Cooper 2012, chapter 3.
2 Quoted as the words of Thomas Prys (1564–1634) in William Rowland, *Tomos Prys O Blas Iolyen 1564–1634*, Cardiff (Gwasg Pifysgol Cymru, 1964), p.61.
3 TNA/PROB 11/152/61, Cooper 2012, p.213, n.125.

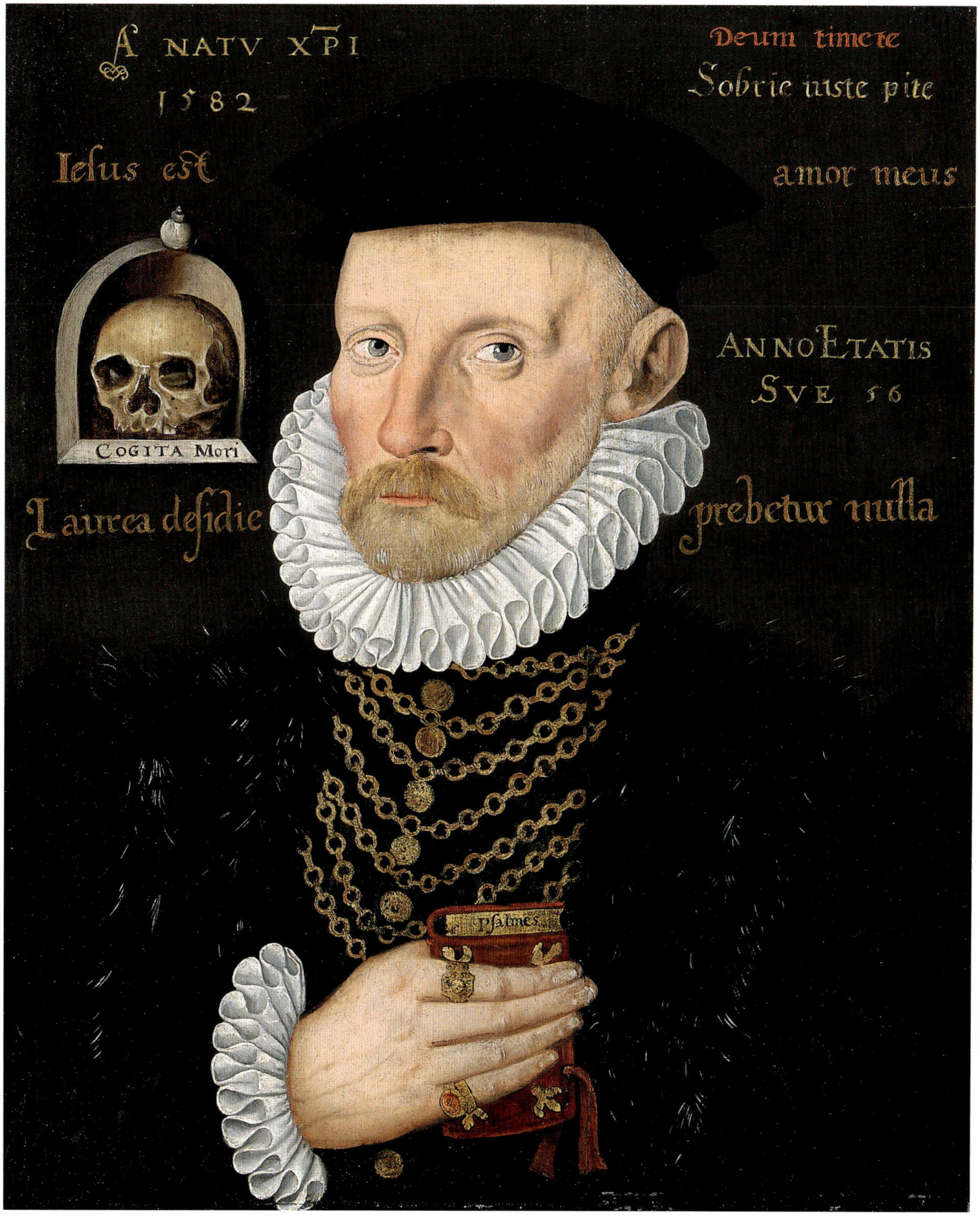

A° NATV XPI
1582
Deum timete
Sobrie iuste pite
Iesus est
amor meus
COGITA Mori
ANNO ETATIS
SVE 56
Laurea desidie
prebetur nulla
psalmes

52

Gamaliel Pye (c.1514–96)

Unknown artist, dated 1596

Oil on panel, 910 × 750mm
Inscribed top left: *AETATIS SVAE 82*; top right: *AN[N]O D[OMI]NI 1596*
Museum of London (2002.74)

The life of the butcher Gamaliel Pye is a good illustration of the potential for opportunism and social mobility in sixteenth-century England. Arriving in London from Nottinghamshire, Pye rose rapidly in the ranks of the Worshipful Company of Butchers to become one of the leading figures in Elizabethan London's expanding meat trade. His commercial abilities are suggested by the fact that he not only bought and slaughtered animals, but came to rear his own cattle and sheep on grazing land bought for the purpose in Surrey. The ability to influence supply and to set prices, and presumably to lease grazing rights, would have given him a considerable advantage.

Shown in this portrait in fashionable yet sober merchant's attire – a black gown and cap – he wears a signet ring with the initials 'GP'.[1] Curiously, the sitter appears to be in his fifties or sixties, though the inscriptions, (which appear to be genuine) record his age in 1596 as eighty-two. Pye's longevity was remarkable at a time when the average life expectancy in the capital was between thirty and forty years.[2]

The desire for profit occasionally led Pye to fall foul of the law. He was twice prosecuted for illegal meat processing, including 'kyllyng of befe on Sondaye before sarvys, 20d', and was later imprisoned for admitting to selling beef and mutton above the official rates.[3] These instances do not appear to have hindered his advancement, however, and Pye was respected enough by his fellow liverymen to be elected warden of the Butchers' Company five times between 1560 and 1572, and senior warden six times between 1575 and 1592. This singular achievement undoubtedly reflected both his wealth and his ability to network and influence his peers. It is possible that the portrait was commissioned to celebrate his standing within the Company.

Pye's opportunism did not prevent generosity to those in need. His will, which was proved in London on 3 August 1596, reveals a notably high level of charitable bequests to the poor.[4] The bulk of his substantial property was left to his widow Margaret and son Edmund, and his will suggests that he was tender-hearted towards family and friends and was a benevolent employer. JE

PROVENANCE

By descent to the Dashwood family, West Wycombe Park; sold 2002 and acquired by the Museum of London.

LITERATURE

Forsyth and Bryson 2006, pp.62–70; Cooper 2012, p.75.

NOTES

1 The sitter in this portrait was identified by Hazel Forsyth and Alan Bryson, and this entry is based on their extensive research (Forsyth and Bryson 2006, p.62f).
2 See Steve Rappaport's survey of the mortality rates of 530 City Freemen in S. Rappaport, *Worlds within worlds, structures of life in 16th-century London* (Cambridge University Press, Cambridge, 1989), pp.69–71. Quoted in Forsyth and Bryson 2006, p.62.
3 G[uildhall] L[ibrary, Butchers' Company Warden's Accounts], MS 6440, vol. 1, fol.67r. From Forsyth and Bryson 2006, p.62.
4 TNA/PROB 11/88/105, fols 62v–64v. Quoted in Forsyth and Bryson 2006, pp.67–8.

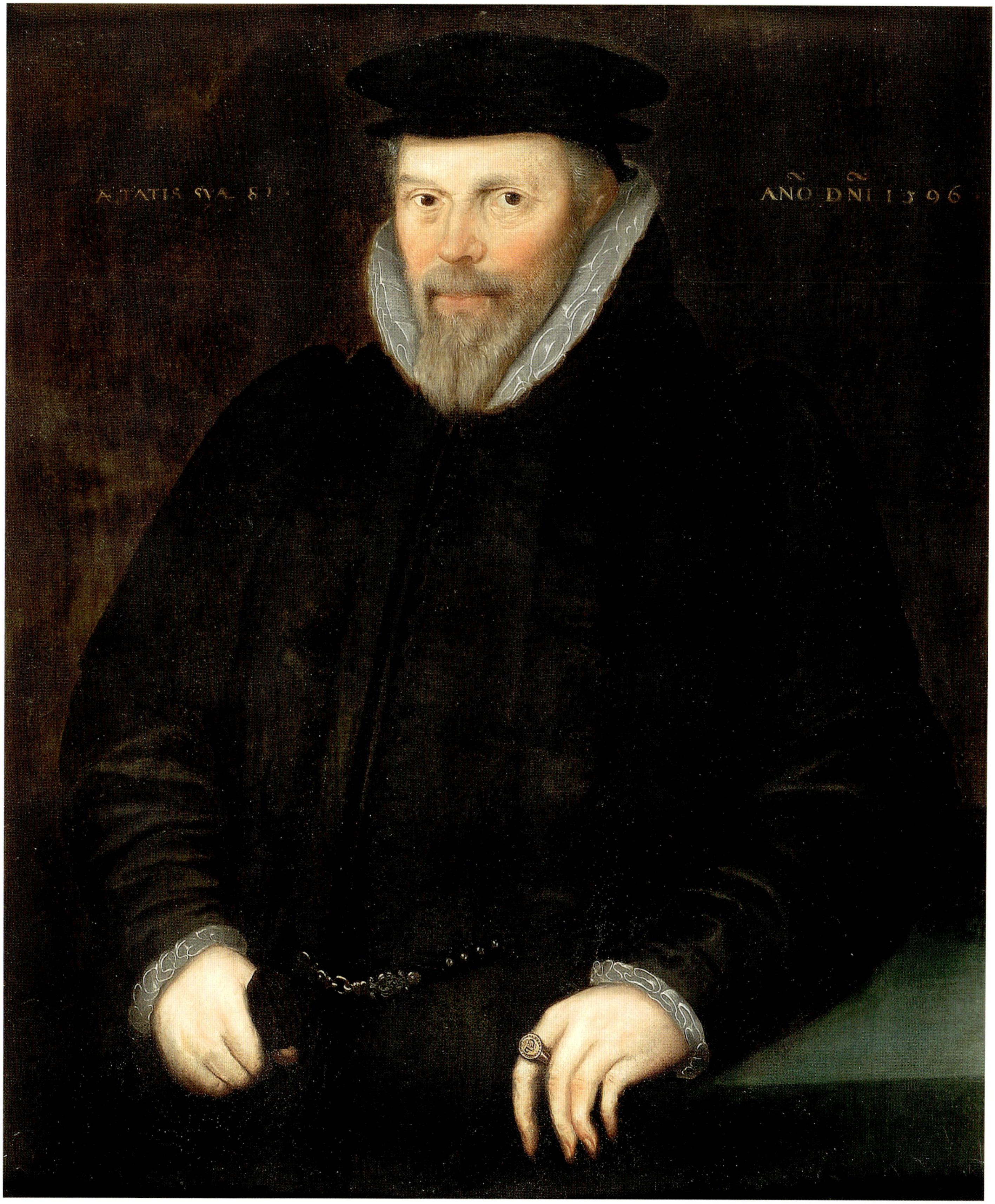
ÆTATIS SVÆ
ANO DNI 1596

53

Joyce Frankland, née Trappes (1531–87)

Unknown English artist, dated 1586

Oil on panel, 628 × 538mm
Inscribed upper left, above the shield: *1586*;
beneath the shield: *Suffer and Serve*
Gonville and Caius College, Cambridge

Not in exhibition

At the time this portrait of the London widow Joyce Frankland was painted, she had suffered numerous tragedies including the loss of both her first husband, Henry Saxey, and her second husband, William Frankland. Most significant of all was the loss of her only son, William Saxey, who died after being thrown from his horse in 1581. Alexander Nowell, Dean of St Paul's, described how he encouraged Joyce to settle on a plan to create scholarships for boys at university, who would serve as '20 good sons to comfort your sorrows' and would 'honour your memory for ever and ever'.[1]

Joyce apparently acted on Nowell's advice and bequeathed a considerable fortune (estimated at around £4,840) in memory of her son, thereby endowing fellowships, scholarships and lectureships at Gonville and Caius College, and Emmanuel College, Cambridge, and at Brasenose College, Oxford. She also bequeathed funds and properties to found a grammar school in Newport, Essex. A model for her philanthropy had perhaps already been provided by her parents, the goldsmith Robert Trappes and his wife Joanna, or Joan, Trappes.[2] In 1568 Joan Trappes had left lands in Kent to support scholars at Lincoln College, Cambridge; a benefaction that was later augmented by Joyce. However, the deed of benefaction to Brasenose stated that preference should always be made to the kindred of the 'Trapp or Saxey' families, suggesting that, in a patriarchal manner, the wealthy widow was above all concerned with perpetuating her own family lineage.[3]

To commemorate these bequests, Joyce bequeathed several portraits of herself, which derive from a sitting in 1586.[4] Like so many portraits of the middling sort, the artist commissioned is unknown. The sitter's pose is carefully orchestrated, with Joyce holding an open timepiece that points to the last hour of the day, a motif that signals her Christian piety, remembrance of death and hope for ultimate salvation. She is soberly dressed and in the context of display in a university setting, her status as a philanthropic widow enabled Joyce to transcend traditional gender definitions, becoming both mother of learning and an honorary gentleman.

TC & AO

PROVENANCE

Bequeathed by the sitter to Gonville and Caius College, Cambridge; first recorded there in 1719.

LITERATURE

Cooper 2012, pp.105–7.

NOTES

1 Venn 1897–1901, vol. III, pp.229–30.
2 Cooper 2012, p.94, figs 90, 91.
3 Ibid., p.107.
4 Other portraits of Joyce survive at Emmanuel College, Cambridge, and at Brasenose College, Oxford, in similar poses. Cooper 2012, pp.106–7.

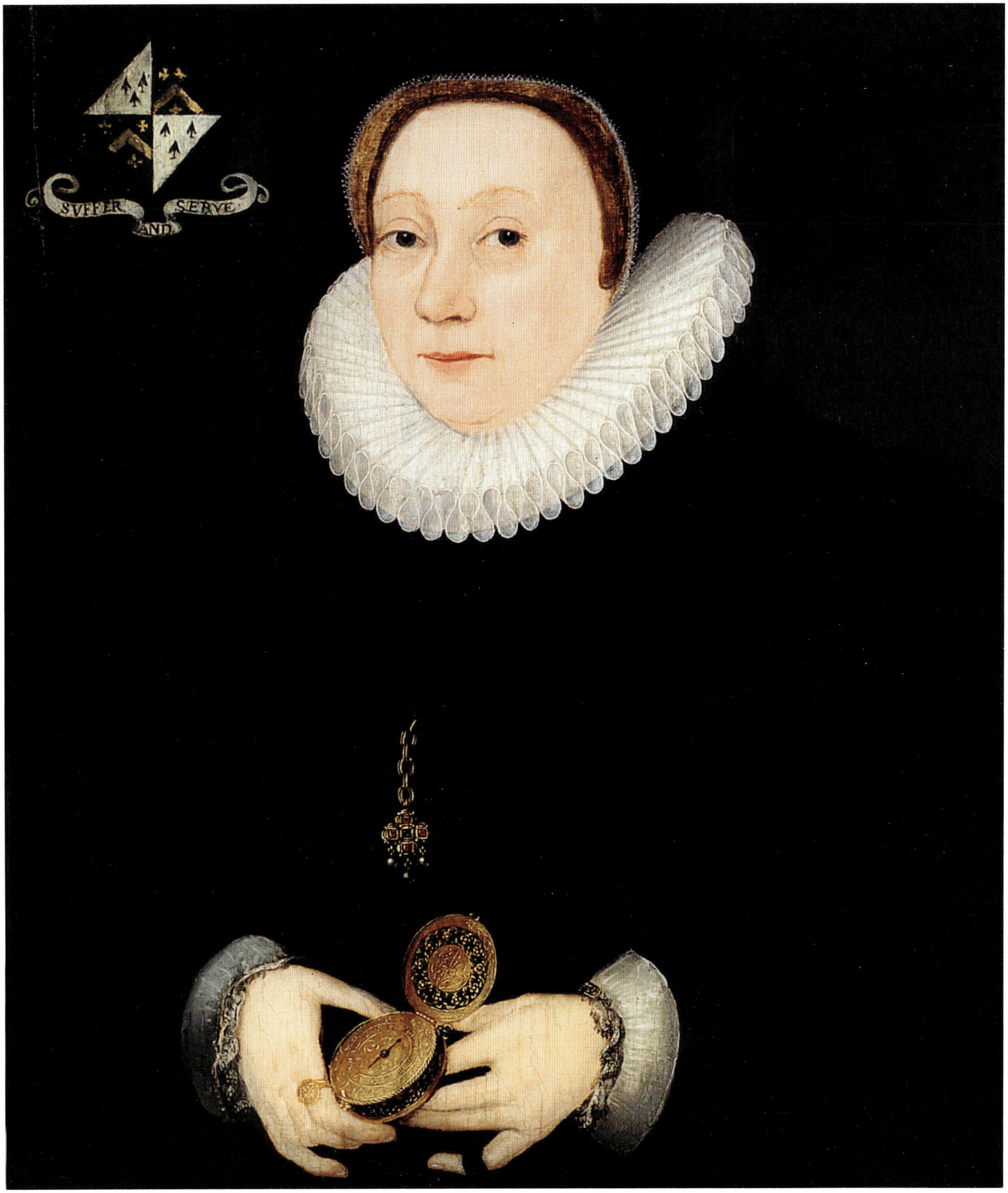
SVFFER AND SERVE

54

A short description of England, Scotland and Ireland (*Corte Beschryuinghe van Engheland, Schotland ende Irland*)

Lucas de Heere, c.1574

Manuscript with illustrations in pen and ink and watercolour with bodycolour, 330 × 320 × 150mm
The British Library, London (Additional MS 28330, f.33, depicting four citizens' wives)

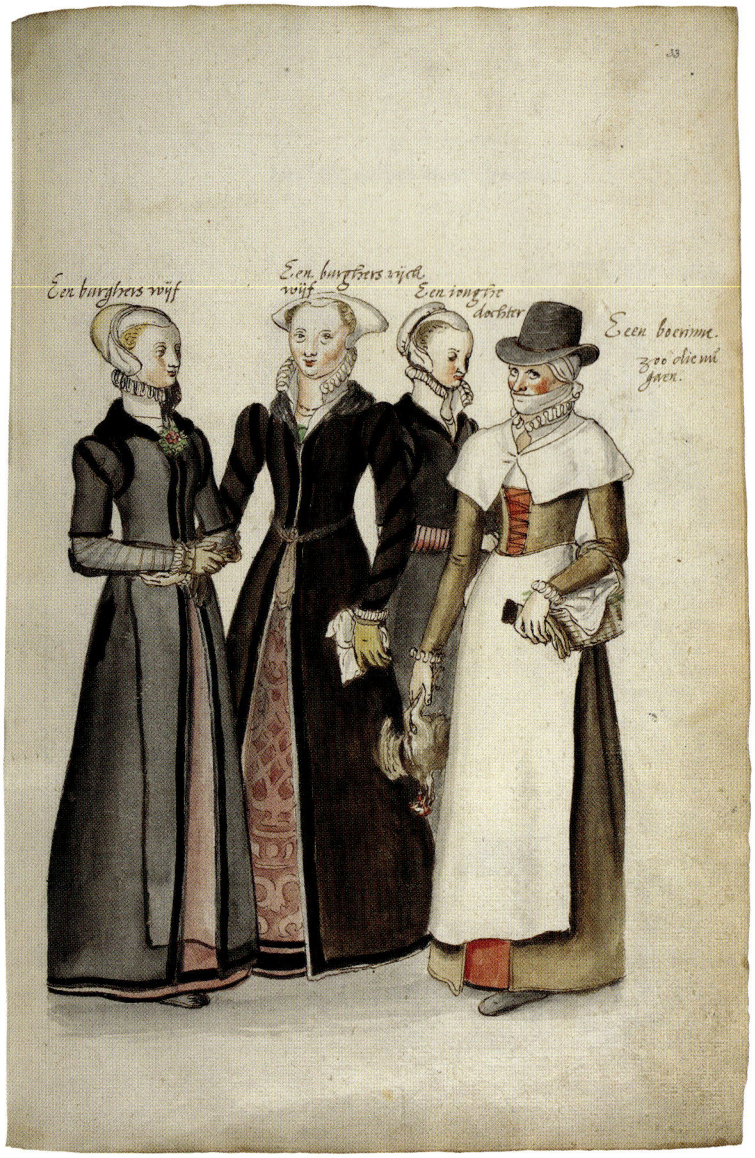

Clothes played an extremely important part in Elizabethan society and, as the most obvious external signifiers of status, they could make or define a citizen. This manuscript includes numerous drawings both of ordinary citizens and of those in the upper echelons of society in England, Scotland and Ireland, apparently based on observations from life, as well as drawings of ancient Britons copied from other sources.

The figures form part of a wider attempt to record the notable features of the British Isles undertaken by Lucas de Heere (1534–84), an exiled Protestant artist from Ghent, who was resident in Britain between about 1566 and 1576. A related manuscript in Ghent contains many of the same figures alongside citizens of the wider world.[1] These manuscripts may have functioned as private pattern books for use among the community of Netherlandish exiles to which de Heere belonged, as similar figures can be identified in *A Fête at Bermondsey* (cat. 4).

On the first of the pages shown here, we see the variations in dress between four women of differing social classes. At the

EXHIBITIONS

Shakespeare: Staging the World, London, British Museum, 2012.

LITERATURE

Chotzen and Draak 1937; Ashelford 1983, p.80; Sloan 2007; Gaudio 2009, pp.24–32; Cooper 2012, pp.66–7.

NOTES

1 *Théâtre de tous les peuples et nations de la terre avec leurs habits et ornaments divers …* (University Library, Ghent, MS 2466).
2 See Susan North, *What the Elizabethans Wore: Evidence from Wills and Inventories of the 'Middling Sort'*, pp.34–41, in the current work.

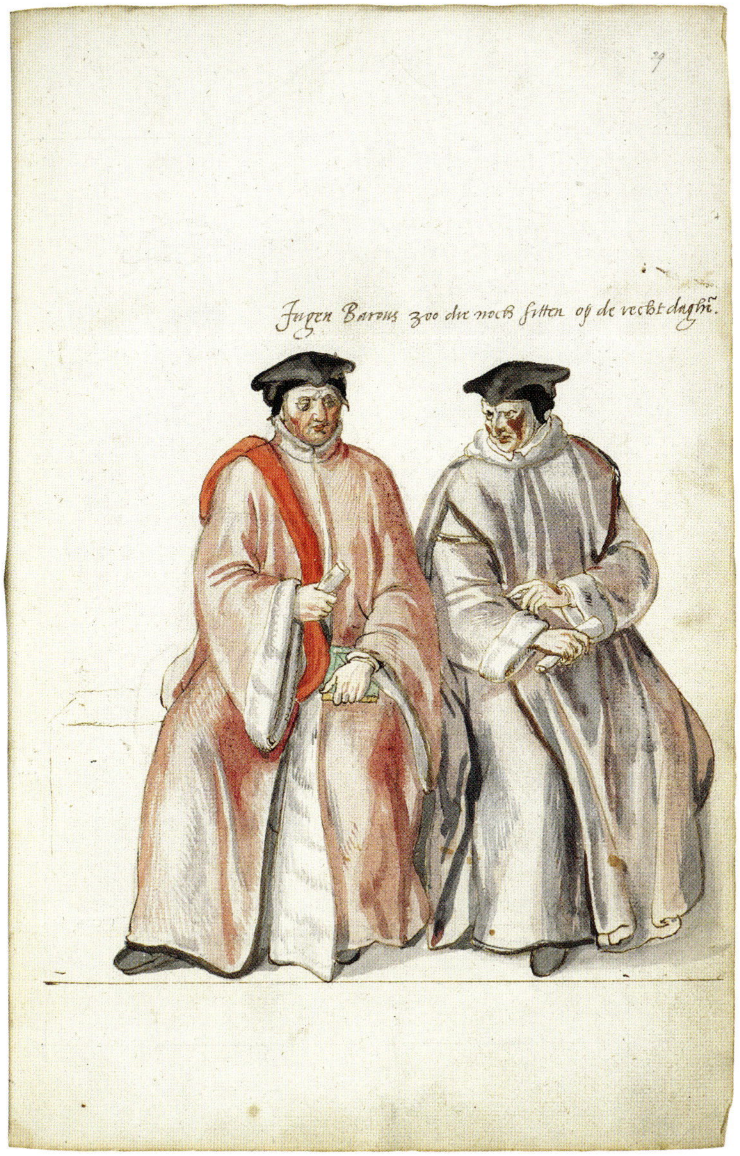

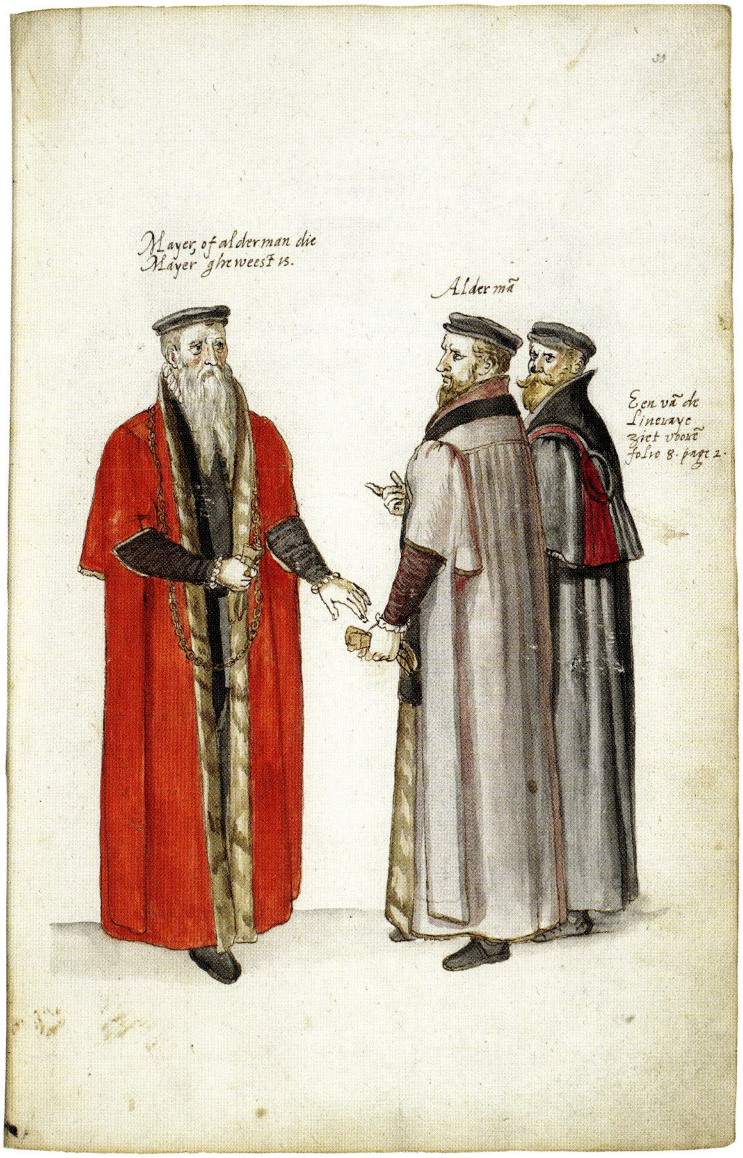

centre are a wealthy citizen's wife and her daughter. Their clothing befits their rank; the mother wears a black gown with a richly brocaded underskirt, while her daughter wears a similar outfit, but with coloured sleeves. At the far left, an ordinary citizen's wife wears a simpler version of their attire; her gown is grey-black with a plain reddish underskirt, a high ruff and a plain coif and cap. The countrywoman at the far right wears a simple brown skirt and bodice, a red underskirt, chemise, and a high black felt hat. She also wears a white apron and a 'chin-clout' (a cloth across her mouth) and carries gloves, demonstrating the ubiquity of gloves across the social classes.

Although the colours of this illustration are slightly faded, it nonetheless demonstrates how darker-coloured garments functioned as a sign of social status.[2] While peasants and members of the lower classes were commonly dressed in the more 'natural' brighter shades of red, brown and plum, wealthy Elizabethan merchants and their wives usually wore black, offset with crisp white ruffs and cuffs. True black fabric was time-consuming and expensive to produce because of the complexity of the dyeing process, giving it an association with luxury. TC & AO

55

The Elizabethan Gold Coinage

a **Six gold sovereigns (£1), initial mark key (1595/6–97/8)**

Diameter approx. 36mm
1844,0425.2713; E.308; 1935,0401.2029-2031 (bequeathed by T.B. Clark-Thornhill); 1946,1004.643 (bequeathed by E.E. Oldroyd)

b **Seven gold half-sovereigns (10s.), initial mark woolpack (1594–95/6)**

Diameter approx. 30mm
1840,1114.2; 1935,0401.2048-2051 (bequeathed by T.B. Clark-Thornhill); 1946,1004.611 (bequeathed by E.E. Oldroyd); 1964,1203.30 (bequeathed by Sir Allen George Clark)

c **Five gold angels (10s.), initial mark A (1583–84/5)**

Diameter approx. 30mm
E.340; 1896,0803.3; 1915,0507.550; 1935,04012081 (bequeathed by T.B. Clark-Thornhill); 1946,1004.613 (bequeathed by E.E. Oldroyd)

d **Five gold crowns (5s.), initial marks crown (1567–70) and woolpack (1594–95/6)**

Diameter approx. 23mm
E.328; 1935,0401.2055-2057 and 2059 (bequeathed by T.B. Clark-Thornhill)

The British Museum, London

In Elizabethan England, access to gold coins in any quantity was usually confined to elite groups, in particular the nobility and the upper levels of the merchant classes. Unusually, there were two standards of gold coin in production: the 'crown' gold of 22-carat fineness and fine or 'angel' gold, which maintained the nearly pure standards of the medieval gold coinage. The angel and the half-sovereign (or demi-sovereign) were both coins worth ten shillings, each containing the same amount of gold, the finer angel being a little lighter.

Elizabethan coin hoards are overwhelmingly of silver coins and represent comparatively moderate levels of wealth. This is normal, since the wealthy could utilise good security arrangements and rarely needed to conceal their treasure. The only significant gold hoards from the reign are quite early and they show a fairly diverse range of material in use with a few medieval survivals, significant quantities of early Tudor gold (re-emerging in the aftermath of the mid-century debasement) and some foreign gold coin, as well as a minority of Elizabeth I's own issues. The 1560s saw a major drive to eliminate foreign gold from English currency, but it is clear that some at least was still available.[1]

Very broadly, the silver coinage of the Elizabethan period was the money of daily life, while gold acted as a store of wealth and the means of large payments. Throughout the later sixteenth century, silver increasingly dominated the currencies of Europe, thanks to New World silver supplies, and gold diminished in proportion within the expanding currency. Nevertheless, it always retained its importance for high-level dealing.[2] BC

LITERATURE

Challis 1978; Challis 1989; Kelleher 2007, pp.210–25.

NOTES

1 See Kelleher 2007.
2 In general, see Challis 1978 and Challis 1989.

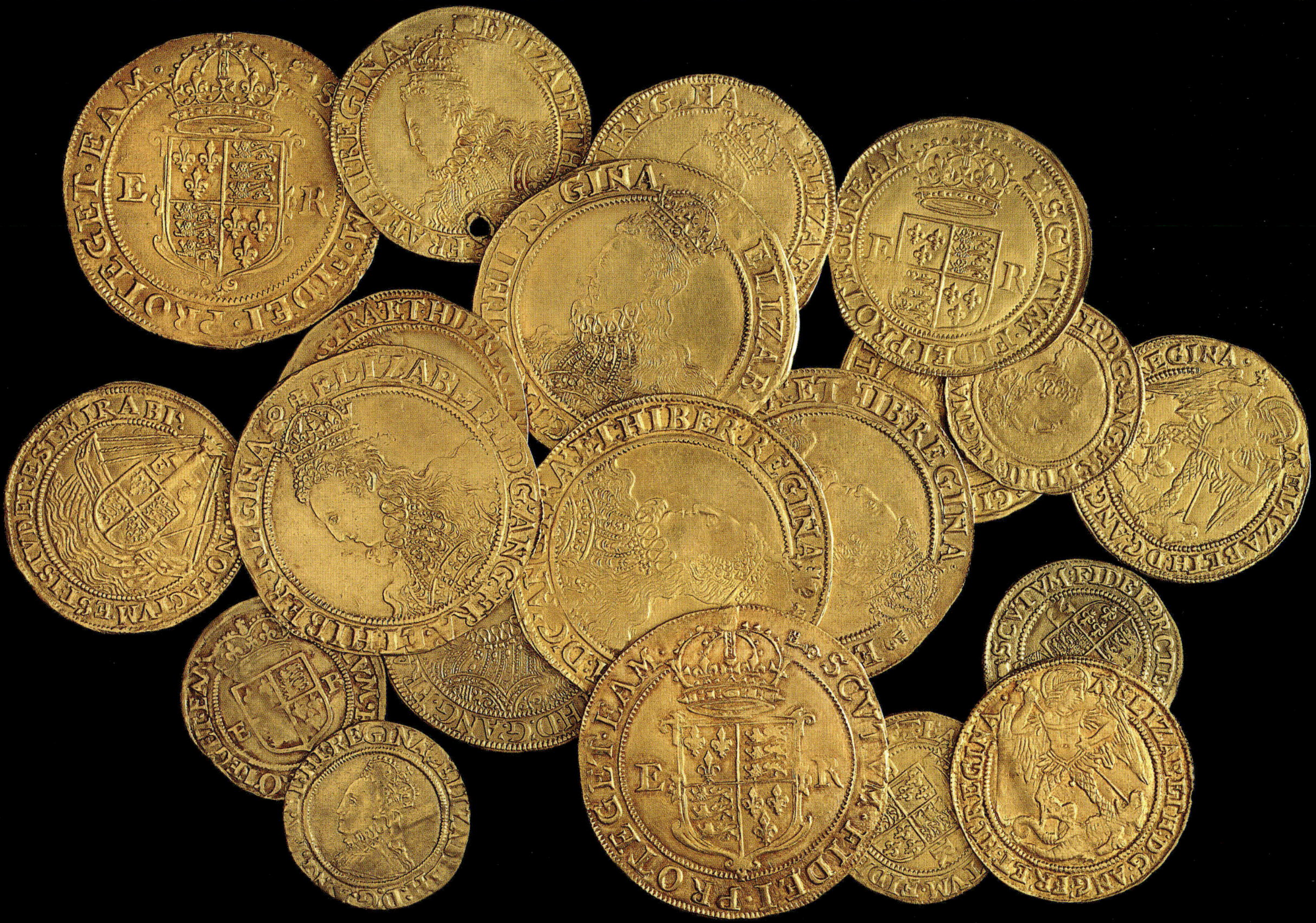

56

Two pairs of gloves

a **Leather and silk embroidered gloves**

England, c.1600–25
Kid leather with silk gauntlets embroidered with coloured silks, silver and silver-gilt threads and spangles, silk ribbon, edged with silver and silver-gilt bobbin lace and spangles; 330mm long
The Glove Collection Trust, courtesy of the Fashion Museum, Bath and North-East Somerset Council
(BATMC GLO 23341 & A (LOAN))

b **Men's leather gloves**

England, c.1600–50
Buff leather; 410mm long
The Glove Collection Trust, courtesy of the Fashion Museum, Bath and North-East Somerset Council
(BATMC GLO 23457 & A (LOAN))

Numerous examples of richly decorative gloves dating from the late sixteenth and early seventeenth centuries survive in museum collections and appear in portraits. The silk embroidered gloves (cat. 56a) are made of the finest kid (goat) leather with gauntlets embroidered with pansies and two different types of roses, and could have belonged to either a man or woman. In portraits of middle-class women, the presence of such accessories may signify their status as married women, as gloves were popular wedding gifts.[1] Although usually shown held in the hands, rather than worn, most of the surviving examples, like those illustrated here, show evidence of wear and soiling. These gloves were clearly not just for show.

Plain leather gloves, with perhaps a decoratively slashed gauntlet, are regularly found in portraits, for example that of Sir Richard Clough (d.1570; cat. 47) and the Countess of Shrewsbury (cat. 28). They represent a more ordinary variety for protecting the hands, which only very rarely survive. The buff leather pair shown here are extremely sturdy, with gauntlets formed of overlapping lobes of pinked skin. The thickness of the leather and lack of silk or metal thread embellishment indicate they were intended for rough usage – either riding and/or a military purpose – and therefore probably belonged to a man.

Probate inventories of glovers from Essex, Derbyshire, Warwickshire and Surrey, dating from the end of Elizabeth I's reign, reveal the range of leathers used for gloves in rural England: doe, buck, calf, sheep and lamb skins, horse and bull hides, and even dog skin.[2] Most of these were bought ready-made as can be seen in the inventory of the London haberdasher William Gynn (cat. 61). The wholesale prices of those in the inventory of James Backhouse of Lonsdale, Yorkshire, ranged from 4 pence to 1 shilling per pair.[3] SN

PROVENANCE

Part of the collection donated to the Worshipful Company of Glovers of London in 1959 by the late Robert Spence. Conserved 1995–9 with help from the HLF.

NOTES

1 Loreen L. Giese, *Courtships, Marriage Customs, and Shakespeare's Comedies* (Palgrave Macmillan, Basingstoke, 2006), p.89.
2 J.M. Bestall and D.V. Fowkes (eds), *Chesterfield wills and inventories 1521–1603*, Derbyshire Record Society, vol. 1, 1977, pp.260–1; D. Marion Herridge (ed.), *Surrey Probate Inventories 1558–1603*, Surrey Record Society, vol. 39, 2005, pp.380–1; Jeanne Jones (ed.), *Stratford-upon-Avon Inventories 1538–1699: I 1538–1625*, Dugdale Society, vol. 39, 2002, pp.195–6; Michael Reed (ed.), *The Ipswich Probate Inventories 1583–1631*, Suffolk Records Society, vol. 22, 1981, p.46.
3 James Raine (ed.), *Wills and Inventories from the Registry of the Archdeaconry of Richmond*, Surtees Society, vol. 26, 1853, p.278.

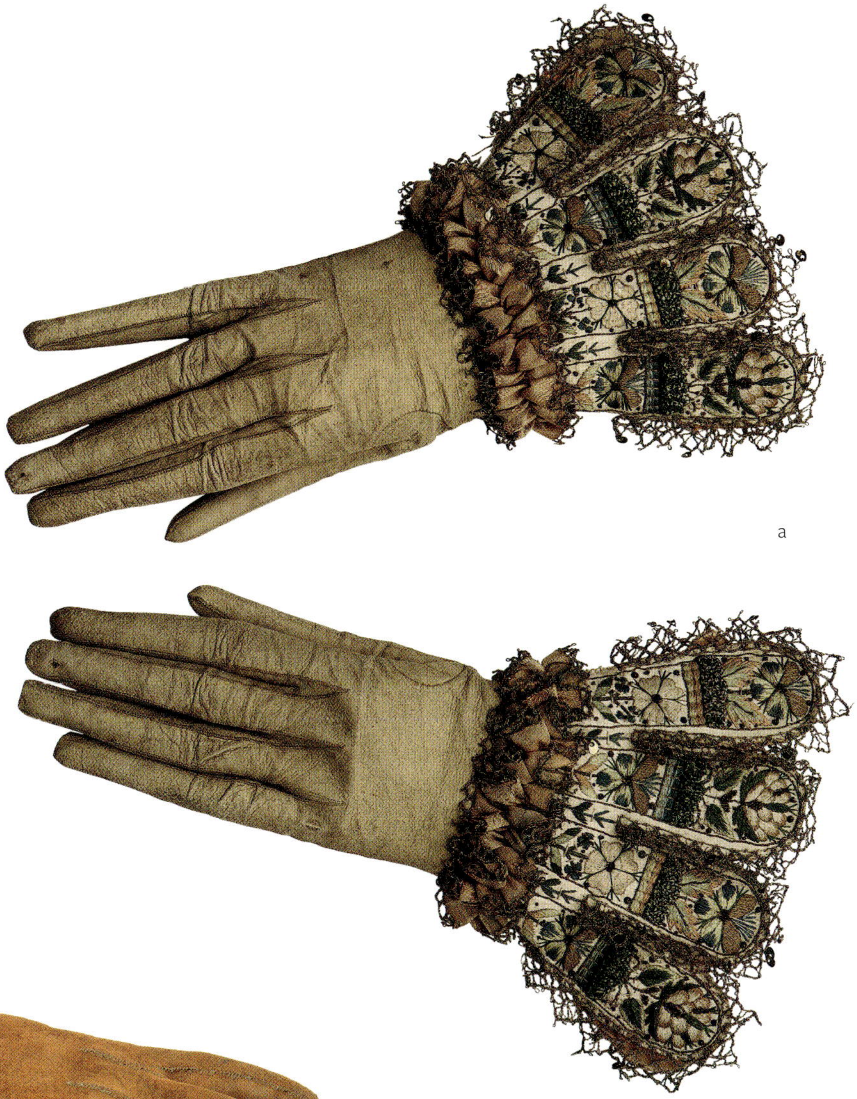

a

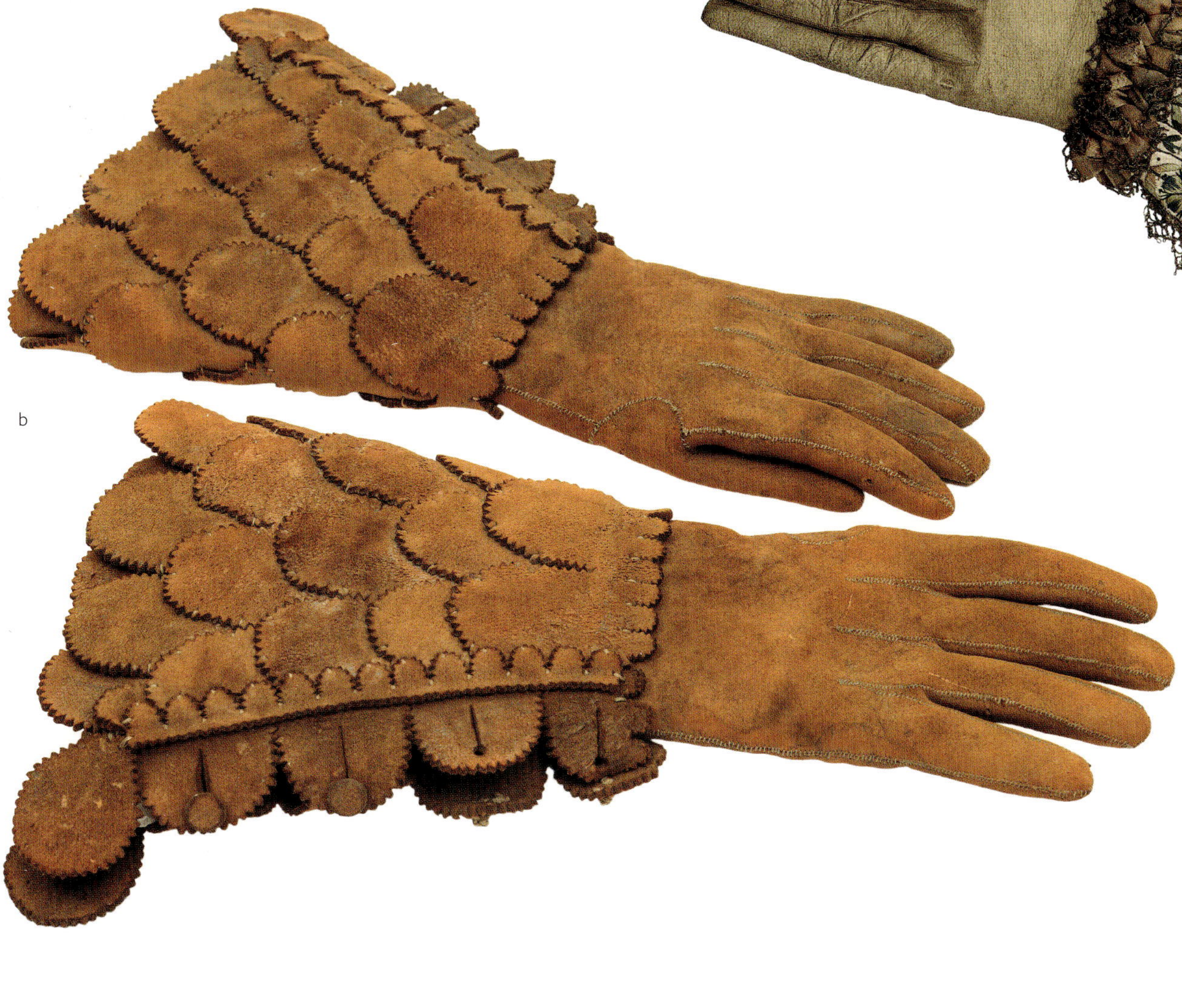

b

57

Merchant and Professional Rings

a **Posy ring, c.1600–25**

England
Gold
Inscribed *KEPE FAYTH TEIL DETHE*
Victoria and Albert Museum, London (M.71-1960)

PROVENANCE

Formerly in the collections of Sir John Evans and Mrs C.J. Longman; given by Dame Joan Evans to the V&A , 1960.

b **Posy ring, c.1525–75**

Western Europe
Gold
Inscribed *+MVLIER. VIRO / SVBIECTA. ESTO*
(Woman is to be subject to man)
Victoria and Albert Museum, London (M.3-1959)

PROVENANCE

Formerly in the collections of Sir John Evans and Mrs C.J. Longman; given by Dame Joan Evans to the V&A , 1960.

c **Signet ring with initials 'HS', c.1525–75**

Western Europe
Silver
Victoria and Albert Museum, London (M.342-1975)

PROVENANCE

Bequeathed by Miss E.M. Begg to the V&A, 1975.

d **Signet ring with initials 'GB', c.1575–99**

England
Silver
Victoria and Albert Museum, London (1375-1903)

PROVENANCE

Purchased from Mr John Jackson, 1903.

e **Signet ring with initials 'DF', sixteenth century**

England
Gold
Ashmolean Museum, Oxford (WA1897.CDEF.F600)

PROVENANCE

Presented to the Ashmolean Museum by Dr C.D.E. Fortnum in honour of Queen Victoria's Diamond Jubilee, 1897.

f **Ring with ship emblem and initials 'RH', c.1600**

England
Gold
Inscribed on reverse of bezel: *A freinds guift*
The British Museum, London (1928,0507.1)

PROVENANCE

Found near London Bridge, 1921; purchased by the British Museum from Dr Laurie A. Lawrence, 1928.

g **Memento mori ring, 1550–1600**

England
Gold, enamel
Inscribed at front of bezel: *+BE HOLD.THE.ENDE*;
around edge of bezel: *RATHER DEATH THAN FALS FAYTH*;
on reverse of bezel: *ML*
Victoria and Albert Museum, London (13-1888)

PROVENANCE

Bequeathed by Miss Charlotte Frances Gerard to the V&A, 1888.

h **Serjeant's ring, 1577**

Richard Pindar, London
Gold
Inscribed: * *LEX + REGIS + PRAESIDIVM*
(Law is the protection of the crown)
The British Museum, London (AF.1747)

PROVENANCE

Formerly Braybrooke Collection; bequeathed by Sir Augustus Wollaston Franks to the British Museum, 1897.

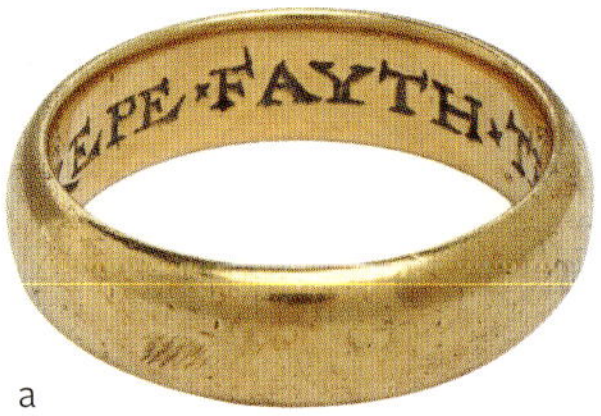

a

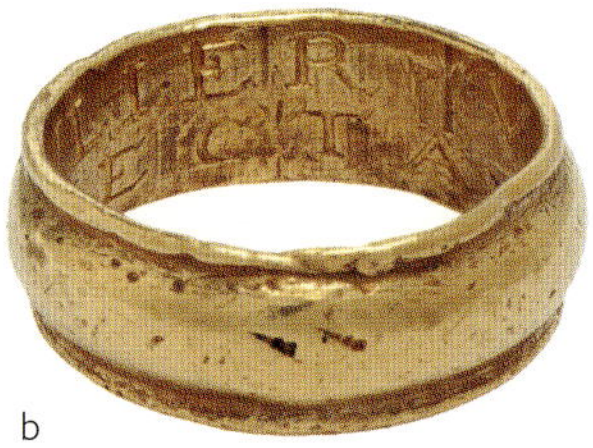

b

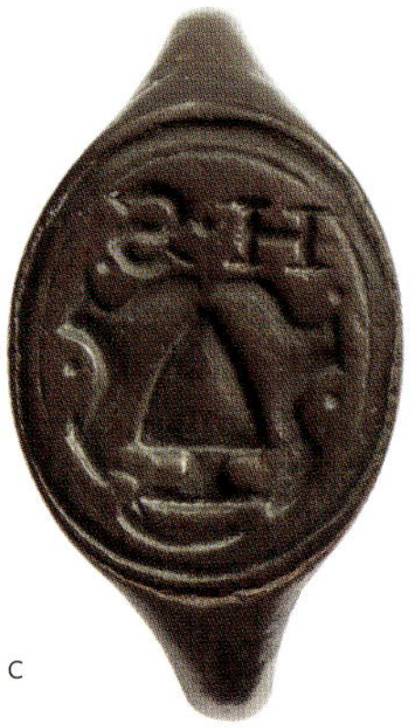

c

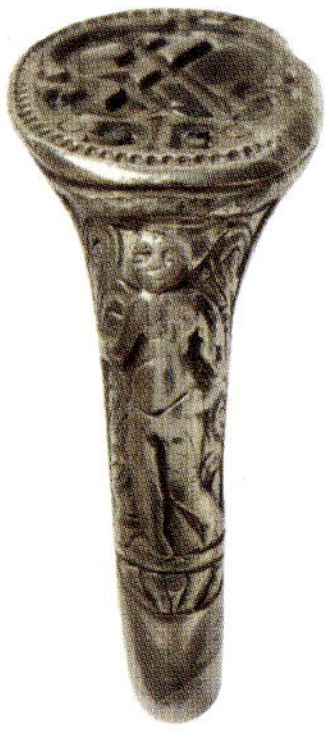

d

LITERATURE

Dalton 1912; Hamilton Baker 1984; Scarisbrick 1994; Scarisbrick 1995; Scarisbrick and Henig 2003; Scarisbrick 2007; Emanuel 2008; Awais-Dean 2012.

We are grateful to Rachel Church (V&A) and Dora Thornton (British Museum) for their help in making the selection, and to Rachel for references to literature.

In Elizabethan England, the middle classes frequently wore rings of many different types in both silver and gold. Popular types included signet rings, which were used to seal and authenticate documents and might be engraved with merchants' marks or imagery related to a man's trade, such as the ship ring. They also served as a means of identification. Posy rings, named after the posy or amorous message that is usually inscribed on the inner surface, were often given by men as love tokens, or to mark a betrothal or marriage. Where the posy refers to the constancy of the wearer (such as 'kepe fayth teil dethe'; cat. 57a) or a wife's status ('woman is to be subject to man'; cat. 57b), it may indicate use in a marriage ceremony. Memento mori rings were worn by the living as a reminder of the transience of life and were popular among merchants to show the futility of their worldly goods. They can be seen in several portraits (including that of Gawen Goodman, cat. 51) and are also frequently mentioned in wills. Common imagery, as shown here (cat. 57g), includes a death's head. Here, the inscription and the initials on its reverse, joined by a true lover's knot, may indicate a second function as a marriage ring.

Serjeants' rings were given to various officials and friends by newly created serjeants-at-law (the highest level of the legal profession, obsolete since 1875). Each ring bore an inscription, usually in Latin, which made reference to the law or the Crown and was particular to the year the serjeants were appointed. Considered as a type of payment upon gaining a privileged position, most of these rings were probably melted down for their gold content, which explains their rarity. NAD

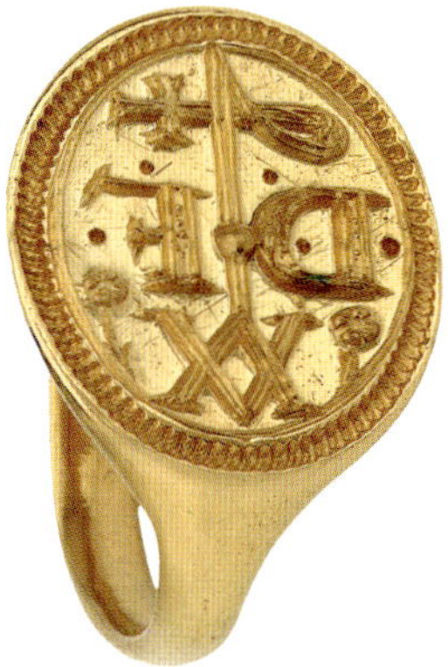

e

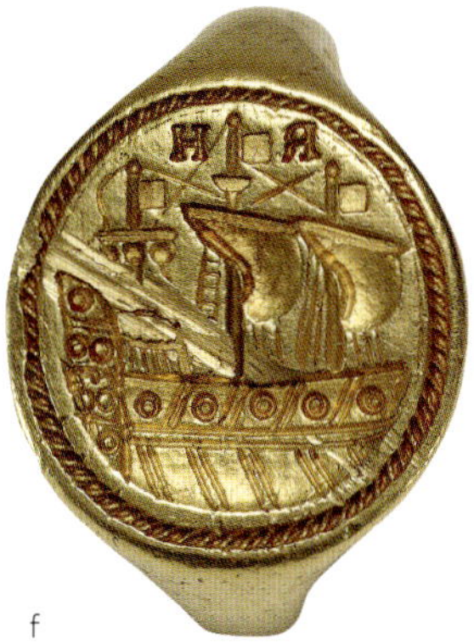

f

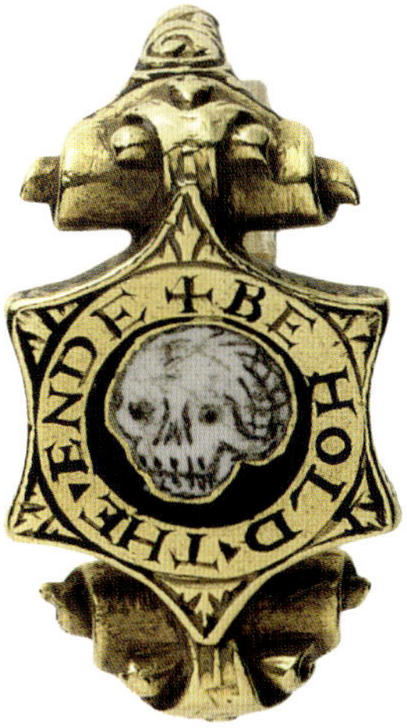

g

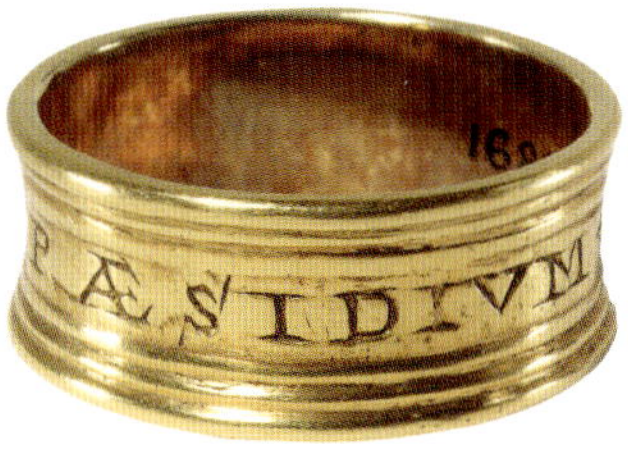

h

60

Set of Drawing Instruments

Bartholomew Newsam, London, c.1565–75

Gilt-brass, steel and wood, 198 × 47mm; depth (gilt-brass case) 83mm
Inscribed on front: *Pax orbi exoptatissima* (Peace most longed for by the world); on right side: *Abundantia Pacis filia* (Abundance is the daughter of Peace); on rear: *Bellum fax mundi* (War is the torment of the world); on left side: *Pauperies Belli filia* (Poverty is the daughter of War)
Signed in cartouche at bottom
The British Museum, London (1912,0208.1)

This is the only surviving example of a set of Elizabethan drawing instruments. The set is contained within a fine gilt-brass case engraved with depictions of Peace, War, Poverty and Abundance on each of its sides. The base of the case is inscribed with the name of the native-born instrument maker Bartholomew Newsam (d.1587), who was active in London from the early part of the reign of Elizabeth I. Although five of the instruments are now missing, the set includes a folding square, a pair of scissors, steel-pointed square scribers, a beam-compass, a sharpening stone, a pencil holder, a set of compasses, a pen, a series of dividers, a pricker, two knives, a drawing pen and a folding rule. All of these instruments are of the very highest quality and would have belonged to either a master-craftsman at the height of his profession, or a wealthy patron with ambitions as a designer. Some Elizabethan courtiers are known to have taken an active role in the planning and design of their building projects. For example, there are a number of extant drawings in the hand of Sir William Cecil, Lord Burghley (cat. 19), in the collections of maps and plans at Hatfield House. Such activities would have required specialist instruments of the type shown here. In November 1607, Burghley's successor as Lord Treasurer, Thomas Sackville, 1st Earl of Dorset, paid 12 shillings for 'Compasses, rulers & other things' from the retailer Thomas Webster.[1] It is probable that this set would have cost considerably more than 12 shillings, and may have been presented as a gift at court.

The practice of drawing for the purposes of both surveying and building had developed substantially over the course of the sixteenth century, leading to important and long-lasting improvements to cartography, navigation, architecture, land surveying and a host of other allied professions. Leonard Digges's *A boke named Tectonicon*, published in 1556, had a profound influence on the use and application of instruments designed for measuring and drawing, and provided improved methods and tables of arithmetical calculation. ET

PROVENANCE

Collection of Dr English; bequeathed by Max Rosenheim to the British Museum, 1912.

LITERATURE

Ward 1981; L'E. Turner 2000; Gerbino and Johnston 2009.

NOTE

1 KHLC MS U269 A1/1.

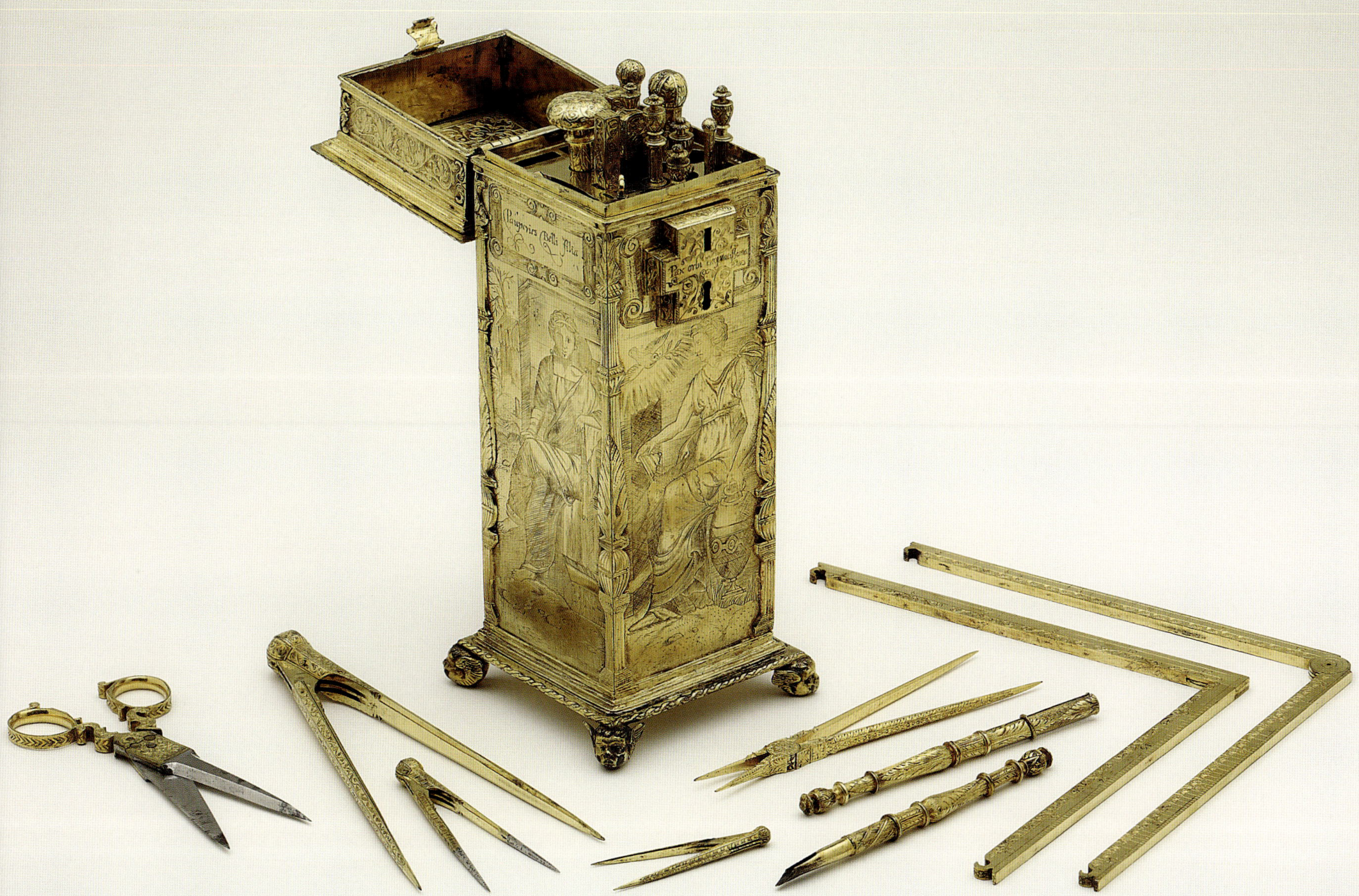

61

Inventory of the Goods of William Gynn, Haberdasher of London (1555–93)

1582

Manuscript, ink on paper, 1444 × 124mm
The National Archives, UK, C 239/48, no.104

This inventory of goods in a London haberdasher's shop lists a vast range of stock from gloves to garters and silks to spectacles. The goods were owned by William Gynn, Haberdasher of St Mary Woolchurch, and the inventory was made in October 1582 in order to recover an outstanding debt.

It gives a very good impression of the choice and variety of goods that were available at the high end of the retail market in Elizabethan London. Over the course of the fifteenth and sixteenth centuries the haberdashery trade in the capital had increased in line with the growing demand for demonstrably expensive clothing accessories.[1] The inventory includes 185 pairs of gloves, of various degrees of finish and quality. The quality of an individual's gloves made an important statement about their wealth and status. As such they were frequently given as gifts at weddings, funerals, and other important events. Gynn catered to every taste, stocking gloves of lambskin, sheep's leather or kid, embroidered with gold, copper, pearls or lace. He also sold billiment lace (used to trim small items) and inkle (linen tape), as well as many different types of fastenings such as pins and laces. This inventory not only lists some 50,000 pins of various types and sizes, but also the 'pynpyllows' or pincushions that were needed for them. In addition, the shop stocked items such as packs of playing cards (14 pence a dozen), hairbrushes (6 pence each) and pictures (eleven, valued altogether at 10 shillings), which were probably bought on impulse by exuberant shoppers.

Gynn was baptised at the Parish Church of Holy Trinity the Less on 25 May 1555.[2] After attending the newly founded Merchant Taylors' School, he established his career as a haberdasher.[3] However, in 1582 his creditors exercised their right to recover goods to pay off a debt of £100 and assessors were sent to appraise his goods up to the value of the debt and thereafter drew up this inventory.[4] Sadly, there is some evidence to suggest that Gynn never recovered from this setback and died in debt. Although a resident of Whitechapel, he was buried on 12 September 1593 in the parish of St Michael Wood Street, which was home to the city's principal debtors' prison. It is perhaps telling that when his brother Wilfred came to make his will in 1603, he made bequests to two London prisons with special provision for those 'which were layd in for dette'.[5] ET

PROVENANCE

Chancery: Extents for Debts, Series II.

NOTES

1 Ian Archer, *The Haberdashers' Company* (Phillimore, Chichester, 1991).
2 LMA, Holy Trinity the Less, Composite register: P69/TRI3/A/01/MS09155.
3 Charles J. Robinson, *A Register of the Scholars admitted into Merchant Taylors' School from A.D. 1562–1874*, vol. 1 (Farncombe & Co., Lewes, 1882), p.4.
4 Martha Carlin, *London and Southwark inventories 1316–1650: a handlist of extents for debts* (Centre for Metropolitan History, Institute for Historical Research, London, 1997).
5 Will of Wilfred Gynne or Gynn, Haberdasher of All Hallows, Lombard Street, City of London. TNA/PROB 11/101/563.

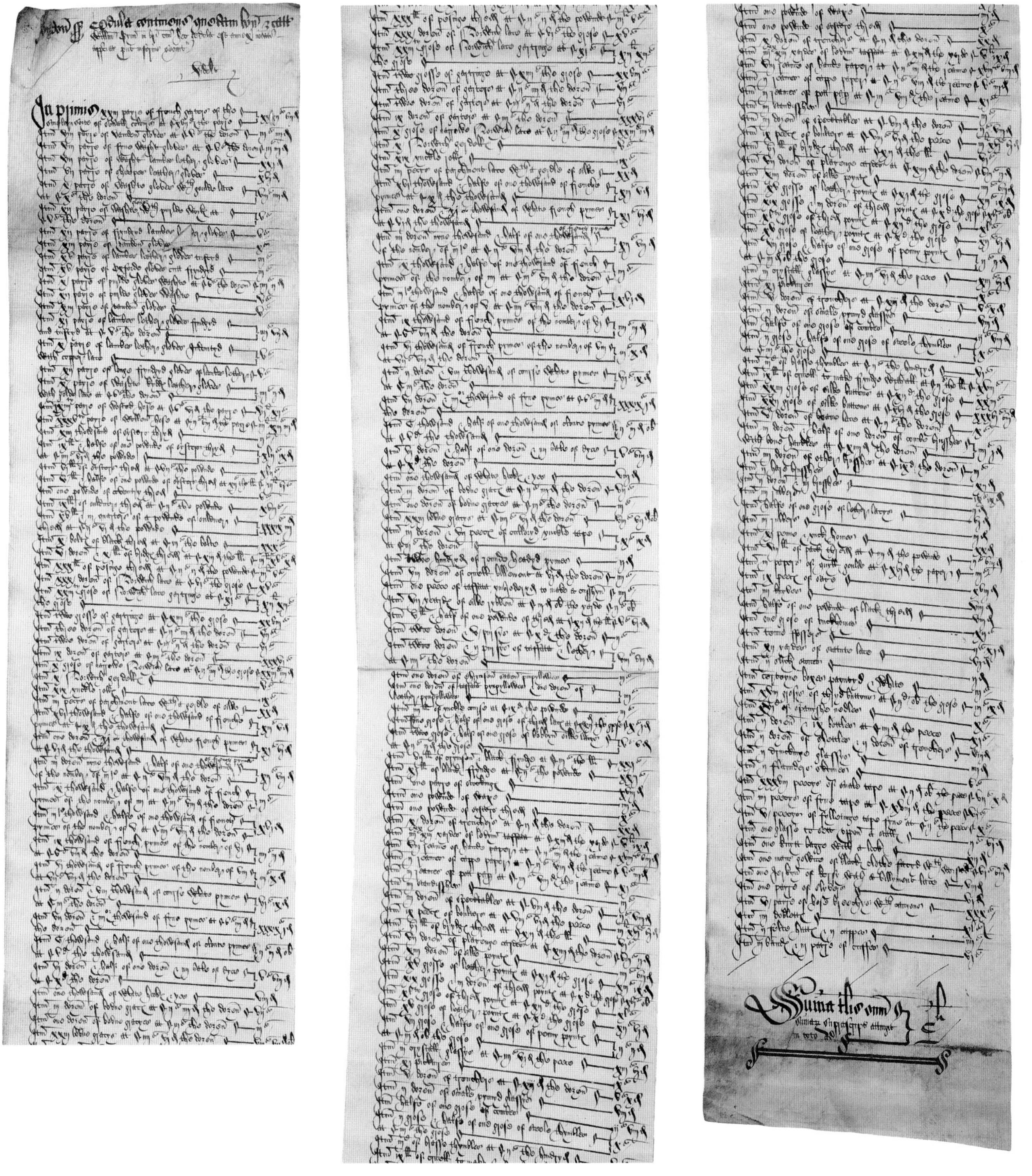

62

Wool Caps

England, 1500–99

Knitted wool
Museum of London (5008, A15260, 5006a, NN8512)

a 5008 diameter 254 mm (crown); width 25 mm (brim)
b A15260 diameter 230 mm (crown); width 25 mm (brim)
c 5006a diameter 210 mm (crown)
d NN8512 diameter 250 mm (crown)

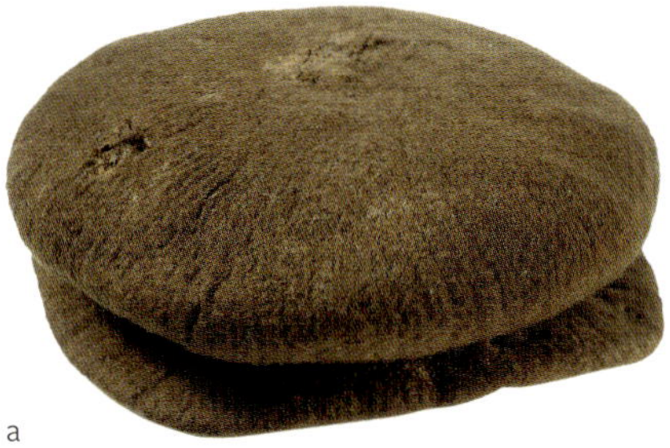
a

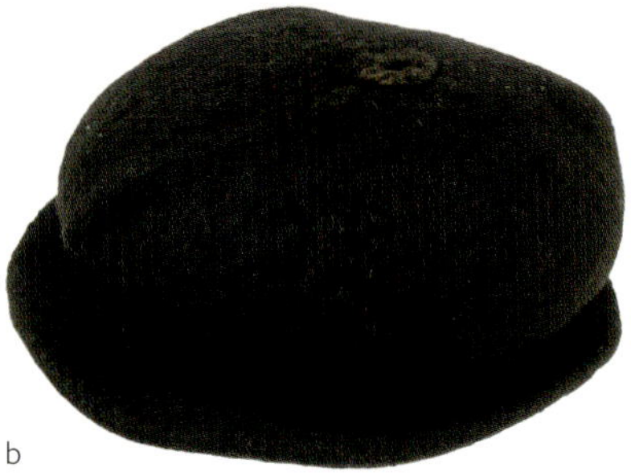
b

The technique of knitting appears to have been introduced into England in the fifteenth century; 'capknytters' are recorded in York as early as 1422.[1] At the beginning of Elizabeth I's reign, woollen caps – knitted, felted, sheared and sometimes decoratively slashed – provided a fashionable yet affordable alternative to the soft velvet 'Milan bonnet' worn by aristocratic men.[2] By 1571, sumptuary law decreed that all non-noble Englishmen should wear English wool caps on Sundays and holidays, a requirement that no doubt led to a decline in the more decorative versions of knitted headwear.[3]

Some of the tools and activities of this trade can be seen in the 1561 inventory of Worcester capper Roger Yelfe, which included 'raw cappes' (long tubes knitted in the round from a single stitch at the crown), dyed and undyed caps, as well as cauldrons, shears, burling irons and pins – the tools for fulling, felting, shearing and cutting them. The 8-pound weight of wool in his shop may have been awaiting distribution to a team of knitters.[4] Most of the surviving knitted caps from the sixteenth century in museum collections have been recovered from archaeological excavations. Chemical analysis reveals that they were originally dyed with a variety of local dyestuffs, such as woad, weld and madder.[5] Styles ranged from simple 'skull' caps with earflaps to the more elaborately brimmed versions shown here. The most luxurious caps often had multiple brims; some were intricately slashed and occasionally decorated with silk ribbons. SN

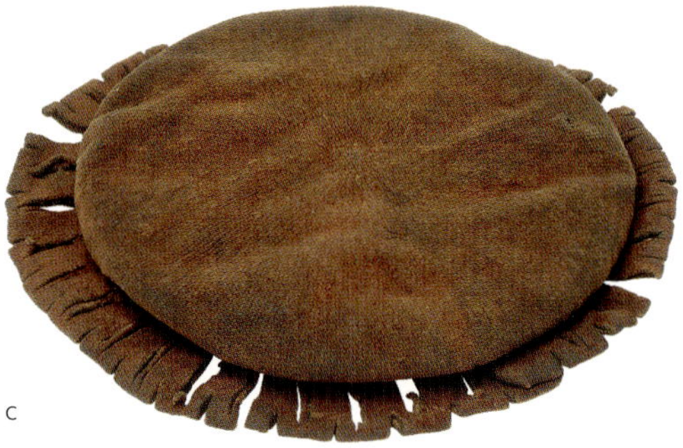
c

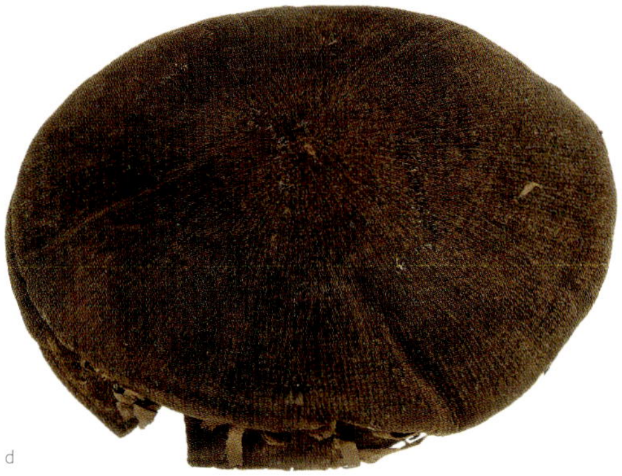
d

NOTES

1 Sandy Black, *Knitting: Fashion, Industry and Craft* (V&A Publishing, London, 2012), p.19.
2 Ibid., p.20.
3 Ibid., p.19.
4 A.D. Dyer, 'Probate Inventories of Worcester Tradesmen, 1545–1614', Worcestershire Historical Society, Miscellany II, 5 new series, 1967, pp.19–20.
5 Julie Gardiner (ed.), *Before the Mast: Life and Death Aboard the Mary Rose* (The Mary Rose Trust, Portsmouth, 2005), p.34.

63

Woman's Waistcoat

England, 1615–20

Linen embroidered with wool
The Vaughan Family Trust, courtesy of the Fashion Museum, Bath and North-East Somerset Council
(BATMC I.03.136 (LOAN))

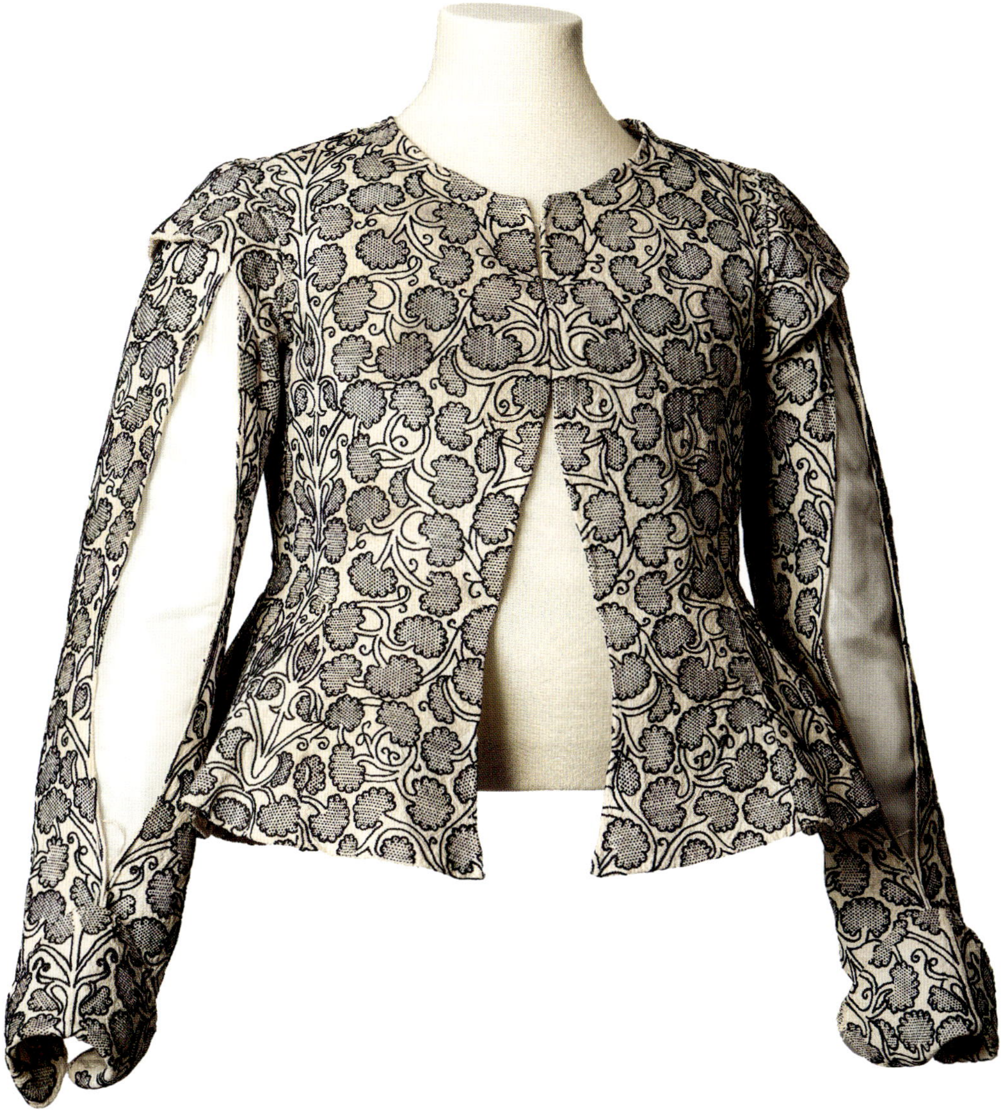

Waistcoats were informal items in the wardrobes of all women in Elizabethan England. They were fitted, but un-boned, garments extending below the waistline and worn with petticoats (skirts) and a loose gown over the top.[1] Aristocratic women, such as Elizabeth Vernon (cat. 27), wore them in private, and their waistcoats were made of silk or linen, decorated with floral embroidery in coloured silks and precious-metal threads. Gentry and middle-class women also owned decorative waistcoats and this Jacobean example is embroidered with wool, indicating that it was a slightly less expensive version of the 'blackwork' embroidery that was executed with silk thread. The scrolling abstract floral design and running-stitch fill seen on this waistcoat are simpler variations of the 'speckling stitch' and naturalistic patterns of early seventeenth-century blackwork.

Waistcoats appear in the wills and inventories of Elizabethan women from the 1570s onward. A Banbury widow, Elizabeth Sly, whose total material goods when she died amounted to only 14 shillings and 11 pence, owned 'a red kyrtull [kirtle or skirt] owld petycotes & A wascot [waistcoat] & A hat & A cap'.[2] Margaret Bourne, a widow of an Essex cleric, bequeathed her 'best silke wastcote' in her will of 1598 and the inventory of Margaret Keelie, widow of a Kent barrister, taken in 1593 listed 'two imbroider'd wastcotes'.[3] SN

PROVENANCE

The Harris of Hayne family, Devon.

NOTES

1 C. Willett Cunnington and Phillis Cunnington, *Handbook of English Costume in the Sixteenth Century* (Faber and Faber, London, 1954), p.171; Ninya Mikhaila and Jane Malcolm-Davies, *The Tudor Tailor: Reconstructing 16th-century dress* (Batsford, London, 2006), p.21.

2 Michael Ashley Havinden (ed.), *Household and Farm Inventories in Oxfordshire, 1550–1590*, Oxfordshire Record Society, vol. 44, 1965, p.65.

3 Melissa Hamnett, 'Fashioning A Self: Issues of Identity Surrounding Women's Dress in England 1590–1640', MA thesis, V&A/Royal College of Art, 2004, pp.140, 148, 151.

64

Thimbles and Pins, late 1500s and early 1600s

England and Germany

Thimbles:
a. Brass, child's with top showing signs of use. Maker's mark probably Nuremberg c.1580–1650 (A26113), height 15mm
b. Brass, band of stars and lozenges. Maker's mark probably Nuremberg c.1580–1650 (A3583), height 16mm

Pins:
Silver, copper and lead alloys (4200, 80.230/12 a, b, c, 86.150/5, 4145 and 80.184, 4–47)

Museum of London

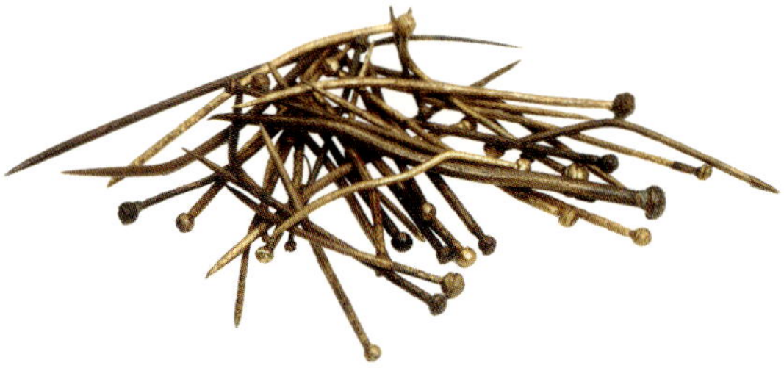

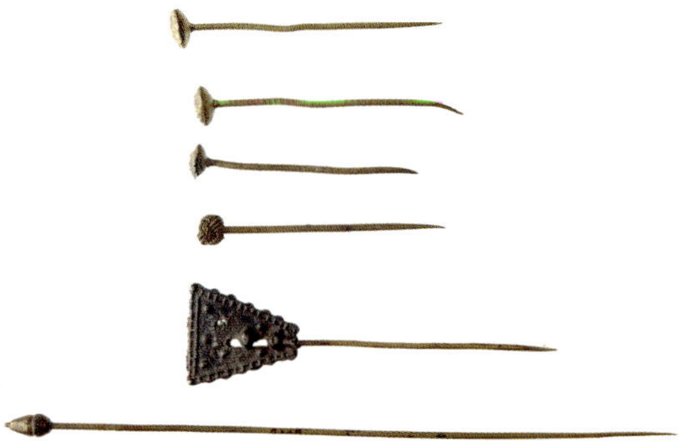

In an age of conspicuous consumption, when people of all classes paid close attention to their dress, fashion and appearance, pins, thimbles and other sewing accoutrements were essential. Pins were routinely used to attach the various elements of sixteenth-century clothing together. Two to three thousand Londoners, mostly paupers, children and the infirm, were employed in pin manufacture, but domestic production could not keep pace with demand and by the end of the century almost £60,000 worth of pins were imported each year.[1]

The portrait of Elizabeth Vernon, Countess of Southampton (cat. 27), shows a pincushion on the table, bristling with black (probably Dutch) iron and brass pins. Similarly decorated pincushions are listed in the Wardrobe Accounts of Elizabeth I, with other references relating to the order and supply of pins suitable for particular items of clothing. In 1565, the royal warrant holder, Robert Careles, supplied 8,000 'great farthingale' pins, 20,000 'middle farthingale' pins, 25,000 'great Velvet' pins and 29,000 'small he[a]d' pins for the Great Wardrobe.[2] Wealthier households set aside 'pin money' and in 1573–4 Sir Henry Sidney (1529–86), of Penshurst Place in Kent, gave the children of his household an allowance of 3 shillings (the equivalent of six days' wages for a kitchen maid) to buy enough pins to last them for six months.[3]

Points, or aglets, of folded sheet brass were fastened to tags or laces to prevent the edges fraying and to facilitate fastening. Some served a purely functional purpose but others were richly embellished and set with gemstones to hang from the hat, sleeve, doublet or bodice. HF

a 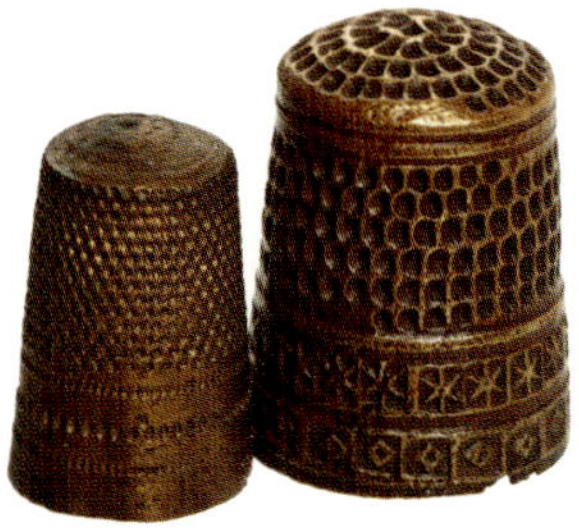 b

PROVENANCE

Numbers 4200 and 4145 found in London Wall; the others from varied archaeological sources.

NOTES

1 BL, Lansdowne MS 84.no. 21.
2 TNA LC5/33, f.60, September 1564.
3 KHLC, De L'Isle Mss (U1475/A56).

65

Buttons, 1500s and early 1600s

England and Europe

a Copper alloy, integral loop (80.469/10)
b Plain silver (87.161/2)
c Copper alloy, front decorated with rosette and petals (86.361/17)
d Silver, with pressed decoration (81.564/58)
e Lead alloy, hollow, the front decorated with
a six-pointed star (81.564/34)
f Lead alloy, decorated with the Mercers' Company
maidenhead (79.319/5)

Museum of London

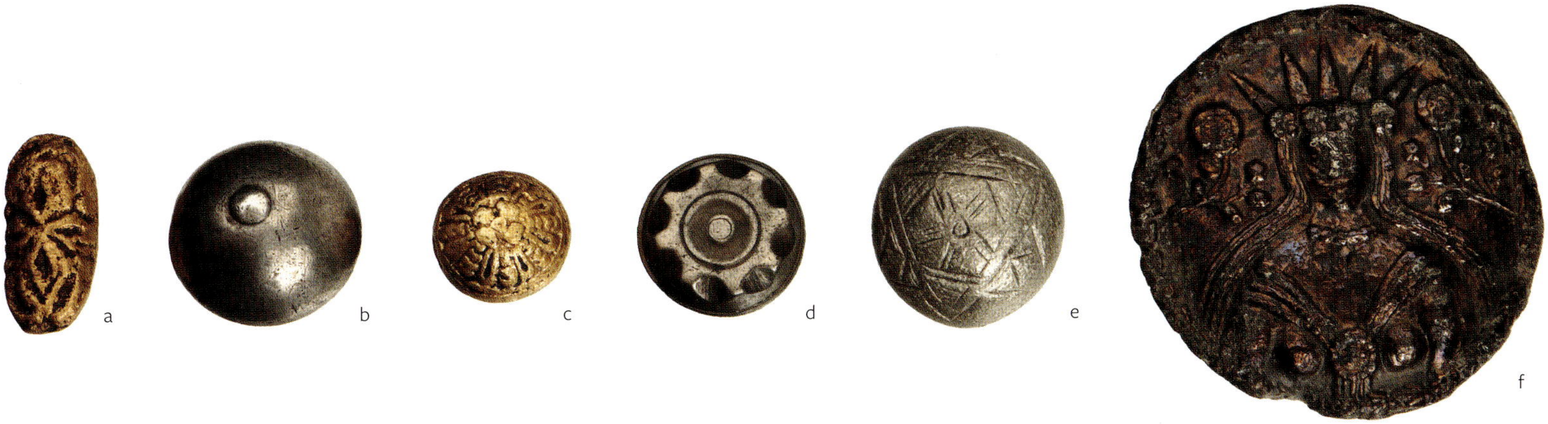

Buttons of many shapes, sizes and materials were used as decorative trimmings and to fasten tight-fitting garments. Most were made in two halves, soldered around the circumference, with a simple loop at the back. The fronts were plain, or decorated with a variety of geometric and foliate motifs, and occasionally also with some kind of whimsical device of particular significance to the owner. One of the buttons shown here, represented by many examples in different metals, depicts the Mercer's Maiden from the arms of the Mercers' Company and was presumably made, and worn, by one of their number as a mark of loyalty and association.

Buttons were a key part of a haberdasher's stock, as can be seen in the inventory of the London haberdasher William Gynn (cat. 61), which mentions over twenty different types of button. They were also given to members of the court and royal household as New Year gifts. Most of the buttons listed in Elizabeth I's Wardrobe Accounts were made from precious metals, suitably bejewelled and enamelled with pansies, pea pods, half-moons and other devices. Some were embellished with half-pearls, mother-of-pearl and hardstones, while others – of acorn shape – formed miniature receptacles for musk and ambergris perfume balls. HF

PROVENANCE
Thames foreshore and other unrecorded London locations.

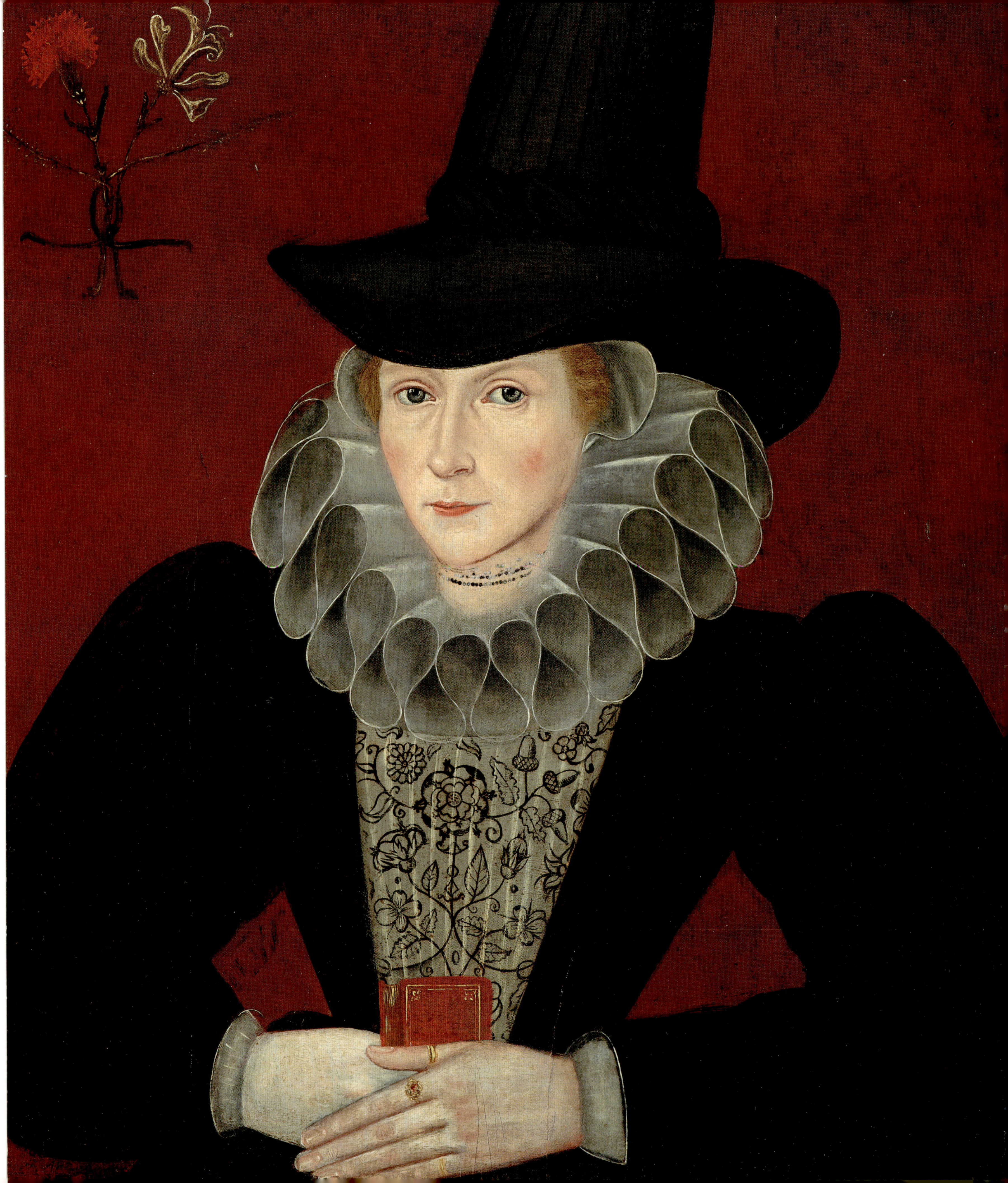

5 PROFESSIONALS, WRITERS AND ARTISTS

The professions of law, medicine and religion flourished in new ways in the Elizabethan period. As urban populations increased, litigation and the need for lawyers expanded, while the sanctioning of clerical marriage created a new phenomenon of family dynasties of clergymen. Lawyers in particular were the subject of criticism for their greed, pride and ability to prolong cases to their own advantage. As with merchants and retailers, there were very significant variations in wealth among professional men; a country clergyman with a small parish could be living on a subsistence income, while some successful London lawyers were easily as wealthy as some of the nobility.

Men who had studied at university, and even some who had not, took up roles in spheres such as teaching, publishing, administration, land surveying and clerical work, while talented authors responded to opportunities by writing plays for the newly established public theatres. The growth of the publishing industry was slower than in some other parts of Europe. Yet, as literacy increased, the demand for books expanded and the publication of printed books in English grew by at least a third in the course of the Elizabethan period.

Increasingly, professional men and others of similar status chose to style themselves as gentlemen, adding the word 'gent' after their names in official documents. Portraits of this group show serious-minded men dressed much like merchants in smart and sober suits of black, but sometimes with Latin mottos or books placed alongside, and newly acquired – or recently revived – coats of arms. Printed portraits of writers were also produced, sometimes for use as frontispieces in printed books, allowing readers to encounter the face of the author for the first time.

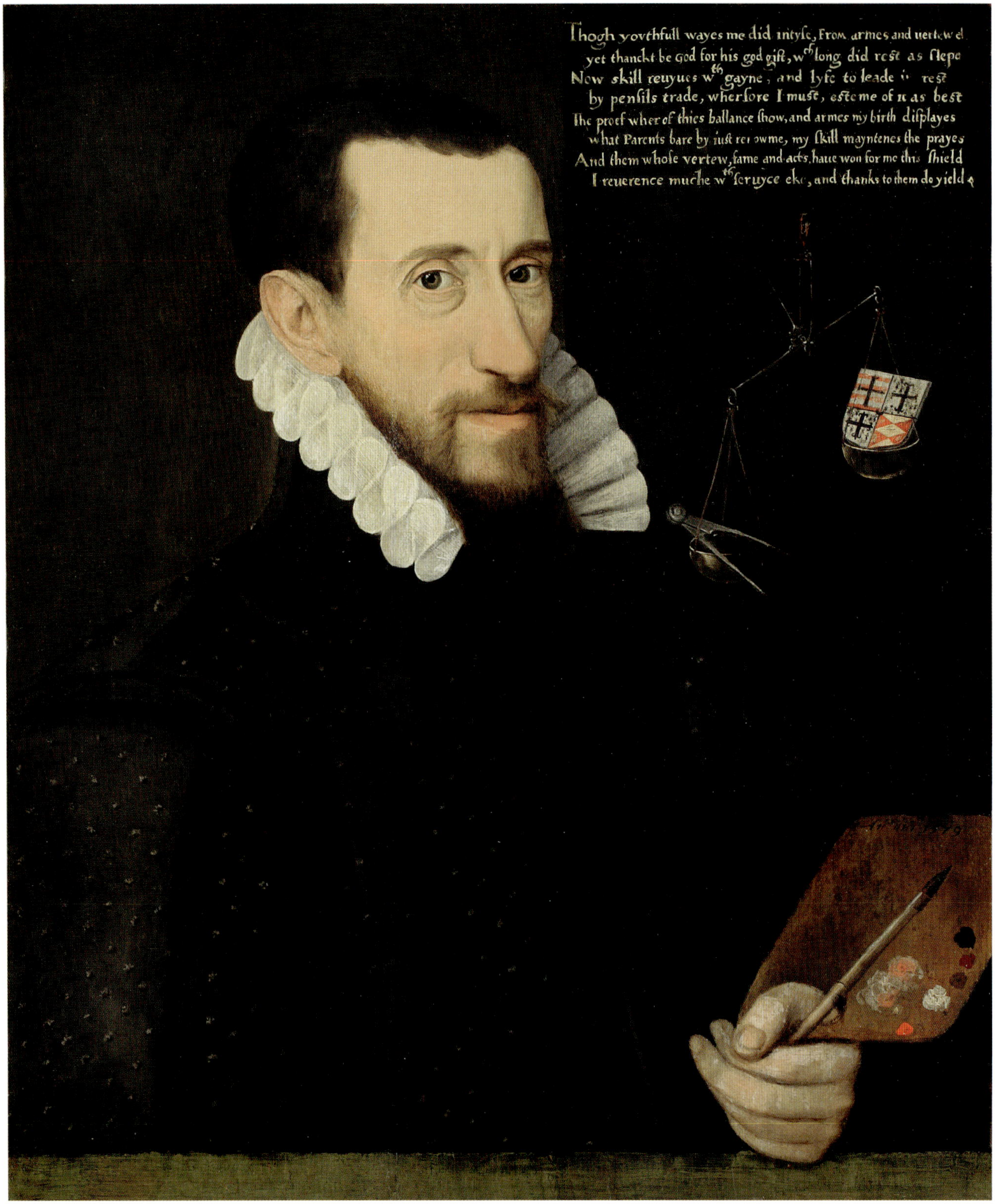
Thogh yovthfull wayes me did intyse, From armes and vertew
yet thanckt be God for his god gift, wch long did rest as slepe
Now skill reuyues wth gayne, and lyfe to leade rest
by pensils trade, wherfore I must, esteme of as best
The proef wher of thies ballance show, and armes my birth displayes
what Parents bare by iust me, my skill mayntenes the prayes
And them whose vertew, fame and acts, haue won for me this shield
I reuerence muche wth seruyce , and thanks to them do yield

67

George Gower (d.1596)

Self-portrait, dated 1579

Oil on panel, 616 × 508mm
Inscribed upper right: *Thogh yovthfull ways me did intyse, From armes and uertew e[ke] | yet thanckt be God for his god gift, wch long did rest as slepe | Now skill reuyues wth gayne, and lyfe to lead in rest | by pensils trade, wherefore I must, esteem of it as best | The proof wherof thies ballance show, and armes my birth displayes | what Parents bare by iust re[n]owme, my skill mayntenes the prayes | And them whose vertew, fame and acts, haue won for me this shield | I reuerence muche wth seruyce eke, and thanks to them do yield*; on top edge of palette: *An[n]o d[omi]ni 1579*
Private collection

This highly unusual portrait depicts Elizabeth I's Serjeant-Painter George Gower, holding the tools of his trade, and is the earliest surviving example of a large-scale self-portrait by a British artist. A grandson of Sir John Gower of Strettenham, Yorkshire, the details of George Gower's artistic training are unknown, but his style indicates that he trained in England. Gower was appointed Serjeant-Painter in 1581 and remained so until his death in 1596, a role that required him to oversee a wide variety of decorative projects, from palace interiors to banners, flags and stage sets for temporary entertainments.[1] He also made an attempt to become the Queen's official portraitist: a draft patent survives from 1583–4, granting the sole right to make Elizabeth's portrait in paintings and prints to Gower and in miniatures to Nicholas Hilliard. However, it is unsigned, and never seems to have been executed.[2] Gower probably ran a reasonable-sized studio and painted portraits of numerous members of the gentry and nobility, including portraits of Sir Thomas Kytson and Elizabeth Cornwallis, Lady Kytson (both 1573; Tate Britain, London; see also fig. 6).

This portrait was painted before Gower's royal appointment and its most striking aspect is that the artist presents himself as both a painter and a gentleman, as his family coat of arms appears in the background. To the left he has included a weighing balance with a compass and the coat of arms on opposing scales. Through this device, Gower argues that artistic skill (represented by the compass) carries more weight than the virtues of birth (signified by the heraldic coat of arms). This interpretation is confirmed by the eight-line verse at the top where Gower argues that his 'pensils trade' or skill holds the same virtue as the military service for which his ancestors were awarded their heraldic badges of honour. This was a remarkable argument in a period during which status acquired by birth – and thus justified by God – underpinned the hierarchical order of society. Gower's inscription might be read as a plea for a meritocracy, but it needs to be understood within the wider debate about the value of painting as a liberal art that was developing throughout sixteenth-century Europe. While scholars and artists on the continent, including Giorgio Vasari in Italy, had already begun to argue for the intrinsic value of artistic authorship, the artist's position in England largely remained that of an artisan or craftsman. It is possible that the portrait may have originally hung in Gower's studio, as an advertisement for his own skill and a means to champion the status of painting. It has been suggested that the picture may have entered the collection of the Fitzwilliam family following a misreading of the heraldry in the eighteenth century.[3]

TC & AO

PROVENANCE

First recorded by Vertue c.1721 as in the collection of John, 2nd Earl Fitzwilliam; thence by descent.

EXHIBITIONS

Between Renaissance and Baroque, Manchester, City Art Gallery, 1965 (125); *The Elizabethan Image*, London, Tate Gallery, 1969–70 (100); *Dynasties: Painting in Tudor and Jacobean England 1530–1630*, London, Tate Gallery, 1995–6 (57), pp.107–8.

LITERATURE

Goodison 1948, pp.261–4; Waterhouse 1948, p.267; Strong 1969a, p.170; Hearn 1995, pp.107–8; Howard 1996, p.33; Hearn, 'Gower, George (d. 1596)', ODNB 2004; Cooper 2012, pp.20–1 and 193.

NOTES

1 Goodison 1948, p.264.
2 Ibid.
3 Waterhouse 1948, p.267.

Portraits of Esther Kello, née Inglis

a **Esther Kello, née Inglis (1570/1–1624)**

Unknown artist, dated 1595
Oil on panel, 746 × 632mm
Scottish National Portrait Gallery, Edinburgh (PG 3556)

b ***Le Livre de l'Ecclesiaste ensemble les Lamentations de Ieremie de la main d'Esther Anglois françoise, a Lislebourg en Ecosse, 1602***

Esther Kello, née Inglis, 1602
Title page of manuscript with self-portrait, pen and ink
National Library of Scotland (MS.20498)

In this unusual portrait of a female artisan (a), the calligrapher Esther Inglis is depicted at around twenty-five years old. Esther was the daughter of French Huguenot émigrés Nicolas and Marie Langlois (anglicised as 'Inglis'), who fled persecution around 1569 and settled in Edinburgh. She was taught the art of calligraphy by her mother and retained a strong sense of her French identity throughout her life, routinely signing her works 'Esther Langlois, Fille Françoise, de Dieppe'. In about 1596, she married the Scottish minister Bartholomew Kello (d.1631). Dated 1595, it is possible that this portrait commemorates her betrothal to Kello, as the flowers found at the upper left, an intertwined carnation (or pink) and a honeysuckle, were common in marriage portraits. The pair lived and worked in Edinburgh during Elizabeth I's reign, then moved to London and Essex under James I before returning to Edinburgh in 1615. This portrait is the earliest of several extant oil portraits.[1]

Inglis produced some fifty-nine manuscripts between 1586 and 1624, many of which were made for elite court patrons, including Elizabeth I, Henry, Prince of Wales, Prince Charles, the poet and courtier Sir David Murray of Gorthy, Antony Bacon, Ludovic Stewart, Duke of Lennox, and Robert Cecil, Earl of Salisbury. Her manuscripts include specimen writing books, secular and religious texts, and books of emblems and arms. Written in a wide range of highly ornamental hands, the books feature decorative introductory pages, headpieces, initials and naturalistic images of flowers and insects that were perhaps influenced by French and Flemish Books of Hours. Many of her manuscripts include her self-portrait, as shown here in the manuscript of *Lamentations* (b), which was dedicated to 'Archibald, Count of Argyle' and includes verses in praise of her by the Scottish Presbyterian divine Andrew Melville. Despite her wealthy clientele and prodigious output, the family was not well off, and when Esther died in Leith in 1624 she was in debt.

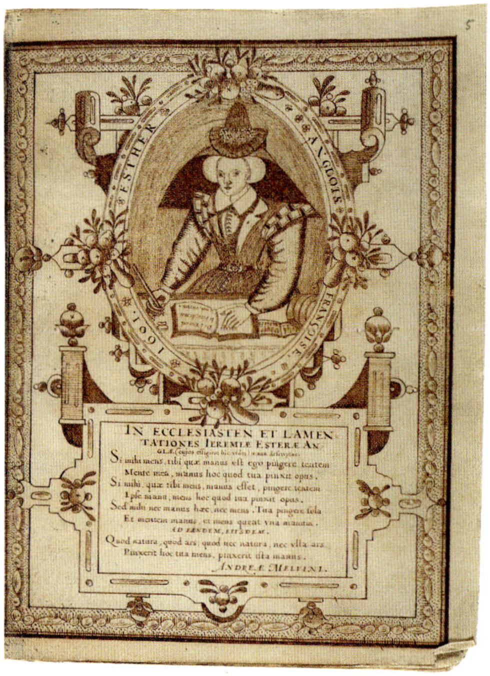

b

More than twenty of these small-scale self-portraits survive, providing evidence of an extensive and idiosyncratic form of 'signature'. Esther Inglis's unique status as a female artist means that this device was probably regarded by her patrons as little more than distinctive and amusing; her deliberate use of her own image as a form of marketing, however, is illustrative of the kinds of developments in portraiture that were taking place throughout the Elizabethan period. TC & AO

PROVENANCE (a)
Gifted by the Society of Antiquaries of Scotland in 2009.

PROVENANCE (b)
Purchased Christie's, 12 December 1986, lot 311.

LITERATURE
Scott-Elliot and Yeo 1990, pp.11–86; Yeo, 'Inglis, Esther (1570/71–1624)', *ODNB* 2004 (accessed online Dec. 2012); Cooper 2012, pp.193–6.

NOTE
1 Two other oil portraits are recorded at Harvard University (Cambridge, Mass.), dated 1606, and Kungliga Biblioteket (National Library of Sweden, Stockholm), dated 1612.

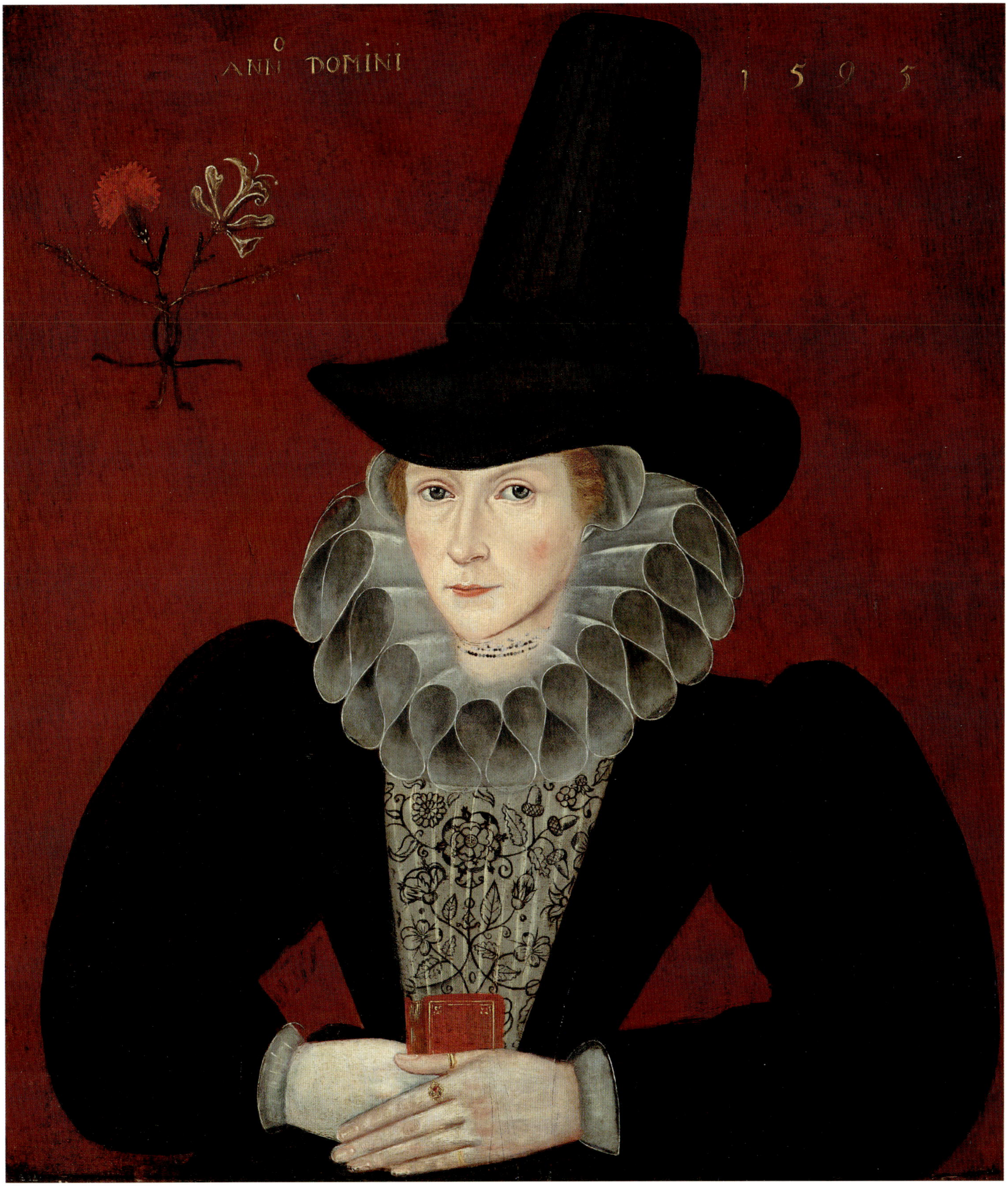

a

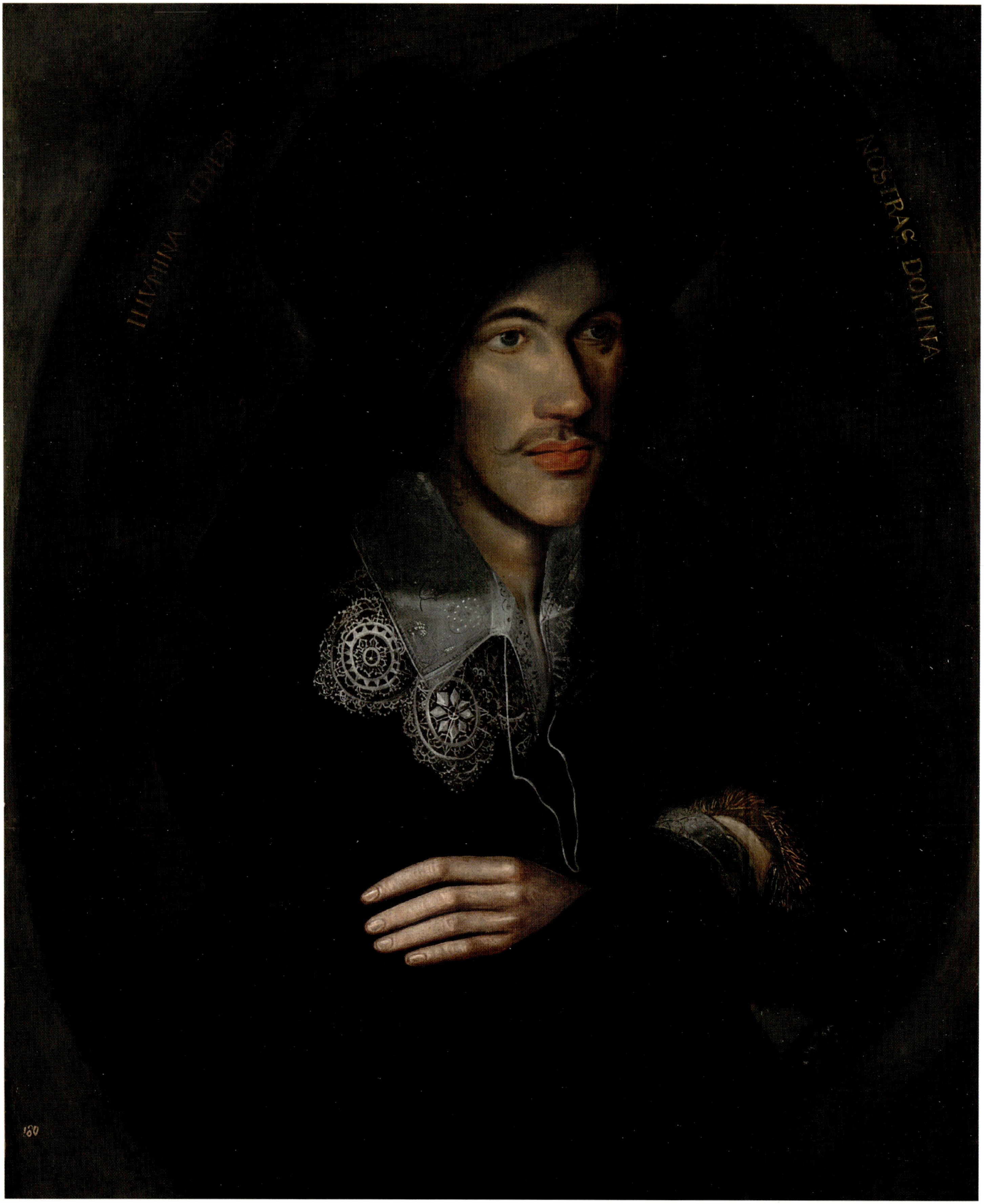
ILLVMINA TENEBR
NOSTRAS DOMINA

71

John Donne (1572–1631)

Unknown English artist, *c*.1596

Oil on panel, 771 × 625mm
Inscribed around the edge of the oval: *ILLUMINA TENEBR*[*AS*] / *NOSTRAS DOMINA* (Lady / or mistress / Lighten my darkness)
National Portrait Gallery, London (NPG 6790)

Many writers in sixteenth-century England were only published after their deaths, and although the writings of John Donne circulated in manuscript form among a small circle of admirers during his lifetime, the first published editions of his *Poems* appeared posthumously, in 1633 and 1635. Born a Catholic, Donne was educated at Oxford and trained in law at the Inns of Court. He was increasingly drawn to the Protestant faith, however, becoming an Anglican priest in 1615 and being appointed Dean of St Paul's in 1621.

This portrait dates from the 1590s, during which time the young Donne was enjoying an intensely creative period while at the Inns of Court, penning the numerous poems, satires and elegies for which he later became famous. This remarkable portrait is one of the earliest of an Elizabethan poet and presents Donne as a melancholic lover. The artist is unknown, but as a writer Donne would have been aware of the performative aspect of representation and must have been closely involved in determining the composition of this portrait.[1] Here he plays the role of a fashionable character type that was particularly associated with literary ability at this date.[2] With his long dark hair and sensuous lips, Donne is romantically handsome. His brooding facial expression and crossed arms, and the manner in which the black cloak is pulled around his body, suggest sulky disaffection with the world. The artful dishevelment of his fashionable, triple-layered lace collar further indicates his preoccupied state, and perhaps also functions as a pun on his name ('unDonne').

The painting relates specifically to the branch of melancholy associated with the infatuated lover, represented on the title page of Robert Burton's *The Anatomy of Melancholy* (1623) by 'Inamorato', a figure in a broad-brimmed, floppy hat.[3] Recent extensive conservation work on this portrait has shown that the highly unusual vertical grey/white brushstroke arising from Donne's exposed chest, just beneath his open shirt, is an original part of the picture. It has been suggested this might represent 'the vapour of melancholy' mentioned in his *Devotions Upon Emergent Occasions* (1623), in which he asks, '[W]hat have I done, either to breed, or to breath these vapors? They tell me it is my Melancholy; did I infuse, did I drinke in Melancholly into my selfe?'[4] Donne's right hand is gloved, but his left hand is bare and illuminated in such a manner that we cannot fail to note his long, elegant fingers; perhaps a reflection of the erotic plea to 'license my roving hands', found in his 'Elegy XIX', written at around the same time. The Latin inscription curving around the top of the painting is a deliberate misquotation of a Christian psalm, 'O Lady, Lighten our darkness'; it further implies that a woman is the source of Donne's melancholia, and suggests that the portrait was painted for a lover or close friend.[5]

Thomas Morton, Bishop of Durham, described seeing what is likely to have been this picture in the private rooms of a member of Lincoln's Inn, sometime between 1595 and Donne's death in 1631.[6] By this time, the portrait was in Donne's possession and his will stated that the picture 'taken in shadows' should be given to 'my honorable and faithful friend Mr Robert Karr of his Majesties Bedchamber' (Robert Ker, later 1st Earl of Ancrum, 1578–1654).[7]

TC & AO

PROVENANCE

Robert Ker, 1st Earl of Ancrum, by descent to the Marquess of Lothian; purchased by the National Portrait Gallery, 2006.

EXHIBITIONS

Searching for Shakespeare, London, National Portrait Gallery, 2006 (80), p.175–6; *Shakespeare: Staging the World*, London, British Museum, 2012 (26).

LITERATURE

Piper 1982, pp.24–31; Gartner Frost 1996, pp.95–125; Patterson 1997, pp.1–35; Edwards 2001, pp.38–40; *Searching for Shakespeare*, National Portrait Gallery, London, 2006, no. 80; Colclough, 'Donne, John (1572–1631)', *ODNB* 2004 (accessed online Nov. 2012); Bate and Thornton 2012, no. 26; Cooper 2012, pp.176–8; Davis, 'The Lothian Portrait of Donne', forthcoming.

NOTES

1 Gartner Frost 1996, p.95; Cooper 2012, p.171.
2 Lawrence Babb, *The Elizabethan Malady: A Study of Melancholia in English Literature from 1580 to 1642* (Michigan State College Press, East Lansing, 1951), pp.73–101.
3 Frost 1996, pp.96–8. Robert Burton, *The Anatomy of Melancholy*, ed. Holbrooke Jackson (The Folio Society, London, 2005).
4 Nick Davis, 'Melancholic Individuality and the Lothian Portrait of Donne', *American Notes and Queries*, vol. 26, issue 1, 2013, forthcoming.
5 Babb, op. cit.
6 Although the wording of the inscription differs, Morton's description of a portrait of Donne 'all envelloed [enveloped] with a darkish shadow, his face and features hardly discernable, with his ejaculation and wish written thereon: Domine illuminae tenebras meas [Lord, light my darkness]' is close enough to suggest that it was the present picture.
7 For a transcript of Donne's will, see Robert Cecil Bald, *John Donne: A Life* (Oxford University Press, Oxford, 1970), pp.563–7.

72

Francis Bacon, later Baron Verulam and Viscount St Alban (1561–1626)

Nicholas Hilliard, c.1578

Watercolour and bodycolour on vellum laid on card, 60 × 47mm
Inscribed along the left-hand edge: *1578 Si tabula daretur digna*;
and along the right-hand edge: *Animum mallem AE*[*tati*][s] *S*[*vae*]*.18*
(It would be preferable if a picture deserving of his mind could be brought about/At the age of 18)
National Portrait Gallery, London (NPG 6761)

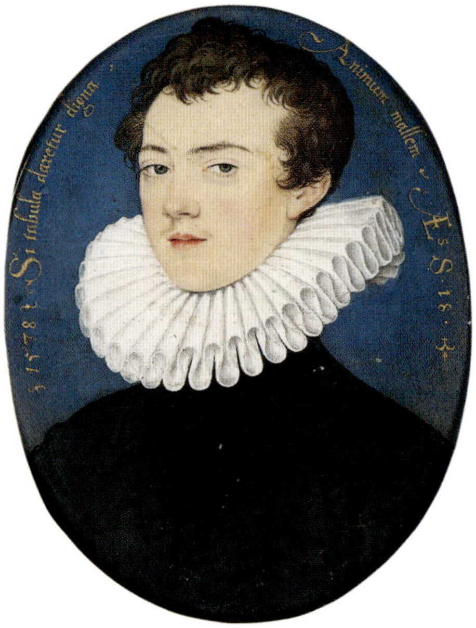

Francis Bacon was the younger son of Sir Nicholas Bacon (1510–79), Lord Keeper to Elizabeth I, and became one of the great intellectual figures of Elizabethan and Jacobean England. This miniature has long been identified as depicting Bacon, whose age matches that of the sitter and for whom the inscription would be particularly apt; by the age of eighteen he had spent over two years at Trinity College, Cambridge, and had entered the Inns of Court. Although all of Sir Nicholas's sons were admitted at Gray's Inn, only Francis took up the law as a profession, perhaps in part because his father had died suddenly while in the process of settling estates for him.

The miniature was painted when both Bacon and the artist Nicholas Hilliard were in France, having travelled there in the entourage of the English Ambassador to the French court, Sir Amias Paulet (*c*.1532–88). It exemplifies Hilliard's graphic and linear style, in which modelling was achieved through subtle hatching in the manner of engravers, as can be seen in the diagonal brushstrokes on the lower lip (detail b) that have been applied over the pale flesh paint in order to give the impression of light falling on the lips. CB

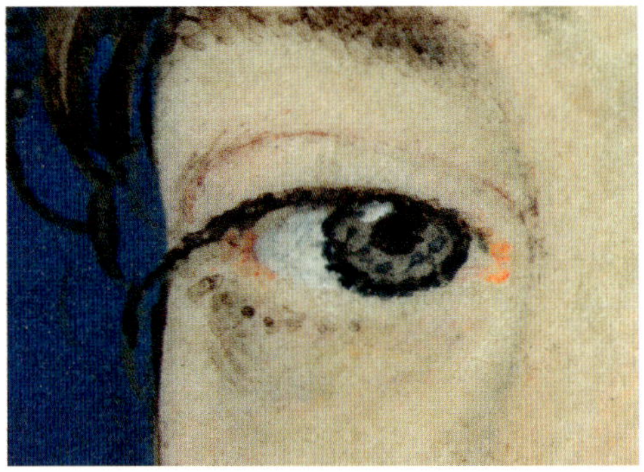

a

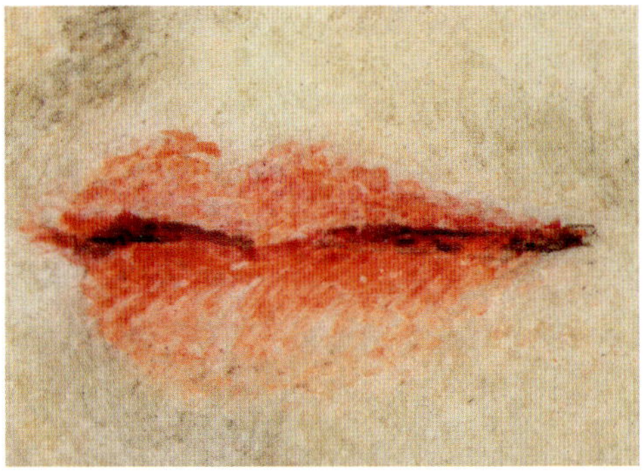

b

PROVENANCE

Said to have come from the French royal collection; James Edwards (1757–1816), 1803; John Adair Hawkins from at least 1825 until at least 1860; D.M. Currie sale, Christie's, 15 May 1903, lot 53, in which the picture was called *Portrait of a Young Gentleman* and bought by Col. H.E. Lindsay; thence by descent in the collection of the Dukes of Rutland; accepted in lieu of tax by H.M. Government and allocated to the National Portrait Gallery, 2006.

EXHIBITIONS

The Shakespeare Exhibition, Stratford-on-Avon, Edinburgh and London, 1964–5 (40); *Age of Shakespeare*, Manchester, Whitworth Art Gallery, 1964 (30); *Searching for Shakespeare*, London, National Portrait Gallery, and New Haven CT, Yale Center for British Art, 2006 (88).

LITERATURE

Blakiston 1949, p.169; Strong 1964, p.337.

73

Edwin Sandys (1519?–88) and his wife Cecily Wilford (d.1611)

Unknown English artist, after 1576

Oil on panel, 292 × 432mm
Inscribed in a later hand: Edwyn Sandys./.A:B:^{P}1576
Bishopthorpe Palace, York

This intimate double portrait of Archbishop Edwin Sandys and his second wife, Cecily Wilford, appears to be one of the earliest portraits of a Protestant bishop alongside his wife. It is recorded as having been painted in their lifetime for their second son, Sir Edwin Sandys, and is likely to have been intended for display within a domestic context.[1]

A zealous reformer, and Vice Chancellor of the University of Cambridge in the reign of Edward VI, Sandys was imprisoned under Mary I, escaped and fled to the continent. He returned to England on the day of Elizabeth I's coronation on 15 January 1559, and within a month had married Cecily, sister of his fellow exile Thomas Wilford. While disappointed in the Elizabethan settlement, in particular the use of vestments, Sandys continued to rise in the Church, becoming Bishop of London (against his wishes) in 1570, and succeeding Edmund Grindal as Archbishop of York in 1576. His appointments doubtless owed something to his close association with both William Cecil, Lord Burghley (cat. 19) and Robert Dudley, Earl of Leicester (cat. 18).

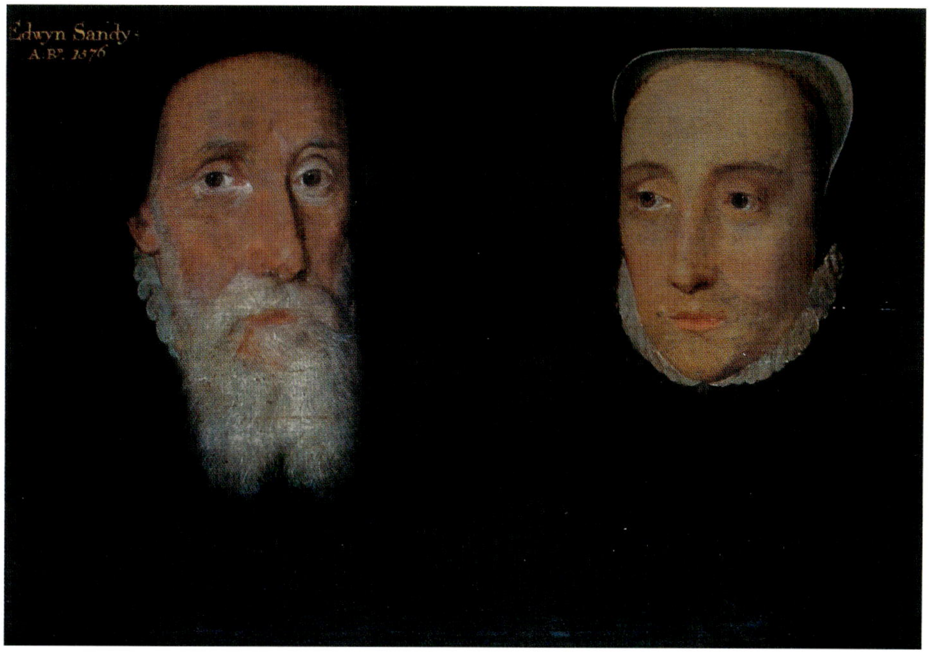

The close focus of the portrait on the couple's features and touching shoulders creates a sense of companionability, though both heads were copied from earlier individual likenesses.[2] Clerical marriage was reluctantly approved by Elizabeth I and the size of Sandys' family – the couple had nine children, seven sons and two daughters – was criticised by some as unpriestly. Sandys' enemy Sir John Bourne, who appreciated Cecily as 'faier, well nurtured, sober and demure',[3] nevertheless thought his lifestyle unsuitable for that of a bishop and complained that Church funds had been used to build a wash house and nursery. JE

PROVENANCE

Bishopthorpe Palace, York; presented by Jordan Sandys in 1721, having been bought from the Earl of Eglington; by descent from Eglington's widow.

LITERATURE

Strong 1969b, vol. 1, p.276 and vol. 2, pl. 543; Ingamells 1972; Ingamells 1981, p.346; Cooper 2012, pp.147–8.

NOTES

1 Note by Jordan Sandys, formerly on the verso, now in the Borthwick Institute, York. Two copies of this portrait are known, one at Ombersley Court, Worcestershire, and the other in the National Portrait Gallery (NPG 1268).

2 The representation of Edwin derives from a portrait dated 1571, when he was Bishop of London (private collection). For that of Cecily, see E.S. Sandys, *History of the Family of Sandys* (Barrow Printing Company, Barrow-in-Furness, 1930), p.88.

3 TNA/SP 12/28/38, quoted by Patrick Collinson, 'Sandys, Edwin (1519?–1588)', *ODNB* (Oxford University Press, Oxford, 2004), p.916 and Cooper 2012, p.147.

74

William Lovelace, 'Serjeant Lovelace' (c.1525/30–77)

Unknown English artist, dated 1576

Oil on panel, 660 × 524mm
Inscribed top right: *AN[N]° D[OMI]NI.1576*;
top left: *VIRTVTE DVCE* (lead by virtue)
Dulwich Picture Gallery, London (DPG 372)

'Serjeant' William Lovelace was a highly successful lawyer, a profession that expanded in the course of the Elizabethan period. Capable, hardworking and loyal, Lovelace is an example of one of the many men who entered the professions from the families of the minor Elizabethan gentry and whose fortunes flourished. He was admitted to Gray's Inn in 1549, called to the Bar in 1551, and in 1567 was appointed Serjeant-at-Law, a small elite order of barristers who held a monopoly on cases in several courts. A committed member of the Protestant establishment, he served alongside the Earl of Pembroke and Bishop Jewell on a major commission for the Establishment of Religion in 1559. He was also active as Member of Parliament for Canterbury in 1563, 1571 and 1572.

Lovelace is shown in his mid-forties, the year before his death, and his expression is serious, guarded and a little world-weary, as befits his role. He is portrayed as a professional man wearing his scarlet legal robes of office and holding a folded parchment document. Lovelace died a wealthy man with several properties in Kent, including a large house in Canterbury with its own small picture 'gallerie', investments in the East India Company, and a wardrobe of expensive doublets and fur cloaks. This portrait is perhaps the 'picture of hymself' recorded in his surviving probate inventory as hanging in the sparsely furnished bedroom in Canterbury.[1] The cause of Serjeant Lovelace's death on 23 March 1577 is unknown but must have been accidental as, in May of the same year, Henry Binneman bought a licence to print *The Brief Course of the Accidents of the Death of Mr. Serjeant Lovelace*, no copy of which has been found.[2] Buried in the nave of Canterbury Cathedral, Lovelace's tomb effigy (also dressed in lawyer's robes) was later destroyed.

The portrait is a rare surviving example of a type that must have been more common in the Elizabethan period. The artist is unknown, and the painting may have been produced by one of the many competent artists' studios in London that undertook both portraits and decorative work in the capital. This portrait has survived partly because it is one of a group of four generations of family portraits that were bequeathed to the Dulwich Picture Gallery in 1686.[3] TC & AO

PROVENANCE

By descent in the family to Richard Lovelace (1617–c.1657); William Cartwright collection; Cartwright bequest to Dulwich College, 1686.

EXHIBITIONS

Mr Cartwright's Pictures: A Seventeenth-Century Collection, London, Dulwich Picture Gallery, 1987 pp.35–9.

LITERATURE

Hall Pleasants 1920, pp.375–92; Waterfield 1987, pp.35–9; Beresford 1998, pp.275–7; Cooper 2012, pp.125–38.

NOTES

1 Cooper 2012, p.125.
2 N.M. Fuidge, 'LOVELACE, William [d.1577] of Bethersden, nr. Ashford and Canterbury, Kent', *The History of Parliament: The House of Commons 1558–1603*, ed. P.W. Hasler, 1981.
3 See Waterfield and Kalinsky 1987, p.35.

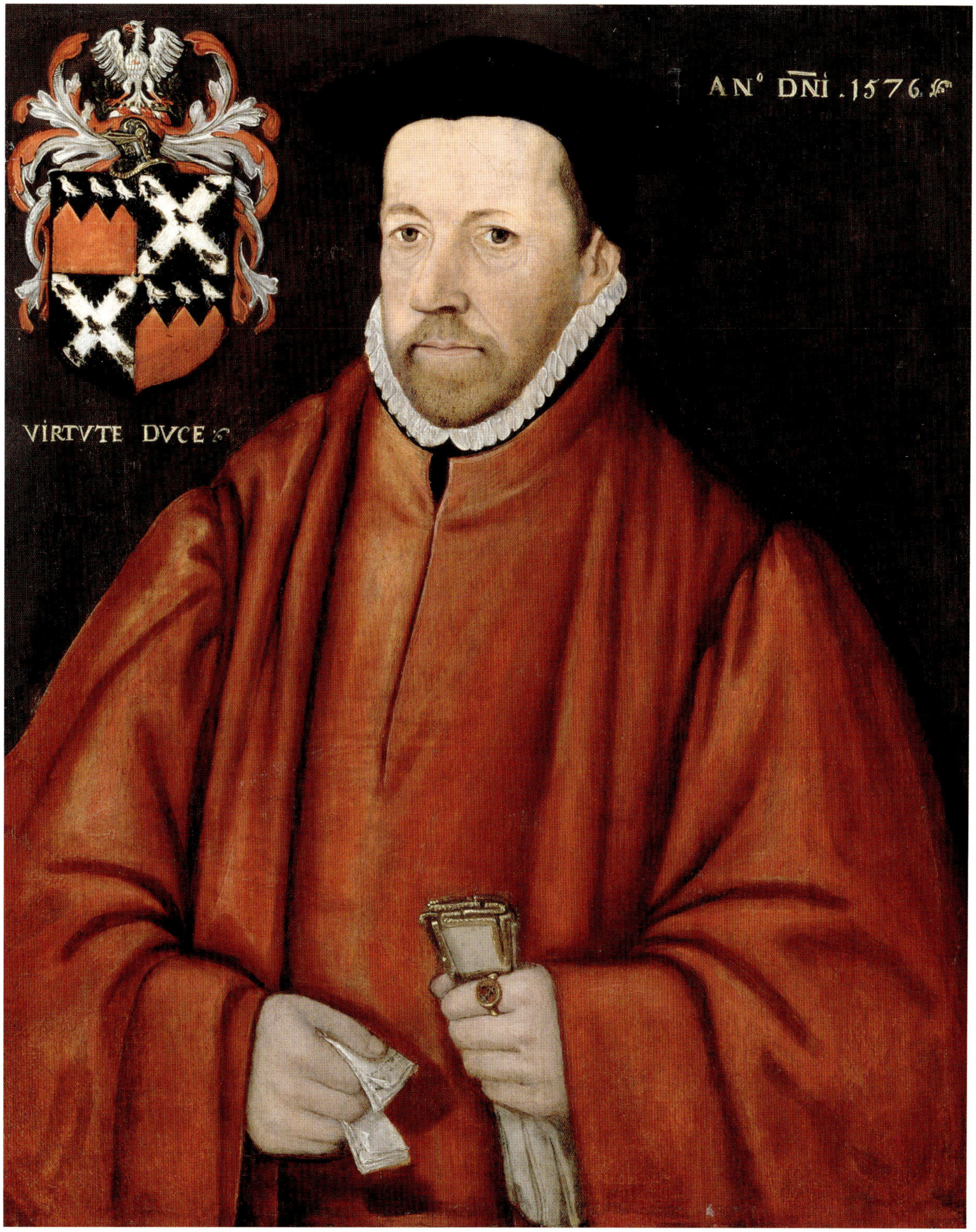

ANº DNI .1576.
VIRTVTE DVCE

75

Henry Birde (1517?–83)

Unknown artist, dated 1583

Oil on panel, 685 × 533mm
Inscribed: A[NN]O D[OMI]NI. *1583/AETATIS.SV[A]E. 66*;
in a different, later, hand: *Mr Henry Birde, Pr[ea]cher*
Norwich Castle Museum & Art Gallery (NWHCM: 1935.130.F)

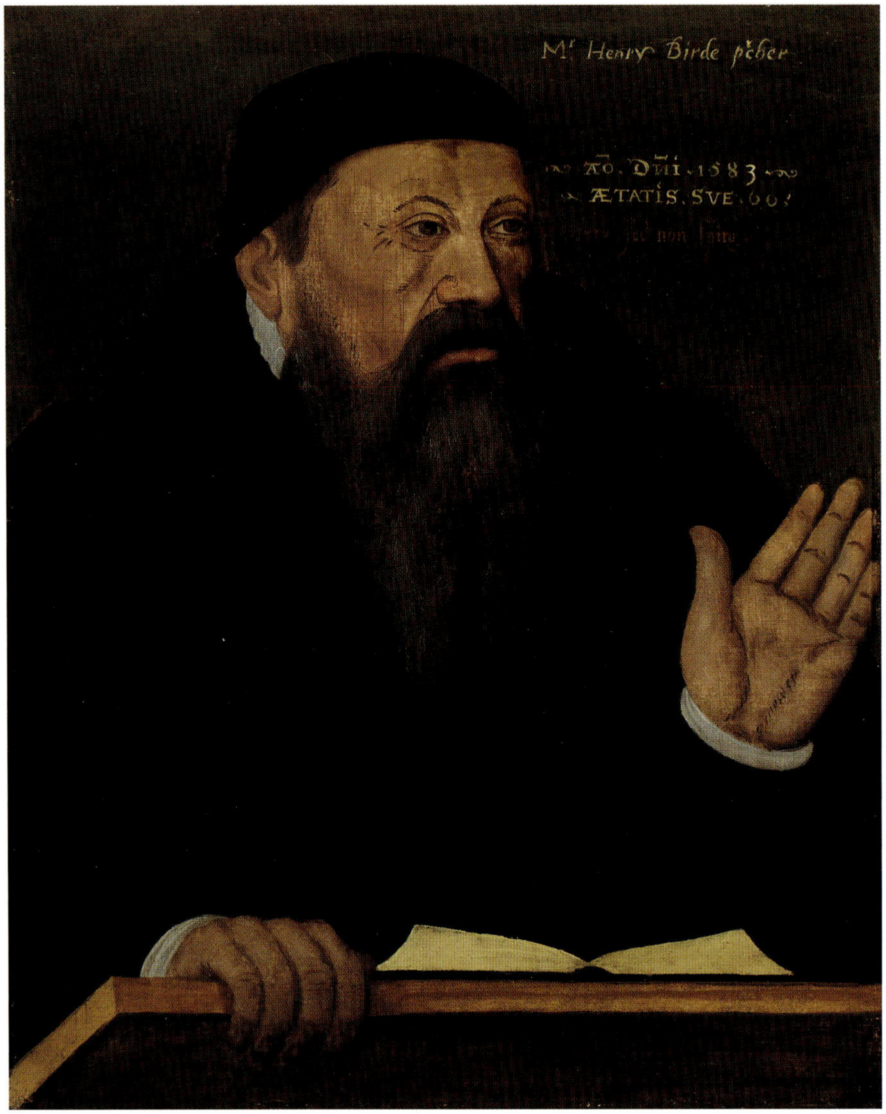

This extremely unusual provincial portrait almost certainly depicts the Norwich clergyman Henry Birde. Like Edwin Sandys (cat. 73), Birde had been exiled abroad during the reign of the Catholic queen Mary I.[1] The Master of a grammar school in the city of Norwich, Birde was 'a reader of the Divinity lecture' at the Cathedral church by 1568.[2] When the dean of the cathedral died in 1573, 'great suit was made' to award the deanery to Birde, who was considered 'a very godly man, and well learned'.[3] He was not successful, but in the same year Birde was included in a commission to examine Catholics in Norwich, along with several others including the Lord Keeper Sir Nicholas Bacon and John Parkhurst, the first Elizabethan Bishop of Norwich. Parkhurst later named Birde in his will as one of his executors.[4] Birde was also remembered among other 'faithfull workemen in the Lords busynes' in the will of alderman John Aldriche (or Aldricke).[5]

The portrait presents him aged sixty-six, in the year of his death. He is shown at a lectern with a book before him, in the act of preaching. One arm is 'outstretched with his palm facing upward as if in speech, and the other clutching the lectern as if to steady his oratory.'[6] The motto 'Spero sed non Spiro' appears to be a play on Cicero's *Dim Spero Spiro* (While I breathe, I hope). Birde was survived by his wife Alice, three sons and one daughter. JE

PROVENANCE

Recorded in the hall of Ridlesworth Rectory, Norfolk, 1805; with the Buxton family by the early twentieth century and presented by Maude Buxton in 1935 to Norwich Castle Museum.

LITERATURE

'Hundred of Giltcross: Ridlesworth', 1805, pp.274–84; Cooper 2012, pp.149–50.

NOTES

1 The escape of 'maister Henrye birde dwelling in Norwich' to avoid persecution is noted in the 1563 edition of John Foxe's *Actes and Monuments*, Book 5, p.1678.

2 NRO/DCN 47/1, fol.396r.

3 Augustus Jessop, *One Generation of a Norfolk House: a contribution to Elizabethan history* (Miller and Leavins, Norwich, 1878), p.47.

4 Ralph Houlbrooke (ed.), *The Letter Book of John Parkhurst, Bishop of Norwich*, Norfolk Record Society, xliii, 1974 and 1975, pp.53, 214–15.

5 TNA/PROB 11/64/302, fol.208r, will of John Aldricke, proved in 1582. Quoted in Matthew Reynolds, *Godly Reformers and their Opponents in Early Modern England, Religion in Norwich c.1560–1643* (Boydell Press, Woodbridge, Suffolk, 2005), p.89.

6 Cooper 2012, p.149.

76

Gregory Martin (1542?–82)

Unknown artist, dated 1573

Oil on panel, 210 × 150mm
Inscribed: *G M / AN[NO DOMINI].AETATIS[SUAE]/1573/31*
St John's College, Oxford

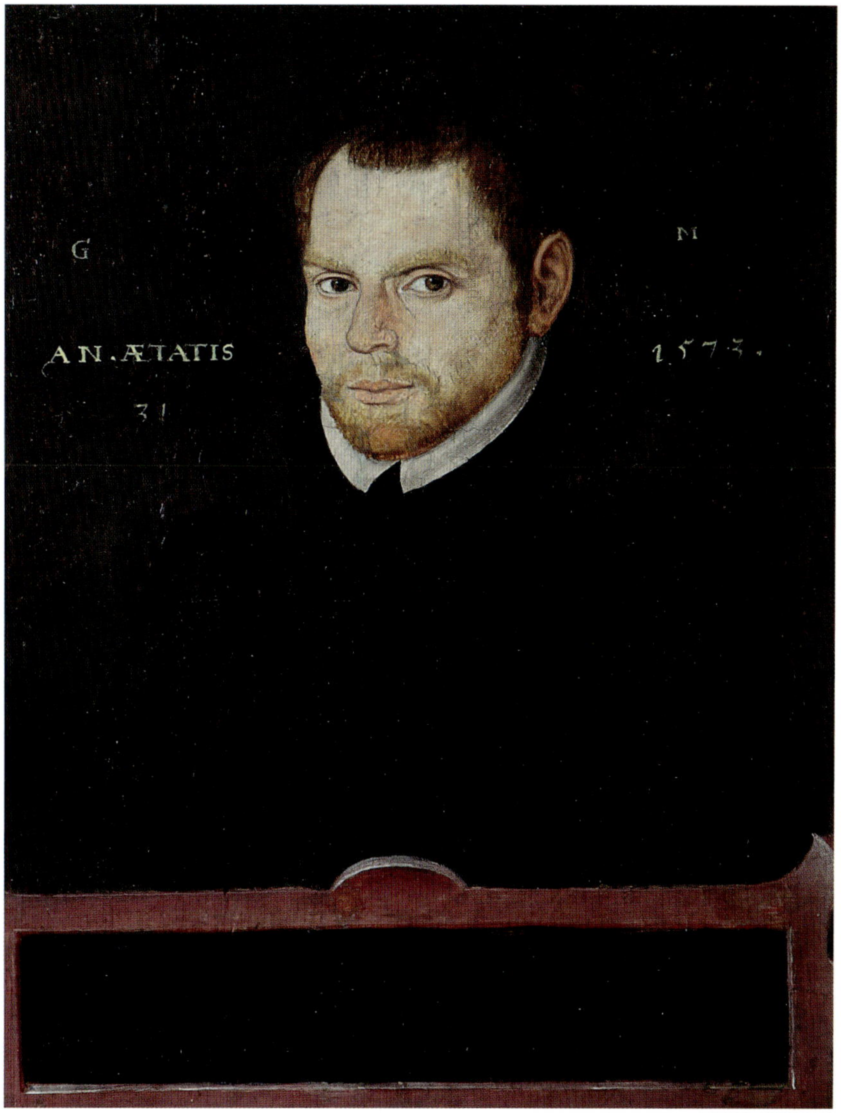

This small panel depicts the Catholic priest Gregory Martin, chiefly remembered today for translating the Catholic Bible into English. His age is given here as thirty-one, making 1542 the likely year of his otherwise unrecorded birth. One of the original scholars of St John's College, Oxford, Martin was an exact contemporary of Edmund Campion, the English Roman Catholic Jesuit priest and martyr. Having resigned his fellowship at St John's in December 1568, he joined the household of Thomas Howard, Duke of Norfolk (cat. 17a), as tutor to his sons, one of whom was Philip Howard, later Earl of Arundel. Within a year the Duke was arrested on suspicion of treason, the Catholic education of his sons one of the many criticisms levelled against him, and Martin fled to the newly founded English College at Douai in France.

Martin's ordination to the priesthood, which took place in Brussels on 21 March 1573, is likely to have been the occasion for this portrait. A second, almost identical, contemporary version of this portrait (by another artist) is in the collection of the Duke of Norfolk.[1] The existence of two such closely related portraits suggests that others may have once existed, perhaps intended as gifts for family, friends or sympathisers. The small scale would have allowed this work to be easily, and discreetly, transported. The purpose of the empty cartouche at the base is unknown, but may have originally been designed to include celebratory text.

Images of Catholic priests may have circulated in England but would have been potentially incriminating objects. There is nothing in this portrait to indicate the religion of the sitter, shown in plain clerical or academic dress and identified by his initials rather than a full inscription.[2] In his *A Treatise of Schisme* (1578) Martin considered the difficulties of English Catholics under Elizabeth I. He exhorted them to behave like Judith in refusing to dine with Holofernes and 'to abstaine altogether from heretical Conventicles'. When a new edition of the work was printed in England in 1584 this appeal was interpreted as inviting the assassination of the Queen and the printer, William Carter, was executed. JE

PROVENANCE
Purchased by Sir Alec Martin from Lewis & Simmons before 1937; presented to St John's College, Oxford, by Sir Alec and Lady Martin through the Art Fund, 1940.

EXHIBITIONS
On loan to the Burlington Fine Arts Club, London, 1937–8.

LITERATURE
Cooper 2012, pp.148–9.

NOTES
1 The portrait was acquired between 1861 and 1890, in which year it is recorded as being lent to a Tudor Exhibition at the New Gallery in London. It first appears in inventories of the collection in 1917. I am grateful to Dr John Martin Robinson for access to both the portrait and the archives at Arundel Castle.
2 Cooper 2012, p.148.

77

The Holie Bible (or *Bishops' Bible*)

Printed by Richarde Jugge, London, published 1568

The Bodleian Libraries, University of Oxford (Bib. Eng. 1568 b.1)

After the Reformation, there was rapid growth in the sales of Bibles in English, leading to a number of new translations. The illegal Tyndale Bible was imported on a large scale in the 1520s, despite the risks importers and readers both took. After Elizabeth I's accession in 1558, Bibles could be sold without fear, which led to several different translations each with their own emphasis. The Geneva Bible (1560) was produced by the more radical Protestants, who had been exiled in Mary I's reign, and included a series of marginal notes designed to direct the reader towards a belief in simplicity of worship, away from ceremonial forms; a non-hierarchical church structure; emphasis on Bible reading; and implacable opposition to Catholicism. This became the best-selling Bible in the late sixteenth and early seventeenth century. It is popularly known as the 'breeches' Bible for its rather charming interpretation of the consequences of the Fall: 'When the eyes of them [Adam and Eve] were opened, and they knewe that they were naked, they sewed figge leaves together, and made themselues breeches' (Genesis 3:7).

This Bible, known as the Bishops' Bible, was published as a response to the Geneva Bible, and was designed by Elizabeth I's bishops to defend a more traditional understanding of the Church as an institution and the relationship between established authority and the people. Like the Geneva Bible, it relied heavily on William Tyndale's translation, as does the 1611 Authorised Version, which was based on the Bishops' Bible, even though the latter is now regarded as a rather wordy, careless and often misleading translation. There are no marginal notes to direct the reader's interpretation, but there are 124 illustrations. It is often asserted that Protestants were much less visual than Catholics in their religious practice, but evidence shows that Protestants were extremely fond of images and pictures to aid worship, placing many at key places in their houses, and it is clear that the Bishops' Bible recognises this aspect of religious devotion.

The pages shown here depict the story of Samson. On the left, Delilah is cutting his hair and so depriving him of his superhuman strength. On the right, we see the shattered pillars in the temple after Samson has pushed them apart to destroy the building, the Philistines forgetting that even though he was blinded, Samson would be dangerous when his hair had grown back. The images serve as a warning against complacency, because the agents of God always find a way to carry out his will and the heathen can never triumph. Both the image and its border were engraved by Virgil Solis (1514–62), a prolific German draughtsman and book illustrator. His monogram can be seen in the lower left corner of the image of Samson and Delilah.[1] AH

NOTE

1 See Hollstein's *German Engravings, Etchings and Woodcuts 1400–1700* (Sound and Vision Publishers, Ouderkerk aan den Ijssel, Netherlands, 2006), LXVI, pp.187–8 and pp.212–13, LXVII, p.54.

13 They aunswered him, saying: No,
but we will bynde thee, & (d) delyuer thee
vnto their handes: but we wyll not
kyll thee. And they bounde hym with
two new cordes, and brought him from
the rocke.

(d) whom god had appointed to be their delyuerer from the yoke of the Philistines.

C
14 And when he came to Lehi, the Phi-
listines showted agaynst him: And the
spirite of the Lord came vpon him, and
the cordes that were vpon his armes,
became as flaxe that was burnt with
fire, for the bandes loosed from of his
handes.
15 And he founde a (e) newe iawe bone
of an Asse, & put foorth his hande, and
caught it, and slue a thousande men
therwith.

(e) That is, of an asse lately dead.

16 And Samson sayde: With the iawe
of an Asse, heapes vpon heapes: with
the iawe of an Asse haue I slayne a
thousande men.
17 And when he had left speakyng, he
cast away the iawe bone out of his
hande, and called the place (f) Ramath
Lehi.
18 And he was sore a thyrst, and called on
the Lord, and sayde: Thou hast geuen
this great victory in the hande of thy
seruaunt: and nowe I must dye for
thirst, and fall into the handes of the vn-
circumcised.
19 But God brake a great tooth that was
in the iawe, & there came water ther-
out, and when he had drunke, his spi-
rite came agayne, & he was refreshed:
wherfore the name thereof was called
vnto this day, The well of the caller
on: which came of the iawe.
20 And he iudged Israel in the dayes of
the Philistines, twentie yeres.

The.xvj.Chapter.

1. Samson carieth away the gates of Azzah. 18. He was deceaued by Delila. 30. He pulleth downe the house vpon the Philistines, and dyeth with them.

A 1 Then went Samson to
Azzah, and sawe there
an harlot, and went in
vnto her.
2 And it was tolde
the Azathites, saying:
Samson is come hy-
ther. And they went about, and layde a
wayte for hym there all nyght in the
gate of the citie, and were styll all the
nyght, saying: In the mornyng whan
it is day, we shall kyll hym.
3 And Samson toke his rest tyll myd-
nyght, and arose at mydnyght, and toke
the doores of the gate of the citie, and
the two postes, and rent them of with
the barre and all, and put them vppon
his shoulders, and caryed them vp to
the top of an hyll, that is before He-
bron.

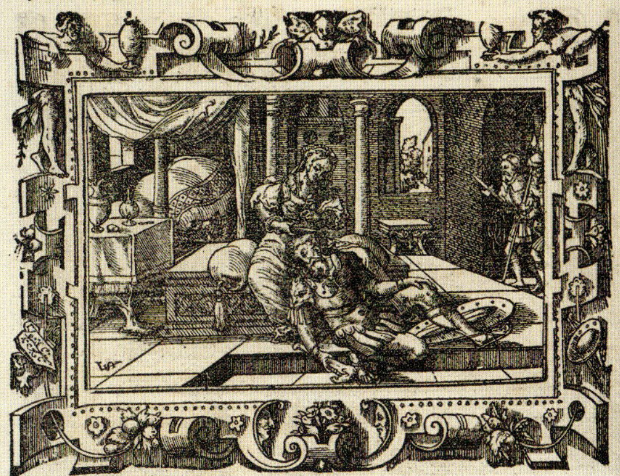

4 And after this, he loued a woman by
the * ryuer of Sorek, whose name was
Dalila.

* Or, playne.

5 Unto whom came the lordes of the
Philistines, and sayde vnto her: (b) Per-
swade him, and see wherin his great
strenght lyeth, and by what meanes we
may ouercome him, that we may bynde
him, and punishe hym: and euery one of
vs shall geue thee a leuen hundred sil-
uer lynges.

(b) Entice him by fayre meanes to tell wherein his strength consisteth.

6 And Dalila sayde to Samson: Oh, tell
me where thy great strength lyeth, and
how thou myghtest be bounde and
brought vnder.
B 7 Samson aunswered vnto her: Yf they
binde me with seuen greene wythes
that were neuer dryed, I shalbe weake,
and be as an other man.
8 And then the lordes of the Philistines
brought her seuen wythes that were
yet greene & neuer dryed, and she bound
hym therwith.
9 (Notwithstanding she had men lying
in wayte with her in the chaumbre):
And she said vnto him, The Philistines
be vpon thee Samson. And immediatly
he brake the cordes, as a stryng of towe
breaketh when it fealeth fire. And so
his strength was not knowen.
10 And Dalila sayde vnto Samson: See,
thou hast mocked me, and tolde me lies:
Now therfore tell me wherwith thou
myghtest be bounde.
11 He aunswered her: Yf they bynde me
with newe ropes that neuer were occu-
pied, I shall be weake, and be as an o-
ther man.
12 Dalila therfore toke newe ropes, and
bounde him therwith, and sayde vnto
him, The Philistines be vpō thee Sam-
son. (And there were lyers of wayte in
the chamber.) And he brake them from
of his armes, as they had ben but a
threade.
13 And Dalila sayde vnto Samson, Hy-
therto thou hast beguyled me, and tolde
me lyes: Yet tell me howe thou mygh-
test be bounde. He sayde vnto her: Yf
thou plattest the seuen lockes of my
head with the threades of the wooffe.
14 And she fastened it with a pynne, and C
sayde vnto him: The Philistines be
vpō thee Samson. And he awaked out
of his sleepe, and went away with the
pynne of the webbe and the wooffe.
15 And she sayde vnto him agayne: How
canst thou saye (c) I loue thee, when
thyne heart is not with me: Thou hast
mocked me this three tymes, and hast
not tolde me wherin thy great strength
lyeth.
16 And as she laye vpon hym with her
wordes, continually vexyng of him, his
soule was encumbred euē vnto ẏ death.
17 And so he tolde her all his heart, & said
vnto her: There neuer came rasor vpon
myne head, for I haue ben a Naza-
rite vnto God, euen from my mothers
wombe: Therfore when I am shauen,
my strength will go from me, & I shall
waxe weake, and be lyke all [other] men.

(c) For so thou vsest to saye, and wouldest haue me to beleue it.
(d) what wretched and miserable thraldome are they in, that can not refrayne the company of the harlot.

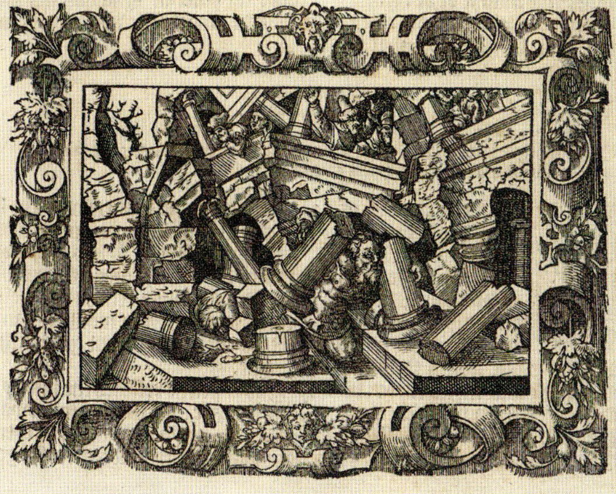

78

Personal Protestant Prayer Books

a **William Seres, *The Primer set furth at large, with many godly and deuoute Prayers***

William Seres for John Wayland, London, 1559
In a sixteenth-century English brown calf binding, tooled in gold, 190 × 140 × 30mm
The British Library, London (C.35.c.19.)

b **H. B. [Henry Bull], *Christian Prayers and Holie Mediations …***

Henry Bull, London, 1570
Bound in an embroidered red velvet with the crest of the Vaughan family, 155 × 100 × 34mm
The British Library, London (C.65k.10.)

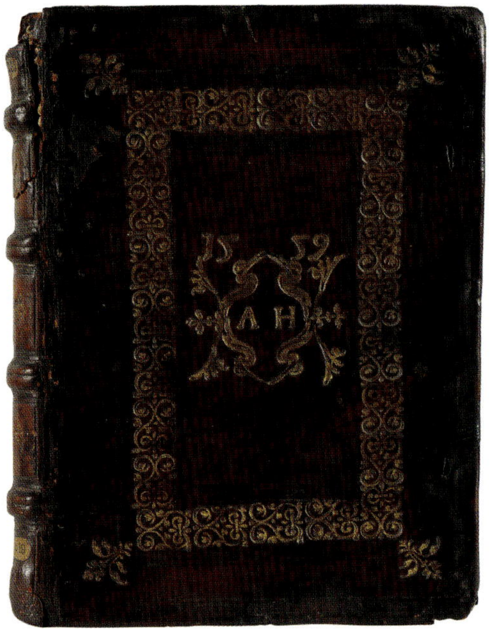

a

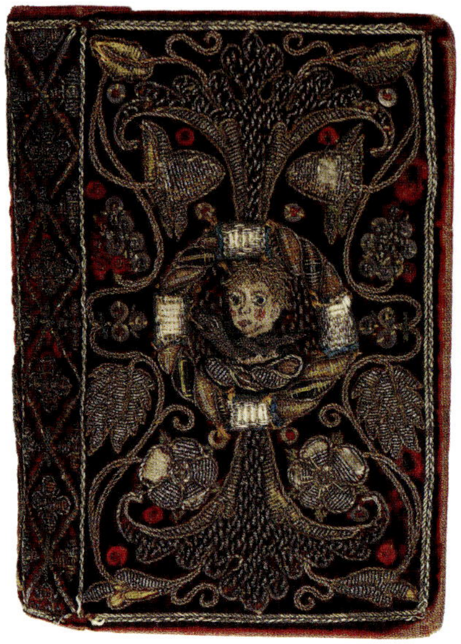

b

Prior to the Reformation, beautifully illustrated small manuals of prayers and Books of Hours, often in manuscript form, were popular with worshippers to facilitate moments of quiet reflection. After the Reformation, personal devotion became especially important and individual spirituality and a personal relationship with God, unmediated by the Church, assumed a greater significance. The nobility, gentry and citizens would often have their own books of prayers and meditations to inspire them to follow the path of virtue and righteousness. By the 1570s, a market for such works had developed and it was relatively easy for families to acquire their own printed books to foster and aid personal worship. As can be seen in the numerous portraits of this period (for example, Gawen Goodman, cat. 51, and Katheryn of Berain, cat. 48), sitters are often represented holding such devotional books.

The books shown here are popular works produced in the first half of Elizabeth I's reign when the Church of England had been re-established as a broad Protestant Church. *The Primer* played a similar role, containing a large collection of prayers in verse and prose for various occasions. Originally in Latin, English versions of such prayer collections were produced for the expanding Protestant audience. This copy was published in the first full year of Elizabeth's reign and from an inscription inside the front cover appears to have belonged to an alderman called 'Hewett', probably Sir William Hewett (1508–67), who became Mayor of London in 1559 and served as alderman from 1550 until 1567.[1]

Christian Prayers and Holie mediations is one of the first of such works, produced by Henry Bull in 1570. Bull was a committed Protestant who was exiled during the reign of Mary I (1553–8), returning armed with a spiritual knowledge that encompassed European religious models as well as native ones. His collection includes prayers from the reigns of Henry VIII and Edward VI, alongside many by European reformers, notably Philip Melancthon (1497–1560), Luther's collaborator and biographer, who helped shape the course of religious devotion in late sixteenth-century Europe. The book contains prayers for every occasion: when you have finished eating; when the sun goes down; when you feel the presence of God; and when repentance is necessary. It also includes instruction on 'the sober usage of the body' and how to make the body subject to the soul. The elaborate decorative binding displays what may be the crest of the Vaughan family, Sheriffs of Carmarthenshire during Elizabeth's reign. AH

NOTE

1 Alfred B. Beaven, *The Aldermen of the City of London* (E. Fisher and Company, London, 1913), vol. 1, p.82; vol. 2, pp.38, 173, 213).

79

Edward Lister (1557–1620)

Unknown English artist, c.1580s–90s

Oil on panel, 905 × 680mm
Royal College of Physicians, London

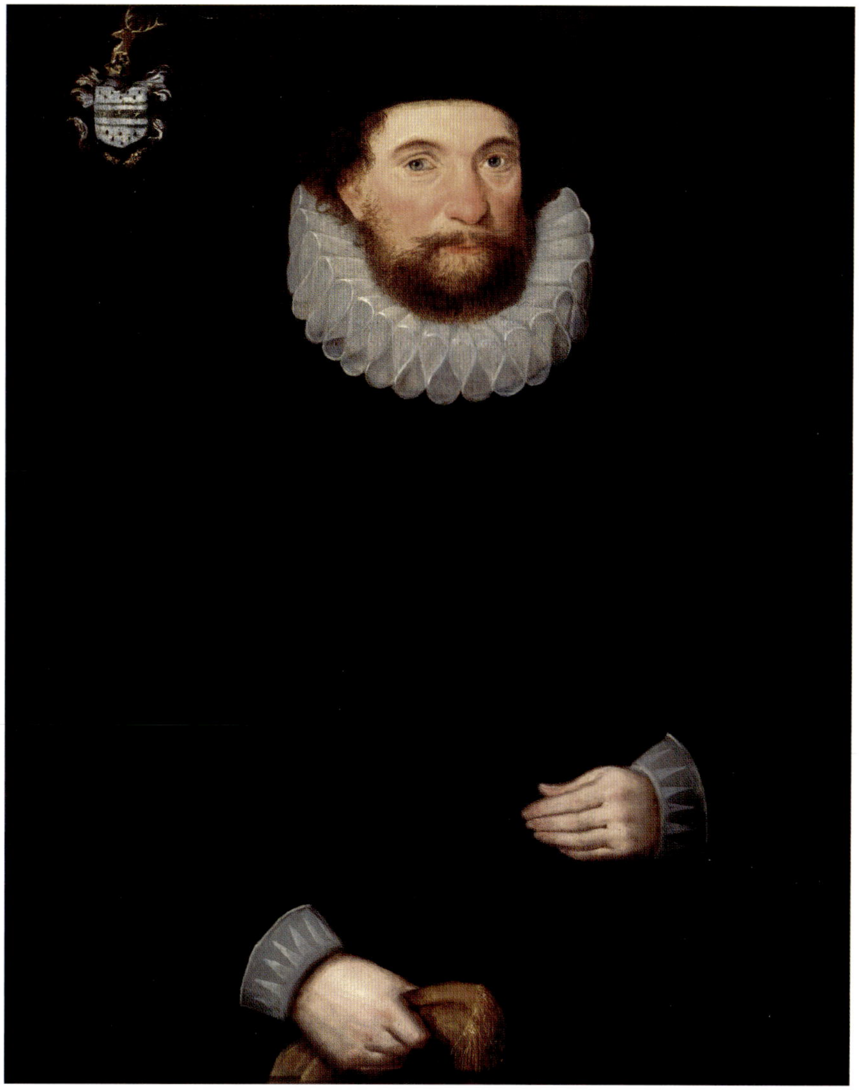

The subject of this portrait has been identified as Edward Lister, who served as Physician-in-Ordinary to both Elizabeth I and James I (from the coat of arms at the top left). The likeness shows a man of middling years with a pleasantly open face, sharp blue eyes, curly brown hair and a full beard. His clothing dates the picture to the late 1580s or 1590s, when he would have been in his thirties or early forties. Lister was only granted arms on 20 April 1602, making it possible that the arms were in use before the grant or that they were added in at a later date.[1] Although Lister's costume has suffered extensive repainting, the paint handling on his face is original and appears to capture his highly individualised features. Born in Wakefield, Yorkshire, to a distinguished medical family, Lister was educated at Eton and then at King's College, Cambridge, before being elected a Fellow of the College of Physicians in 1594. He held many offices in the College; chosen as Censor six times, he was Treasurer from 1612 to 1618. The role of Physician-in-Ordinary was a prestigious one. Caring for the monarch while diseases such as plague, sweating sickness, typhus, scurvy and leprosy swept through England would have been challenging, especially as medical personnel were expected to travel as part of the royal entourage. Lister is recorded as living in the parish of St Mary Aldermanbury, London, and he described himself in his will as 'Edward Lister of London Esquire, Doctor of Phisique', demonstrating that his professional identity was closely bound to his status as a gentleman.[2]

It is not clear why this portrait was commissioned, or where it originally hung; it may have been a personal commission, as it was not acquired by the College of Physicians until after 1926. On 27 February 1593 Lister married Anne Farmery, a doctor's daughter and the widow of a fellow collegian, in the parish church, and it is possible the picture was commissioned around this time. There is evidence that portraits were displayed at the College of Physicians, as in 1596 they announced a novel profit-making scheme: any member or 'noble person' could display his portrait or coat of arms on payment of £10. The premises in Amen Corner were destroyed in the Great Fire of London in 1666, and only two seventeenth-century portraits – those of Dr William Harvey and Dr Simeon Foxe (now lost) – were recorded as being saved.[3] TC & AO

PROVENANCE

Purchased by the Royal College of Physicians as a portrait of a Martin Lister (c.1638–1712) sometime after 1926.

LITERATURE

Wolstenholme and Piper 1964, pp.262–3; Lane Furdell 2001, pp.82–3; Moore, 'Lister, Edward (1557–1620)', rev. Rachel E. Davies, *ODNB* 2004 (accessed online Jan. 2013).

NOTES

1 Wolstenholme and Piper 1964, p.262.
2 Cooper 2012, p.159.
3 Wolstenholme and Piper 1964, preface.

80

John Banister (1532/3–99?) Delivering an Anatomy Lecture

Unknown artist, dated 1581

Oil on paper or oil on gouache and varnished, 338 × 432mm
Inscribed top left: *Anatomia Scientiae dux est / aditumque ad dei agnit*[*i*]*o* = / *nem pra*[*e*]*bet / Joh*[*a*]*nnes Banister Aetatis / sui Anno 48* (Anatomy is [considered] the chief of knowledge, and leads the way to understanding God. John Banister aged 48); top right: *Anno Domini 1581* (The year of the Lord 1581); below arms to left: *Tendit in ardua virtus* (The road to virtue is hard); below arms to right: *De prascientia* (On the foreknowledge of God)
University of Glasgow Library (MS Hunter 364 V 1.1.)

John Banister was recognised in his lifetime as one of the great Elizabethan surgeons. At a time when surgeons had a lower status than that of physicians, he championed the idea that the knowledge of medicine was essential for surgical training. He appears to have trained in his native Nottingham, and later at the University of Oxford, and he became a member of the Company of Barbers and Surgeons in 1572. He served as a surgeon to the army of the Earl of Warwick in 1563 and in the mid-1580s to the Earl of Leicester in the Netherlands. In 1593 he was licensed to practice both medicine and surgery by the College of Physicians following an insistent letter of recommendation from the Queen, who described him as 'our well beloved John Banister, Gent', who had 'of long time practiced the art of Chirurgerie in sundrie places of our realm' having done 'much good to many persons.'[1]

This rare and remarkable image shows Banister at the age of forty-eight in the process of delivering the Visceral anatomy lecture in 1581. Anatomy lectures, focusing on the dissection of different parts of the body, took place four times a year at Barber-Surgeons' Hall, and were attended by both members of the company and invited guests. The painting was originally part of a bound manuscript, which included numerous illustrations or 'tables', many of which survive, such as that describing the tools used for dissection shown with a dead pig and dog and a live monkey (fig. 31). In this group portrait, several of the men in attendance to the right have the character of portraits rather than generic figures and can be identified as the Masters of Anatomy, one holding a probe and the other a knife. To the far right, wearing a furred gown, is the Master of the Company, Robert Mudesley. Banister himself is shown wearing a black doublet and cloak, together with a gold pendant jewel with a drop pearl and five rings, indicating his wealth and status. The principal participants wear white protective armbands. In reality they would also have worn aprons, which may have been left out to show the status of their clothes. The open book to the left has been identified as a page from *De re anatomica* (Paris, 1559) by the Italian anatomist Realdo Colombo.[2] The coats of arms depicted in the book are the personal arms of the Banister family and the Company of Barbers and Surgeons, indicating that the volume was probably created for Banister's personal use, perhaps as a teaching tool. Banister published numerous treatises, which show that he treated a variety of diseases such as ulcers, pleurisy, syphilis and diseases of the eye. Many of his writings were compilations of standard European authorities, albeit translated into English and with clarifications and corrections.

TC

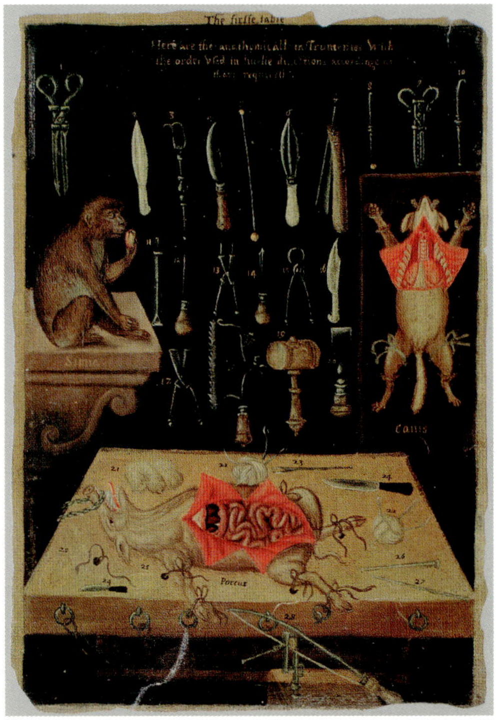

FIG. 31
From *Anatomical Tables* by John Banister
English School, 1500s

PROVENANCE

Hunterian Bequest, 1807.

LITERATURE

Power 1913, pp.6, 18–36; Buckland Wright 2008, pp.95–116.

NOTES

1 Buckland Wright 2008, p.105.
2 Ibid., p.98.

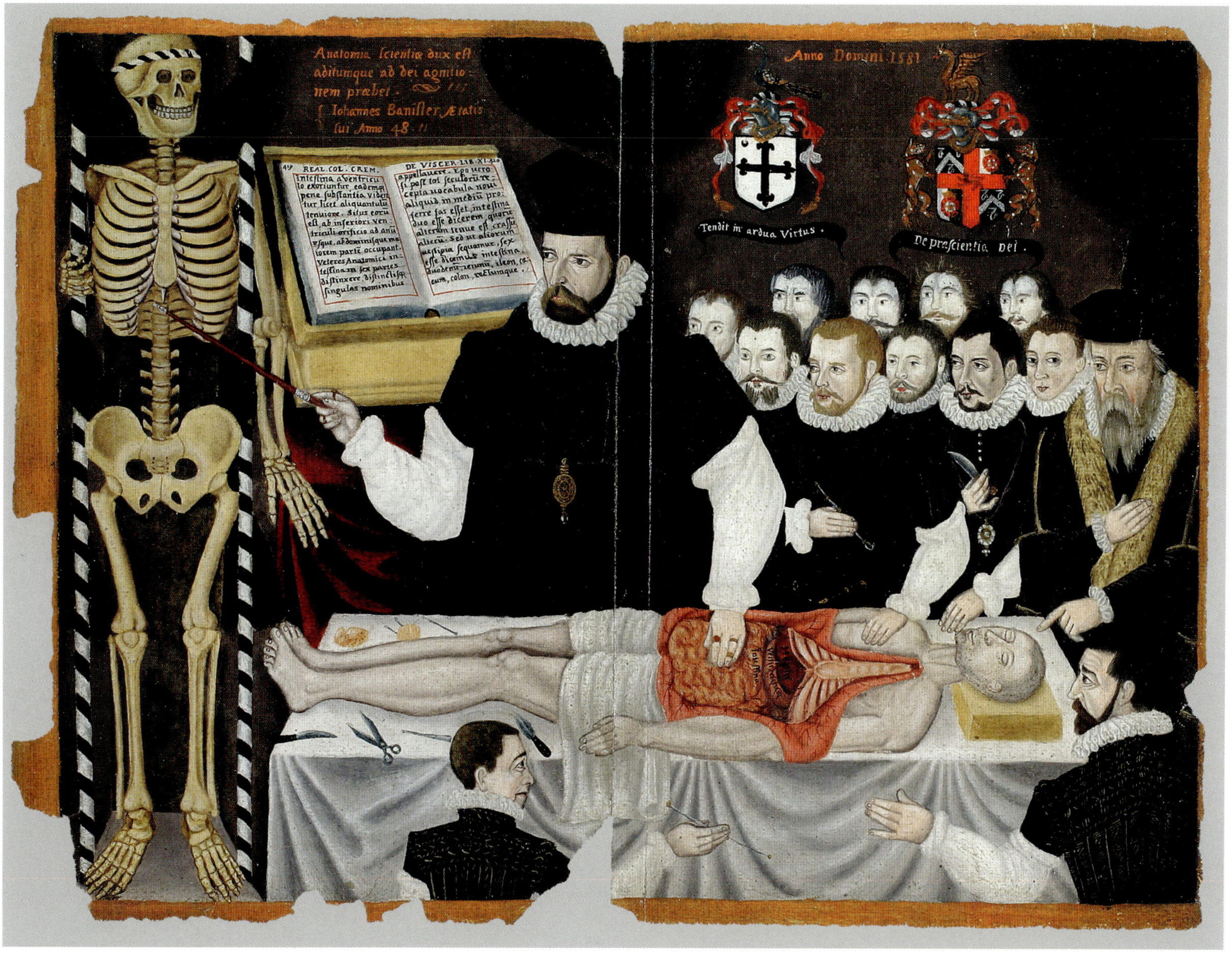
Anatomia scientiæ dux est aditumque ad dei agnitionem præbet.
Iohannes Banister Ætatis sui Anno 48.
Anno Domini 1581
REAL. COL. CREM.
DE VISCER. LIB. XI.
Tendit in ardua Virtus.
De prascientia Dei.

81

Song Books by Thomas Whithorne

a **Thomas Whithorne, *Songes for three, fower and fiue voyces***

John Day, London, 1571
140 × 183 × 10mm
The British Library, London (K.4.C.2)

b **Thomas Whithorne, *Cantus and Bassus of Duos, or Songs for two voices***

Thomas Este, London, 1590
140 × 205 × 8mm
The British Library, London (K.4.C.3)

There was considerable debate about the appropriate place of music in Elizabethan England: while some thought music essential to 'refresh the minde' and make one better able to bear labour, numerous critics influenced by ardent Protestant thought were highly critical of its influence.[1] Following the Reformation in England, however, church congregations were encouraged for the first time to sing new music during services, rather than the old liturgical chants. The Elizabethan period also saw a rise in amateur music popularised by the sale of ballad sheets – often on topical moralising subjects – as well as songbooks.

The composer, music and dancing master Thomas Whithorne (or Whythorne) (*c.*1528–96, fig. 15) was unusual in financing the publication of several secular songbooks of his own compositions, designed for middle-class audiences. Originally from Ilminster in Somerset, Whithorne studied at Magdalen College, Oxford and left without a degree, later becoming clerk to the writer John Heywood (1496/7 – in or after 1578), at which point he learned to play the virginals and lute, and began to write poetry. However, Whithorne is better known as the author of a remarkable early autobiography, written with phonetic spelling around 1576, which describes his early life as a servant among wealthy households, including Lord Ambrose Dudley and many unidentified patrons. His narrative describes numerous disappointments in both love and his professional life, and provides a wealth of detail about Elizabethan family lives and personal relationships.

These songbooks, dating from the beginning and end of Whithorne's career, were designed for domestic use, providing households without instruments with music to be sung in groups, as a type of early madrigal. His *Songes for three, fower, and fiue voyces* was produced in booklets for the separate voice parts, the part-book shown here being for the contratenor. His *Duos, or Songs for two voices* also includes a woodcut portrait of Whithorne, especially commissioned for this volume. The Latin inscription beneath translates as 'sharp but not too sharp', punning both on his name – with the word 'thorn' within it – and on the musical sharp sign. His music is rarely played and is little known today; it is not considered to rank alongside that of his better-known contemporaries including William Byrd, John Dowland and Thomas Tallis. TC

NOTE

1 John Milsom, 'Music Politics and Society', in *A Companion to Tudor Britain*, ed. Robert Tittler and Norman Jones (Oxford, Wiley Blackwell, 2004), pp.492–508, p.492 (quoting John Case, *The Praise of Musicke*, 1586).

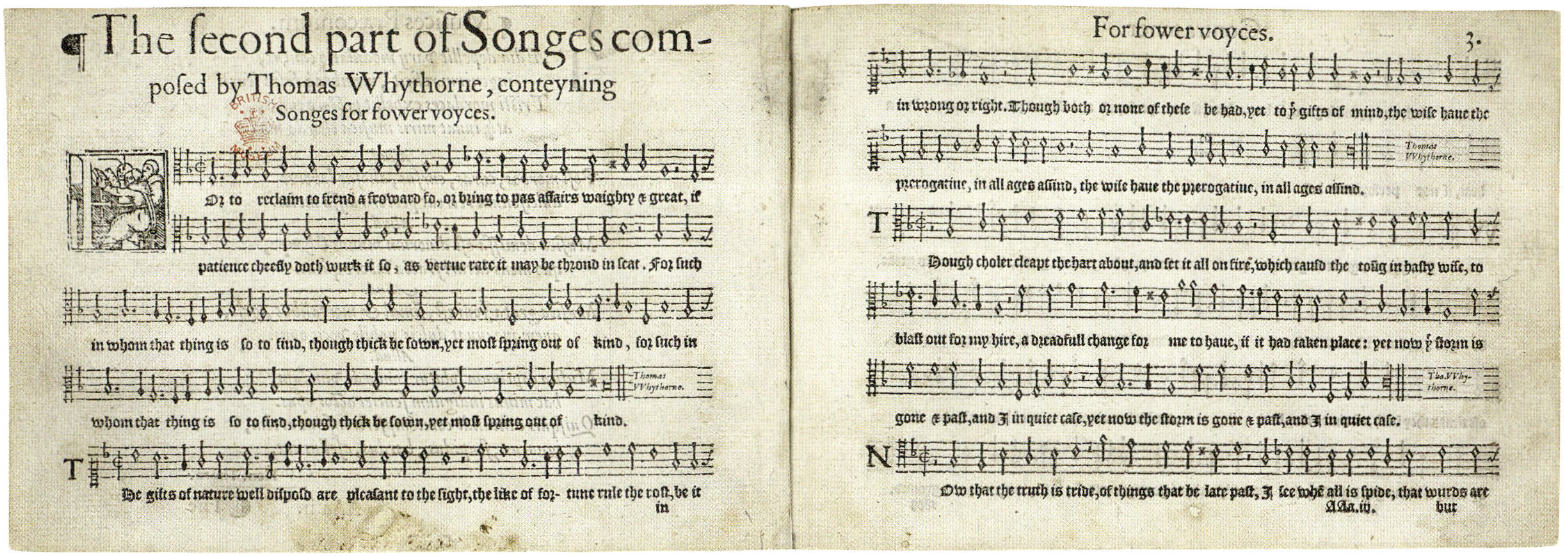

a

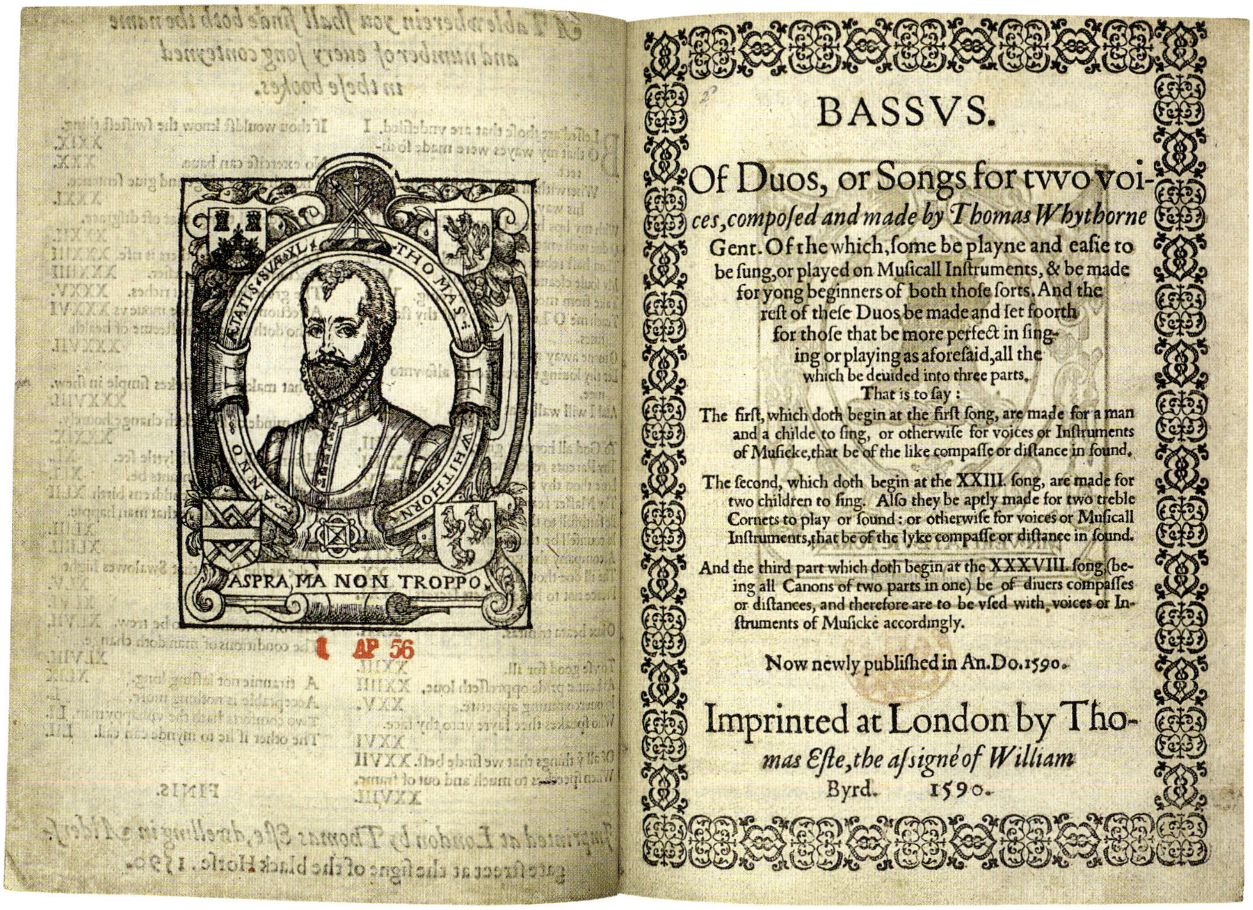

BASSVS.

Of Duos, or Songs for tvvo voices, *composed and made by Thomas Whythorne* Gent. Of the which, some be playne and easie to be sung, or played on Musicall Instruments, & be made for yong beginners of both those sorts. And the rest of these Duos be made and set foorth for those that be more perfect in singing or playing as aforesaid, all the which be deuided into three parts. That is to say:

The first, which doth begin at the first song, are made for a man and a childe to sing, or otherwise for voices or Instruments of Musicke, that be of the like compasse or distance in sound.

The second, which doth begin at the XXIII. song, are made for two children to sing. Also they be aptly made for two treble Cornets to play or sound: or otherwise for voices or Musicall Instruments, that be of the lyke compasse or distance in sound.

And the third part which doth begin at the XXXVIII. song (being all Canons of two parts in one) be of diuers compasses or distances, and therefore are to be vsed with, voices or Instruments of Musicke accordingly.

Now newly published in An. Do. 1590.

Imprinted at London by Thomas *Este, the assigné of William* Byrd. 1590.

b

82

a **John Gerard, *The Herball, or, A Generall Historie of Plantes***

John Norton, London, published 1597
With original hand colouring, 335 × 220mm
The Bodleian Libraries, University of Oxford (L.1.5.Med)

b **John Gerard (c.1545–1612)**

after an unknown artist
William Rogers, 1598
Line engraving, 186 × 149mm
National Portrait Gallery, London (NPG D2756)

John Gerard was a renowned herbalist and member of the Company of Barbers and Surgeons.[1] His *Herball* was his best-known work and became one of the most widely owned texts in the English language. It was dedicated to William Cecil, Lord Burghley (cat. 19), whose gardens in The Strand, London, and at Theobalds in Hertfordshire were designed under Gerard's supervision. The book was intended to set forth 'the description, place, time, names, nature, and vertues of all sorts of herbs for meate, medicine, or sweet-smelling use etc.' Gerard included plants from the New World, as well as from his own garden in Holborn, but in essence the text is an English translation of a highly popular herbal published in 1554 by the Flemish scholar Rembert Dodoen.

Both the 'virtues' and the 'hurts' are given for each plant where applicable. Some of the folklore contained in the recipes now seems extraordinary, such as the suggestion that the radish root, 'stamped with honey and the powder of a sheepes hart dried, causeth haire to grow in short space' (p.185), or that leeks dull the sight and cause 'troublesome and terrible dreams' (p.139). Others, such as the use of mint for pains of the head and stomach, we might recognise today. The beautiful peonies illustrated here, and found 'in our London gardens', had no special medicinal benefit but were valued for the delights they offered the senses.

This presentation edition was a gift from the Queen's publisher, John Norton, to the Bodleian in 1601. *The Herball* contains more than 1,800 woodcuts, most of which Norton bought in Frankfurt. They were individually coloured by hand to imitate the correct natural colours of the plants. The portrait of Gerard shown here formed the frontispiece to another, uncoloured, edition of *The Herball*. He is shown aged fifty-three holding the flower of the potato plant, which he was the first person to record in print in a plant catalogue of 1596. William Rogers (*fl.*1584–1604), regarded as one of the finest of early English engravers, was responsible both for engraving the portrait and designing the title page of the book. Sadly, both title page and portrait from the hand-coloured Bodleian edition have been stolen (fig. 32). JE

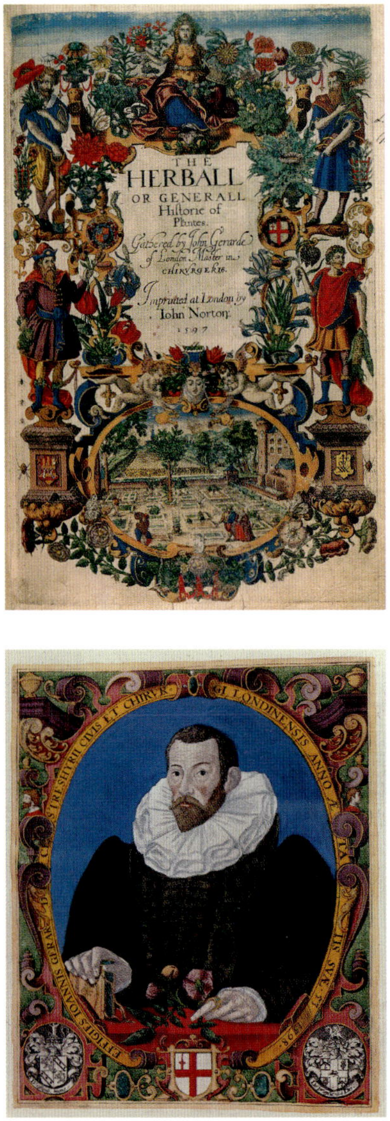

FIG. 32
Title page and portrait from *The Herball*, 1597.

PROVENANCE (a)
Purchased 1966 with the aid of the Friends of the National Libraries and the Pilgrim Trust.

PROVENANCE (b)
Acquired by the National Portrait Gallery, London from the Martin Collection, 1861.

NOTE
1 As the Barber-Surgeons' Company was known between 1540 and 1745.

and another called *Pæonia promiſcua ſeu neutra*, Baſtarde, Misbegotten, or neither of both, but as it were a plant participating of the male and female, one double Peionie with white flowers, and a fourth kinde bearing ſingle white flowers.

1 *Pæonia mas.*
Male Peionie.

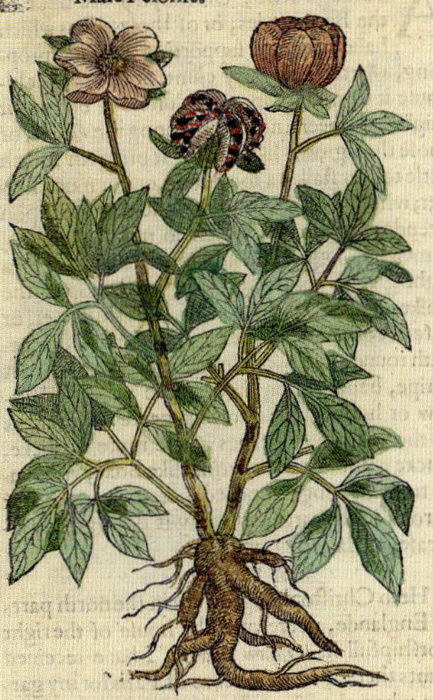

2 *Pæonia fœmina.*
The female Peionie.

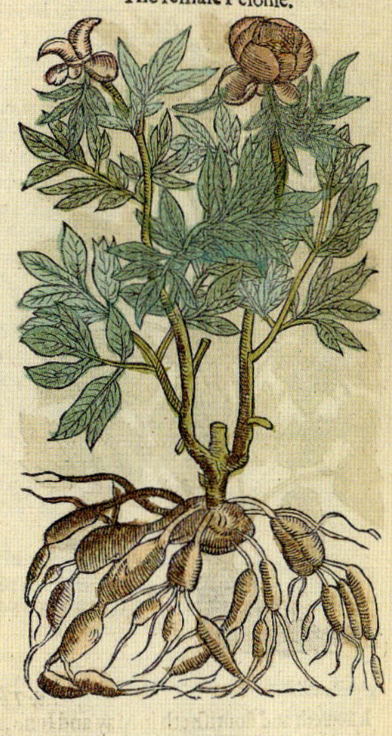

✻ The deſcription.

1 THe firſt kinde of Peionie (being the male, called *Pæonia mas*, in Engliſh male Peionie) hath thicke red ſtalkes a cubite long: the leaues be great and large, conſiſting of diuers leaues growing or ioined togither vpon one ſlender ſtem or ribbe, not much vnlike the leaues of the Walnut tree, both in faſhion and greatnes; at the top of the ſtalks grow faire large red flowers verie like roſes, hauing alſo in the midſt yellow threds or thrums, like them in the Roſe called *Anthera*; which being vaded and fallen away, there come in place three or fower great coddes or huskes which do open when they be ripe; the inner part of which cods are of a faire red colour, wherein is contained blacke ſhining and poliſhed ſeedes, as big as a Peaſe, and betweene euerie blacke ſeede is couched a red or crimſon ſeed, which is barren and emptie. The roote is thicke, great and tuberous, like vnto the common Peionie.

2 There is a kinde of Peionie, called of *Dodonæus Peonia fœmina prior*, of *L'Obelius Pæonia fœmina*, in Engliſh female Peionie, which is ſo well knowne vnto all that it needeth not any deſcription.

3 The thirde kinde of Peionie (which *Pena* ſetteth foorth vnder the name *Pæonia fœmina Polyanthos, Dodonæus Pæonia fœmina flos multiplex*, in Engliſh double Peionie) hath leaues, rootes, and flowers like the common female Peionie, ſaue that his leaues are not ſo much iagged, and are of a lighter greene colour: the rootes are thicker and more tuberous; and the flowers much greater, exceeding double, of a very deepe red colour, in ſhape and faſhion very like the great double Roſe of Prouence, but greater and more double.

4 There

4 There is found another ſort of the double Peionie not differing from the precedent in ſtalkes, leaues, or rootes: this plant bringeth foorth white flowers wherein conſiſteth the difference.

3 *Pæonia fœmina multiplex.*
Double red Peionie.

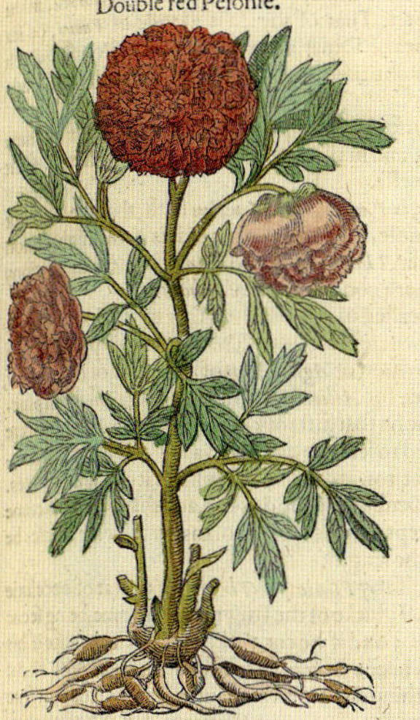

4 *Pæonia fœmina polyanthos flore albo.*
The double white Peionie.

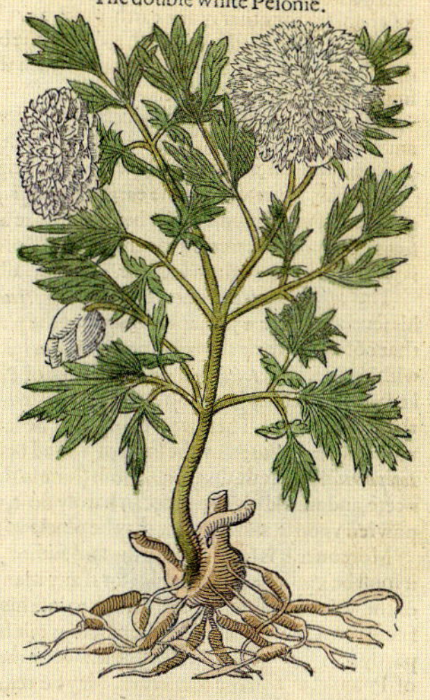

✻ The deſcription.

There is another kinde of Peionie (called of *Dodonæus Pæonia fœmina altera*, but of *Pena Pæonia Promiſcua ſeu neutra*: in Engliſh Maiden or Virgine Peionie) that is like vnto the common female Peionie, ſauing that his leaues and flowers are much ſmaller, and the ſtalkes ſhorter, and beareth red flowers, and ſeede alſo like the former.

We haue likewiſe in our London gardens another ſort bearing flowers of a pale whitiſh colour, very ſingle, reſembling the female wilde Peionie, in other reſpects like the double white Peionie.

✻ The place.

All the ſorts of Peionies do grow in our London gardens, except that double Peionie with white flowers, which we do expect from the lowe countries of Flaunders.

The male Peionie groweth wilde vpon a conie berrie in Betſome, being in the pariſh of Southfleete in Kent, two miles from Graueſend, and in the grounde ſometimes belonging to a Farmer there called *Iohn Bradley*.

✻ The time.

They flower in May, the ſeede is ripe in Iuly.

✻ The names.

The Peionie is called in Greeke παιονία: in Latine alſo *Pæonia*, and *Dulcifida*: in ſhops *Pionia*: in high Dutch Peonien blumen: in low Dutch Past bloemen: in French *Pinoine*: in Spaniſh *Roſa del monte*: in Engliſh Peionie: it hath alſo many baſtarde names, as *Roſa fatuina, Herba Caſta*, of ſome *Lunaris*, or *Lunaria Pæonia*: bicauſe it cureth thoſe that haue the falling ſicknes, whom moſt men do call *Lunaticos*, or Lunaticke. It is called *Idæus Dactylus*: which agreeth with the female Peionie,

a

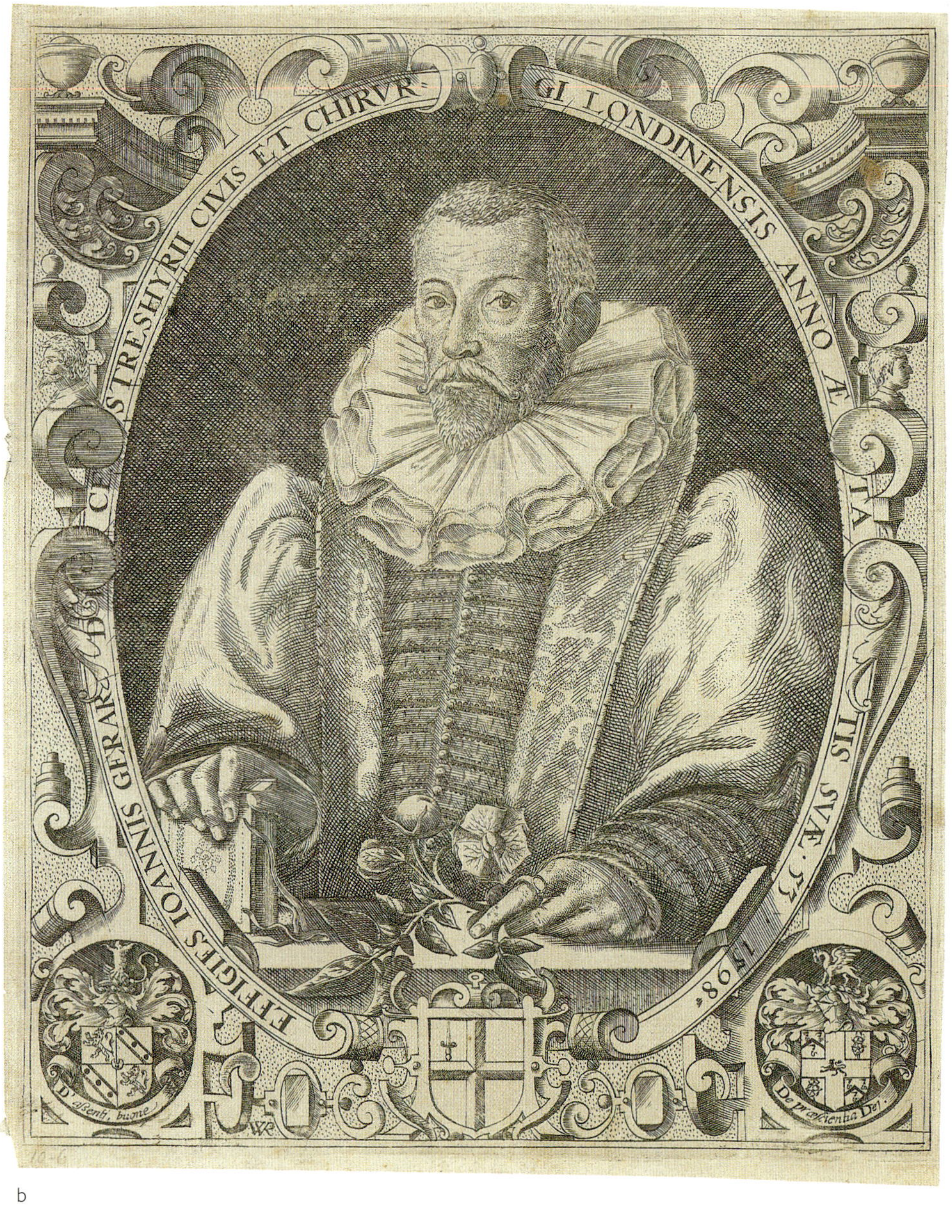
EFFIGIES IOANNIS GERAR
CESTRESHYRII CIVIS ET CHIRVR-
GI LONDINENSIS ANNO Æ
TA TIS SVÆ. 53
1598.
De Prœscientia Dei.

b

83

John Day (1521/2–84)

Unknown artist, dated 1562

Woodcut, 282 × 180mm
The British Museum, London (1896,1230.73)

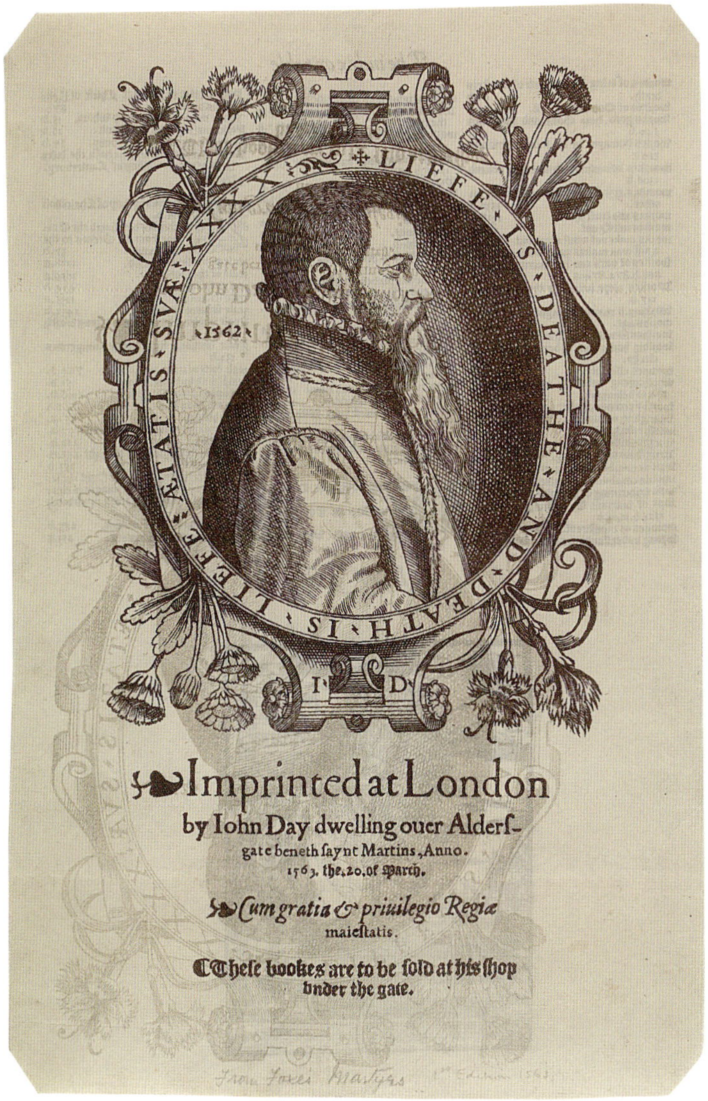

The reputation of the eminent printer John Day rests on his involvement in the largest and most ambitious publishing project ever undertaken in England, the production of John Foxe's *Acts and Monuments of the Church of England* – popularly known as the *Book of Martyrs*. Committed to the Protestant cause, Day was briefly imprisoned under Mary I, but flourished following the accession of Elizabeth I. In a period when English printing was still relatively under-developed in comparison to the European industry, Day's work was characterised by technical assurance and typographical sophistication, which may be attributed to his reliance on foreign workmen. Supplying England's growing reading public with affordable copies of popular, small-format evangelical books such as psalters and books known as alphabet primers or ABCs made Day wealthy, but it was his involvement in the *Book of Martyrs* that brought him fame.

First published in 1563, Foxe's *Book of Martyrs* drew together a wealth of contemporary testimonies on the persecution of Protestants under the Catholic Church. The book was officially sponsored from the outset; William Cecil (cat. 19) oversaw its production and by 1571 an order had been issued for it to be set up in every cathedral and in the houses of senior clergy. The book's significance was akin to that of the Bible, and its success ensured that a Protestant interpretation of the Reformation triumphed for centuries to come. Day was responsible for the striking appearance of the vast book, which was lavishly illustrated with fifty woodcuts designed in collaboration with Flemish artists.[1]

This portrait in profile is dated 1562, the year before the first publication of the *Book of Martyrs*, and was inserted at the end of the book, ensuring that Day's name would forever be associated with this ground-breaking work.[2] The woodcut records his age and includes the motto 'Life is death and death is life', reflecting on the importance of Christian salvation. AO

PROVENANCE

Acquired by the British Museum, 1896.

LITERATURE

King 2006; Evenden 2008; Evenden and Freeman 2011.

NOTES

1 King 2006, pp.162–95.
2 The date of the portrait has led scholars to argue that Day was reluctant to commission any images until printing was about to begin (Evenden and Freeman 2011, p.114).

and lyke order for hir Children, and goodes in effect
as followeth viz She beinge sicke and dowbtinge that
she shoulde not lyve sent for william Holland of the
same Towne one of the pure maisters of her maiesties
navie who came to her, And then she saide vnto him
in effect viz she desiered him to be a father to her
children till the cominge home of her saide husband from
beyond the Seas, And she desiered the saide
william Holland that yf god shoulde call her saide
husbande oute of this worlde before his returne
home, Then that he the saide Holland woulde be
their saide children governour till they come to age
And further she desiered & willed the saide willi
Holland to receave home Arretries the
some of six score poundes due by obligacon att
michaellmas then next followinge with all other
goodes and dettes belonginge to her saide
husband or her, And to kepe and dispose them
to the vse of her children yf her husbande did not
returne home Beinge then present

6 WORKING PEOPLE AND THE POOR

The vast majority of the population of England and Wales in the 1500s were, of course, working people, but few portraits or images of such men and women were ever produced.

Average life expectancy in the Elizabethan period was less than forty years, and high infant mortality rates indicate that many families would have lost children at an early age through illnesses or poverty. Years of bad harvests, particularly in the 1590s, caused widespread hardship including famine in some parts of the country. However, social tensions were eased by shared Christian values. Although there was a rise in private chapels at this period, the nature of parish life meant that in communities across the country the rich and poor alike usually worshipped at church together. Charity was an essential Christian duty and many of those who could afford to do so regularly gave to the poor.

Some of the most advantaged among this group were those who gained citizenship in towns, following the completion of apprenticeships in a recognised skill or craft such as carpentry, ironmongery and masonry, or the preparation and sale of goods or groceries, which were regulated by guilds. Citizenship brought key economic and political rights in towns, as well as access to schooling and support in old age. Although debt could be a problem, most of this group would have led lives free from poverty.

Far less visible in history are the labouring poor, men and women who washed clothes, worked the land, fished the seas, cleaned the streets and carried water, or those who fought in the ranks of the army or navy. Over the course of Elizabeth I's reign the government made repeated attempts to improve local provision for the poor and urban censuses began to be undertaken to help assess local needs. However, there were also harsh penalties for vagrancy and refusal to work for lawful wages could result in being whipped.

84

Sea-Going Clothing

England, c.1590–1650

Linen, 1380 × 750mm
Museum of London (53.101/1)

This remarkable ensemble may represent the survival of a rare early outfit for going to sea. It is very difficult to date, given the lack of anything else with which to compare it. In Cesare Vecellio's costume book *Habiti Antichi et Moderni di tutto il Mondo* (1598), an illustration of an English sailor shows a similar outfit with loose-fitting, pull-over upper garment and full breeches (fig. 33). Both of these items have been sturdily and repeatedly patched and mended with a variety of materials, and were clearly heavily worn. Spots of tar suggest encounters with the rigging of any one of a variety of boats or vessels.

There was no official uniform for ordinary seamen in the Navy until 1857 and while eighteenth-century sea-going clothing was particularly distinctive, there are very few descriptions of what fishermen and sailors wore before the 1650s.[1] It is assumed that they wore variations of everyday dress – as warm and waterproof as natural materials could be made, amply cut to allow for active movement, but not so loose as to entangle in any rigging or equipment. The full breeches may be what was referred to in the late sixteenth century as 'slops' or 'galligaskins'.[2] By the 1650s, sailors' 'slops' mirrored the fashionable loose, petticoat breeches that all men wore, so this ensemble is likely to be earlier in date.

Information from wills and probate inventories of Elizabethan 'mariners' confirms the use of special clothing for the sea. For example, in his will dated 1576, 'master and maryner' Edmund Shaldforthe of Newcastle left his nephew 'a whysell with a chyne of sylver with my sea gowne and all the rest of my sea close, and a bagge with a lock of sylver'.[3] This is the closest one can get to documentation of the kind of the clothes shown here. The survival of this outfit is probably due to its inclusion in the 'studio wardrobe' of history painters Frank Moss Bennett (1874–1952) and John-Louis-Ernest Meissonier (1815–91). Both were painters known for their meticulous attention to historical detail. SN

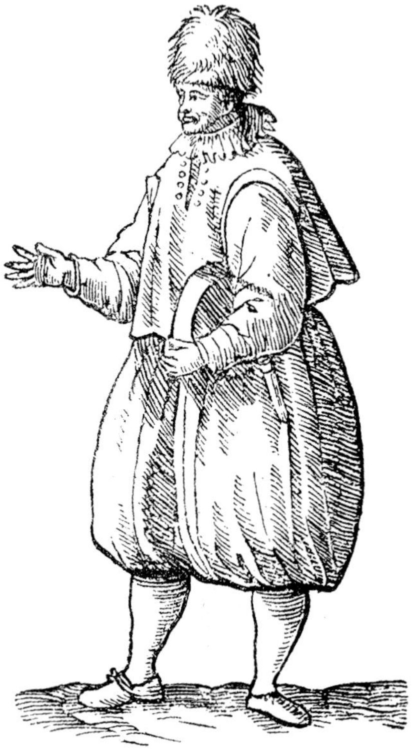

FIG. 33
'An English Sailor' from *Habiti Antichi et Moderni di tutto il Mondo*
Cesare Vecellio, 1598

PROVENANCE

Bought in 1953 by the Museum of London from the daughter of history painter Frank Moss Bennett (1874–1952). Many of the props used in Bennett's studio came from another history painter, Jean-Louis-Ernest Meissonier (1815–91). Previous history unknown.

NOTES

1 Dudley Jarrett, *British Naval Dress* (London, J.M. Dent and Sons, 1960), pp.15–18.
2 C. Willett Cunnington and Phillis Cunnington, *Handbook of English Costume in the Sixteenth Century* (London, Faber and Faber, 1954), p.195.
3 J.C. Hodgson (ed.), *Wills and Inventories from the Registry at Durham, part III*, Surtees Society, vol. 112, 1906, p.78.

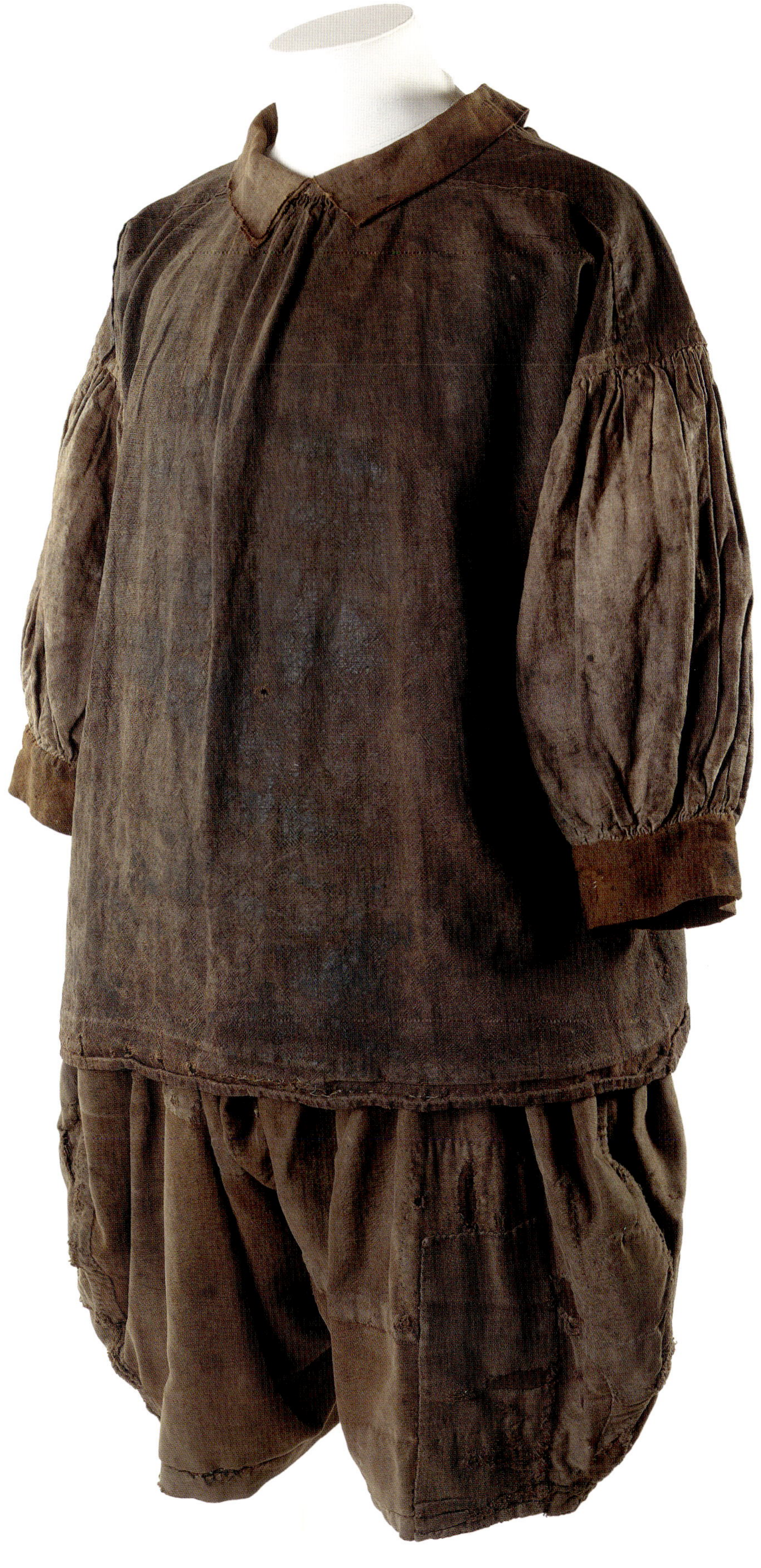

85

Child's mitten

England, c.1501–99

Knitted wool
Length 130mm; width 70mm (including thumb piece)
Museum of London (A 1989)

In addition to a luxury industry producing silk-knitted hose and gloves in the sixteenth century, there were craftsmen and women making a variety of practical socks, stockings, sleeves, mittens, gloves and headwear, knitted in sturdy wools.

Knitting was part-time work that could be done in conjunction with other rural activities and domestic tasks. Knitting needles were portable and inexpensive.[1] For these reasons, teaching poor children to knit was repeatedly encouraged by Elizabethan economic and social reformers. One reported that a child of seven could earn up to four shillings a week knitting.[2] This little mitten not only covered the hand of an Elizabethan child, but may also have been made by one. SN

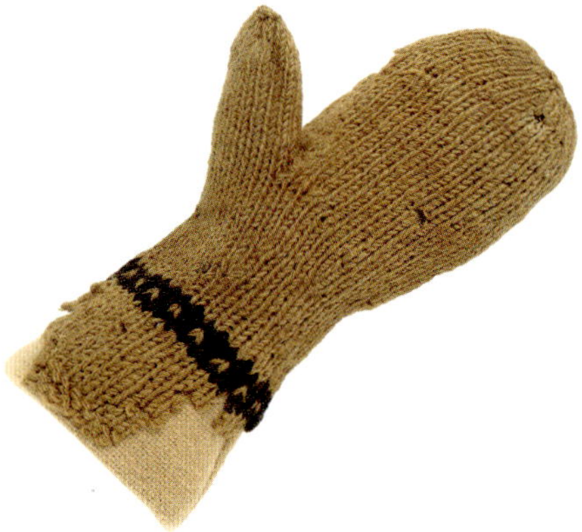

NOTES

1 Joan Thirsk, 'The Fantastical Folly of Fashion: The English Stocking Knitting Industry, 1500–1700' in *The Rural Economy of England: Collected Essays* (London, Hambledon Press, 1984), pp.244–5.

2 Richard Rutt, *A History of Hand Knitting* (London, Batsford, 1987), pp.76–7.

86

Earthenware Drinking Vessels

England, late sixteenth century

Tyg: height 65mm, diameter (rim) 75m; jug: height 256mm, diameter 115mm; goblet: height 130mm, diameter 79mm
Museum of London (A 15256, A 28361, 5898)

During the reign of Elizabeth I the range of eating and drinking vessels increased dramatically, becoming ever more specialised as new foods and beverages, and ways of preparing and serving them, were introduced. Simple earthenware pots, with a splash of green or yellow glaze for decoration, began to replace traditional vessels of wood. They were attractive, durable, easy to clean, and above all cheap – which meant they were in great demand. The pots shown here are typical examples of the sorts of wares found in London homes, alehouses and taverns. The two-handled tyg was probably used for communal drinking and the jug for serving at table.

Red earthenware cooking pots and jugs were made in Essex or imported from the Netherlands, but the whitewares were made in the vicinity of Farnham Park on the Surrey/Hampshire border. Bulk orders were placed by the City livery companies for their feasts and dinners, and vast numbers of 'grene pottes' for beer and wine were despatched to London for the use of the gentlemen of the Inns of Court. The Benchers and Barrister's Clerks were required to provide their own pots at their own expense but, in 1596, the records show that the Middle Temple gardener, Philip Wallis, received a daily allowance for bread and four or more 'green pots' of beer for his dinner and supper. HF

PROVENANCE

London Wall; Red Lion Market; Gray's Inn Road, London.

LITERATURE

Matthews and Green 1969, pp.1–17.

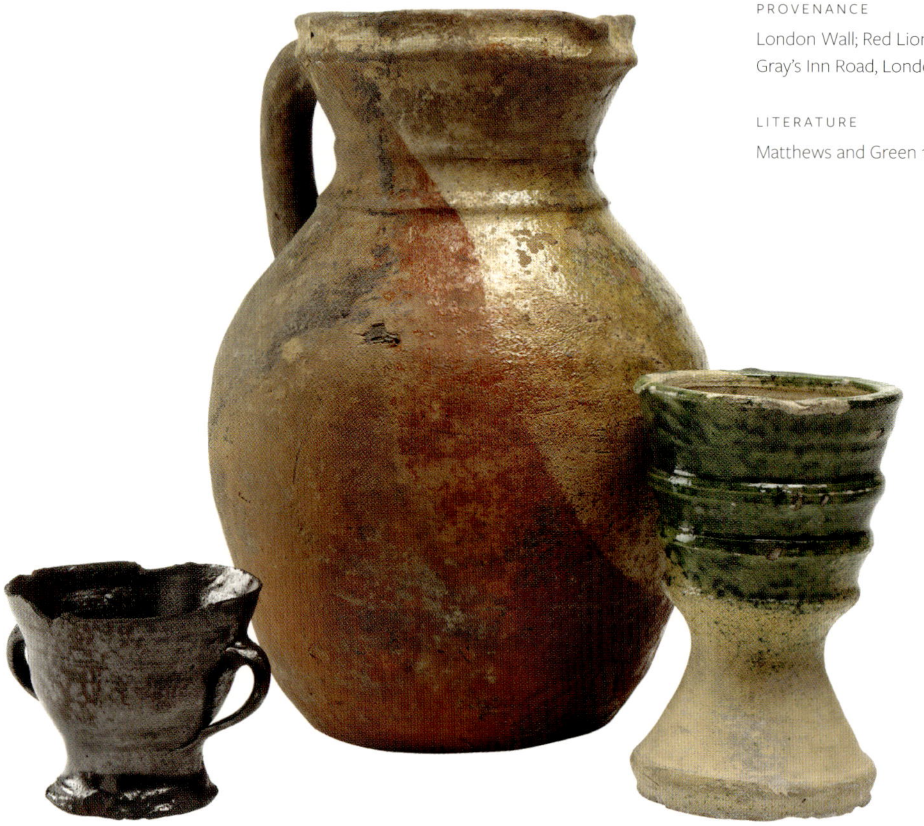

87

Will of Susan Baker (d.1583)

Dated 1583

Manuscript, ink on paper
City of London Metropolitan Archives
(DL/C/B/005/MS 09172/012A Will Number 64)

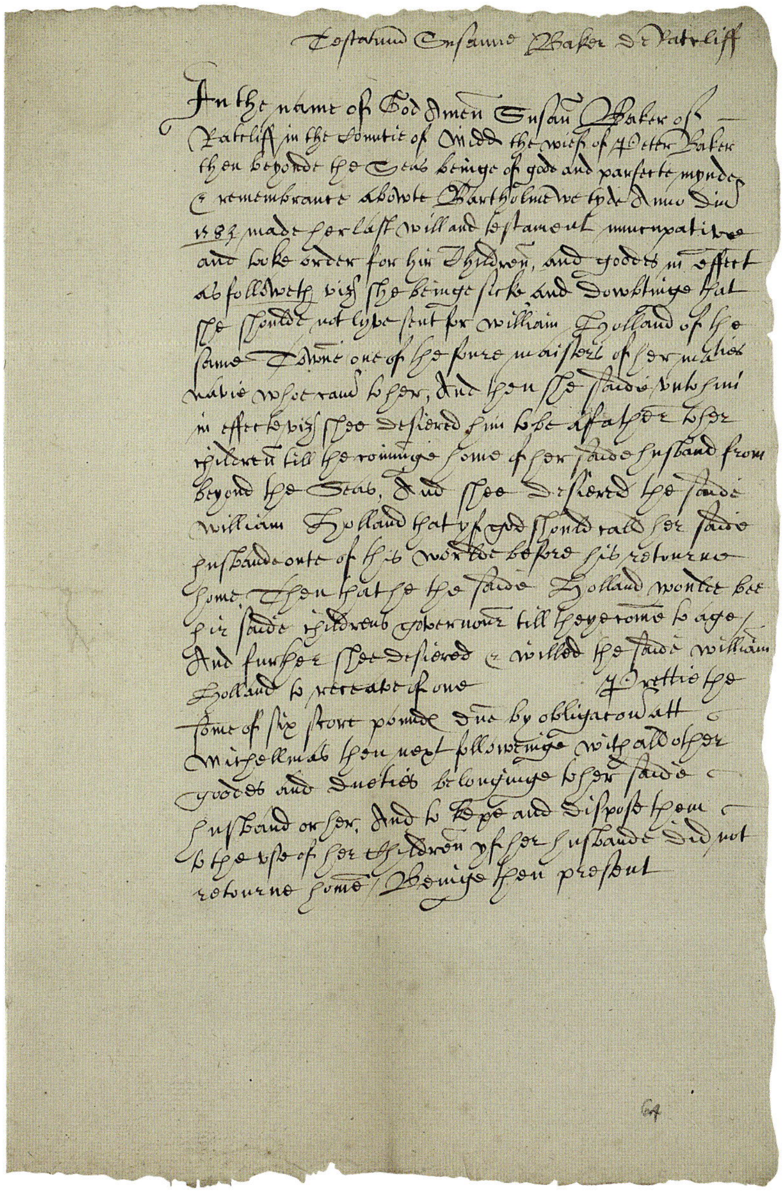

This unusual document sets out the last wishes of a woman named Susan Baker, who died in 1583. She was the wife of a seaman named Peter Baker, and their story gives a strong sense of the hardships suffered by Elizabethan families with members who worked and fought at sea. Susan was the daughter of William Holland (d.1587), one of the officers of the Queen's Navy. She married Peter Baker in April 1568 at their Parish Church of St Dunstan and All Saints, Ratcliff.[1] This was a notoriously overcrowded and bawdy district to the east of the city of London, heavily populated with labourers and sailors who sought employment at the nearby docks. Although the will gives little information about the extent of her wealth or possessions, it is unlikely that they amounted to a great deal. Elizabethan seamen often earned just 4 pence a day, which was less than half the average wage of an unskilled labourer.

The document is what is known as a nuncupative will; a verbal statement made in the absence of a written will and delivered in the presence of a witness who recorded the intentions of the testator. It was made on the last day of her life, 24 August 1583, at a time when Susan, 'being sicke and dowtinge [doubting] that she should not lyve [live], sent for william holland of the same Towne … [saying] unto him in effect viz shee desiered him to be a father to her children till the cominge home of her said husband from beyond the Seas'. She was buried the day afterwards at her parish church, on 25 August 1583.[2]

Sadly, Peter Baker never returned home. He died at some point between April 1584 (the date of his last recorded letter home) and 6 March 1585, when his own will was proved. During this time he learned of the loss of both his wife and two of his young children. Writing to William Holland from abroad, Baker entrusted his father-in-law with 'a care unto mye poore children that are lefte', namely Susan who was six years old, Peter who was five, and Christopher who was nearly four.[3] Their grandfather and guardian William Holland died two years later. He made no mention of these children in his will.[4] ET

PROVENANCE

Commissary Court of London.

NOTES

1. LMA, St Dunstan and All Saints, Register of Marriages, P93/DUN/264.
2. LMA, St Dunstan and All Saints, Register of Burials, P93/DUN/274.
3. LMA, St Dunstan and All Saints, Register of Marriages, P93/DUN/255.
4. Will of William Holland, TNA/PROB 11/70/218.

Chronology

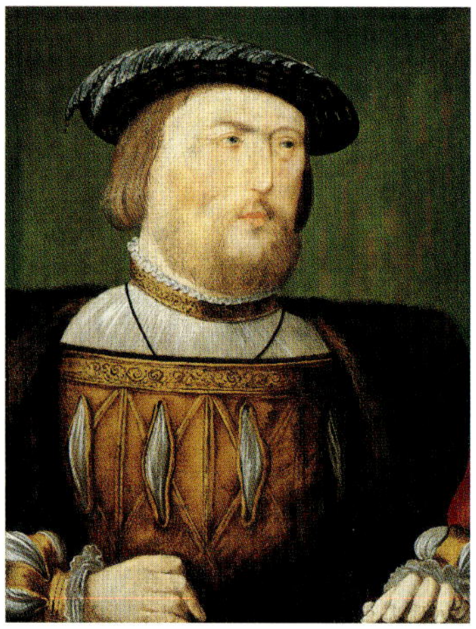

FIG. 34 King Henry VIII

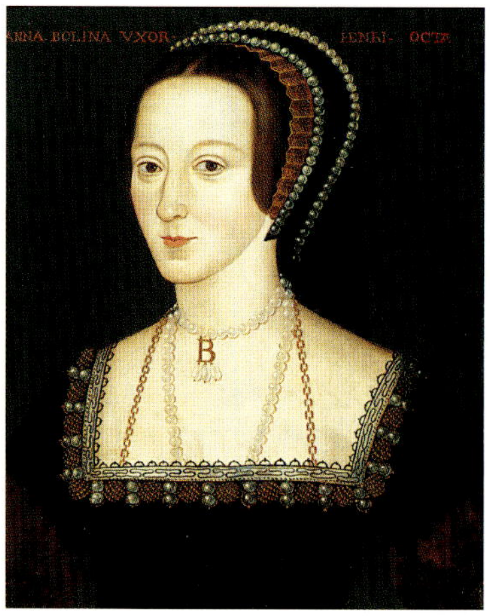

FIG. 35 Anne Boleyn

Events in England, Wales and Scotland
(❖ CULTURAL/LITERARY/SCIENTIFIC EVENTS)

Events overseas

1533
HENRY VIII divorces Catherine of Aragon and marries ANNE BOLEYN.
Their daughter ELIZABETH is born at Greenwich Palace (7 September).

Spain conquers Incan Empire.

1534
Parliament introduces Act making the King Supreme Head of the Church of England.

1536
Anne Boleyn executed; Henry VIII marries Jane Seymour.
MARY and Elizabeth Tudor excluded by Act of Succession.

❖ Death of the humanist scholar Desiderius Erasmus in Basel (b.1466, Rotterdam).

1537
Jane Seymour dies after the premature birth of a son (the future EDWARD VI).

1538
Henry VIII excommunicated by Pope Paul III.

1539
All parish churches required to have English-language Bibles.

1540
Henry VIII marries Anne of Cleves and the marriage is annulled; Henry marries Catherine Howard.
Thomas Cromwell executed.

1541
Henry VIII declared King of Ireland by Dublin Parliament.

❖ Michelangelo completes the *Last Judgement* fresco on the altar wall of the Sistine Chapel, Rome.

1542
Catherine Howard executed.

1543
Henry VIII marries Catherine Parr.
MARY STUART crowned Queen of Scotland.

❖ Death of Hans Holbein in London (b.1497, Augsburg).
❖ Andreas Vesalius publishes pioneering research into human anatomy.

1545
The Mary Rose sinks in the Solent.

1546

German Reformer Martin Luther dies in Eisleben (b.1483).

1547
❖ Birth of Nicholas Hilliard (d.1619).
Death of Henry VIII; accession of his son Edward VI (aged 9), under the protectorate of his uncle Edward Seymour, Earl of Hertford, then named Duke of Somerset.

Death of Francis I (b.1494); Henry II succeeds as King of France.

1549
THOMAS CRANMER'S *Book of Common Prayer* published (first Edwardian prayer book signals the passing of the Catholic mass).

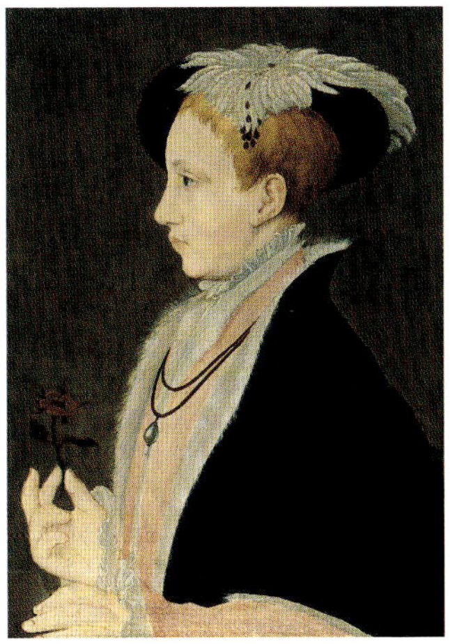

FIG. 36 King Edward VI

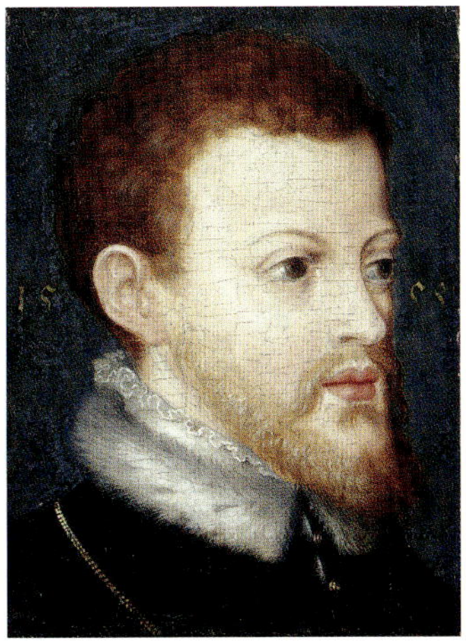

FIG. 37 Philip II, King of Spain

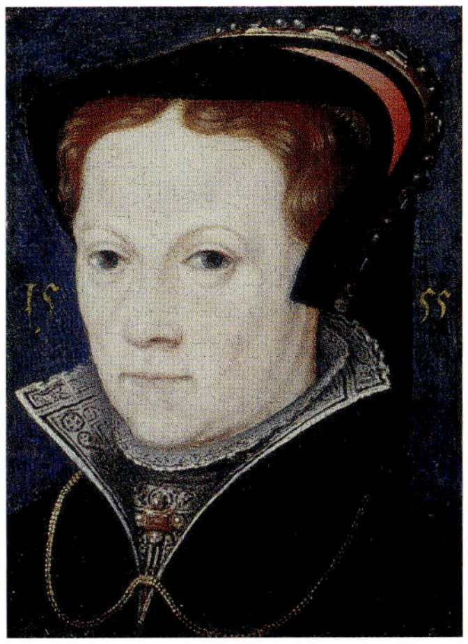

FIG. 38 Queen Mary I

1550
With Treaty of Boulogne, England abandons Boulogne and France withdraws from Scotland. London altars are replaced by communion tables.

❖ Giorgio Vasari publishes *The Lives of the Artists* in Italy.

1552
Protector Somerset executed for treason.

1553
Death of Edward VI from tuberculosis.
Lady Jane Grey proclaimed Queen and reigns for 9 days.
Accession of Mary I.
Persecution of Protestants from 1553 to 1558.

1554
Mary I marries PHILIP OF SPAIN.
Lady Jane Grey executed; Princess Elizabeth imprisoned in the Tower of London.

1555
Commencement of burnings of Protestants, including Bishops Latimer and Ridley in Oxford.
John Hawkins begins slave trading.

Philip of Spain becomes ruler of the Netherlands.

1556
Thomas Cranmer burned at the stake.
Widespread dearth and famine.

Charles V abdicates and his son, Philip II, becomes King of Spain.

1557
England declares war on France.

1558
England loses Calais; death of Mary I.

ACCESSION OF ELIZABETH I
(17 November).

WILLIAM CECIL, 1ST BARON BURGHLEY (cat. 19) appointed Principal Secretary of State.
Major influenza epidemic kills ten per cent of population.

1559
Elizabeth I's coronation at Westminster Abbey (15 January).
Elizabeth's first Parliament;
Parliament presses the Queen to marry.
Acts of Supremacy and Uniformity passed renouncing papal authority in England but adopting a less radical liturgy than in 1552.
MATTHEW PARKER becomes Archbishop of Canterbury.

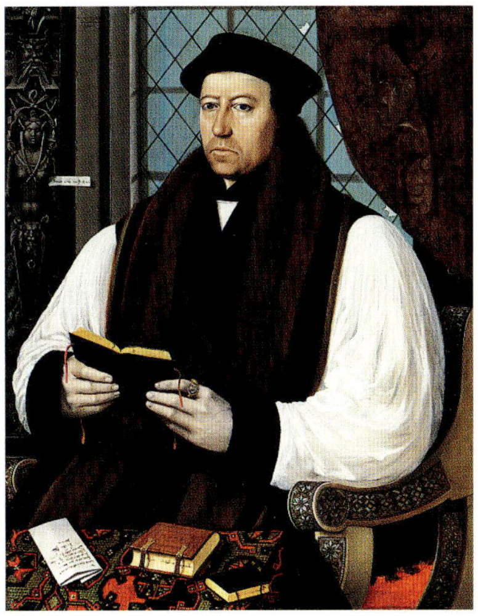

FIG. 39 Thomas Cranmer

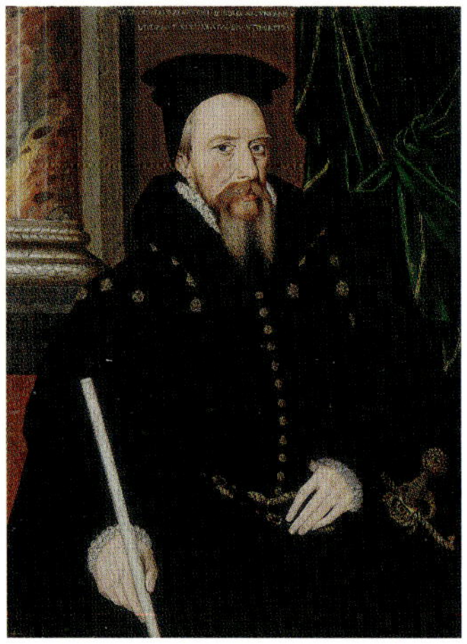
FIG. 40 William Cecil, 1st Baron Burghley

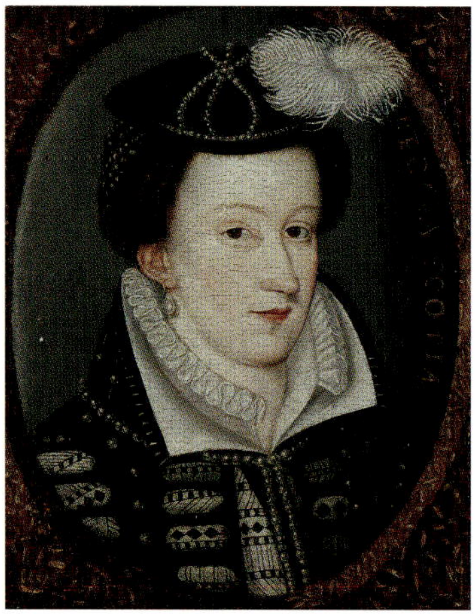
FIG. 41 Mary, Queen of Scots

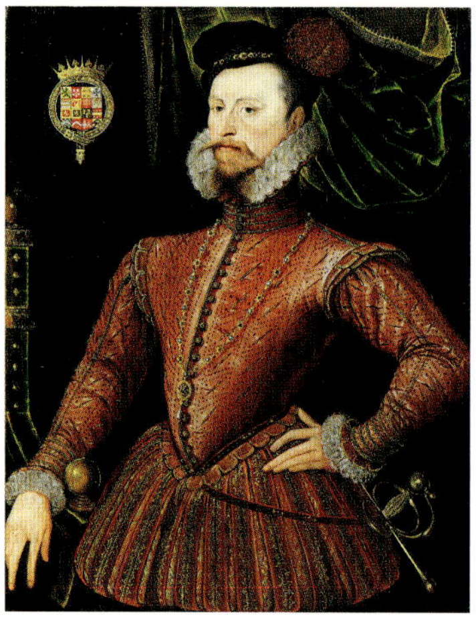
FIG. 42 Robert Dudley, 1st Earl of Leicester

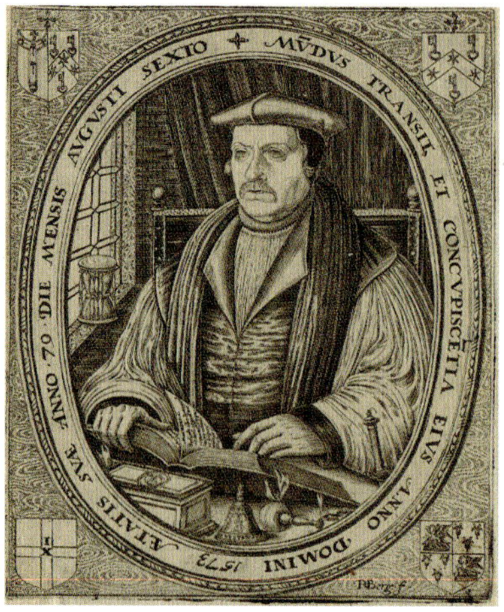
FIG. 43 Matthew Parker

Francis II dies (b.1544); Charles IX succeeds as King of France with Catherine de' Medici as Regent.
Publication of the Geneva Bible.

1561
Spire and parts of the roof of St Paul's Cathedral destroyed by lightning.
❖ Publication of Thomas Hoby's English translation of Baldassare Castiglione's *The Courtier*.

❖ Tulips first brought to Europe.

1562
Elizabeth I ill at Hampton Court with an almost-fatal bout of smallpox.
Total re-coinage helps restore confidence in the economy.

1563
Church of England establishes the Thirty-Nine Articles of Religion.
Around 17,000 Londoners die of the plague; Elizabeth I moves her court to Windsor.
Graduates, schoolmasters and MPs are required to take the Oath of Supremacy.
The Statute of Artificers lays out new rules of labour, prices and wages.
❖ John Foxe's *Acts and Monuments* (Foxe's 'Book of Martyrs') published (cat. 83).

Protestant heresies condemned at the Council of Trent.

1564
❖ Birth of WILLIAM SHAKESPEARE (d.1616) and Christopher Marlowe (d.1593).
Queen's visit to the University of Cambridge.
ROBERT DUDLEY created Earl of Leicester.

❖ Michelangelo dies in Rome (b.1475).
❖ Galileo born in Pisa (d.1642).

1565
Widowed Mary, Queen of Scots, marries Henry Stewart, Lord Darnley.

1566
Murder of David Rizzio, Mary, Queen of Scots' private secretary, and the birth of her son JAMES (later VI of Scotland and I of England).
Sumptuary Law prohibits the wearing of particular clothes/cloth (also 1571).

Election of Pope Pius V.

1567
Murder of Lord Darnley; Mary, Queen of Scots marries James Hepburn, Earl of Bothwell, causing a rebellion and is forced to abdicate in favour of her young son, with the Earl of Moray as Regent.
The Bible is published in Welsh.

Spain suppresses revolt in the Netherlands; Duke of Alva arrives in the Netherlands, heralding onset of religious persecution and new waves of immigration to England.

1568
William Cecil orders the seizure of Spanish bullion ships at Plymouth and Southampton, and the Spanish respond by seizing English merchant ships docked in Antwerp.
Mary, Queen of Scots, flees to England and is imprisoned by Elizabeth I.
Publication of Archbishop Matthew Parker's *Bishops' Bible* (cat. 77).

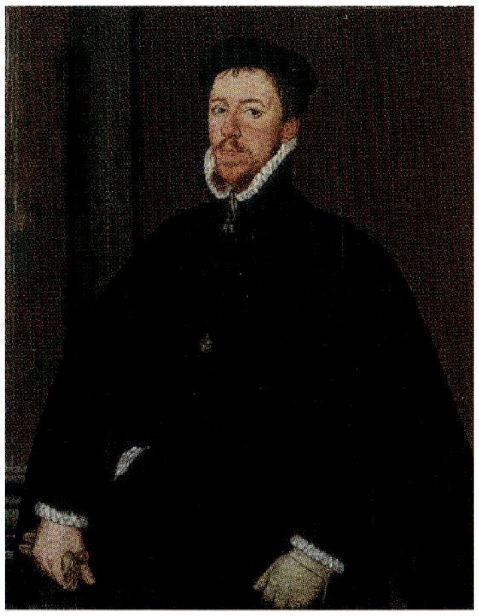

FIG. 44 Thomas Howard, 4th Duke of Norfolk

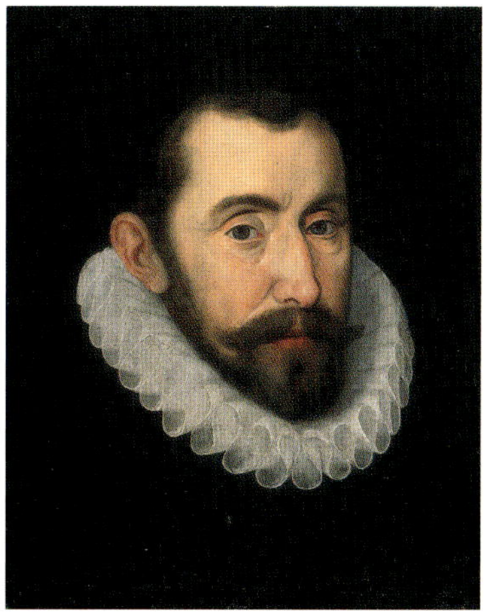

FIG. 45 Sir Francis Walsingham

1569
Roman Catholic-inspired rebellion called the 'Northern Rising' in northern England.
THOMAS HOWARD, DUKE OF NORFOLK (cat. 17), arrested on suspicion of treason and imprisoned in the Tower of London.

❖ Death of Pieter Bruegel the Elder in Brussels (b. *c.*1525)
Gerardus Mercator develops system of cartographic projection.

1570
Execution of 450 participants in 'Northern Rising'.
Pope Pius V issues Regnans in Excelsis, excommunicating Elizabeth I.
Elizabeth considers marriage to Henry, Duke of Anjou.
❖ Publication of Roger Ascham's *The Scholemaster*.
❖ Translation of Euclid's *Elements of Geometry*, with a preface by John Dee.

❖ Spain imports potatoes from the Americas.

1571
Elizabeth visits Thomas Gresham's Exchange (completed 1569) and it is rechristened the Royal Exchange (see cat. 46).
Ridolfi Plot discovered (to overthrow Elizabeth and replace her with Mary, Queen of Scots).
Sir William Cecil is created Lord Burghley.

1572
Elizabeth I and Catherine de' Medici sign the Treaty of Blois (a defensive alliance of England and France against Spain).
Execution of Duke of Norfolk for his part in the Ridolfi Plot.
❖ Nicholas Hilliard paints a portrait miniature of Elizabeth I (cat. 16).
❖ Birth of John Donne (d.1631; cat. 71) and BEN JONSON (d.1637).

St Bartholomew's Day massacre (August 24): Huguenots massacred by Catholics in Paris. Dutch War of Liberation begins and William of Orange is elected Stadholder.
Sir Francis Drake seizes Spanish treasure in West Indies.

1573
SIR FRANCIS WALSINGHAM becomes Secretary of State (with Sir Thomas Smith) and principal spymaster.

1575
Elizabeth I declines the sovereignty of the Netherlands.
Elizabeth visits Earl of Leicester at Kenilworth while on progress.
Arrival of first seminary priests into England.
❖ Publication of Christopher Saxton's *County Atlas of England and Wales*.
❖ Elizabeth grants a twenty-one-year monopoly on polyphonic music, and a patent to print and publish music to Thomas Tallis and William Byrd.

1576
❖ Martin Frobisher (cat. 21) begins first of three voyages to find the Northwest Passage.
❖ First commercial building used exclusively for drama, 'The Theatre', built in Shoreditch.
Calls for Houses of Correction to punish 'idle' poor and set them to work.

Antwerp sacked by mutinous Spanish troops.
Rudolf II becomes Holy Roman Emperor.
❖ Death of Titian in Venice (b. *c.*1488–90).

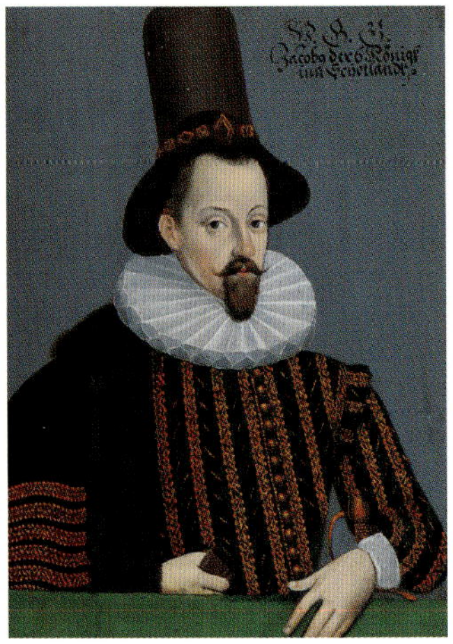

FIG. 46 King James I of England and VI of Scotland

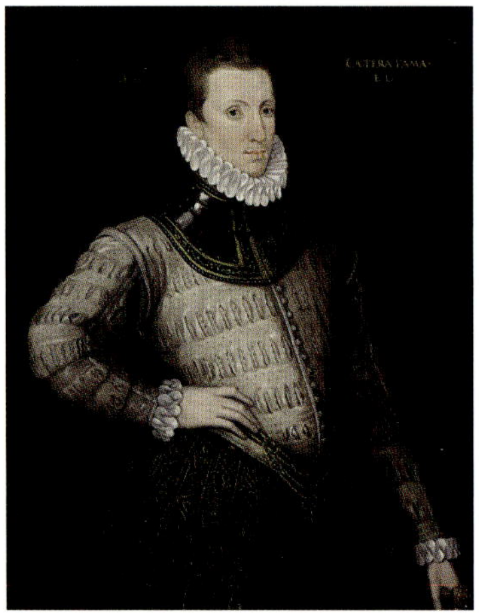

FIG. 47 Sir Philip Sidney

1577
Christopher Hatton (cat. 20) is knighted and made Vice-Chamberlain of the Royal Household.
❖ Francis Drake (cat. 24) sets out in *The Pelican* on the voyage that is to become his circumnavigation of the globe.
❖ Raphael Holinshed's *Chronicles of England, Scotland, and Ireland* is published.

1578
James VI, aged eleven, seizes authority in Scotland, but Regent Morton resumes control.
Robert Dudley secretly marries Lettice Knollys.

1579
Treaty of alliance with the Dutch, under William of Orange.
Elizabeth I entertains ideas of marriage with Francis, Duke of Anjou.
❖ George Gower paints his self-portrait (cat. 67).
❖ Sir Thomas North publishes translation of Plutarch's *Lives of the Noble Grecians and Romans.*

1580
❖ Francis Drake returns to England triumphant after circumnavigating the globe.
❖ Edmund Spenser's *Shepheardes Calendar* is published.

❖ Publication of Montaigne's first *Essays.*

1581
Francis Drake is knighted.
Foundation of the Turkey Company after embassy of Richard Staper and Edward Harborne to Ottoman Empire (1578–9).
John Dee and Edward Kelley start their 'mystical experiments'.
Controversial execution of the Jesuit Edmund Campion.
❖ Publication of Richard Mulcaster's *Positions Concerning the Training up of Children.*
❖ The surgeon John Banister is depicted in a portrait delivering an anatomy lecture (cat. 80) at the Royal College of Surgeons, London.

1582
Duke of Anjou leaves England after the failure of marriage negotiations with Elizabeth I.

First English colony in Newfoundland.
Pope Gregory XIII reforms the calendar in Catholic Europe.

1583
Throckmorton Plot to place Mary, Queen of Scots, on the English throne is discovered.
❖ SIR PHILIP SIDNEY'S *Apology for Poetry* is published.

1584
Expulsion of the Spanish ambassador for complicity in the Throckmorton Plot, and bond of association directed against the accession of Mary, Queen of Scots, to the English throne.
❖ Elizabeth commissions the second Great Seal, designed by Nicholas Hilliard.

William of Orange (b.1533) is assassinated in Delft.
Walter Ralegh (cat. 22) annexes Virginia.

1585
Walter Ralegh (cat. 22) is knighted.
Anglo-Dutch treaty of alliance is signed, whereby Elizabeth I agrees to send troops (5,000 foot soldiers and 1,000 cavalry) to aid the Dutch against the Spanish.
❖ Cambridge University Press founded.

Sixtus V elected Pope.

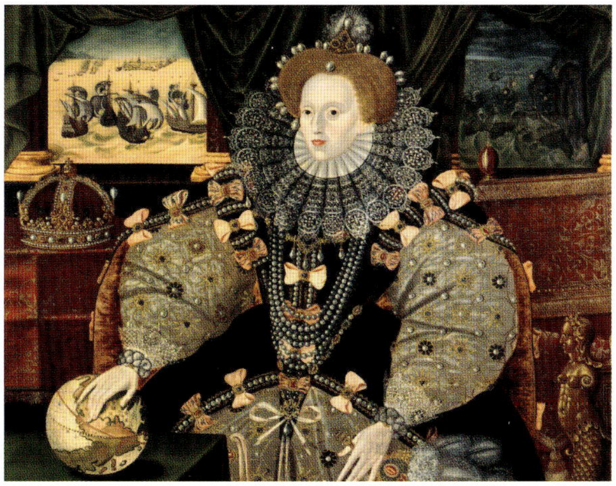

FIG. 48 Elizabeth I (known as the 'Armada Portrait'), c.1588

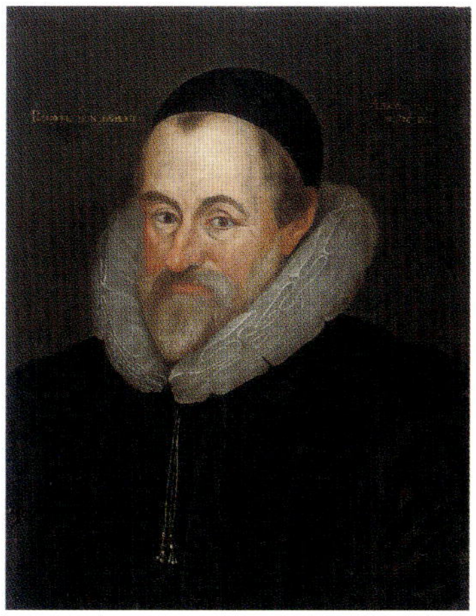

FIG. 49 William Camden

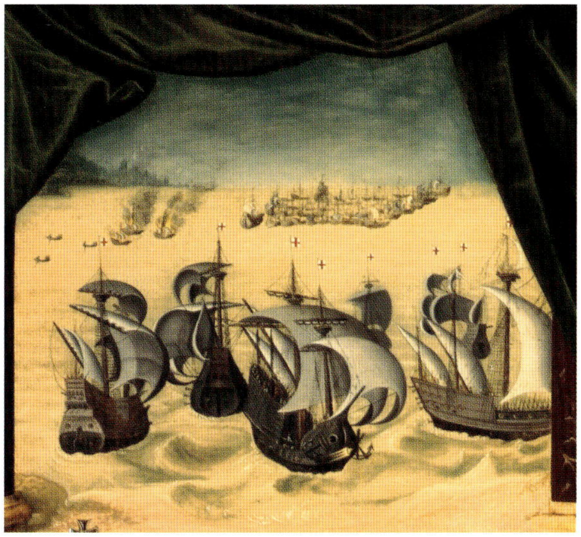

Detail of fig. 48 showing the English ships in the foreground

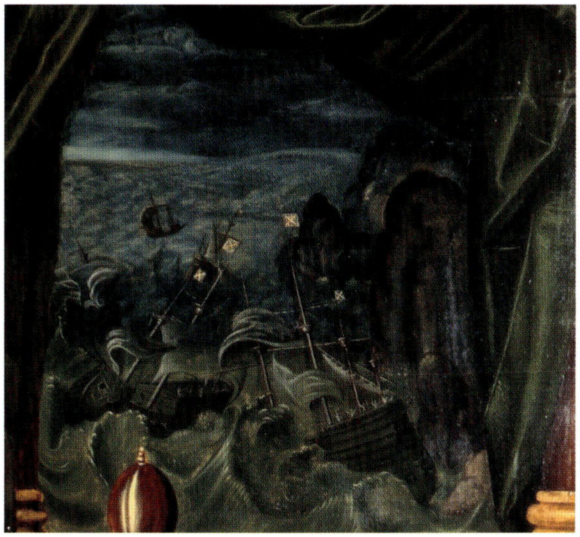

Detail of fig. 48 showing the sinking of the Spanish ships and the destruction of the Armada

1586

Babington Plot to assassinate Elizabeth I and replace her with Mary, Queen of Scots, is discovered by Sir Francis Walsingham.
Trial and conviction of Mary begins at Fotheringay Castle.
Death of the Catholic martyr Margaret Clitherow (b.1556) who, having refused to plead, suffers the penalty of being crushed to death.
Death of Philip Sidney (b.1554), who had been wounded in the Netherlands.
❖ WILLIAM CAMDEN publishes *Britannia*, a history of Britain.

1587

Elizabeth I reluctantly authorises the execution of Mary, Queen of Scots.
Elizabeth appoints Robert Devereux, Earl of Essex (cat. 26) as her Master of the Horse.
❖ The Rose Theatre is established in Southwark.
❖ Marlowe's *Tamburlaine* is performed.

Walter Ralegh founds the ill-fated colony at Roanoke, Virginia.

1588

Spanish Armada sets sail for England (May) and is defeated (August).
Elizabeth rallies troops at Tilbury (August) amid fears of Spanish invasion; storms off Ireland destroy twenty-five Spanish ships (September).
English merchants found the Guinea Company to traffic slaves from Africa's Guinea coast.
Death of Robert Dudley (b.1532/3).
❖ Thomas Hariot publishes *A Brief and True Report of the New Found Land of Virginia*.

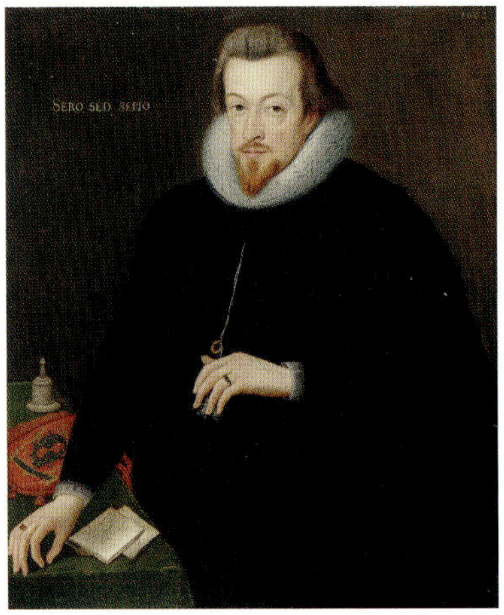

FIG. 50 Robert Cecil

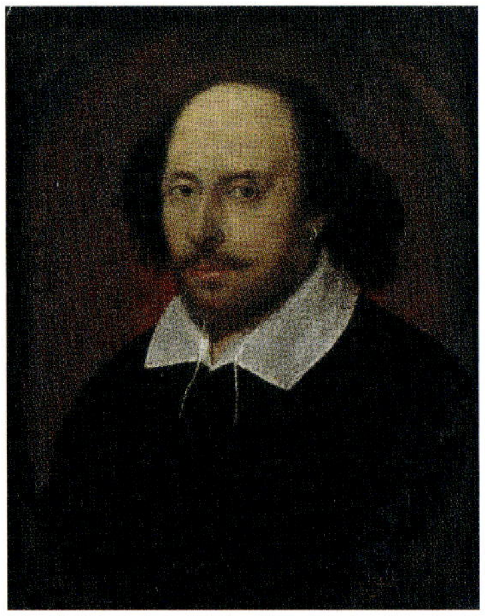

FIG. 51 William Shakespeare

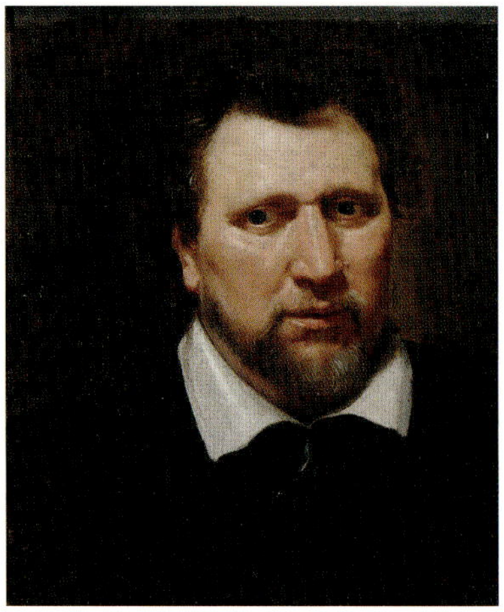

FIG. 52 Benjamin Jonson

1589
James VI of Scotland marries Princess Anne of Denmark.

Catherine de' Medici (b.1519) dies and Henry III (b.1551) is murdered; the Protestant Henry of Navarre claims the French throne.

1590
❖ Publication of the first books of Edmund Spenser's epic allegorical poem *The Faerie Queene*.
❖ Building of Hardwick Hall, Derbyshire, commences (see fig. 4).

❖ Dutch craftsman Zacharias Janssen invents compound microscope.

1591
ROBERT CECIL is knighted and made a Privy Councillor.
Death of Sir Christopher Hatton (b.1540) (cat. 20).

1592
Ralegh imprisoned in the Tower for marrying Elizabeth Throckmorton, one of Elizabeth's ladies-in-waiting.
❖ Thomas Kyd's *Spanish Tragedy* is published.

1593
Robert Devereux, Earl of Essex (cat. 26), made Privy Councillor.
Fairs, feasts, plays and games forbidden for fear of disorder and plague.
Parliament debates status of immigrants (victims of persecution or economic migrants?).
❖ Christopher Marlowe is stabbed to death in a tavern brawl.
❖ Shakespeare's *Venus and Adonis* is published.
❖ Philip Sidney's *New Arcadia* is published.
❖ Marlowe's *Doctor Faustus* is performed.
❖ First books of Richard Hooker's *Laws of Ecclesiastical Polity* are published.

1594
Elizabeth's physician, Roderigo Lopez, hanged for treason.
❖ Shakespeare's *Rape of Lucrece* and his first play, *Titus Andronicus*, are published.

Henry IV (Henry of Navarre) crowned King of France

1595
❖ Ralegh sails from England in search of El Dorado.
Provost Marshall appointed to oversee London policing following rioting and civil unrest.
Tyrone's Rebellion against the advance of the English state in Ireland begins, lasting until 1603.
Riots in Southwark among apprentices and masterless men.
❖ Shakespeare's sonnets circulate in manuscript form.
❖ Around this date John Donne writes his poems the 'Satires' and early 'Elegies', and sits for a portrait in the 'shadows' (cat. 71).

1596
Death of Sir Francis Drake (b.1540) at sea.
Sir Robert Cecil appointed Principal Secretary of State.
One of the worst harvests of the century, with food riots in Kent and the abortive Oxfordshire rising.

English fleet captures and sacks Cadiz.

1597
Earl of Essex made Earl Marshal.
Most severe famine of the century in north-west England.
❖ John Dowland publishes the first of three books: 'Songes or Ayres of Foure Partes for the Lute' (pub. 1597, 1600, 1603).
❖ John Gerard's *Herball, or, A Generall Historie of Plantes* is published (cat. 82).

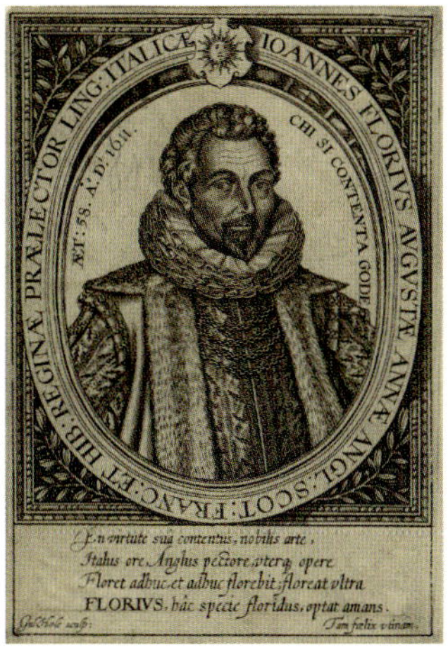

FIG. 53 John Florio

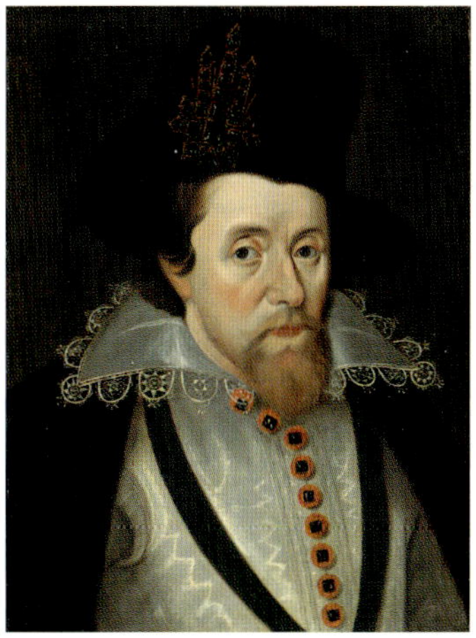

FIG. 54 James I and VI

❖ First collection of *Essays* by Sir Francis Bacon (cat. 72) is published.

A second Spanish armada, bound for Ireland, is wrecked in the Bay of Biscay.

1598
Death of Lord Burghley (b.1520).
Parliament enacts important legislation for relief of the poor and punishment of vagrants (with a refinement in 1601), setting policy for the next 250 years.
Elizabeth Vernon and Henry Wriothesley, 3rd Earl of Southampton, marry in secret (see cat. 27).
❖ John Stow's *Survey of London* is published.

Death of Philip II of Spain (b.1527); accession of Philip III.
Edict of Nantes gives rights to French Huguenots.

1599
Birth of Oliver Cromwell (d.1658).
Robert, Earl of Essex, is placed in charge of an army to suppress Irish rebels, and instead signs an unauthorised truce with the Earl of Tyrone.
Elizabeth I deprives Essex of his titles and places him under house arrest.
❖ Globe Theatre opens in Southwark.

1600
Birth of Charles, son of James VI of Scotland (later Charles I of England; d.1649).
East India Company founded with a charter granted by Elizabeth I.
Elizabeth attends the wedding of Henry Somerset, Lord Herbert of Chepstow, and Lady Anne Russell (cat. 1).
Elizabeth refuses renewal of the sweet wine monopoly, which underpinned the Earl of Essex's finances.
❖ Actor Will Kemp dances from London to Norwich.

1601
Elizabethan 'Poor Law' is codified.
Earl of Essex and conspirators commission special performance of *Richard II*, possibly Shakespeare's, at the Globe.
Essex's Rebellion fails and he is executed.

Anglo-Dutch forces defend Ostend against Spanish invasion.

1602
Elizabeth I noted to be infirm.
❖ Bodleian Library opens with 2,000 volumes; entry restricted to graduates.

1603
Elizabeth I dies at Richmond Palace (24 March), and the Tudor dynasty ends.
James VI emerges as her successor, although Elizabeth's intentions regarding the succession remain ambiguous to the end.
Submission of Tyrone.
❖ Shakespeare's *Hamlet* is published.
❖ JOHN FLORIO'S translation of Montaigne's *Essays* is published.

1604
James VI adopts title 'King of Great Britain, France and Ireland'.

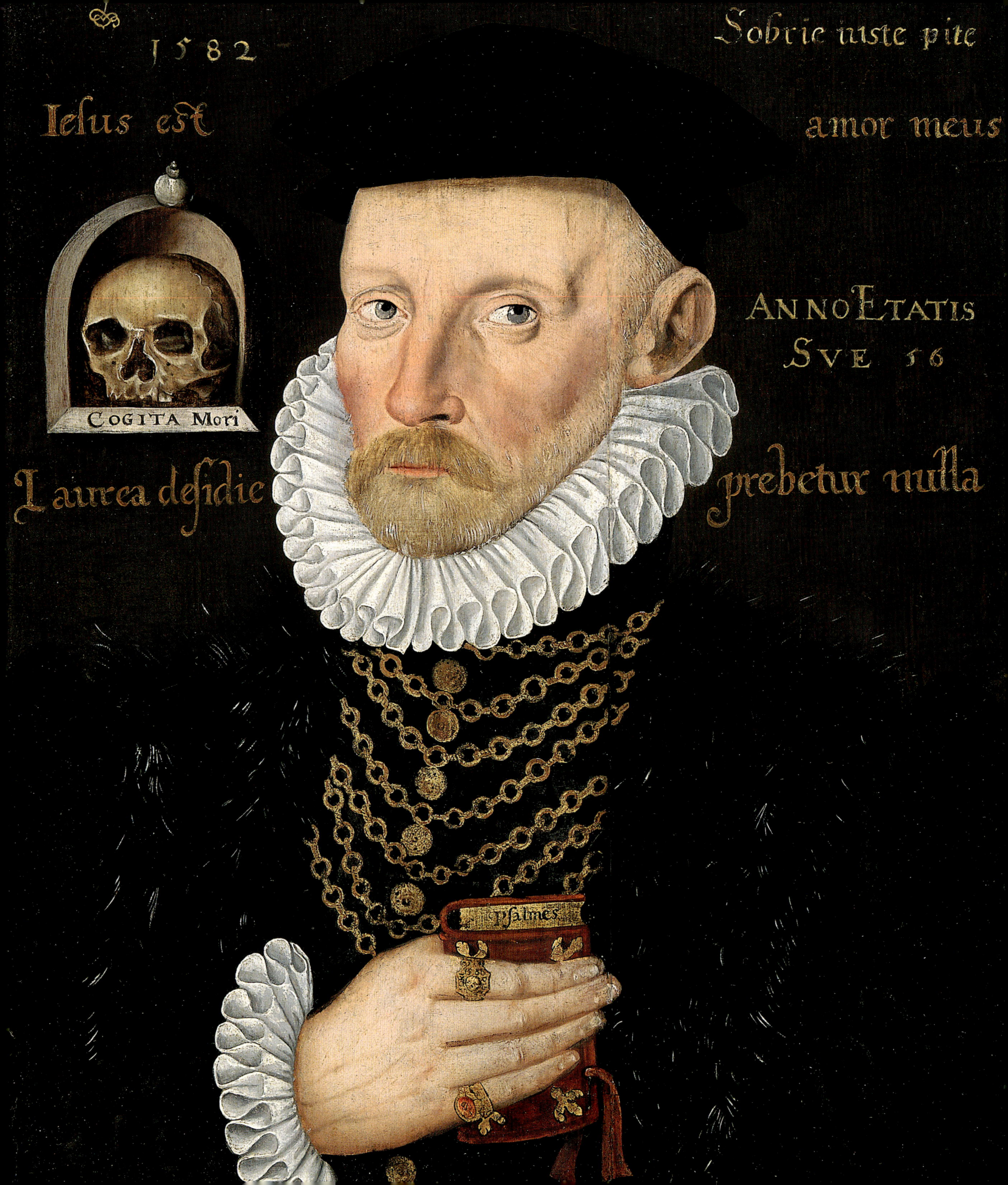
1582
Sobrie iuste pie
Iesus est
amor meus
ANNO ETATIS
SVE 56
COGITA Mori
Laurea desidie
prebetur nulla
psalmes

Select Bibliography

William Addison, *Audley End* (Dent, London, 1953)

David Armitage, 'The *Procession Portrait* of Queen Elizabeth I: A Note on Tradition', *Journal of the Warburg and Courtauld Institutes*, 53, 1990

Jane Ashelford, *A Visual History of Costume: The Sixteenth Century* (Drama Book Publishers, New York, 1983)

Jane Ashelford, *The Art of Dress: Clothes and Society 1500-1914* (National Trust, London, 1996)

Erna Auerbach and C. Kingsley Adams, *Paintings and Sculpture at Hatfield House* (Constable, London, 1971)

Erna Auerbach, 'Holbein's Followers in England', *Burlington Magazine*, XCIII, 1951

Erna Auerbach, 'Portraits of Elizabeth I', *Burlington Magazine*, XCV, 1957

Erna Auerbach, *Nicholas Hilliard* (Routledge and Kegan Paul, London, 1961)

Natasha Awais-Dean, *Bejewelled: The Male Body and Adornment in Early Modern England* (unpublished PhD thesis, University of London, London, 2012)

Natasha Awais-Dean, 'A Gem in the Archives' in Jewellery History Today (forthcoming, Autumn 2013)

John Ballinger, 'Katheryn of Berain. A Study in North Wales Family History', *Y Commrodor*, XL, 1929

Peter Barber, *London: A History in Maps* (London Topographical Society in association with the British Library, London, 2012)

Jonathan Bate and Dora Thornton, *Shakespeare: Staging the World* (British Museum Press, London, 2012)

Arthur Beer, 'Astronomical Dating of Works of Art', *Vistas in Astronomy*, 9, 1967

Richard Beresford, *Dulwich Picture Gallery: Complete Illustrated Catalogue* (Unicorn Press, London, 1998)

Rev. Herbert E.D. Blakiston, 'The Oxford Exhibition of Historical Portraits', *Burlington Magazine*, XIV, 1904

Noel Blakiston, 'Nicholas Hilliard as a Traveller', *Burlington Magazine*, XCI, 1949

Ian Blanchard, 'Gresham, Sir Thomas (*c*.1518–1579)' (*Oxford Dictionary of National Biography*, Oxford University Press, Oxford, 2004)

Ian Blanchard, 'Clough, Richard, d.1570' (*Oxford Dictionary of National Biography*, Oxford University Press, Oxford, 2008)

Francis Blomefield, 'Hundred of Giltcross: Ridlesworth', *An Essay towards a Topographical History of the County of Norfolk: volume 1* (printed for William Miller by W. Bulmer & Co., 1805)

D.H. Boalch, *The Manor of Rothamsted* (Rothamsted Experimental Station, Harpenden, 1953)

Lord Braybrooke, *The History of Audley End* (S. Bentley, London, 1836)

I.D. Brown and C.H. Comber, 'Portrait punches used on the hammered coinage of Queen Elizabeth I', *British Numismatic Journal*, 58, 1988

Chris Buckland Wright, 'John Banester 1533–1610' in Ian Burn (ed.), *Notable Barber Surgeons* (Worshipful Company of Barbers, London, 2008)

C.E. Challis, 'Mint officials and moneyers of the Tudor period', *British Numismatic Journal*, 45, 1975

C.E. Challis, *The Tudor Coinage* (Manchester University Press, Manchester, 1978)

C.E. Challis, *Currency and the Economy in Tudor and early Stuart England*, The Historical Association, New Appreciations in History 4, London, 1989

C.E. Challis, 'The introduction of coinage machinery into the Royal Mint by Eloy Mestrell, part 1', *British Numismatic Journal*, 59, 1989

Dr Th. M. Chotzen and Dr. A.M.E. Draak, *Beschrijving der Britsche Eilanden, door Lucas de Heere* (Antwerp, 1937)

Helen Clifford, 'Archbishop Parker's Gifts of Plate to Cambridge', *Burlington Magazine*, CXXXIX, no. 1126, January 1997

David Colclough, 'Donne, John (1572–1631)', *Oxford Dictionary of National Biography* (Oxford University Press, Oxford, 2004)

B.J. Cook, 'Humphrey Cole at the Mint', in *Humphrey Cole: Mint, Measurement and Maps in Elizabethan England*, ed. S. Ackermann, BM Occasional Paper no. 126, British Museum, London, 1998

Tarnya Cooper, *Memento Mori Portraiture: Painting, Protestant Culture and the Patronage of the Middle Elites in England and Wales 540–1630* (unpublished D.Phil thesis, University of Sussex, 2001)

Tarnya Cooper, *A Guide to Tudor and Jacobean Portraits* (National Portrait Gallery, London, 2008

Tarnya Cooper, *Citizen Portrait: Portrait Painting and the Urban Elite of Tudor and Jacobean England and Wales* (Yale University Press, London and New Haven CT, 2012)

J.L. Cor, 'The portraits of the Cecils', in *William Cecil, Lord Burghley*, Historical Monographs, 1904

Pauline Croft, 'The "Mule" Portrait of Lord Burghley', Bodleian Library Record, vol. 20, April–October 2007

Lionel Cust, 'The Painter HE: Hans Eworth', Walpole Society, II, 1913

Lionel Cust, 'The Portraits of Sir Walter Ralegh', Walpole Society, VIII, 1920

O.M. Dalton, *Catalogue of the Finger Rings: Early Christian, Byzantine, Teutonic, Mediaeval and Later; Bequeathed by Sir Augustus Wollaston Franks, in which are included the other rings of the same periods in the Museum* (British Museum Press, London, 1912)

Nick Davis, 'Melancholic Individuality and the Lothian Portrait of Donne', *American Notes and Queries*, vol. 26, issue 1, 2013, forthcoming.

Olga Dmitrieva and Tessa Murdoch (eds), *Treasures of the Royal Courts: Tudors, Stuarts and the Russian Tsars* (V&A Publishing, London, 2013)

Susan Doran, *Monarchy and Matrimony: The Courtships of Elizabeth I* (Routledge, London, 1996)

Susan Doran (ed.), *Elizabeth*, exh. cat., National Maritime Museum, London, 2003

David N. Durant, *Bess of Hardwick: Portrait of an Elizabethan Dynast*, rev. edn (Peter Owen, London, 1999)

D.L. Edwards, *John Donne: Man of Flesh and Spirit* (Continuum, London and New York, 2001)

Mark Emanuel, *The Surviving Rings of the Serjeants at Law* (privately printed, London, 2008)

English Embroidery in the Metropolitan Museum 1580–1708: 'Twixt Art and Nature, exh. cat., Metropolitan Museum, New York, 2008

Elizabeth Evenden, *Patents, Pictures and Patronage: John Day and the Tudor Book Trade* (Ashgate, Farnham, 2008)

Elizabeth Evenden and Thomas Freeman, *Religion and the Book in Early Modern England* (Cambridge University Press, Cambridge, 2011)

David Evett, *Literature and the Visual Arts in Tudor England* (University of Georgia Press, Georgia, 1990)

E. Farrer, *Catalogue of Norfolk and Suffolk Portraits: the Gift of The Late H.H. Prince Frederick Duleep Singh* (Thetford, printed by Henry Green, 1927)

Hazel Forsyth and Alan Bryson, 'Gamaliel Pye, Citizen of London. A newly discovered 16th-century City portrait', *British Art Journal*, vol. VI, no.1, 2006

Kate Gartner Frost, 'The Lothian Portrait: A Prologmenon', *John Donne Journal*, 15, 1996

Michael Gaudio, 'The truth in clothing: the costume studies of John White and Lucas de Heere' in Kim Sloan (ed.), *European Visions: American Voices*, British Museum Research Publication no. 172 (British Museum, London, 2009)

The Genealogye of the Worshippfull and auncient familie of the Heskaythes of Ruffourd in Lancashire (printed privately, London, 1869)

Anthony Gerbino and Stephen Johnston (with Gordon Higgot), *Compass and Rule: Architecture as Mathematical Practice in England 1500–1750* (Yale University Press, London and New Haven CT, 2009)

J.A. Gere and Philip Pouncey, *Italian Drawings in the Department of Prints and Drawings in the British Museum: Artists Working in Rome, c.1550 to c.1640* (British Museum, London, 1983)

Mark Girouard, *Hardwick Hall*, rev. edn (National Trust, London, 1999)

Clare Gittings, *The National Portrait Gallery Book of Elizabeth I* (National Portrait Gallery, London, 2006)

Philippa Glanville, *Silver in Tudor and Early Stuart England: A Social History and Catalogue of the National Collection, 1480–1660* (Victoria and Albert Museum, London, 1990)

Elizabeth Goldring, 'Talbot [née Hardwick], Elizabeth [Bess; called Bess of Hardwick], countess of Shrewsbury (1527?–1608)', *Oxford Dictionary of National Biography* (Oxford University Press, Oxford, 2004)

J.W. Goodison, 'George Gower, Serjeant Painter to Queen Elizabeth', *Burlington Magazine*, 1948

J.W. Goodison, *Catalogue of Cambridge Portraits* (Cambridge University Press, Cambridge, 1955)

Richard Goulding, 'Wriothesley Portraits', Walpole Society, VIII, 1919–20

J. Hall Pleasants, 'The Lovelace Family and its Connections', *The Virginia Magazine of History and Biography*, vol. 28, 1920

John Hamilton Baker, *The Order of the Serjeants at Law* (Selden Society, supplementary series, London, 1984)

Bernard Harris, 'A Portrait of a Moor', in *Shakespeare Survey*, no. 11, ed. Allardyce Nicoll (Cambridge University Press, Cambridge, 1958)

P.W. Hasler, *The History of Parliament: The House of Commons, 1558–1603* (HMSO, London, 1981), vol. III

Edward Hawkins, compiled by Augustus Franks and Herbert Grueber (eds), *Medallic Illustrations of the History of Great Britain and Ireland to the death of George II*, 2 vols (British Museum Press, London, 1885), vol. I

J.F. Hayward, *Swords and Daggers* (HMSO, London, 1963)

J.F. Hayward, *The Art of the Gunmaker, Volume 1, 1500–1660*, 2nd edn (Barrie and Rockliff, London, 1965)

Karen Hearn (ed.), *Dynasties: Painting in Tudor and Jacobean England 1530–1630*, exh. cat., Tate Gallery, London, 1995

Karen Hearn, 'Gower, George (d.1596)', *Oxford Dictionary of National Biography*, (Oxford University Press, Oxford, 2004)

Arthur Mayger Hind, *Engraving in England in the Sixteenth and Seventeenth Centuries* (Cambridge University Press, Cambridge, 1952), vol. 1

F.W.H. Hollstein, *The New Hollstein: Dutch and Flemish etchings, engravings and woodcuts 1450–1700*, Part II (Roosendaal: Koninklijke Van Poll, Amsterdam, 1993), vol. 31

G.J. Hoogewerff, *De Noord-Nederlandsche Schilderkunst*, 1941–2 (ÕS-Gravenhage, The Hague, 1941–2), vol. IV

Maurice Howard, The Tudor Image (Tate Publishing, London, 1996)

Earl of Ilchester, 'Queen Elizabeth's Visit to Blackfriars: June 16, 1600', Walpole Society, IX, 1920

John Ingamells, *Catalogue of Portraits at Bishopthorpe Palace* (Borthwick Institute Publications, York, 1972)

John Ingamells, *The English Episcopal Portrait 1559–1835: a catalogue* (Paul Mellon Centre for Studies in British Art, London 1981)

Gervase Jackson Stops (ed.), *The Treasure Houses of Britain: 500 Years of Private Patronage and Art Collecting* (Yale University Press, London and New Haven CT, 1985)

Lisa Jardine, *The Awful End of Prince William the Silent, The First Assassination of a Head of State with a Handgun* (HarperCollins, London, 2005)

R. Kelleher, '*Gold is the strength, the sinnewes of the world*: continental gold and Tudor England', *British Numismatic Journal*, 77, 2007

F.M. Kelly, 'Queen Elizabeth and her Dresses', *Connoisseur*, CXIII, 1944

John N. King, 'Queen Elizabeth I: Representations of the Virgin Queen', *Renaissance Quarterly*, vol. 43, 1990

John N. King, *John Foxe's 'Book of Martyrs' and Early Modern Print Culture* (Cambridge University Press, Cambridge, 2006)

Elizabeth Lane Furdell, *The Royal Doctors 1485–1714, Medical Personnel at the Tudor and Stuart Courts* (University of Rochester Press, Rochester, 2001)

William Leahy, *Elizabethan Triumphal Processions* (Ashgate, Farnham, 2005)

Sophia Lee and Dominic Naish, *The Vintners' Catalogue of Plate* (Vintners' Company, London, 1996)

Marika Annikki Leino, *Italian Renaissance Plaquettes in Context* (unpublished PhD thesis, University of London, 2004)

Santina M. Levey, *The Embroideries at Hardwick Hall: a catalogue* (National Trust, London, 2007)

Santina M. Levey and Peter K. Thornton, *Of Household Stuff: the 1601 Inventories of Bess of Hardwick* (National Trust, London, 2001)

Ger Luijten (ed.), *Remigius and Frans Hogenberg*, compiled by Ursule Mielke (Sound & Vision, Netherlands, 2009)

Wallace T. MacCaffrey, 'Cecil, William, 1st Baron Burghley (1520/21–1598)', *Oxford Dictionary of National Biography* (Oxford University Press, Oxford, 2004

L.G. Matthews and H.J. Green, 'Post-Medieval Pottery of the Inns of Court', Post-Medieval Archaeology, vol. 3, 1969

James McDermott, *Martin Frobisher: Elizabethan Privateer* (Yale University Press, London, 2001)

James McDermott, 'Frobisher, Sir Martin (1535?–1594)', *Oxford Dictionary of National Biography* (Oxford University Press, Oxford, 2004)

Oliver Millar, *The Tudor, Stuart and Early Georgian Pictures in the Collection of Her Majesty the Queen* (Phaidon Press, London, 1963)

Norman Moore, 'Lister, Edward (1557–1620)', rev. Rachel E. Davies, *Oxford Dictionary of National Biography* (Oxford University Press, Oxford, 2004)

'The Norfolk Archaeological Society Excursion to Thetford and Fersfield', *Norfolk Archaeology*, vol. 24, September 1929, p.15

F. O'Donoghue, *Catalogue of engraved British portraits preserved in the Department of Prints and Drawings in the British Museum* (British Museum, London, 1908–25), vol. II

Charles Oman, *Catalogue of Rings in the Victoria and Albery Museum* (Victoria and Albert Museum, London, 1930)

Angus Patterson, *Fashion and Armour in Renaissance Europe: Proud Lookes and Brave Attire* (V&A Publications, London, 2009)

Annabel Patterson, 'Donne in Shadows: Pictures and Politics', *John Donne Journal*, 16, 1997

Andrew Pettegree, 'Day [Daye], John (1521/2–1584), printer and bookseller', *Oxford Dictionary of National Biography* (Oxford University Press, Oxford, 2004

David Piper, *The Image of the Poet: British Poets and their Portraits* (Clarendon Press, Oxford, 1982)

Elizabeth Pomeroy, *Reading The Portraits of Elizabeth I* (Shoe String Press, North Haven CT, 1989)

Mrs R.L. Poole, *Catalogue of Oxford Portraits*, 4 vols (Oxford Historical Society, Oxford, 1912), vol. I

Mrs R.L. Poole, expanded by Kenneth Garlick, *Catalogue of Portraits in the Bodleian Library* (Bodleian Library, Oxford, 2004)

A.E. Popham, 'Georg Hoefnagel and the Civitates Orbis Terrarum', *Maso Finiguerra*, 1936, vol. I

D.A. Power, 'Notes on early portraits of John Banister of William Harvey and the Barber Surgeons visceral lecture in 1581', Proceedings of the Royal Society of Medicine, 1913, 6

Princely Magnificence: Court Jewels of the Renaissance, 1500-1630, exh. cat., Victoria and Albert Museum, London, 1980–1

Rev. W.G. Proctor, 'Notes on the Hesketh Pedigree', *Transactions of the Historic Society of Lancaster and Cheshire for the Year 1910*, New Series, XXVI, Liverpool, 1911

Graham Reynolds, *Nicholas Hilliard & Isaac Oliver* (Victoria and Albert Museum, London, 1971)

Graham Reynolds, *English Portrait Miniatures* (Cambridge University Press, Cambridge, 1988)

Aileen Ribeiro, *The Gallery of Fashion* (National Portrait Gallery, London, 2000)

Aileen Ribeiro, *Fashion and Fiction: Dress in Art and Literature in Stuart England* (Yale University Press, London and New Haven CT, 2003)

Enid Roberts, 'Katheryn of Berain [called Mam Cymru]', *Oxford Dictionary of National Biography* (Oxford University Press, Oxford, 2008

Walter Rye, *An Autobiography of an Ancient Athlete and Antiquary* (privately published, Norwich, 1916)

Margaret Sax, 'The recognition and nomenclature of quartz materials with specific reference to engraved gemstones', *Jewellery Studies*, 7, 1996

Diana Scarisbrick, *Jewellery in Britain 1066–1837: A Documentary, Social, Literary and Artistic Survey* (Michael Russell, Norwich, 1994)

Diana Scarisbrick, *Tudor and Jacobean Jewellery* (Tate Publishing, London, 1995)

Diana Scarisbrick, 'Sir Thomas Gresham and the Grasshopper Rings', *The Royal Exchange*, ed. Ann Saunders (London Topographical Society, London, 1997)

Diana Scarisbrick and Martin Henig, with an introduction by James Fenton, *Finger Rings, from Ancient to Modern* (Ashmolean Museum, Oxford, 2003)

Diana Scarisbrick, *Rings: Jewelry of Power, Love and Loyalty* (Thames & Hudson, London, 2007)

George Scharf, *Catalogue of Pictures at Knowsley Hall* (Bradbury, Agnew & Co., London, 1875), Supplement

Timothy Schroder, 'Lord Burghley's silver spice dishes', *Apollo*, February 2004

Timothy Schroder (ed.), *The Gilbert Collection at the V&A* (V&A Publishing, London, 2009)

A.H. Scott-Elliot and Elspeth Yeo, 'Calligraphic Manuscripts of Esther Inglis (1571–1624): A Catalogue', *The Papers of the Bibliographical Society of America*, 84, 1990

Searching for Shakespeare, exh. cat., National Portrait Gallery, London, 2006

Kevin Sharpe, *Selling the Tudor Monarchy: Authority and Image in Sixteenth-Century England* (Yale University Press, London and New Haven CT, 2009)

Kim Sloan, *A New World: England's First View of America* (British Museum Press, London, 2007)

Roy Strong, *Portraits of Queen Elizabeth I* (Clarendon Press, Oxford, 1963)

Roy Strong, 'Nicholas Hilliard's Miniature of Francis Bacon Rediscovered and other Minutiae', *Burlington Magazine*, CVI, no. 736, 1964

Roy Strong, *The English Icon: Elizabethan and Jacobean Portraiture* (Paul Mellon Foundation for British Art, in association with Routledge & Kegan Paul, London, 1969) (a)

Roy Strong, *Tudor and Jacobean Portraits in the National Portrait Gallery*, 2 vols (HMSO, London, 1969) (b)

Roy Strong, *The Cult of Elizabeth* (Thames & Hudson, London, 1977)

Roy Strong, *Artists of the Tudor Court: The Portrait Miniature Rediscovered, 1520–1620* (Victoria and Albert Museum, London, 1983) (a)

Roy Strong, *The English Renaissance Miniature* (Thames & Hudson, London, 1983) (b)

Roy Strong, 'The Leicester House miniatures: Robert Sidney, 1st Earl of Leicester and his circle', Shorter Notices, *Burlington Magazine*, CXXVII, no. 991, October 1985

Roy Strong, *Gloriana: The Portraits of Queen Elizabeth I* (Thames & Hudson, New York, 1987)

Henry Symonds, 'English mint engravers of the Tudor and Stuart periods', *Numismatic Chronicle*, 4th series, 13, 1913

Hugh Tait, *The Golden Age of Venetian Glass* (British Museum Press, London, 1979)

Hugh Tait (ed.), *Five Thousand Years of Glass* (British Museum Press, London, 1991)

R.K.R. Thornton and T.G.S. Cain (eds), *A Treatise concerning the Arte of Limning by Nicholas Hilliard* (Carcanet Press, Manchester, 1981)

Victor Tourneur, 'Steven van Herwijck', *Numismatic Chronicle*, 5th series, II, 1922

Edward Town, 'A Biographical Dictionary of London Painters 1547–1625', *Walpole Society* (forthcoming, 2014)

The Treasure Houses of Britain, exh. cat., National Gallery of Art, Washington DC, 1985

Gerard L'E. Turner, *Elizabethan Instrument Makers: The Origins of the London Trade in Precision Instrument Making* (Oxford University Press, Oxford, 2000)

John Venn (ed.), *Biographical History of Gonville and Caius College*, 7 vols (Cambridge University Press, Cambridge, 1897–1901), vol. III

J. & J.A. Venn, *Alumnni Cantabrigienses: A Biographical list of all known students, graduates and holders of office at the University of Cambridge, from the earliest times to 1900* (Cambridge University Press, Cambridge, 1927)

R.J.B. Walker, *Audley End, A Catalogue of Pictures* (HMSO, London, 1973)

F.A.B. Ward, *A Catalogue of European Scientific Instruments in the department of Medieval and later Antiquities of the British Museum* (British Museum, London, 1981)

Giles Waterfield, *Mr Cartwright's Pictures, A Seventeenth-Century Collection*, exh. cat., Dulwich Picture Gallery, London, 1987–8

E.K. Waterhouse, 'A note on George Gower's self portrait at Milton Park', *Burlington Magazin*e, XC, 1948

Anthony Wells-Cole, *Art and Decoration in Tudor and Jacobean England: The Influence of Continental Prints, 1558–1625* (Yale University Press, London and New Haven CT, 1997)

Anthony Wells-Cole, 'Scissors-and-paste in two paintings of Elizabeth I', *Burlington Magazine*, 1317, 2012

E. Wollaston Knocker, *Dover Corporation. Insignia, seals, plate, mayors, officers, honorary freemen, Town Hall portraits, pictures, windows and charities* (printed by A. Ezra, Dover, 1898)

Gordon Wolstenholme and David Piper, *The Royal College of Physicians of London: Portraits* (Churchill, London, 1964)

Stephen Wright, 'Frankland, Joyce (1531–1587)', *Oxford Dictionary of National Biography* (Oxford University Press, Oxford, 2004)

Frances Yates, *Allegorical Portraits of Queen Elizabeth I at Hatfield House*, Hatfield House Booklet no. 1, 1952

Frances Yates, *The Valois Tapestries*, 2nd edn (Routledge & Kegan Paul, London, 1975)

Elspeth Yeo, 'Inglis, Esther (1570/71–1624)', *Oxford Dictionary of National Biography* (Oxford University Press, Oxford, 2004)

Picture Credits

The National Portrait Gallery would like to thank the copyright holders for granting permission to reproduce works illustrated in this book. Every effort has been made to contact the holders of copyright material, and any omissions will be corrected in future editions if the publisher is notified in writing. Credits for figures are given below. Dimensions for figures are given height × width (mm), where available.

FIG. 1: *Joan Alleyn*, unknown English artist, 1596. Oil on panel, 791 × 632mm. Photo: by permission of the Trustees of Dulwich Picture Gallery (DPG 444).
FIG. 2: *The Hornby Castle Set of early Kings and Queens*, unknown artists, late sixteenth century–*c.*1620. Oil on panel, various measurements (see below). Photos © National Portrait Gallery, London. Purchased 1974.
King William I ('The Conqueror') (NPG 4980(1)), 568 × 414mm, uneven;
King Henry I (NPG 4980(2)), 584 × 444mm, uneven;
King Stephen (NPG 4980(3)), 579 × 447mm;
King Henry II (NPG 4980(4)), 571 × 418mm, uneven;
King John (NPG 4980(5)), 578 × 451mm;
King Edward II (NPG 4980(6)), 580 × 450mm, uneven;
King Edward III (NPG 4980(7)), 584 × 448mm, uneven;
King Richard II (NPG 4980(8)), 578 × 449mm, uneven;
King Henry IV (NPG 4980(9)), 580 × 445mm, uneven;
King Edward IV (NPG 4980(10)), 572 × 448mm;
King Edward V (NPG 4980(11)), 578 × 444mm;
King Richard III (NPG 4980(12)), 570 × 448mm, uneven;
King Henry VII (NPG 4980(13)), 572 × 445mm, uneven;
King Henry VIII (NPG 4980(14)), 582 × 450mm, uneven;
Anne Boleyn (NPG 4980(15)), 564 × 441mm, uneven;
Queen Mary I (NPG 4980(16)), 572 × 451mm.
FIG. 3: *Death and the Maiden*, English School, dated 1570. Oil on board, 650 × 490mm. Photo: by permission of the Shakespeare Birthplace Trust.
FIG. 4: *The Long Gallery at Hardwick Hall, Derbyshire*. Photo © National Trust Images/Nick Guttridge.
FIG. 5: see cat. 10
FIG. 6: *Elizabeth Knollys, Lady Layton*, attributed to George Gower, 1577. Oil on panel, 686 × 610mm. Courtesy Montacute House, Somerset. Photo: © National Trust Images/Derrick E. Witty.
FIG. 7: *Sir Henry Lee*, Anthonis Mor (Antonio Moro), 1568. Oil on panel, 641 × 533mm. Photo © National Portrait Gallery, London (NPG 2095). Given by Harold Lee-Dillon, 17th Viscount Dillon, 1925.
FIG. 8: *Woodcut of Elizabeth I*, unknown artist, late 1500s. Photo: © The Ashmolean Museum, University of Oxford (WA.B.l.17 Sutherland).
FIG. 9: *John Isham, Warden of the Mercers' Company*, unknown English artist, *c.*1567. Oil on panel, 1080 × 820mm. Photo: courtesy Lamport Hall, Northamptonshire.
FIG. 10: *Dr King preaching at Old St Paul's before James I*, John Gipkyn, 1616. Oil on panel. Photo: courtesy Society of Antiquaries of London, UK/The Bridgeman Art Library.
FIG. 11: Frontispiece to *The Third and Last Part of Conny-catching. With the new deuised knauish arte of foole-taking. The like coosnages and villanies neuer before discouered*, Robert Greene, 1592. Photo: reproduced by permission of The Huntington Library, San Marino, California.
FIGS 12 AND 13: details from *A Fête at Bermondsey* (cat. 4), Joris Hoefnagel, *c.*1568–70. Courtesy the Marquess of Salisbury, Hatfield House. Photos: © National Portrait Gallery, London.
FIG. 14: *The Family of Henry VIII: An Allegory of the Tudor Succession*, Lucas de Heere, *c.*1570–5. Oil on panel, 1312 × 1840mm. Photo © National Museum of Wales.
FIG. 15: *Thomas Whithorne*, unknown English artist, dated 1569. Oil on panel, 423 × 364mm. Photo: courtesy Beinecke Rare Book and Manuscript Library, Yale University.
FIG. 16: *Chester Cathedral, Consistory Court*. Photo: © Stephen Craven. Reproduced by permission of the Dean & Chapter of Chester Cathedral.
FIG. 17: *The 'Stang Ride' or 'Skimmington Ride' plasterwork panel in the Great Hall at Montacute House, Somerset*. Photo: © National Trust Images/Nadia Mackenzie.
FIG. 18: 'A Puritan Family' from *The Whole Psalms in Four Parts*, English School, 1563. Woodcut. Photo: © Private Collection/The Bridgeman Art Library.
FIG. 19: *Alice Barnham and Her Sons Martin and Steven*, English School, 1557. The Berger Collection at the Denver Art Museum. Photo: provided by the Denver Art Museum.
FIG. 20: *Statues of the Nine Worthies on the East Front at Montacute House, Somerset*. Photo: © National Trust Images/Andrew May.
FIG. 21: *Robert Sidney, 1st Earl of Leicester*, unknown artist, *c.*1588. Oil on canvas, 991 × 794mm. Photo © National Portrait Gallery, London (NPG 1862). Purchased 1920.
FIG. 22: see cat. 30
FIG. 23: detail from *A Fête at Bermondsey* (cat. 4), Joris Hoefnagel, *c.*1568–70. Courtesy the Marquess of Salisbury, Hatfield House. Photo: © National Portrait Gallery, London.
FIG. 24: Youth's jerkin of pinked leather, *c.*1560. 520 × 450 × 305mm. Photo: © Museum of London (36.327).
FIG. 25: detail from *A Fête at Bermondsey* (cat. 4), Joris Hoefnagel, *c.*1568–70. Courtesy the Marquess of Salisbury, Hatfield House. Photo: © National Portrait Gallery, London.
FIG. 26: detail from *A Fête at Bermondsey* (cat. 4), Joris Hoefnagel, *c.*1568–70. Courtesy the Marquess of Salisbury, Hatfield House. Photo: © National Portrait Gallery, London.
FIG. 27: Gerardus Mercator and Jodocus Hondius, after an unknown artist, mid-seventeenth century. Line engraving, 385 × 445mm. Photo: © National Portrait Gallery, London (NPG D26294). Given by the daughter of compiler William Fleming MD, Mary Elizabeth Stopford, 1931.
FIG. 28: detail from *Elizabeth I* (cat. 8), unknown Continental artist, *c.*1575 (NPG 2082). Photo: © National Portrait Gallery, London.
FIG. 29: see cat. 20
FIG. 30: *Monument to Peter Cappone from the south wall of the north chancel in St Olave's Church, Hart Street, London*, unknown artist, *c.*1800. Watercolour on paper, height 420mm. Photo: courtesy City of London, London Metropolitan Archives.
FIG. 31: *Dissection instruments from* Anatomical Tables by John Banister, English school, sixteenth century. Glasgow University Library, Scotland (Ms Hunter 364 Table I). Photo: © Glasgow University Library, Scotland/The Bridgeman Art Library.
FIG. 32: *Title page and author portrait from* The Herball (engravings by William Rogers), John Gerard, 1597. Engraving. The Bodleian Libraries, The University of Oxford (L.1.5. Med (Cons. Res. 5)). Photos: courtesy The Bodleian Libraries, The University of Oxford.
FIG. 33: *'An English Sailor' from* Habiti Antichi et Moderni di tutto il Mondo, Cesare Vecellio, 1598. Engraving. Photo: courtesy Universal History Archive/Getty Images.
FIG. 34: *King Henry VIII*, unknown Anglo-Netherlandish artist, *c.*1535–40. Oil on panel, 584 × 445mm. Photo: © National Portrait Gallery, London (NPG 3638). Given by Sir Geoffrey Langdon Keynes, 1948.
FIG. 35: *Anne Boleyn*, unknown artist, *c.*1533–6. Oil on panel, 543 × 416mm. Photo: © National Portrait Gallery, London (NPG 668). Purchased 1882.
FIG. 36: *King Edward VI*, studio of William Scrots, *c.*1546. Oil on panel, 473 × 279mm. Photo: © National Portrait Gallery, London (NPG 442). Purchased 1877.
FIG. 37: *Philip II, King of Spain*, after Titian, 1555. Oil on panel, 86 × 64mm. Photo: © National Portrait Gallery, London (NPG 4175). Given by Edward Peter Jones, 1960.
FIG. 38: *Queen Mary I*, after Anthonis Mor (Antonio Moro), dated 1555. Oil on panel, 86 × 64mm. Photo: © National

Portrait Gallery, London (NPG 4174). Given by Edward Peter Jones, 1960.
FIG. 39: *Thomas Cranmer*, Gerlach Flicke, 1545. Oil on panel, 984 × 762mm. Photo: © National Portrait Gallery, London (NPG 535). Transferred from the British Museum, 1879.
FIG. 40: William Cecil, 1st Baron Burghley, unknown Anglo-Netherlandish artist, 1560s. Oil on panel, 953 × 718mm. Photo: © National Portrait Gallery, London (NPG 2184). Purchased 1928.
FIG. 41: *Mary, Queen of Scots*, unknown artist, *c.*1560–92. Oil on panel, 251 × 191mm. Photo: © National Portrait Gallery, London (NPG 1766). Purchased 1916.
FIG. 42: *Robert Dudley, 1st Earl of Leicester*, unknown Anglo-Netherlandish artist, *c.*1575. Oil on panel, 1080 × 826mm. Photo: © National Portrait Gallery, London (NPG 447). Purchased 1877.
FIG. 43: *Matthew Parker*, Remigius Hogenberg, published 1573. Line engraving, 115 × 93mm (paper size). Photo: © National Portrait Gallery, London (D25183). Given by the daughter of compiler William Fleming MD, Mary Elizabeth Stopford, in 1931.
FIG. 44: *Thomas Howard, 4th Duke of Norfolk*, unknown Anglo-Netherlandish artist, 1565. Oil on panel, 1032 × 802mm. Photo: © National Portrait Gallery, London (NPG 6676). Purchased with help from the Art Fund and National Heritage Memorial Fund, 2004.
FIG. 45: *Sir Francis Walsingham*, possibly after John de Critz the Elder, *c.*1587. Oil on panel, 375 × 298mm. Photo: © National Portrait Gallery, London (NPG 1704). Purchased 1913.
FIG. 46: *King James I of England and VI of Scotland*, unknown artist, *c.*1590. Oil on panel, 203 × 143mm. Photo: © National Portrait Gallery, London (NPG 1188). Purchased 1899.
FIG. 47: *Sir Philip Sidney*, unknown artist, *c.*1576. Oil on panel, 1139 × 840mm. Photo: © National Portrait Gallery, London (NPG 5732). Purchased with help from The Art Fund, 1984.
FIG. 48: *Elizabeth I, Armada Portrait*, George Gower, *c.*1588. Oil on panel, 1050 × 1330 mm. Photo: reproduced by kind permission of His Grace the Duke of Bedford and the Trustees of the Bedford Estates.
FIG. 49: *William Camden*, by or after Marcus Gheeraerts the Younger, 1609. Oil on panel, 565 × 419mm. Photo: © National Portrait Gallery, London (NPG 528). Transferred from the British Museum, 1879.
FIG. 50: *Robert Cecil, 1st Earl of Salisbury*, John de Critz the Elder, 1602. Oil on panel, 902 × 734mm. Photo: © National Portrait Gallery, London (NPG 107). Given by David Laing, 1860.
FIG. 51: *William Shakespeare*, attributed to John Taylor, *c.*1600s. Oil on canvas, feigned oval, 552 × 438mm. Photo: © National Portrait Gallery, London (NPG 1). Given by Francis Egerton, 1st Earl of Ellesmere, 1856.
FIG. 52: *Benjamin Jonson*, Abraham van Blyenberch, *c.*1617. Oil on canvas, 470 × 419mm. Photo: © National Portrait Gallery, London (NPG 2752). Purchased 1935.
FIG. 53: *John Florio*, William Hole, published 1611. Engraving, 168 × 133mm (paper size). Photo: © National Portrait Gallery, London (NPG D31841). Given by Henry Witte Martin, 1861.
FIG. 54: *King James I of England and VI of Scotland*, after John de Critz the Elder, *c.*1606. Oil on panel, 572 × 419mm. Photo: © National Portrait Gallery, London (NPG 548). Transferred from the British Museum, 1879.

EXHIBITION WORKS

1 (and p.6). John Wingfield Digby, Sherborne Castle Estates. Photo: courtesy Sherborne Castle, Dorset.
2. Llyfrgell Genedlaethol Cymru/The National Library of Wales, Aberystwyth (MAP 05391). Photo: Supplied by Llyfrgell Genedlaethol Cymru/The National Library of Wales, Aberystwyth.
3. The British Library (Sloane MS 2596 f.52). Photo: © The British Library Board.
4 (and p.45). The Marquess of Salisbury, Hatfield House. Photo: reproduced by permission of the Marquess of Salisbury, Hatfield House.
5. Lent by Her Majesty Queen Elizabeth II (RCIN403446). Photo: Royal Collection Trust/© Her Majesty Queen Elizabeth II 2013.
6. National Portrait Gallery, London (NPG 6947). Purchased 2012. Photo: © National Portrait Gallery, London.
7. The Trustees of the British Museum, London (PD Gg. I-1417). Photo: © The Trustees of the British Museum.
8 (and p.56). National Portrait Gallery, London (NPG 2082). Purchased 1925. Photo: © National Portrait Gallery, London.
9.The Marquess of Salisbury, Hatfield House. Photo: reproduced by permission of the Marquess of Salisbury, Hatfield House.
10. Hardwick Hall, The Devonshire Collection (National Trust inventory number: 1129128). Acquired through the National Land Fund and transferred to the National Trust in 1959. Photo: © National Trust/Robert Thrift.
11. The Trustees of the British Museum (1862-1213.1). Photo: © The Trustees of the British Museum.
12. Lent by kind permission of the University of Cambridge. Photo: courtesy the University of Cambridge.
13. Dover Museum and Bronze Age Boat Gallery. Photo: courtesy Dover Museum and Bronze Age Boat Gallery.
14. The Trustees of the British Museum (1914, 0926.1). Photo: © The Trustees of the British Museum.
15 a, b, c and d. The Trustees of the British Museum. b donated by the Bank of England; c (also p.1) bequeathed by Sir Allen George Clark; d bequeathed by T.B. Clark-Thornhill. All photos: © The Trustees of the British Museum.
16. National Portrait Gallery, London (NPG 108). Purchased 1860. Photo: © National Portrait Gallery, London.
17 a. Private Collection. Photo: courtesy Private Collection.
17 b. From the private collection of Lord Braybrooke, on display at Audley End House, Essex (English Heritage). Photo: © English Heritage.
18. National Portrait Gallery, London (NPG 4197). Purchased with help from The Art Fund, the Pilgrim Trust, H.M. Government and an anonymous donor, 1961. Photo: © National Portrait Gallery, London.
19. The Bodleian Libraries, University of Oxford (LP 38). Photo: courtesy The Bodleian Libraries, University of Oxford.
20. Northampton Borough Council, Northampton Museum and Art Gallery. Photo: courtesy Northampton Borough Council, Northampton Museum and Art Gallery.
21. The Bodleian Libraries, University of Oxford (LP 50). Photo: courtesy The Bodleian Libraries, University of Oxford.
22. National Portrait Gallery, London (NPG 7). Purchased 1857. Photo: © National Portrait Gallery, London.
23. The Marquess of Salisbury, Hatfield House. Photo: reproduced by permission of the Marquess of Salisbury, Hatfield House.
24. National Portrait Gallery, London (NPG 4851). Purchased with help from The Wolfson Foundation and H.M. Government, 1971. Photo: © National Portrait Gallery, London.
25. National Portrait Gallery, London (NPG 5994). Accepted in lieu of tax by H.M. Government and allocated to the Gallery, 1988. Photo: © National Portrait Gallery, London.
26. National Portrait Gallery, London (NPG 6241). Accepted in lieu of tax by H.M. Government and allocated to the Gallery, 1994. Photo: © National Portrait Gallery, London.
27. The Buccleuch Collection. Photo: courtesy The Buccleuch Collection.
28. Hardwick Hall, The Devonshire Collection (National Trust inventory number: 1129165). Acquired through the National Land Fund and transferred to the National Trust in 1959. Photo: © National Trust Images.
29. The Bute Collection at Mount Stuart. Photo: courtesy The Bute Collection.
30. The Burghley House Collection. Photo: courtesy The Burghley House Collection.
31. Privately owned. Photo: courtesy Private Collection.
32. Private Collection. Photo: courtesy Private Collection, Belgium.
33. Edward Harley Esq. Photo: courtesy Edward Harley Esq.
34. University of Birmingham, Research and Cultural Collections (A0427). Photo: courtesy University of Birmingham.
35. Ancient House, Thetford – Norfolk Museums and Archaeology Service. Photo: courtesy Norfolk Museums and Archaeology Service.
36 (and p.78). The British Library (Additional MS 44026). Photo: © The British Library Board.
37. Victoria and Albert Museum, London (M.949-1983). Purchased with the assistance of the National Heritage Memorial Fund. Photo: © Victoria and Albert Museum, London.
38. Victoria and Albert Museum, London (M.51-1947). Bequeathed by Francis Mallett. Photo: © Victoria and Albert Museum, London.
39 a. The Trustees of the British Museum (A.F.1943). Photo: © The Trustees of the British Museum.
39 b. The Ashmolean Museum, University of Oxford (WA1897.CDEF. F468). Presented by C.D.E. Fortnum in honour of Queen Victoria's Diamond Jubilee, 1897. Photo: courtesy The Ashmolean Museum, University of Oxford.
39 c. Victoria and Albert Museum, London (201-1906). Photo: © Victoria and Albert Museum, London.
39 d. The Ashmolean Museum, University of Oxford (WA1897.CDEF. F596). Presented by C.D.E. Fortnum in honour of Queen Victoria's Diamond Jubilee, 1897. Photo: courtesy The Ashmolean Museum, University of Oxford.

39 e. The Ashmolean Museum, University of Oxford (WA1897.CDEF. F475). Presented by C.D.E. Fortnum in honour of Queen Victoria's Diamond Jubilee, 1897. Photo: courtesy The Ashmolean Museum, University of Oxford.
40 a. Victoria and Albert Museum, London (M.7-1982). Purchased with the assistance of The Art Fund. Photo: © Victoria and Albert Museum, London.
40 b. The Trustees of the British Museum, London (1915,1216.134). Photo: © The Trustees of the British Museum.
41 a. The Rosalinde and Arthur Gilbert Collection on loan to the Victoria and Albert Museum, London. Photo: © Gilbert Collection.
41 b. Victoria and Albert Museum, London (M.665-1910). Salting Bequest. Photo: © Victoria and Albert Museum, London.
42 a. Victoria and Albert Museum, London (2143-1855). Photo: © Victoria and Albert Museum, London.
42 b. The Burrell Collection, Glasgow Museums (29.310). Photo: © CSG CIC Glasgow Museums Collection.
42 c. The Ashmolean Museum, University of Oxford (WA1947.191.324, bequeathed by Francis Mallet, 1947). Photo: courtesy The Ashmolean Museum, University of Oxford.
43. The Trustees of the British Museum (AF.3134). Photo: © The Trustees of the British Museum.
44 a. Hardwick Hall, The Devonshire Collection (National Trust inventory number: 1129780). Acquired through the National Land Fund and transferred to the National Trust in 1988. Photo: © National Trust Images/John Hammond.
44 b. Hardwick Hall, The Devonshire Collection. Acquired through the National Land Fund and transferred to the National Trust in 1988. Photo: © National Trust Images.
45 (and p.130). National Portrait Gallery, London (NPG 352). Purchased 1872. Photo: © National Portrait Gallery, London.
46. The Trustees of the British Museum, London (1863, 114.692). Photo: © The Trustees of the British Museum.
47. Private Collection. Photo: courtesy Private Collection.
48. National Museum of Wales, Cardiff (NMWA 19). Photo: courtesy National Museum of Wales, Cardiff.
49. The Churchwardens of St Olave Hart Street, London. Photo: courtesy The Churchwardens of St Olave Hart Street, London.
50 a, b and c. Lawes Agricultural Trust. Photo: courtesy Lawes Agricultural Trust.
51. National Museum of Wales, Cardiff (NMWA 3453). Photo: courtesy National Museum of Wales, Cardiff.
52. Museum of London (2002:74). Photo: © Museum of London.
53. (Not in exhibition) Gonville and Caius College, Cambridge. Photo: by permission of the Master and Fellows of Gonville and Caius College, Cambridge.
54. The British Library (Additional MS 28330, f.33, depicting four citizens' wives). Photo: © The British Library Board.
55 a. The Trustees of the British Museum (1844,0425.2713; E.308; 1935,0401.2029-2031 (bequeathed by T.B. Clark-Thornhill)); 1946,1004.643 (bequeathed by E.E. Oldroyd)). Photo: © The Trustees of the British Museum.
55 b. The Trustees of the British Museum (1840,114.2; 1935,0401.2048-2051 (bequeathed by T.B. Clark-Thornhill); 1946,1004.611 (bequeathed by E.E. Oldroyd); 1964,1203.30 (bequeathed by Sir Allen George Clark)). Photo: © The Trustees of the British Museum.
55 c. The Trustees of the British Museum (E.340; 1896,0803.3; 1915,0507.550; 1935,04012081 (bequeathed by T.B. Clark-Thornhill); 1946,1004.613 (bequeathed by E.E. Oldroyd)). Photo: © The Trustees of the British Museum.
55 d. The Trustees of the British Museum (E.328; 1935,0401.2055–2057 and 2059 (bequeathed by T.B. Clark-Thornhill)). Photo: © The Trustees of the British Museum.
56 a and b. The Glove Collection Trust, courtesy of the Fashion Museum, Bath and North-East Somerset Council (a: BATMC GLO 23341 & A (LOAN); b: BATMC GLO 23457 & A (LOAN)). Photo: courtesy the Fashion Museum, Bath and North-East Somerset Council.
57 a, b, c and d. Victoria and Albert Museum, London (a: M.71-1960; b: M.3-1959; given by Dame Joan Evans) (c: M.342-1975; bequeathed by Miss E.M. Begg) (d: 1375-1903). Photos: © Victoria and Albert Museum, London.
57 e. The Ashmolean Museum, University of Oxford (WA1897.CDEF. F600). Photo: courtesy The Ashmolean Museum, University of Oxford.
57 f. The Trustees of the British Museum, London (1928,0507.1). Photo: © The Trustees of the British Museum.
57 g. Victoria and Albert Museum, London (13-1888). Bequeathed by Miss Charlotte Frances Gerard. Photo: © Victoria and Albert Museum, London.
57 h. The Trustees of the British Museum (AF.1747). Photo: © The Trustees of the British Museum.
58. Private Collection. Photo: courtesy Private Collection.
59. Museum of London (A 6940). Photo: © Museum of London.
60. The Trustees of the British Museum (1912,0208.1). Photo: © The Trustees of the British Museum.
61. The National Archives, UK (c 239/48, no.104). Photo: courtesy The National Archives, UK.
62 a, b, c and d. Museum of London (a: 5008; b: A15260; c: 5006a; d: NN8512). Photos: © Museum of London.
63. The Vaughan Family Trust, courtesy of the Fashion Museum, Bath and North-East Somerset Council (BATMC I.03.136 (LOAN)) Photo: courtesy the Fashion Museum, Bath and North-East Somerset Council.
64 a, b and c. Museum of London (a: A26113; b: A3583; c: 4200, 80.230/12 a, b, c, 86.150/5, 4145 amd 80.184, 4–47). Photos: © Museum of London.
65 a, b, c, d, e, f. Museum of London (a: 80.469/10; b: 87.161/2; c: 86.361/17; d: 81.564/58; e: 81.564/34; f: 79.319/5). Photos: © Museum of London.
66 a. The Worshipful Company of Vintners. Photo: courtesy The Worshipful Company of Vintners.
66 b. Trinity Hall, Cambridge. Photo: courtesy Trinity Hall, Cambridge.
67 (and p.2). Private Collection. Photo: courtesy Private Collection.
68. National Portrait Gallery, London (NPG 4852). Purchased with help from H.M. Government, 1971. Photo: © National Portrait Gallery, London.
69. The Trustees of the British Museum (M.6869). Photo: © The Trustees of the British Museum.
70 a (and p.172). Scottish National Portrait Gallery (PG 3556). Gifted by the Society of Antiquaries in Scotland, 2009. Photo: courtesy Scottish National Portrait Gallery.
70 b. National Library of Scotland (MS.20498). Photo: courtesy National Library of Scotland.
71. National Portrait Gallery, London (NPG 6790). Purchased with help from the National Heritage Memorial Fund, The Art Fund, Lord Harris of Peckham, L.L. Brownrigg, The Portrait Fund, Sir Harry Djanogly, The Headley Trust, The Eva and Hans K. Rausing Trust, The Pidem Fund, Mr O. Damgaard-Nielsen, Sir David and Lady Scholey and numerous Gallery visitors and supporters, 2006. Photo: © National Portrait Gallery, London.
72. National Portrait Gallery, London (NPG 6761). Accepted in lieu of tax by H.M. Government and allocated to the Gallery, 2006. Photo: © National Portrait Gallery, London.
73. Bishopthorpe Palace, York. Photo: courtesy of The Church Commissioners.
74. Dulwich Picture Gallery, London (DPG 372). Photo: reproduced by permission of the Trustees of Dulwich Picture Gallery, London.
75. Norfolk and Norwich Museums Service (NWHCM: 1935.130F). Photo: © Norfolk Museums and Archaeology Service (Norwich Castle Museum & Art Gallery).
76. The President and Fellows of St John's College, Oxford. Photo: © Lee Atherton.
77. The Bodleian Libraries, University of Oxford (Bib. Eng. 1568 b.1). Photo: courtesy The Bodleian Libraries, University of Oxford.
78 a and b. The British Library, London (a: C.35.c.19; b: C.65k.10). Photo: © The British Library Board.
79. The Royal College of Physicians. Photo: © The Royal College of Physicians.
80. University of Glasgow Library (MS Hunter 364 V 1.1). Photo: courtesy University of Glasgow Library.
81 a and b. The British Library (a: K.4.C.2; b: K.4.C.3). Photos: © The British Library Board.
82 a. The Bodleian Libraries, University of Oxford (L.15.Med). Photo: courtesy The Bodleian Libraries, University of Oxford.
82 b. National Portrait Gallery, London (NPG D2756). Purchased 1966. Photo: © National Portrait Gallery, London.
83. The Trustees of the British Museum (1896,1230.73). Photo: © The Trustees of the British Museum.
84. Museum of London (53.101/1b). Photo: © Museum of London.
85. Museum of London (A 1989), Seymour Lucas Collection. Photo: © Museum of London.
86. Museum of London (5898; A 15256; A 28361). Photo: © Museum of London.
87 (and p.200). City of London Metropolitan Archives. Photo: courtesy City of London Metropolitan Archives; LMA: DL/C/B/005/MS09172/012A no. 64.

Index

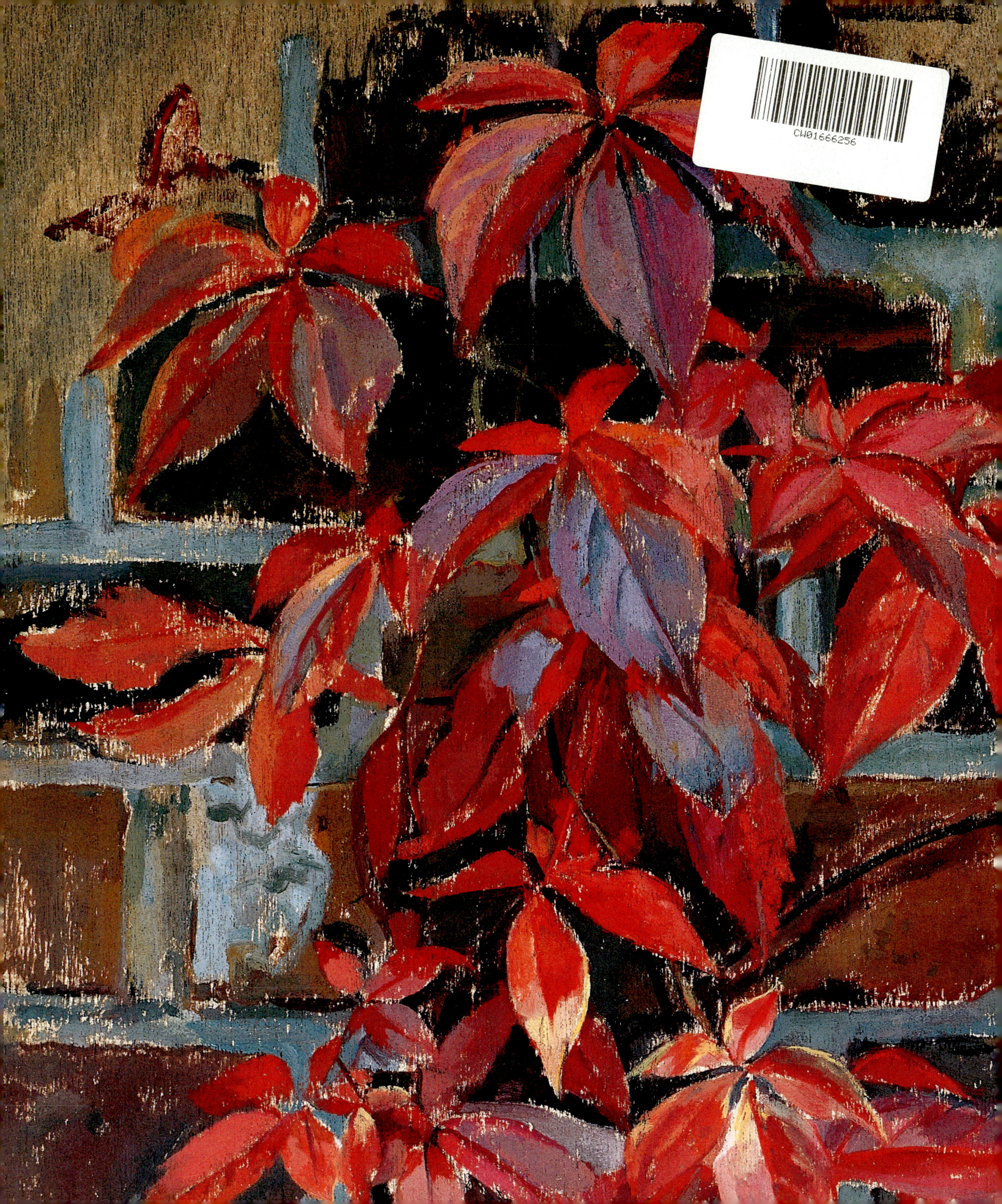

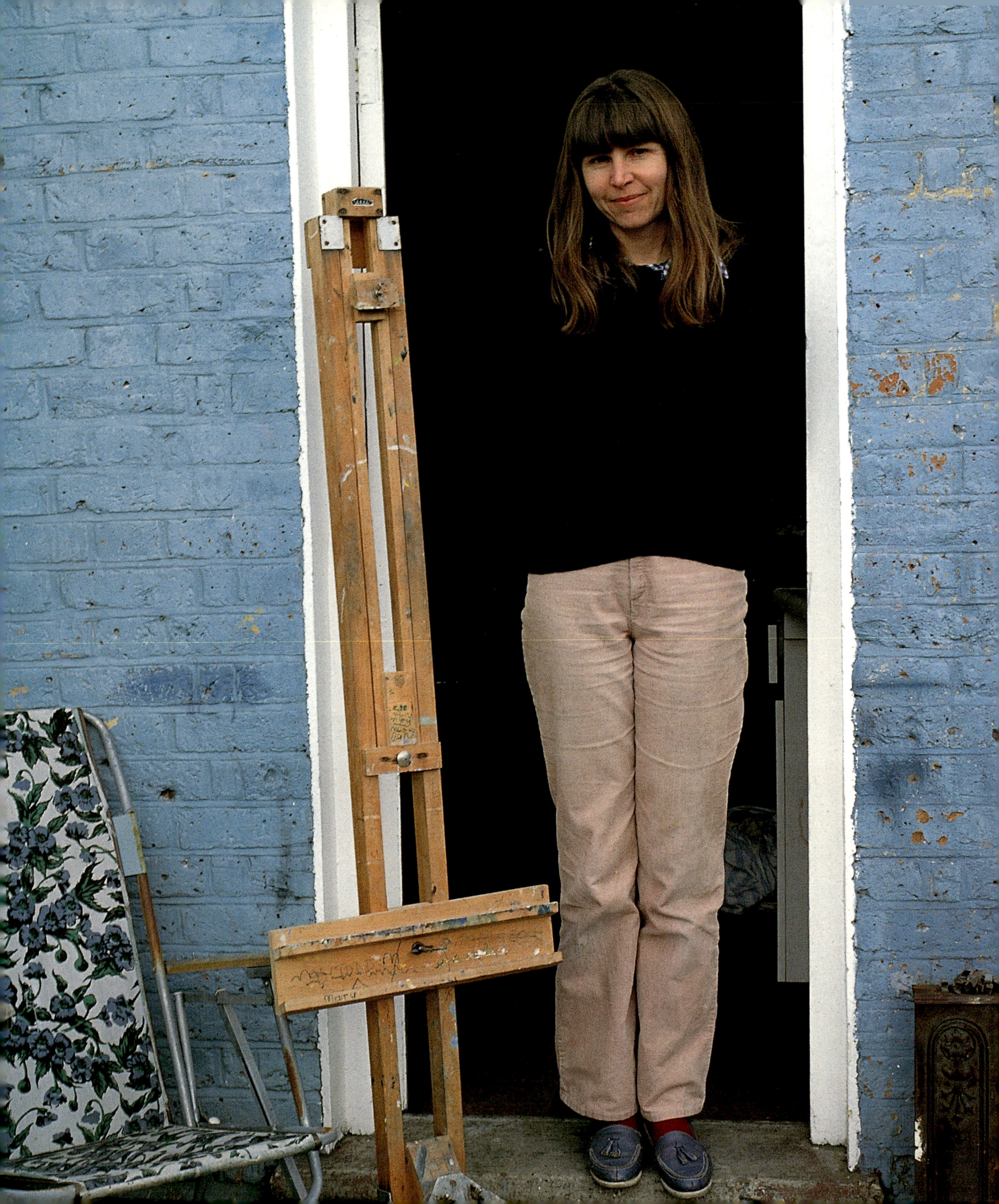

DAPHNE TODD

paint and principle

Daphne Todd.

The Life and Work of
Daphne Todd OBE, PPRP, NEAC

Jenny Pery

Jenny Pery

THE STUDIO
FINE ART PUBLICATIONS

First published in 2008 by Studio Fine Art Publications

ISBN 978-1-905883-27-1

British Library Cataloguing-in-Publication-Data

A CIP data record for this book is available from the British Library

David Messum Fine Art Limited
The Studio
Lords Wood
Marlow
Buckinghamshire SL7 2QS
T: 01628 486565
F: 01628 890205
www.messums.com

Printed by
DG3 Europe ltd, Docklands, London.
T: 020 7531 0500
www.dg3.com

Studio Publications is part of
David Messum Fine Art Ltd

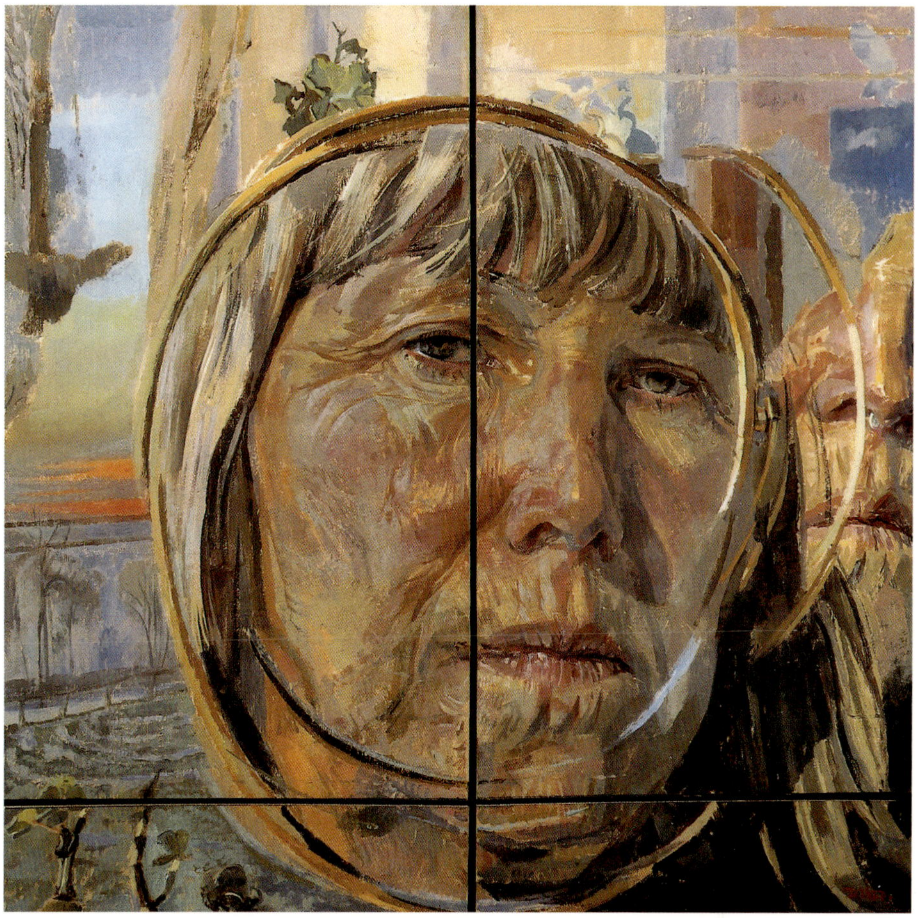

[1] *Me in a Magnifying Mirror*, 2001
40.6 x 40.6 cms 16 x 16 ins

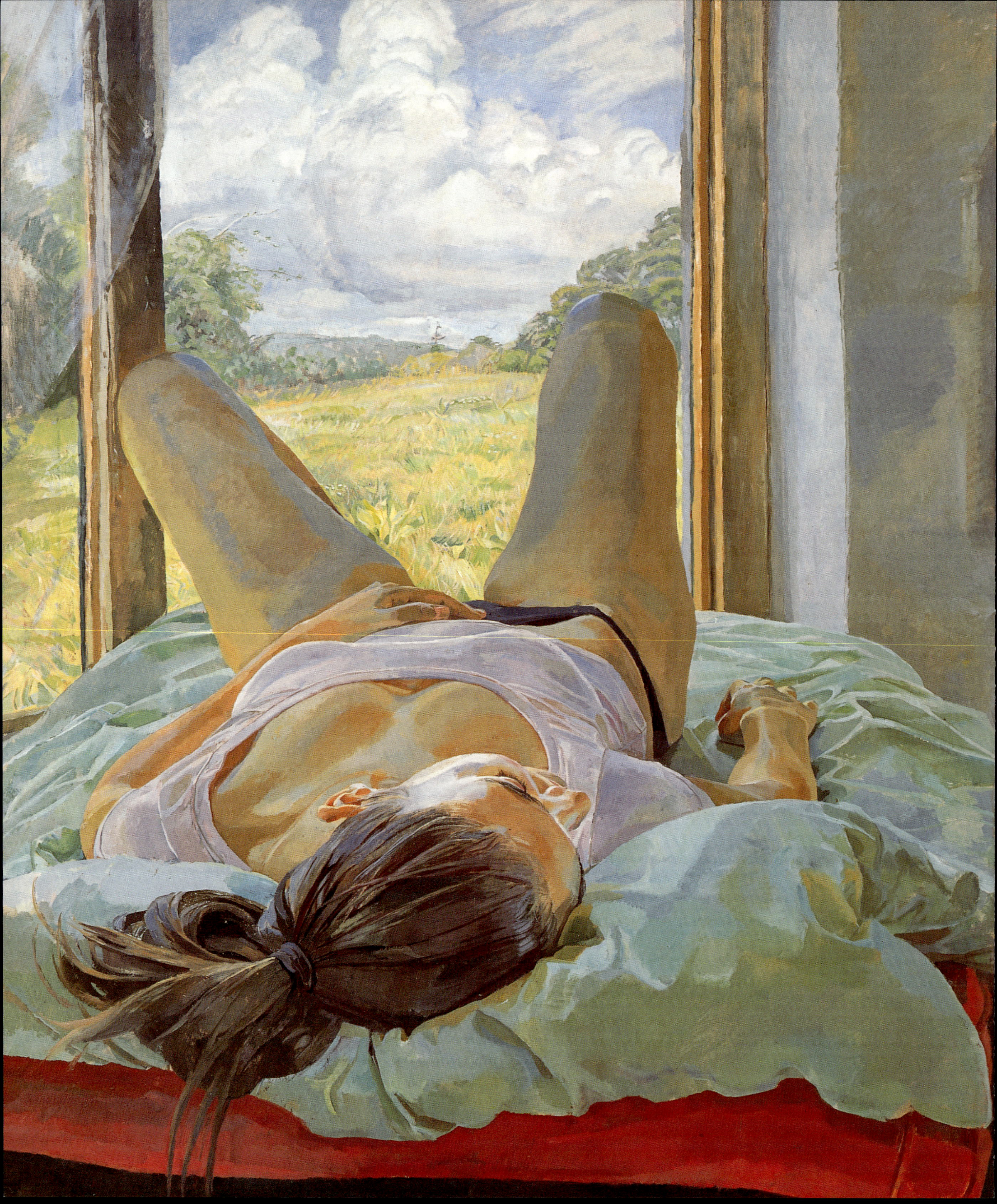

DAPHNE TODD is one of Britain's most distinguished contemporary painters. She is also a member of that exclusive and diminishing minority that paints entirely from life. Her work invites comparison with some of the grandees of representational painting - Euan Uglow and Patrick George, and, in a previous generation, Stanley Spencer. Perhaps the contemporary painter nearest to her in spirit is the equally distinguished John Wonnacott. Todd's work, like theirs, contains far more than simple representation, far more than an accurate eye and an understanding of paint can produce. She brings a human curiosity and appreciation to each subject she confronts, missing nothing, but selecting what seem to her the most significant items. In her portraits as well as in her other work, she often reinvents the motif, creating a multiplex version of the truth she sees. She is adventurous while remaining utterly truthful.

Todd's deservedly high reputation as a figurative painter of the utmost integrity and commitment has been hard won. It is built on years of dogged persistence, often working in artistic isolation, swimming against the tide of fashion. The many obstacles she has had to overcome in her development as a painter seem only to have increased her determination to produce work of the highest quality. Along the way she has also made major contributions to the fields of art education and administration, and her energetic presence in the field of portraiture has been an important factor in reviving the popularity of the painted portrait, which has faced a slow but steady decline since the advent of photography. Born with a natural talent and determined from early youth to become an artist, painting at the highest possible level has been the driving force in Daphne Todd's life. Now at the height of her career, she is confidently in command of her chosen medium.

'When I paint I feel I am stroking the surfaces that I see. Fundamentally it's all about looking and describing the surfaces.' [1] Although Daphne Todd's artistic ideology is based on the simple desire to paint what she sees, there is considerably more to it than that. She sees beneath the surfaces and into the heart of the pots, plants or dreaming heads that she depicts. Her paintings are suffused with incandescent light. The colour is high-key, oil paint thinly applied in soft flickering touches that create tiny tonal jumps. The surfaces seem to vibrate with pent-up energy. All her subjects are in a state of change - people, places or objects that are ageing, weathering, eroding, hovering between

[2] *Landscape Between Legs*, 2004
94 x 76.2 cms 37 x 30 ins

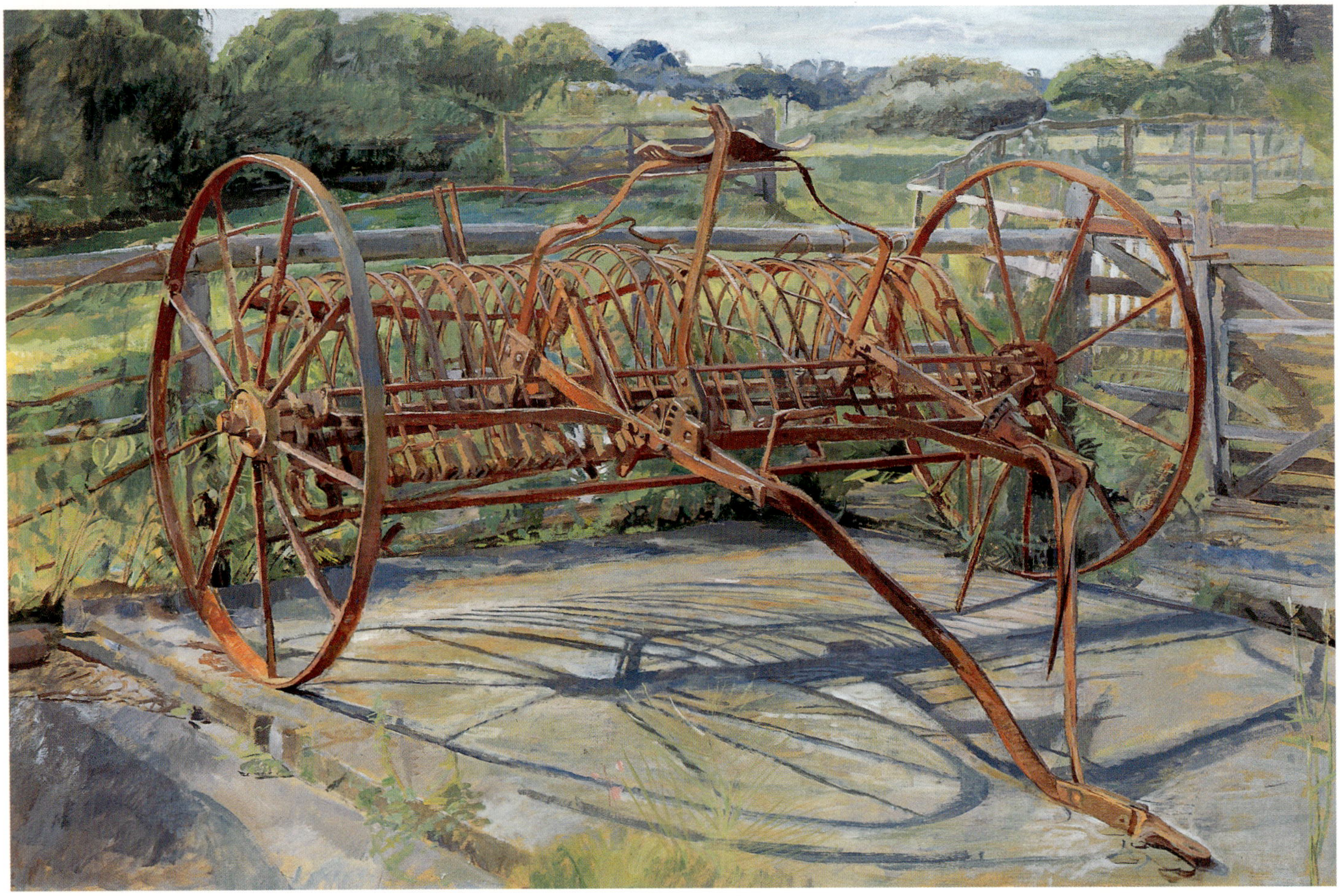

[3] *Old Hay Rake*, 2003
58.4 x 88.9 cms 23 x 35 ins

genesis and decay. Their colour and tonality give the impression of life glimpsed through a fine gauze veil. In her studio work especially, there is a sense of *à la recherche du temps perdu*. A blue or yellow haze, colours of memory, overlies much of the imagery. In most of her paintings the sense of loss and longing is strong.

Daphne Todd's impressive oeuvre to date covers a remarkable range, although her public reputation is built on her portraits. She did not set out, however, to be a portrait-painter, but simply to paint 'what's there'. Committed to figuration from the start, she is first and foremost a painter of the world around her. Commissioned portraits are supplemented by a large body of work made at home in her vast, airy barn/studio on her farm in Sussex. Into her familiar surroundings come models, and these wistful, dreaming presences furnish Todd with the figures for enigmatic genre pictures, about, as she puts it 'the way things were'. Alongside these are landscapes and outdoor still-lifes, intimate paintings of plants and pots and walls and the bric-a-brac of country life.

[4] *Ron and Ray Pett, Rotherfield Butchers*, 1989
127 x 101.6 cms 50 x 40 ins

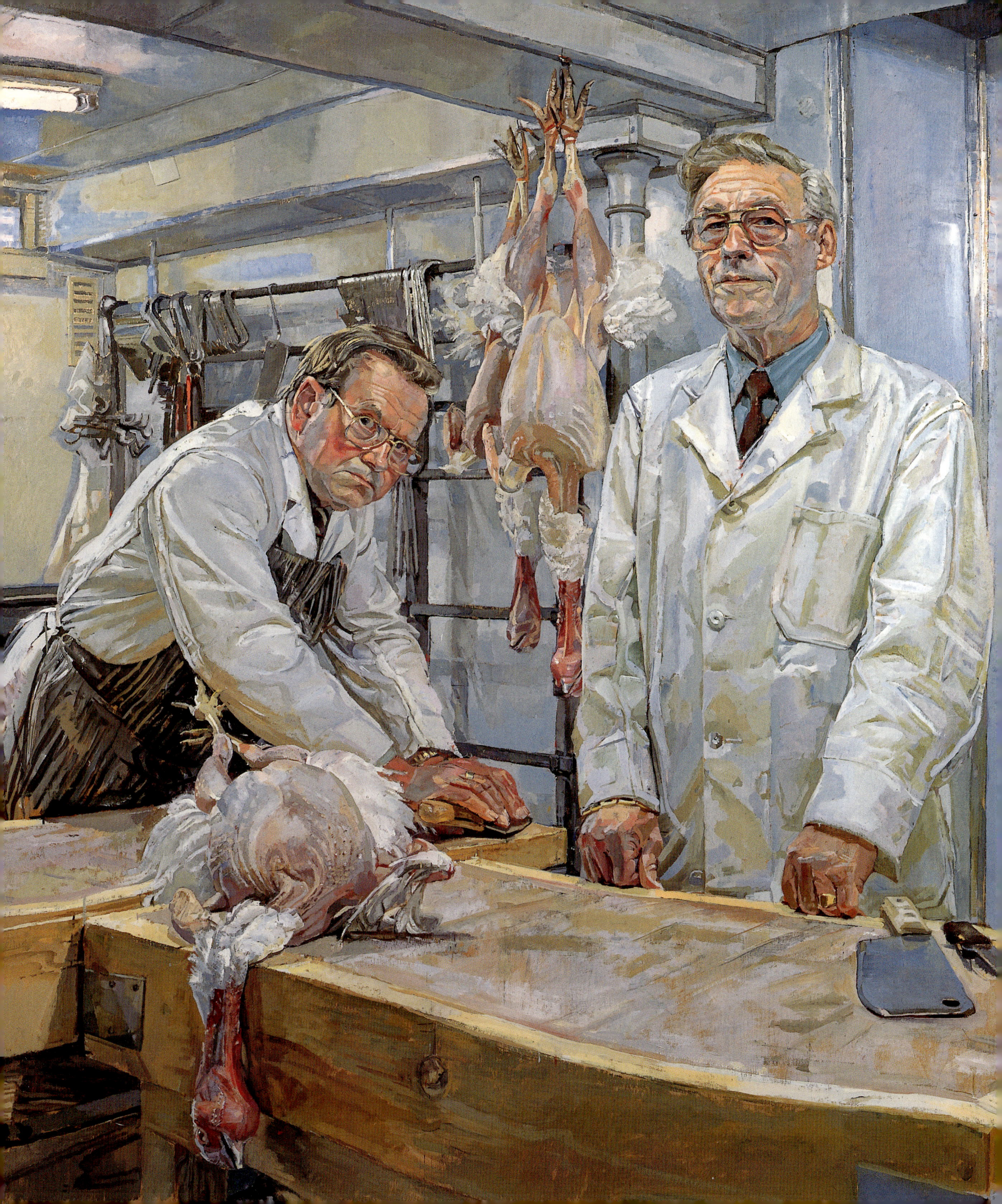

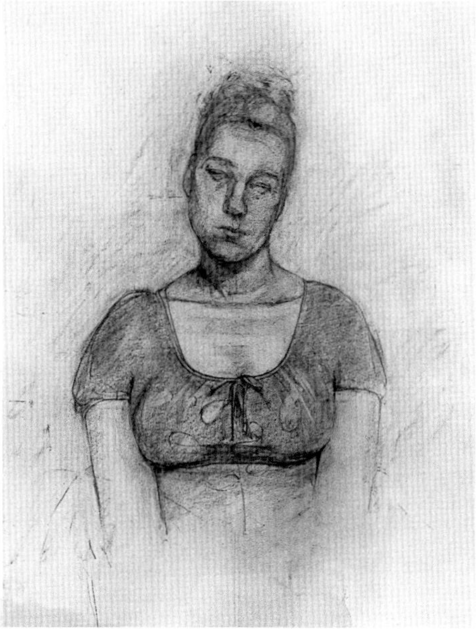

Sara, 1969

Being a superb draughtsman, no subject seems to daunt her and she is able to handle complex imagined compositions while still working directly from life.

Daphne Todd has always drawn naturally and well. As far back as she can remember she was drawing with a pencil, and good accurate drawing underlies all her work. As she says, 'I came to art through drawing. I was always going to do art. I was always the best at school and got all the art prizes'. [2] By the time she reached secondary school she had already decided to be an artist, although neither she nor her parents had any idea what that might involve. Although she was told that a distant relative used to paint night scenes of the Lancashire cotton mills from memory, there were no artists in her extended family. The only painting in her parents' house was a small reproduction of an interior by Pieter de Hooch, cut out of a magazine and framed in passé-partout. To see work by the old masters she had to join a private library, full of musty old books. There she pored over pictures by Michelangelo and Leonardo da Vinci, falling in love with Leonardo's long flowing beard in his self-portrait drawing.

Daphne Todd's parents both came from Lancashire. Her maternal great-grandparents were very poor, having to scrimp and save and even to share their tea-leaves with relatives in the street. Her grandparents began work, aged thirteen, in the cotton mills, and Daphne's mother, Annie Mary Lord (born in 1908), recalled how the men hated the work in the mills, which they considered fit only for women, but were forced to take it as no other work was available at the time. Every so often they would go on the booze and fail to come home, leaving their families without food. There were stories of beaten wives and starving children. Her mother remembers her grandmother who was illiterate, and also her own childhood in a millworker's house with the privy at the bottom

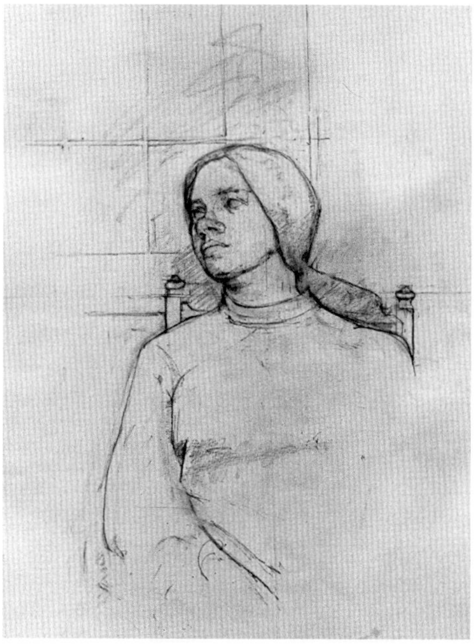

Christine Looking Up, 1970

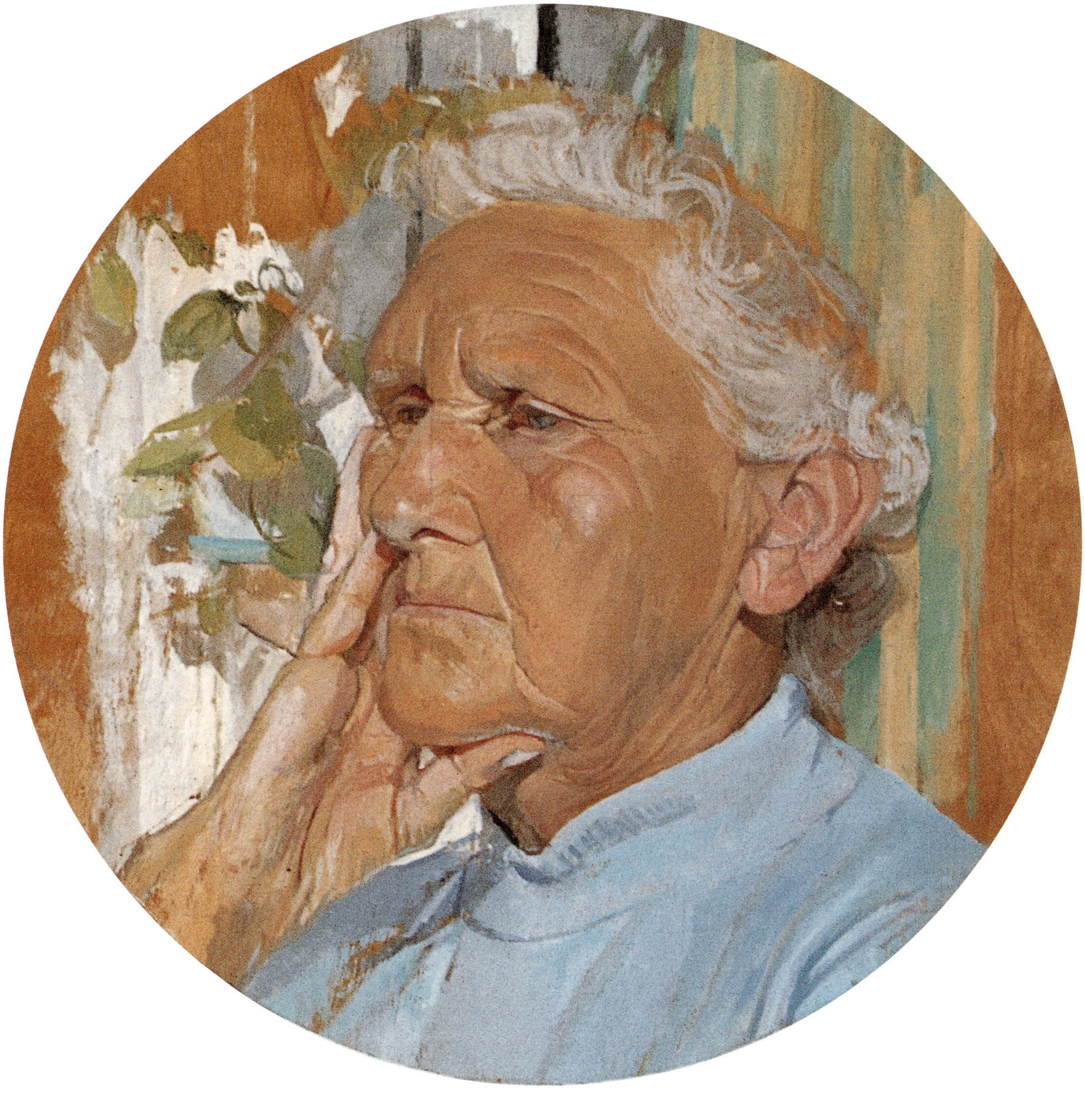

[5] *The Artist's Mother,* 1975
dia. 25.4 cms 10 ins

[6] *Beech Cathedral*, 2002-4
154.9 x 121.9 cms 61 x 48 ins

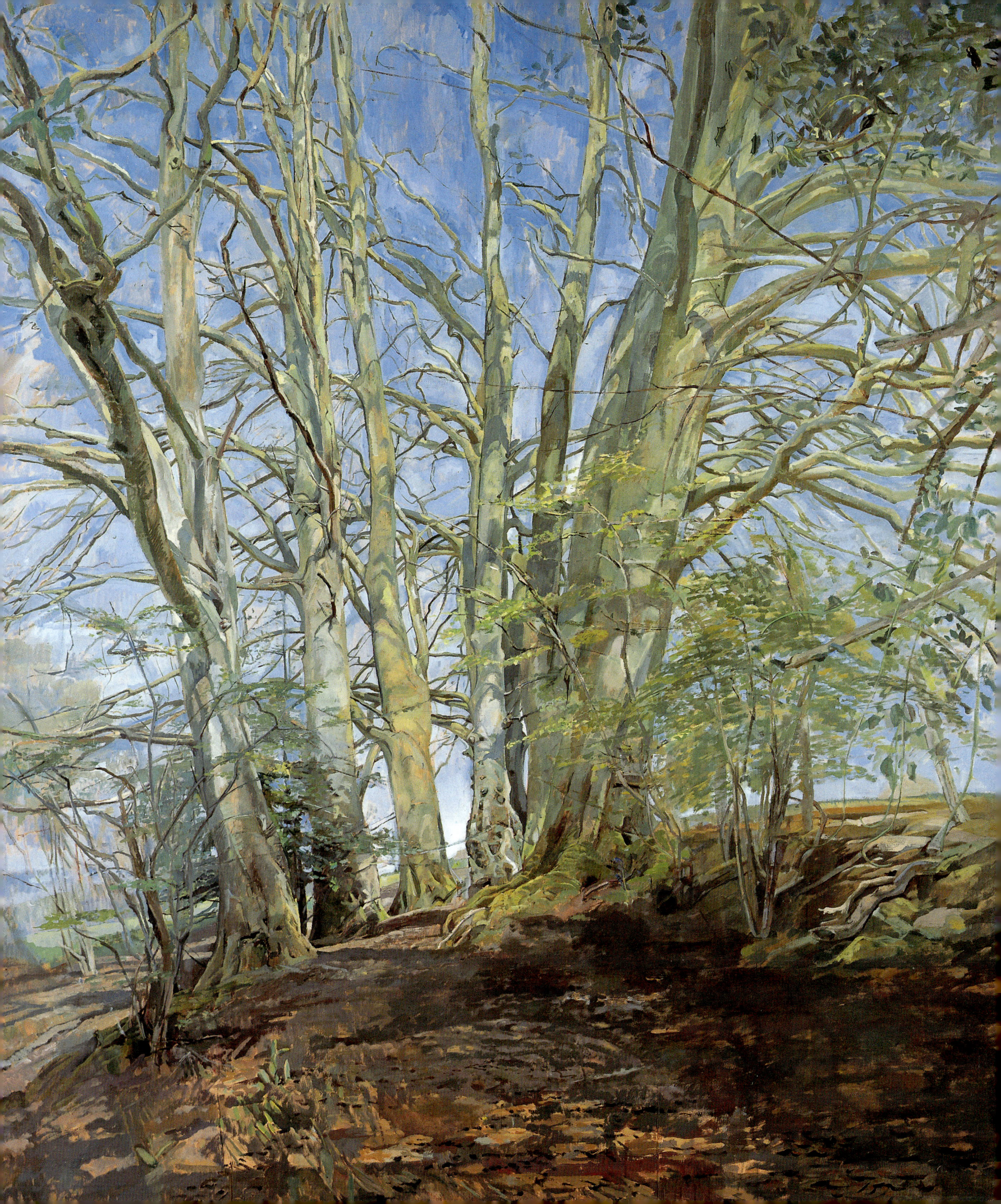

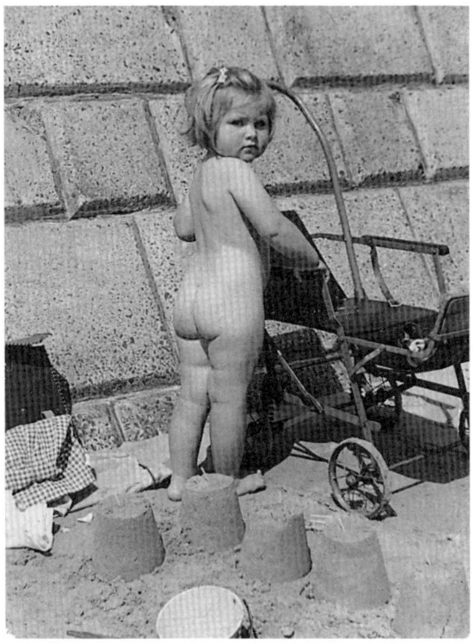

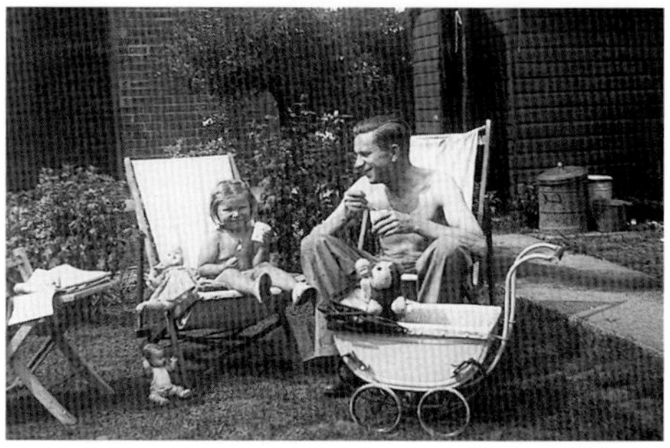

of the garden and the night soil being taken away. Annie Lord's parents then moved from the mills to become owners of a shop which was divided into two parts, one selling sweets and the other tripe. From this they progressed to a fish-and-chip shop, and then her father became a small-time stockbroker. In order to pick up business he joined the local Conservative Club, at the same time starting to drink heavily. He died of drink at the age of fifty-two.

Clockwise from top left:
Daphne Jane Todd as a child;
Daphne with her father, 1949;
With John at Bexhill, 1952;
Daphne's father Frank Todd and his brothers.

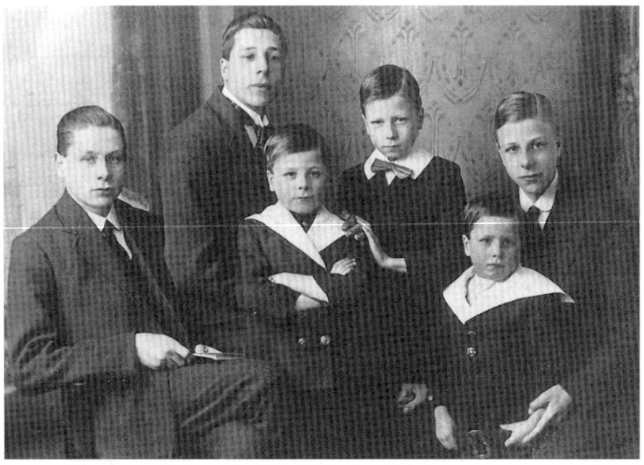

Daphne Todd's father, Frank Todd, was born in Bolton in 1912, the youngest of six boys. His father had worked as a salesman in a haberdasher's shop. Frank Todd was intelligent but by nature so shy and quiet that he refused to become even a corporal during the war, despite much encouragement. After the war the Todd family moved to Yorkshire where Frank worked as a municipal accountant in the local treasurer's office. It was in York that Daphne was born on 27 March 1947. When she was three years old her father took the family to Kent to obtain a better position within local government. There he made good and eventually became deputy treasurer of Canterbury. A son, John, was born in Kent in 1950. Daphne's earliest memory is of the long train journey south from Yorkshire to Kent. She attended primary schools in Canterbury (St Christopher's and St Stephen's), but when the family moved to Whitstable she continued her schooling at the Endowed School and later commuted to the Simon Langton Grammar School for Girls in Canterbury.

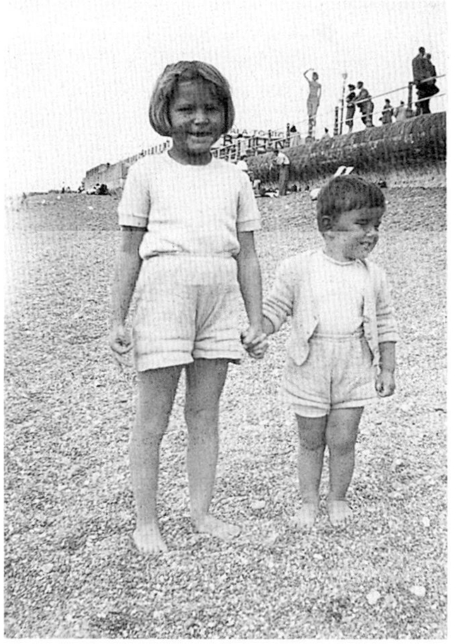

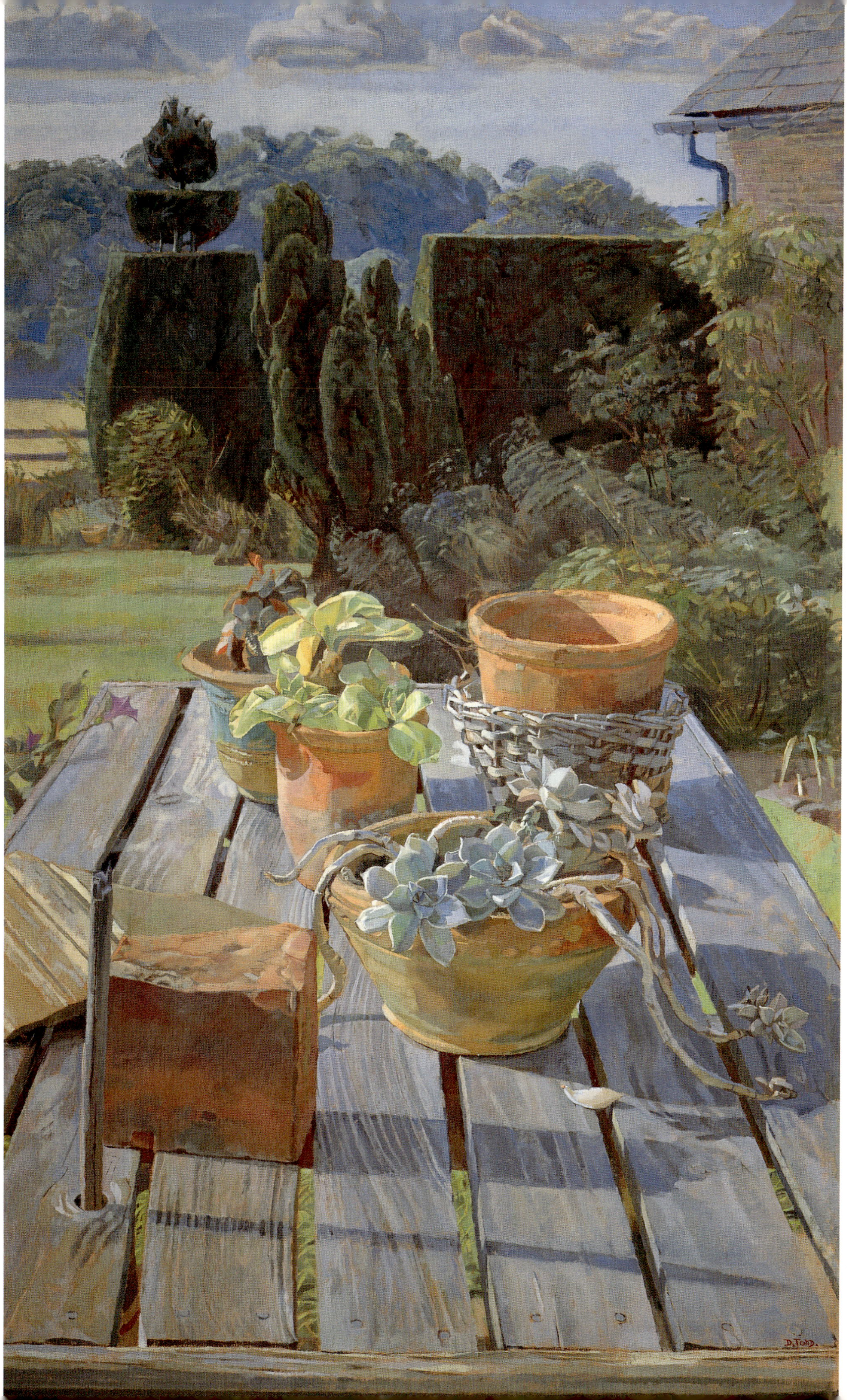

[7] *Garden Still-Life*, 2000
101.6 x 58.4 cms
40 x 23 ins

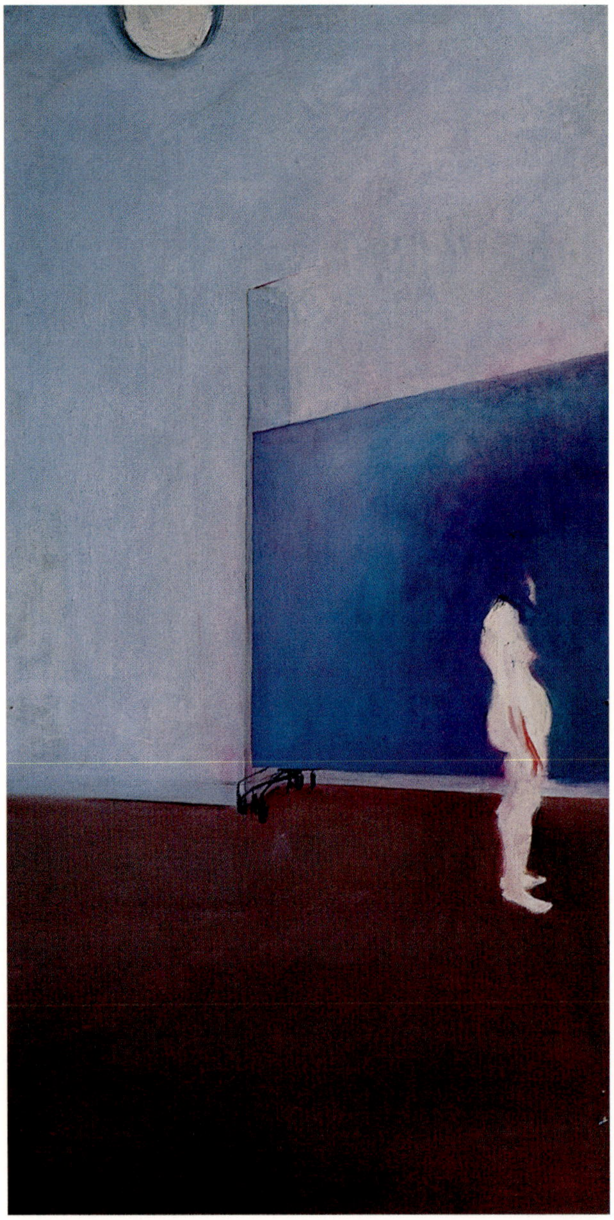

[8] *Standing Nude*, 1965
121.9 x 61 cms 48 x 24 ins

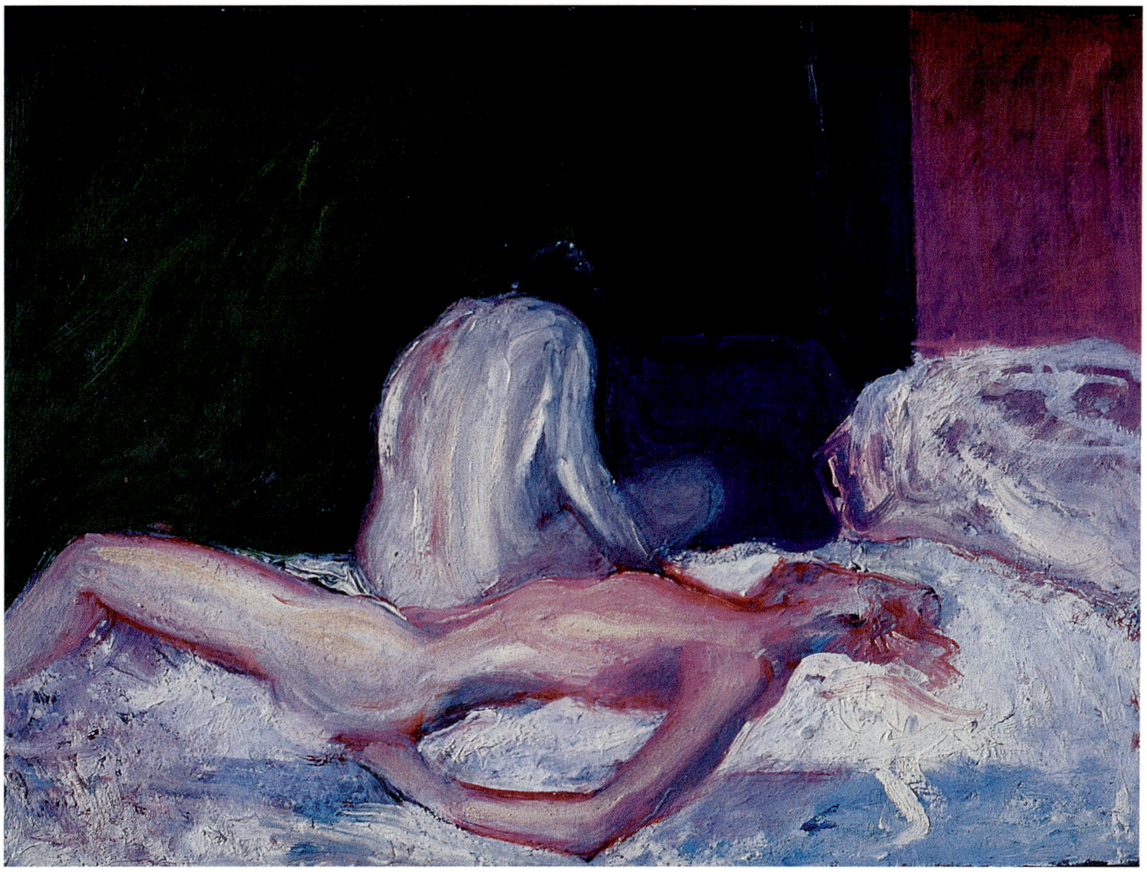

[9] *Two Figures on a Bed, Painted from Memory*, 1965
30.5 x 40.6 cms 12 x 16 ins

Todd did well at school but maintains that she was not taught anything in art lessons. The teaching consisted of giving the girls a subject such as 'The Wedding' to paint and leaving them to get on with it. From the beginning, however, her work stood out, and one of her paintings was sent to a televised art programme called The Sketch Club and was shown on television. This was her first oil, using the paint from a painting-by-numbers set that she had been given. Finding the painting by numbers far too boring, she used the little pots of paint to make an imaginary picture of a farm, and also a portrait of her friend Linda.

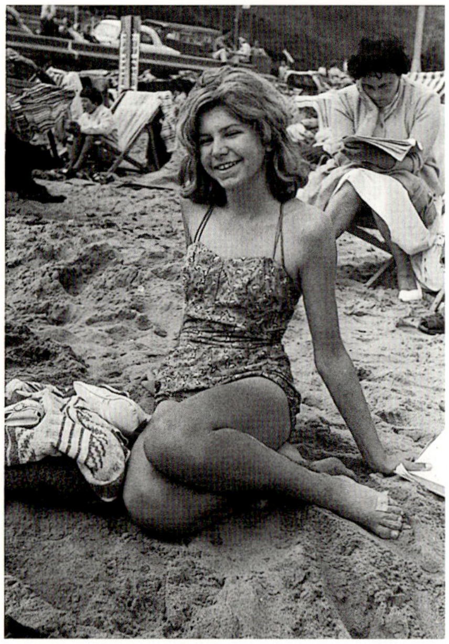

Daphne, Shanklin, Isle of Wight, 1962

By the time Todd reached the sixth form she was doing a good deal of painting and drawing, mostly from observation – portraits of friends and family – as well as cycling to the country and the coast for landscapes and collecting twigs and flowers and shells for still lifes. At school she hid in the Art Room to avoid games, which she detested, becoming by far the most committed painter in the school. When a local store organised a competition for a big painting of a Crucifixion, intended to be a team effort, she fell out with the other girls and painted it all herself.

The grammar school suited Todd well. She passed all the necessary exams and also did a lot of acting, especially with the Lindley Players, a local amateur dramatic society. In the holidays she went camping with school friends or made use of her family beach hut at Whitstable, named 'Daydreams' after her father's nickname for her - 'Daffy Daydreams'. When the time came to leave school it was generally agreed that she should go to art school. She was conscious, however, of her ignorance of art history. From books Todd had picked up a smattering of knowledge, and in her A-level exams had described Leonardo da Vinci as 'transcendental' at 'sfumato' and 'chiaroscuro' without having the least idea what the words meant.

Todd's parents supported her desire to go to art school, seeing it as a genteel sort of life for their daughter, but had no idea how or where she should apply. A book about Victor Pasmore had given her the idea that the Slade School of Art was the best place to go, and right from the start she had wanted the best. The headmistress thought she was unlikely to get in, and Todd was further daunted by the recent arrival at school of another girl who was also applying for the Slade. This girl came from a good family with real paintings in their house and her father had already taken her to meet the tutors at the Slade. Todd agonised about the chances of being offered a place in the face of such competition. Her

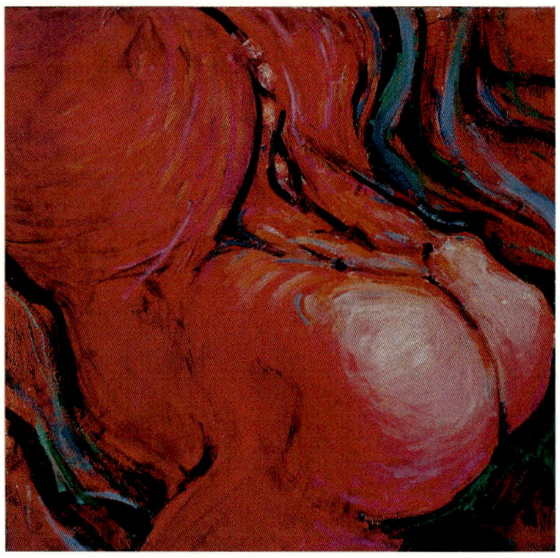

[10] *Bottom* 1965
121.9 x 121.9 cms 48 x 48 ins

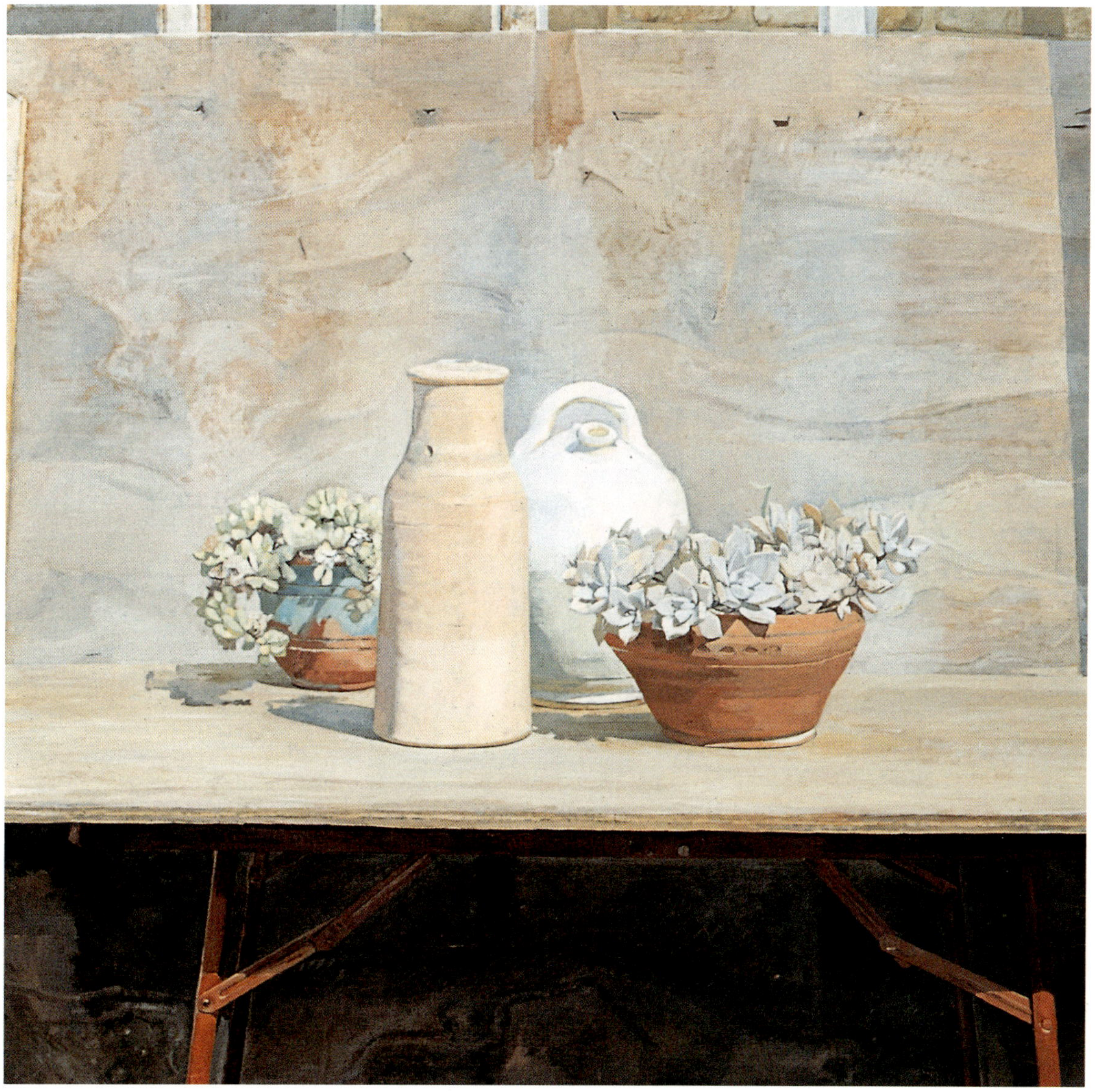

[11] *"Spanish" Still-life*, 1979
76.2 x 76.2 cms 30 x 30 ins

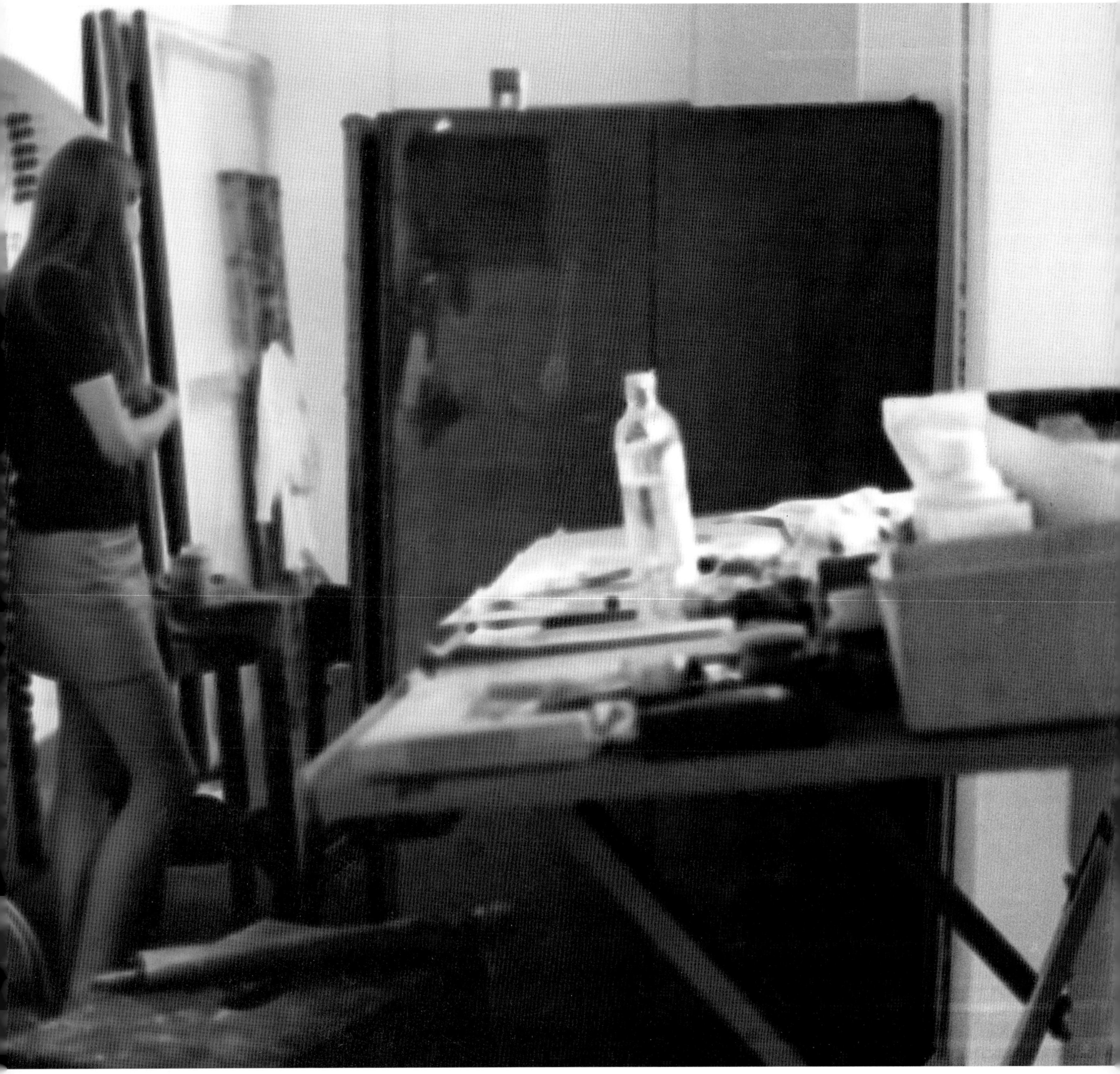

Final year at the Slade, 1970

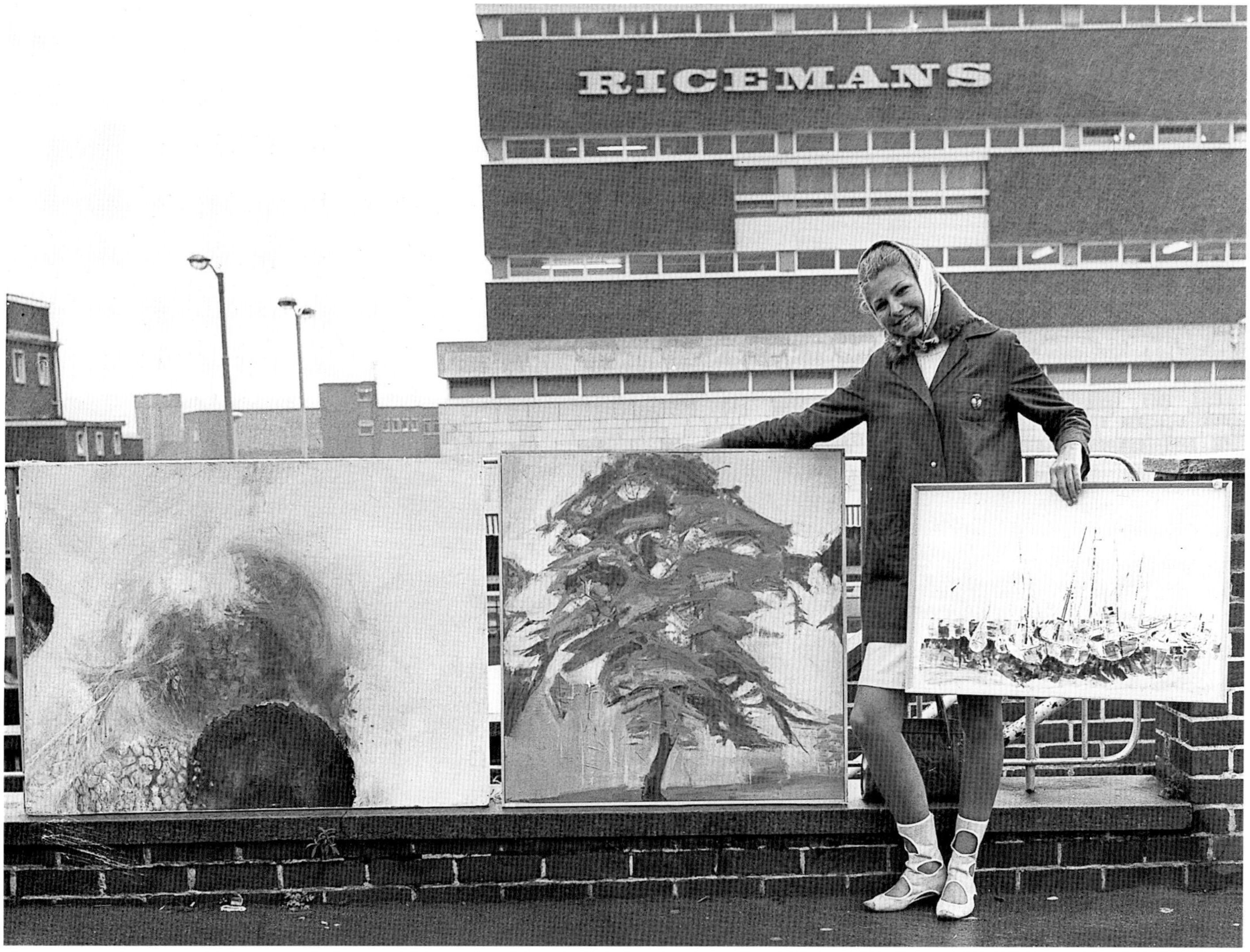

On the railings, Canterbury, 1965

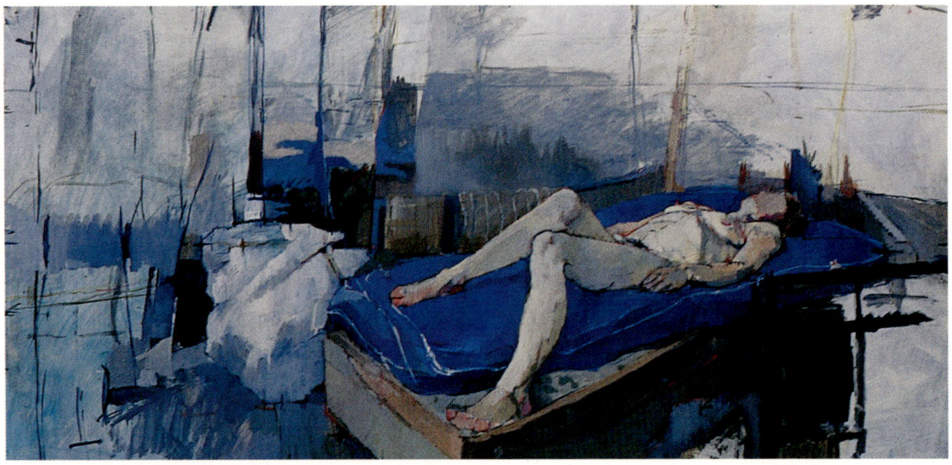

[12] *Life Study, Second Year at the Slade*, 1966
61 x 121.9 cms 24 x 48 ins

own father said he was not the right sort of man to be able to help. Both parents had previously accompanied her to an interview at Hornsey School of Art, and it had been a miserable experience for all of them. Since her cause would not be helped by her father's presence, with characteristic courage and determination she telephoned the Slade herself to ask if she could go and talk to one of the tutors there.

At the Slade Ian Tregarthen Jenkin, Professor Sir William Coldstream's second-in-command, looked through Daphne's portfolio and helped her sort out a suitable collection of drawings for her interview. He weeded out the drawings of nudes done at Canterbury Art College, where she had started attending evening and Saturday classes, and selected the more personal work that she had done at home, particularly a drawing of a cabbage that Todd had spent almost the whole of Christmas Day and Boxing Day working on to avoid sitting slumped in front of Christmas television. Armed with a portfolio full of this work and dressed in a suit, with her hair up, she was able to approach her interview with confidence. She was accepted and in 1965, aged eighteen, she left home for London and the next six years at the Slade.

During her first year at the Slade Todd lived in College Hall, Malet Street (a University College Hall of Residence), but after that she moved to the Slade hostel in Cartright Gardens where the rent began at £18 a term. For the next five years it was there that she stayed during term-time. At the Slade her undergraduate tutor was Maurice Field, whom she remembers as teaching nothing apart from how to lay out colours; he seemed to regard his charges as little girls, not young women. During Todd's post-graduate years Keith Vaughan was her tutor; he proved

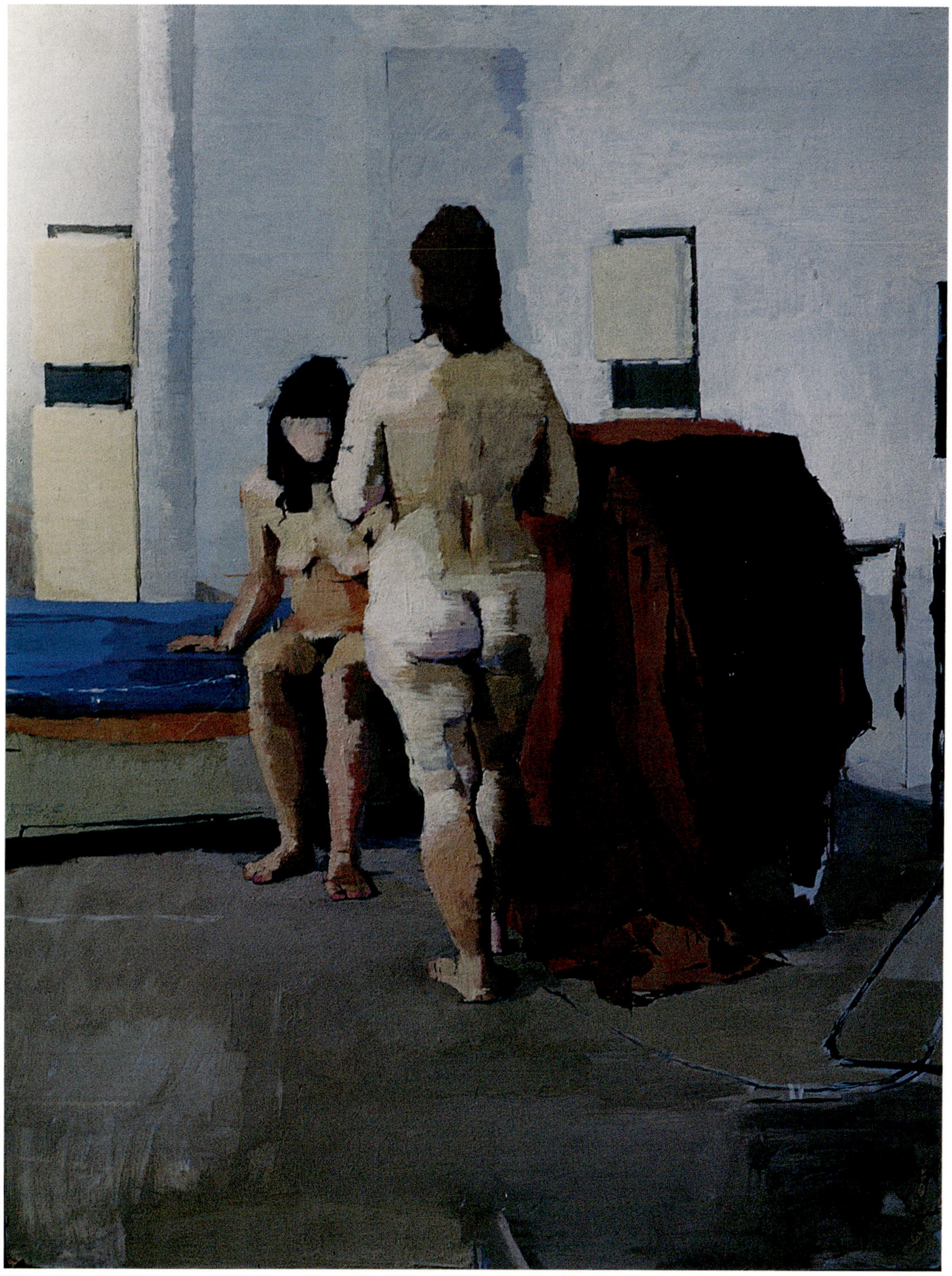

[13] *Life Room, Second Year at the Slade*, 1966
61 x 45.7 cms 24 x 18 ins

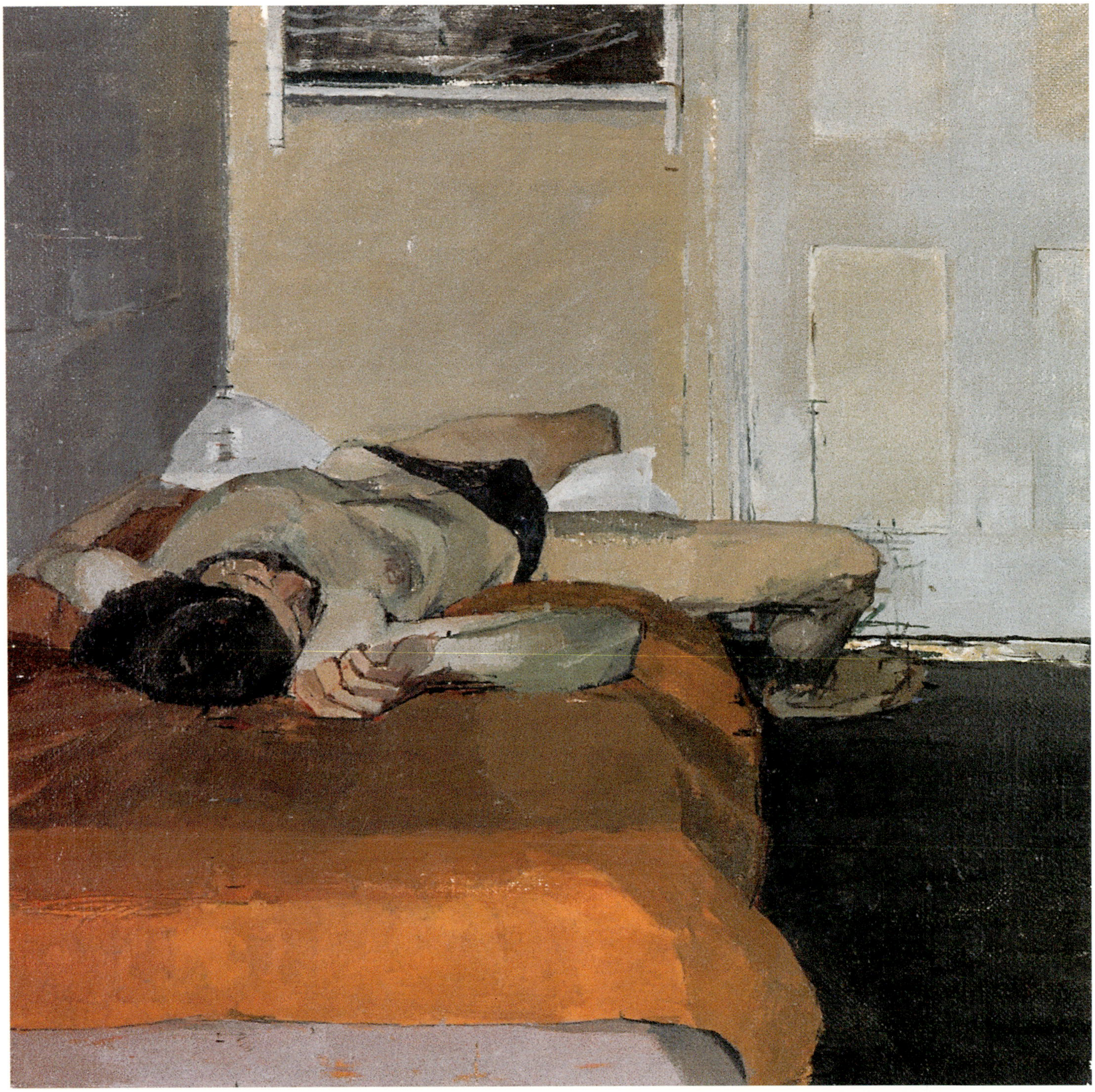

[14] *Boy on a Bed, (Jim)*, 1967
45.7 x 45.7 cms 18 x 18 ins

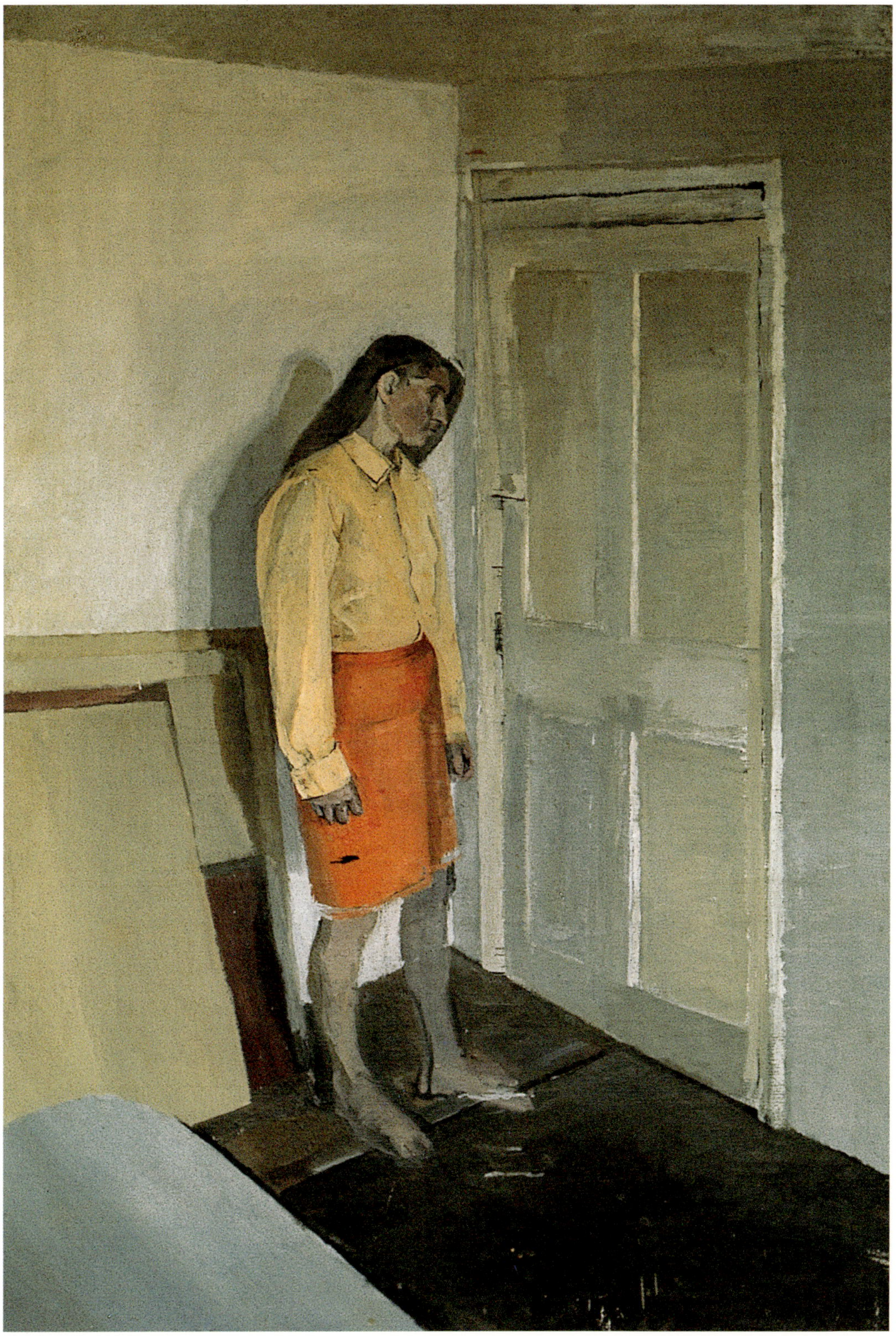

[15] *Carol by the Door,* 1968
152.4 x 121.9 cms 60 x 48 ins

equally useless as he was only interested in boys. Apart from a single tutorial when he showed interest in a drawing of one model superimposed upon another, she had little contact with him and never saw him in the studios. Patrick George, who was in charge of the first year, twice a week arranged a series of exercises and practical experiments with colour theory. 'I remember Patrick George giving us an exercise when everything had to be considered as more, or less, grey, and most of the work I did at the Slade was greyish. But I loved Cézanne and also Chardin, a colourist who makes one colour sing against another, lovely juicy buttery paint.' [3] The most useful teaching came on Fridays, when Euan Uglow came to teach Life Drawing. For the remaining two days of the week the students worked independently. During Todd's time at the Slade William Coldstream only taught her once, in her second year. 'He was very good. He sat on my stool swinging his legs, measured what I had been measuring and told me it was like algebra. I had done an unmeasured drawing which I had thrown on the floor and he compared the two, saying "that's art as well, you know"'. [4]

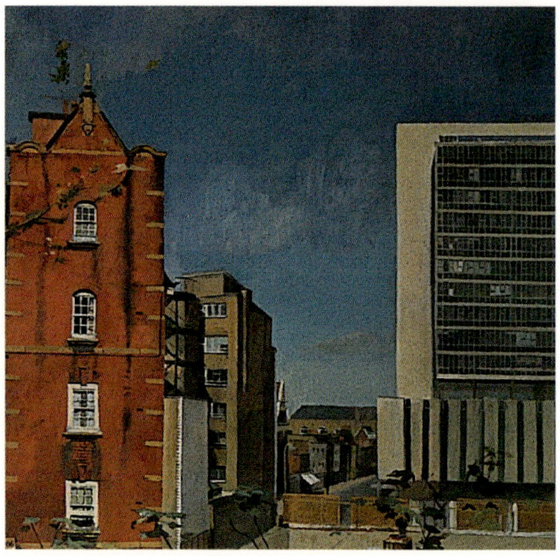

[16] *A View from the Slade Hostel, Cartright Gardens*, 1967
61 x 61 cms 24 x 24 ins

There was good advice to be had from other tutors. Perspective was no longer taught but, having encountered problems with depicting space, Todd persuaded B.A.R. (Sam) Carter to revive his lectures on the subject. Although he was regarded as the world expert, his expertise was no longer used. It was difficult to persuade other students to attend his talks, and his audience often consisted of two people, Todd and her best friend Janet Buckle (nee Womersely - who now lives in Doncaster and is a noted painter of mining scenes). Although Todd never used geometric perspective for depicting three dimensions on two, she found it useful to understand what it was in order to discard it. Also useful was the series of lectures on the Psychology of Perception, presented instead of Anatomy which was no longer taught as such, and another on Methods and Materials given by Arthur (later Sir Arthur) Lucas, Chief Restorer at the National Gallery.

Todd found the anatomy study she needed in the Life Room, where models posed for three weeks at a time with a variety of tutors including Jeffrey Camp, Robert Medley (who commented 'this girl knows what she wants') and, once, Michael Andrews. Most students worked in the General Room, where abstract colour-field work was then popular and 'Happenings' were beginning. The Life Room was regarded as an

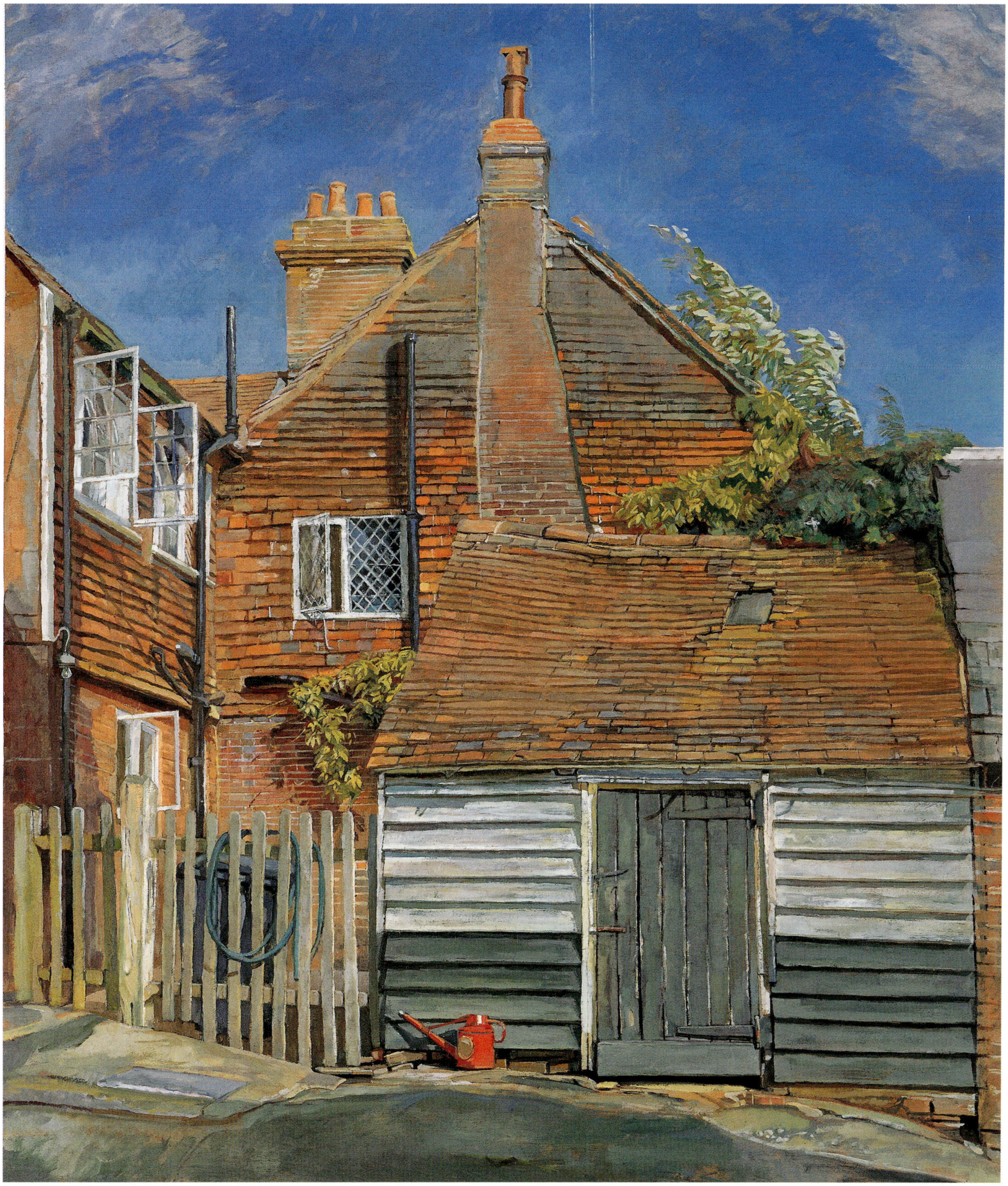

[17] *House in the Heat,* 2003
83.8 x 66 cms 33 x 26 ins

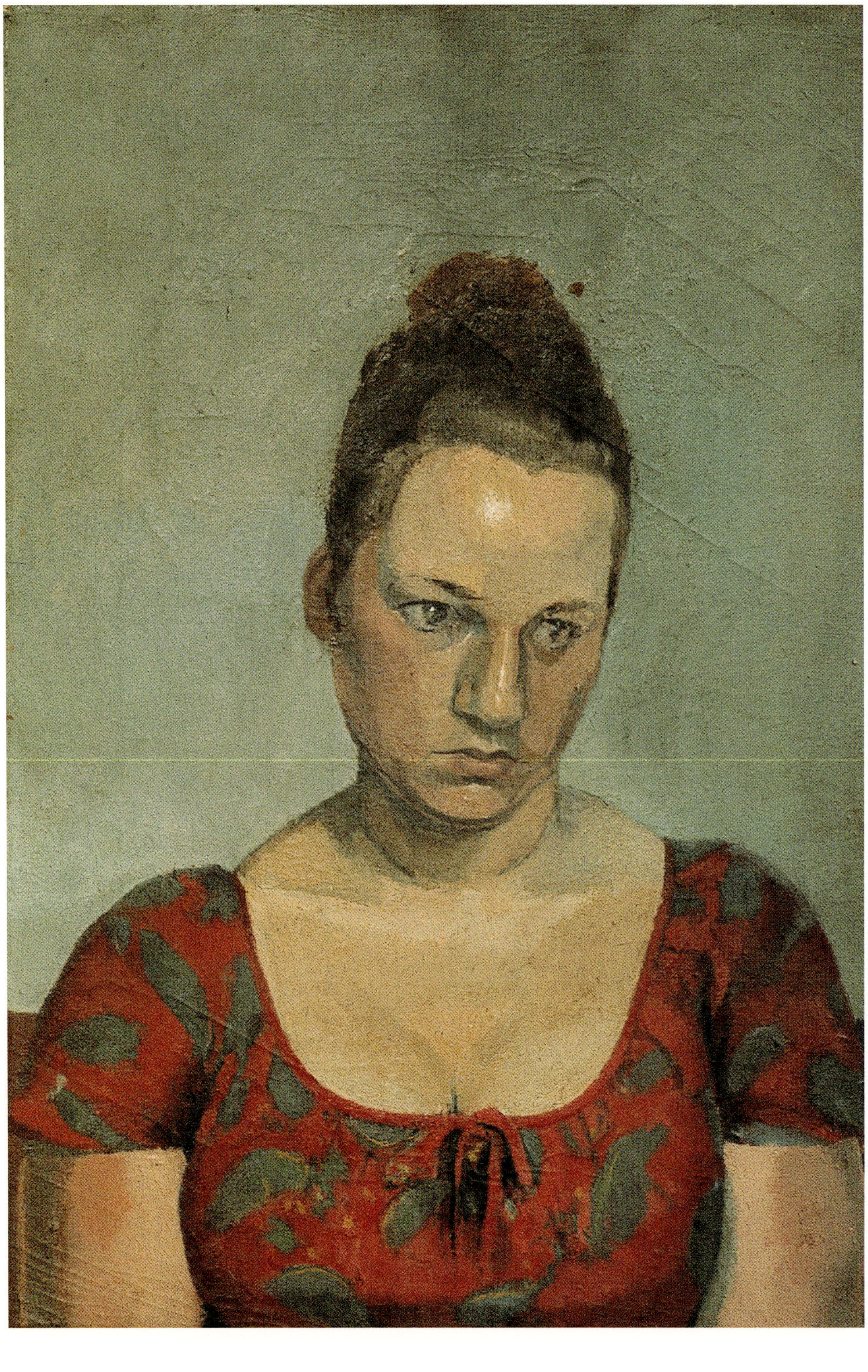

[18] *Sara John*, 1969
45.7 x 30.5 cms 18 x 12 ins

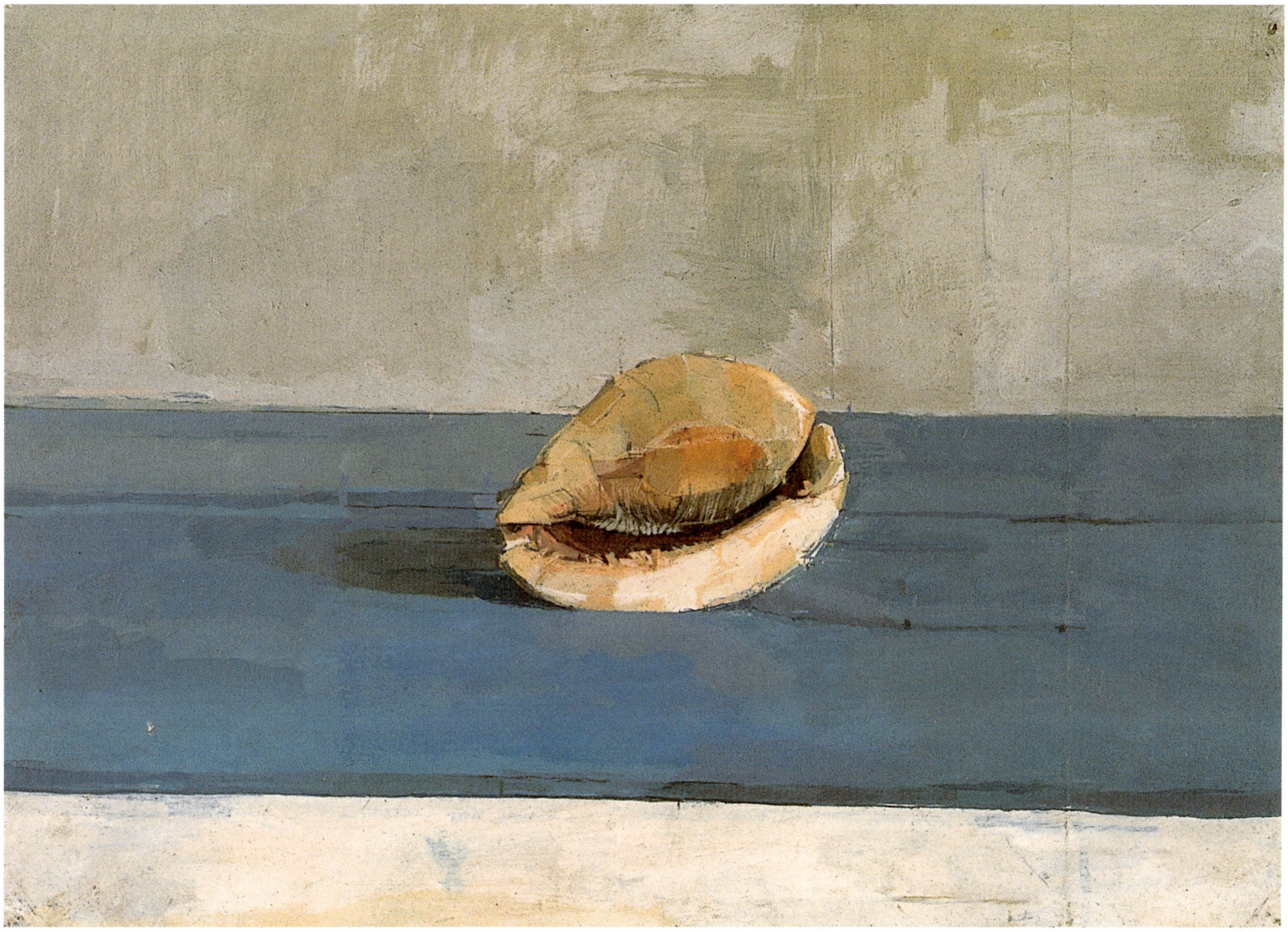

[19] *Shell on a Blue Cloth*, 1967
27.9 x 38.1 cms 11 x 15 ins

anachronism, left over from a previous era, although one of the smart places to be was in Frank Auerbach's studio, which had a life model. Todd tried to do a drawing in there but found it oppressive. 'Everyone painted like Auerbach and I thought I could do something different. The whole place was dripping in grey paint - everybody's easel had a heap of grey paint beside it scraped up – silent except for grunting, very intense, and nothing to do with looking. I like to be able to describe surface, but not there – you had to be committed to that way of life before you went in'. [5] Representational painters at the Slade divided into two camps, Auerbach's or Uglow's. Although Auerbach did work from observation, he and students such as John Virtue and Peter Prendergast were concerned with the dynamic relationship between perceived objects. There was no interest in colour or the way light affected the surface of objects. Todd's love of surface soon drew her into Uglow's 'camp'. However, the many different approaches to be found within the Slade broadened Todd's outlook. She shocked her parents, accustomed to the tasteful watercolours of roses that she used to make at home, with the series of large paintings of bottoms that she took home after her first term. These also shocked the clientele of the local pub, The Long Reach, where, while working as a barmaid to earn money during the holidays, she had been asked to display her pictures.

It was at the Slade that Todd discovered the artistic direction that she would follow. From the start her work stood out, and she collected several prizes – The British Institute Award for Figurative Painting, the Tonks Drawing Prize and the intercollegiate David Murray Award for landscape painting. She further widened her horizons by trips abroad with Slade friends in the holidays, visiting Paris, where she spent days and days in the Louvre and the Jeu de Paume just looking at paintings; Grenoble; Ingres at Besancon; the Renaissance wonders of Florence; the Vatican in Rome. Later she drove two friends, Susan Engledow and Christine Adams (both still painters) to Holland and Belgium, camping in her little tent, to visit the Vermeers, Van Eycks, Rembrandts, Rubens's studio, and the Van Goghs. During her second long vacation she took off with a non-driving friend, Susan Timmis, in an ancient van purchased for £30 especially for the trip, to the Ardèche in the south of France to paint. They lived in Todd's old tent in a vineyard on a hill. There they each worked on three paintings, made at different times of day – morning, afternoon, and evening. One of Todd's paintings made there,

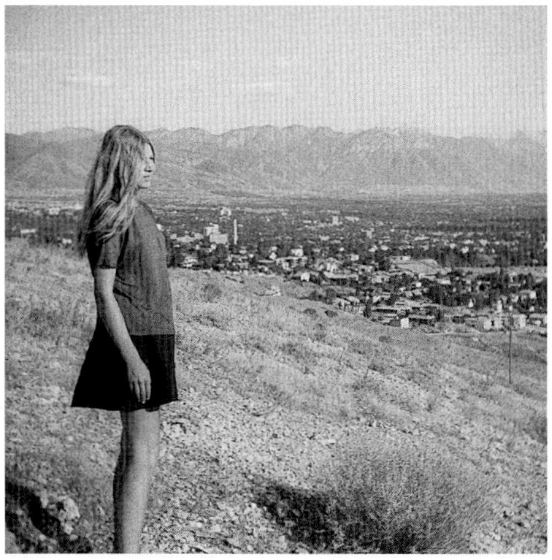

Daphne Todd, Salt Lake City 1968

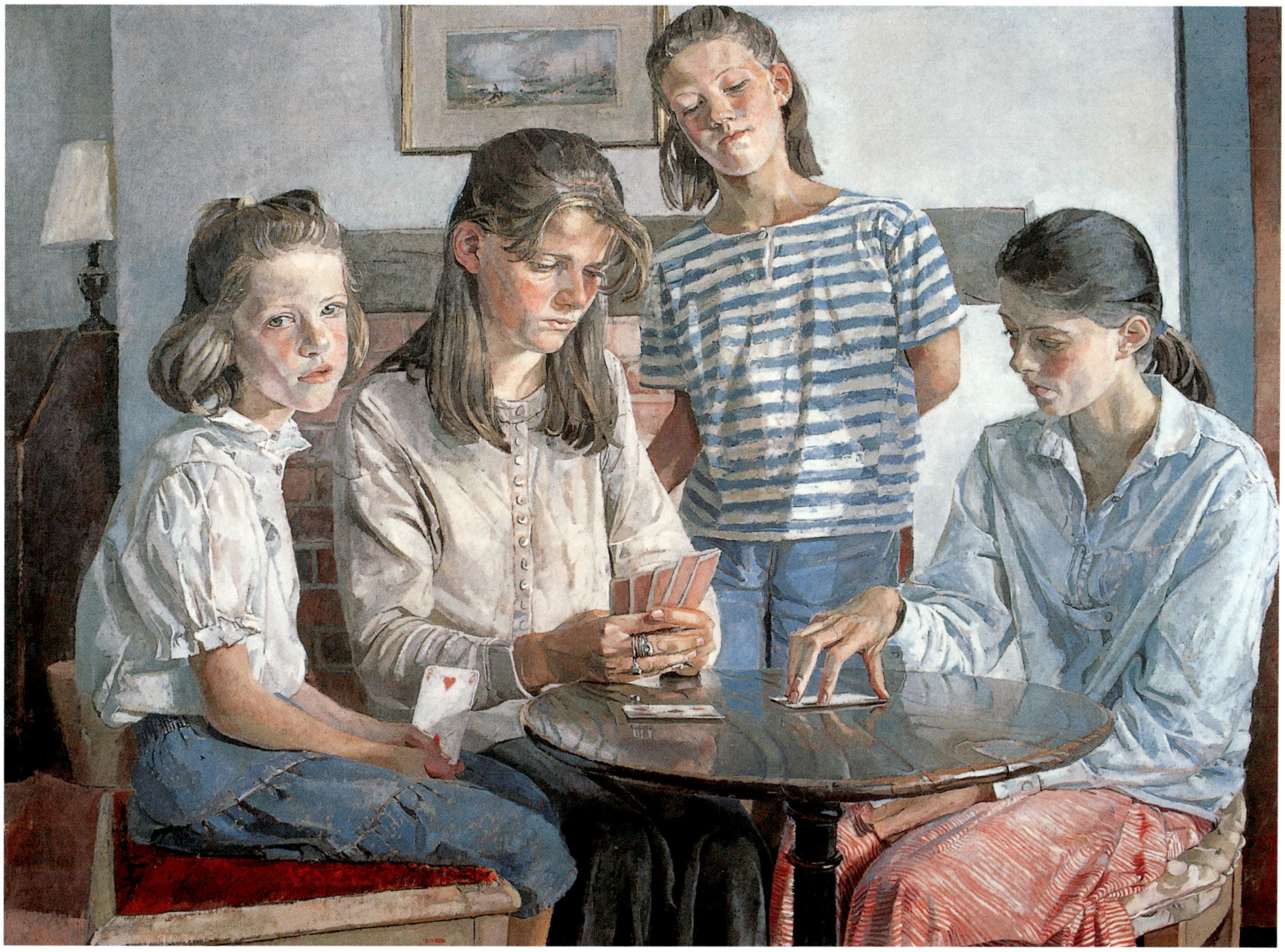

[20] *The Daughters of Giles Curtis,* 1989
121.9 x 91.4 cms 48 x 36 ins

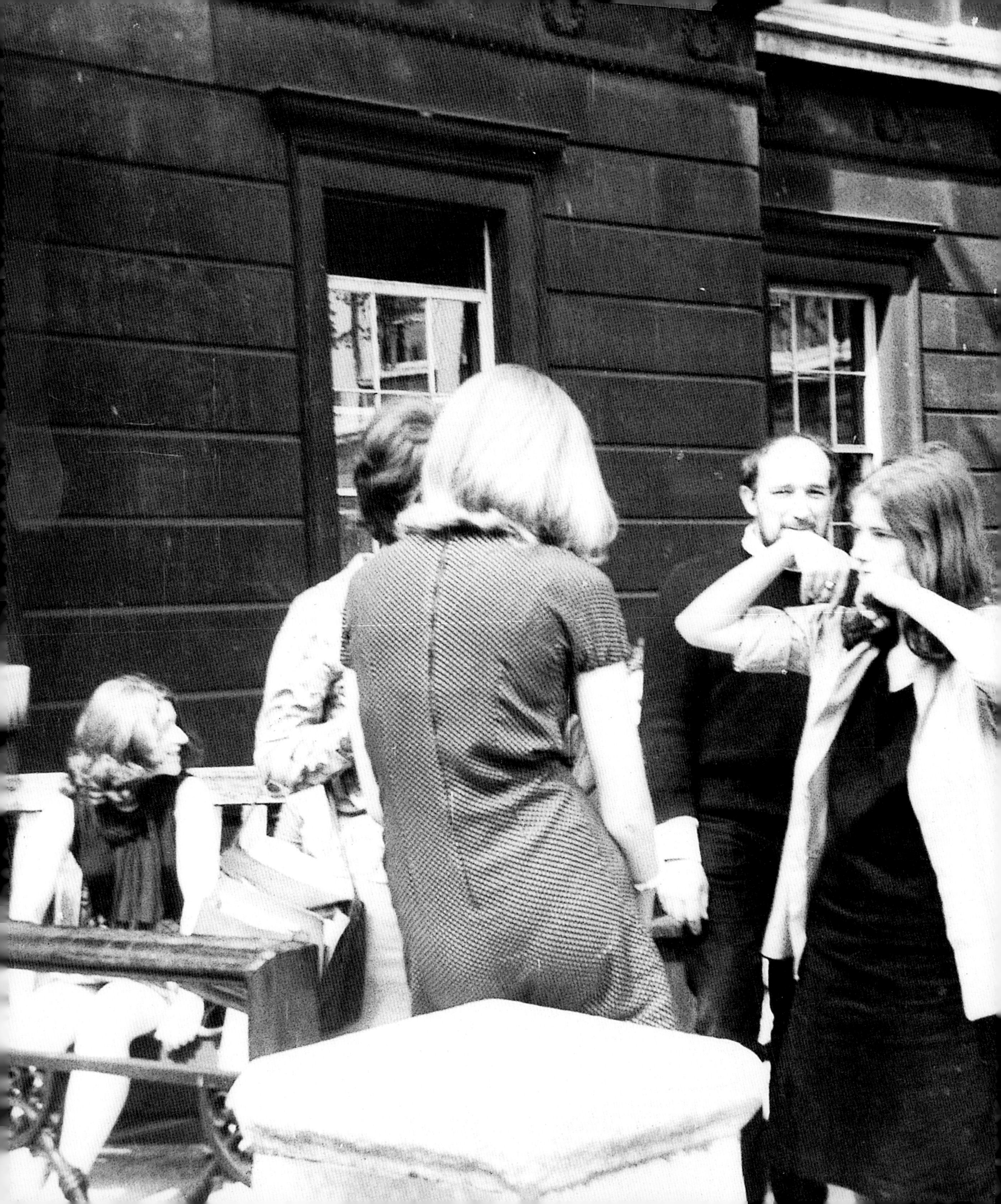

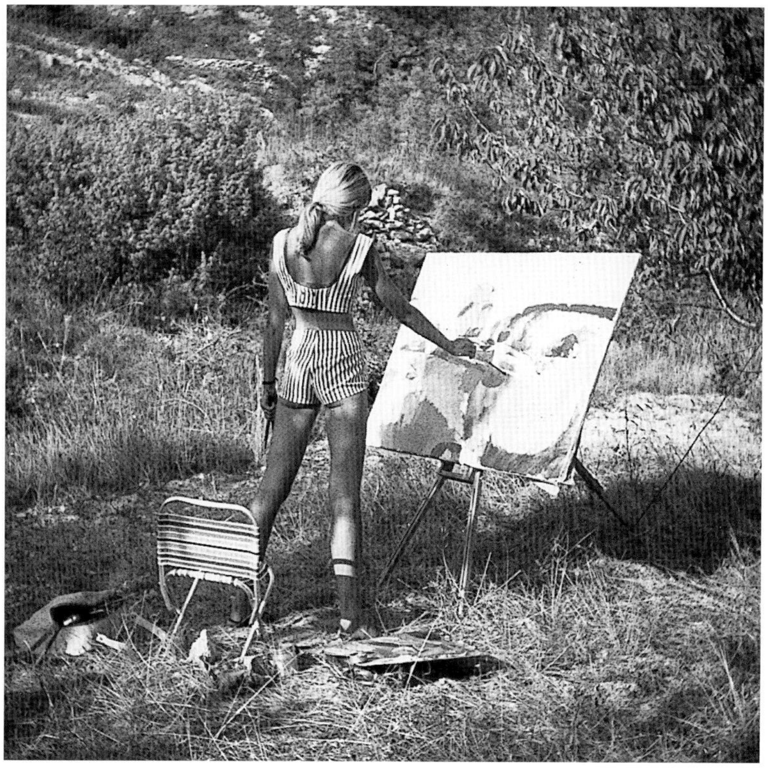

Left:
Daphne Todd (back view) with Euan Uglow outside the Slade, 1965

Above:
Painting in Ardèche, France, 1967, her first painting to be exhibited at the Royal Academy

Rocks at Saint Martin (1967), was the first piece of her work accepted by the Royal Academy, for the 1969 Summer Exhibition.

The following year, in the long vacation of 1968, she went alone to the United States and spent some weeks painting in the notorious Chelsea Hotel in New York, then travelled around Colorado and the mid-West, scaring herself but also teaching herself to be self-reliant. Her three-month solo trip around the USA and Mexico was to prove as life-changing as any event in her career. She looked at marvellous paintings: Cézanne at the Metropolitan Museum in New York, Titian and Vermeer at the Isabella Stuart Gardner Museum in Boston, and Rembrandt at the Frick. She was beaten up and raped, she ran out of money, slept on buses and in shelters, accepted hospitality from strangers, and became ill in Mexico. At the Hotel Chelsea, which was full of mad characters, she made six paintings to fulfil the conditions of the David Murray prize which had funded her travels. These included a portrait of a Frenchman smoking which, committed to the hotel's safe while she travelled, was subsequently lost. The self-imposed risk and adventure of these long vacations enlarged her horizons and and greatly increased her self-confidence.

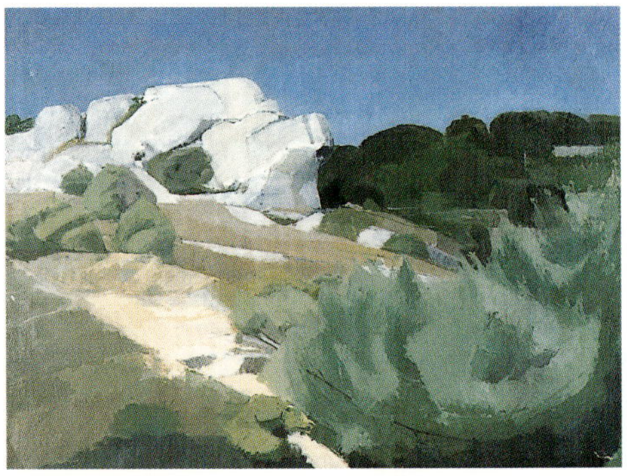

[21] *Rocks at St Martin*, 1967
121.9 x 91.4 cms 48 x 36 ins

For Todd the years at the Slade were seminal. Not only did they expand her horizons and sharpen up her drawing to the prevailing very high standard, but they brought her into the orbit of Euan Uglow, whose influence had a crucial effect on both her life and her work. If Uglow had not shown an early interest in her she might not have fallen so hopelessly in love with him. But she soon became aware of his interest, which crystallised during her first summer term. Todd had been looking at a small exhibition of student drawings in the Slade offices while Uglow and Patrick George were discussing them behind a screen. She thought that Uglow had said something dismissive about her work – 'they're just shaded drawings' - and then the pair went on to discuss who they might take to the wine bar they were heading for. They were probably 'on the pull' for models rather than girlfriends, as it was fairly common practice for the tutors in art colleges in general to look over each new student intake and sort them out amongst themselves, to paint them or to sleep with them. Each innocent new intake of students was of course unaware of this. Daphne Todd's name came up, with those of her friends Janet Buckle and Susan Engledow, and Patrick George was delegated to give her a lift to the Strand. He appeared to chat her up on

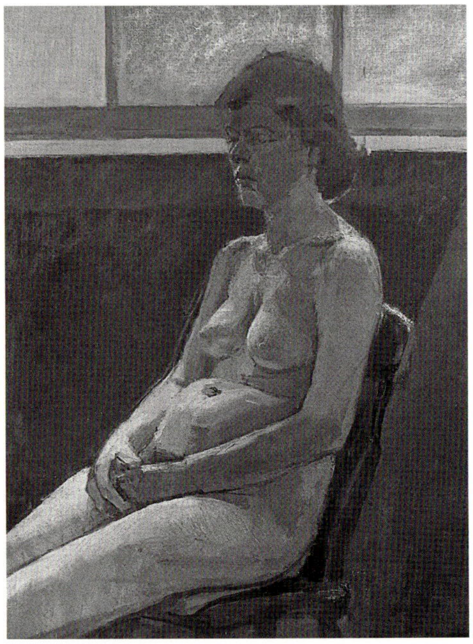

Miss Burke against the light, 1967

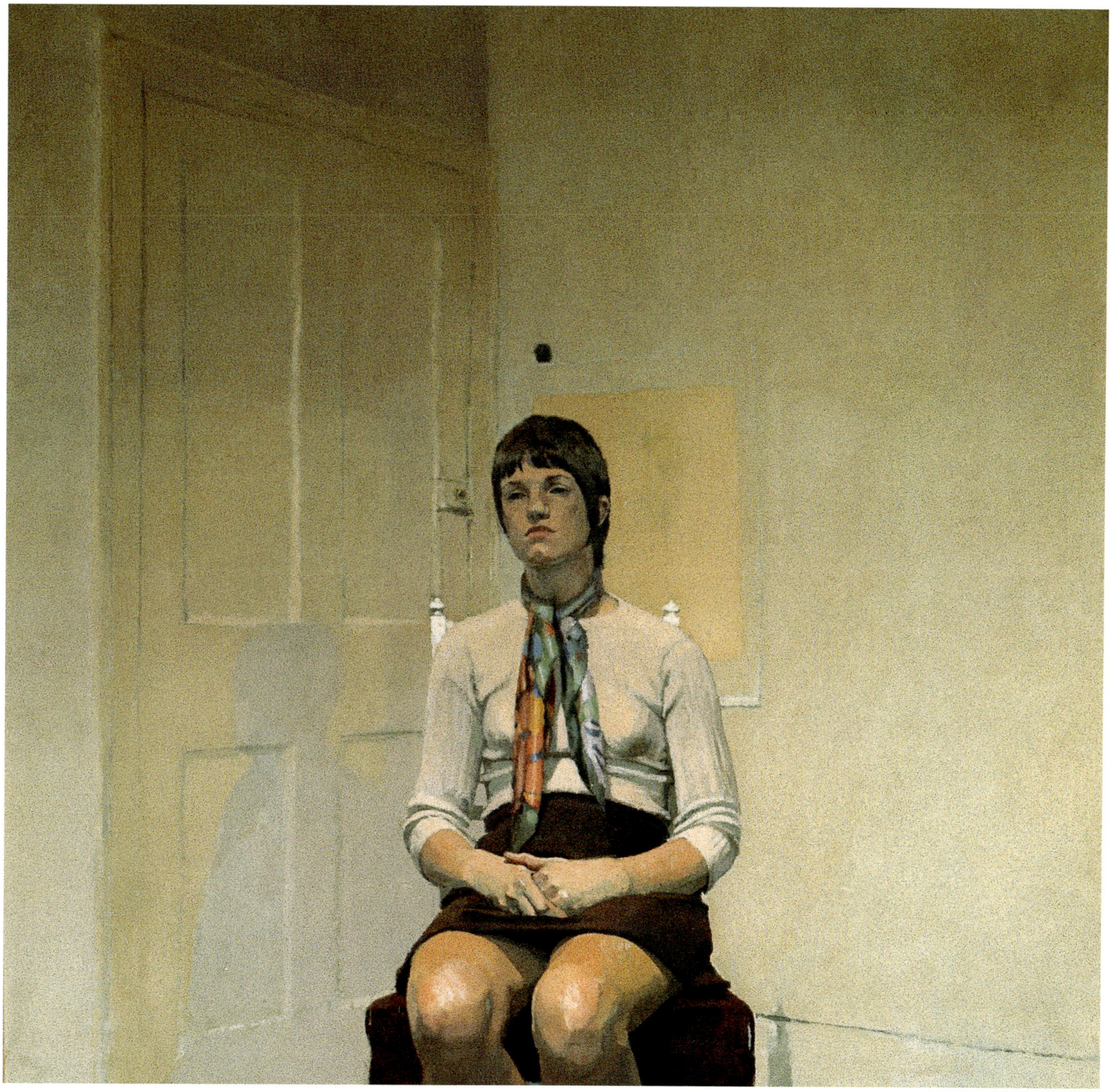

[22] *Vivien, Knees,* 1971
106.7 x 106.7 cms 42 x 42 ins

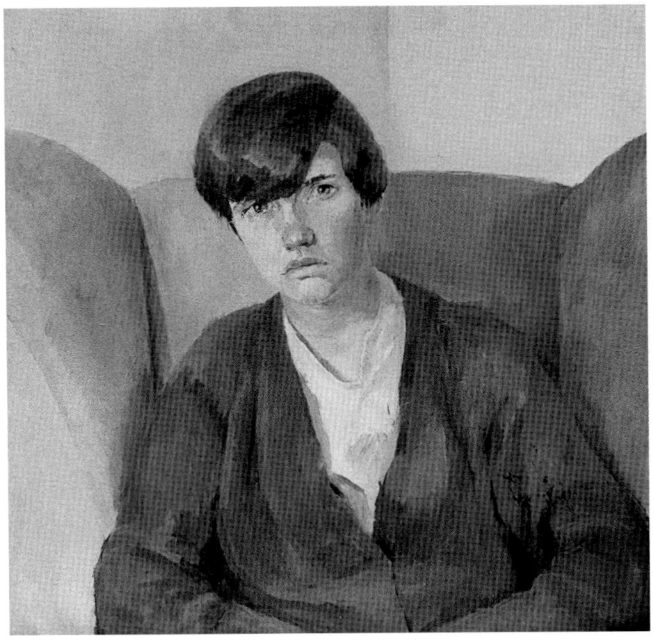

Vivien Gardner, 1965
24 x 24 ins

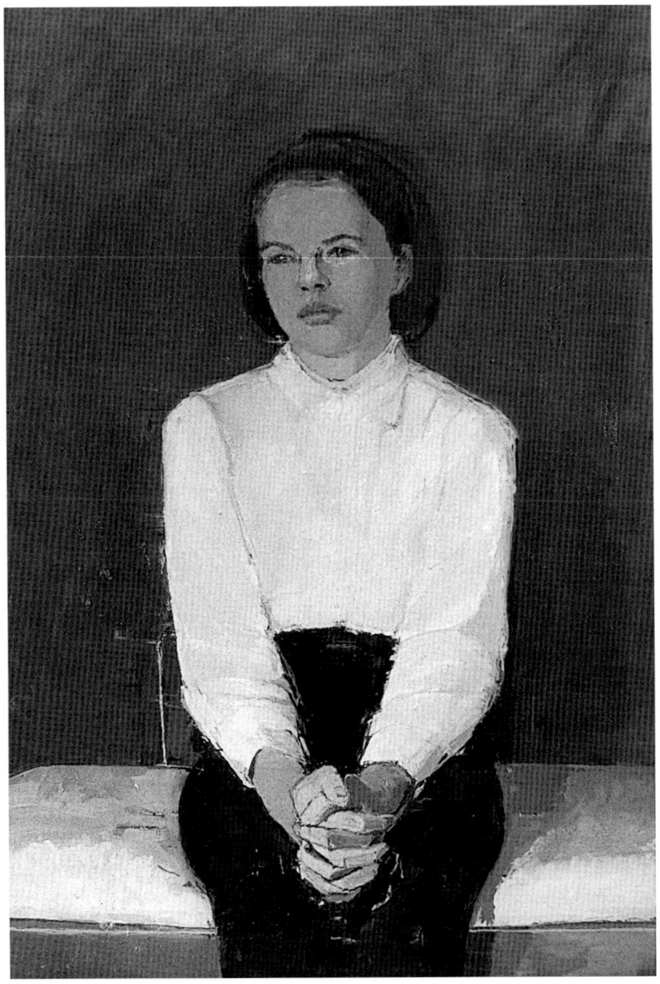

Hilary Gardner, 1966
36 x 24 ins

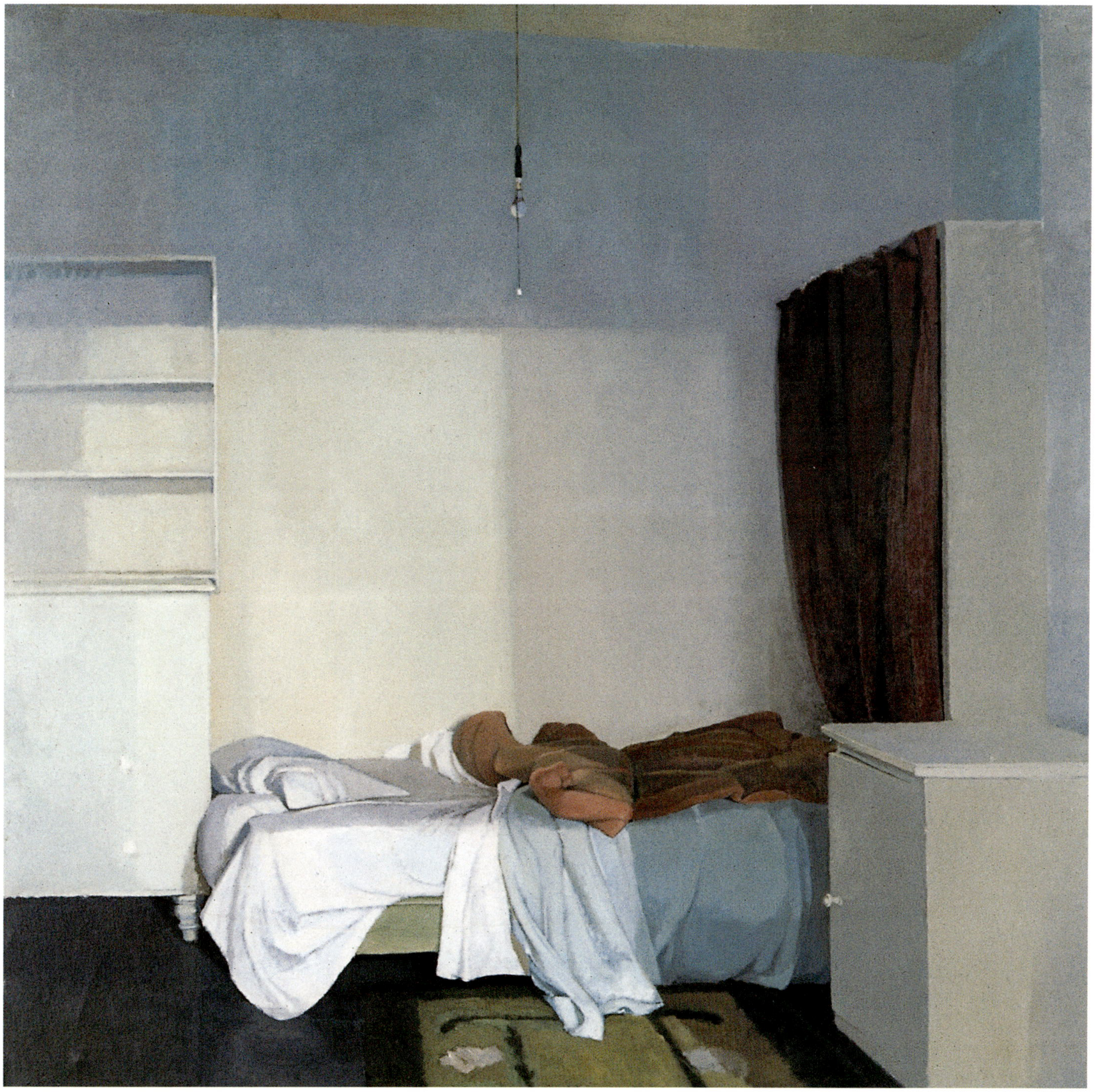

[23] *Bed*, 1969/70
121.9 x 121.9 cms 48 x 48 ins

the way but it was obvious that she could not take her eyes off Uglow. She had recently been struck by Uglow's painting in a small staff exhibition to show students their tutors' work. Until then she had had no means of knowing the sort of work he did, although he taught the first year drawing every Friday. One hot day Uglow organised his class to go drawing in Regents Park. Nobody did any work and the day turned into a sort of bacchanalia. Todd remembers lying in the grass and finding Uglow nearby; also running across a great space and being felled by him with a rugger tackle. He then invited her to a party at Anthony Eyton's house in Brixton. Because she had invited her parents to London to be taken to a theatre, she could not get to the party until very late. Staying until the very end and sitting alone on the stairs, she heard Eyton in the kitchen asking Uglow 'Why don't you take her home to bed? She clearly wants you to'. Uglow demurred, but then relented and took her back to his house. Later in the year Uglow included Todd in supper parties with visiting tutors at Bertorelli's in Charlotte Street, where she was made to feel that it was a special privilege for her, a mere first-year student, to be admitted to this august company.

This was the start of a five-year relationship into which Todd put her heart and soul. Uglow had been married very briefly and was already separated from his wife. Although he kept Todd a secret from his old-fashioned mother and from some of the staff at the Slade, her understanding was that she was the only girl in his life. Together they went out frequently with Uglow's friends and colleagues – Myles Murphy, Craigie Aitchison, Geri Morgan, Jeffrey Camp and Laetitia Yhap, Peter and Maria Snow, Patrick George, Tom Espley, Anthony Eyton, Patrick Symons and the psychiatrist Nicholas Brown, among others. At the beginning of her second year at the Slade Todd started posing for Uglow for the painting *Nude from Twelve Regular Vertical Positions from the Eye*, which was to win first prize in the John Moores Liverpool Exhibition 8 in 1972. Uglow wanted a tall thin model for this one-off experiment in visual perception. In his Battersea studios he had arranged two background areas, one with polystyrene tiles on the back wall and one with squares of coconut matting, and he tried Todd out, standing on a cupboard, in front of both backgrounds before starting work. Todd 's strong principles made her take the posing very seriously, and she was wary of her nudity being inappropriately exploited, although it quickly became clear that Uglow was more interested in

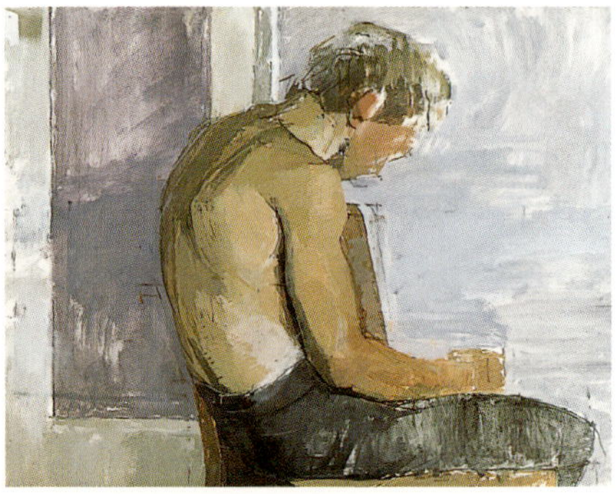

[24] *Back (John)*, 1967
61 x 76.2 cms 24 x 30 ins

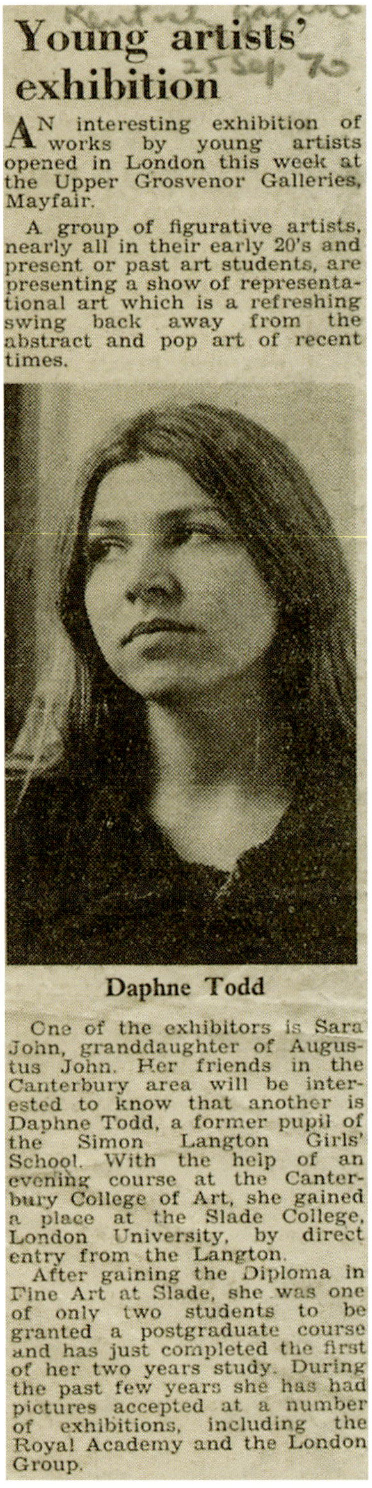

Young artists' exhibition

AN interesting exhibition of works by young artists opened in London this week at the Upper Grosvenor Galleries, Mayfair.

A group of figurative artists, nearly all in their early 20's and present or past art students, are presenting a show of representational art which is a refreshing swing back away from the abstract and pop art of recent times.

Daphne Todd

One of the exhibitors is Sara John, granddaughter of Augustus John. Her friends in the Canterbury area will be interested to know that another is Daphne Todd, a former pupil of the Simon Langton Girls' School. With the help of an evening course at the Canterbury College of Art, she gained a place at the Slade College, London University, by direct entry from the Langton.

After gaining the Diploma in Fine Art at Slade, she was one of only two students to be granted a postgraduate course and has just completed the first of her two years study. During the past few years she has had pictures accepted at a number of exhibitions, including the Royal Academy and the London Group.

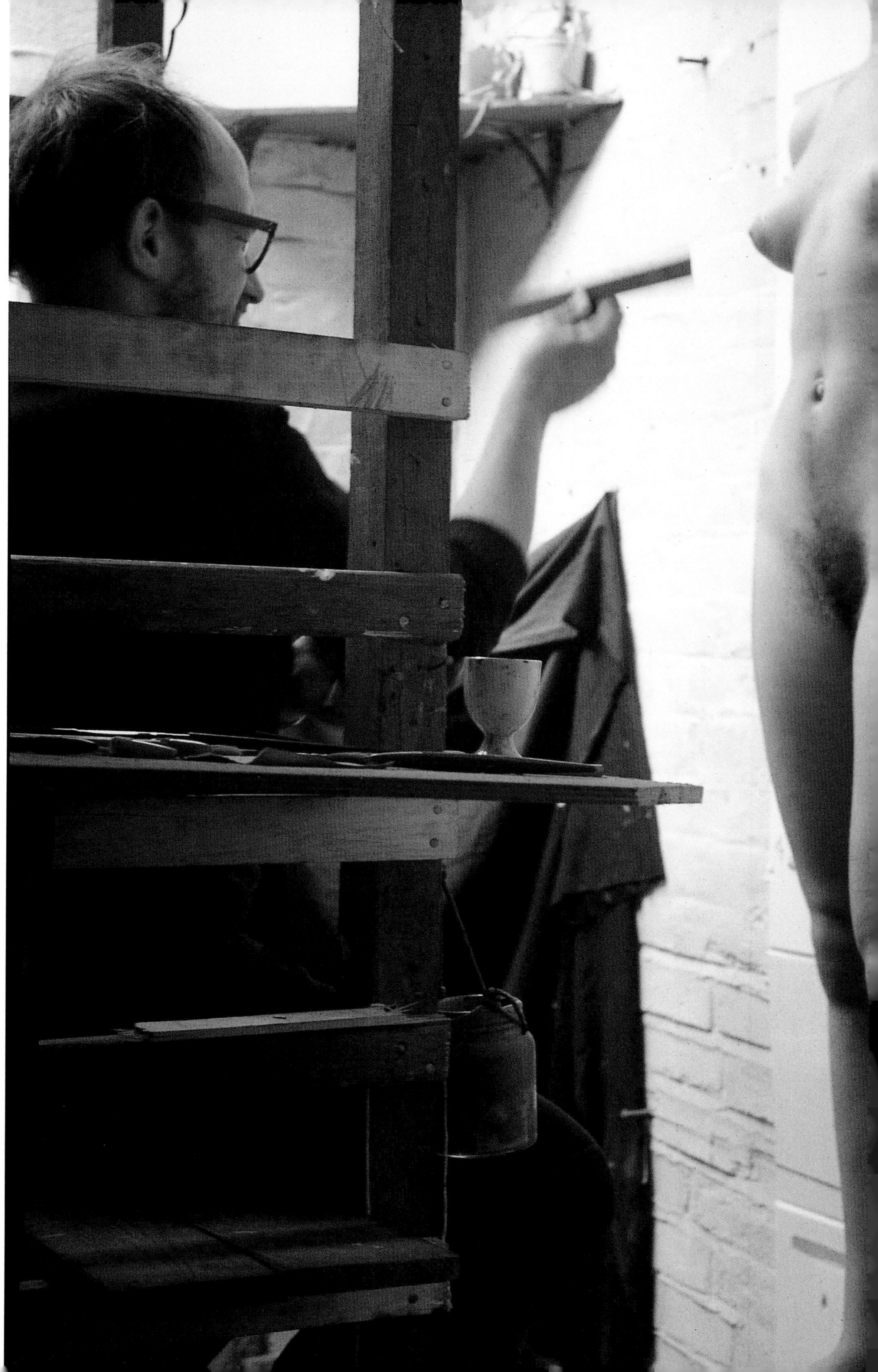

Daphne Todd with Euan Uglow modelling for *Nude from Twelve Verticle Positions from the Eye*

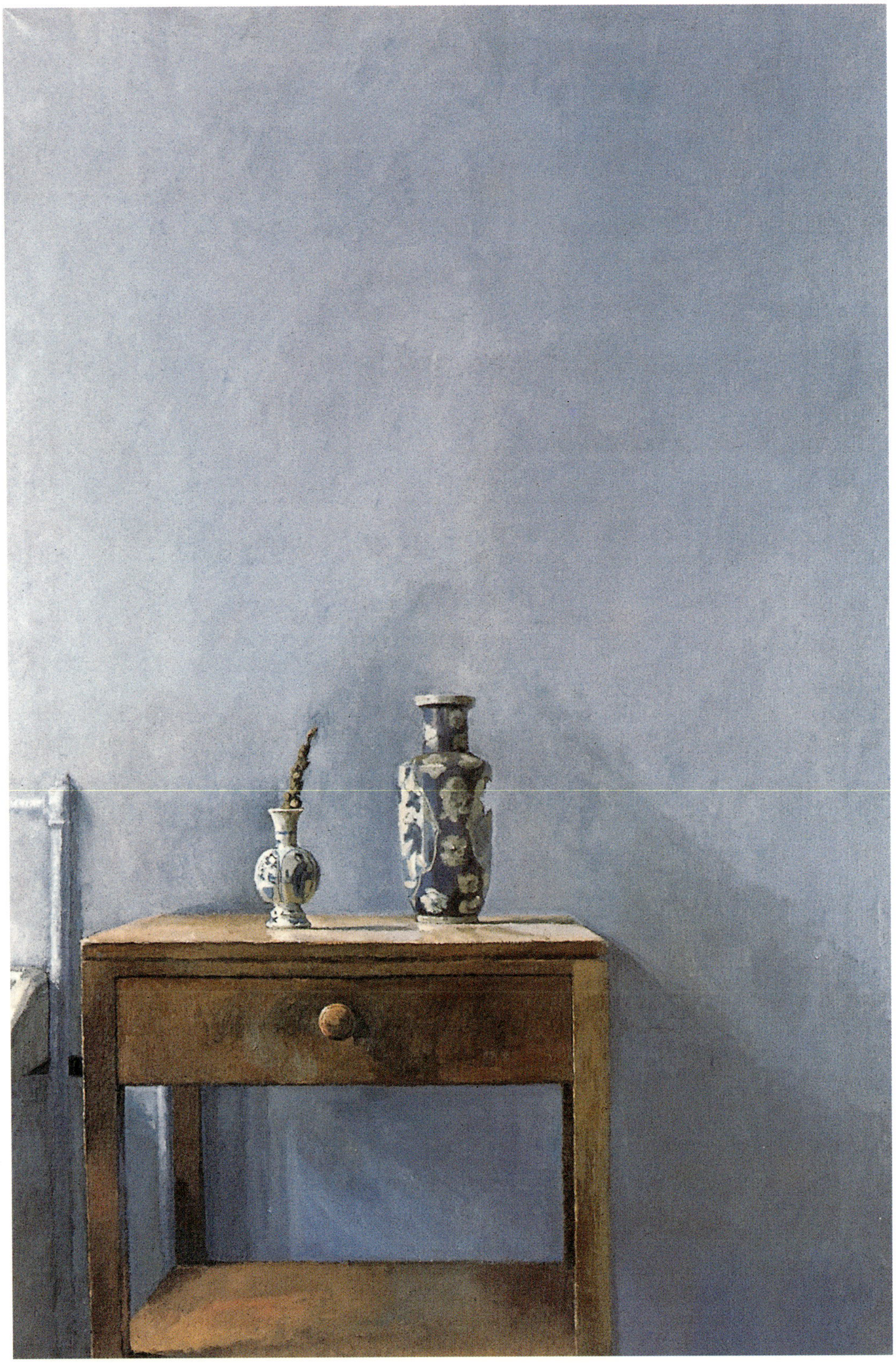

[25] *Blue Still Life*, 1970
90.2 x 59.7 cms 35½ x 23½ ins

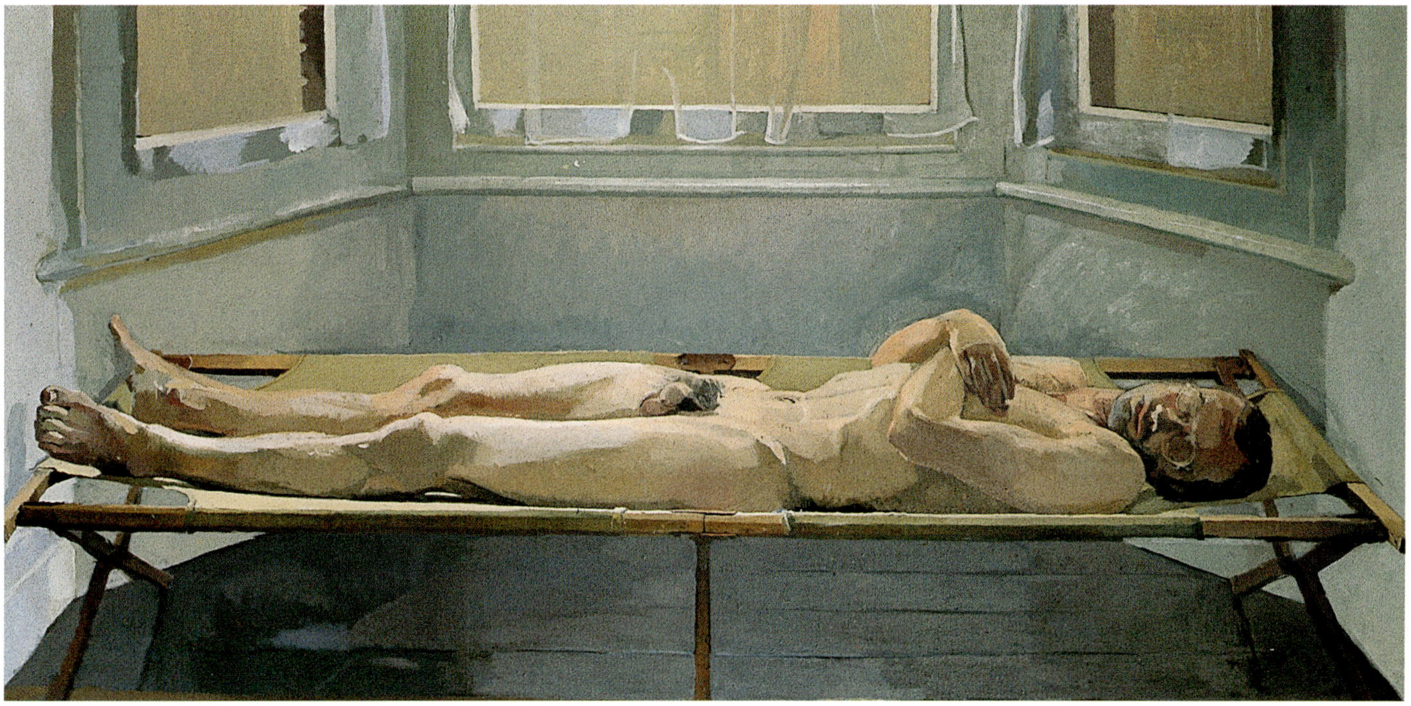

[26] *Male Nude (Peter), Prone,* 1973
61 x 121.9 cms 24 x 48 ins

painting than anything else. She posed for two sessions a week for four hours each and was paid £2 a week. After the day's work she and Uglow would usually go out together. Sometimes her visits would overlap with those of another model, because Uglow was also working on a picture of a nude walking – *Large Nude Walking Towards You* - but he took care to keep his models apart so that they did not chat. *Nude from Twelve Vertical Positions from the Eye* took eighteen months to complete, with Todd posing even in the holidays (apart from part of the long summer vacation). In the end she stopped it when the work was exhibited (uncompleted in Uglow's view) at the Marlborough Gallery, because she could see that Uglow would have gone on for years if she had allowed it (his *Large Nude Walking* took five years to complete).

Uglow always needed absolute accuracy in regaining the pose before he started work. Todd would often stand in position for an hour and no work would be done until Uglow believed in the pose enough to make the next mark. When he did start he painted in a frenzy, working as fast as he could. He had rigged up a seat on scaffolding so that he could change his eye level, but he always started with the big toe at eye level, so the feet received more attention than anything else. After a year and a half the face had almost nothing on it. He forbade Todd to sunbathe or to wash off the positioning marks that he had made on her body. Although she did sit in the bath with her bottom and feet in water she carefully washed around the marks. She believed implicitly that it was necessary to the art and that she was doing it for a higher purpose.

During her five-year liaison with Uglow Todd absorbed his way of painting, coming to understand his artistic concerns completely and at first modelling her own painting on his. As she recalled, 'I had gone to the Slade thinking I liked Pasmore, figurative Pasmore, and I had got to know how Coldstream painted and I liked that sort of painting. That's the way I went, but I'm much more human than Uglow, partly because I understand what he was about. I know that my first statement will never be the final statement – I'm not trying to find some empirical underlying truth, like algebra – although that comes into my work a bit because things have to be related, I will stop when I say to myself "I'd like that to be an arm in the way I see an arm". I feel over surfaces, and if the arm is a bit hairy I often start with the hair although it may eventually go because I know I can't say it any more. I'm more likely to start with an expression on a face, going for something as a human being

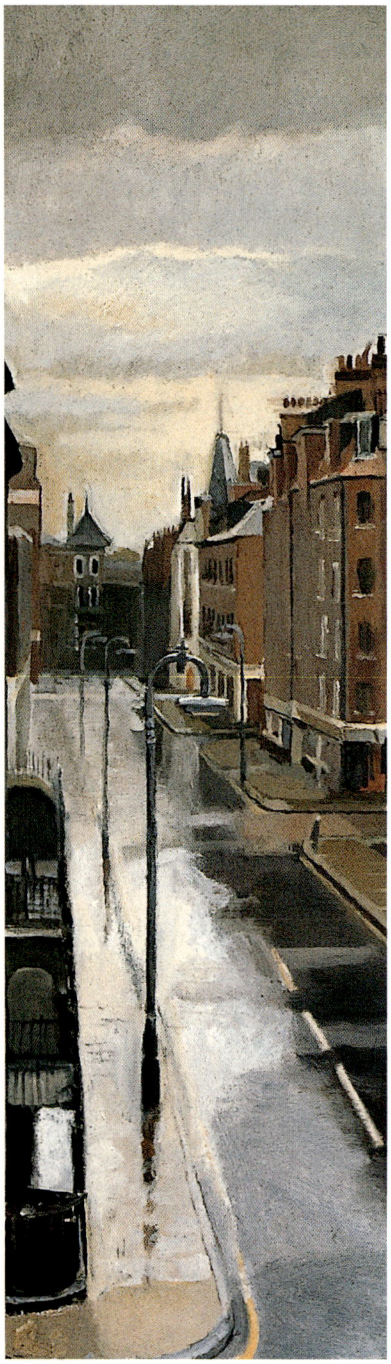

[27] *View from Slade Hostel – Sandwich Street in the Rain*, 1970
50.8 x 20.3 cms 20 x 8 ins

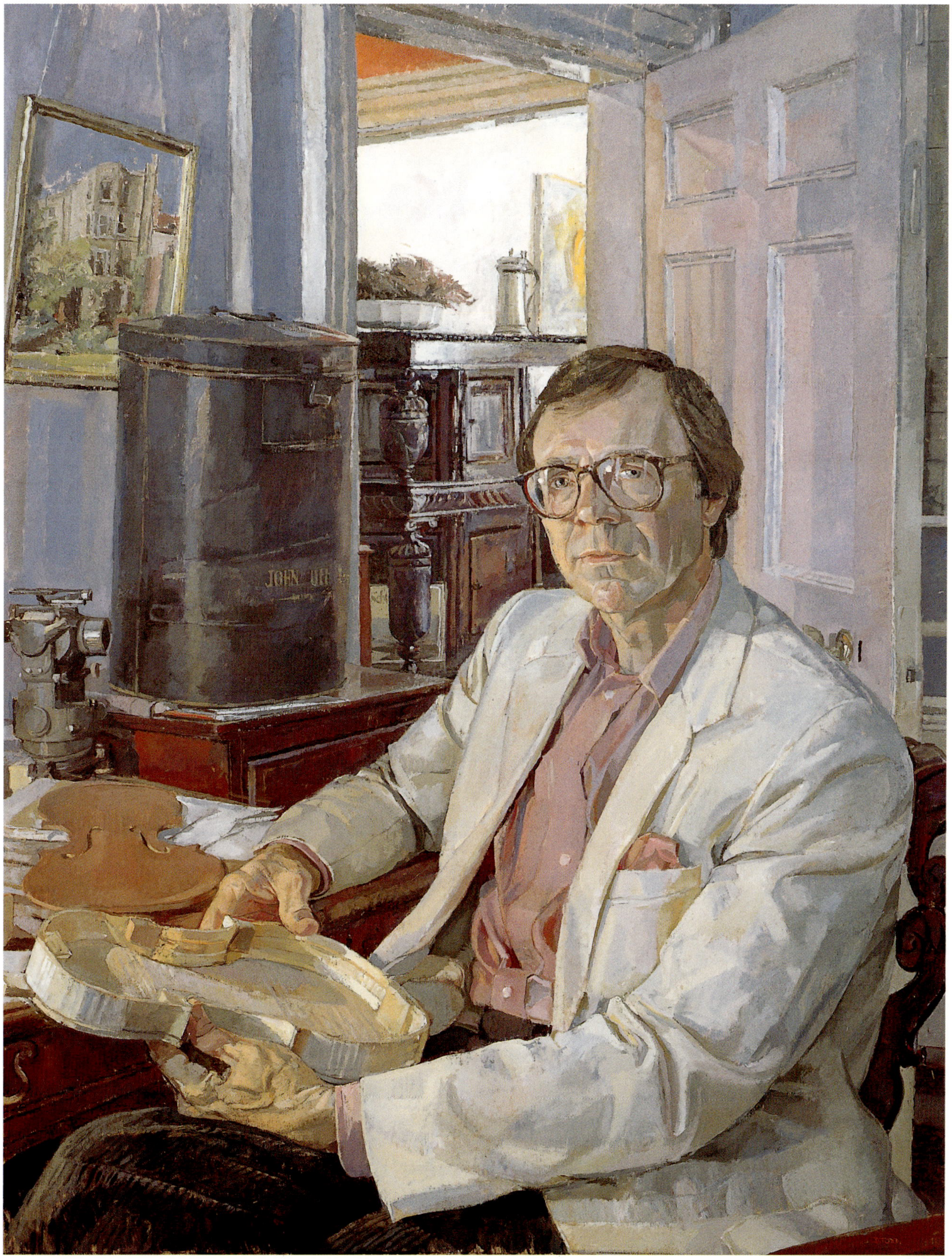

[28] *Professor John Uff CBE, QC*, 1992
101.6 x 76.2 cms 40 x 30 ins

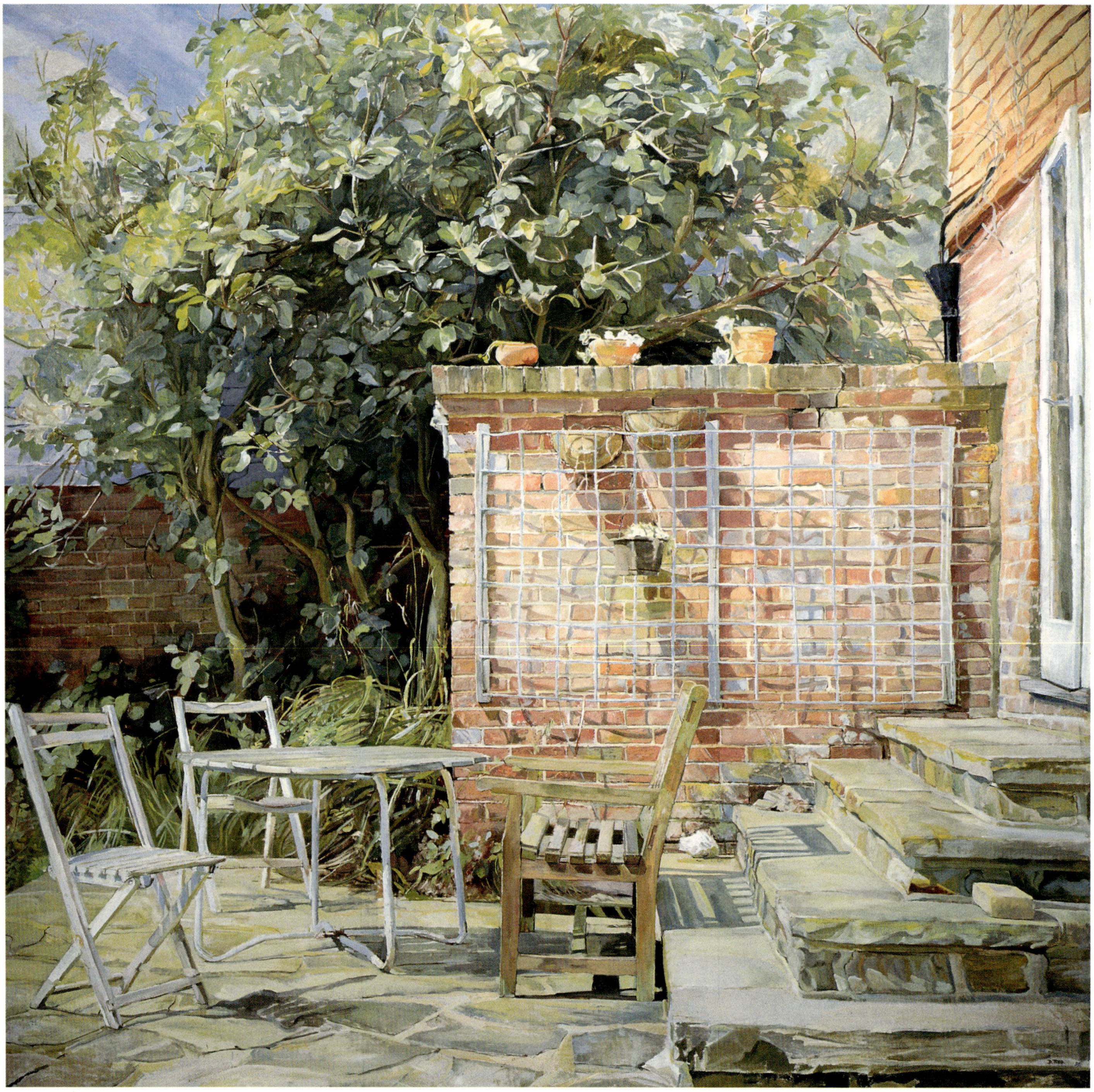

[29] *The Terrace*, 1985
121.9 x 121.9 cms 48 x 48 ins

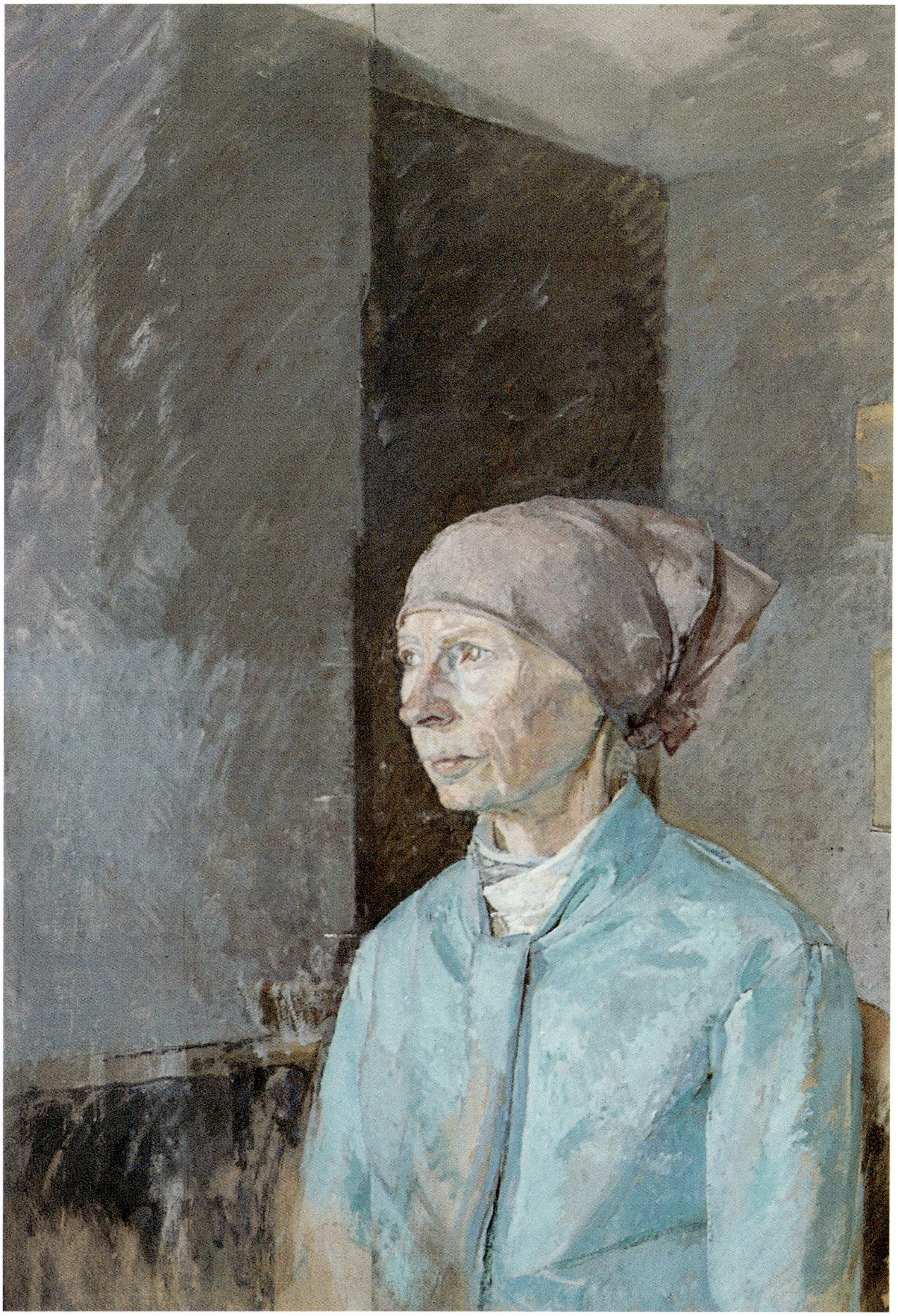

[30] *Florence Crawford,* 1980
76.2 x 50.8 cms
30 x 20 ins

goes for it, a nose or a cheek or a funny twist of the mouth. Uglow was not interested in real people - I think he used models partly because it kept him on the ball – if you've got a human being turning up it keeps you painting. '[6]

Throughout her time at the Slade Todd met Uglow once or twice a week and although she did not expect him to marry again, knowing he was wedded to his art, she assumed that their relationship would continue throughout their lives. All her friends expected her to marry him. When his rejection came she was utterly devastated. She had become irritated by being on call at all times of day or night, although at first it had been exciting rushing across London in a taxi with a coat over her nightdress to see him, or cycling all the way from Cartright Gardens in Euston to Clapham. She decided to test the relationship by accepting other engagements, and was therefore not always available when he telephoned. Possibly Uglow saw this as a way out, but he behaved cruelly. Todd was showing fourteen of her drawings and paintings at an exhibition entitled *Young Artists of Today*, sponsored by Women's Realm magazine, at the Upper Grosvenor Galleries. As the first non-student exhibition at which she was well represented, it was clearly important to her and she was longing to share her success with Uglow. But he turned up late to the Private View bringing a tall blonde girl with him, and then left with hardly an acknowledgement.

Todd was aghast at his behaviour, and had no idea what to do about it. Abandoned by the man she thought of as 'the most wonderful man in the world', she wanted to die. 'I decided that I couldn't go on living. I went home to the Slade hostel and got out on to the roof to throw myself off, but there were some palings and I thought "supposing I am impaled on those but don't die, it would be horrendous". So then I went back to my room to gas myself and I tried just breathing it in but it didn't work and I tried to catch the gas in a plastic bag but that didn't work. After a bit I gave up. I got drunk on gin and tonics every day for a fortnight. Although I was only in my twenties the fact that Euan had gone off with an even younger girl made me feel terrible, washed-up and worthless. I felt extreme pain. I had wanted to go to the Slade because it was the best place, and there he was, clearly one of the best things there, and also interested in me. He was my first love, the one for me. Nothing would ever be the same again, and I wept every day for a year.'[7]

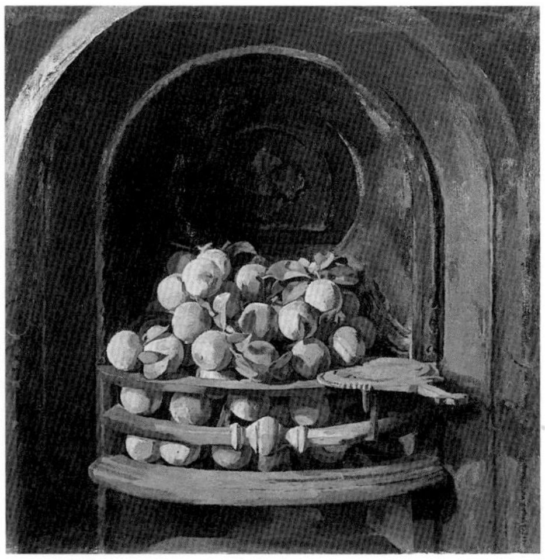

Artificial Oranges in a Grate, 1971/2

To Daphne Todd Euan Uglow was a god and a genius. He was

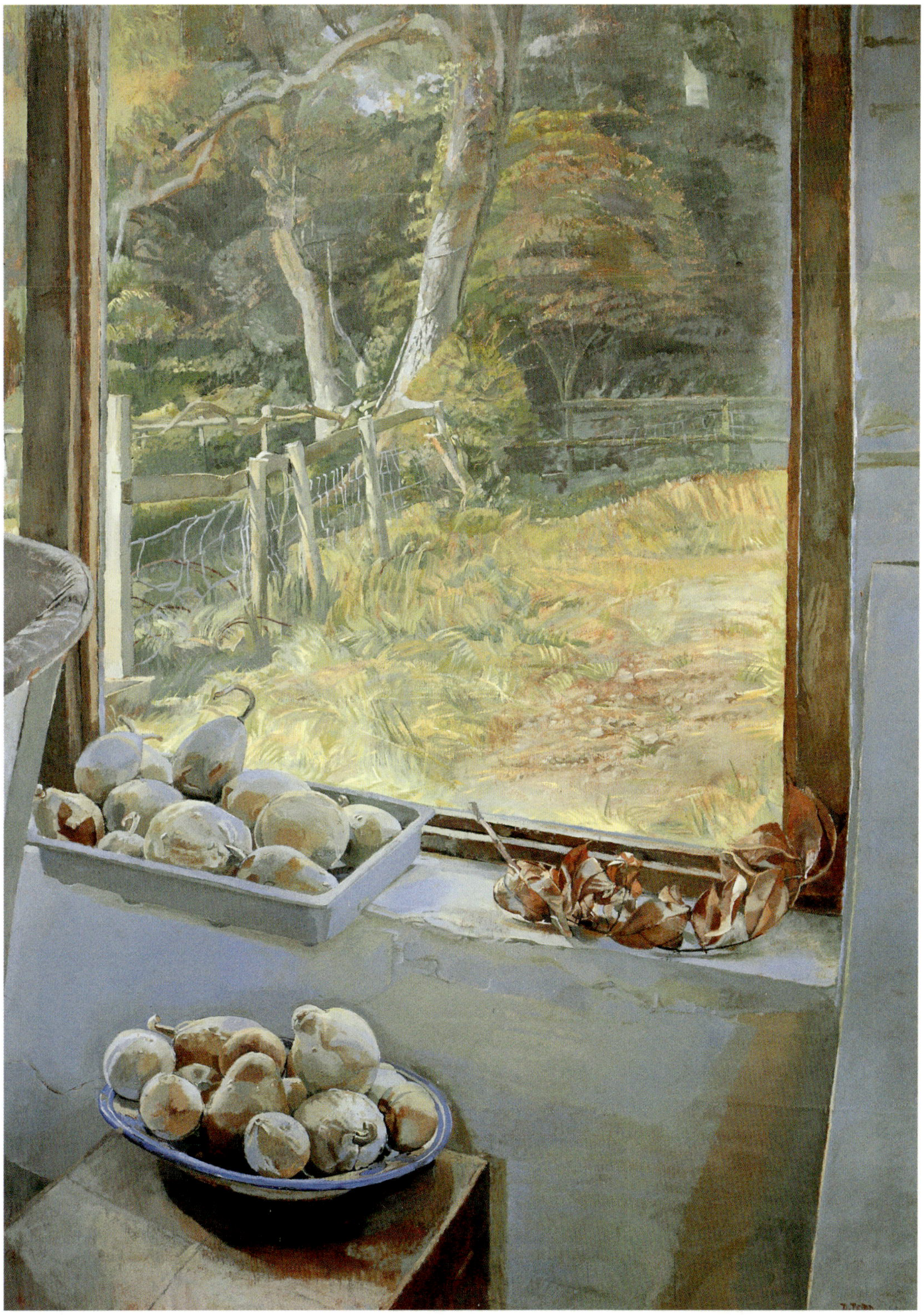

[31] *Inconsequential View,* 2004
101.6 x 71.1 cms 40 x 28 ins

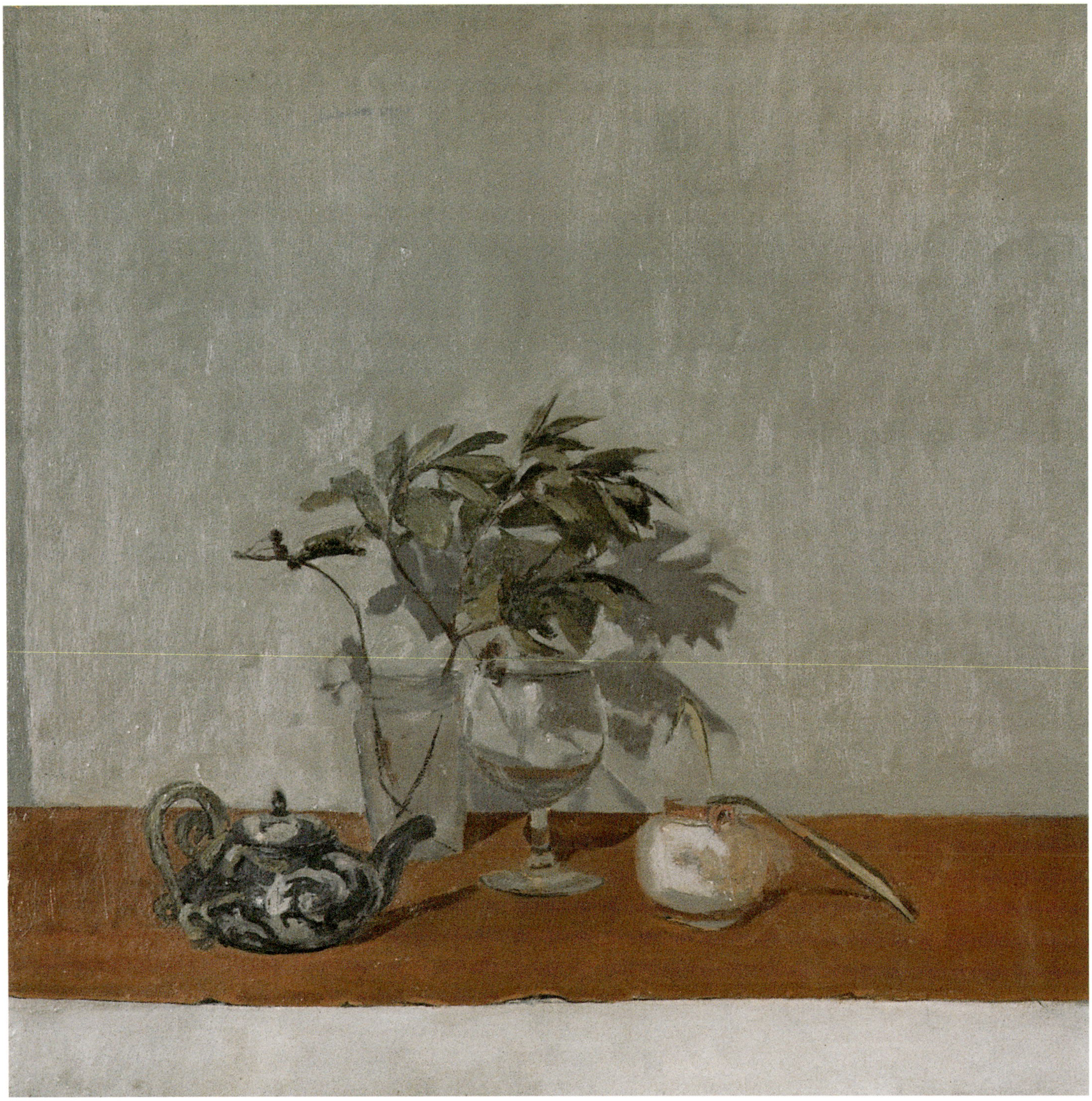

[32] *Still Life with Arbutus,* 1967
61 x 61 cms 24 x 24 ins

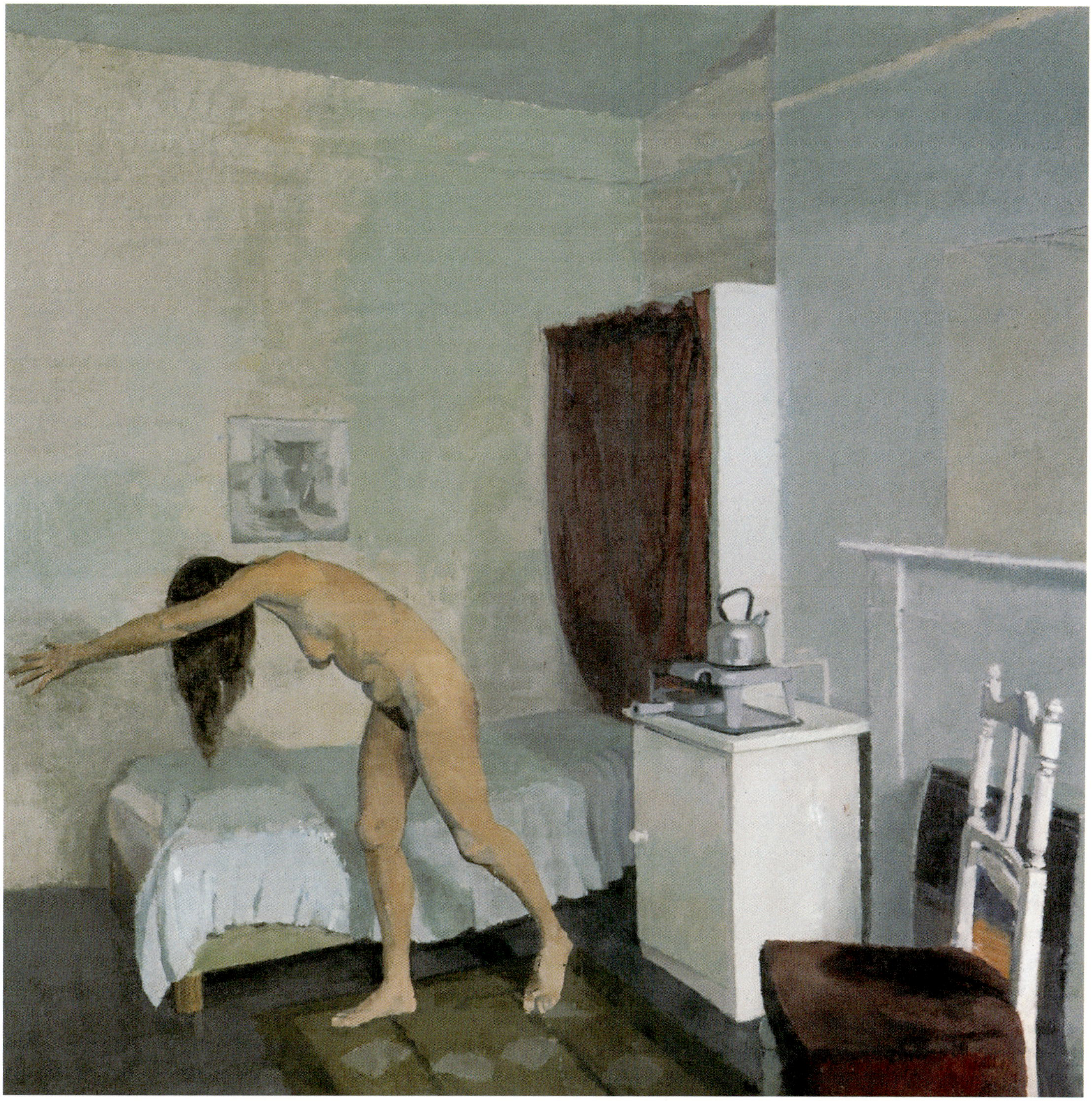

[33] *Carol, Reaching,* 1970
76.2 x 76.2 cms 30 x 30 ins

clearly the source of energy within his circle of friends, who all referred to him as The Master. They deferred to him, although he was as critical of them as of all other painters, even of Coldstream who had taught him from boyhood. He regarded Coldstream's methods as too 'hit and miss', whereas he would go on and on measuring until he achieved the perfect result. Coldstream would leave uncertainty on show whereas Uglow wanted certainty – the *certezza* that Eyton would often mention. Although he drank too much, drove like a maniac, and womanised while fiercely protecting himself from becoming ensnared, he was strictly moral about painting. Each painting must have a 'big idea' and must never be 'knitting' or 'filling in'. The idea, not the ideal, was important and his intense optical analysis became a search for 'irrefutable data', for the archetype behind the transient subject.

Todd's understanding of art was transformed by her association with Uglow. 'I learnt a lot from watching Euan and seeing the painting he did of me, seeing how he did it. He was very intense and passionate about it, and although they look smooth paintings, the paint would be put on with a whoosh and mixed like that as well. Everything was done like that.' [8] During the years with him she was able to evaluate his ideas and working methods and to select those tenets of his philosophy that suited her, and thus to free her own vision as a painter. 'You'd imagine that his painting had to be truthful to the subject, but it wasn't quite as simple as that. In the tall nude the marks that went in from the side were initially made out of brown paper to cover the bits you can't see because of the cone of vision, but he didn't describe them as brown paper – they became painted strips. In the end he was just making a picture. He painted a rose, and I said "all the colours are too bright". It was all keyed up and nothing to do with copying the colours. I learnt eventually that I didn't want to do what he did, but his style became a prop for many people. If you've got no other thought in your head, you can always start measuring and put some dots and dashes down. I still measure, but I don't want it to be about the process but about the subject. Leaving the fixing marks in is not what a thing looks like, it's just a language. Euan's paintings don't become the sort of surfaces that you see, they remain at one remove, an analogy of what he is seeing. He is not interested in texture; he never describes skin. There is nothing hairy about Euan's hair. In my view it's not like what you see at all, it's extracting and trying to distil something from what you see, not what you see in the

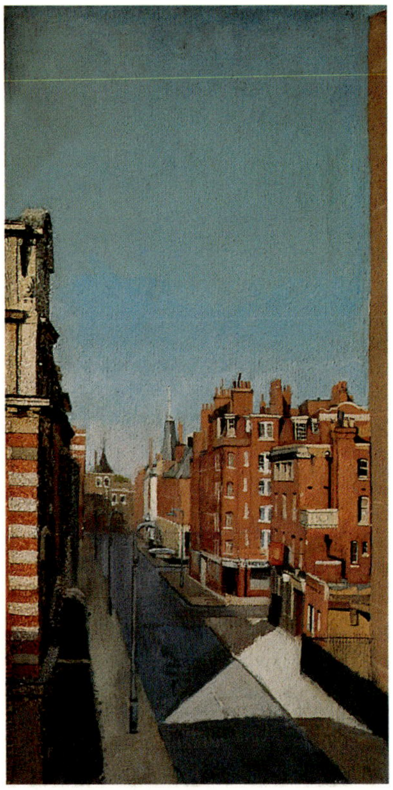

[34] *A View from Cartright Gardens, Late Sun*, 1970
61 x 30.5 cms 24 x 12 ins

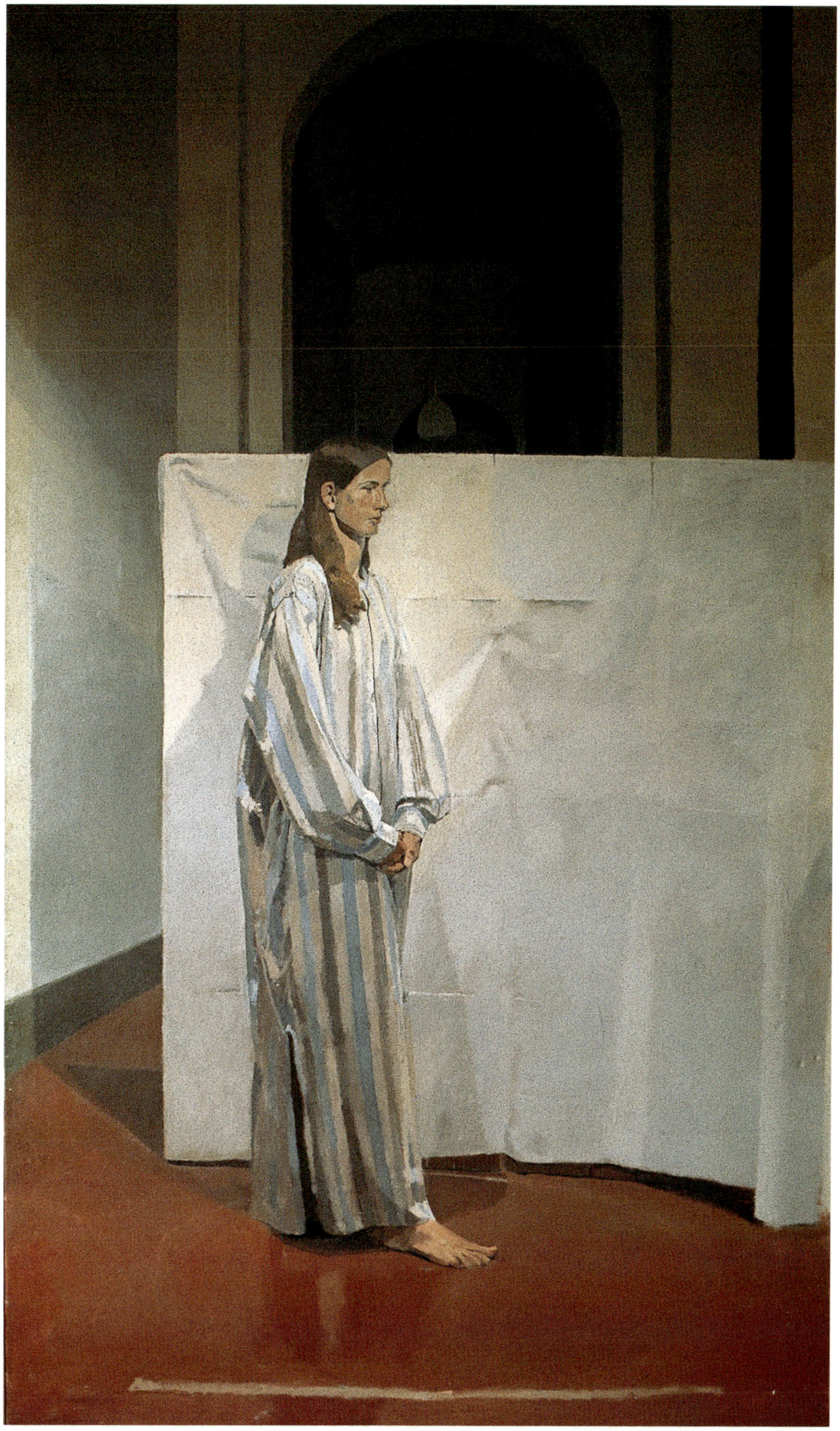

[35] *Susan in my Nightshirt*, 1971
243.8 x 121.9 cms 96 x 48 ins

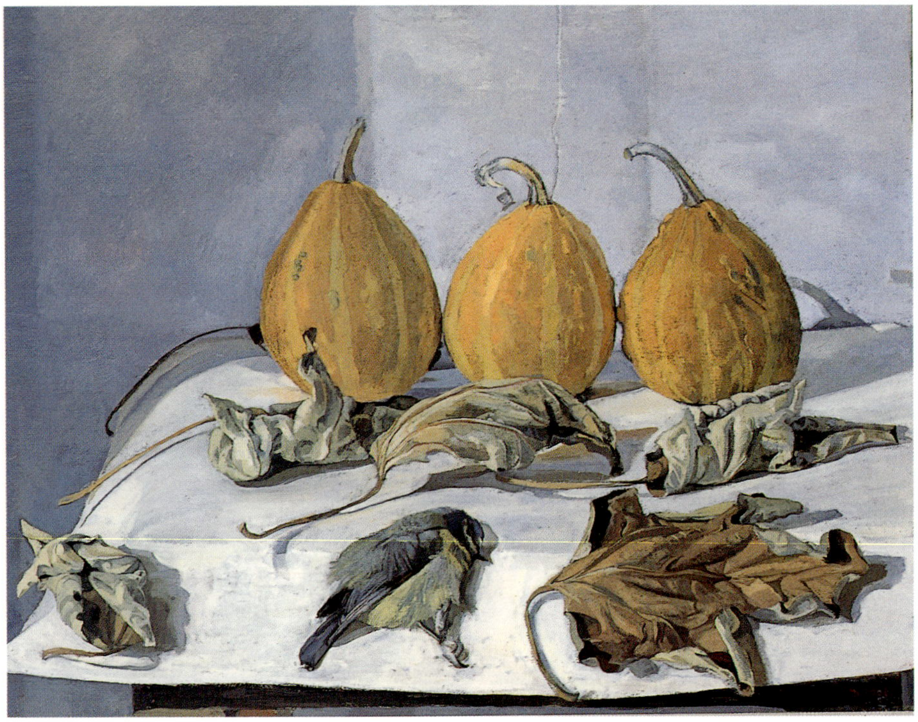

[36] *Gourds and Leaves with Dead Blue Tit*, 1999
33 x 43.2 cms 13 x 17 ins

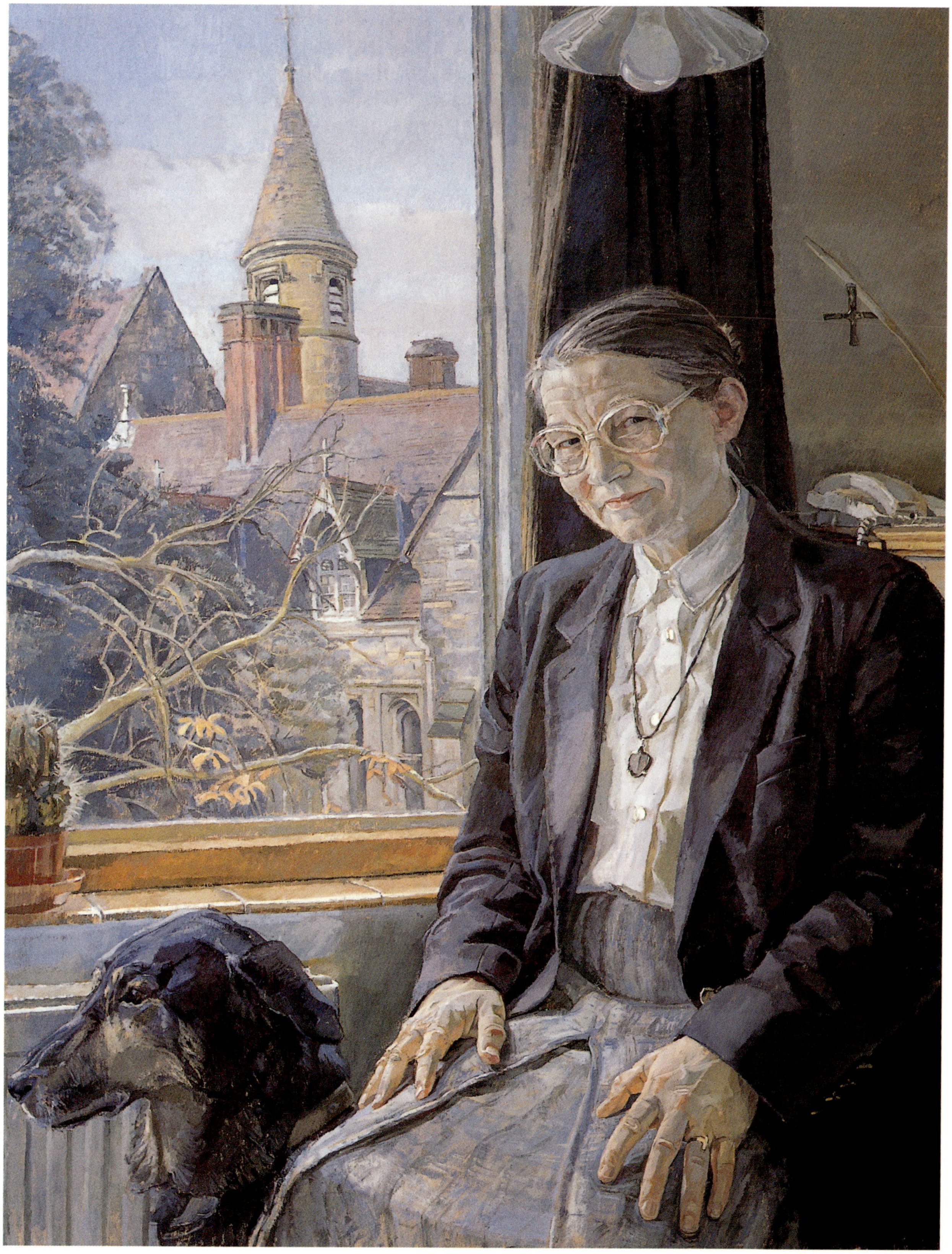

[37] *Sister Jean Sinclair, Headmistress, St Leonards Mayfield School, with Bill*, 1995
76.2 x 63.5 cms 30 x 25 ins

way you see it. In order to cancel distortions he makes new distortions. Because painting has had to justify itself compared to photography, a picture has to make something new on a flat surface. You don't keep your eye still in one place, you can't do that any more, you have to choose what you are looking at. Euan felt himself lost if he didn't have something to look at, so found his own ways of dealing with those opposing realities – the reality out there where you can see vast amounts of detail. You've only got a limited palette, you've got limited tones, a flat surface on which it has to go down, so you make choices. I don't think Euan was interested in real life as such – painting was a power thing and I think he enjoyed the power. Nobody talks about his rather kinky side - he would not wish it to be seen as kinky, but of course it was. He had power over all these women who were prepared to take their clothes off and give their time to him for hours and hours every week over a period of years in extremely uncomfortable positions.' [9]

After her break-up with Uglow, Todd, weeping every day, picked up the pieces of her shattered life and with characteristic grit got through her final term at the Slade, collecting her postgraduate diploma in 1971. To stop the tears flowing she completed the paintings for her finals with the help of sedatives prescribed by the Student Health Service. When the time came to leave the Slade she assumed that she would earn her living as the previous generation had done, more by part-time teaching than by selling paintings. While still a post-graduate student she had done a little teaching at Heatherley's Art School and also at the Byam Shaw School of Art, earning £5 an hour for the work. The Byam Shaw regularly employed a student teacher from the Royal College of Art, the Academy Schools and the Slade, but Todd was the only teacher that they kept on.

The job at Heatherley's originally came through the Principal, John Walton, whom Todd had met through a quasi-commission when he was looking for a student to make a copy for the Peel Club of the John Peel portrait in the National Portrait Gallery. Painting portraits had always interested her. She had painted some fine full-length studies of friends at the Slade, one of which, *Diane with Mouth Open*, was exhibited alongside work almost entirely by Academicians at the Royal Academy in 1973. At the Slade, however, the prevailing view was that portraiture was a lesser form of art. 'Face painting' was considered an activity devoid of ideas, and commissioned portraitists were regarded as paid toadies. Although

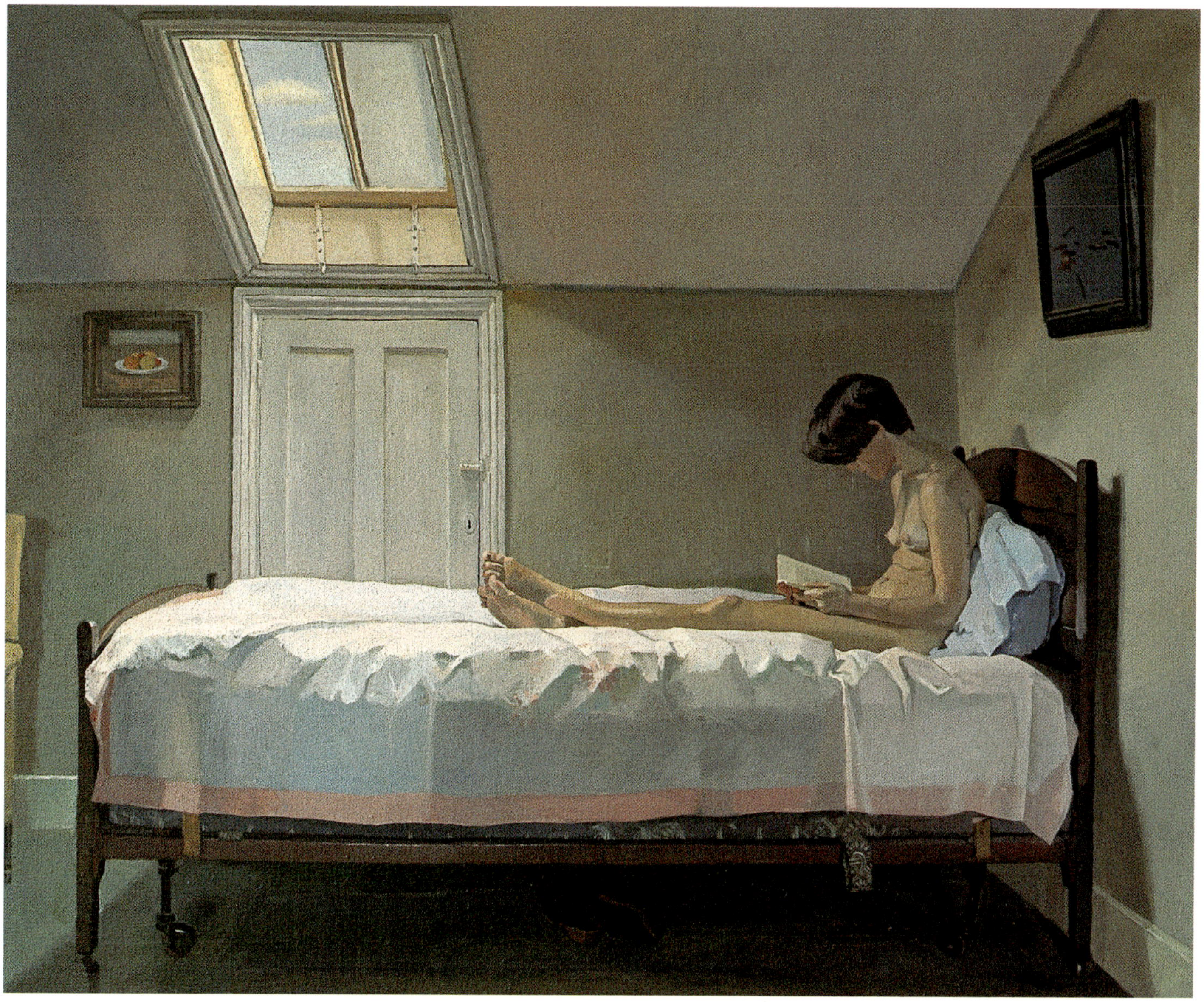

[38] *Vivien Reading on my Bed*, 1972/3
91.4 x 121.9 cms 36 x 48 ins

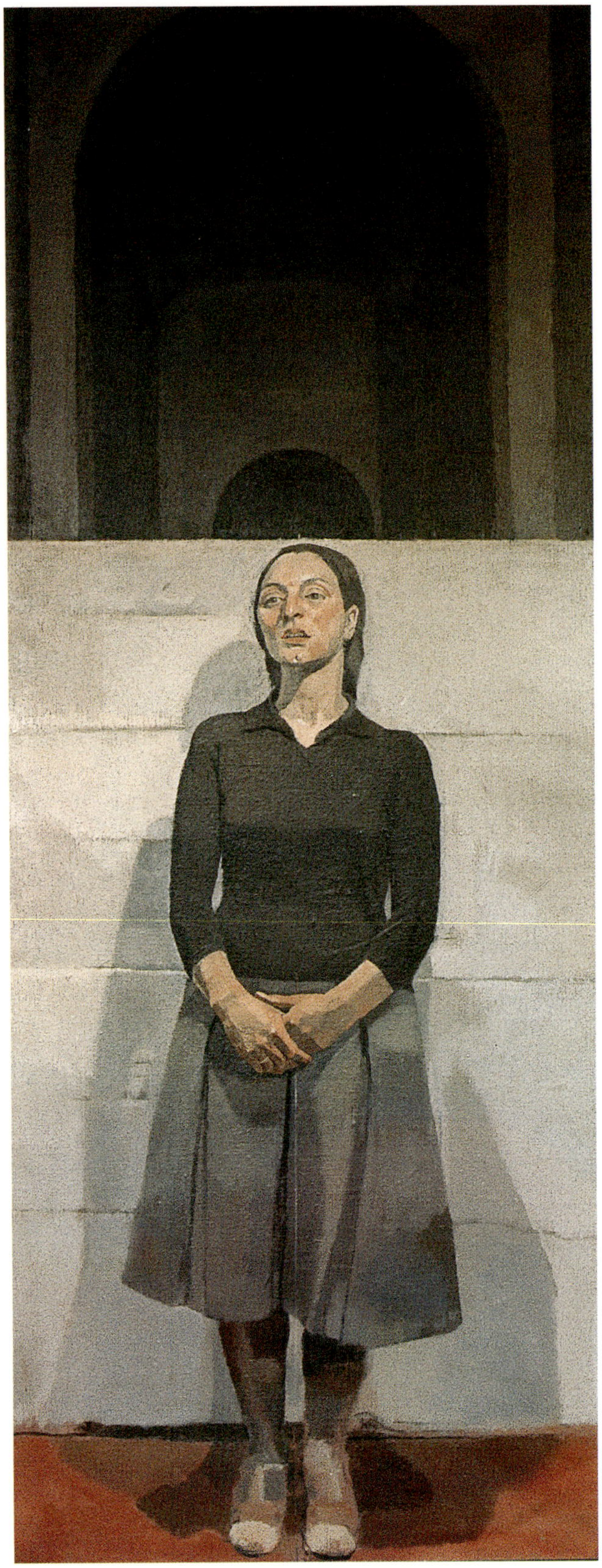

[39] *Diane with Mouth Open, No 1,* 1971
152.4 x 61 cms 60 x 24 ins

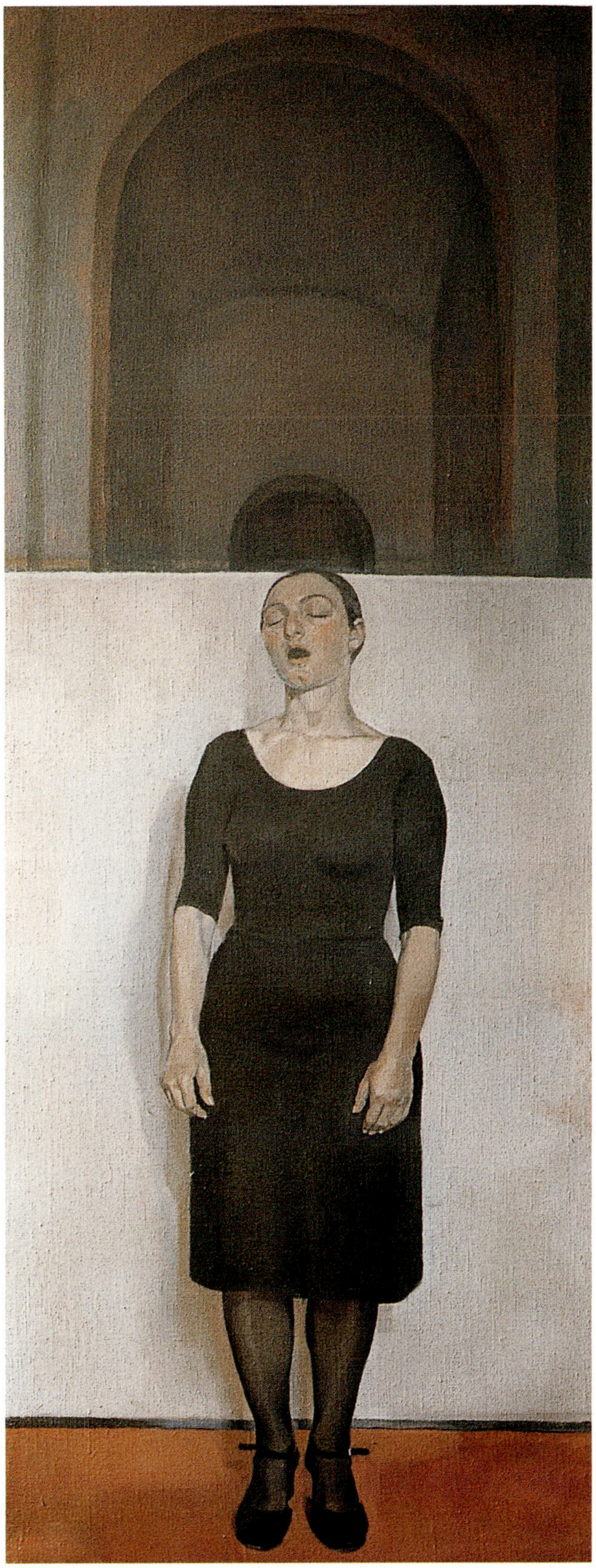

[40] *Diane with Mouth Open, No 2,* 1971/2
152.4 x 61 cms 60 x 24 ins

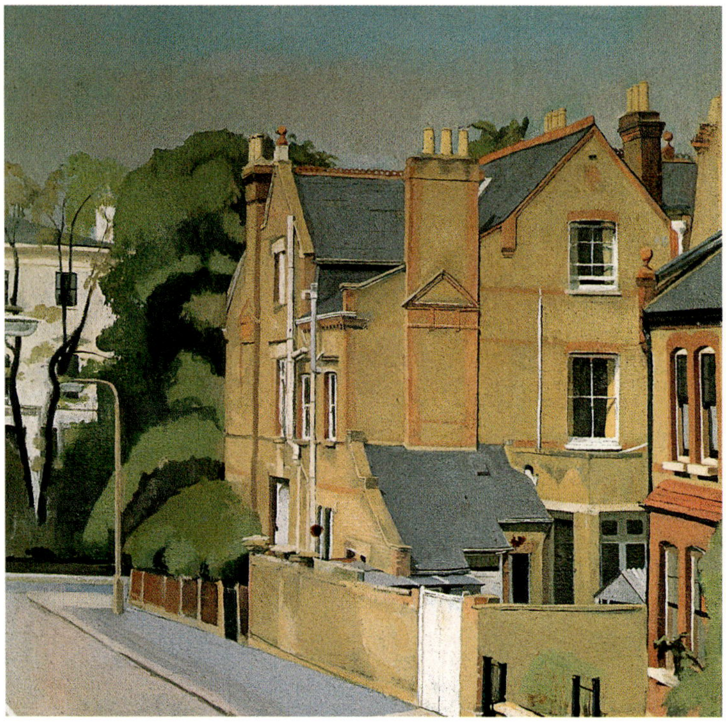

[41] *Clapham Park,* 1971-72
61 x 61 cms 24 x 24 ins

a 'plant and portrait room' remained at the Slade, scarcely anybody besides Todd went into it and it was soon painted black to provide a background for 'happenings' by students such as Stuart Brisley.

Todd's first foray into commissioned portraiture had come in her second student year. The Hon. Robert Pomeroy wanted his two sons painted and he selected Todd to perform this task after seeing her work at the Slade. During the Easter holidays she was packed off to stay in the Pomeroys' substantial house in Somerset. Uglow lent her his folding easel, assuring her everything would be fine. But for Todd it was a nightmare. 'I had only painted friends, measured à la Slade, and that's no way to deal with little boys. By the end of the week I was bouncing them on the bed, sitting them down for two minutes, rushing around to paint. The worst thing was the social side. The family were invited to dinner with a neighbouring countess and I had nothing but my painting clothes except for a little dress. Everyone else was in long dresses. I was stroppy; the two men either side of me talked about social portrait painters they assumed I would know. I had never heard of them and was infuriated. I knew about Titian etc but nothing about these nondescript people they mentioned.' [10] The experience was, however, to prove valuable. Todd learnt that she could deliver a good picture

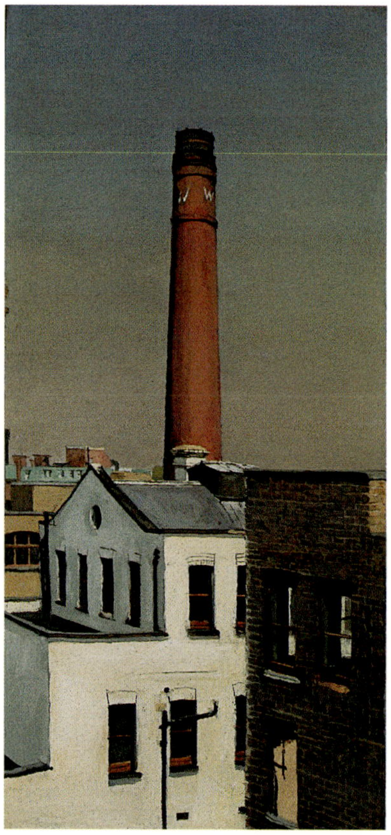

[42] *Townscape with Beige Factory Chimney* , 1971-72
30.5 x 15.2 cms 12 x 6 ins

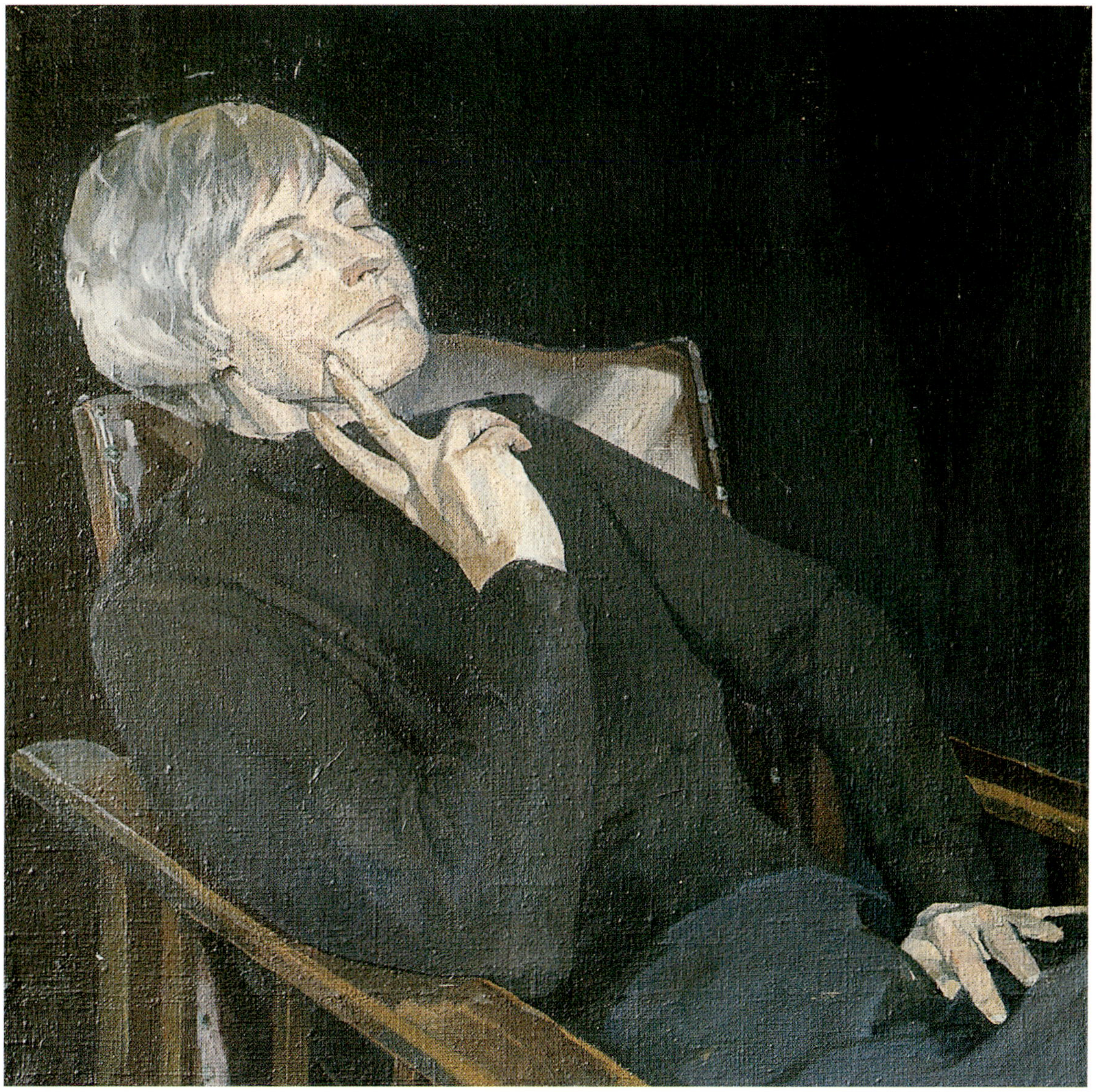

[43] *Mrs Peter Diggory,* 1973
61 x 61 cms 24 x 24 ins

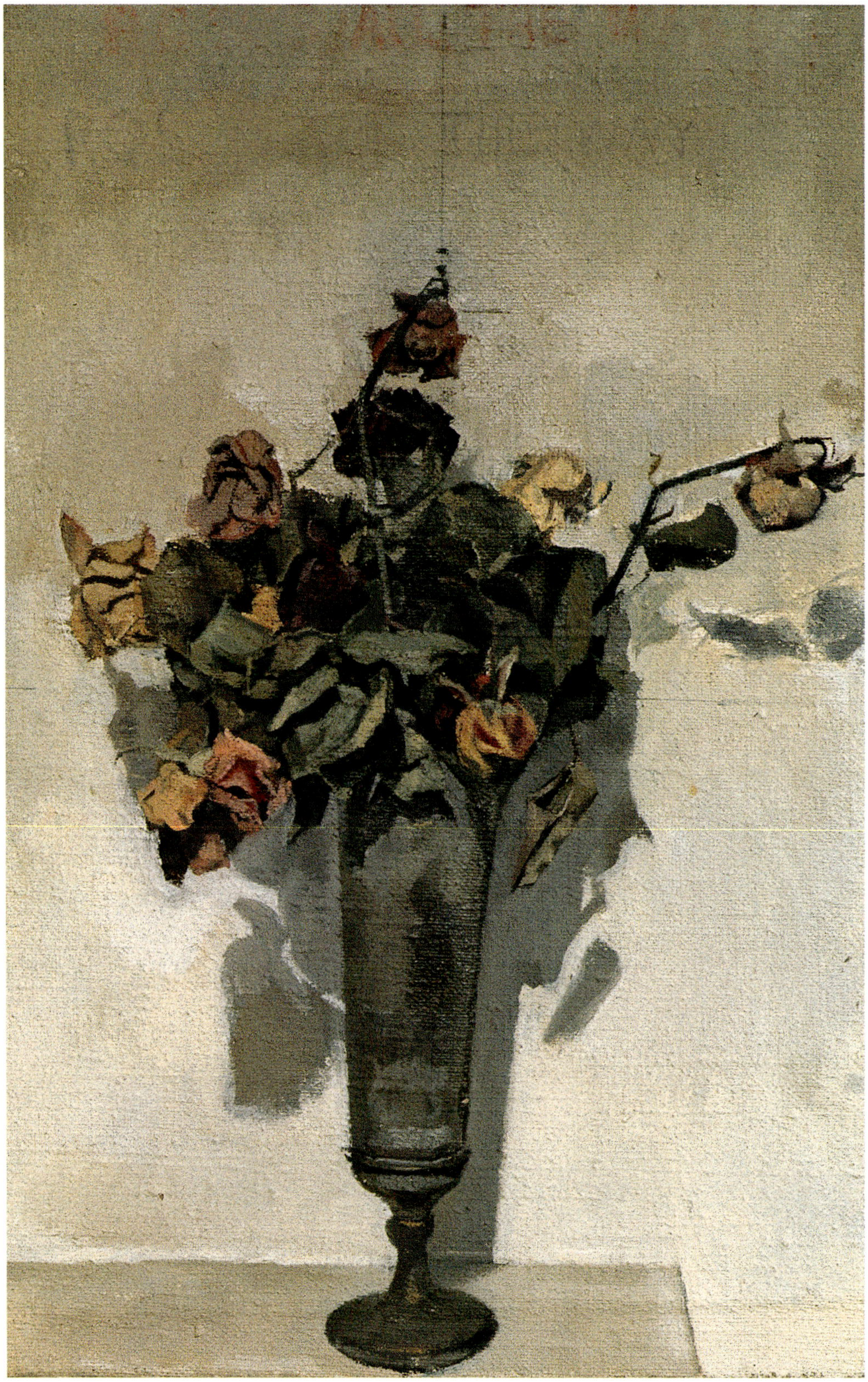

[44] *Roses all the Way?* 1972
45.7 x 30.5 cms 18 x 12 ins

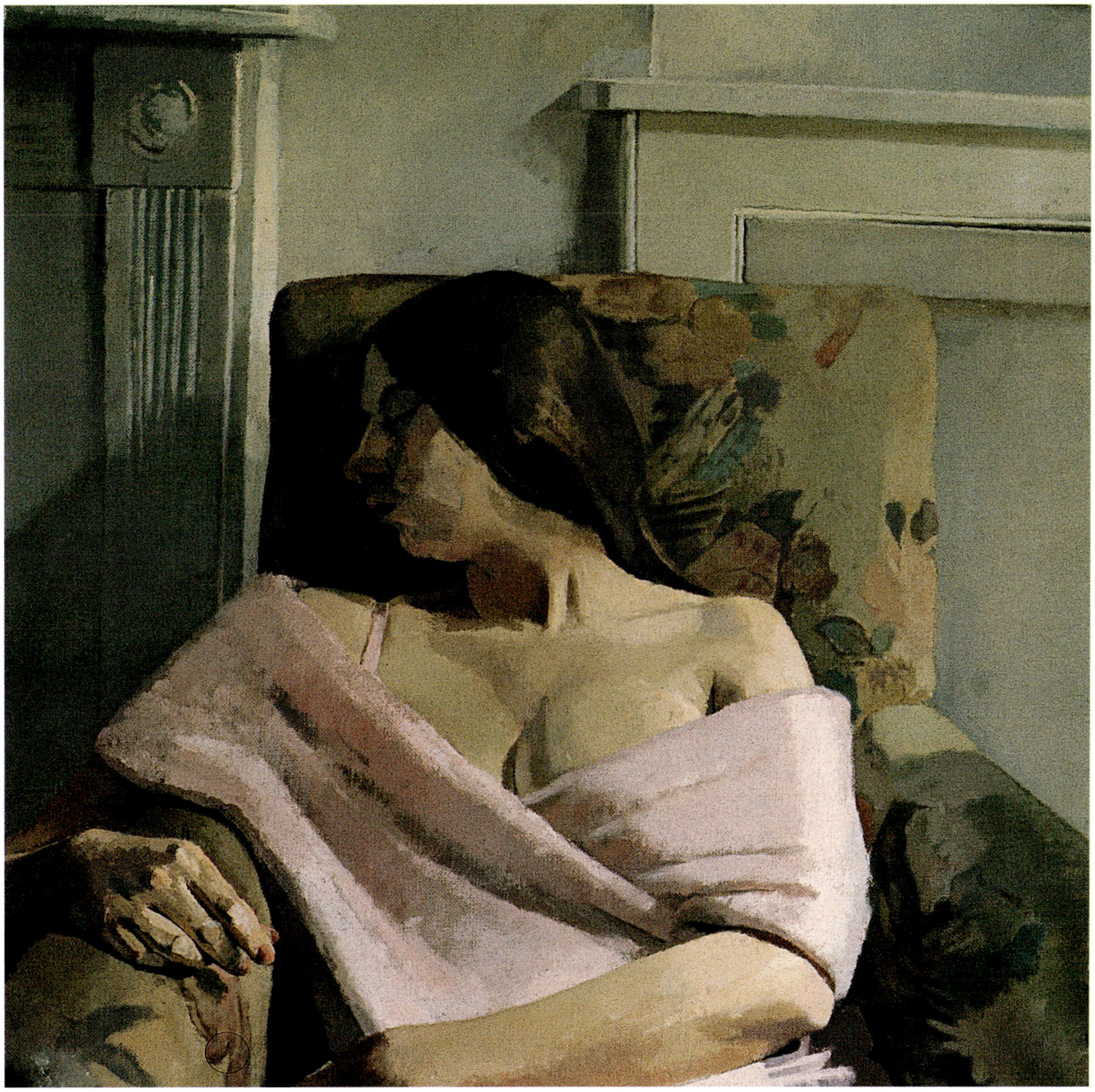

[45] *Girl in a Pink Shawl,* 1971
61 x 61 cms 24 x 24 ins

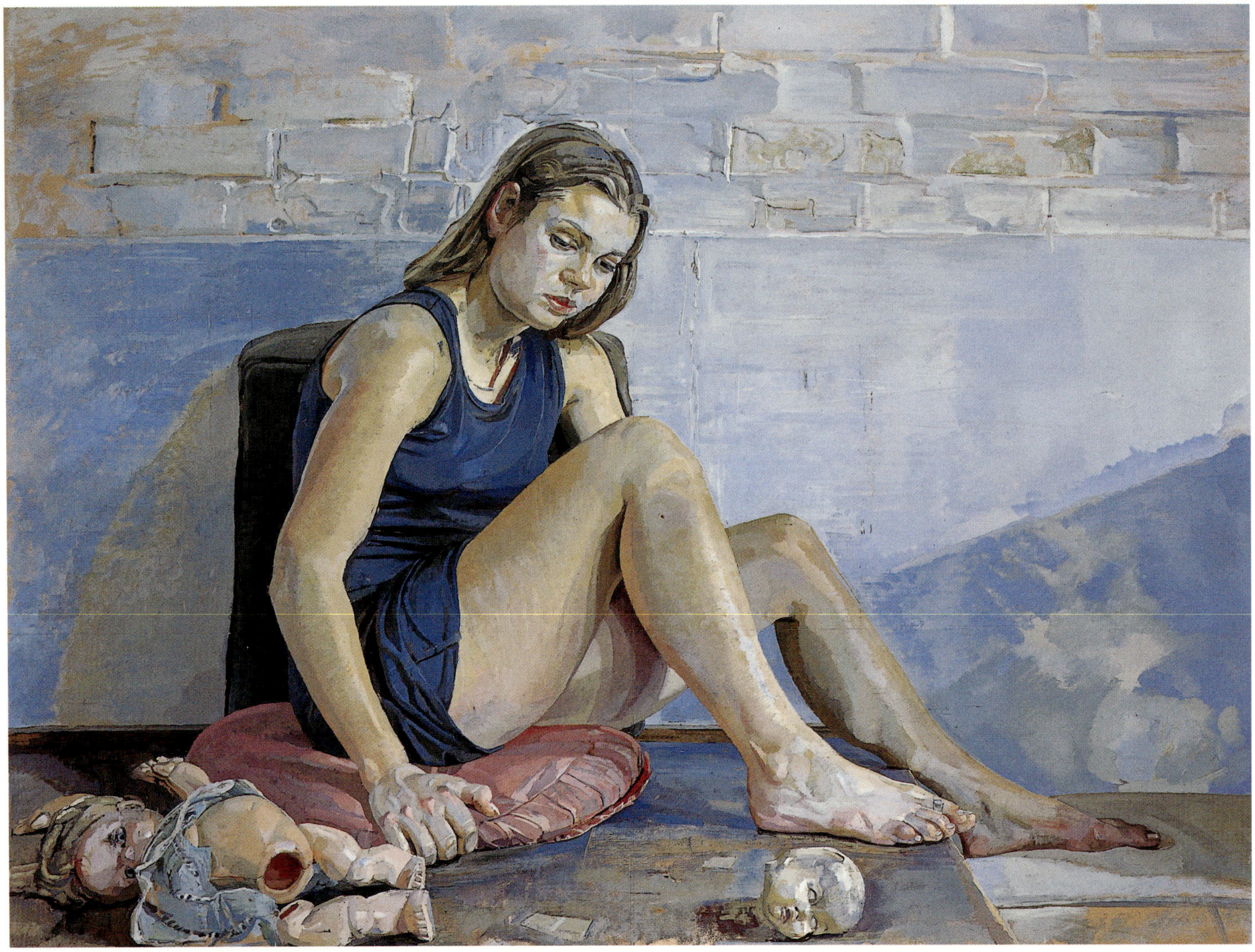

[46] *Dolls*, 1999
96.5 x 127 cms 38 x 50 ins

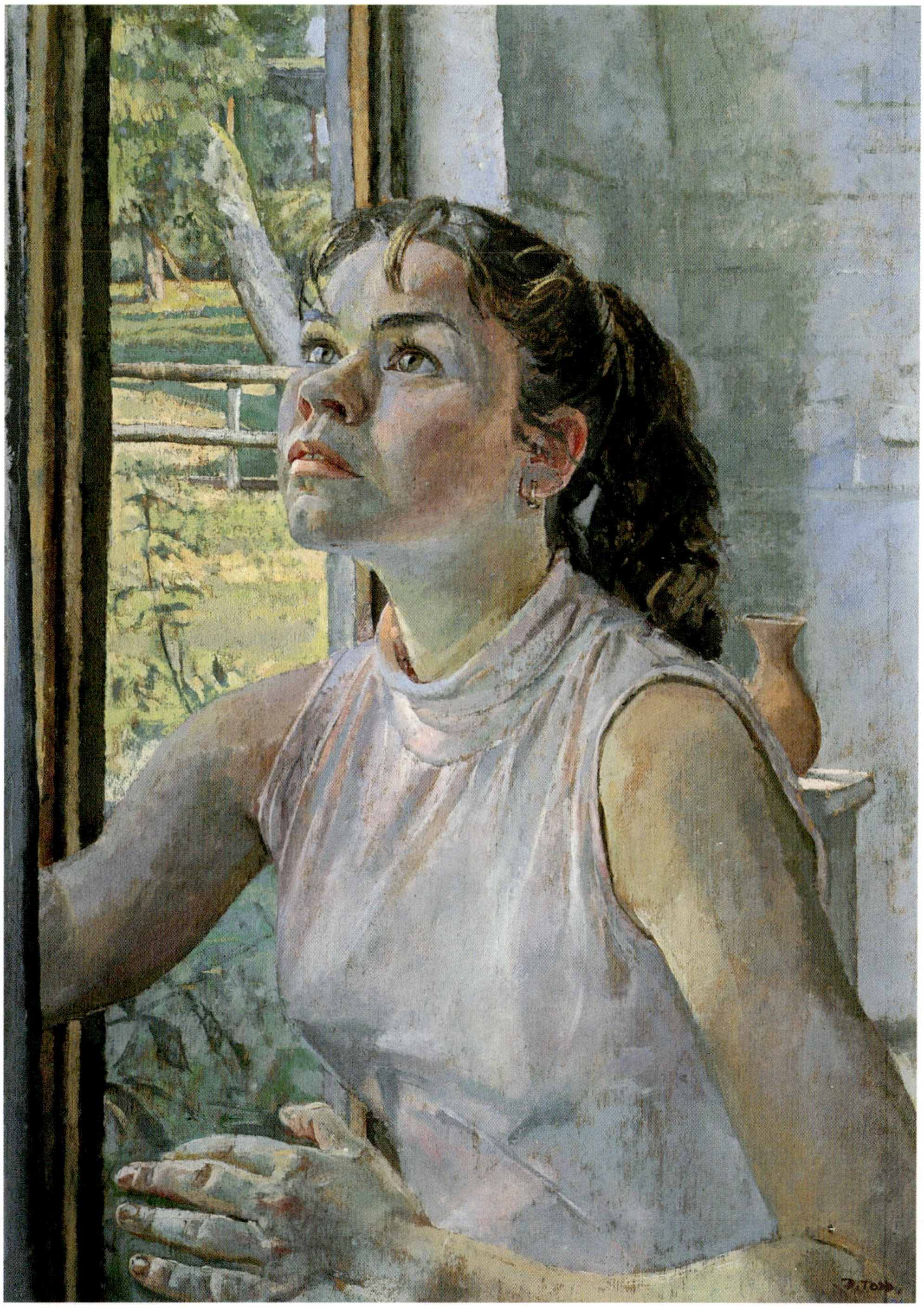

[47] *Girl Looking Up,* 2002
53.5 x 38.1 cms 21 x 15 ins

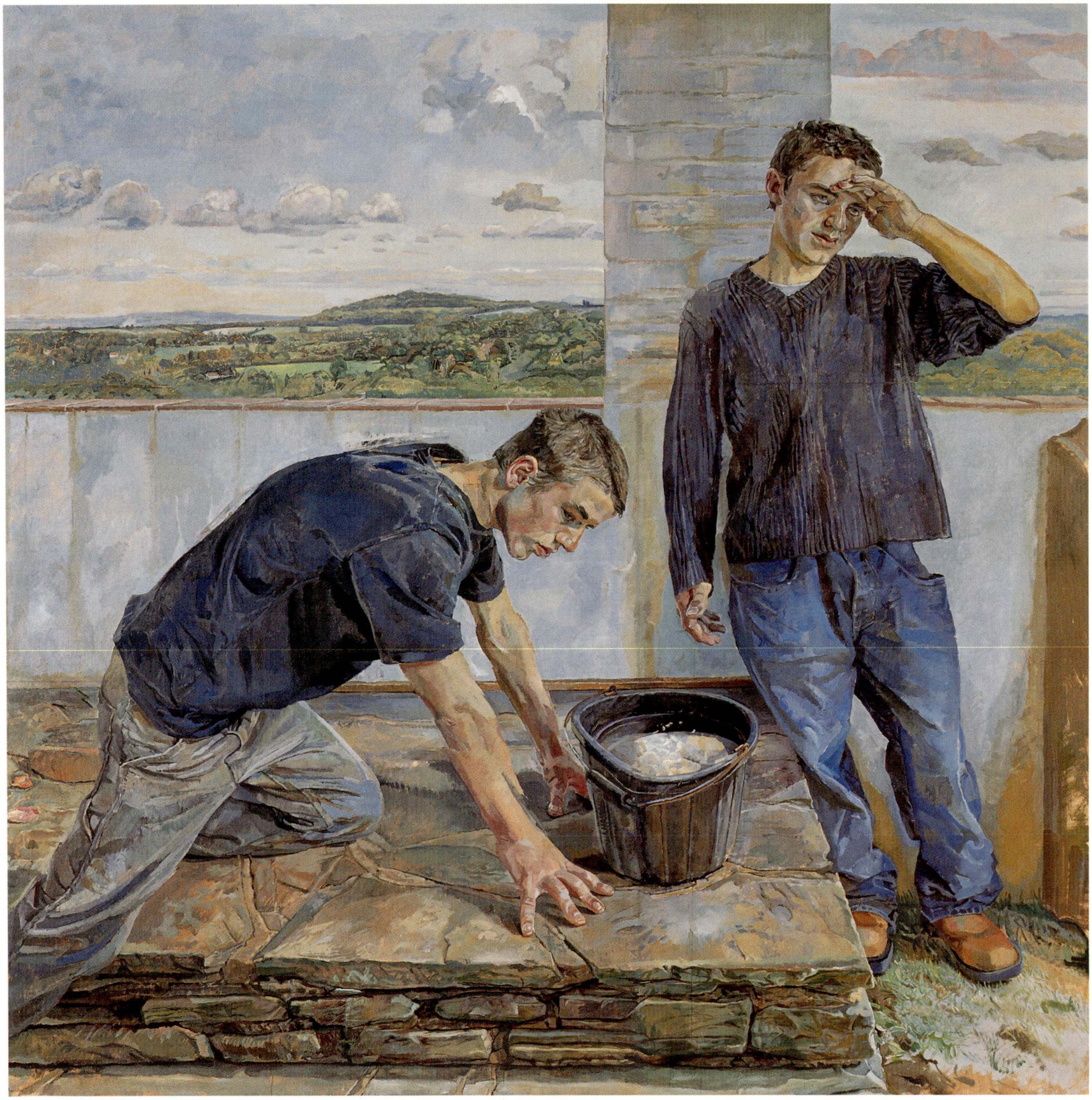

[48] *Eclipse,* 2003
152.4 x 152.4 cms 60 x 60 ins

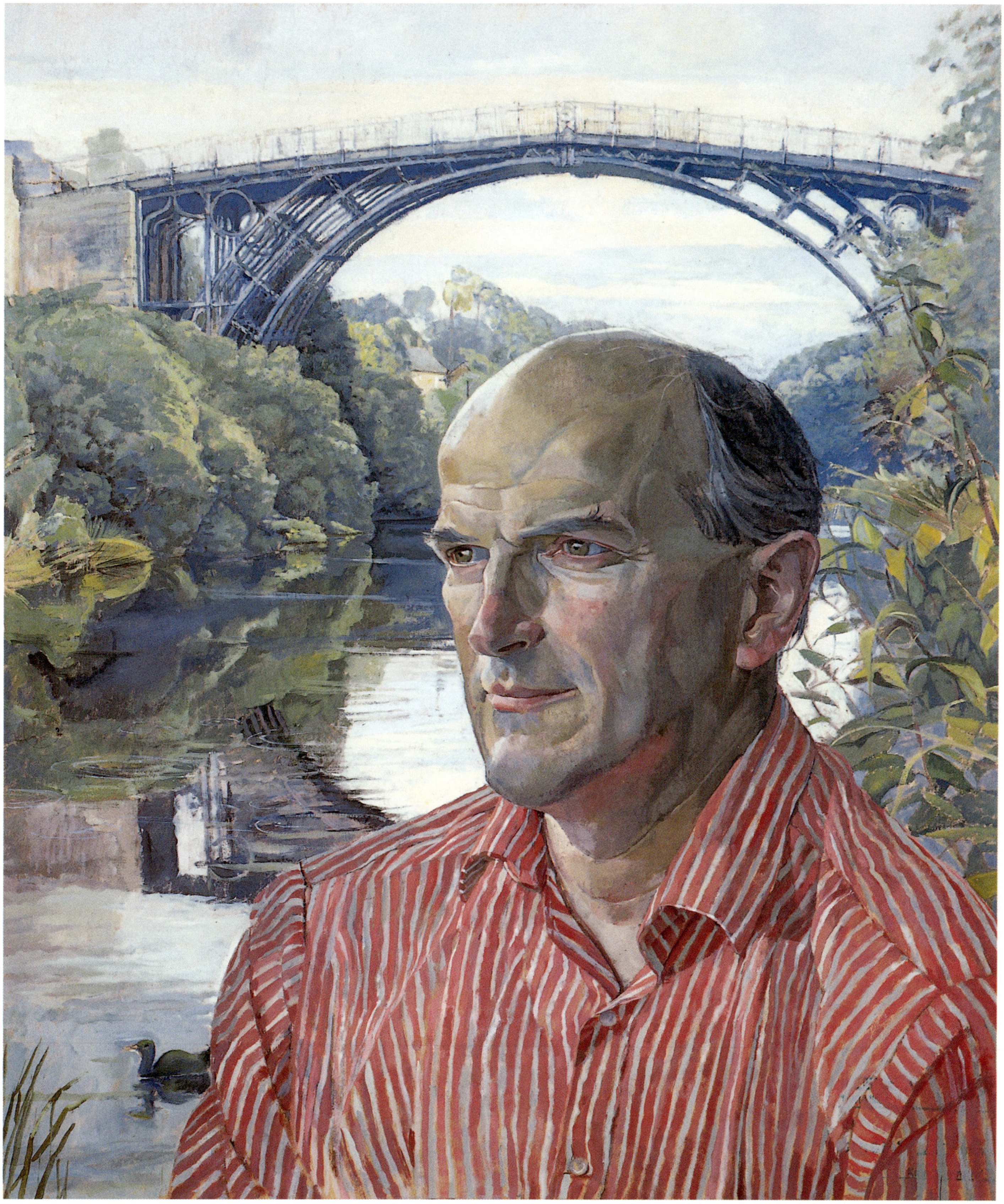

[49] *Sir Neil Cossons*, 1992
61 x 50.8 cms 24 x 20 ins

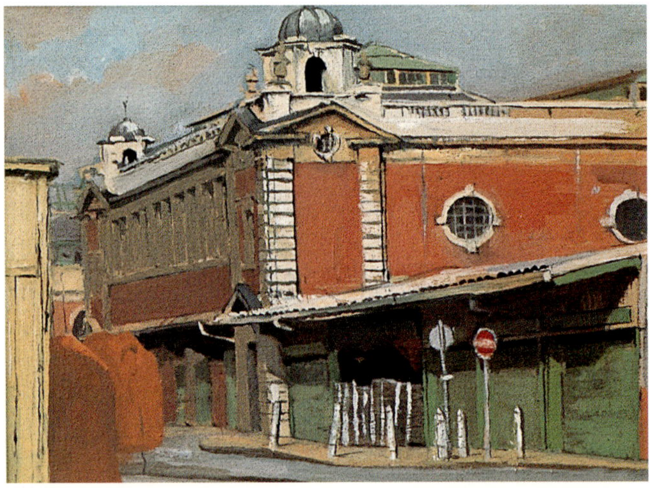

[50] *Covent Garden*, 1973
10.2 x 15.2 cms 4 x 6 ins

however difficult the circumstances, and none of the commissions that followed this one would ever seem so daunting. And her efforts bore unexpected fruit, one of the little Pomeroy boys becoming a painter himself.

Todd's painting was attracting attention in wider fields than the Slade. In 1972 Michael Shepherd, then Art Critic for the Daily Telegraph, commented: 'I was arrested in a mixed exhibition by the almost metaphysical presence of one of Daphne Todd's paintings demonstrating her interest in the powers of colour…' [11] He included work by Todd alongside that of Francis Bacon, Michael Andrews, Lucien Freud and Graham Sutherland in his Critic's Choice Exhibition of

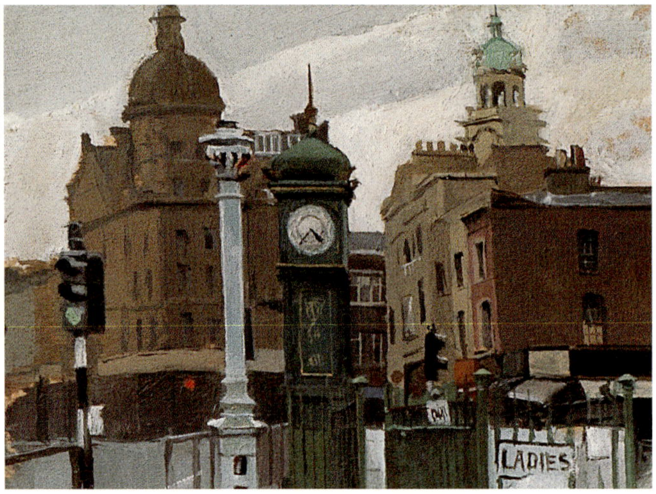

[51] *Angel, Islington*, 1973
10.2 x 15.2 cms 4 x 6 ins

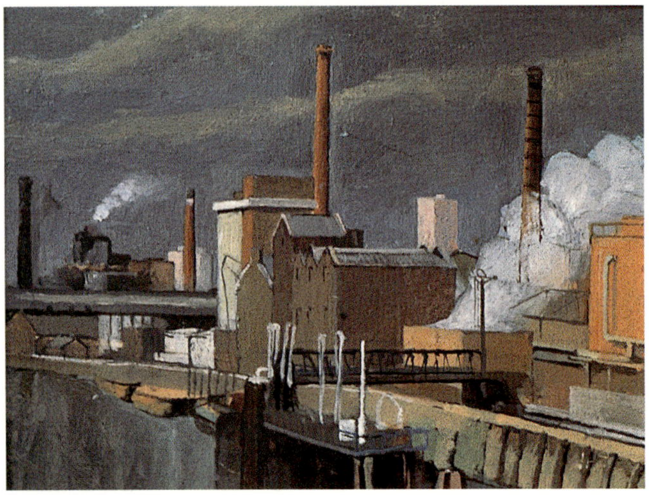

[52] *Wandsworth Bridge*, 1973
10.2 x 15.2 cms 4 x 6 ins

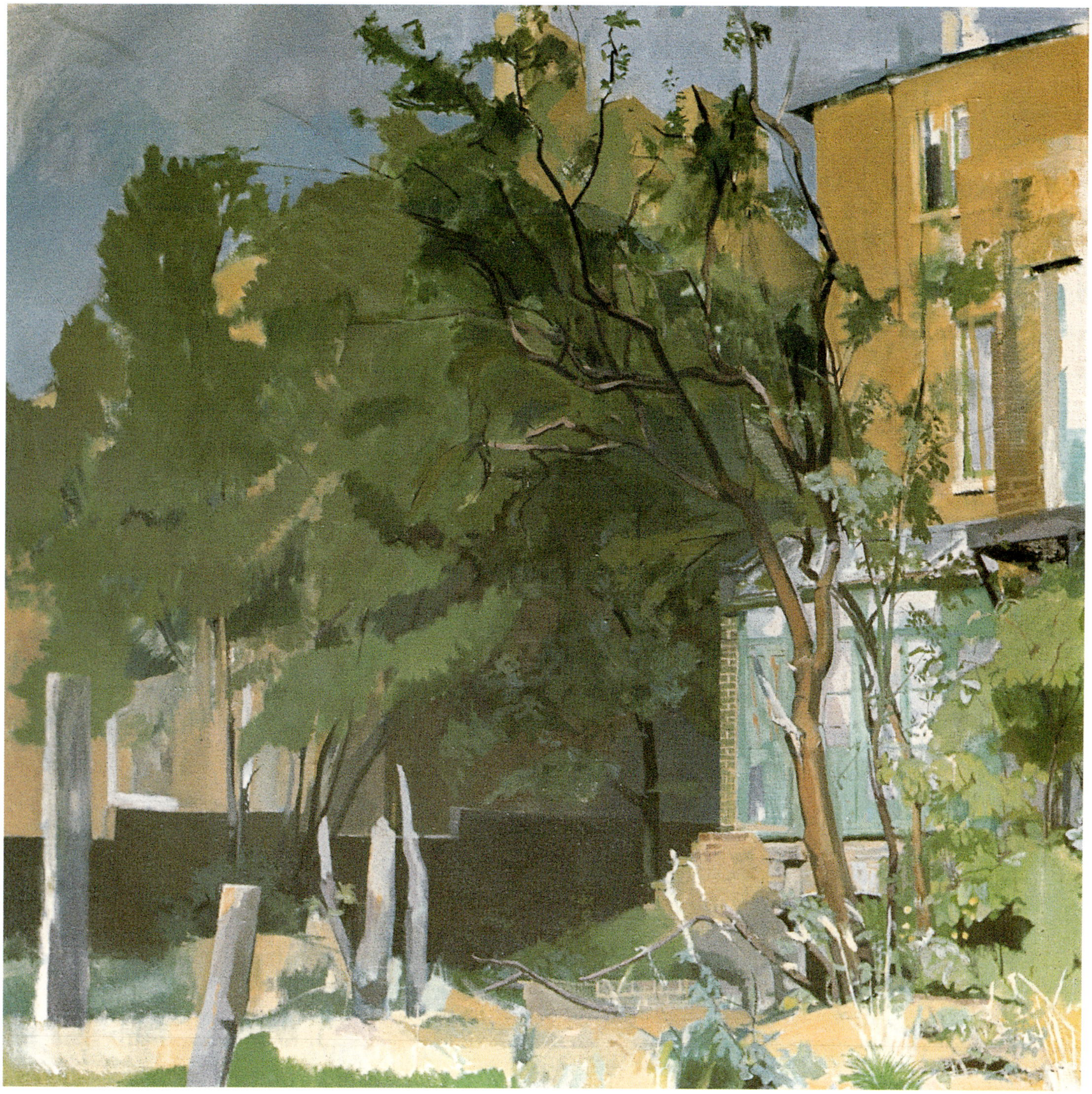

[53] *Clapham Garden*, 1972
76.2 x 76.2 cms 30 x 30 ins

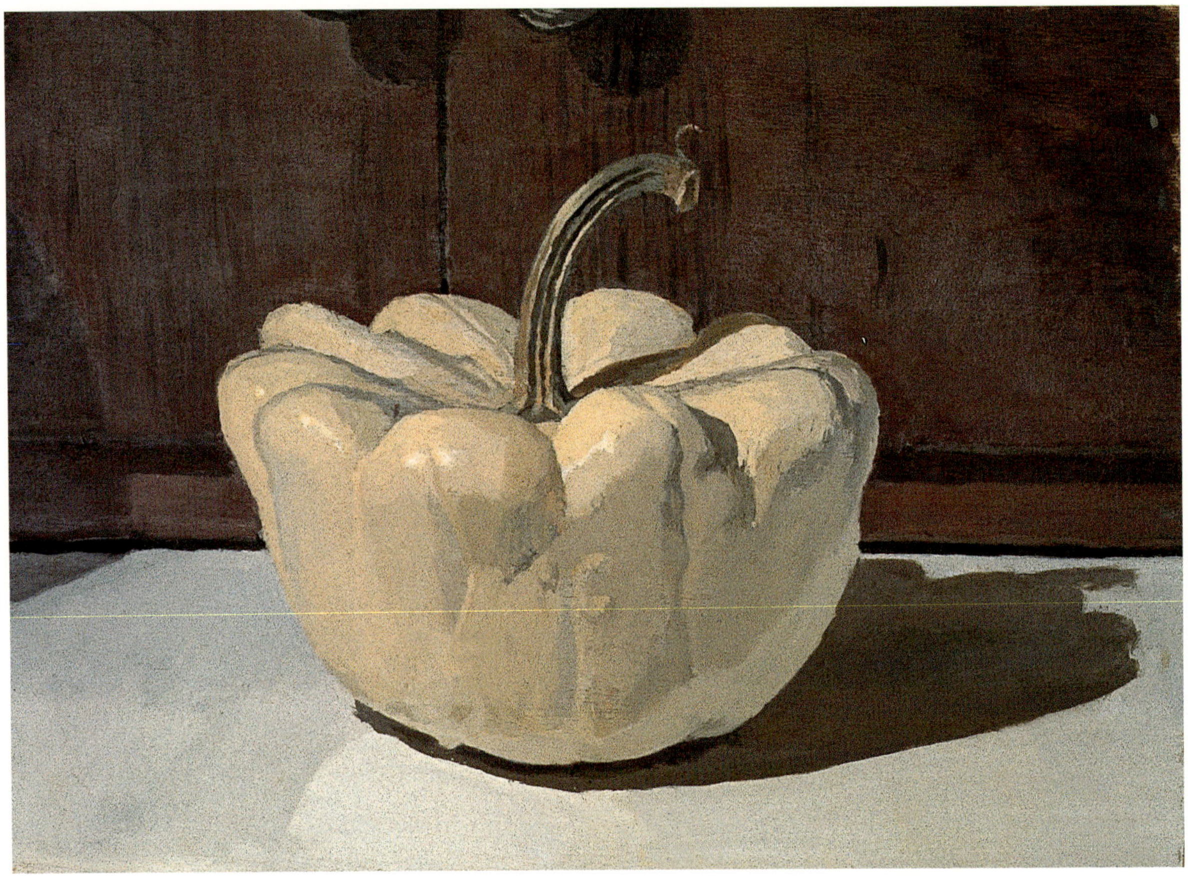

[54] *Custard Marrow,* 1973
19.1 x 22.9 cms 7½ x 9 ins

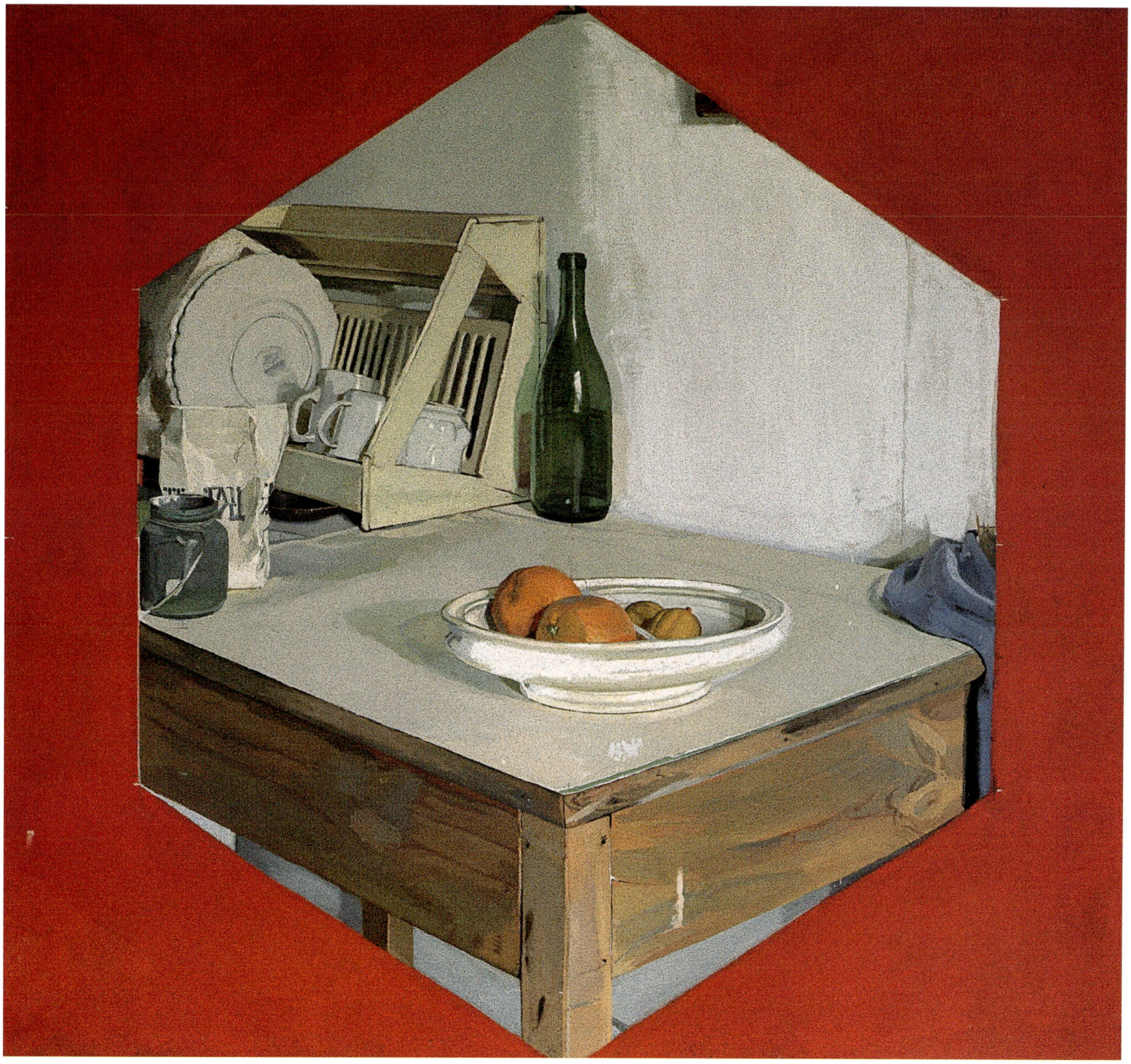

[55] *Red Still-life,* 1972
60 x 69.9 cms 26 x 27½ ins

that year. In later years he several times singled out Todd's work for praise in his annual review of the Royal Academy Summer Exhibition.

After a year in London, living in the garret of a house with sitting tenants that she had bought in Thornbury Road in Clapham, teaching and still weeping over Uglow, Todd precipitated herself out of her despair by buying a minivan and driving 900 miles to Spain to paint landscapes. Her Slade friend Susan Engledow had married a man with Spanish connections. The couple had an unaltered plot with two houses and an olive grove in the middle of Madrid, and they allowed her to camp in the olive grove. She travelled on her own and had so many terrifying experiences with the van breaking down that she frightened herself out of her grief. Instead she fell in love with Spain. For some of the summer she camped in her trusty old canvas tent in Madrid but found the plot too artificial as a painting ground. Driving out to the Guaderrama mountains, she started painting there, but one particularly large painting looking down into a valley lit by the setting sun proved too challenging. As she had made an excellent start on it she drove all the way back the following year to complete it, but, still unable to cope with the vast expanse and with the constantly changing light, she felt she had ruined it. After three months at the same painting ground, this time living in her van (her old tent had finally been destroyed by a herd of cattle walking through it), working on many landscapes as well as a paying a small boy to pose in the landscape (*Boy in Landscape*, exhibited at the Royal Academy in 1974), she suddenly found a way to paint, using as a base birch plywood sized with two coats of rabbit skin glue to make the tooth sharper. She had once before experimented with painting on wood panel when it was the only thing to hand in France (a painting later bought by Ian Tregarthen Jenkin). She disliked the way the surface of canvas stretched under her hand, especially in sun and wind, and she needed to be able to work close to the picture surface, as if drawing. Although she had won prizes for drawing at the Slade she had felt that her painting was 'somehow lacking'. Painting on wood seemed to be the answer. 'The wood showed me a way to paint as if it were drawing and to do what I do when I am drawing. One has to allow oneself to copy and be precise – being precise

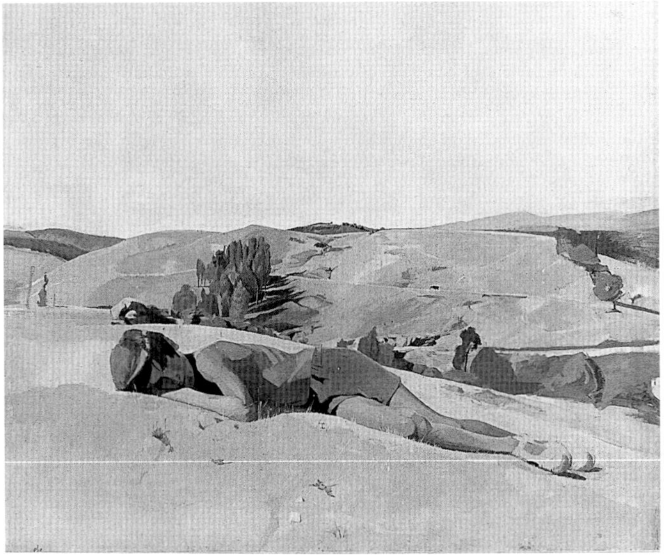

Boy in a Spanish Landscape, 1973

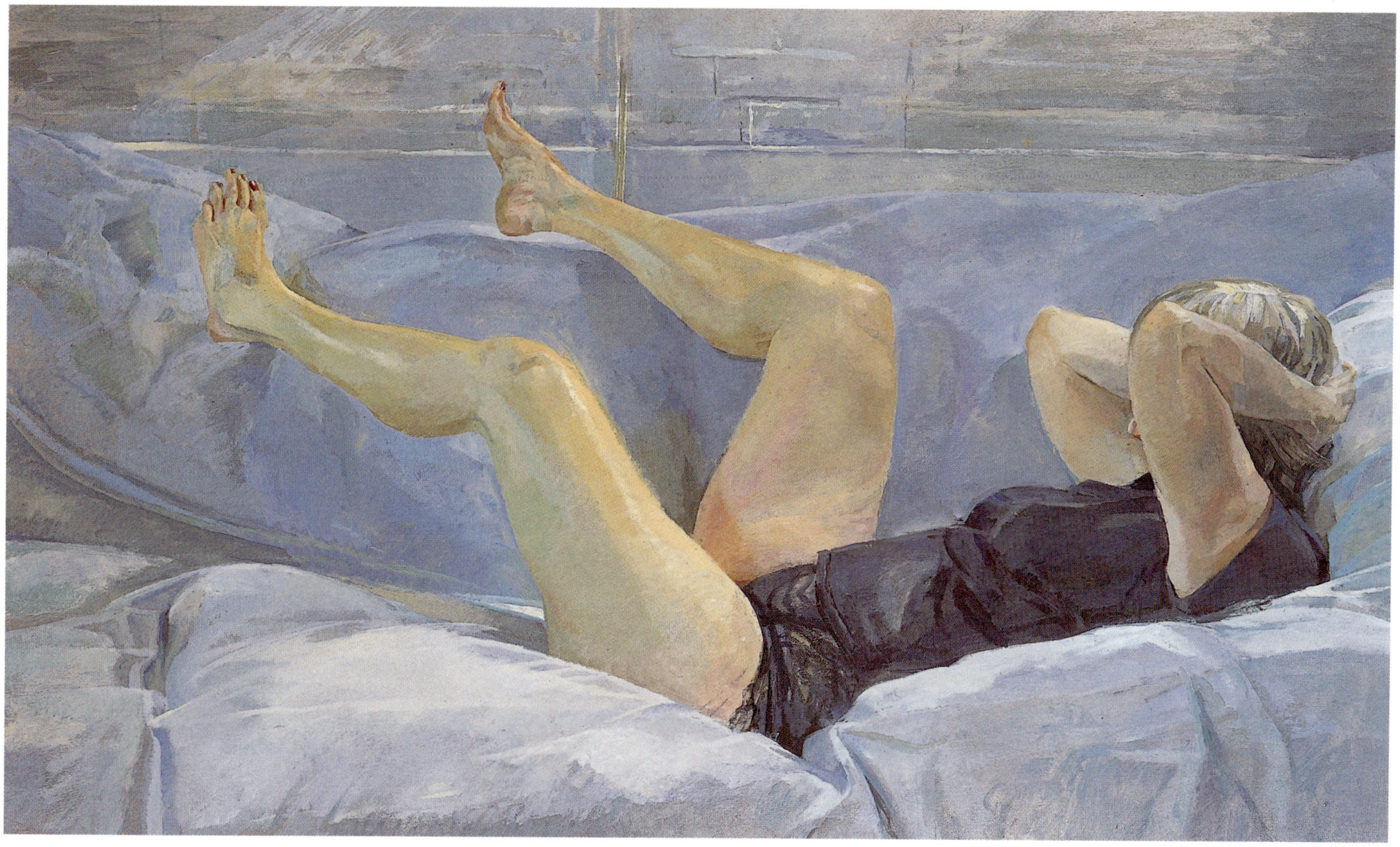

[56] *Legs, Landing*, 2006
47.6 x 76.8 cms 18¾ x 30¼ ins

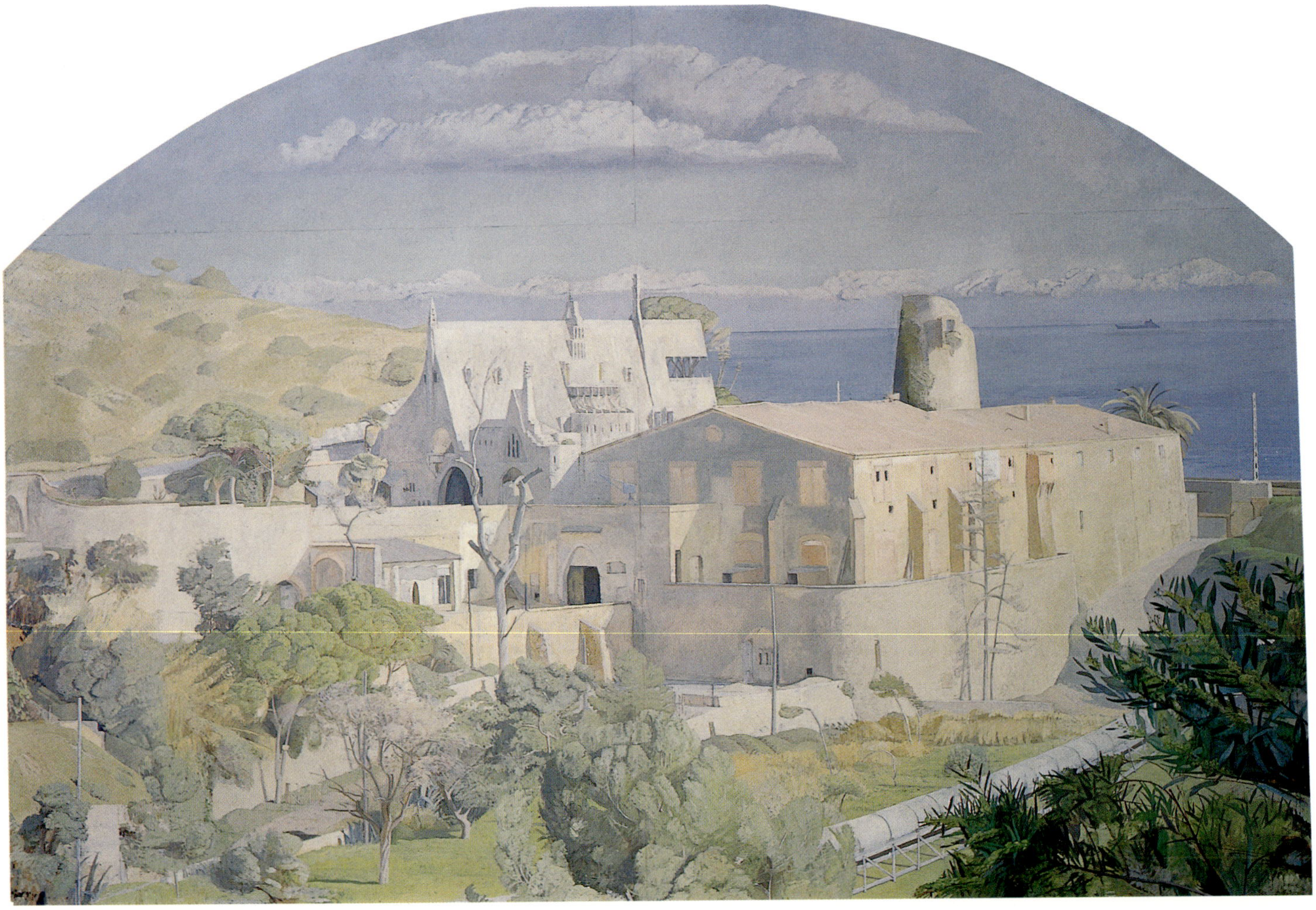

[57] *Gaudi at Garraf, with Industrial Tube, Spain*, 1976
203.2 x 304.8 cms 80 x 120 ins

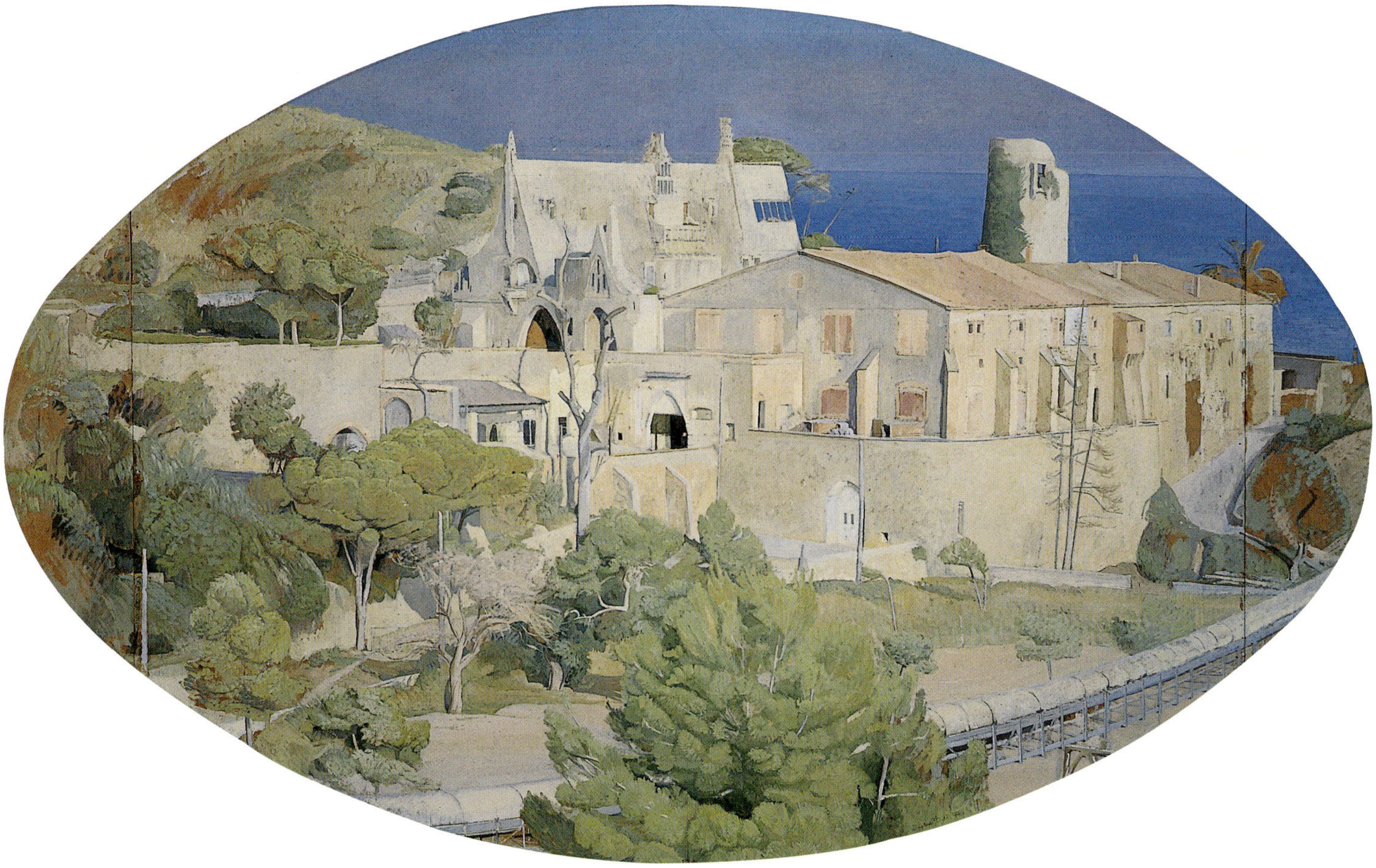

[58] *Gaudi at Garraf, with Industrial Tube II, Spain,* 1977
119.4 x 177.8 cms 47 x 70 ins

and using a sable brush and resting on your finger made it a lot easier. With wood you can just snap pieces off and add pieces or put two pieces together. I started the trend in plywood. You can have big paintings and pack them in your minivan, rolled up round the side, and you can sit at them – I prefer to sit as it is quite tiring standing. Also sitting keeps the eye steadier and because I am not walking backwards and forwards I can see the subject and the painting at once and paint it like it is. It is like painting on the side of a drum and as long as you have a bendy ruler to transfer measurements it works perfectly well. When I left the Slade and went to Spain I felt as if I had learnt to paint. The drawing I did at the Slade was in pencil on white paper, but once I had learnt to paint I felt that all I was doing was stroking things down as they looked. It was a revelation that I was allowed, or had allowed myself, to do something so simple.' [12]

The Spanish paintings seemed almost to come to completion by themselves. Todd painted a large, detailed landscape of a cement works in pale tones as if seen through cement-laden air. 'It was all so clear, I felt that all I had to do was paint these things – I didn't have to have an idea, all I had to do was put down what was there. I went out on a great long jetty where they unloaded the cement, and I parked my minivan and I had the board strapped to the side of the van. It took weeks going back at the same time each day. I left two bits unpainted because I thought I needed the orange of the board, but those bits will eventually go black. All the gesture disappeared when I started painting the things themselves. The landscape, *Gaudi at Garraf with Industrial Tube* (96" x 144"), was the biggest painting I have ever done. They were all shown at the Royal Academy Summer Exhibition. There won't be any more of them because I couldn't paint like that now. The way I touch the board is different now.' [13]

These Spanish paintings seemed to flow off her brush, making her high with excitement. Many painters experience this 'high' while painting (Todd knew that Uglow did) and for her it first happened in Spain. 'I had gone up into the middle of a plain in the middle of nowhere, and I was aware of having an orgasm while painting. You get to a stage in painting when you are in it, everything is flowing, and it takes you by surprise. There is

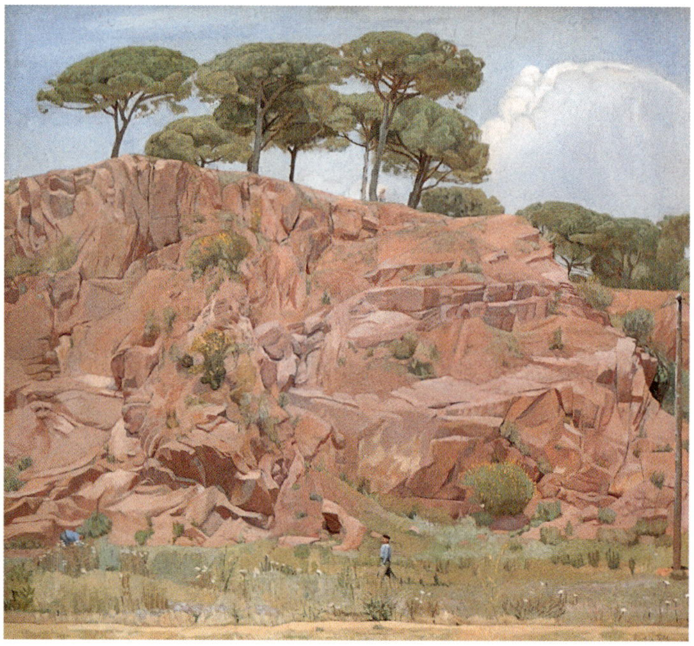

[59] *Pink Rocks, Castel del Fels, Spain*, 1975
76.2 x 79.4 cms 30 x 31¼ ins

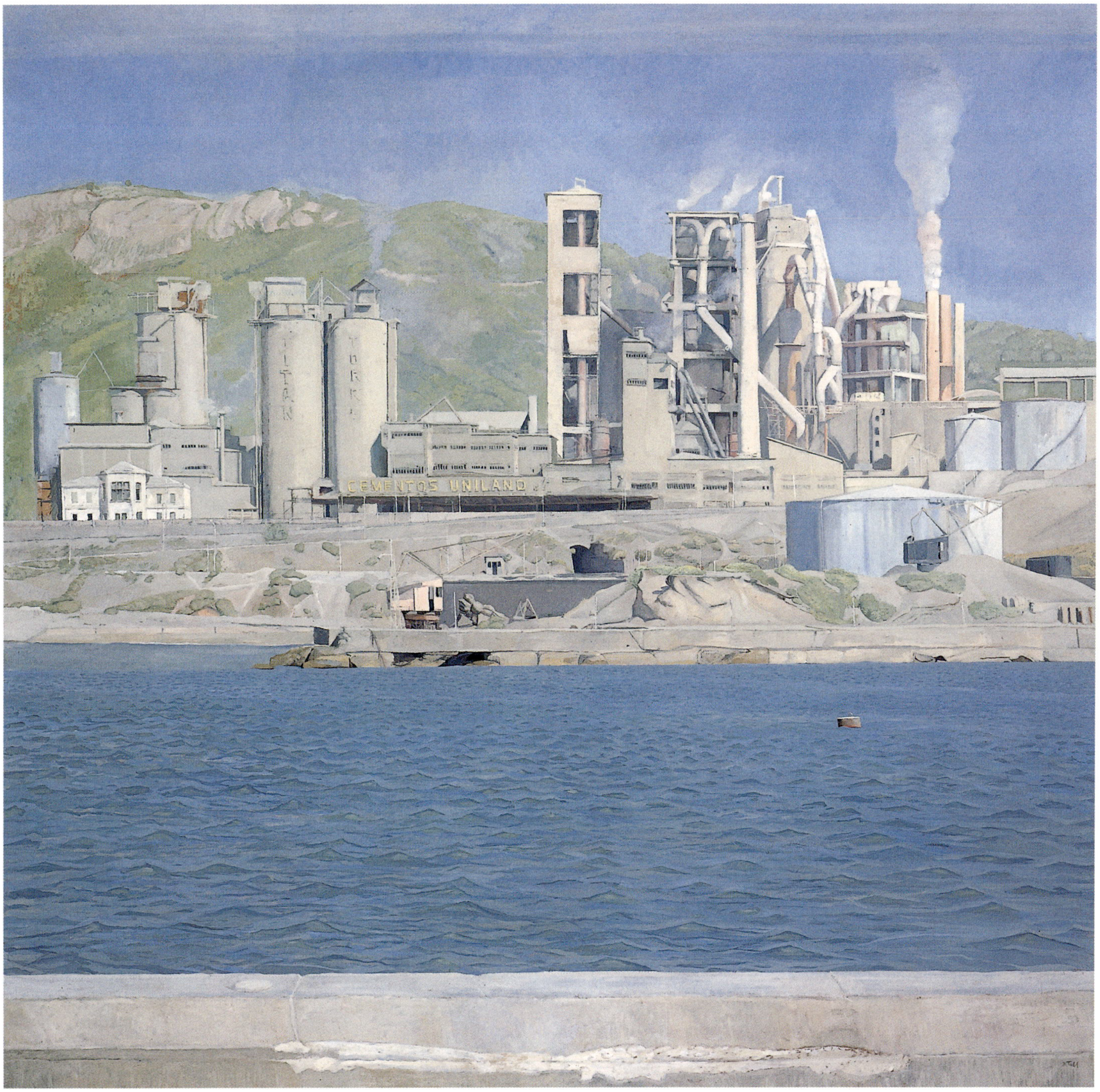

[60] *Cement Factory across Water, Valcarca, Spain,* 1976
127 x 127 cms 50 x 50 ins

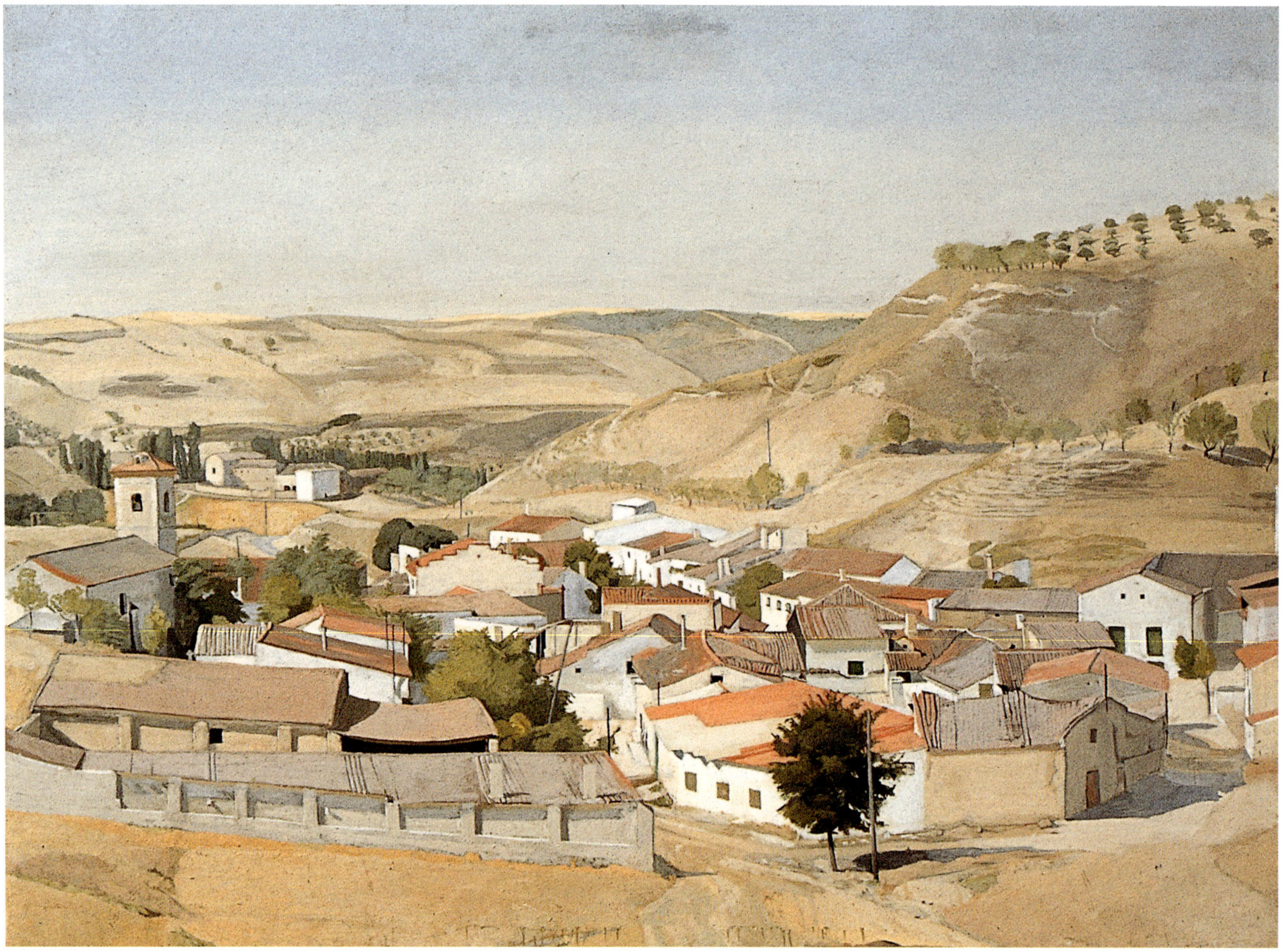

[61] *Village near Alcalã,* 1974
76.2 x 97.8 cms 30 x 38½ ins

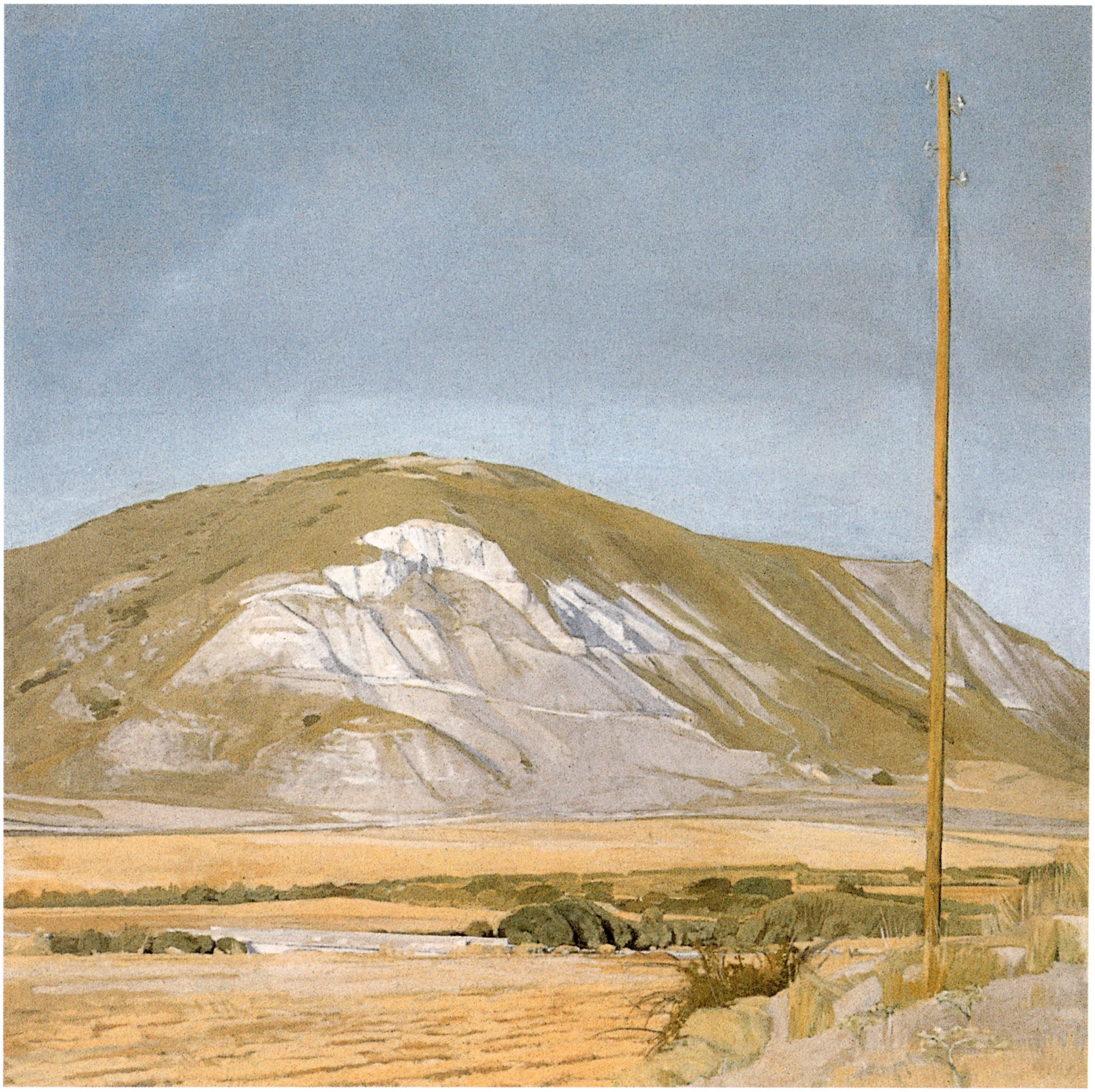

[62] *Hill near Alcalā*, 1974
91.4 x 91.4 cms 36 x 36 ins

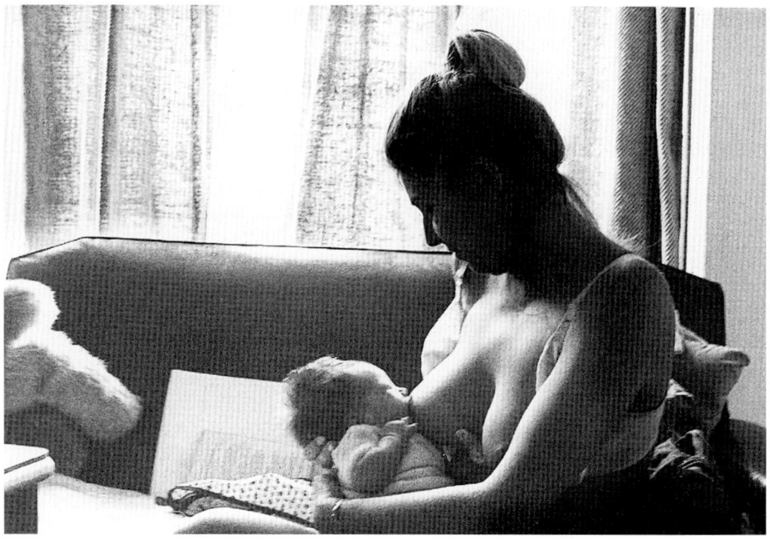

Daphne and Mary, 1977

a sexual content in all good painting just as it is a sexual act to put on paint. It needs saying, because women are a bit prudish about it.'[14] Todd believes that sexual arousal can come through the eye, that the retina has a particularly sensitive spot on it. Looking at something very hard, especially at colour, can produce a strong sexual high. Many years later, according to the Cambridge Chronicle she caused a flutter of dismay at Girton College in Cambridge, when, in an after-dinner speech, she referred to the 'G-spot in the eye'.

Returning to Spain for a third summer to redeem her life through painting, Todd met the accountant Graham Spurgeon. Separated from his wife, he had a job in Barcelona and wanted to continue living in Spain. He fell in love with Daphne Todd and, after making numerous flying visits to see her in England, he asked her to live with him. Knowing that she would never meet anyone like Uglow again, Todd decided in her pragmatic way that this might reasonably enable her to get on with the rest of her life. She was fond of Graham and persuaded herself that she loved him, although her emotions were still numb from the break-up with Uglow. But she was twenty-eight and wanted a baby. She felt that Graham would be an adequate father, and that the two of them could make a life together. As she reorganised her life, painting landscapes all through the day and coming back in the evening to make a meal and have a drink, Graham seemed a pleasant companion. She lived with him in Spain for two years, first in Castel del Fels, then in Garraf, near Barcelona, every year driving back to London with her crop of landscapes to submit to the Royal Academy. But by the time two years had passed Spurgeon had become an alcoholic and had lost his job in Spain.

When Todd knew she was having a baby she decided to return to England, and Spurgeon returned to live with her in the ground-floor flat of her Clapham house. The upper floors were still let, as they had been for the previous two years, affording Todd a small income which enabled her to pay her own way, something she has always regarded as important. Spurgeon eventually found a good job in England but was fretful, life in South London having none of the attractions of Spain. In 1978, in order to try and save their foundering relationship, they bought

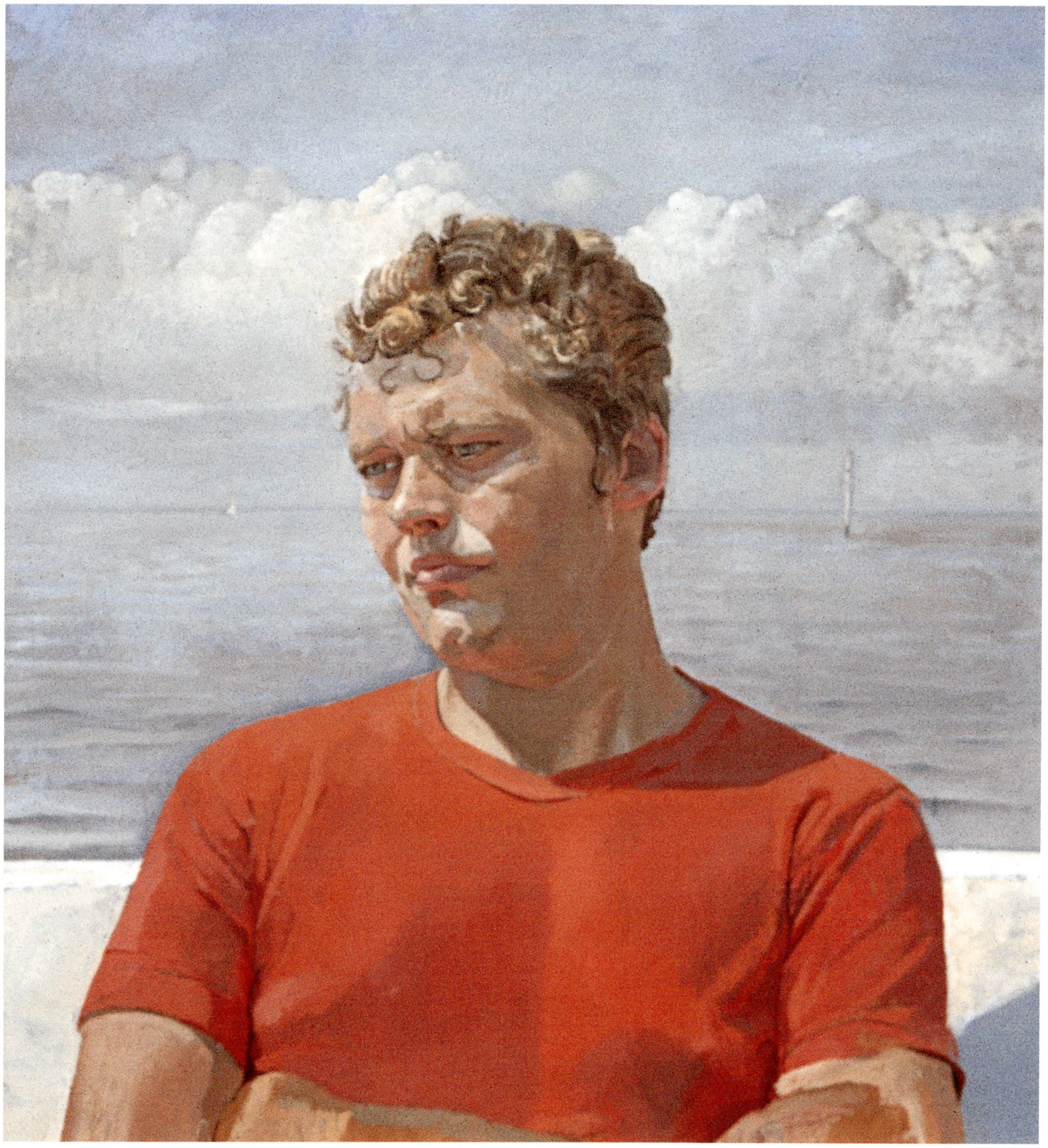

[63] *Graham Spurgeon*, 1976
49.5 x 45.1 cms 19½ x 17¾ ins

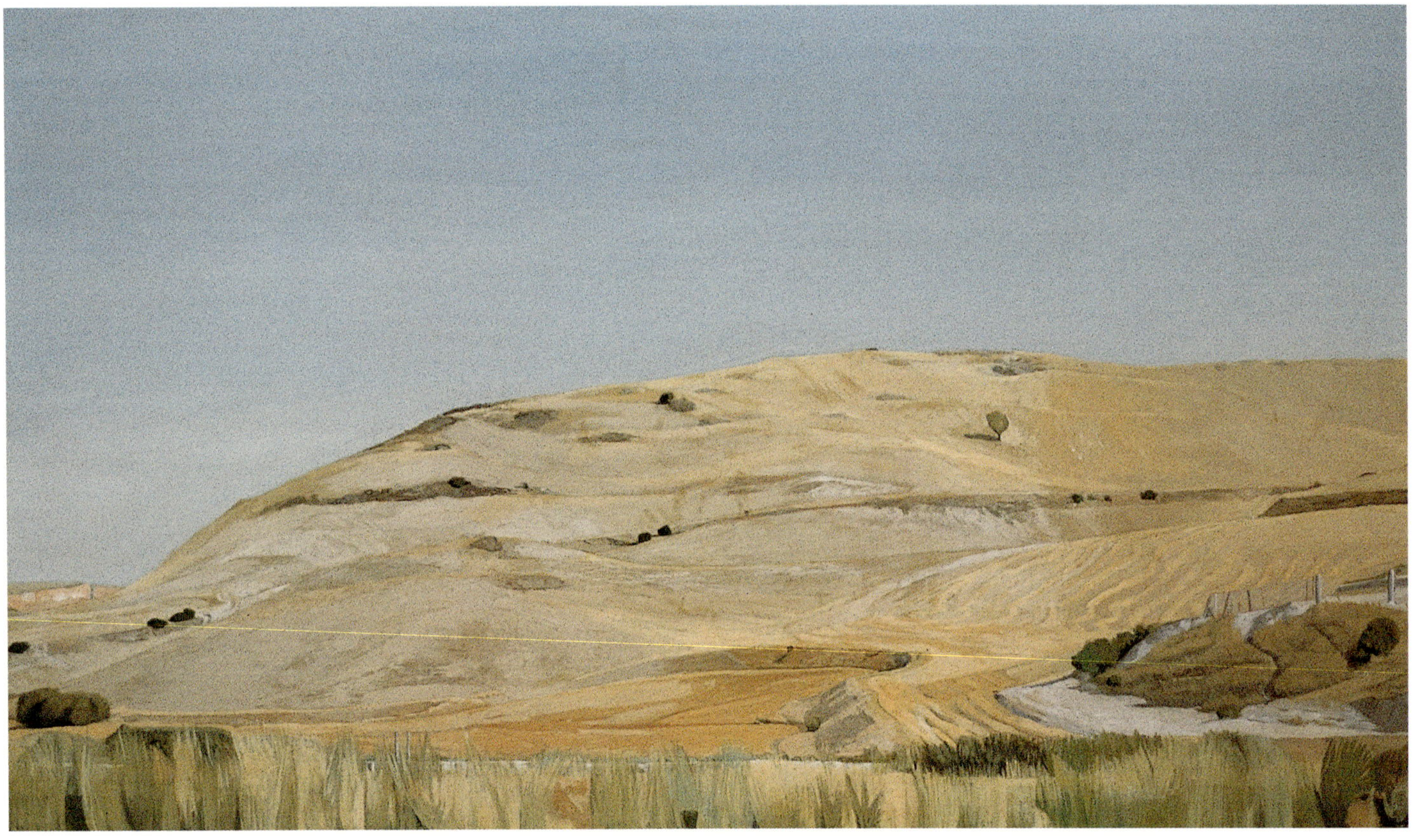

[64] *Bare Hill, Alcalã, Spain*, 1974
62.2 x 95.3 cms 24½ x 37½ ins

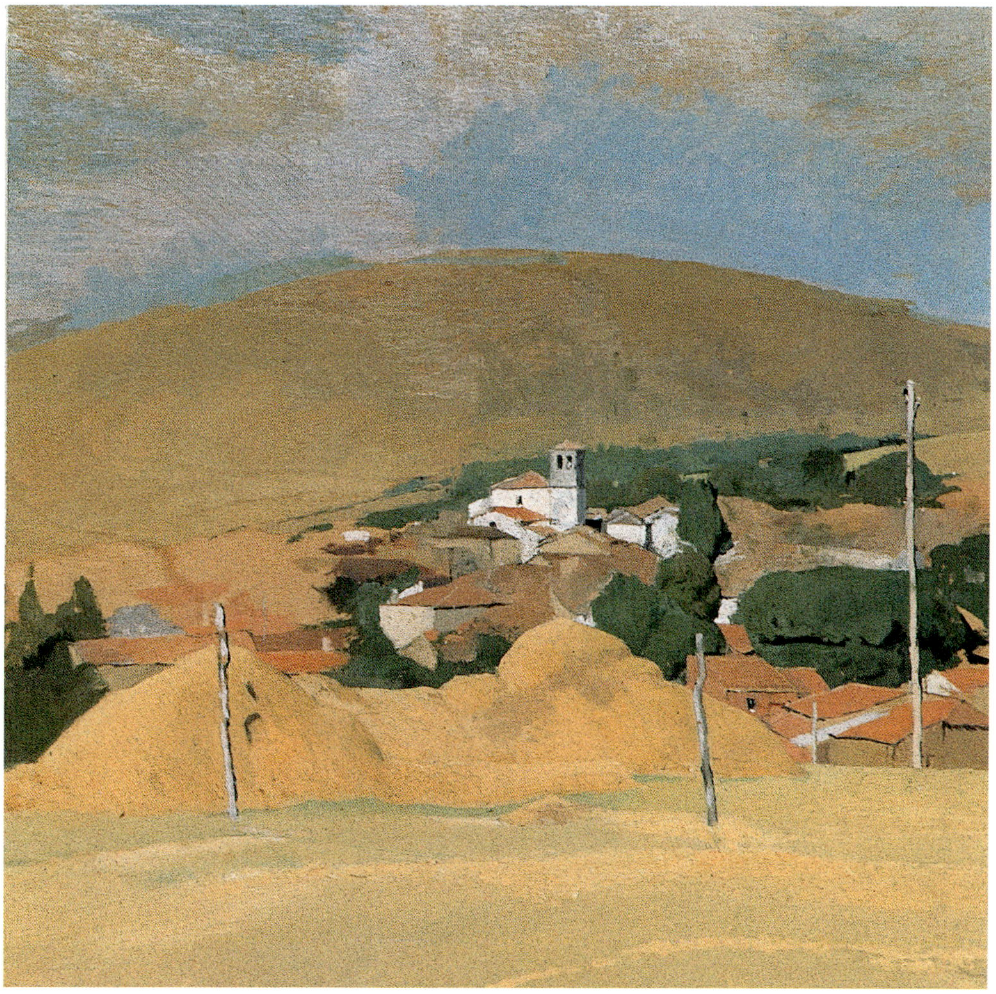

[65] *Canencia, Spain,* 1973
30.5 x 25.4 cms 12 x 10 ins

a house together in New Cross. During this time Todd began painting outdoor still-lifes in sunlight, to remind herself of Spain. She has continued to work on outdoor still-lifes to the present day, although the paintings, in cooler hues, now look more English. Painting the changing outdoor light keeps her on her toes, excellent practice for the rapid decisions that portrait-painting necessitates.

In New Cross things soon went wrong. Spurgeon lost his new job and, drunk all the time, was becoming dangerous. The baby Mary, born in 1977, was at risk. A painting, *Dark Room*, made in Thornbury Road, features Mary as a toddler (twice), the dog (recently out of quarantine), and Spurgeon's legs in a drunken doze. This was one of the first of the composite paintings made from life that have become part of Todd's repertoire. She was painting with dedication, but Spurgeon was becoming an increasing liability, and she was once again faced with putting together a new life. This meant getting an injunction and throwing Spurgeon out. Despite the difficulties and the custody battles that she had to fight over her baby, Todd was not resentful, never feeling that Spurgeon had given her a hard time. She felt, rather, that it was he who had been unfortunate in meeting her at a time when she was emotionally numb. She therefore never asked for, and never received, any maintenance. As soon as she decided to finish the relationship she felt wonderfully free, with the added bonus of a lovely baby.

With a small loan from her mother Todd bought out Graham Spurgeon's share of the house and went back to teaching at Heatherley's to earn a living for herself and her daughter, juggling childcare with a Slade friend (the restorer Christine Kirkwood) who lived nearby. It was at Heatherley's that she met Lieutenant-Colonel P.R.T. (Terry) Driscoll, who had retired from the army and was combining farming in Sussex with acting as part-time Bursar of the Art School. She liked him immediately, appreciating his reliability and loyalty, traits she associated with service people generally. Perhaps at last she had found the company of someone that she could trust and rely on absolutely. After a four-year courtship Daphne Todd and Terry Driscoll married on 31 August 1984, with a wedding reception at Salter's Green Farm, Driscoll's home in Sussex. Mary, when

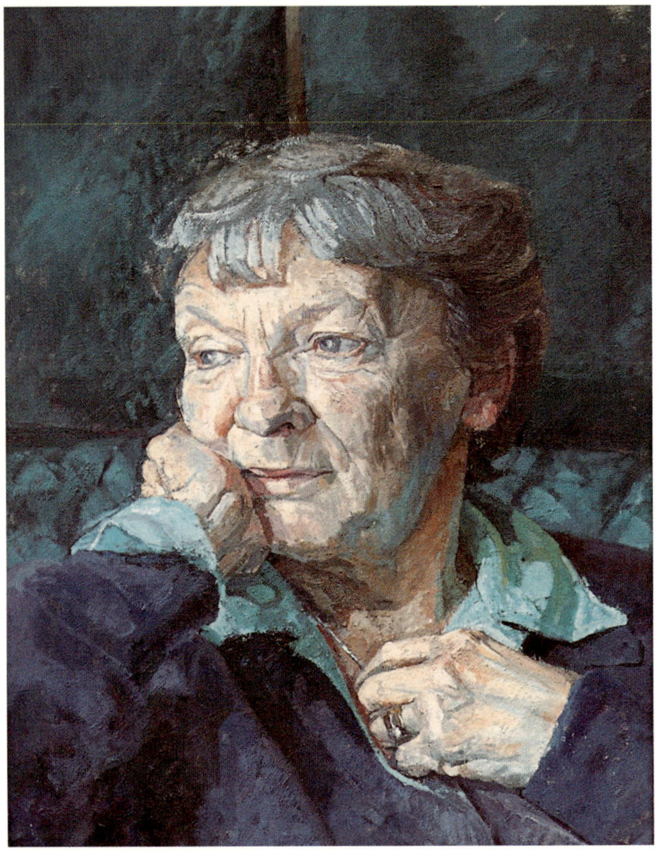

[66] *Iris Morris*, 1979
40.6 x 30.5 cms 16 x 12 ins

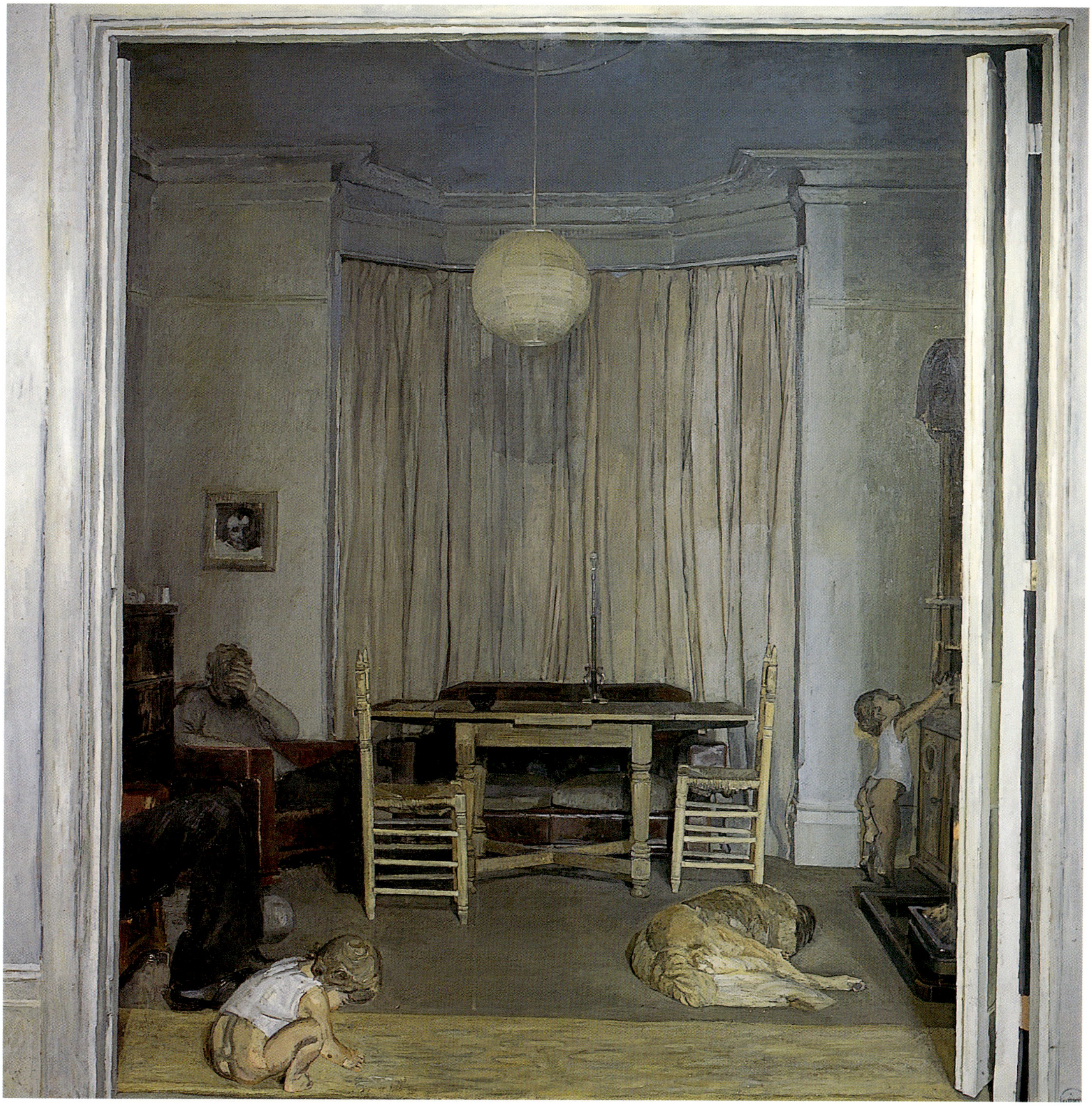

[67] *Dark Room*, 1978
152.4 x 152.4 cms 60 x 60 ins

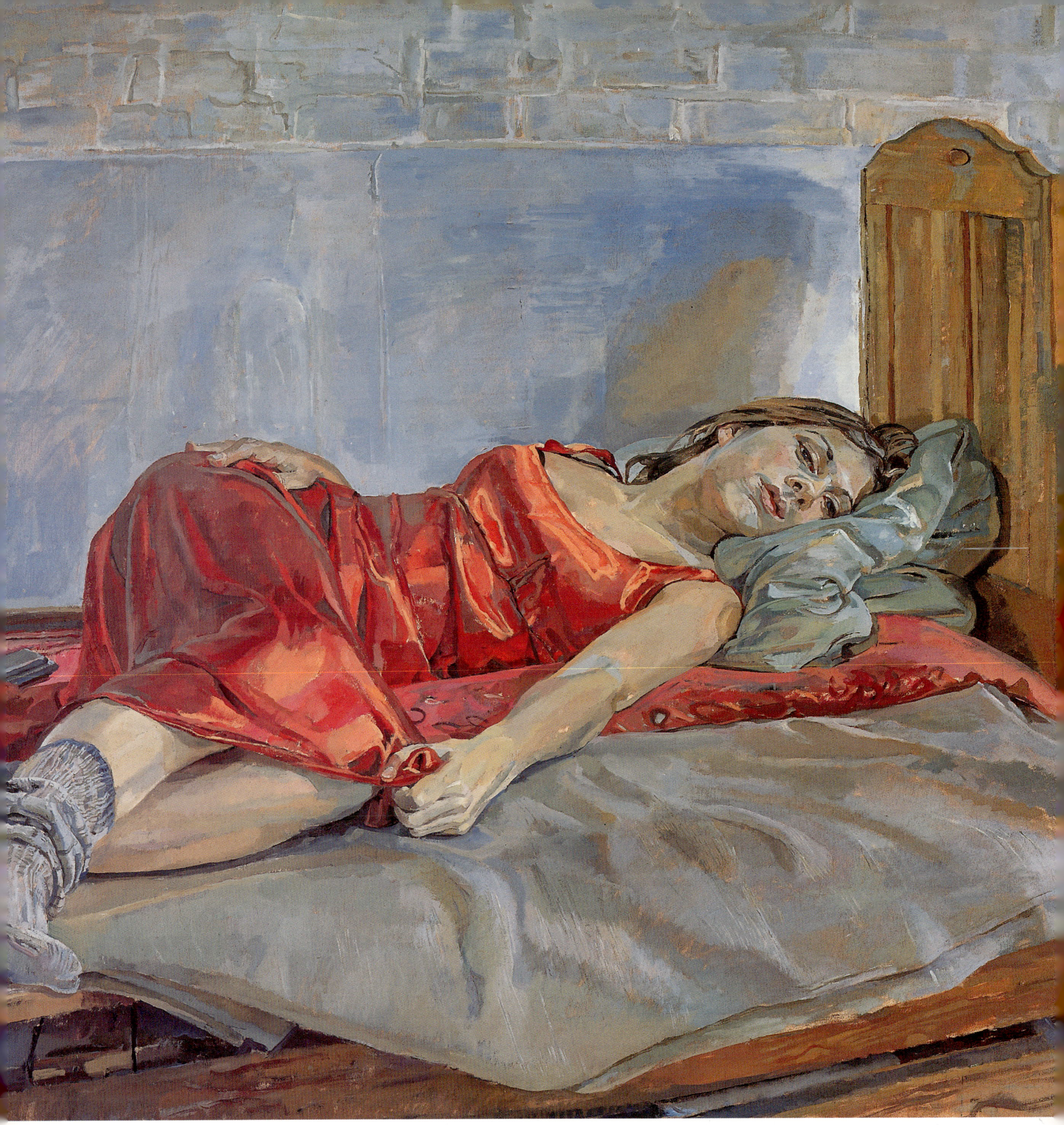

[68] *After the Wedding Party*, 2002
86.4 x 81.3 cms 34 x 32 ins

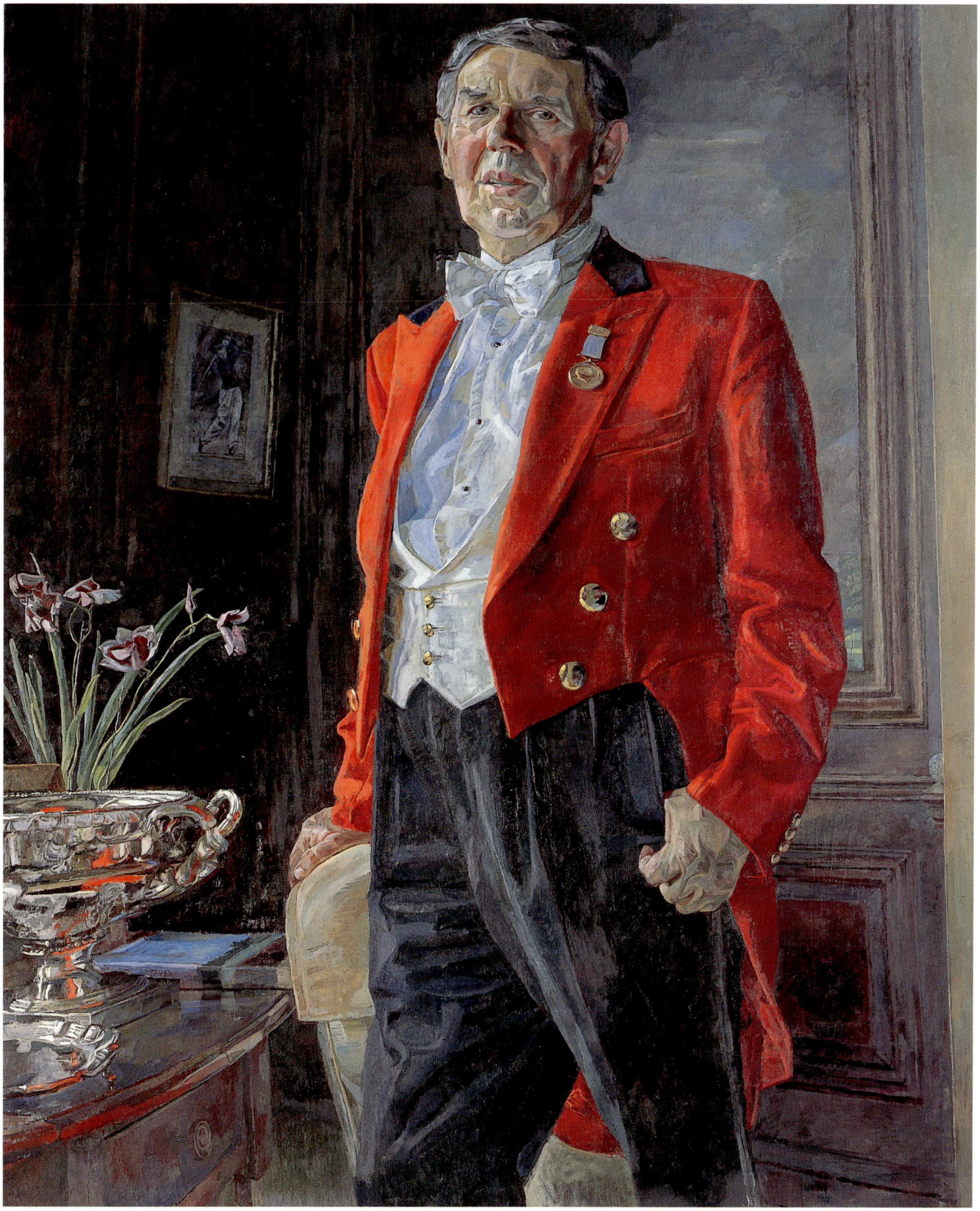

[69] *Michael Lunt, Captain, Royal and Ancient Golf Club*, 2007
127 x 101.6 cms 50 x 40 ins

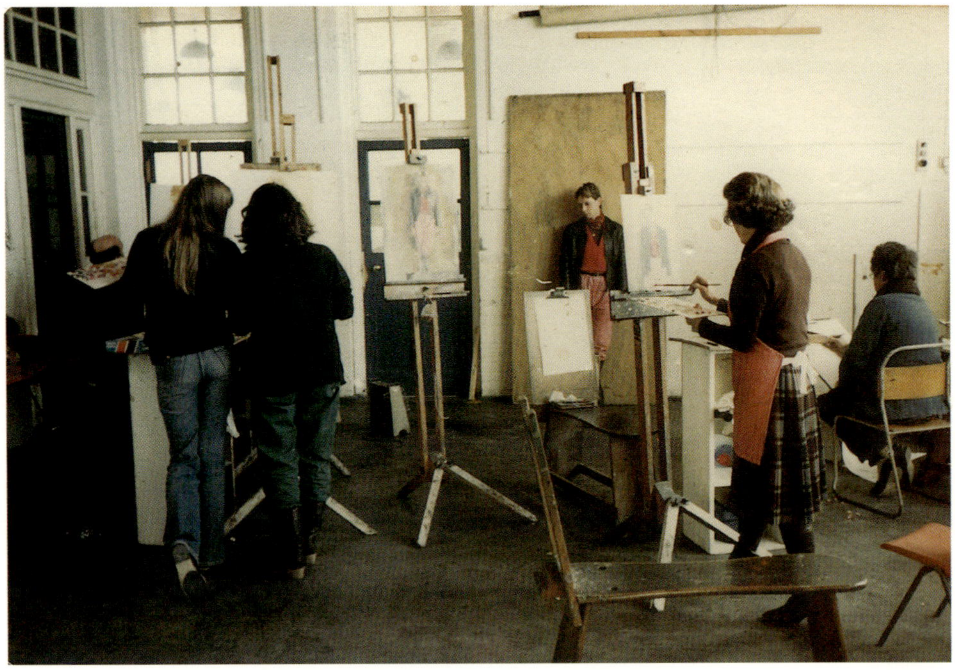

Teaching at Heatherley's

only two years old, had enquired 'You're my Daddy now aren't you?' Within three years of their marriage Terry Driscoll legally adopted Mary.

The Heatherley School of Fine Art has provided a vital stable base for Todd for over thirty years. She knew it well from part-time teaching while still a student at the Slade, before her future husband began to work there. Founded in 1845, Heatherley's is the oldest independent art school in London and one of the few that focuses on figurative painting and sculpture. It was originally formed by a group of students who, jibbing at the restrictions placed upon them by the Government School of Design in Somerset House, started a separate class in Dickenson's Drawing Gallery in Maddox Street. 'Dickenson's' became 'Leigh's' under the principalship of James Matthews Leigh, and then 'Heatherley's' under the leadership of his assistant Thomas J Heatherley, who ran it for thirty years. Burne Jones, Rossetti, Millais, Lord Leighton, Sir Edmund Poynter, Russell Flint, Walter Crane, Sickert, Michael Ayrton, Shepherd of Winnie-the-Pooh fame, and Churchill are amongst its former students. The fact that it was the first art school to admit women on equal terms with men was important to Todd; she was only too conscious of the latent bias against women artists, and aware of Uglow's opinion, shared by other Slade tutors, that women

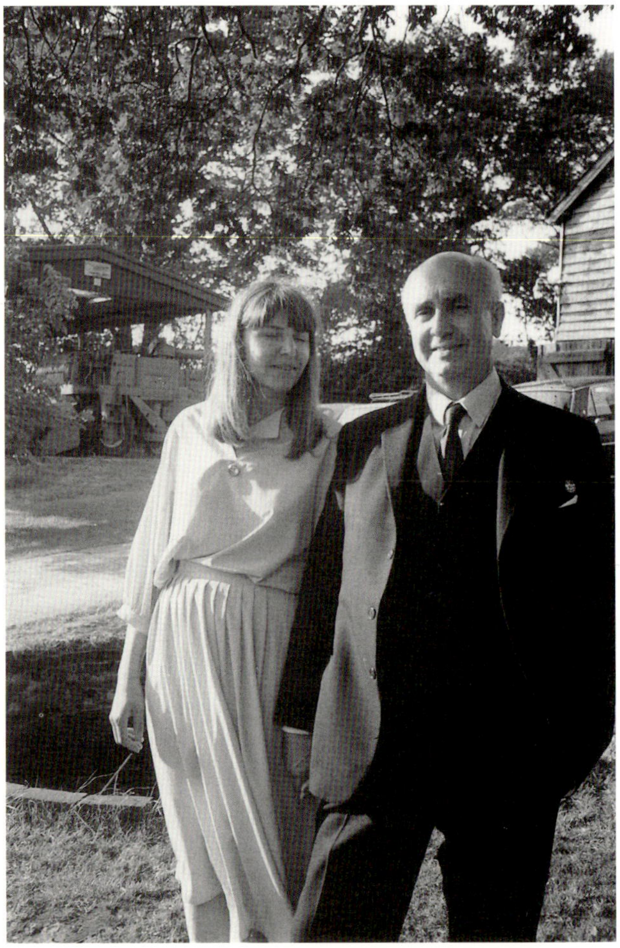

Daphne and Terry's Wedding Day, 31st August 1984

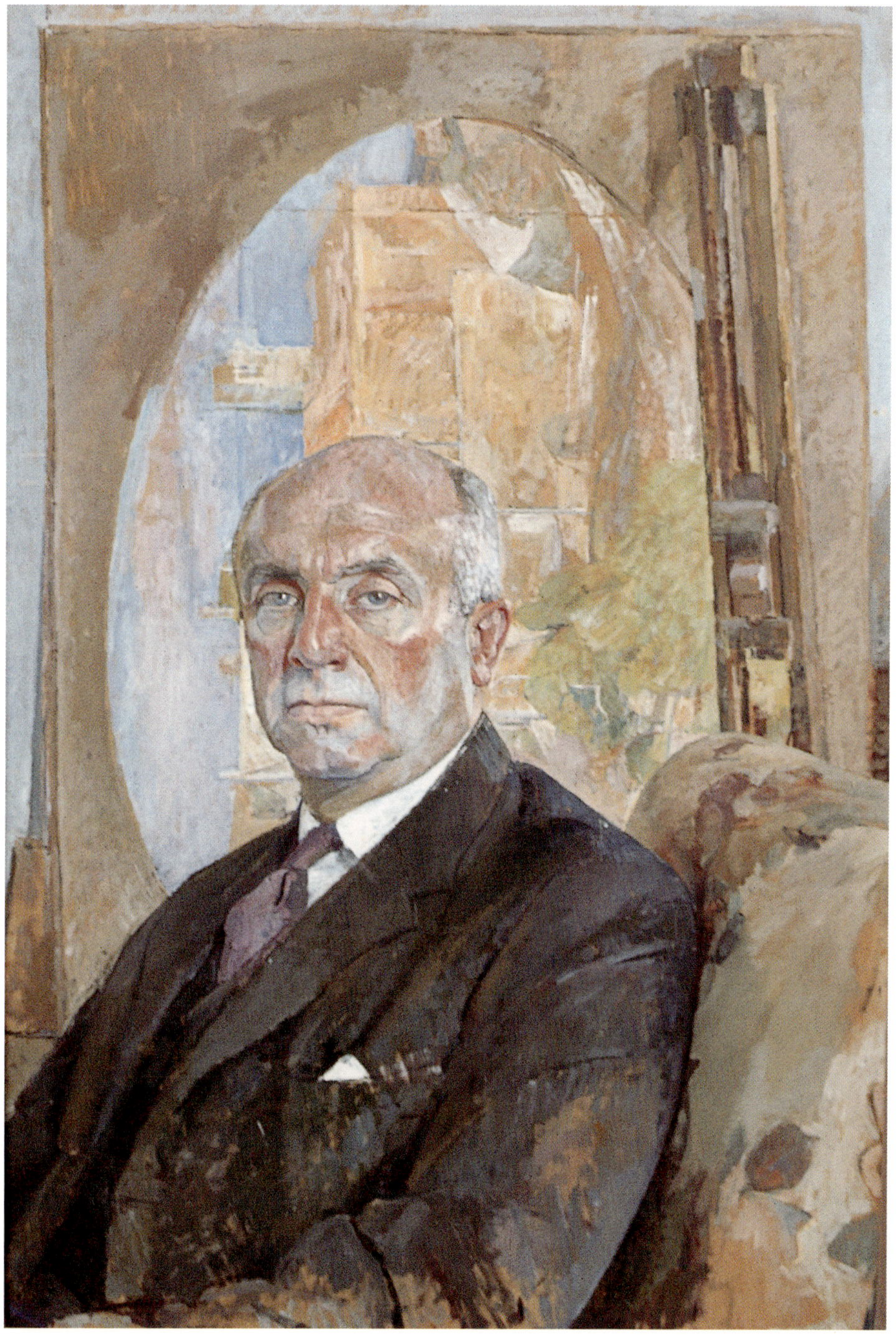

[70] *Lt. Col. P.R.T. Driscoll,* 1981
76.2 x 50.8 cms 30 x 20 ins

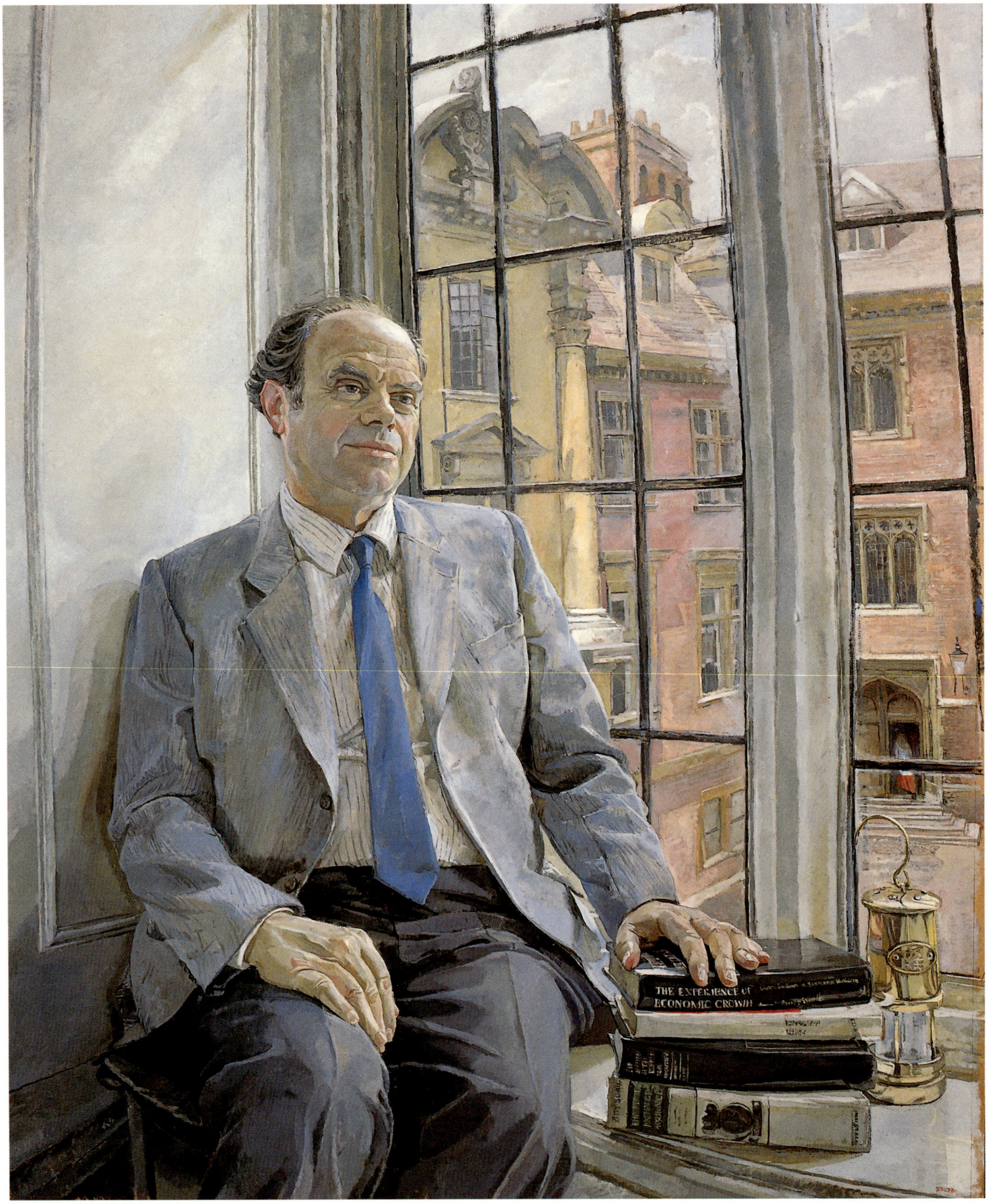

[71] *Professor Barry Supple, FBA, The Master, St Catharine's College, Cambridge,* 1991
127 x 101.6 cms 50 x 40 ins

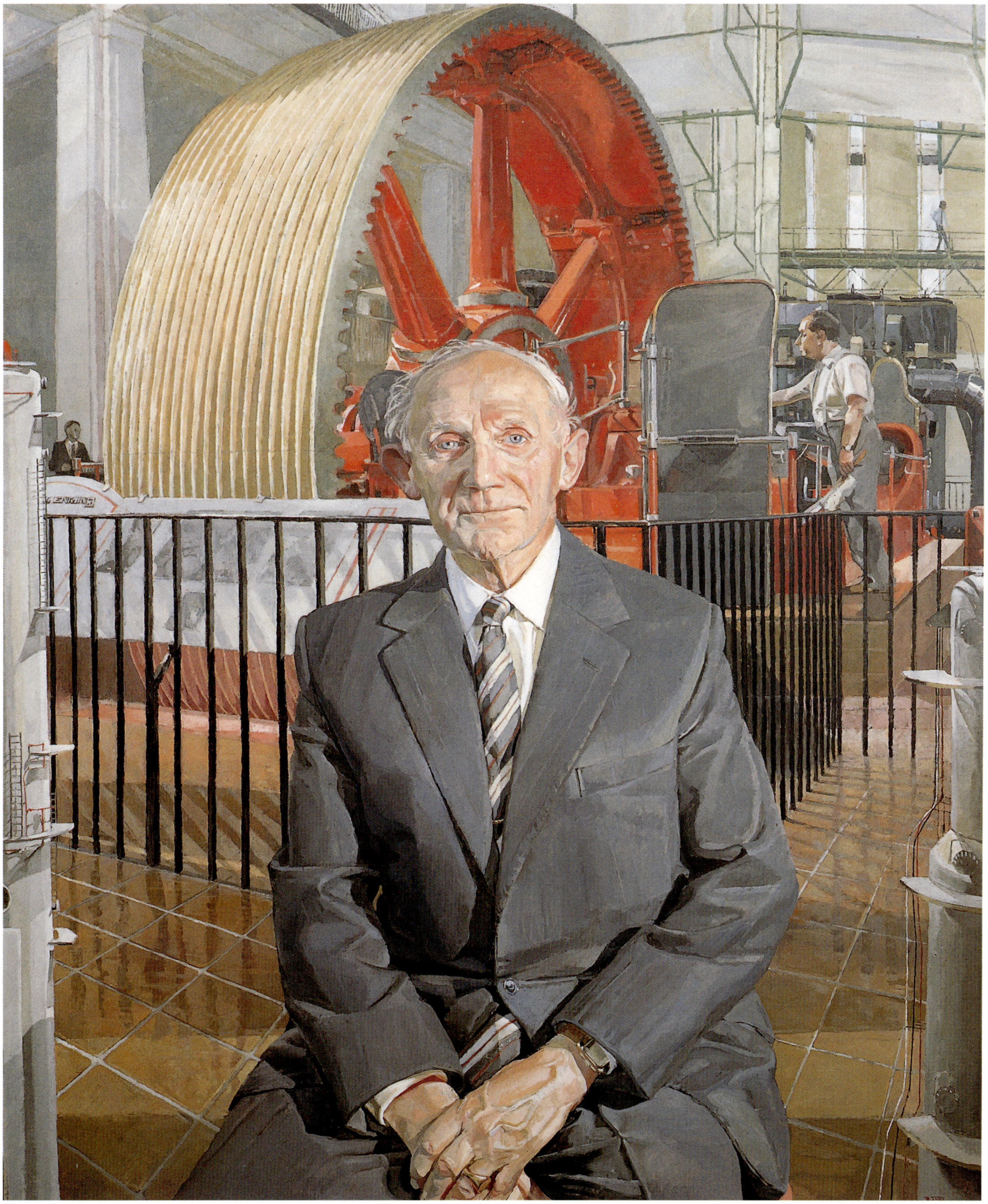

[72] *Sir Austin Pearce, Chairman, Trustees of the Science Museum,* 1990
127 x 101.6 cms 50 x 40 ins

'couldn't really do it'. Indeed, so often was this topic aired at the Slade that a fellow-student, John Virtue, bet her (in writing) £100 that she would not still be an artist in twenty years' time.

Daphne Todd proved as useful to Heatherley's as the art school was to her. In 1980 she had been appointed Director of Studies and over the following six years the number of students trebled. She was instrumental in introducing the Diploma in Portraiture, one of the three full-time courses that the school now offers, and also in maintaining the 'Open Studio' which anybody who wants to do Life Drawing can attend for a small fee.

Todd's teaching experience had begun during her two post-graduate years, before her time at Heatherley's. Those two years had served her better than a teacher training degree. She had been determined to take up the offer of a postgraduate place at the Slade (only two places were awarded that year to Slade undergraduates) despite her parent's refusal to sign the required forms. They had been alarmed, during Daphne's undergraduate years, by her nude posing and by her racketing about the world for months at a time, and they wanted her to return to Whitstable and become an art teacher at her old school. Without the requisite signatures she received no postgraduate grant and had to make ends meet by posing for evening classes, serving in Harrods on Saturdays and holidays, and teaching. Besides Heatherley's, she taught Local Authority evening classes at Dalston and Norwood, and to gain experience did some Voluntary Art Therapy at Friern Barnet Mental Hospital. Thinking that she might eventually have to teach in a school, she took some pottery classes, which she hated. But she was nothing if not resourceful, and after a while had the idea of running her own Saturday life classes in Heatherley's splendid purpose-built studios in Gordon Square. John Walton allowed her to do so provided her classes were financially independent and free to the school's own students. Todd hired her own models and occasionally a second teacher. It was hard work and financially barely broke even but the experience of organising the models and keeping the interest of the students was invaluable.

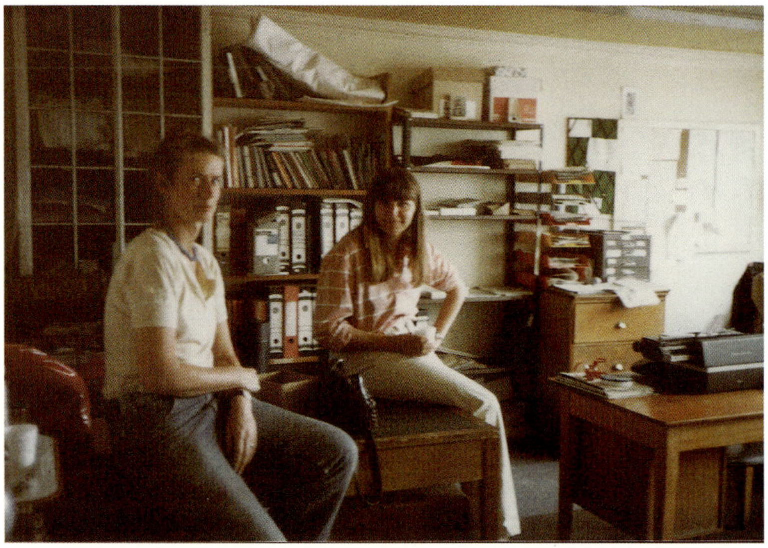

Susan Engledow and Daphne Todd
in the office at Heatherley's

When Todd returned from Spain and needed a job Walton invited her back to take over as Director

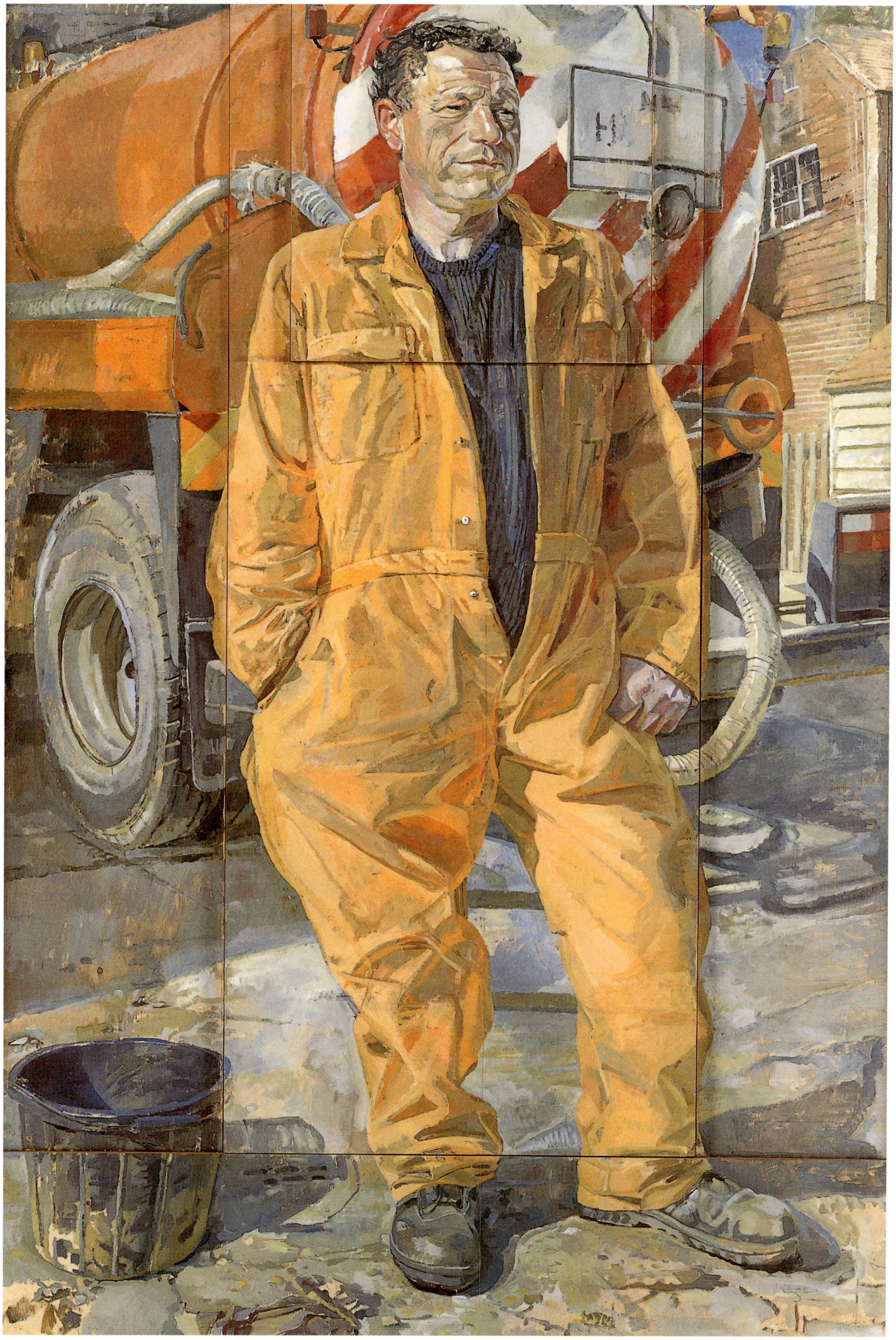

[73] *Trevor Tasker, Cesspit Emptier,* 1999
60 x 40 ins
152.4 x 101.6 cms

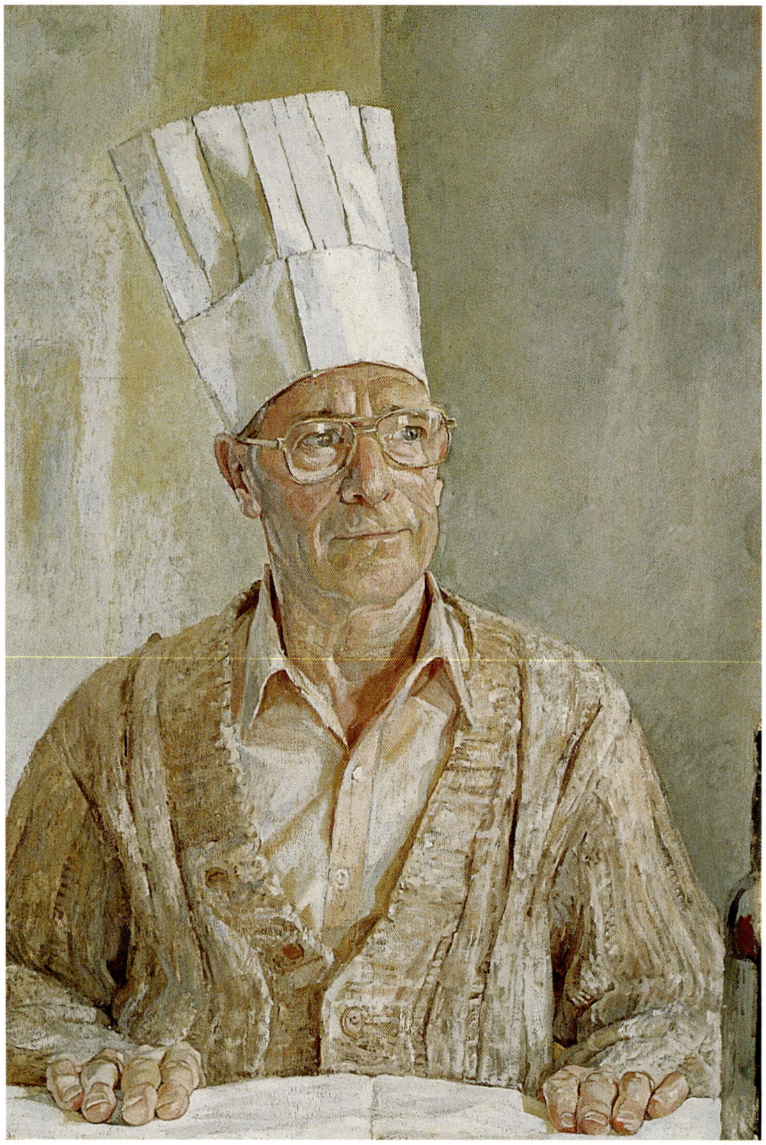

[74] *Reg in a Chef's Hat,* 1983
40.6 x 30.5 cms 16 x 12 ins

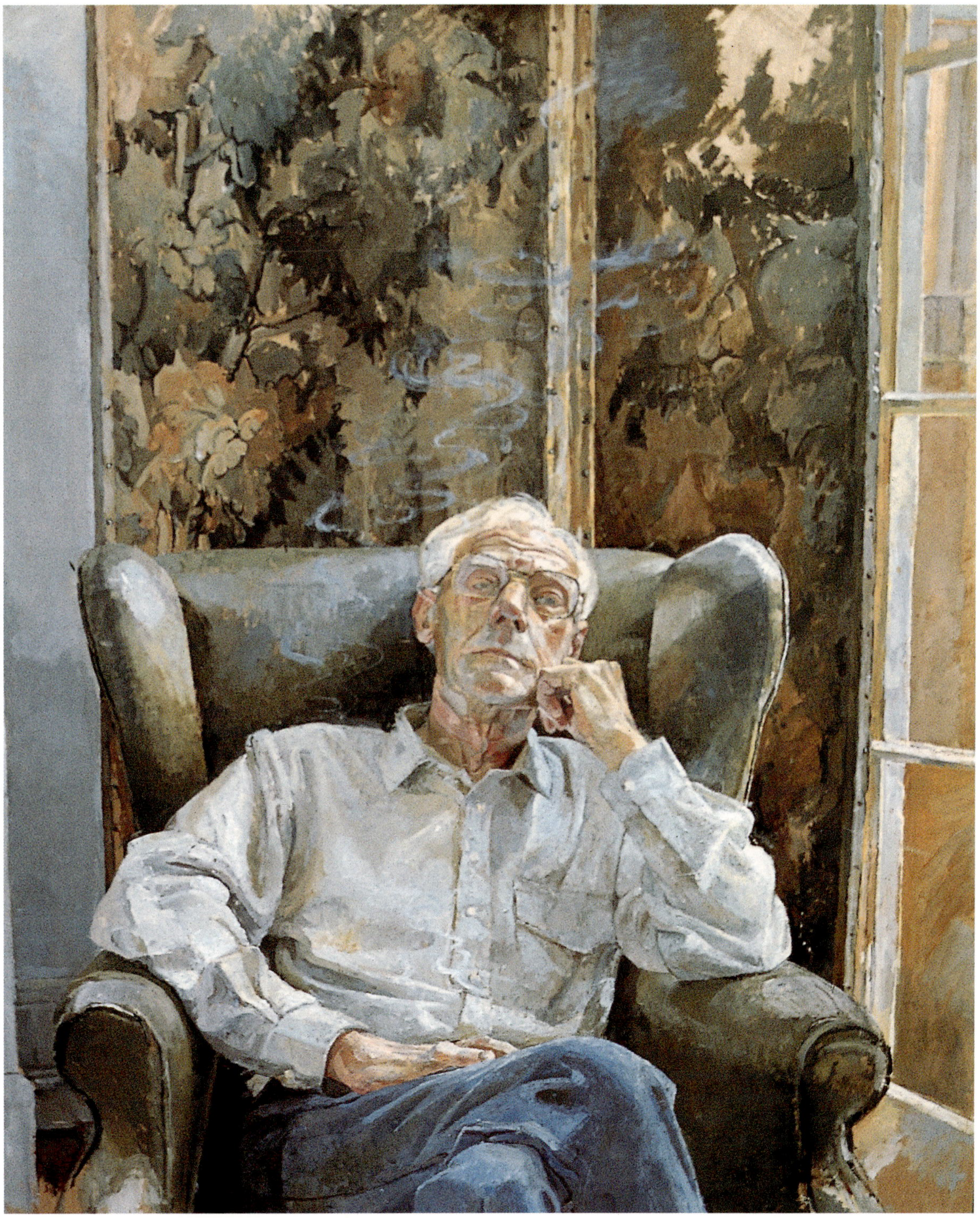

[75] *Mr Christmas,* 1983
71.1 x 59.7 cms 28 x 23½ ins

of Studies, a post she had very briefly held before. With this remit she was determined to change Heatherley's from what was effectively a Foundation Course into something more substantial. Against the wishes of some tutors she required all the students to both study life drawing and exhibit at least one life drawing in the school exhibition, even if that was not their strong point. 'The public have to know that the students are being taught something and you can't always tell if it's all happy-splashy stuff. Everyone has an eye for proportion in a human being. I did change Heatherley's because I'm pretty pragmatic and strong-willed and if I wanted something to happen it jolly well happened.' [15]

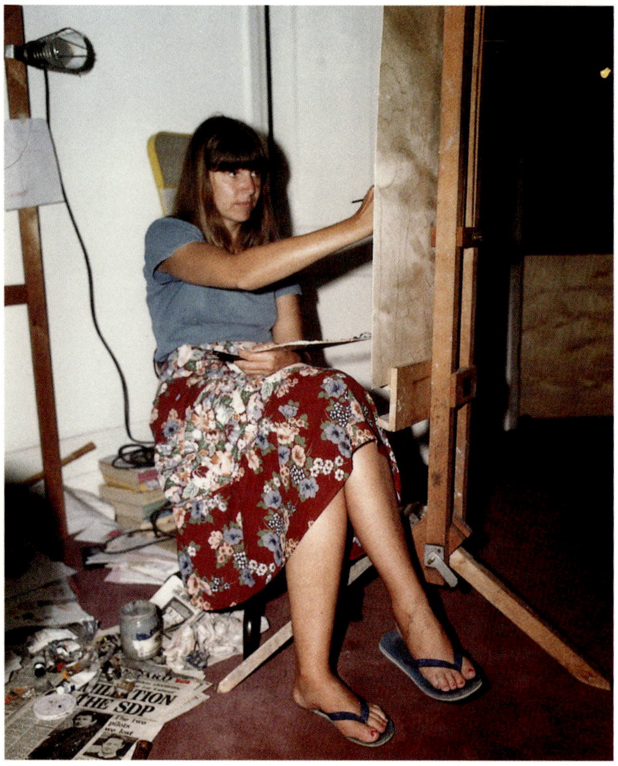

Daphne Todd painting Mr Christmas

The Portrait Diploma course, led by Susan Engledow, has been very successful, attracting keen students unable to find what they want in the state sector. Heatherley graduates exhibit with the Royal Society of Portrait Painters, the BP Portrait Award and the Society of Portrait Sculptors. Todd has been closely involved, first as a teacher, then as Director of Studies and, since 1987, as a Trustee, in many of the changes at Heatherley's. Never afraid of confrontation, she has recently been instrumental in fighting, and winning, a difficult, often acrimonious, three-year battle over the school's relocation to new premises following the threat of a compulsory purchase order from the Royal Borough of Kensington and Chelsea. The money offered by the Borough was not enough to relocate satisfactorily and their bullying attitude prompted Todd to seek help from the influential contacts she had made through painting portraits. Conrad Dehn QC, a former sitter, pointed the way to the most appropriate Learned Counsel. The offer from the Borough was then increased from three to five million. Trustees hesitated to take the risk of overseeing the new development themselves, but, after receiving a copy of a hard-hitting article that Todd had written for *Jackdaw*, Anya, Lady Sainsbury, another former sitter, came to the rescue with the recommendation of a complete team of reliable architects and developers. Heatherley's is due to move to its new custom-built location in Lots Road, Chelsea, in 2008. This battle exacted intense efforts from those at the epicentre, with two crates of papers to wade through and as many as twenty-six meetings to attend in one of the three years. 'Most

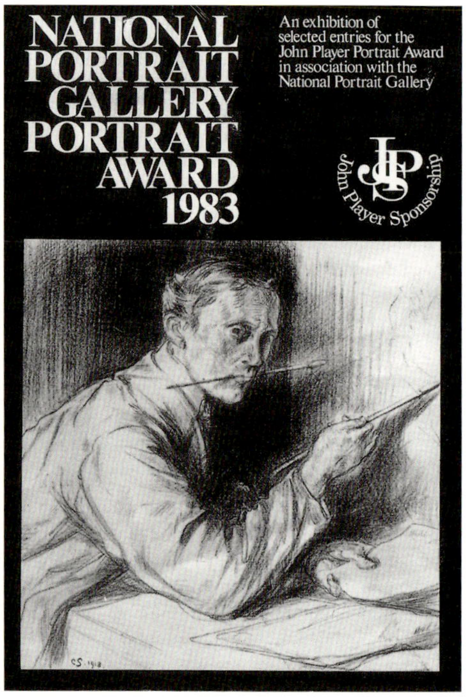

Daphne Todd wins 2nd prize and £750 with *Mr Stonor, Waiting*

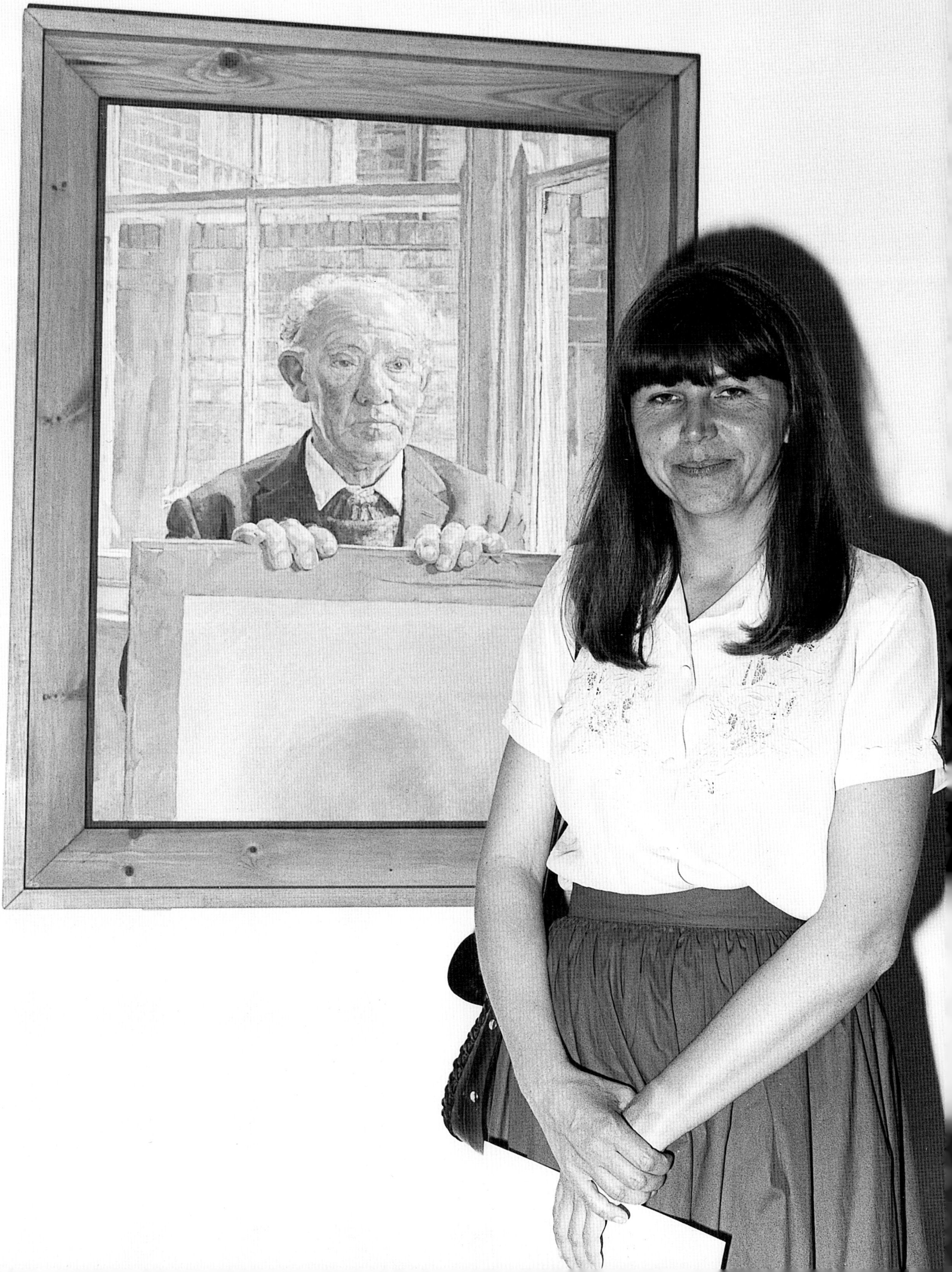

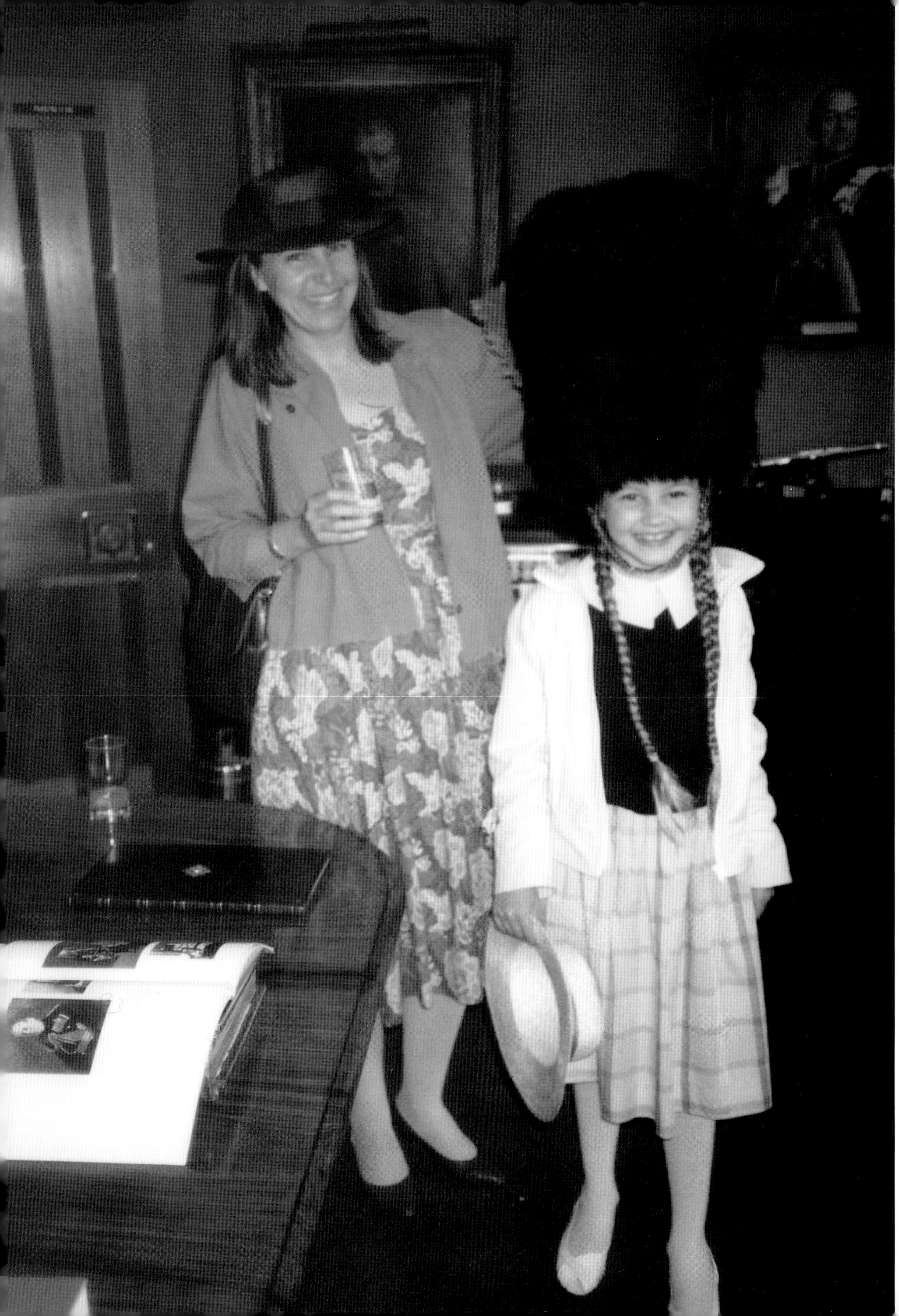

Daphne and Mary
at Headquarters of
the Irish Guards

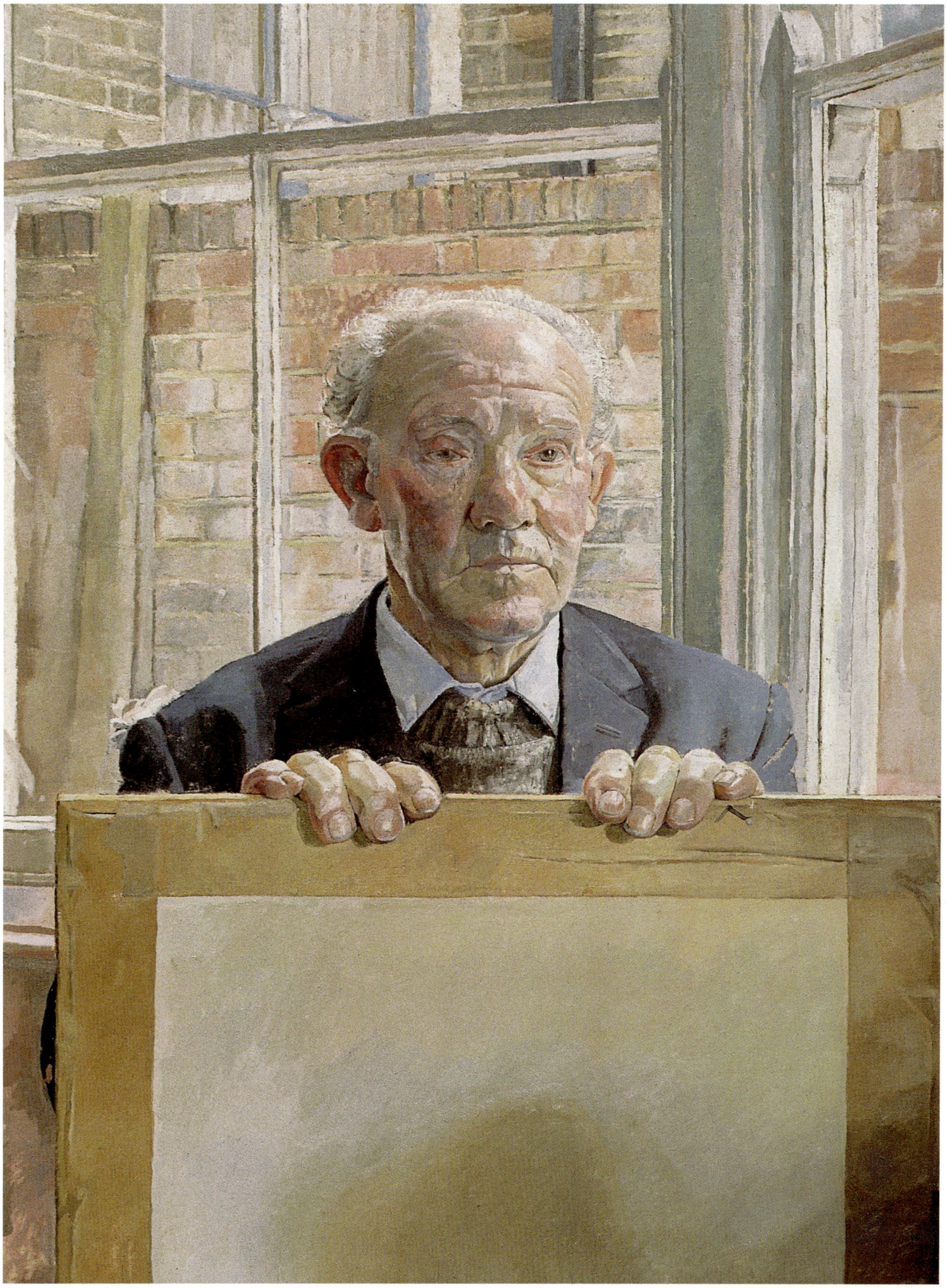

[76] *Mr Stoner, Waiting*, 1982
76.2 x 55.9 cms 30 x 22 ins

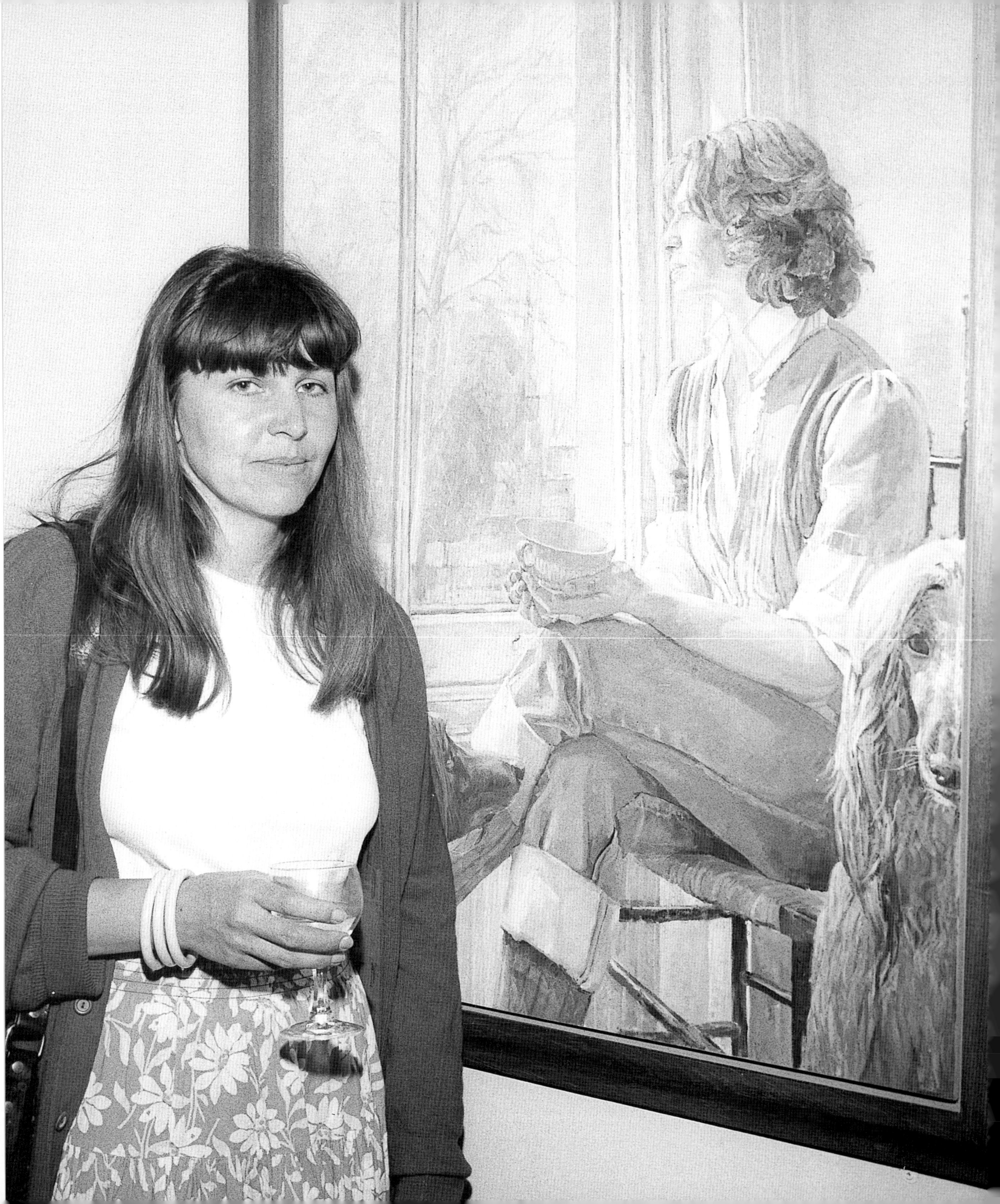

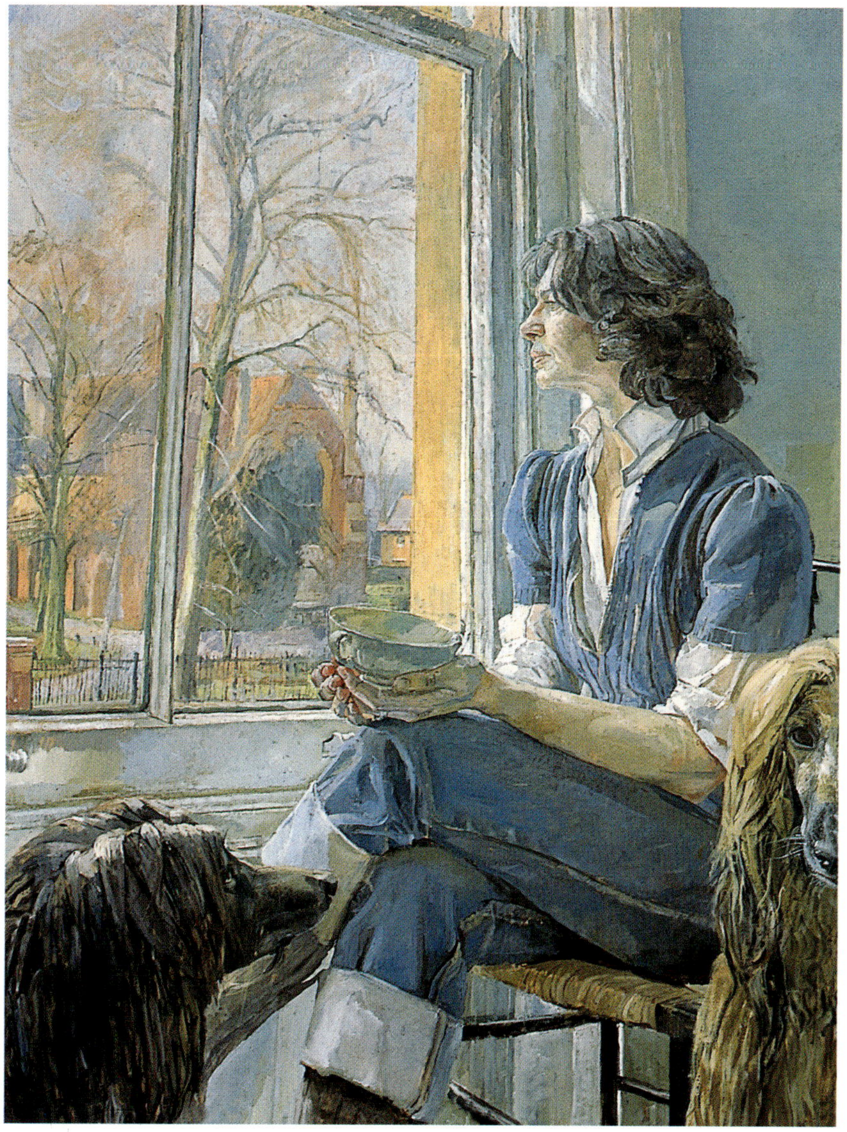

[78] *Lonely Lady, Dr Polly Matzinger,* 1984
101.6 x 76.2 cms 40 x 30 ins

Opposite:
At the National Portrait Gallery, 1986, with *Lonely Lady: Dr Polly Matzinger*

daughter, to the Trooping of the Colour and the Saint Patrick's Day Parade. At this time, although she had painted a few informal portraits, she had not set up as a portrait painter and had no idea what to charge for the picture. As the John Player Second Prize had been £750 her fee for this portrait was £750.

In 1984 Todd was elected to membership of the New English Art Club. She had exhibited with the New English as a non-member for several years and been nominated by them as a finalist for the Hunting Prize on more than one occasion prior to her election. She had also exhibited with the Royal Institute of Oil Painters and the Royal Society of British Artists to good effect but her slow rate of production induced her to be selective, and she judged the New English as representing the higher painterly quality with which she wished to associate. She was too busy with fighting custody battles over Mary to take an active part in their organisation, but after election to membership of the Royal Society of Portrait Painters in 1985, she began to devote some of her spare time to this Society's cause. Her success in the 1984 John Player Award had been partly responsible for her election as a member. In 1985 she received a Special Commendation at the John Player Award for the painting *Lonely Lady* (Dr Polly Matzinger), in the same year winning first prize (then £5000) in the Hunting Group National Art Prize (now the Hunting/Observer Award) with the painting *Four Spanish Chairs*, a painting of four cheap hypermarket chairs she had brought back from Spain and painted in her kitchen in New Cross during the period of fighting to retain custody of Mary. The prize money enabled her to convert one of the barns on the Driscoll farm into the beautiful airy forty-foot-long studio she has worked in ever since.

In 1985, besides winning the Greater London Council Prize at the Royal Festival Hall for the painting *Reg in a Chef's Hat*, now in the Arts Club collection, portrait commissions began to flow in to such an extent that there was little time left for teaching. She was also playing the part of a farmer's wife - herding bullocks, helping weigh and inject them, helping to get the hay in and stack it, dealing with the two sheep (used as lawnmowers) and gouging maggots from their wounds when they got struck by the fly.

The many demands on her time have not diminished Todd's output of work. In the past two decades she has drawn or painted over two hundred portraits besides her other work. Her sitters have come from

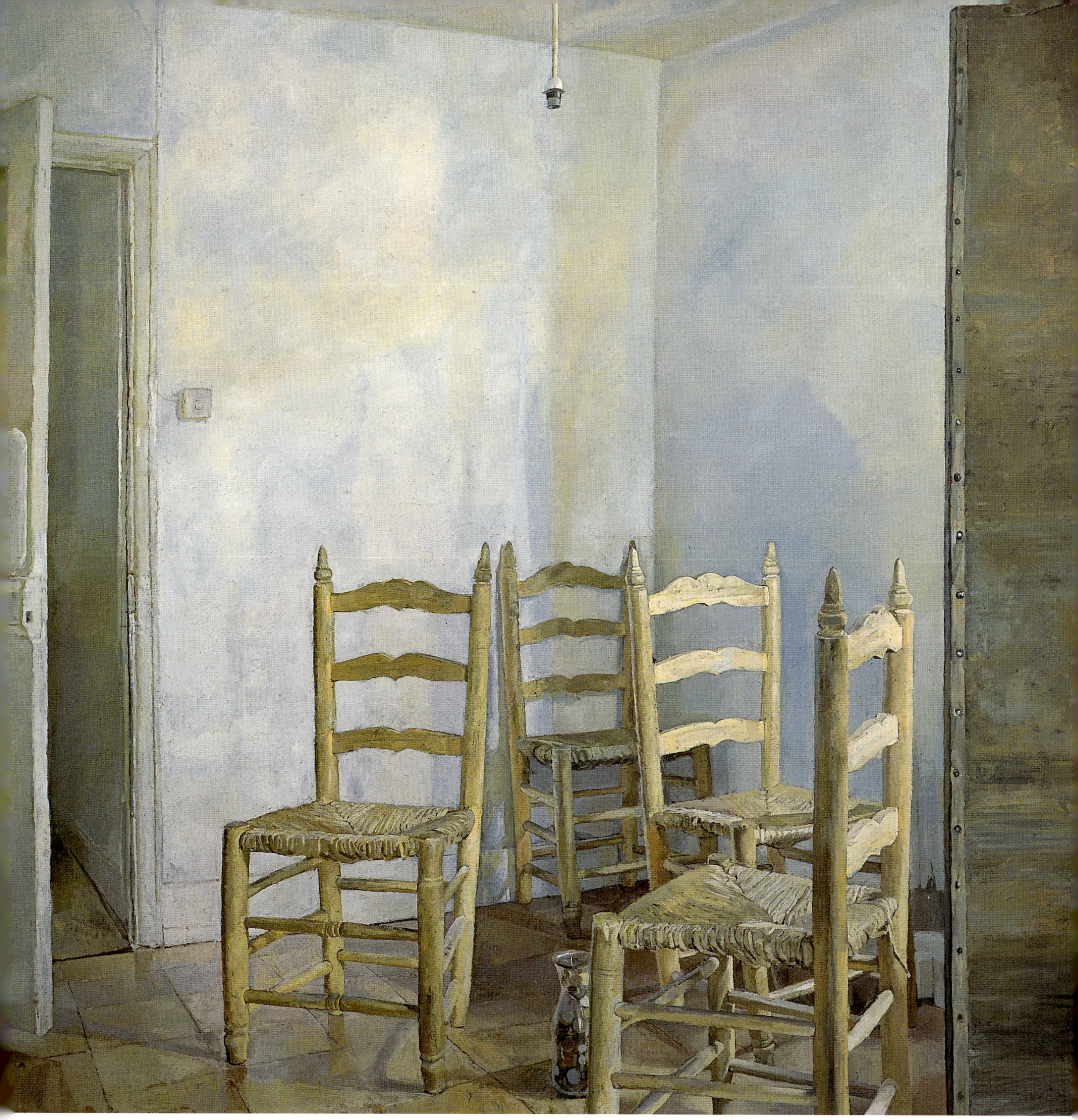

[79] *Four Spanish Chairs*, 1984
121.9 x 121.9 cms 48 x 48 ins

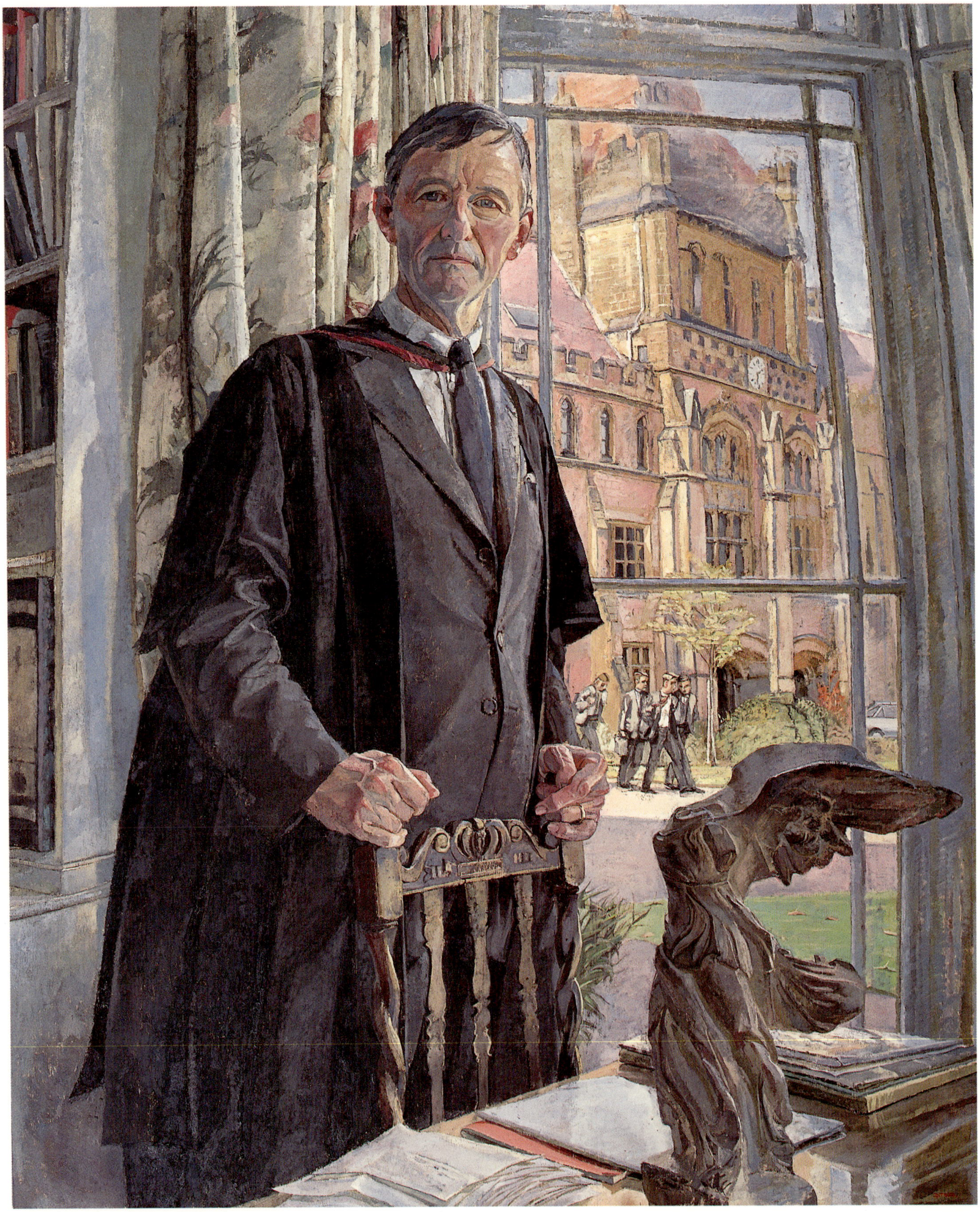

[80] *Christopher Everett, Headmaster, Tonbridge School,* 1989
121.9 x 91.4 cms 48 x 36 ins

Opposite: [81] *Roger Webb: Roger and Dee and Half of Me,* 1996
61 x 50.8 cms 24 x 20 ins

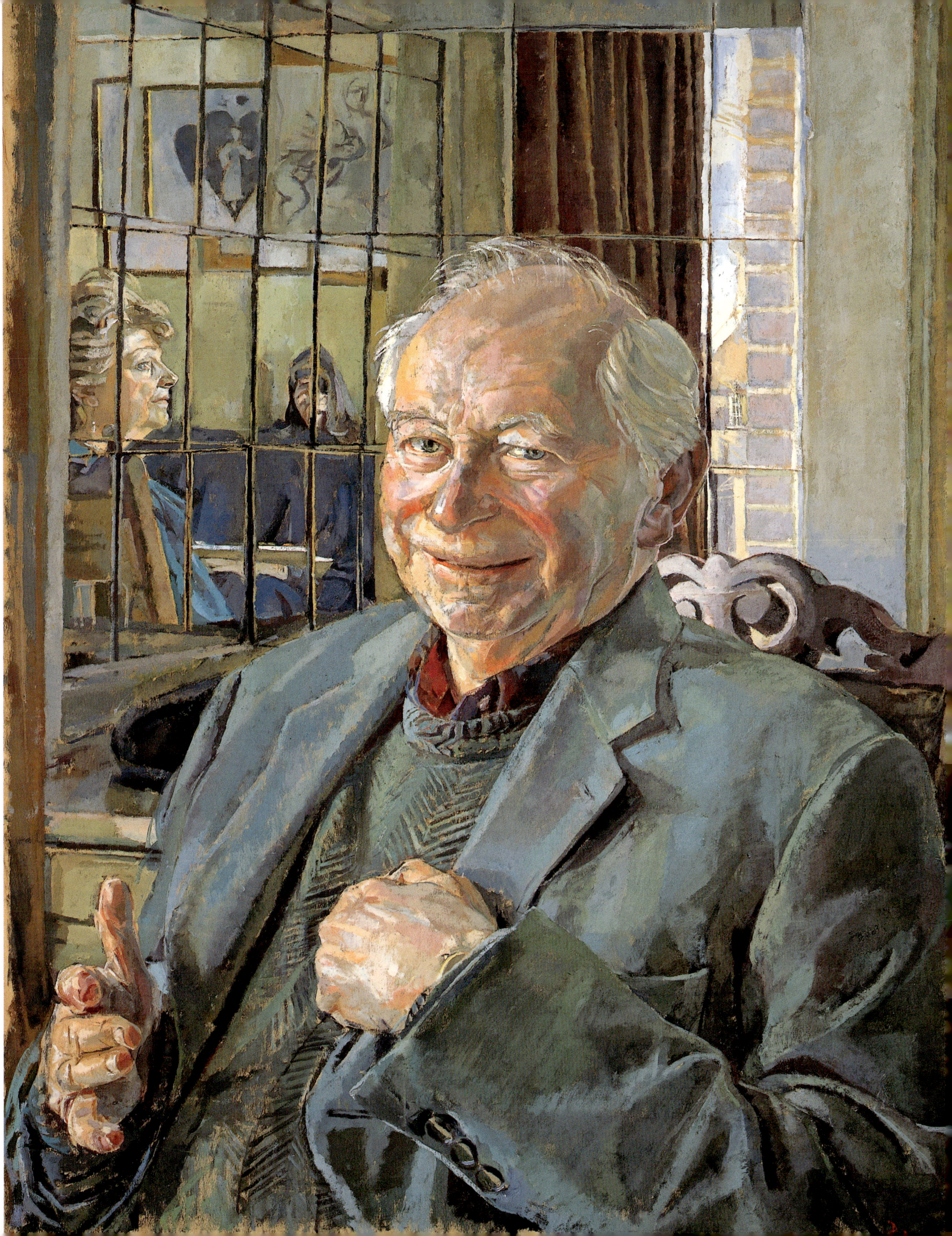

many different backgrounds in public and private life. Each commission presents a new set of problems to be solved and she enjoys the buzz of setting up the pose, trying to see each person afresh in their own habitat. She prefers to paint her sitters in their own spaces, finding that on the rare occasions that they come to her studio she does not know how to deal with the background. She tries to find a background appropriate to the sitter, believing that a true portrait is not necessarily just the head, but that body and background are important. She always works directly from life and, unlike most contemporary portrait painters, never uses photographs, even for details of the clothing. As she points out: 'A lot of people don't realise that a photograph doesn't record what we see, but records a lot of things that we haven't seen ourselves. You can look at a photograph and see all sorts of things in the background that you didn't know were there, and recorded in the way you don't see them. You look at foliage and see blurry things in a photograph whereas when you look at foliage yourself you don't see blurry things because you focus on each bit of it. People don't realise that a photographic record is not what they are seeing. If the photographer is an artist he can make haunting images but they are not the same as what the human eye sees.' [18]

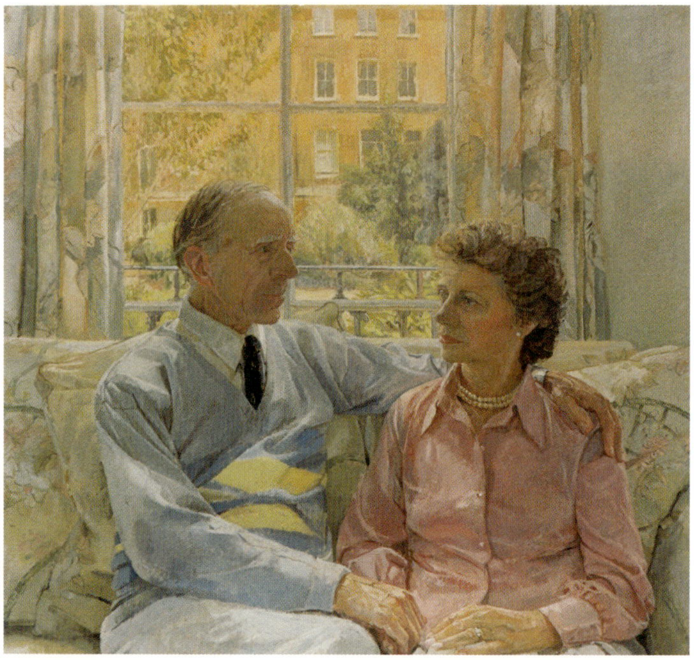

[82] *Sir Kirby and Lady Laing,* 1988
76.2 x 101.6 cms 30 x 40 ins

Todd's portrait commissions vary considerably. If they are for colleges the size is prescribed to fit alongside others and in general they cannot be too experimental. Sometimes the size is dictated by the budget. Todd does not often meet her sitters before she goes to paint them, although occasionally she is vetted by a committee beforehand. On her first visit all her senses are alert. 'I usually start by watching the subject while looking for a room with suitable light that won't disrupt their life too much. I like to have a new background each time that I can make a picture with. Where Euan would set himself problems – for instance, this is going to be about the diagonal – I wouldn't want to do that, I wouldn't want to specify a problem and then try and resolve that equation. I would rather react to what is there, the sort of shapes the sitter is making, the sort of body language they are using, latching onto a curve of the head or an upper lip, something that strikes me as being particularly different and peculiar to them. Whatever you put down leads on to the next thing and the painting leads you on. You might go

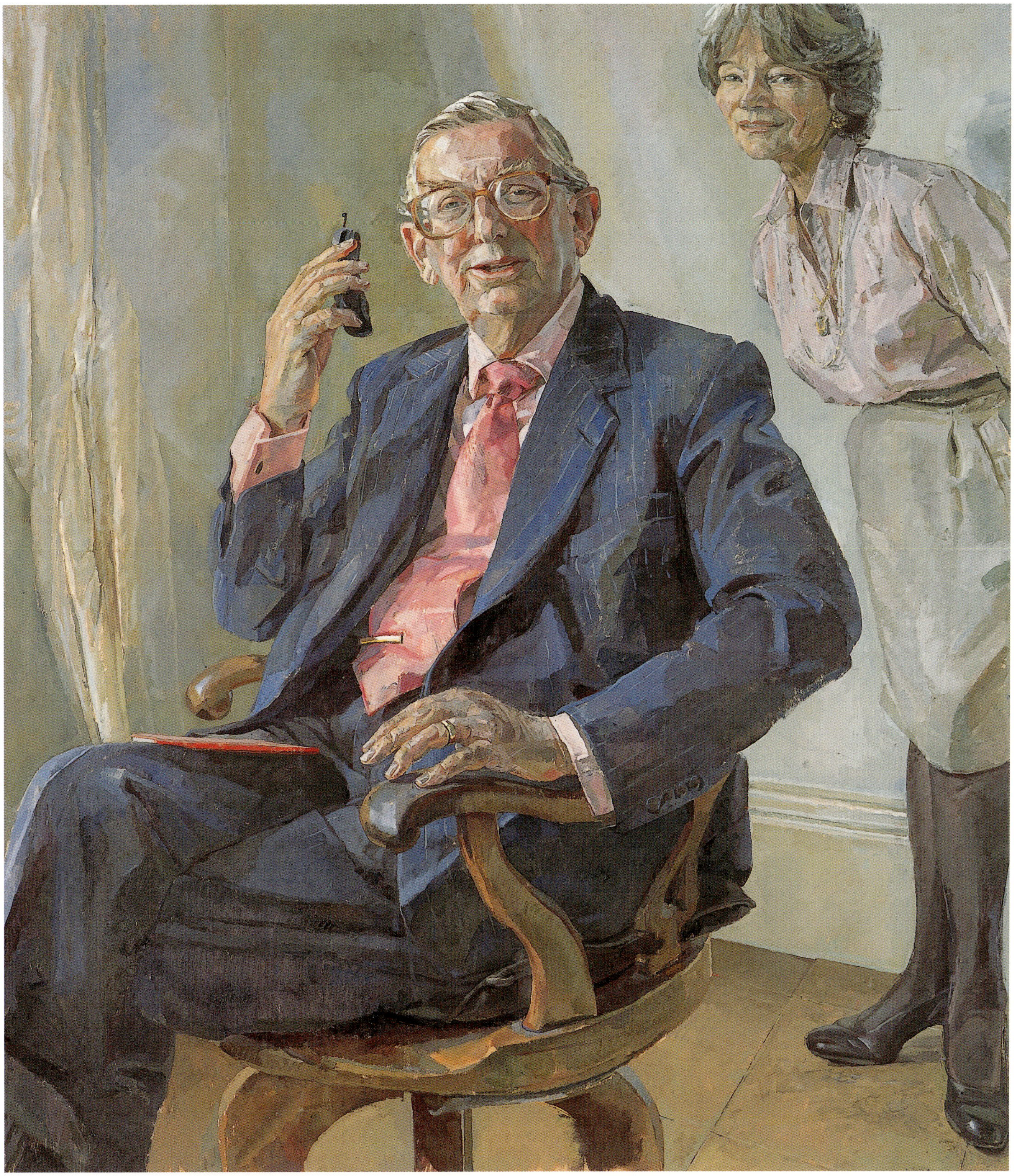

[83] *Lord Sainsbury with Lady Sainsbury Popping In,* 2000
127 x 101.6 cms 50 x 40 ins

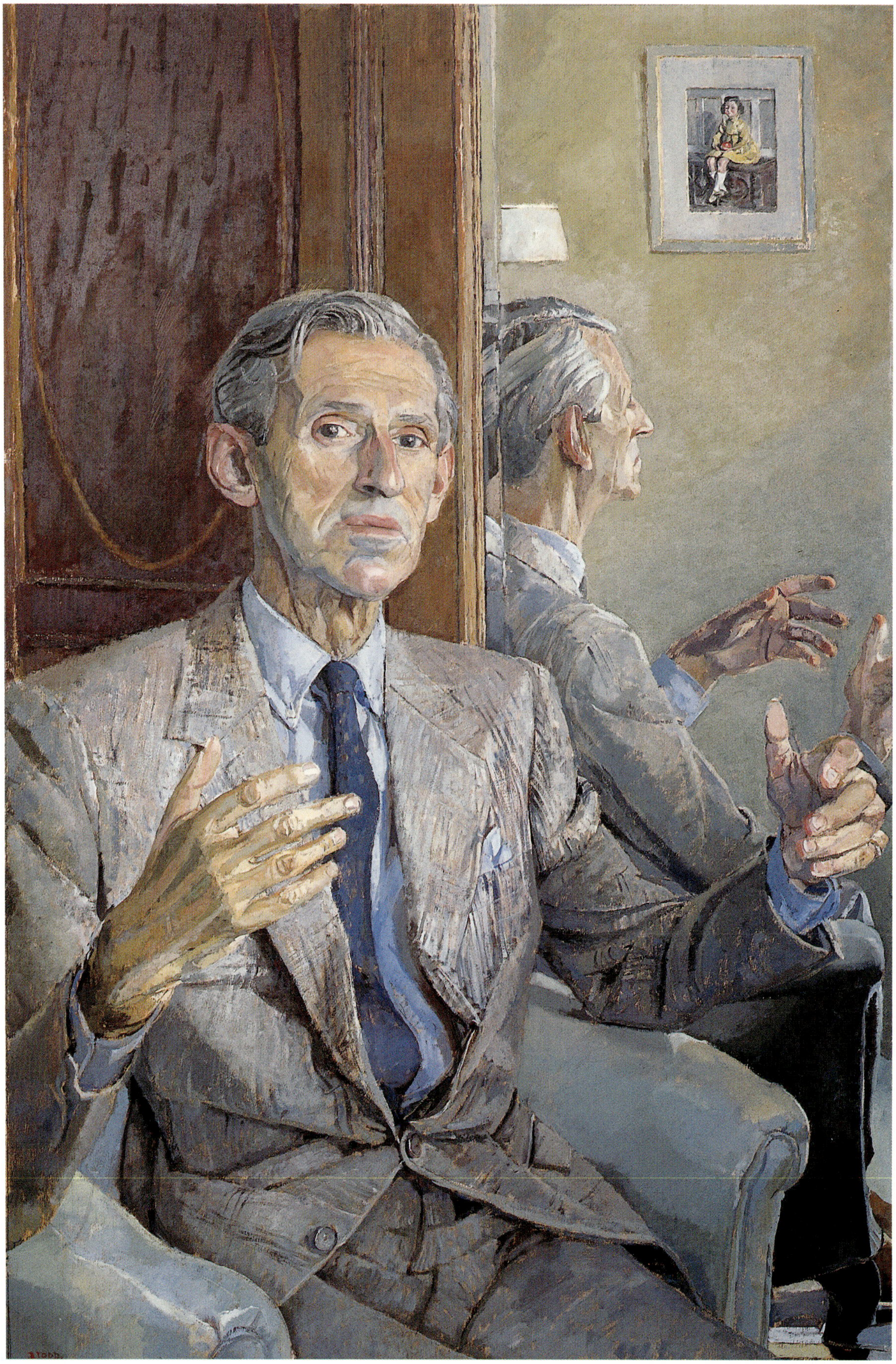

[84] *Baron Klingspor,*
1991
76.2 x 63.5 cms
30 x 25 ins

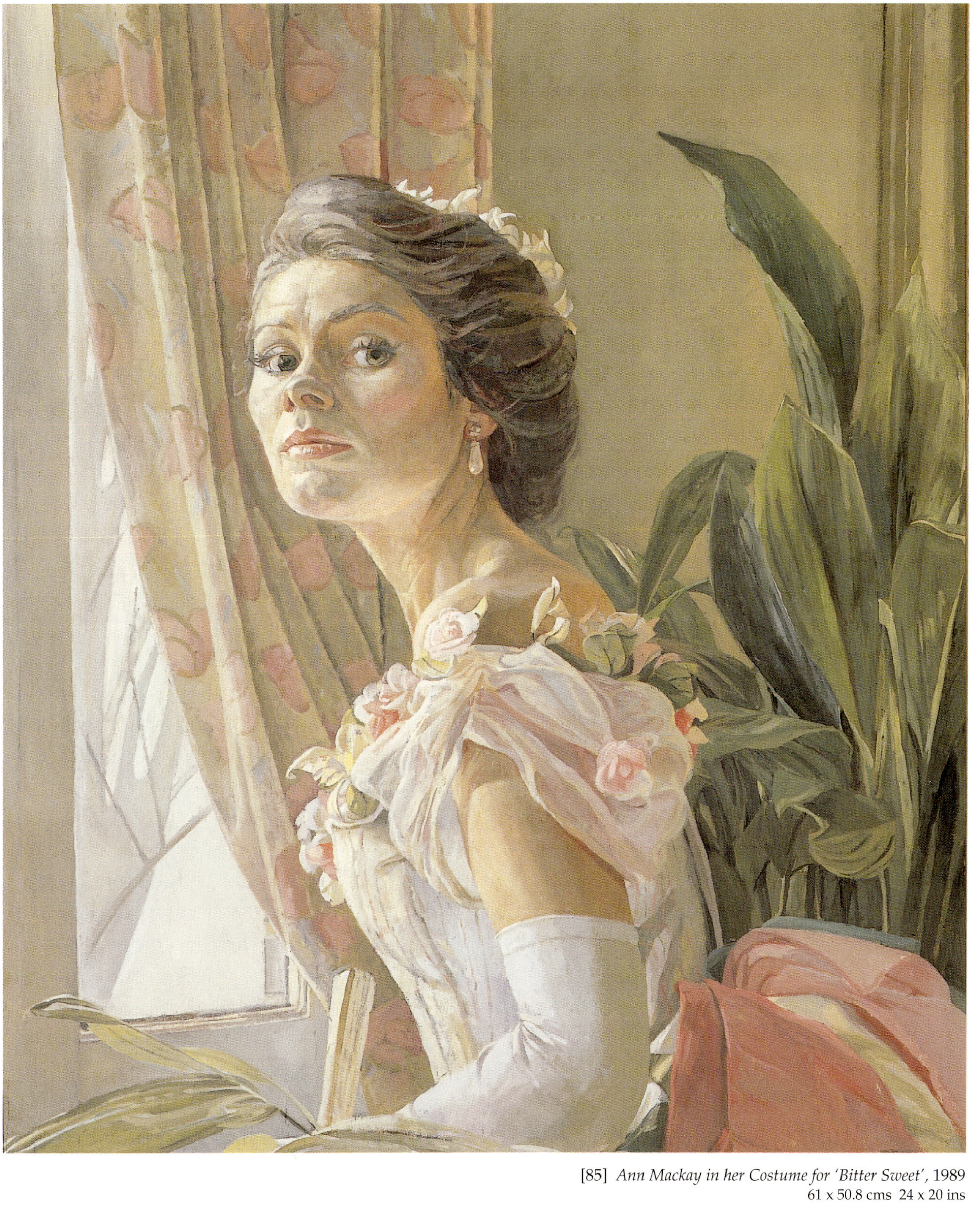

[85] *Ann Mackay in her Costume for 'Bitter Sweet'*, 1989
61 x 50.8 cms 24 x 20 ins

back and destroy all those things, but you are in the mesh of seeing what's out there as well as seeing what you have put down as well. It's a sort of ping-pong.' [19]

As Todd is acutely aware, the portrait-painter not only looks and records but also 'feels' the sitter, reacting to him (or her) in human terms and to some extent relating his shape to his or her own body shape. Portraiture is therefore invariably a dialogue between two people, the portrayer and the portrayed. The underlying language and the 'touch' of the portrait reveals much about the artist. Human responses of sympathy or antipathy, visual and tactile responses to the sitter's outward appearance, the selection of some characteristics and omission of others, all the choices deriving from the artist's own predilections, go to make the finished picture. A strong sense of the artist's presence imbues all good portraits, giving them an immediacy that carries across the centuries. It is the proliferation of hackneyed and pedestrian portraits, where the artist's input is minimal, that has given portraiture a bad name. But any portrait by Titian or Rembrandt renders absurd the idea that it is a lesser form of art. Some of the world's best paintings present one man's view of another, and because everybody knows what it is to be human, these pictures have an effect on the viewer that other subjects cannot create. Because photography has largely removed the emotional input of the artist from images of people, people have become accustomed to seeing faces depicted without feeling. The directly painted image, however, is a good conveyor of feeling, and a good portrait has a magical ability to transmit to the viewer the artist's understanding of the human condition.

Finding that her own reputation as a portrait painter was growing, Todd was concerned to raise the profile of contemporary portraiture. With this as her hidden agenda, her organisational skills made her an invaluable member of the Royal Society of Portrait Painters. The Society had a long and proud history. Founded in 1891 by twenty-four artists dissatisfied with the selection policy of the Royal Academy, then the only major showplace for new work in London, these eminent Victorian painters staged annual exhibitions concentrating solely on portraiture. Amongst the early members were Sir John Everett Millais, George Frederick Watts, John Singer Sargent, James McNeill Whistler, Dame Laura Knight, Solomon J Solomon, the Hon John Collier, Arthur Hacker, Herman G Herkomer and the cartoonist Leslie Ward, better

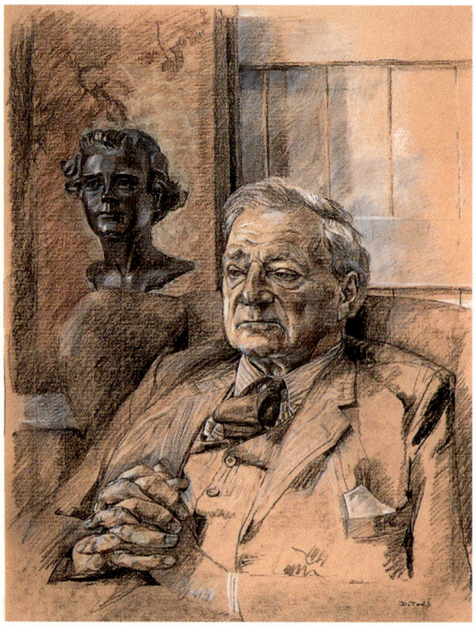

[86] *The Rt Hon the Earl Kitchener of Khartoum & Broome TD, DL*, 1994
76.2 x 61 cms 30 x 24 ins

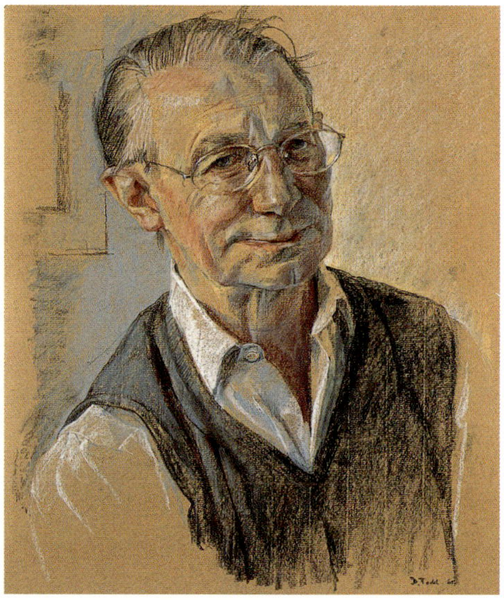

[87] *Lord Fellowes*, 2004
40.6 x 30.5 cms 16 x 12 ins

Opposite:
Daphne Todd with H.R.H. The Prince of Wales at The Royal Society of Portrait Painters, 2000

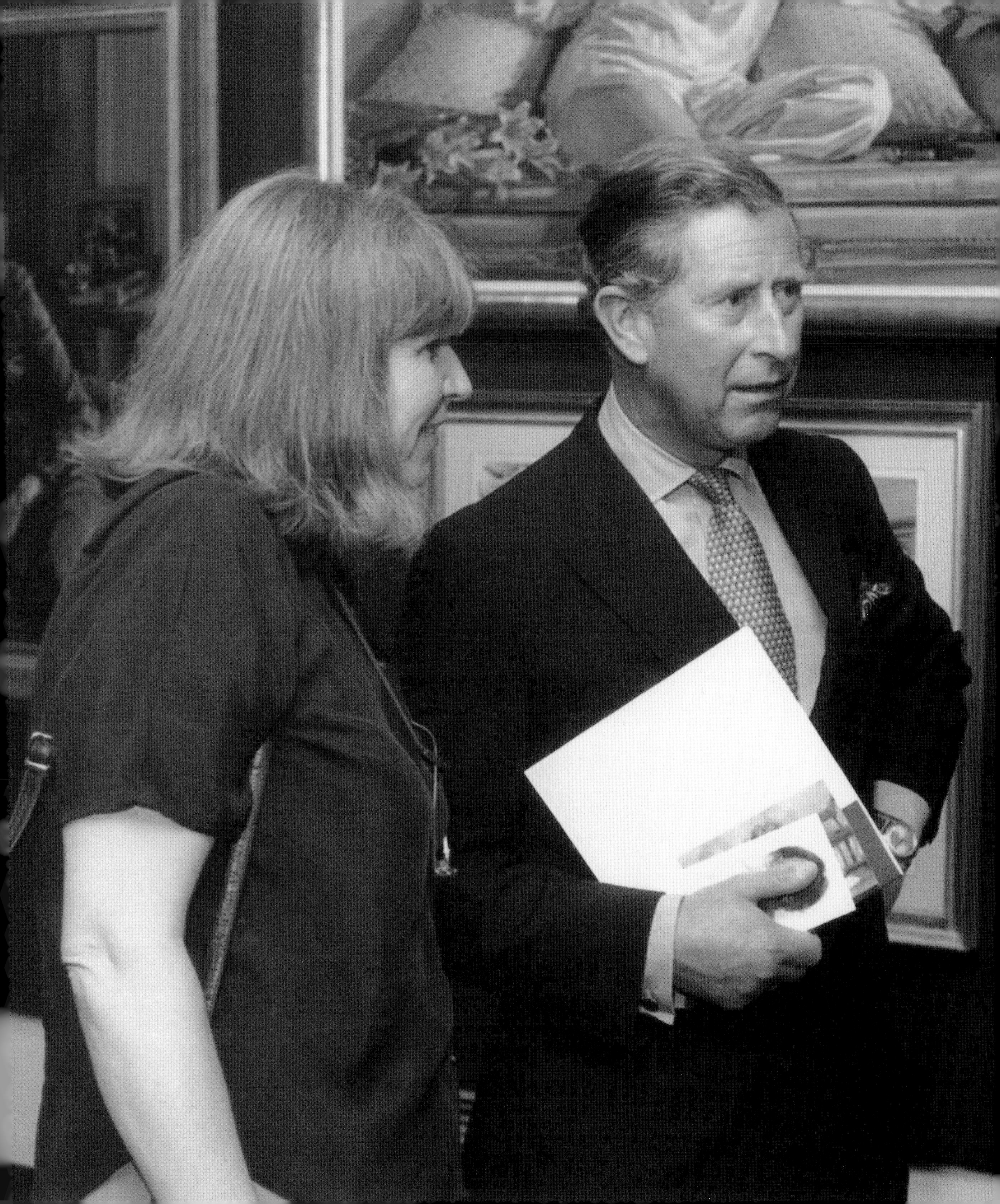

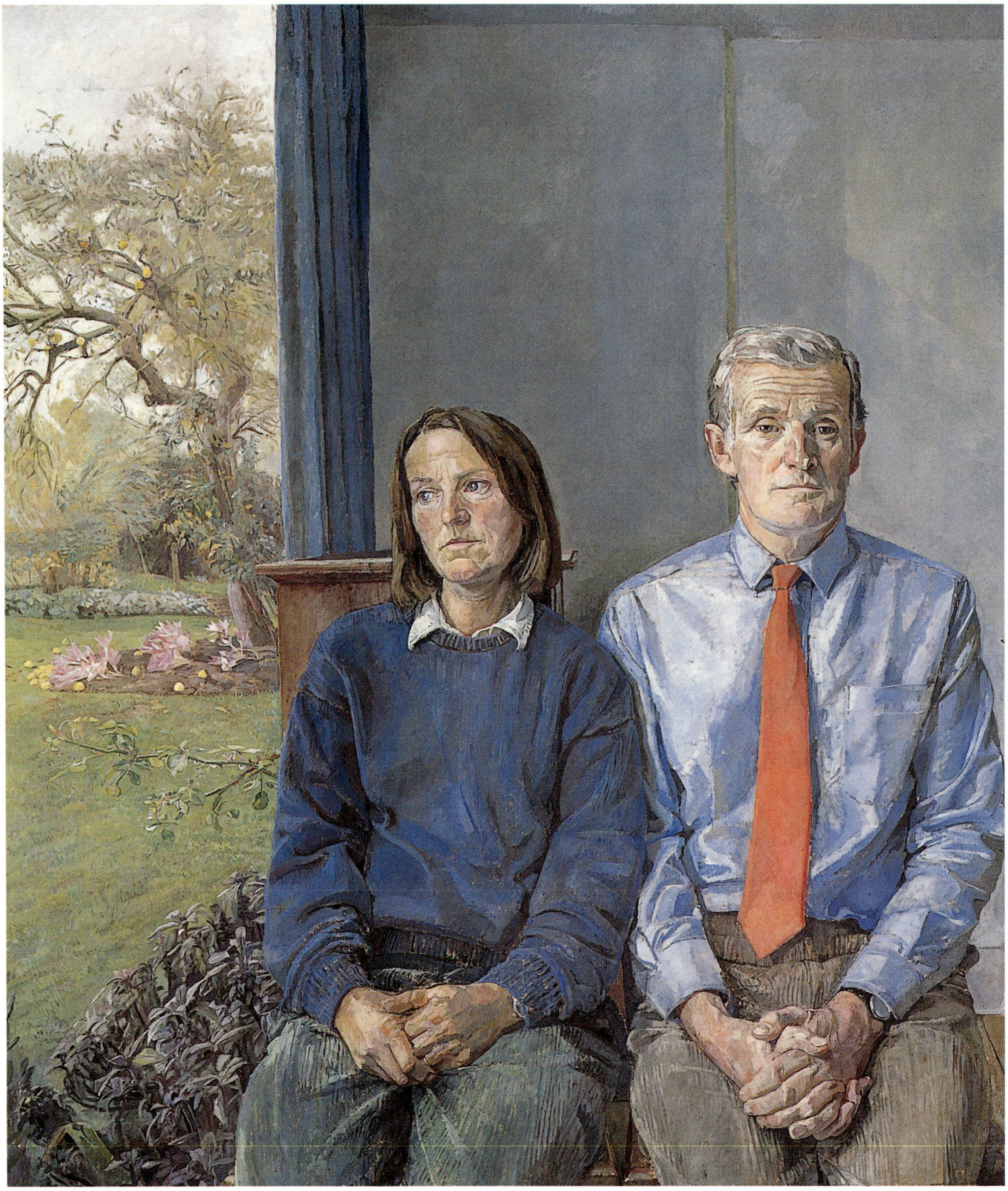

[88] *A Close Couple: S & O Mathews*, 1990
121.9 x 91.4 cms 48 x 36 ins

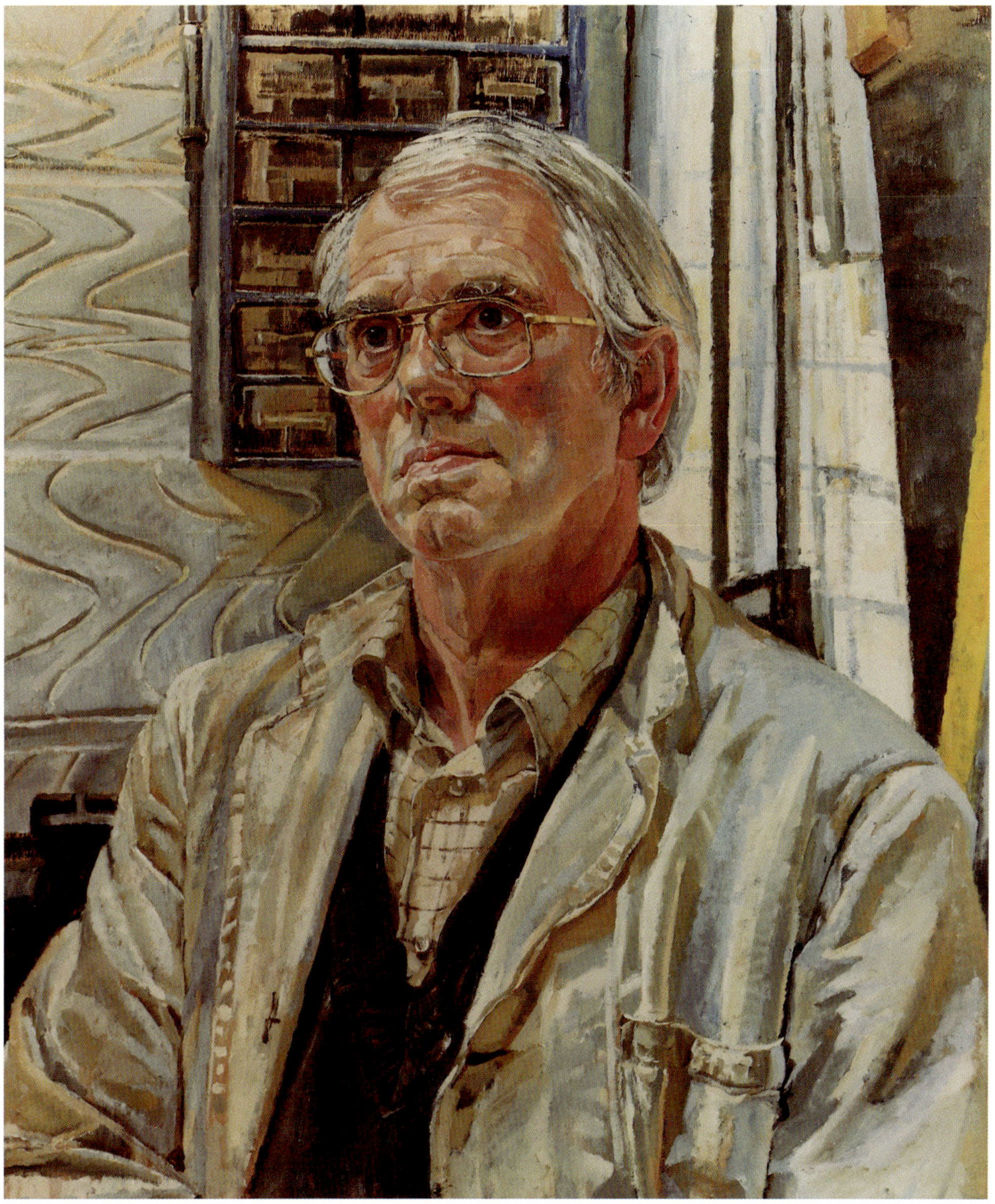

[89] *The Rev Peter Gant in his Workshop,* 1998
72.4 x 63.5 cms 28½ x 25 ins

known as 'Spy'. At the Coronation exhibition in 1911 George V conferred the status of a Royal Society to the Society. It became an important addition to London's social scene and initially each president was knighted. Dedicated portrait painters moved in exalted social circles and perhaps only History Painting then took precedence over portraiture in the hierarchy of art. Conditions changed after the Second World War, with fewer requests for portraits and many businesses or associations turning to photography for their required records. The age-old tradition of painting people began to be marginalized and by the 1980s the Royal Society of Portrait Painters was seen as a backwater, ignored by the art critics.

Todd felt that something ought to be done about this, and that she could help the Society, which should not merely jog along, hiding behind old traditions and refusing innovative work and thus attracting only bad painters to its membership. Her teaching and administrative experience, as well as her north-country 'nous', were very useful, and she was full of suggestions. After two years on the Council she enquired what the Society was planning to do about its approaching centenary. Although this had not previously been mentioned David Poole, then President, had it in mind and asked Todd to chair the Centenary Sub-Committee. For the centenary in 1991 this committee organised an historical exhibition of work by past members, borrowed from major art collections around the country.

In 1994 Todd was elected to be both the youngest and the first female President of the Royal Society of Portrait Painters. Although membership had, unusually, been open to women since the Society's foundation, none had the top job and at the time of Todd's election June Mendoza was the only other woman member. There was a certain amount of skirmishing over Todd's appointment, but she won the day. She was ambitious for the Society, wanting it to look outwards and reach its fingers into all spheres. She also wanted to include portraits that were not necessarily commissions but simply good paintings of people, to make the Society more concerned with art and less with the social network. With this in mind she invited Tom Phillips and John Wonnacott (both now CBEs) to join as Honorary Members. She also set up an Advisory Committee of top representatives from each section of British society and instituted an annual dinner to which influential people were invited. It was at her specific invitation that Lord Morris of Castle Morris

Changing Faces offers support to those with facial disfigurement. James Partridge, its dynamic Director, himself underwent reconstructive surgery following extensive burns in his youth. During Todd's presidency the RSPP began to donate a free evening to the charity during the society's annual exhibition at the Mall Galleries. Changing Faces now awards a substantial prize for "the portrait that is most powerful in the way that its subject communicates with the viewer."

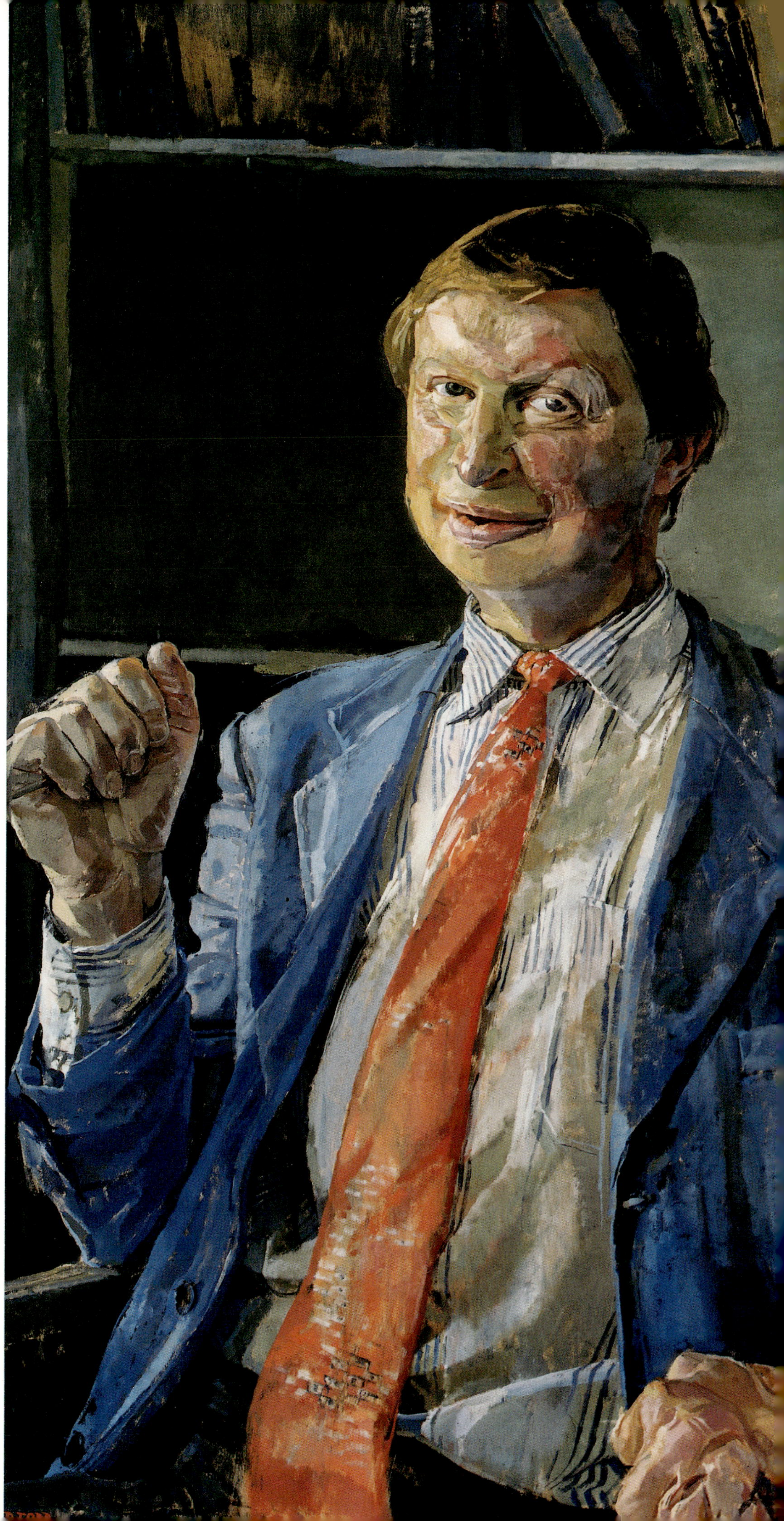

[90] *James Partridge OBE, Director of 'Changing Faces'*, 2005
101.6 x 61 cms 40 x 24 ins

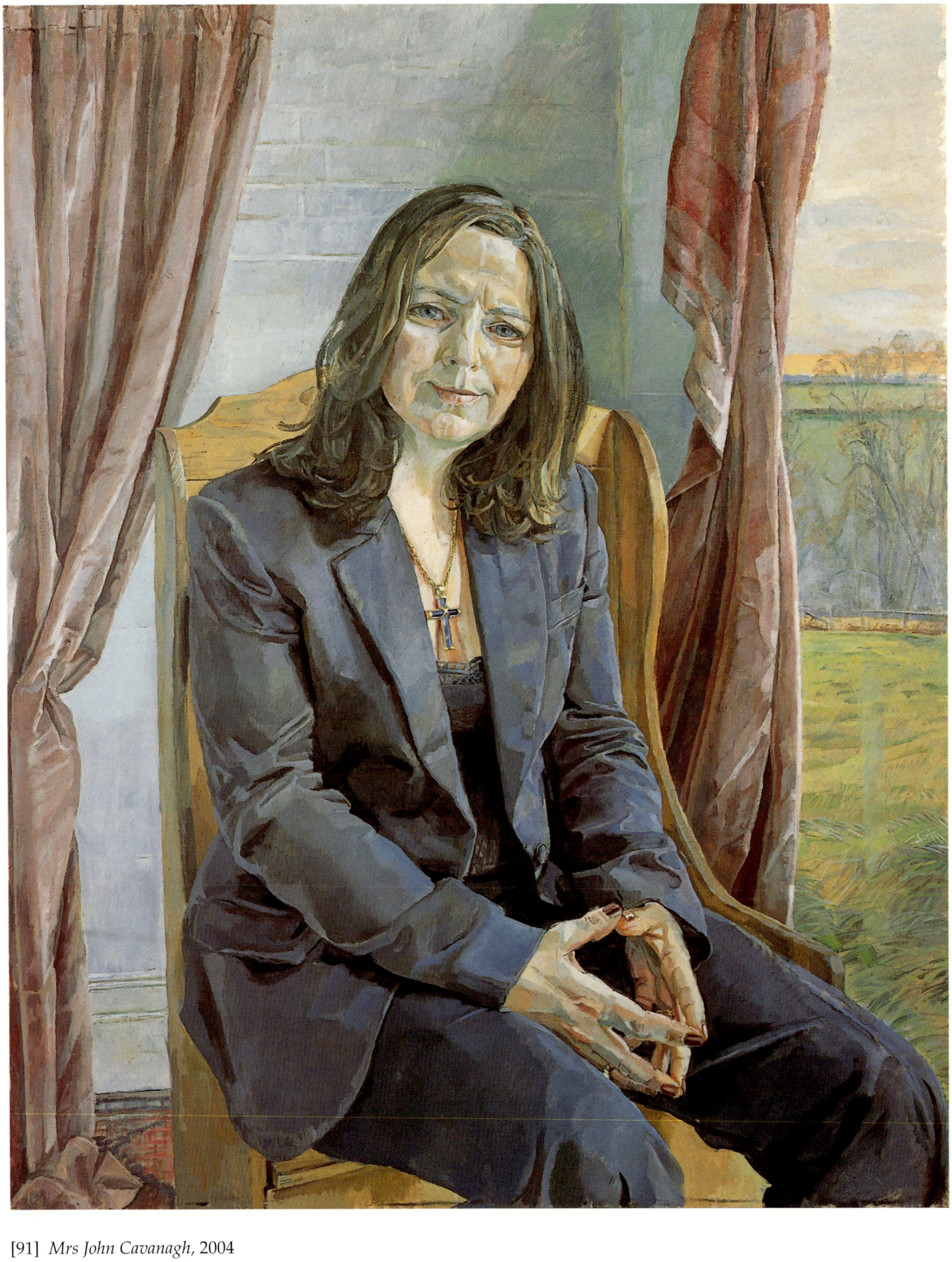

[91] *Mrs John Cavanagh,* 2004
91.4 x 71.1 cms 36 x 28 ins

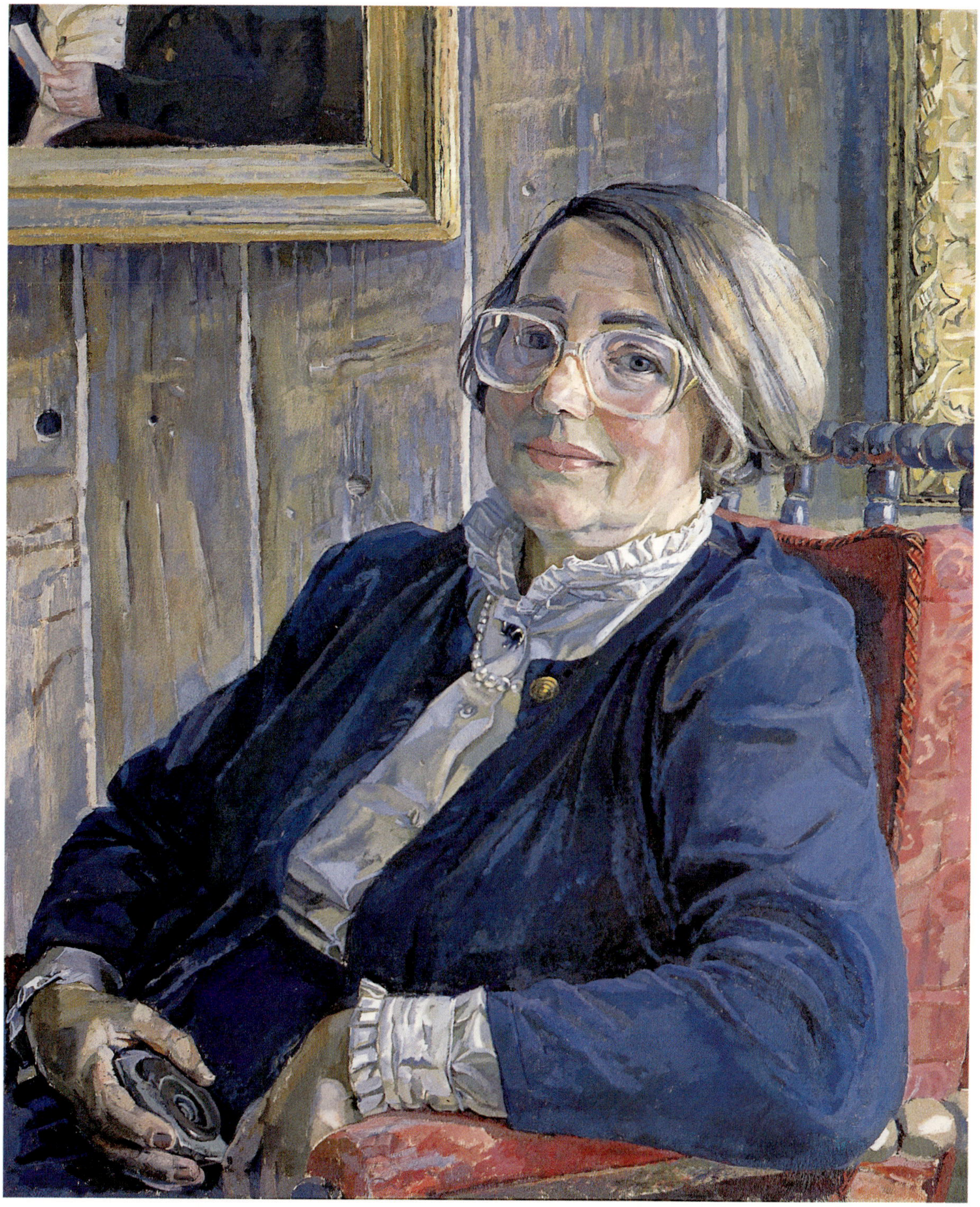

[92] *Mrs Nicholas Bagshaw,* 1996
61 x 45.7 cms 24 x 18 ins

(representing Education), Lord Armstrong (the Civil Service), Lord Deedes (the Press), Sir Christopher Ondaatje (Finance) and Lord Fellowes (the Palace) became members of the Advisory Board of the Society. With their help the Society became much more dynamic, championing representational painting in what is still a somewhat hostile climate. Several prestigious annual prizes or awards for portraiture were introduced. Sir Christopher Ondaatje, a former sitter of Todd's, generously funded the Ondaatje Prize, and through the good offices of Peter Kuhfeld His Royal Highness the Prince of Wales sponsored a new prize for drawing. The Society felt able to offer a little modest patronage of its own and dedicated a rent-free evening during its annual exhibition to the charity Changing Faces, which helps those with facial disfigurements. When Todd's presidency ended in 2000 the members of the Advisory Board asked that she remain as one of them, and the Society was delighted to grant their wish.

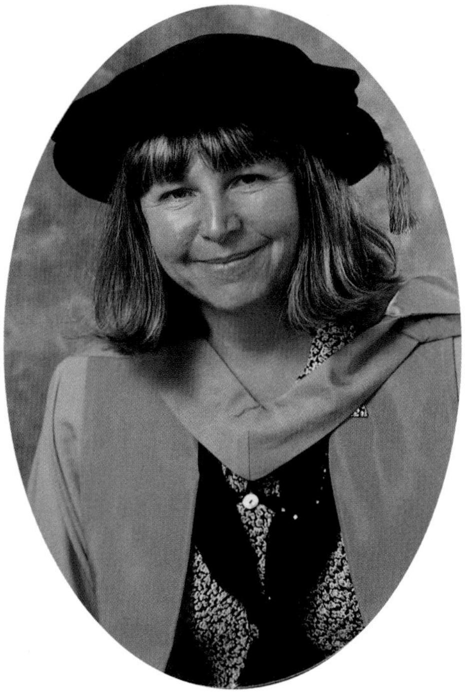

Honorary Doctorate ,
De Montfort University, 1998

The Royal Society of Portrait Painters is now thriving, with between forty and sixty active members, and selecting from seven hundred entries for each annual exhibition. Unlike the BP Award, which exhibits mainly non-commissioned paintings of people, the Society caters particularly for portrait painters who are dealing with commissions all the time. Its exhibitions provide a showcase from which commissions arise, and they also help to educate, inform and entertain the public.

Daphne Tood is awarded the OBE. With Mary and Terry at Buckingham Palace, 2002

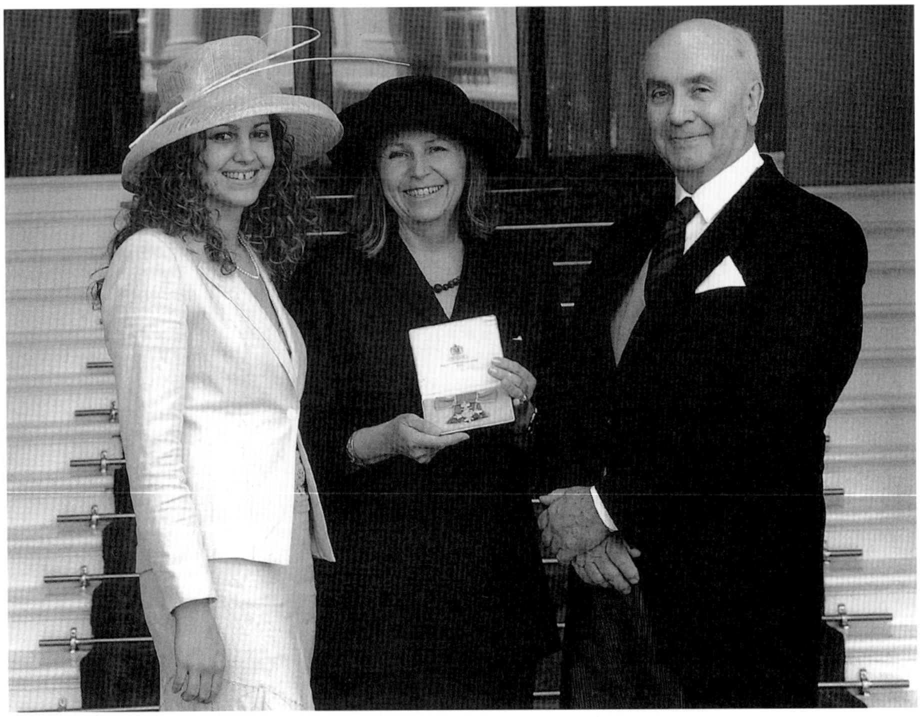

In 2000, while she was President, Todd organised a special exhibition, *People's Portraits*, which started at the Mall Galleries and toured the country for two years. Members had been asked to submit non-commissioned paintings of 'ordinary people' in a variety of different occupations. For this exhibition Todd painted the composite picture, *Mr Tasker, Cesspit Emptier*, standing in front of his sewage tanker. She chose him 'because he looked personable and I thought there may not be many cesspit cleaners in the future. He was utterly hopeless at posing. Originally I was going to pose him outside by his tanker, but he couldn't

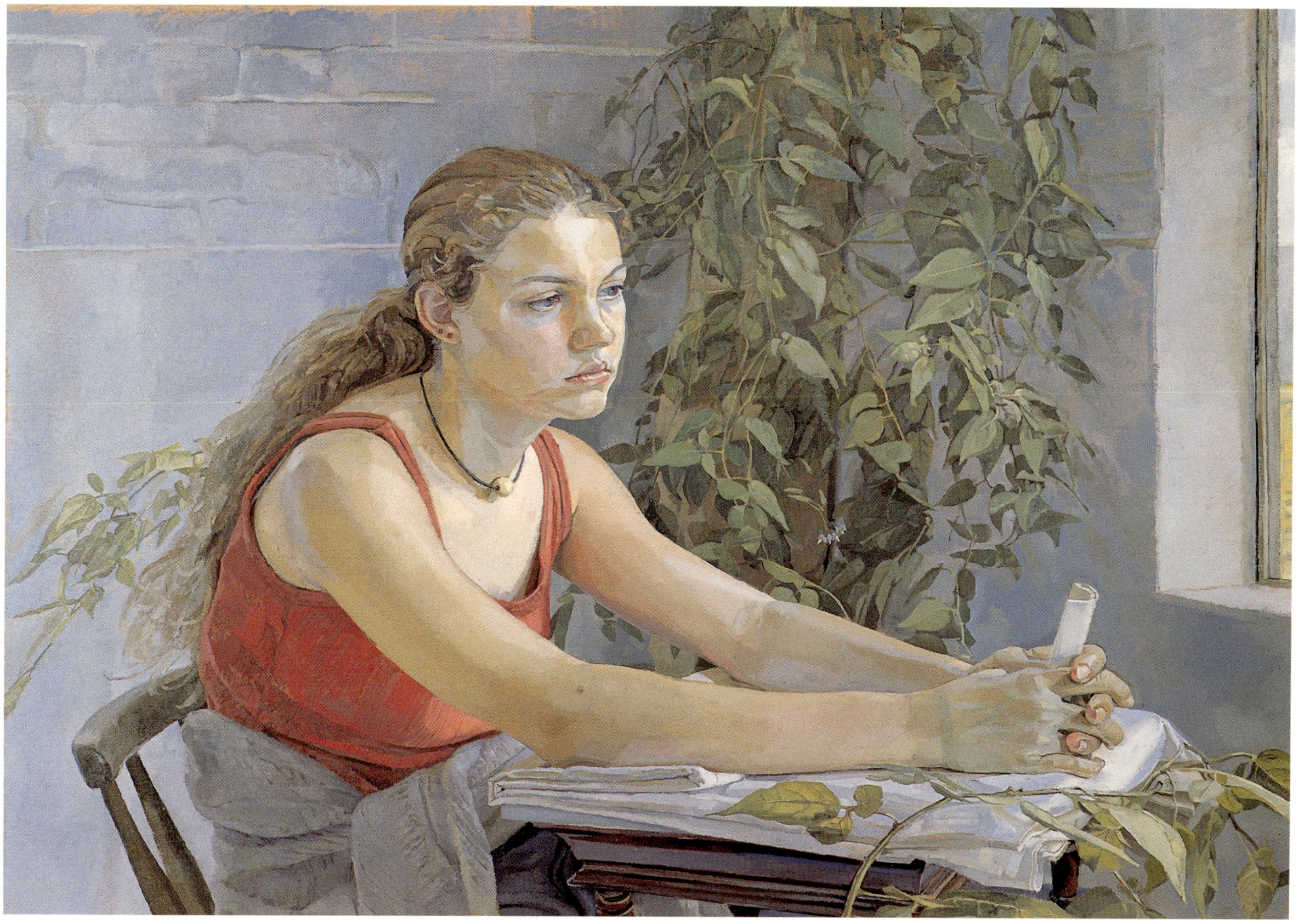

[93] *Mary Driscoll, aged 16,* 1993
63.5 x 86.4 cms 25 x 34 ins

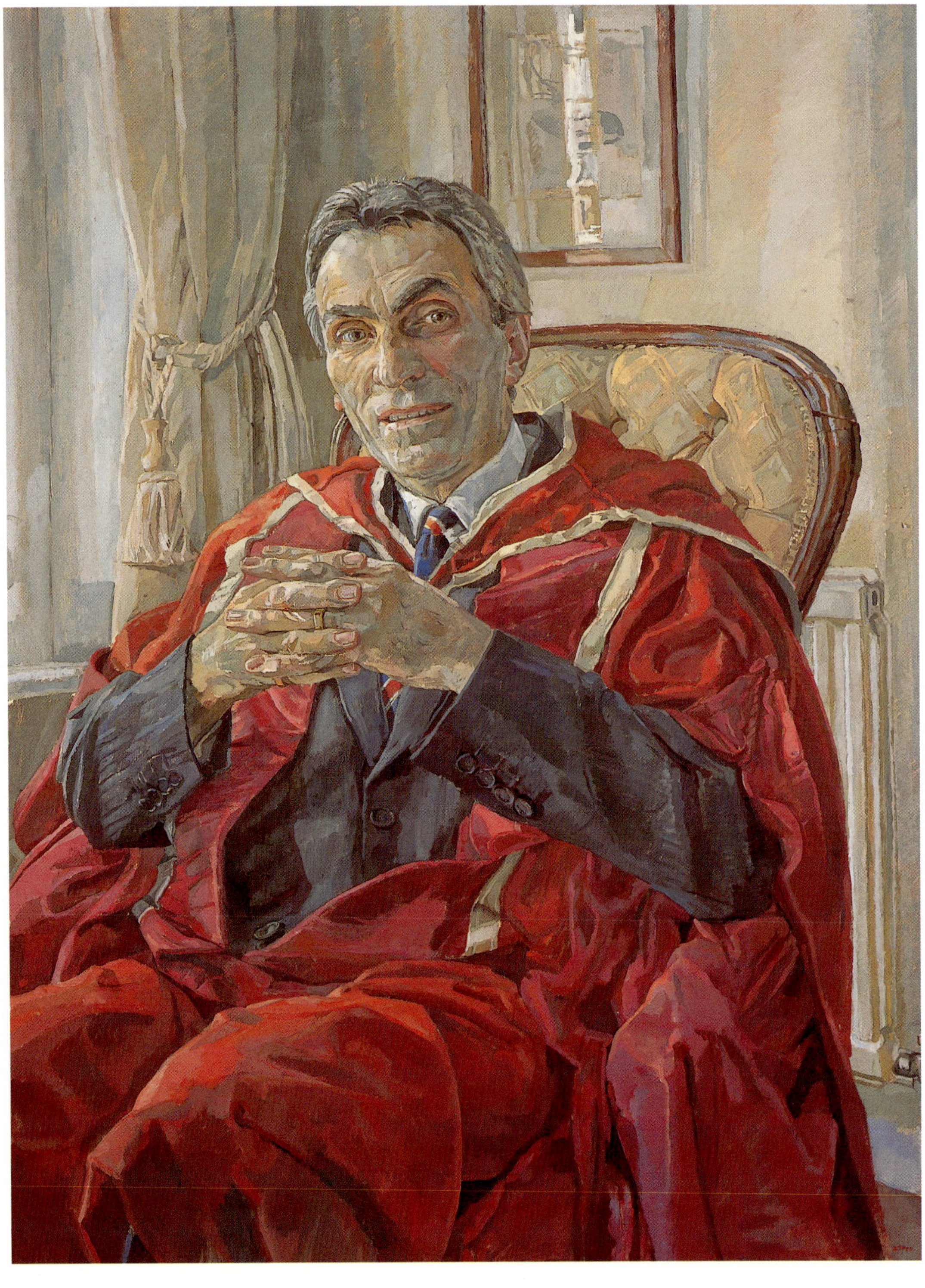

[94] *Professor Peter Mortimore OBE, Director, Institute of Education,* 2003
96.5 x 71.1 cms 38 x 28 ins

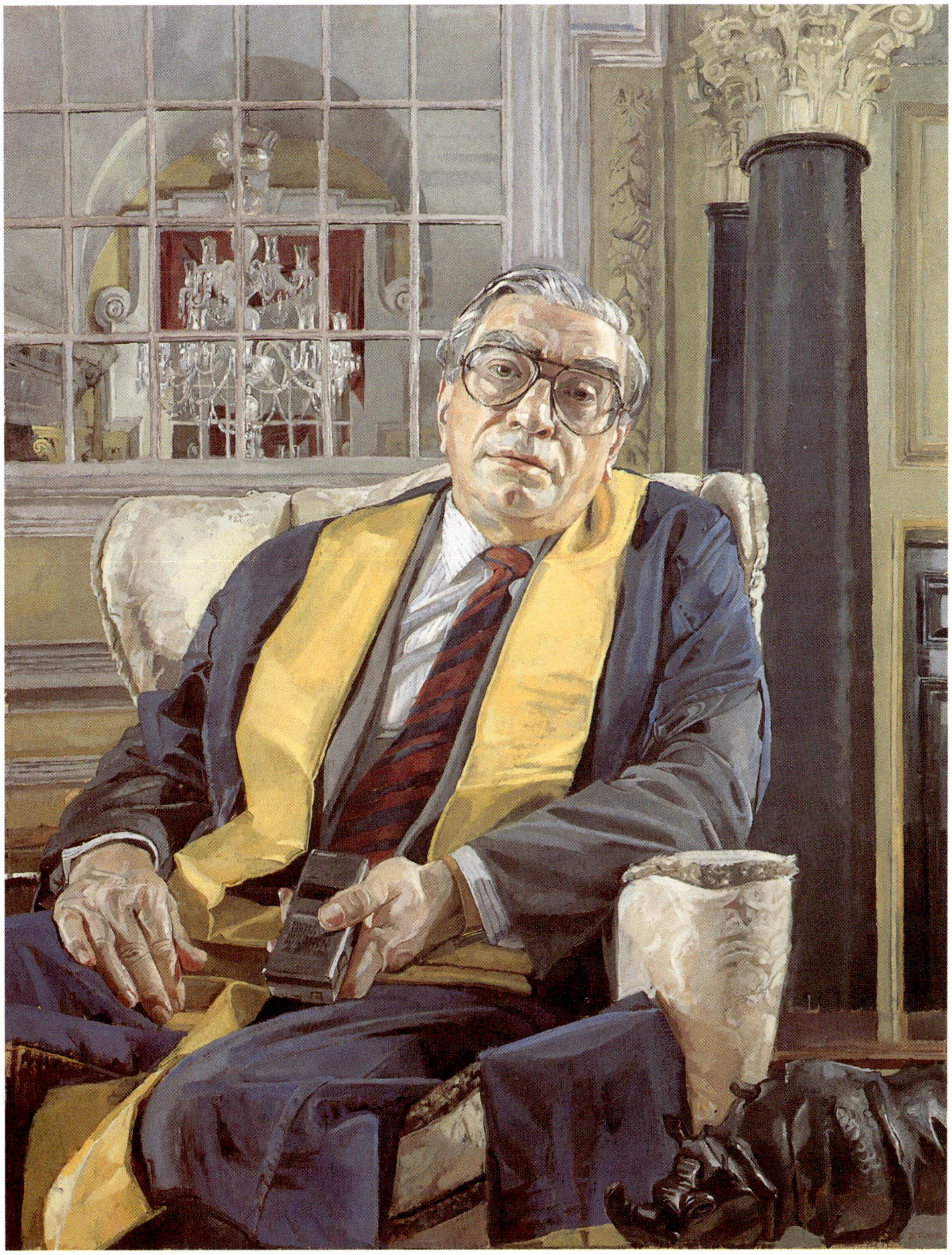

[95] *Dr Ian Field CBE, Secretary British Medical Association,* 1994
101 x 76.2 cms 40 x 30 ins

keep still, the sun came in and out, the wind blew, so I decided just to do a head. I started a head in the studio and he got a bit better at posing, and as he was wearing wonderful orange overalls I got him standing up and doing a bit more and then I thought of putting the bits together. The whole standing figure, with the tanker, was done it bits – partly inside and partly outside. I liked that way of working, but you have to be clear that it is done in this way, it's wrong if you pretend it isn't. You want the mechanics of perception to be visible in the finished portrait. It's as true as I can make it to the whole experience, which is the important thing. Truth to a particular experience is not in the brief of many portrait painters today.' [20]

For Todd *Mr Tasker* was ground–breaking because it was her first experiment with working on different panels and piecing the picture together. With the core of the *People's Portraits* exhibition, it was donated to the Society, to form the first collection of work they had ever had. When Todd was prospecting for a permanent site to show this collection she mentioned it to Dame Marylin Strathern, Mistress of Girton College, Cambridge, whose portrait she was painting. Dame Marilyn jumped at the idea of housing it at Girton, and organised the considerable funding required to display the collection professionally. There it has a permanent home, open to the public every afternoon. Every year Girton College gives a reception to the Society, and, at the current President Andrew Festing's suggestion, the collection is augmented by new members of the Royal Society of Portrait Painters, who donate a painting of someone in an occupation that would not normally be portrayed.

The Royal Society of Portrait Painters has played an important part in Daphne Todd's life. It was indirectly through the Society and her fellow portrait-painter Anthony Williams, that Todd first attracted the attention of the art dealer David Messum, who has brought her non-commissioned work before a wider public.

In the past two decades Todd has done much for the administration of the arts. She was able to create a link between Heatherley's and the Royal Society of Portrait Painters, which became one of the outside examiners for the only Portrait Diploma in the country, the course that she had instigated. Having been made one of the very first female liverymen of the Worshipful Company of Painter-Stainers since 1248, she is also involved in organising the Lynn Painter-Stainer Prize exhibition, specifically for representational painting, in their livery hall.

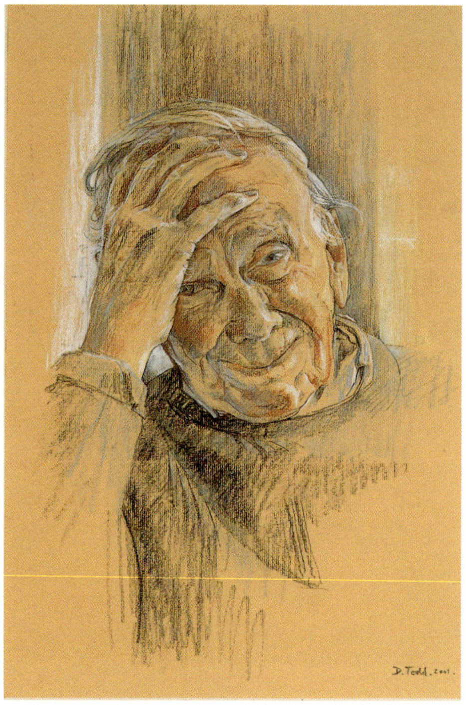

[96] *Lord Deedes*, 2001
40.6 x 30.5 cms 16 x 12 ins

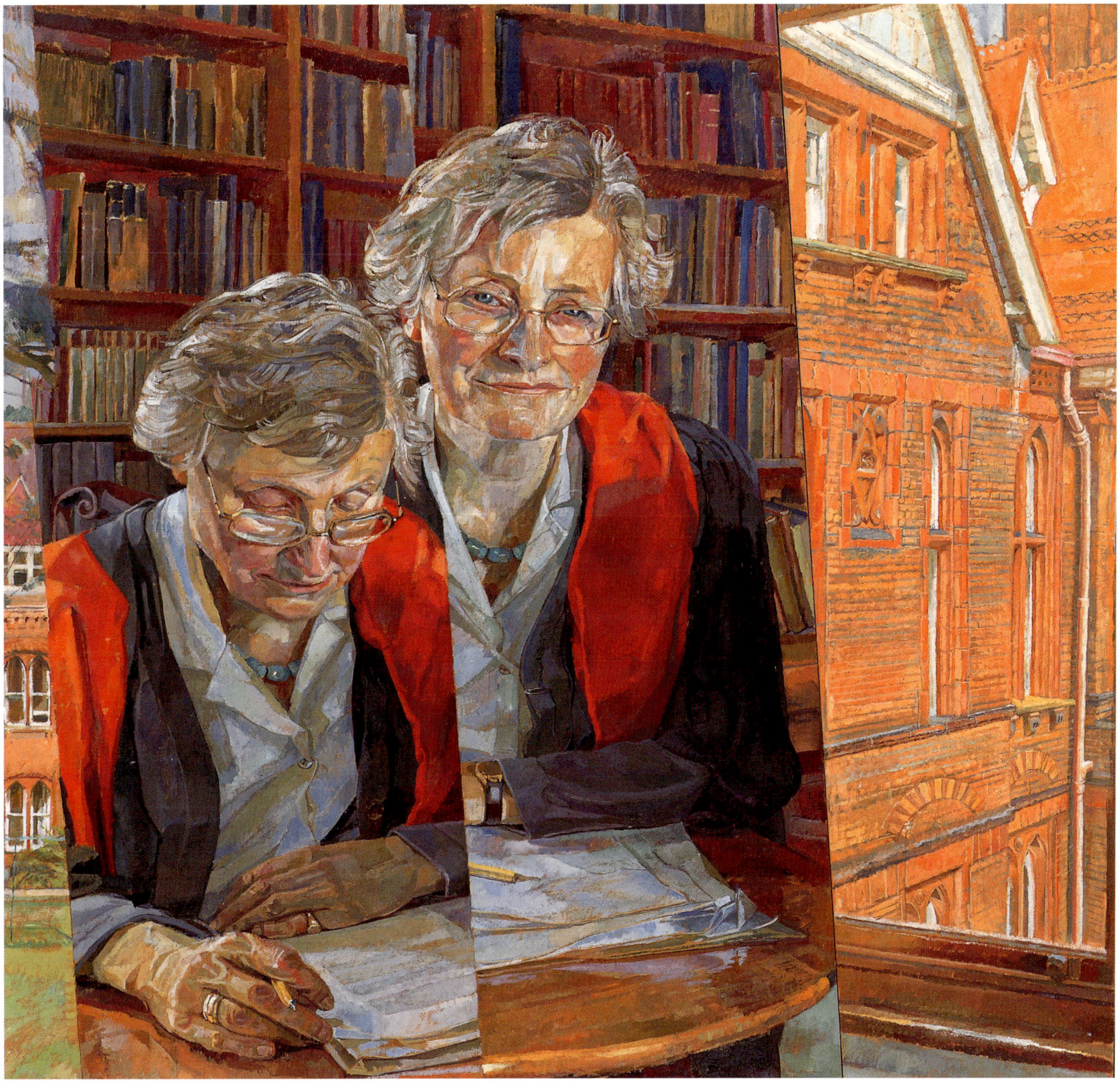

[97] *Dame Marilyn Strathern DBE FBA, Mistress of Girton,* 2000
76.2 x 63.5 cms 30 x 25 ins

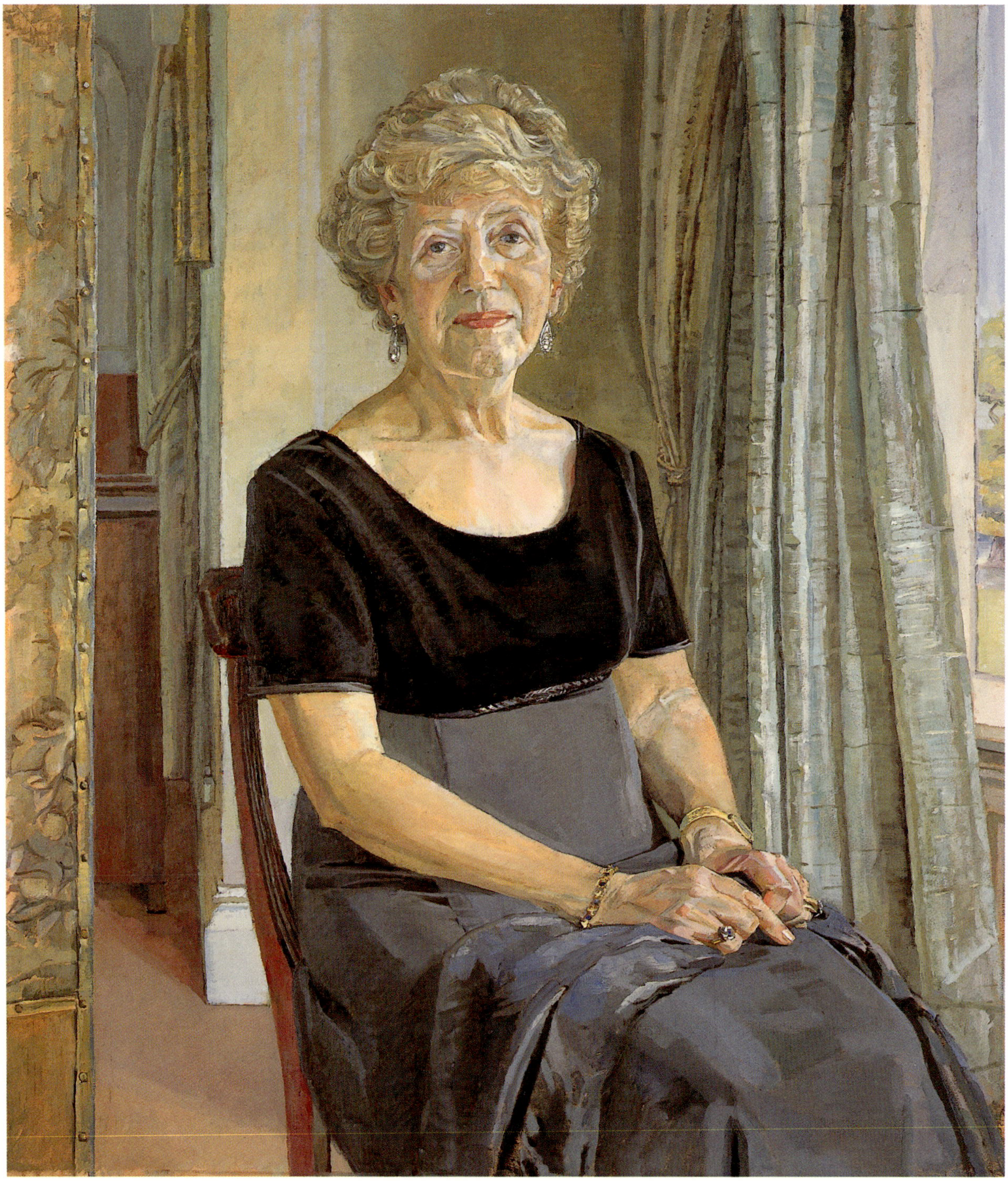

[98] *Margaret, Lady Carter,* 1998
102.9 x 77.5 cms 40½ x 30½ ins

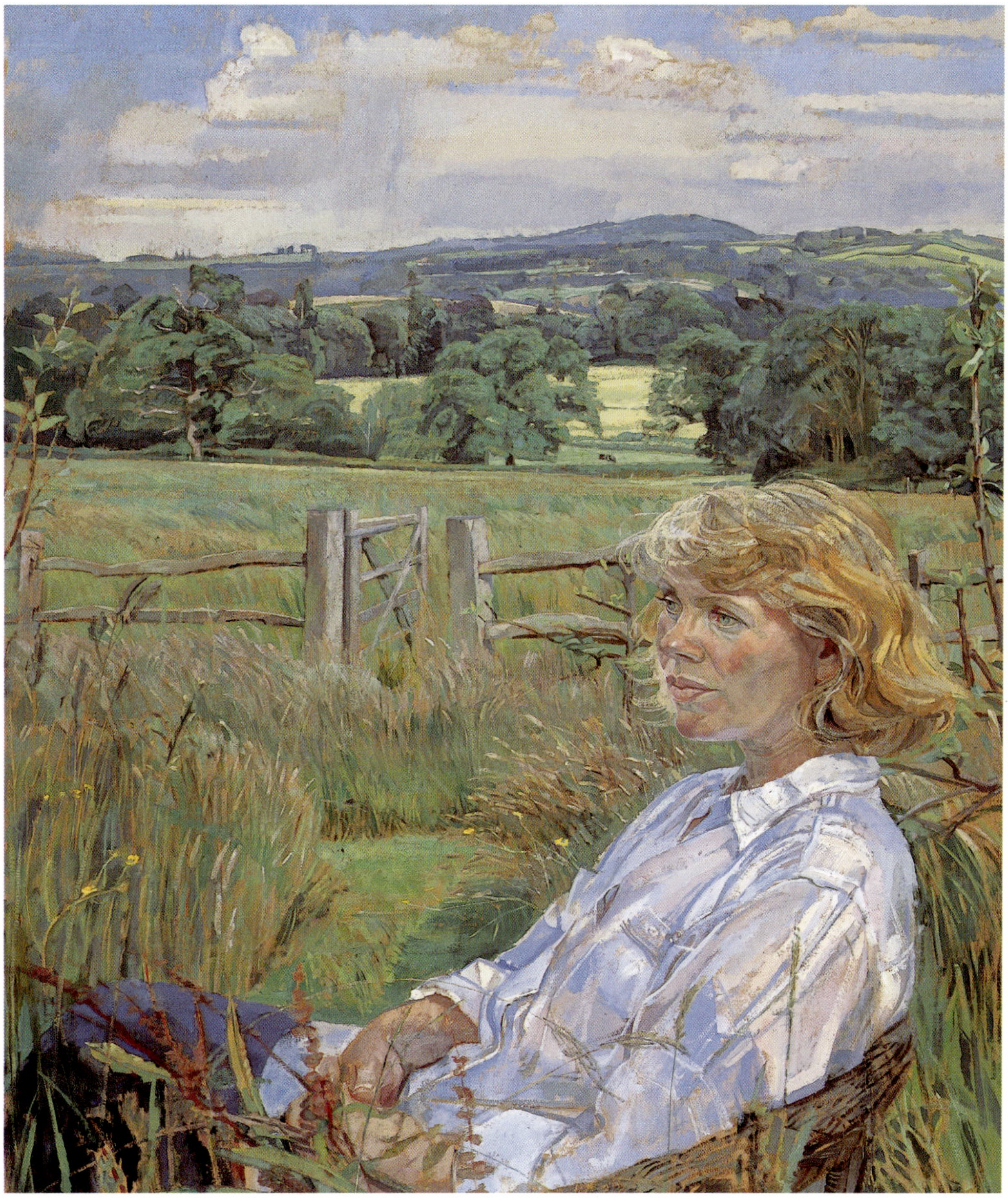

[99] *Mrs Crispian Collins*, 1997
61 x 61 cms 24 x 24 ins

She has become very much a mover and shaker in the art world, often invited to speak as well as to adjudicate. Her word counts, and she has become an effective champion of the art she admires. She is not afraid to tackle the sacred cows of the time and to leap to the defence of her colleagues, as is testified in a characteristically punchy letter to The Daily Telegraph about the Myra Hindley picture in the exhibition *Sensation* at the Royal Academy in 1997 (over which John Ward, a former Vice-President of the Royal Society of Portrait Painters, resigned). 'Sir, John Ward is a hero. So are the other three Royal Academicians whose resignations you have reported. You can argue about whether or not the stuff in Sensation is art until the cows come home to be dissected by Damien Hirst. That is not the point. The point is that relatives of children tortured and killed in the most horrifyingly debased way are very much alive and have made it clear that they are tortured by the so-called 'portrait' of Hindley (and perhaps its proximity to statues of naked children covered in genitalia). We are human beings first, artists second. Academicians who failed to control the doings of the paid employee should be ashamed of themselves. As individuals they surely would not treat injured people so callously. Why do it collectively in the name of art? It is surely ironic that this 'portrait', a blow-up of a photograph albeit in hand-shaped dots, is defended, while Ward is criticised for painting too many portraits for the good of his oeuvre. Ward's portraits, especially his groups and his girls, are surely among the most distinguished of his generation… Portraiture is not only one of the most difficult of disciplines, it has also produced some of the world's most universally acknowledged masterpieces… The RA will be the poorer without John Ward, but he was right to go. If we want the Academy to stand for something decent, the rest of us should terminate our Friends' subscriptions forthwith. ' [21] Todd's efforts on behalf of sense and decency and good art have not gone unnoticed. She was awarded an Honorary Doctorate of Arts by De Montfort University in Leicester in 1998 and an OBE in 2001.

Todd averages between six and eight portraits a year, and still makes time for her non-commissioned work, for administration, and for running the house and organising the family. For many years Daphne Todd and her husband have provided a home for both their elderly mothers – for over twenty years in the case of her mother-in-law, who died aged ninety-eight. Her own mother, now ninety-nine, has been

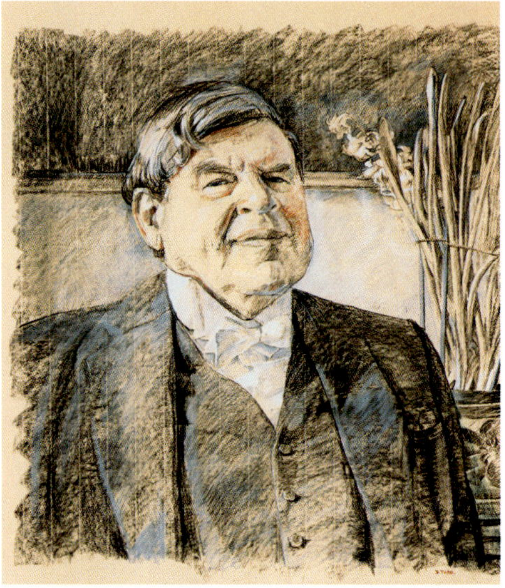

[100] *Tim Card, Vice Provost, Eton College,* 1998
68.6 x 61 cms 27 x 24 ins

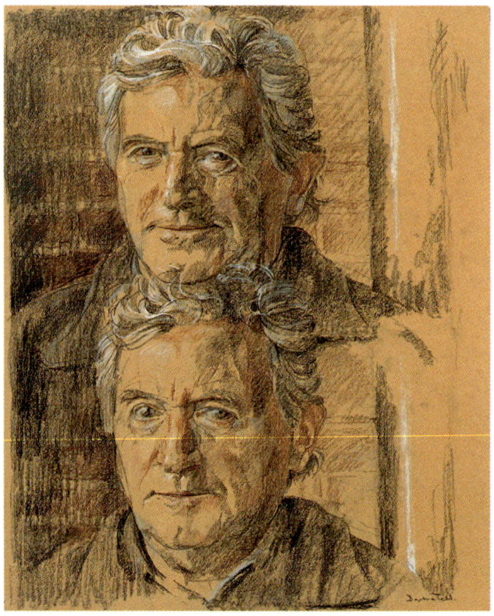

[101] *Dan Colman,* 2002
61 x 40.6 cms 24 x 16 ins

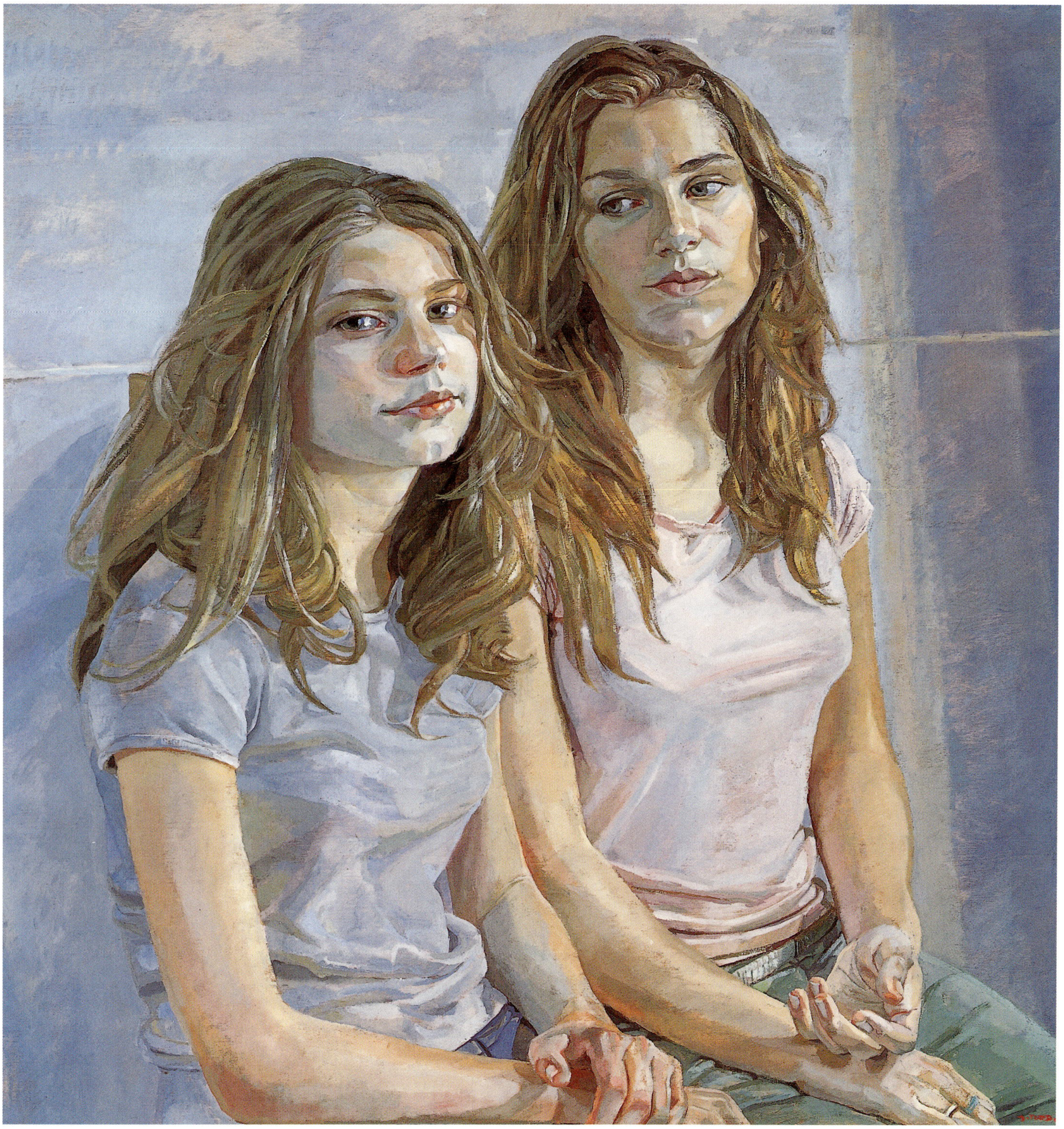

[102] *Alice and Sefi*, 2005
61 x 57.2 cms 24 x 22½ ins

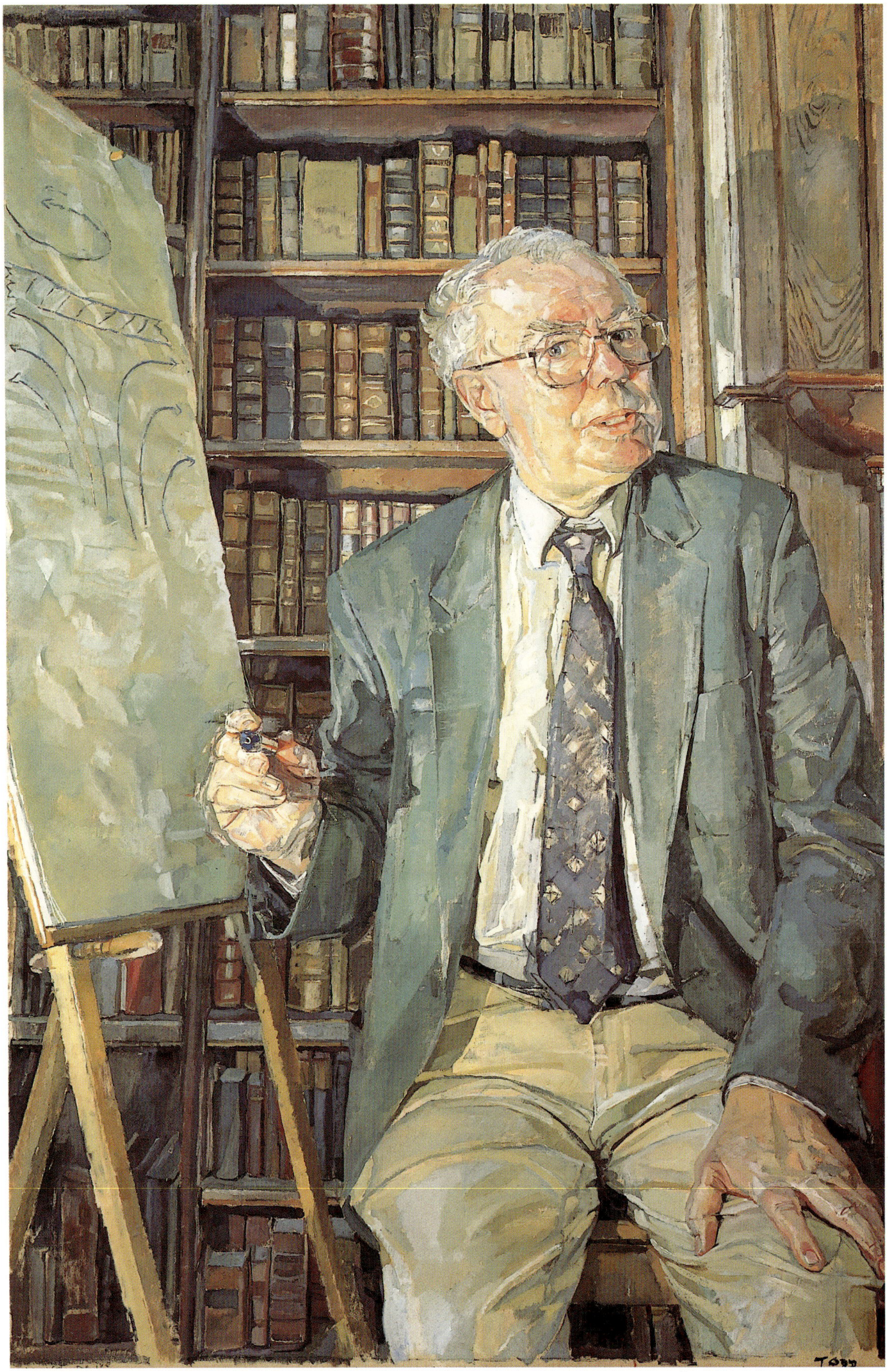

[103] *Professor John Albery FRS, Master, University College, Oxford*, 1997
114.3 x 76.2 cms 45 x 30 ins

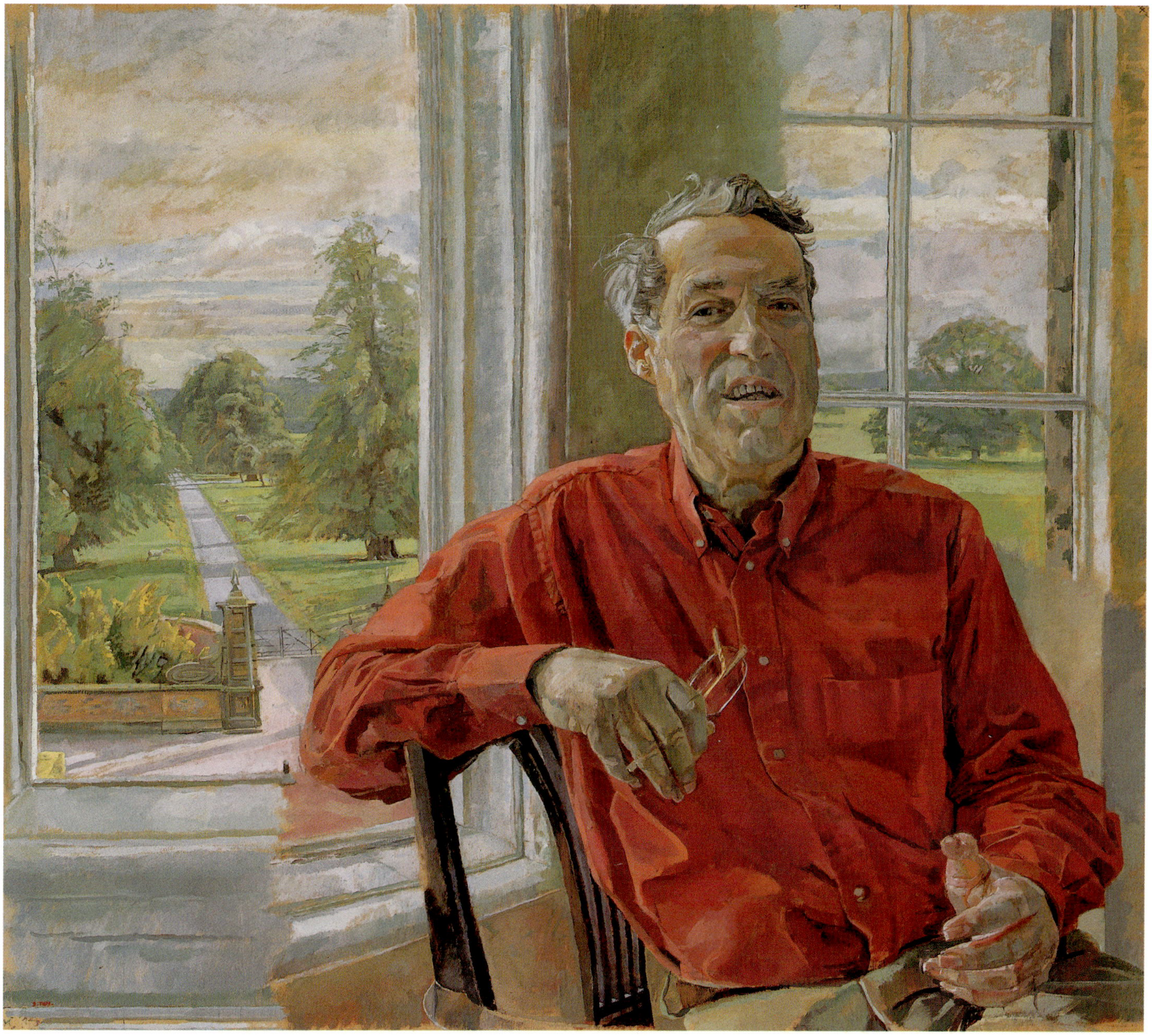

[104] *Charles Foster Esq, Arley Hall,* 2004
76.2 x 63.5 cms 30 x 25 ins

with them for fourteen years. Todd is herself fiercely independent and proud to be so. She has always been self-supporting financially and domestically, doing all her own housework and gardening. 'Coming from a lower middle class background, I didn't know anybody who had cleaners or any help. I do my own housework and always have. Portraits have made me a living and sent Mary to private school and I'm pleased about that, but I haven't got a pension. I think I'll die painting, as Cézanne did. I think it's good to know your future is in your own hands. It makes you do things that you might not otherwise do, and that's not a bad thing. Money is always desperately embarrassing. Everyone asks: who are you painting at the moment, and how much? It's none of their business. It's how you are painting that's relevant, not who and how much.' [22]

As each portrait commission poses new problems, Todd tries to approach each with an open mind. Sometimes the picture gets off to a flying start, sometimes there are complications. A commission by the Abbey National Building Society for a portrait of Lord Tugendhat at first seemed daunting, because he presented such a cool, business-like exterior. But his office opposite Baker Street Station offered marvellous views in two directions, out towards London zoo and over to the Post Office Tower, and his position at his desk between the windows became a sort of grid reference. When he came into his office he always took off his jacket and rolled up his sleeves. Todd painted him like this, with his security pass around his neck.

To Todd the space around the sitter is very important. 'You go into their space, and it's not just them, it's them in their space.' [23] For Dame Marilyn Strathern's portrait she painted a diptych, two heads on one panel and the view from her window at Girton College on the other. This was of a red brick wall, covering everything inside her room in a warm red glow. Dame Marilyn wrote of sitting for the portrait in the Cambridge Review: 'Daphne was extraordinarily open and generous. She shared with me the emerging picture, which I was able to observe as it happened, and described what she was doing with the colour… Coordination and composition seemed to summon themselves through the simplest application, except that it was not simple at all. As she explained, each individual application must work alongside all the other applications, in their company so to speak, and it is from this that the effectiveness of the colouring comes. There has to be, she implied, a

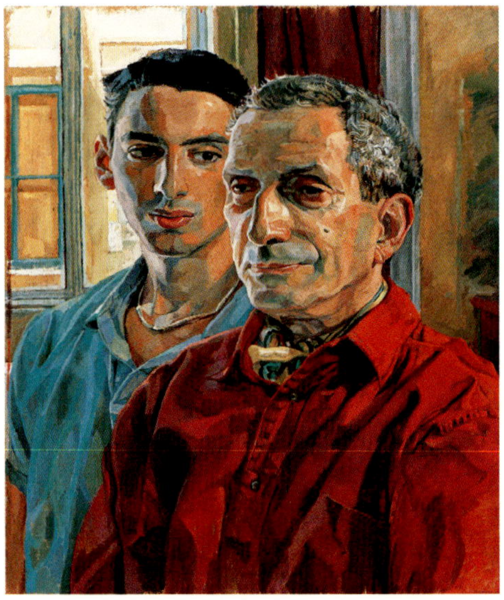

[105] *Maurice & James Minzly*, 2001
61 x 50.8 cms 24 x 20 ins

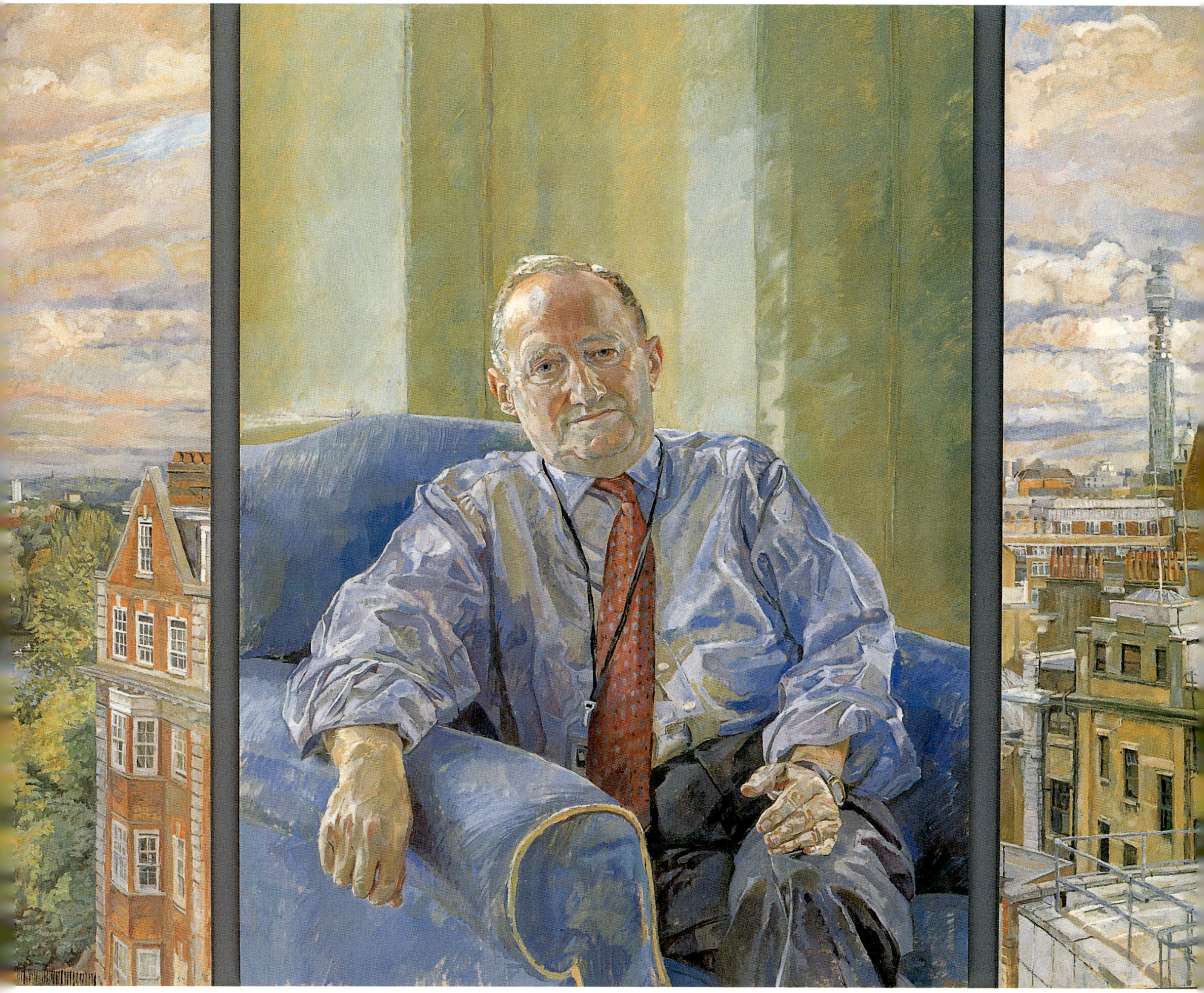

[106] *Lord Tugendhat at the Abbey National,* 2001
triptych 106.7 x 132.1 cms 42 x 52 ins

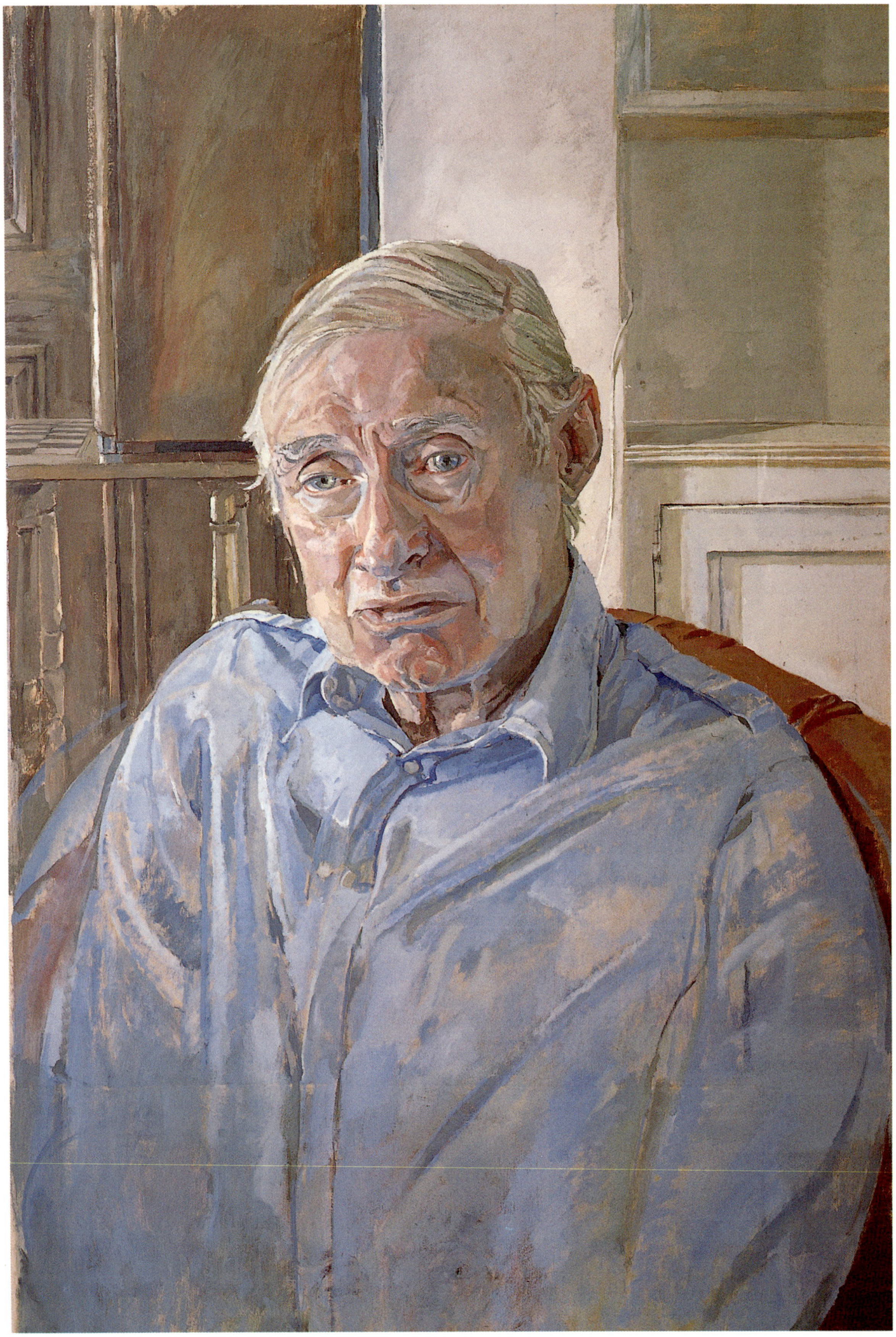

[107] *Unresolvable Painting of Spike Milligan, Looking Haunted*, 1995
88.9 x 60.5 cms
35 x 23⅞ ins

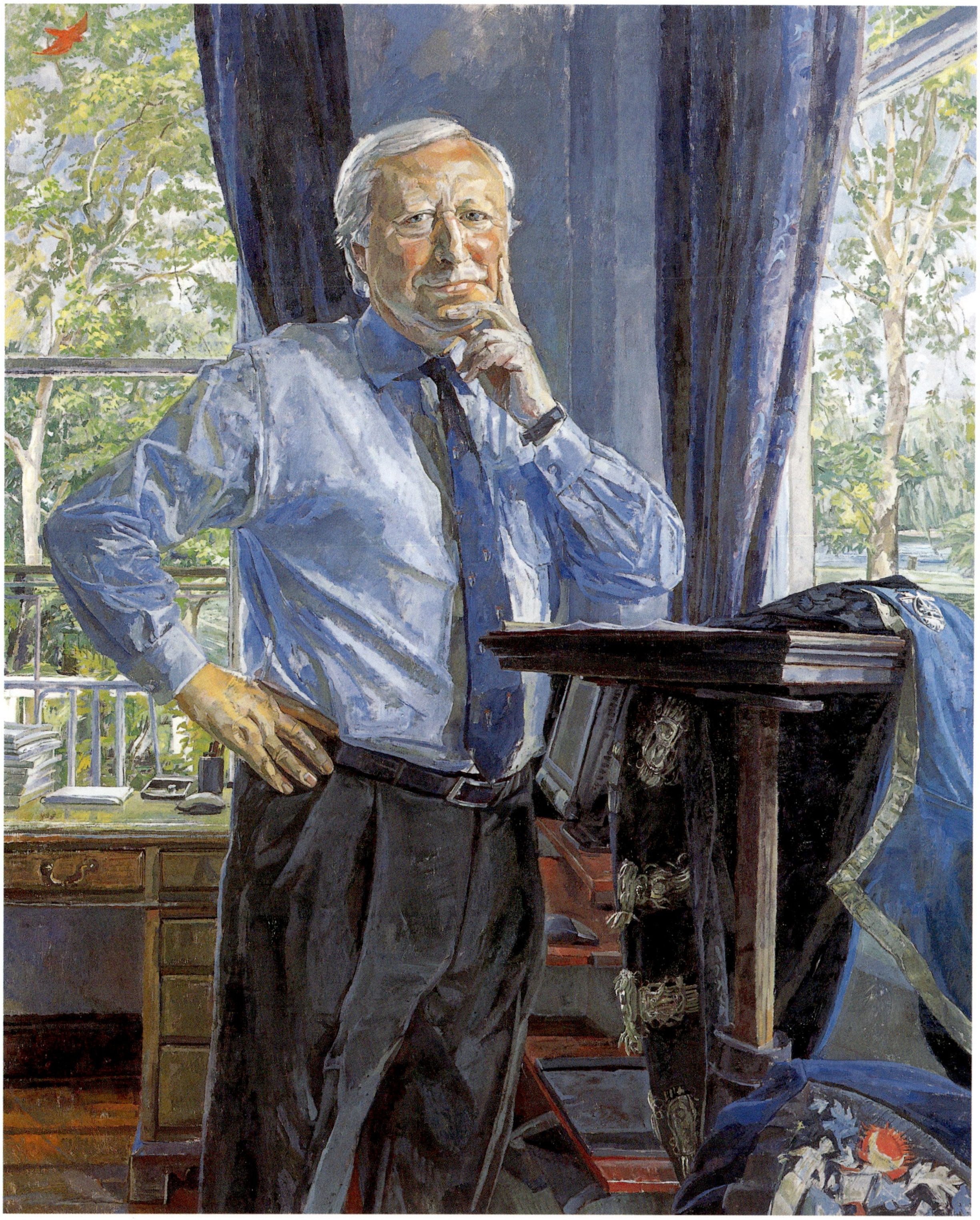

[108] *Professor Allan Templeton, President, Royal College of Obstetricians and Gynaecologists,* 200
106.7 x 86.4 cms 42 x 34 ins

constant translation between what is observed and the place that each minute brushstroke is going to have within the frame.' [24]

Todd's concern to place the sitter in a telling environment was apparent in her portrait of the mezzo-soprano Dame Janet Baker, commissioned by the National Portrait Gallery. As Dame Janet recorded, 'Daphne wanted to paint me at my home. She looked around the house for somewhere suitable, and decided in the end that we should do it in the attic of all places, which was not very tidy and not very clean and was absolutely stifling in the heat. She planted me on a chair in a long dress and wanted me to hold the score I was learning at the time – it was some Chausson, as I recall. Any score I was working on I used to carry with me everywhere, and this one was terribly tatty and battered. I thought it would have been better to hold something new, but Daphne wanted a sense of realism. She told me when she started painting that "I'm not a painter who flatters", and my heart sank. It wasn't that I wanted to be flattered, but nor did I want to be exaggeratedly unlike myself. The finished painting did come as quite a shock, because it seemed to me that she had painted the person I was destined to become. I don't simply mean that she made me look older, but somehow there was a gravitas that was certainly a part of me but which I had not completely acquired.' [25]

The portrait of Bill Holland, Head of Universal records, also evolved from first impressions. 'I had done one head and then I saw another one, and then another. Although it's not one expression blending into another as in a film, you get more of an idea of the person through seeing several expressions. Each head has its own bit of background, patched together. He was playing CDs at the time and tears were pouring down his cheeks. I painted the CDs from life. The last couple of days I was there from 9am to 6pm without any real break and they kept bringing me sandwiches. He would go away to have a rest and I would carry on.' [26] This painting's circular composition of four sentient, thinking heads spinning around an imaginary axis is superbly resolved.

Sir Christopher Ondaatje, whom Todd has painted several times, made a perspicacious evaluation of her portraiture. 'A third portrait now hangs in the National Portrait Gallery. The results of her efforts still entice both criticism and praise – but no-one can possibly deny that her images reveal an amazing amount of truth. It is almost as if she has gouged out my soul with her fingers and then, using some magic,

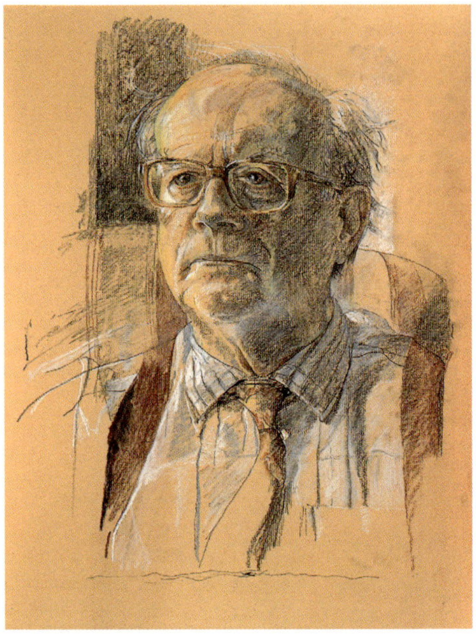

[109] *Lord Ashburton KG KCVO DC*, 1999
38.1 x 27.9 cms 15 x 11 ins

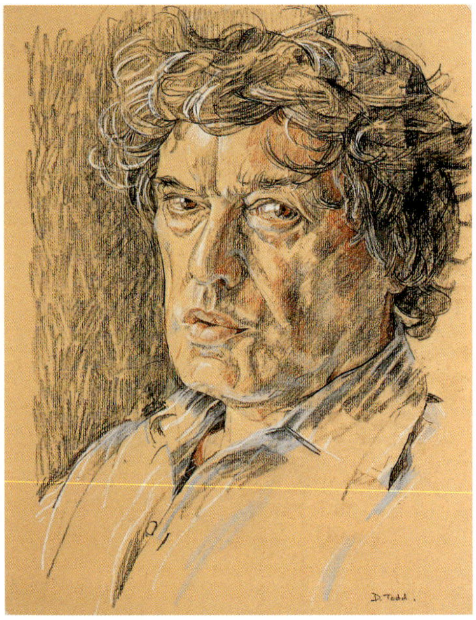

[110] *Sir Tom Stoppard OM*, 2002
40.6 x 30.5 cms 16 x 12 ins

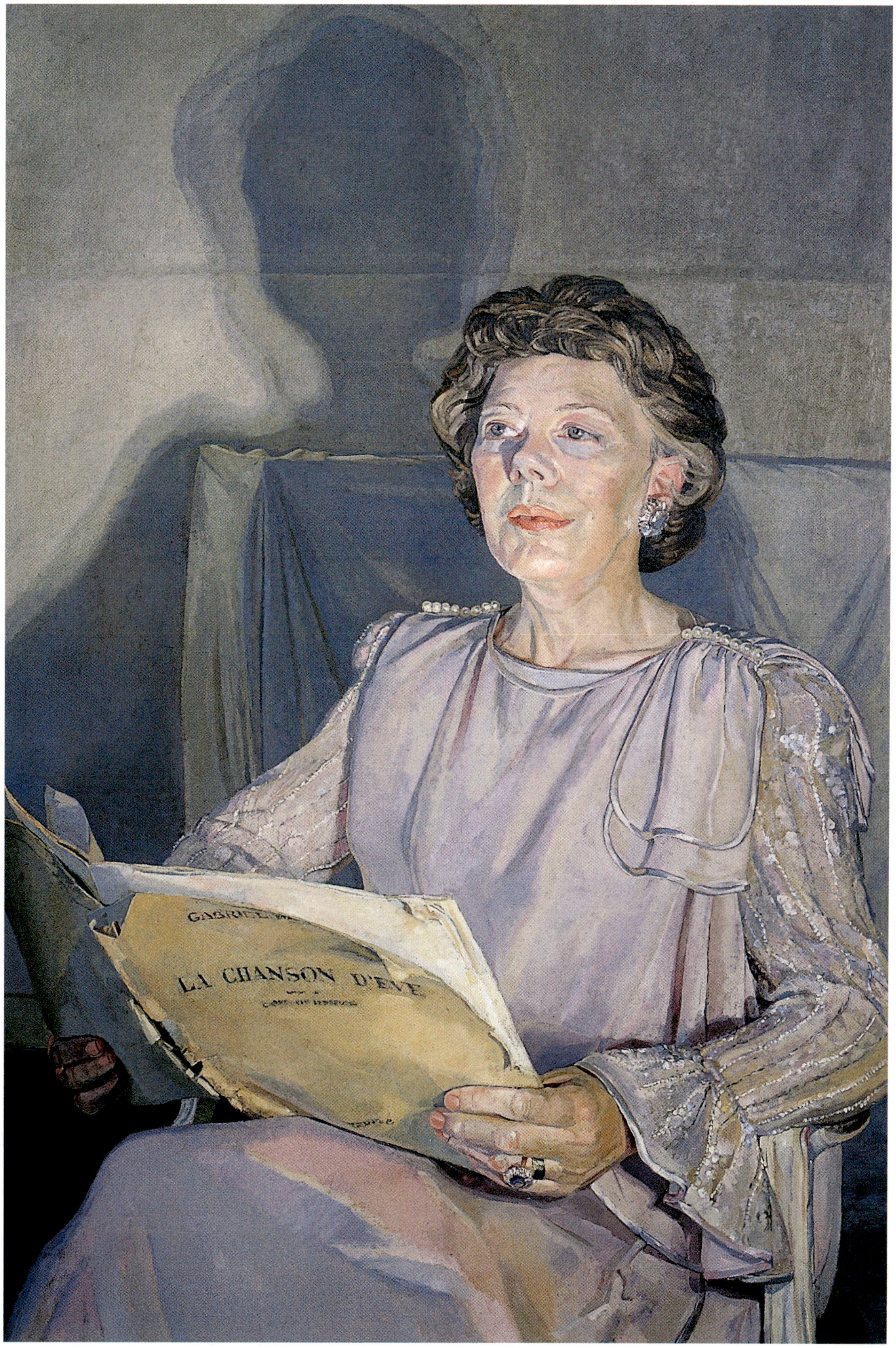

[111] *Dame Janet Baker DBE,* 19
91.4 x 61 cms 36 x 24 ins

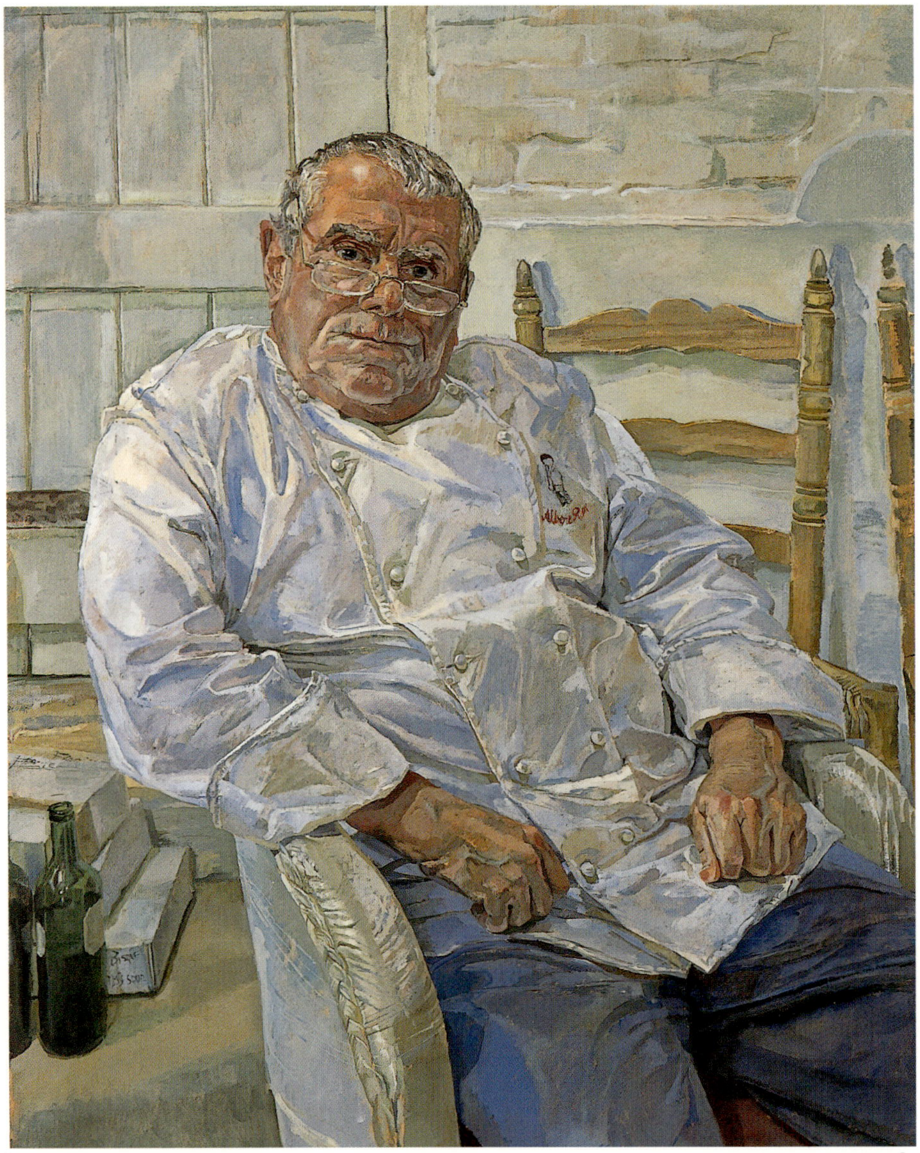

[112] *Albert Roux OBE, Le Gavroche*, 2003
86.4 x 68.6 cms 34 x 27 ins

Opposite:
[113] *The Chef and Butler, Lincoln College, Oxford*, 2007
121.9 x 91.4 cms 48 x 36 ins

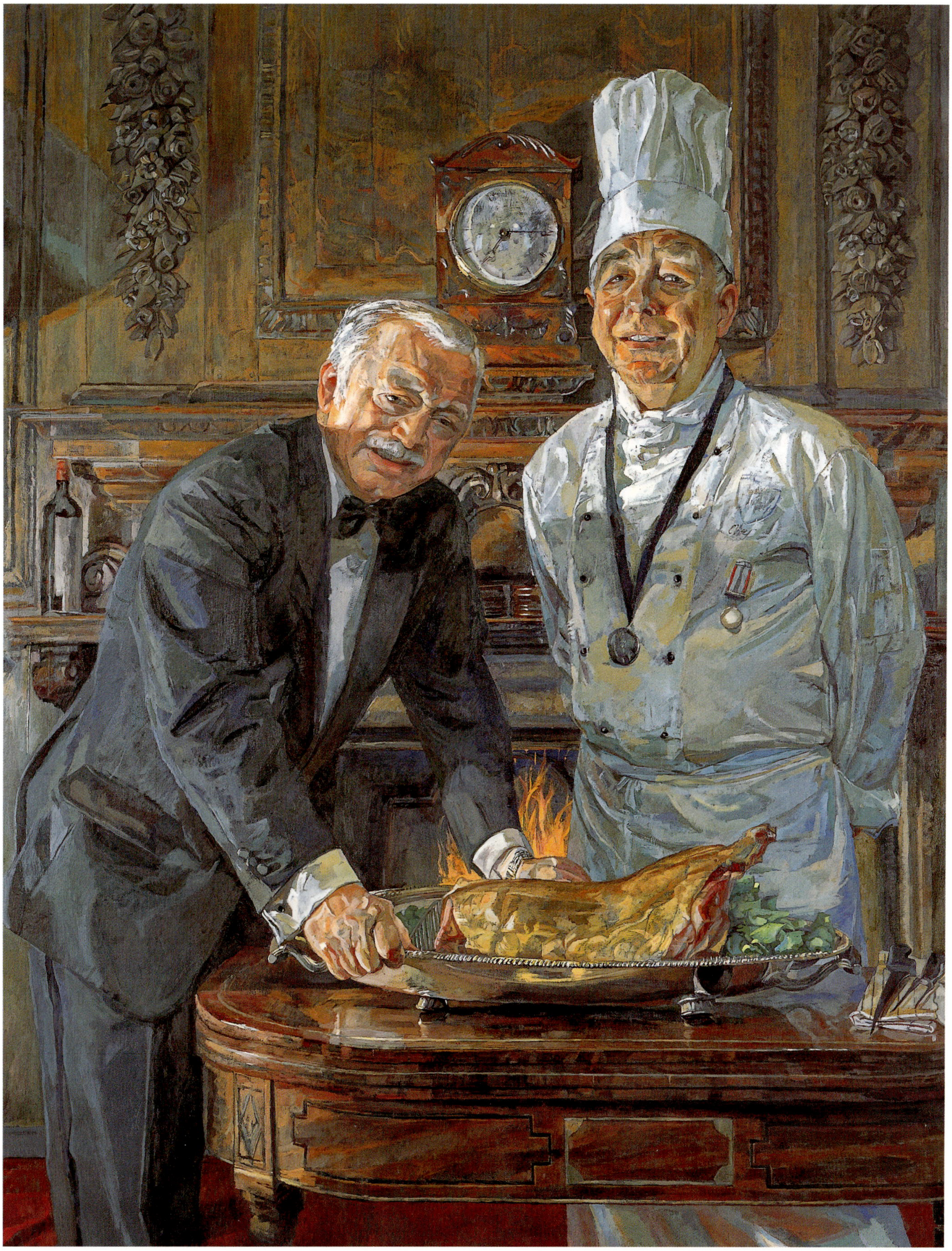

smeared it on her canvas. One needs a certain amount of courage to allow Daphne to do this. She misses nothing. It is difficult to hide… She is currently one of the best established mid-career artists of her generation with an unforgiving analytical eye but with a clear humanity as well, good at revealing unseen attributes of an individual's personality and responding to the precise mood and atmosphere of the English landscape.' [27]

Lord Morris of Castle Morris wrote, in a letter to Todd, about her drawing of him which he used as the cover for his book: 'I could see new things in it all the time… I was nervous, easily intimidated, defensive, and it was many years before I perfected the disguise made up of being "on guard", able to make any opponent laugh or look silly, trusting no-one, and giving the general impression that I believed I was as good as the next man. The picture registers all that, the look in the eyes, and the marvellous ambiguity in the line of the lips, THOUGH ONLY I COULD POSSIBLY SEE IT. Certainly, you could not have known it, or expressed it in words, and not even my close family could describe it. It is a marvellous image, the work of an artist of real stature and brilliant penetration, deep sensitivity and masterly technical skill. I love looking at it and in a strange way I am proud of it.' [28]

In an electrifying recent portrait of the art critic William Packer Todd felt free to do what she wanted because he was also a painter. She did not want to think about composition but just to dive in and paint. She started with a small board for the head, but the presence of his body was so insistent that she added it on another board, and pieced the two together on different levels. The doubled-up image emphasises the different focal points as well as suggesting more space. A recent portrait of Andrew Wilton, from the Tate, is similarly irregular. 'I started it in the same way as with Packer, with the head, and semi-incised where I might want to add to it. During the second sitting a beautiful young man appeared in red pyjamas and sat at his feet. He went into the picture so the concept changed, but try as I might I could not get to the edges of the background, so I cut them out. Because birch veneer can be cut anywhere it means you can start in the way that's natural to you.' [29]

Always working directly from life, Todd is critical of portraits that appear to mimic photographic exposures. 'A photograph tends to bleach out the lit areas, in lamplight for example, whereas in real life when you look at a lit area you see more, not less, so you can tell what is about a

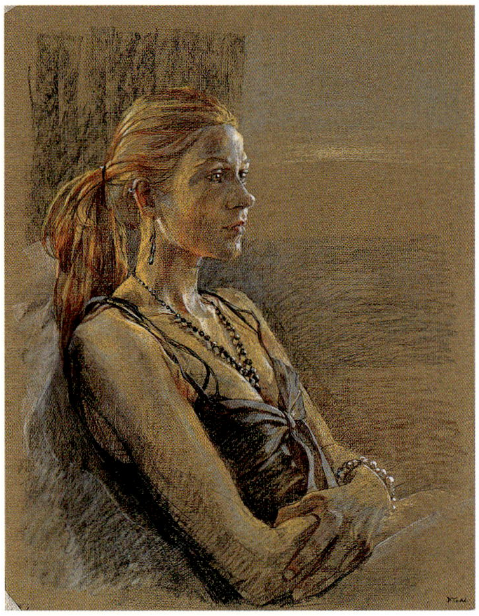

[114] *Daisy Collins,* 2007
61 x 40.6 cms 24 x 16 ins

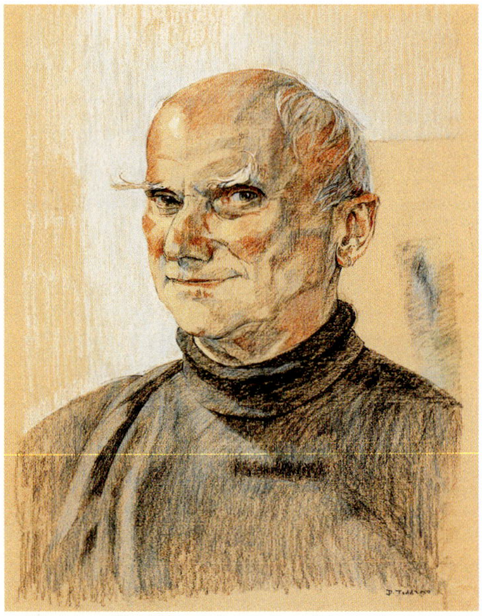

[115] *Lord Morris of Castle Morris,* 2000
45.7 x 27.9 cms 18 x 11 ins

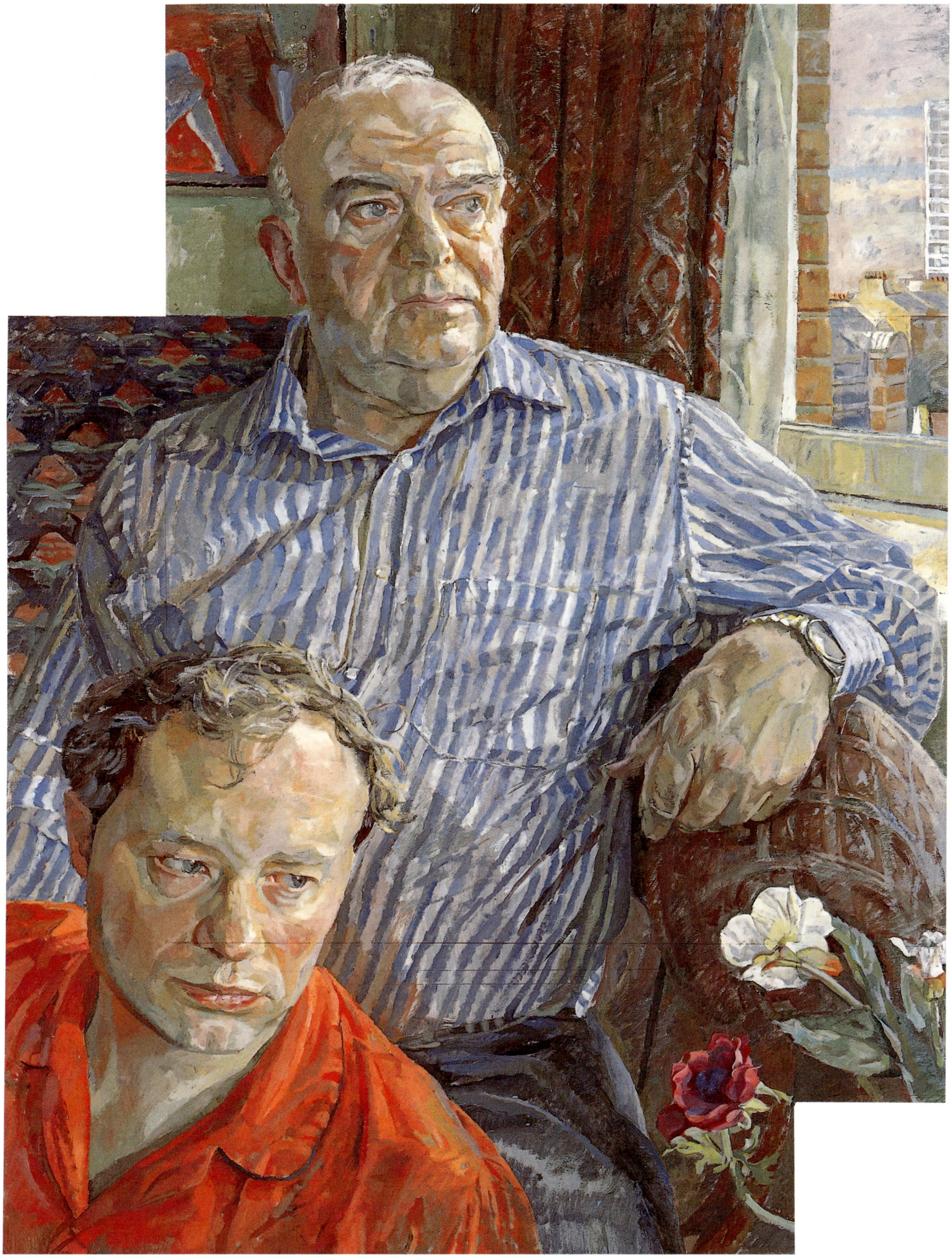

[116] *Andrew Wilton with Russell in Red Pyjamas,* 2007
71.1 x 58.4 cms 28 x 23 ins

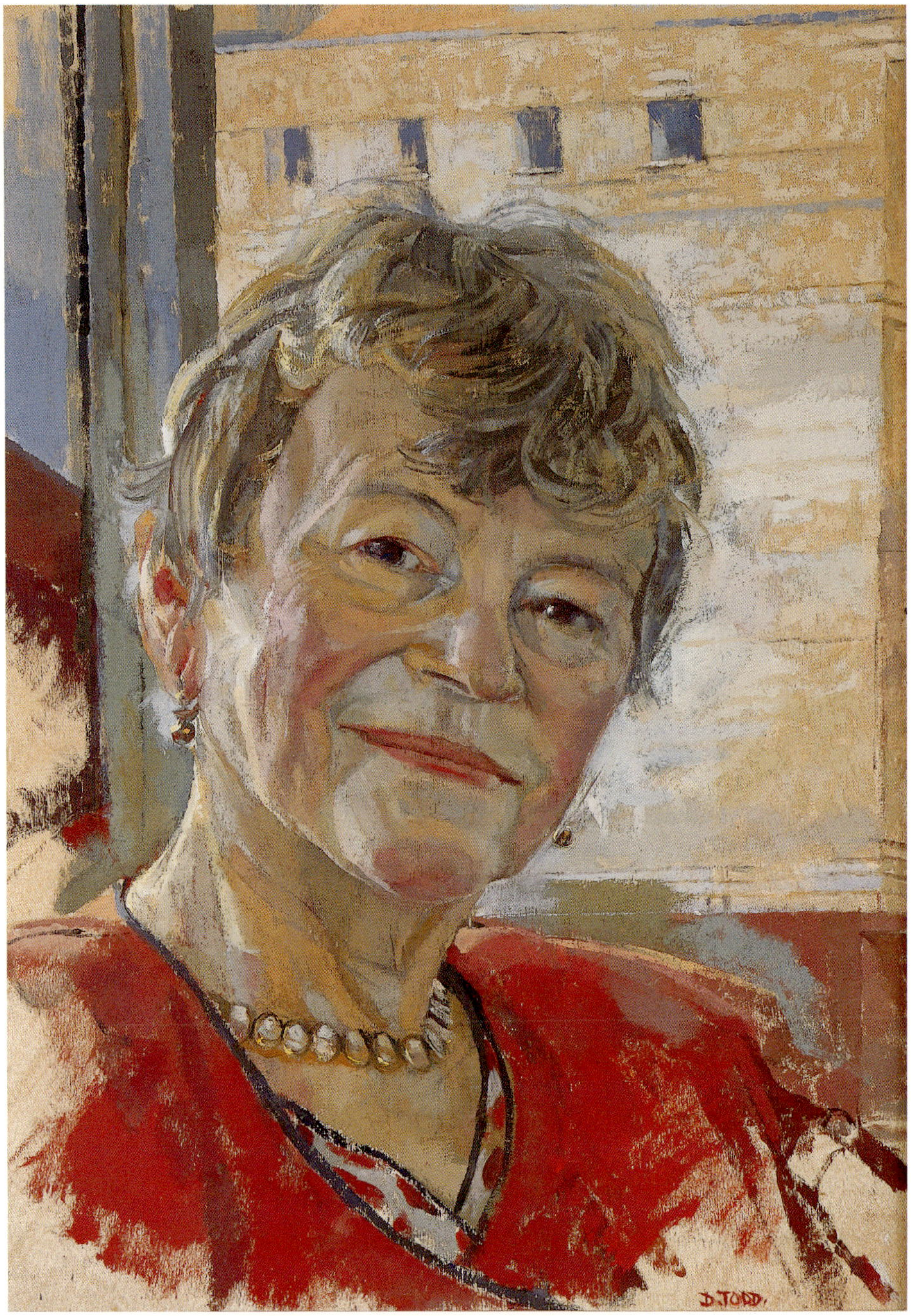

[117] *Head Study, Dame Anne Mueller,* 2000
c. 45.7 x 30.5 cms 18 x 12 ins

Opposite:
[118] *Dame Anne Mueller DCB, First Chancellor, De Montfort University,* 1996
152.4 x 101.6 cms 60 x 40 ins

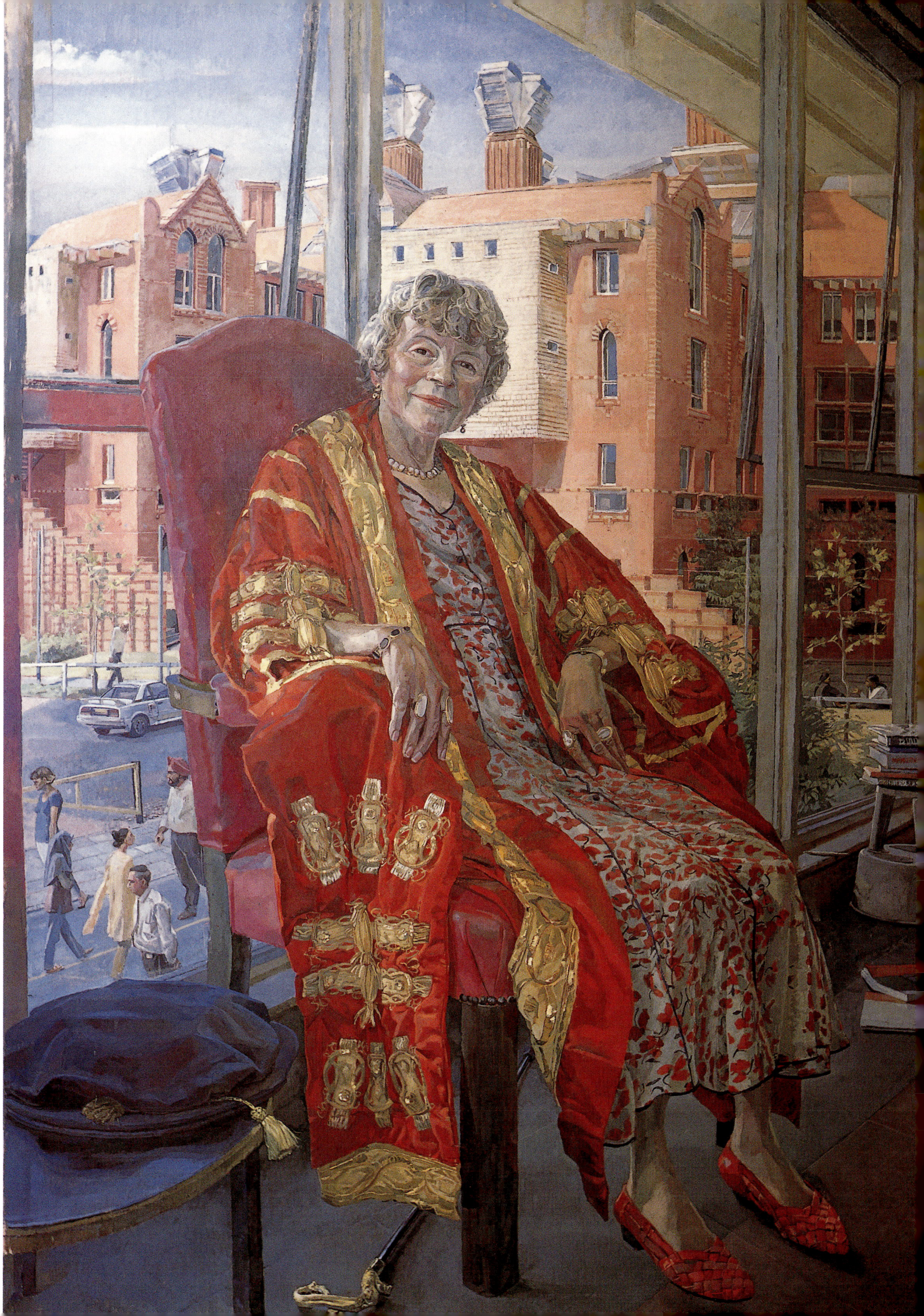

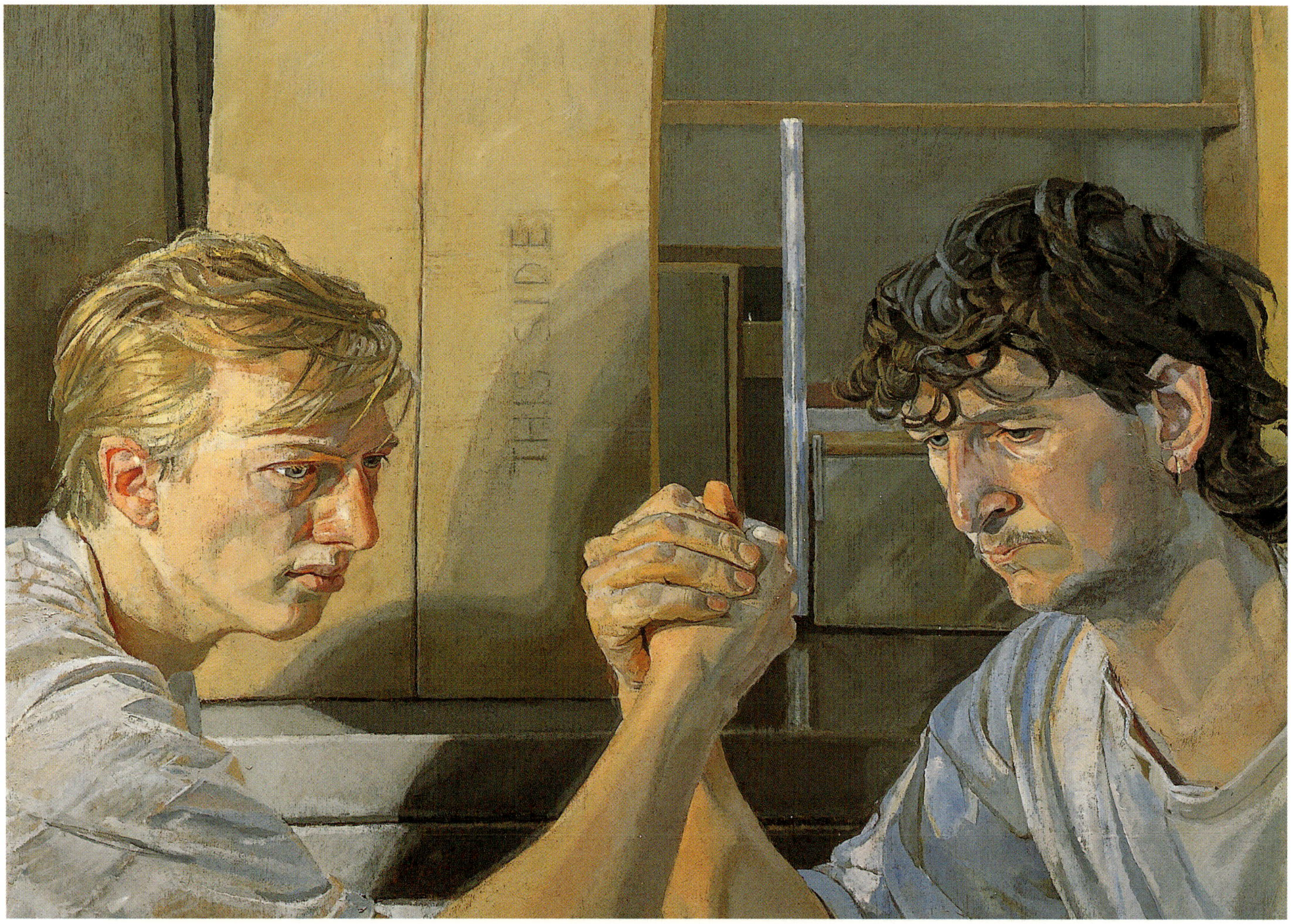

[120] *Contest,* 1992
45.7 x 63.5 cms 18 x 25 ins

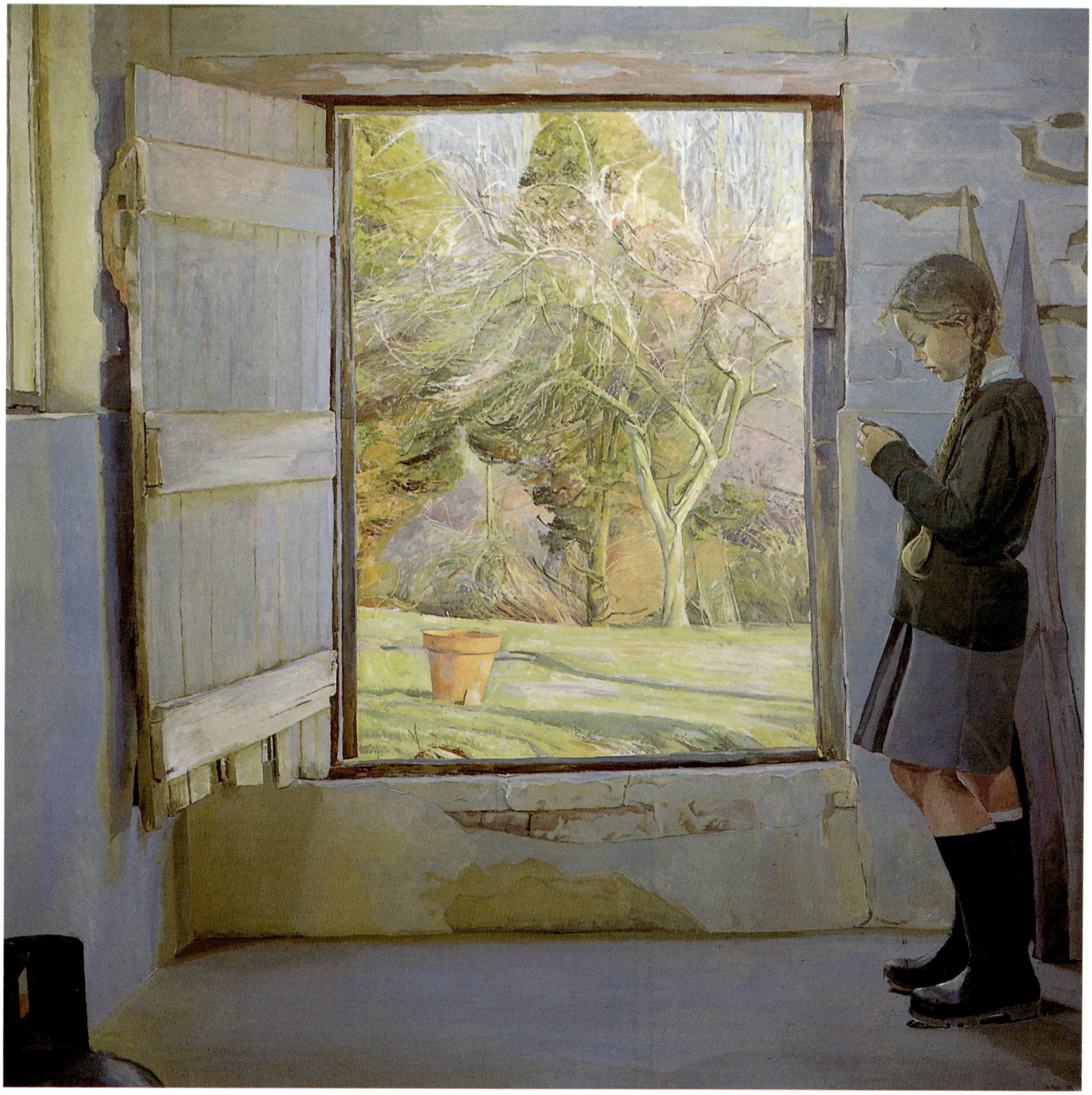

[121] *Mary by the Barn Door,* 1985
121.9 x 121.9 cms 48 x 48 ins

hedge with the fields beyond. The view is out of the window, down the garden, through the trees and far away. The models are family and friends, flaked out after a party, playing cards, just sitting. In short, of whoever or whatever happens to be there, registered by a quietly edgy eye, sharply drawn and crisply painted.' [31]

Liz Rideal, curator of the exhibition *Mirror Mirror*, writing of Todd's *Self-Portrait*, picked up on Todd's concern with rendering the complexity of her perceptions truthfully, and also on her ability to juggle the various elements in her life. 'Todd has often been preoccupied with framing the subject within the space of the picture plane, as in her portrait of the tall figure of Christopher Ondaatje in the National Portrait Gallery's collection, caught (almost jammed) within the doorway of his library. In her self-portrait the round magnifying mirror acts as a centralising device separating the various aspects of her life; outside the sunset of a Sussex landscape and the watery pool of her farm, and inside the abstract colours of the different parts of life – the "real" (outdoor, outer, physical) versus the "abstract" (inside internal, cerebral). It is a bold and knowing work, specific, powerful, complex yet modest in scale. It is typical in palette, with the familiar and strange mixture of oranges with pinks and indigo/violets that have become her trademark.' [32]

Daphne Todd is a painter first, a portraitist second. The surfaces she studies, whether in a landscape, a still life or a human head, present her with the same painterly problems. A tree, a flower-pot, an arm or hand, are subjected to the same intense scrutiny as the features of a face, the musculature of a head creating similar rhythms in paint to those of wind-lashed trees or weather-worn buildings. Todd approaches a human head in exactly the same way as any other subject, having no set method or preconceived idea. To do so would be totally against her principles. As she says, 'deliberately not having a view is an important part of it. One shouldn't be thinking too much. I want to be neutral and receptive. Each time there is a new set of surfaces to explore. It's like doing a performance, with a certain amount of adrenalin running, making snappier judgements and there's the sitter watching you all the time. I like to know where things are going to be – I think you have to compose – I do sometimes start with the left eye as you are not meant to. I think you place your first mark where it is meant to be against the corners of the painting, but I don't necessarily plot everything. I now paint on a grey ground so that I can whizz the paint on and not have to

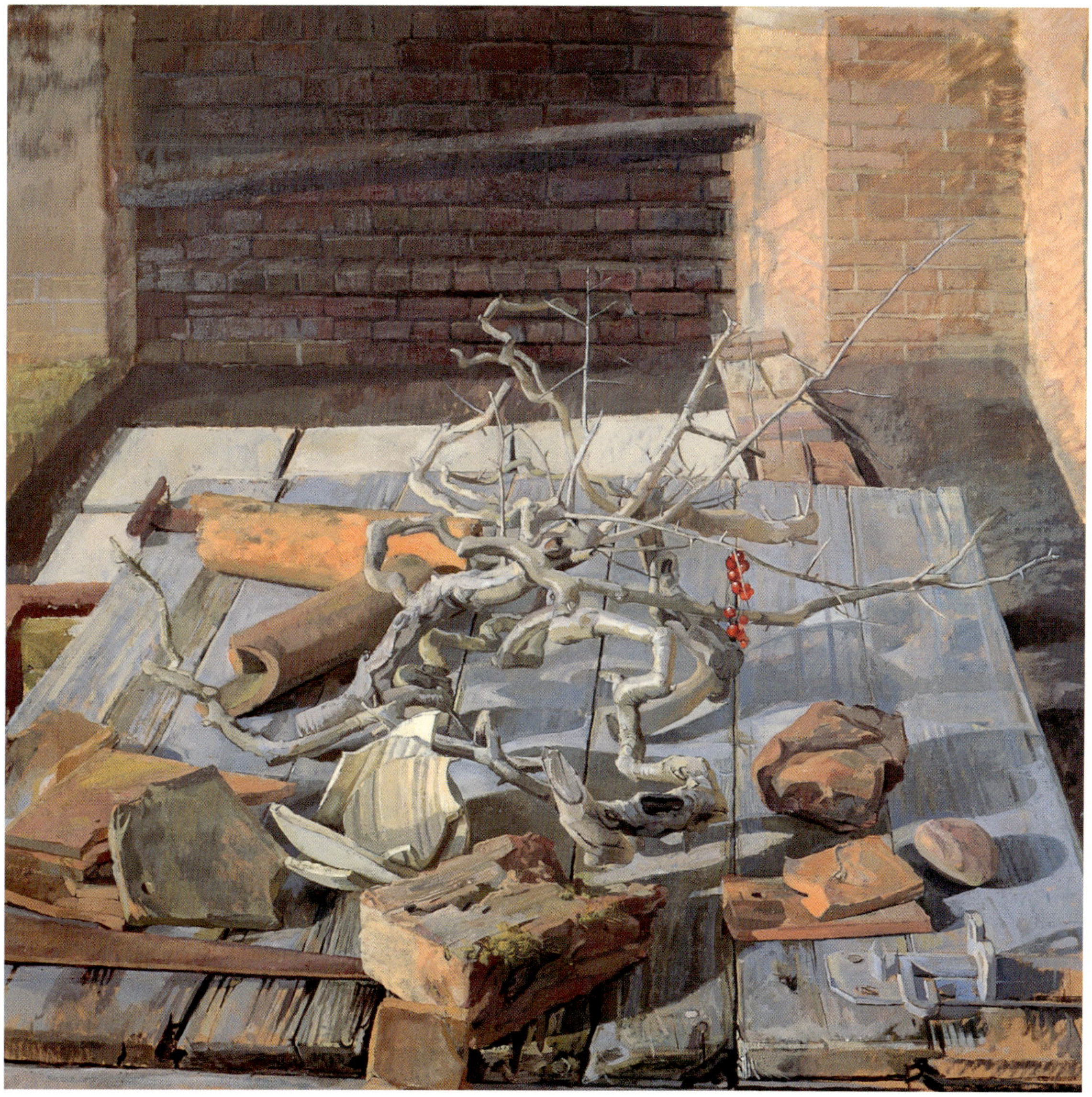

[122] *Crown of Thorns*, 1988
71.1 x 71.1 cms 28 x 28 ins

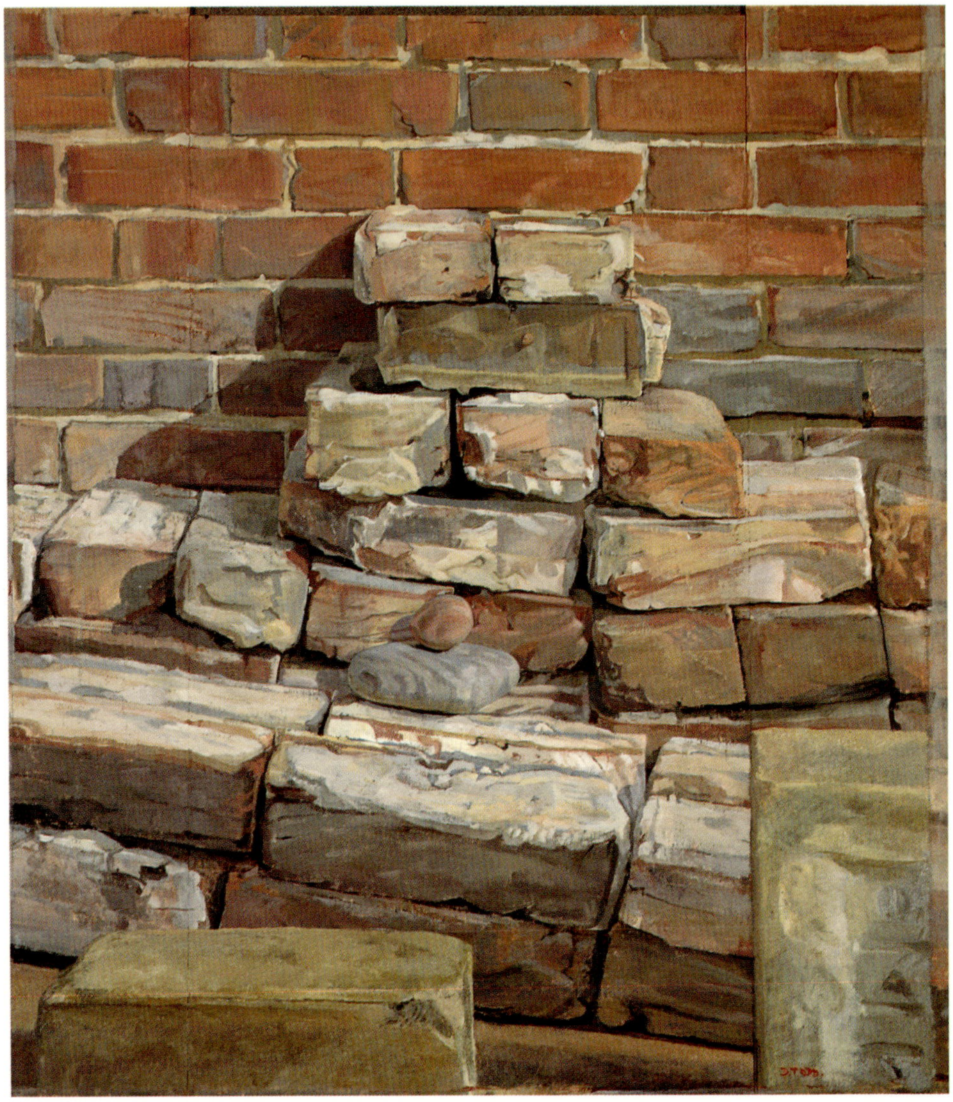

[123] *Bricks and Stones,* 2000
58.4 x 50.8 cms 23 x 20 ins

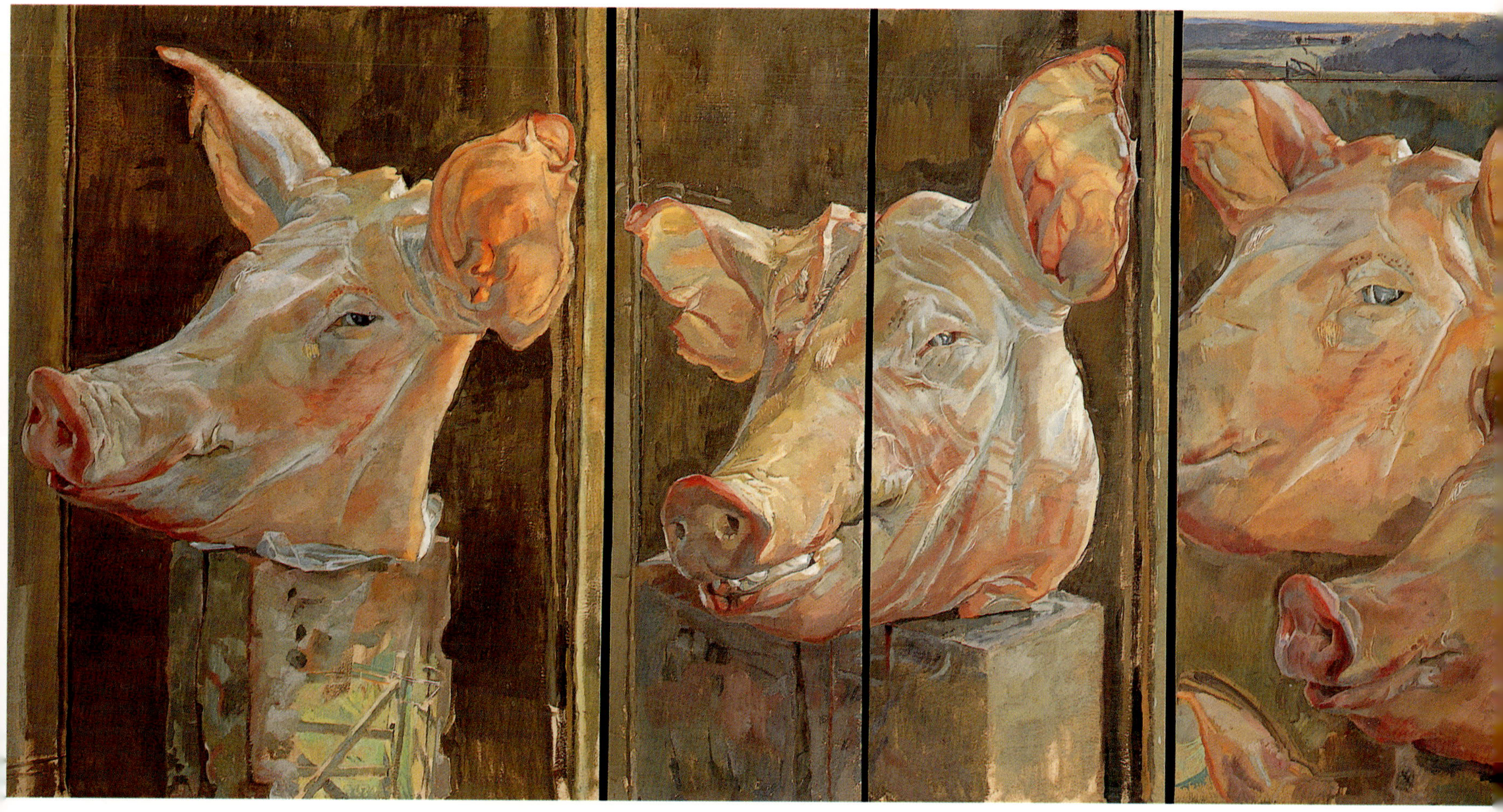

[124] *Oh, Pink Piggy,* 2004
45.7 x 86.4 cms 18 x 34 ins

fill in the tiny paint gaps later. I can leave bits out and let the grey shine through, so it's more like drawing.' [33]

Although the commissions continue to roll in, and her tally of portraits continues to rise, Todd does not regard herself in any way as a traditional portrait-painter. 'I'm not thinking about tradition, I'm just looking. There are portrait painters who are trying to make paintings to look like other paintings and I'm not. I'm taking the raw material and thinking how can I catch something from this and make a painting out of it. How do you catch all these bits that are floating past you at speed, disappearing, changing all the time? Sadly, I don't think this way of working is the norm any more as it's not being taught in our schools. There may be little pockets where actually looking at things is being kept alive, and sorting out these problems of getting three dimensions into two and how to deal with your psychological take on it as well as the purely mechanical reality of what's out there. It's a very very rich experience and because of its richness each person will get a different set of criteria out of it and automatically be original.' [34]

Daphne Todd clearly loves paint, although she is concerned to keep it lean and try not to 'build' texture with it. She uses paint as a draughtsman, skimming the surface of her boards with delicate, feathery marks. Her eyes dart over her subjects and the profusion of marks put down in response to what she sees coalesce to produce images that glitter with vivid life. The profusion of marks that animates the surfaces of her pictures also produces a brittle quality, emphasised by the light tonality and unusual colour combinations. Whereas Victorian portraitists rescued form from the gloom of dark backgrounds, Todd creates form by following the fall of light and keeping everything as light as possible. But despite the high-key colour her paintings have a sharp edge of anxiety. There is a gleam and crackle to the paint, as if her intense vision were generating static electricity. Although her paintings avowedly record simple visual fact, we sense that there is a complex inner world adding force to the observed image. We are confronting a looking-glass world where enigmatic dramas are being played out and things are not quite what they seem. In her studio Todd moves between her inner and her outer world, looking, thinking, questioning, remembering and resolving.

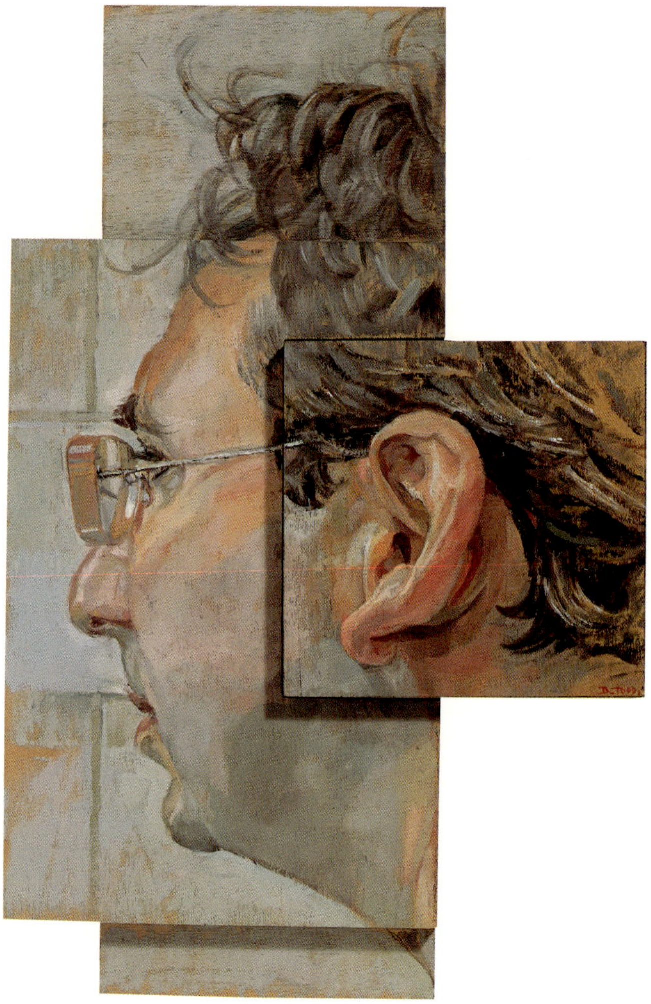

[125] *Mark Sanders: The Ear,* 2002
22.9 x 12.7 cms 9 x 5 ins

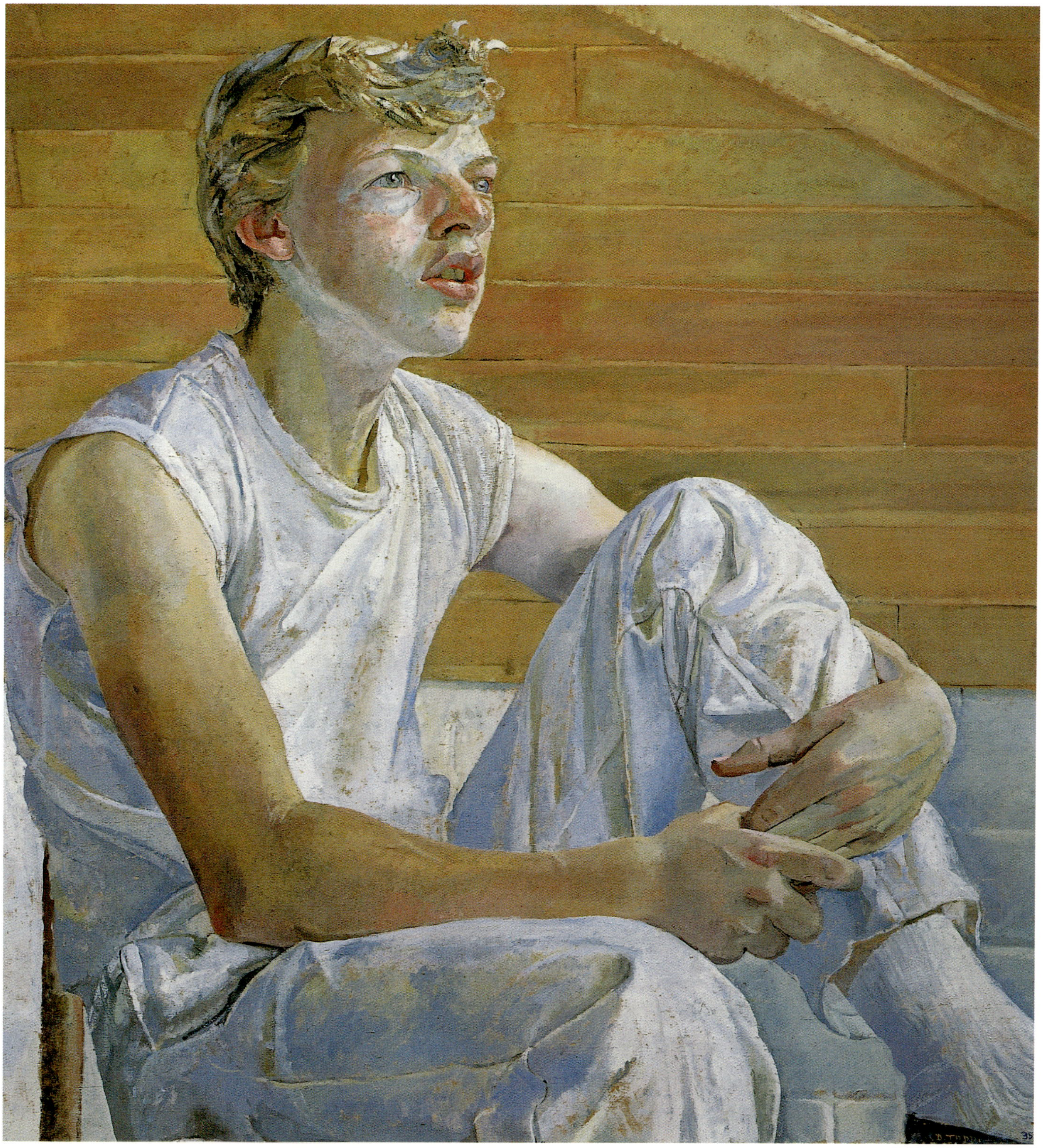

[126] *Boy in White*
63.5 x 58.4 cms 25 x 23 ins

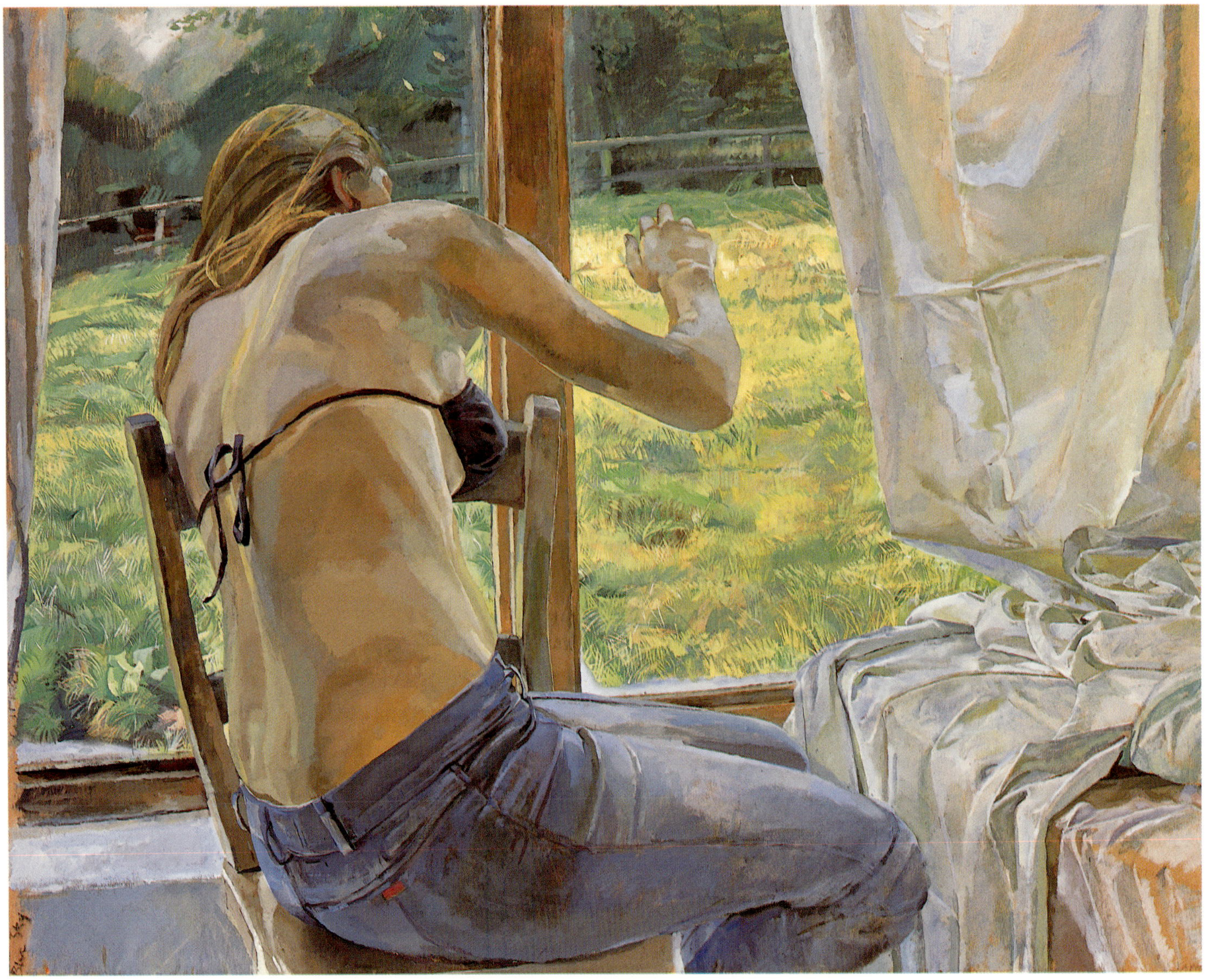

[127] *Is He Coming?* 2005
71.8 x 88.3 cms 28¼ x 34¾ ins

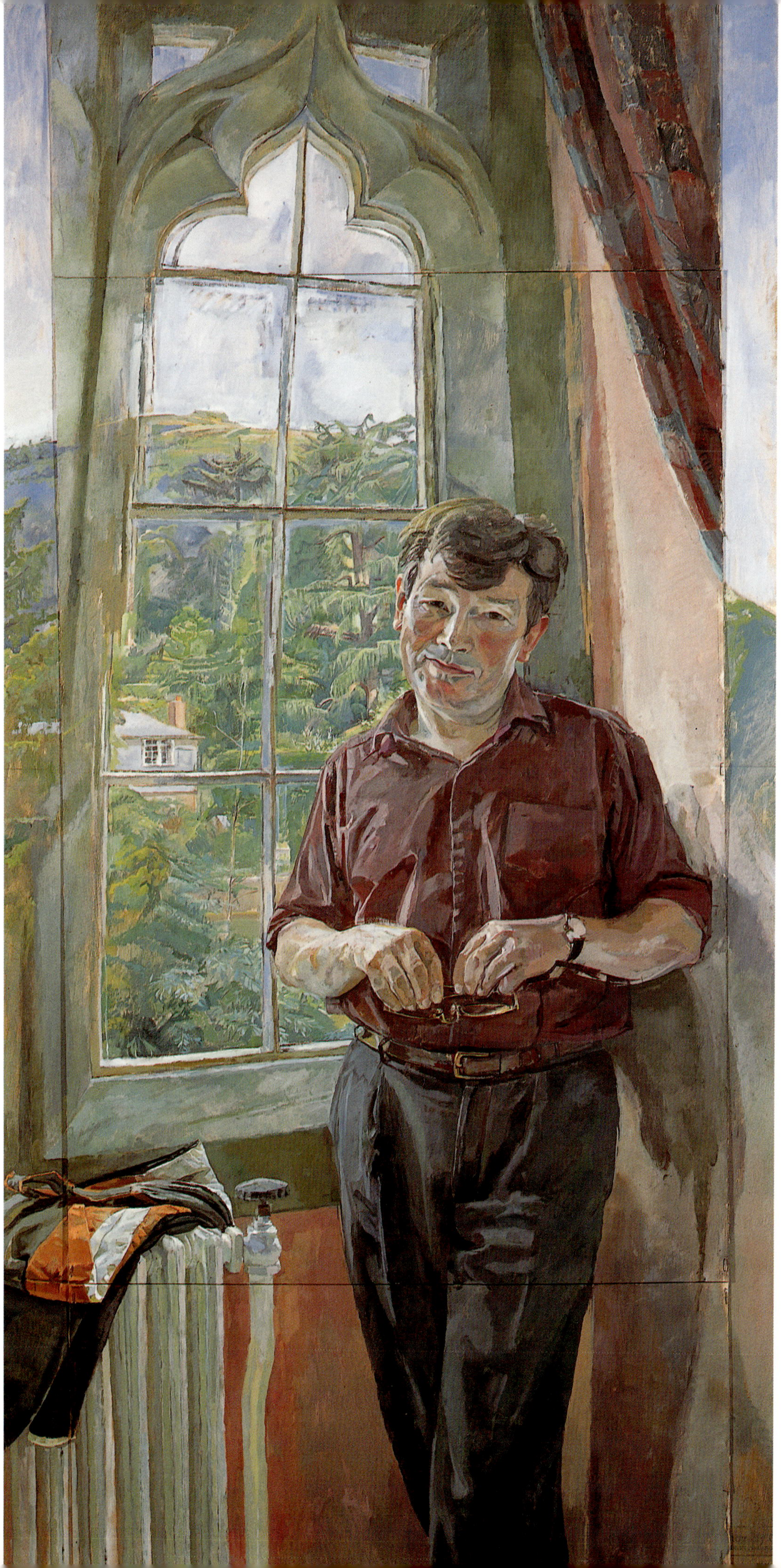

[128] *Hugh Carson, Headmaster, Malvern College*, 2005
167.6 x 190.5 cms
66 x 75 ins

(Photographed before the panels were professionally mounted at differing levels.)

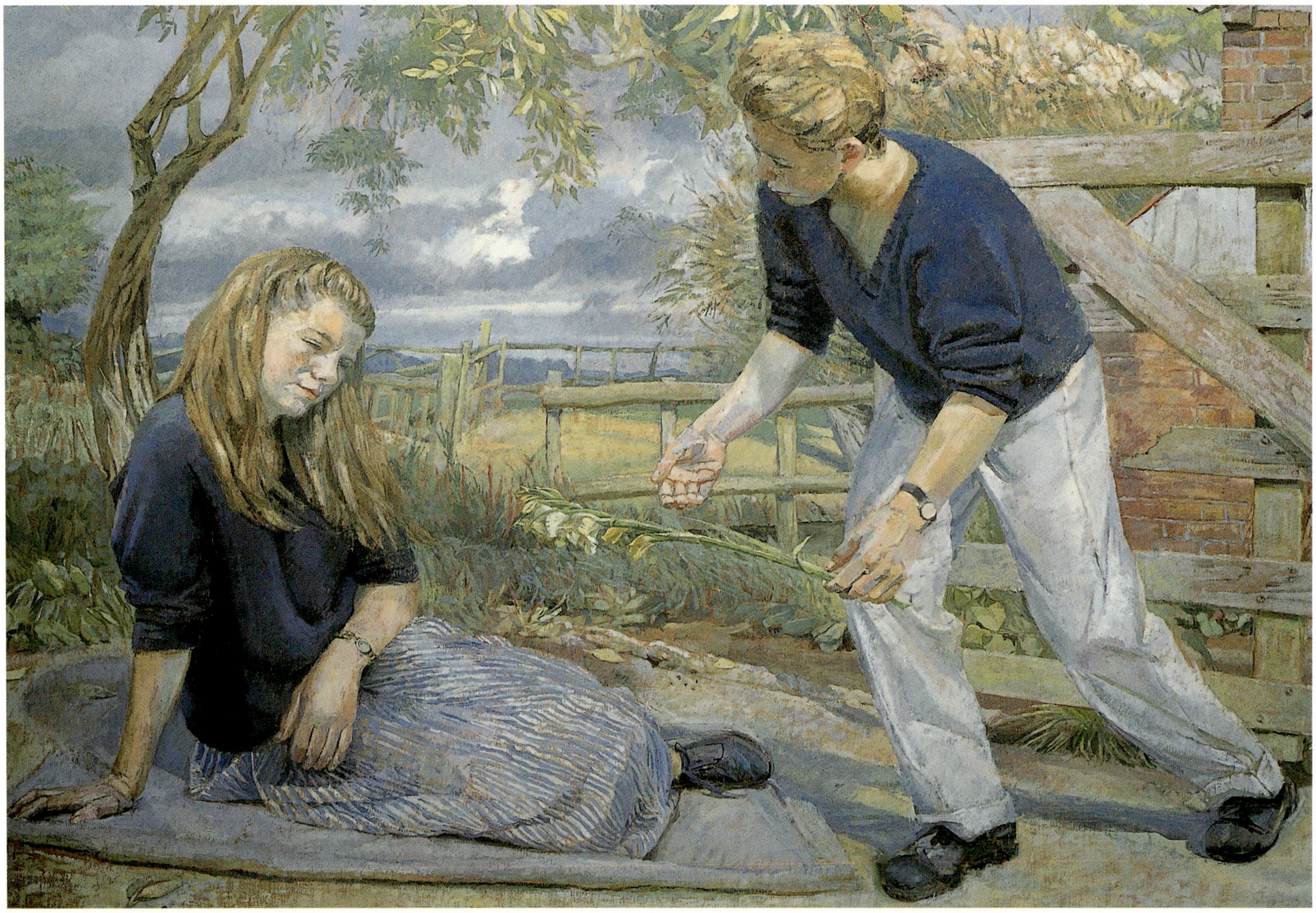

[129] *Two Figures and a Flower*, c.1995
67 x 101 cms 27½ x 39½ ins

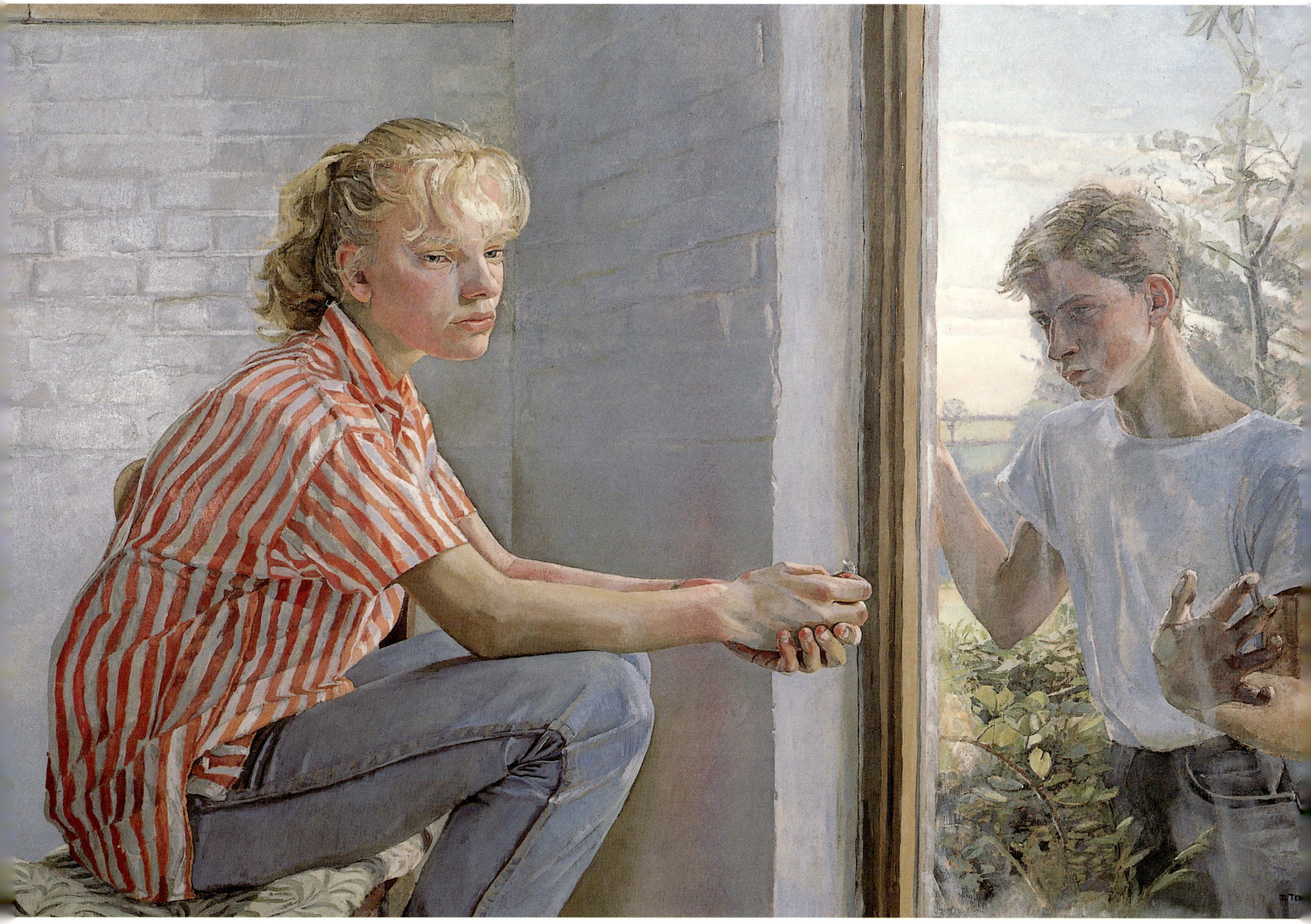

[130] *Boy Looking In,* 2000
71.1 x 106.7 cms 28 x 42 ins

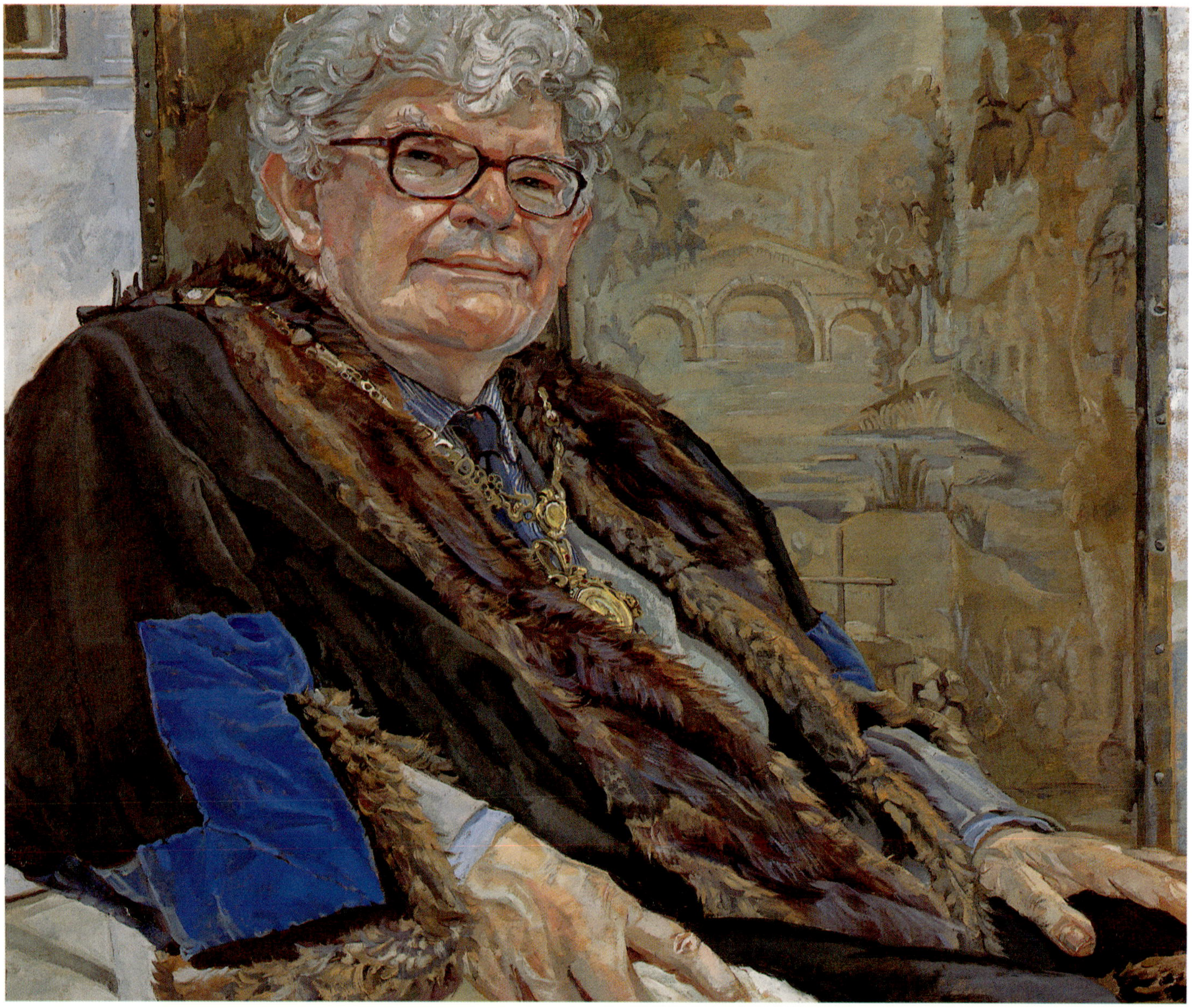

[131] *Arnold Stevenson, Past Master, Worshipful Company of Painter-Stainers,* 2002
53.3 x 63.5 cms 21 x 25 ins

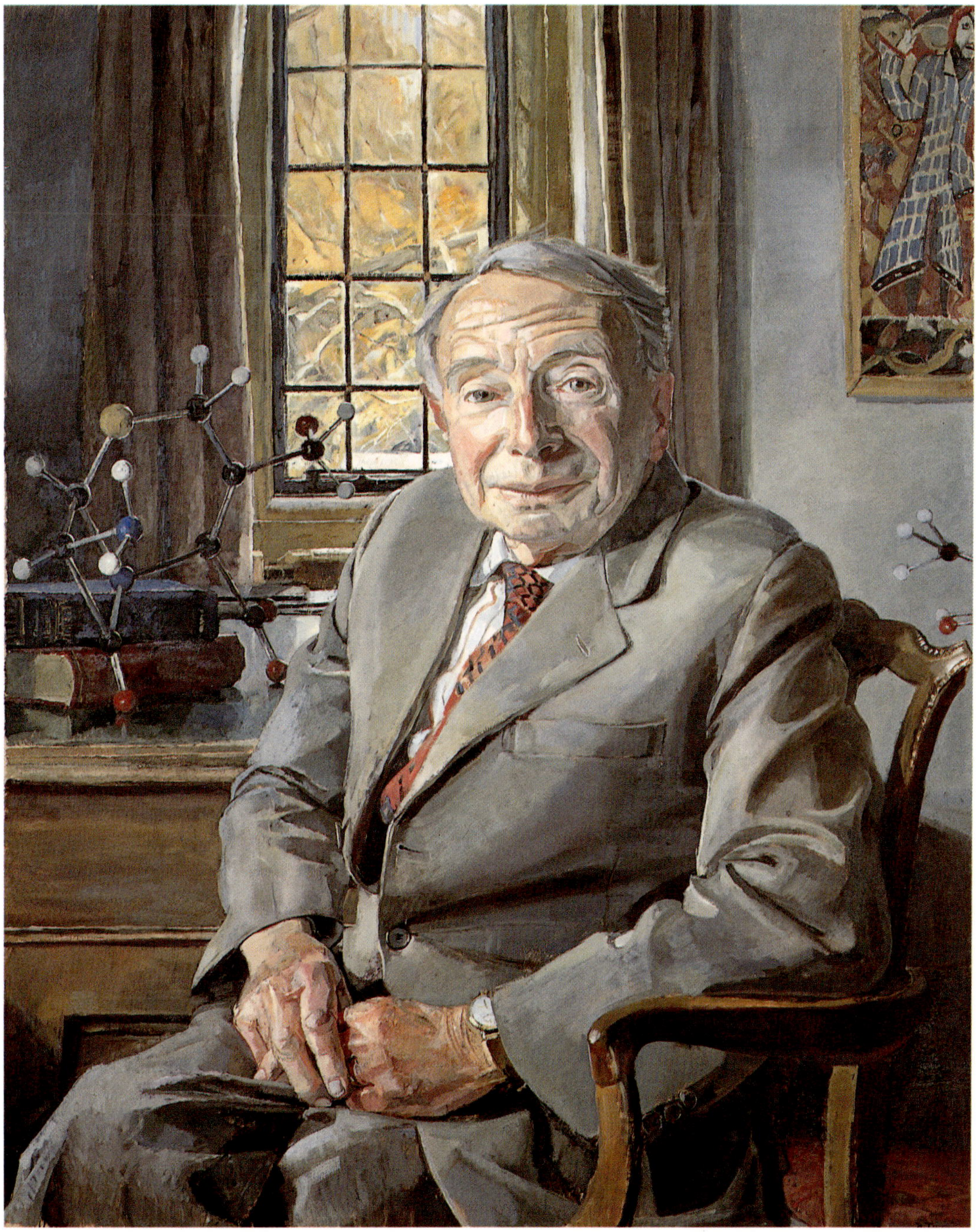

[132] *Sir Edward Abraham*, 1991
91.4 x 71.1 cms 36 x 28 ins

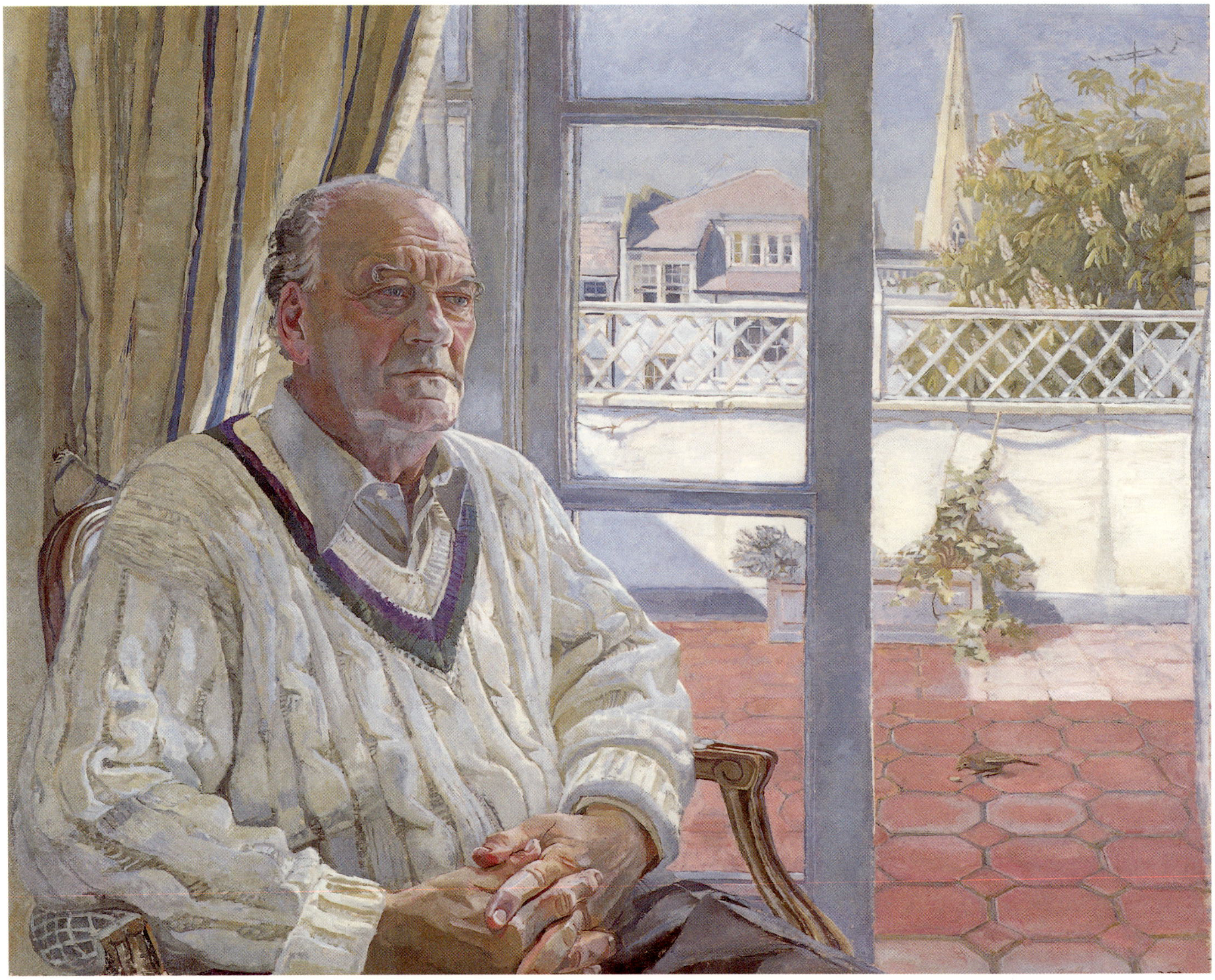

[133] *Lord Pennock,* 1990
71.1 x 91.4 cms 28 x 36 ins

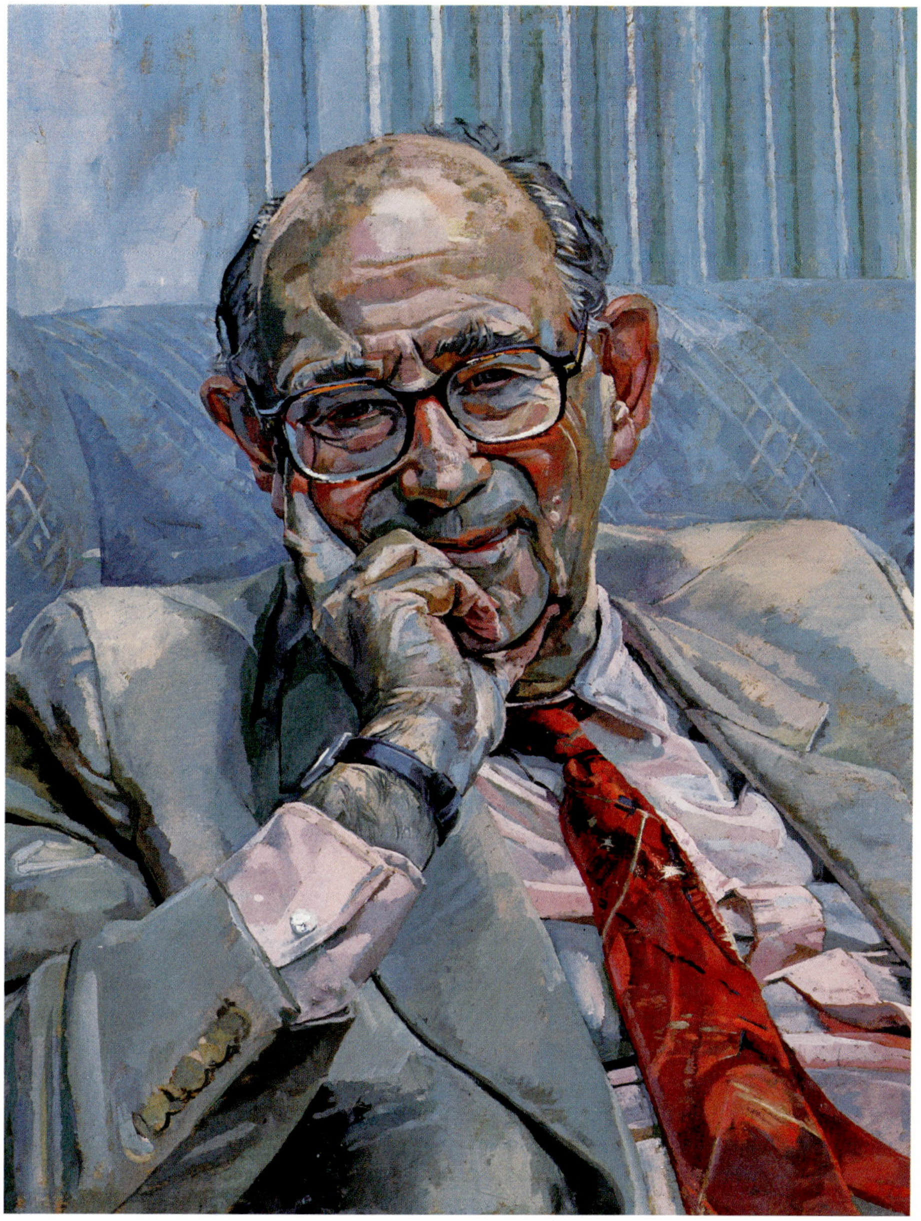

[134] *Conrad Dehn QC,* 2001
50.8 x 40.6 cms 20 x 16 ins

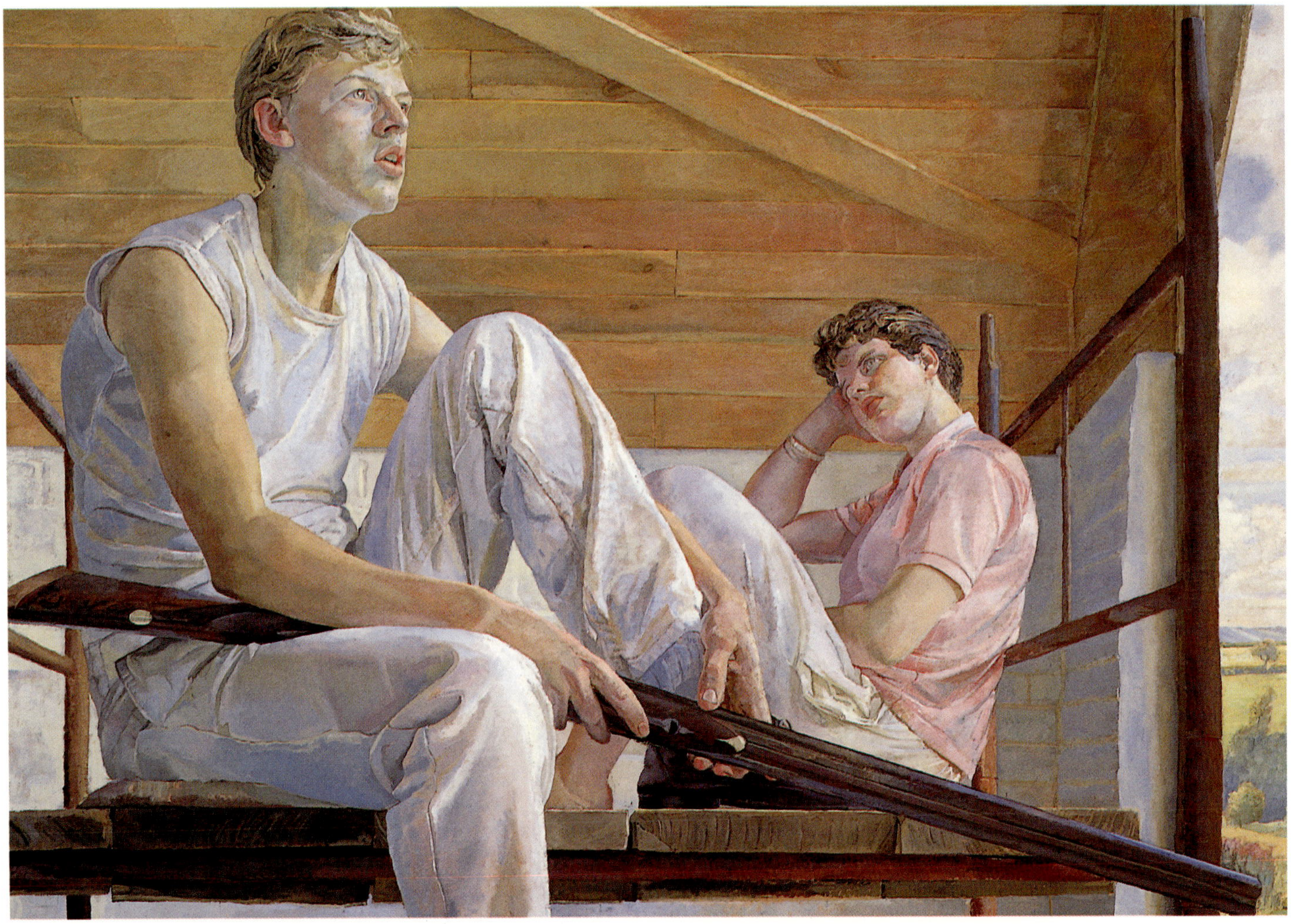

[135] *Summer Dreaming*
91.4 x 121.9 cms 36 x 48 ins

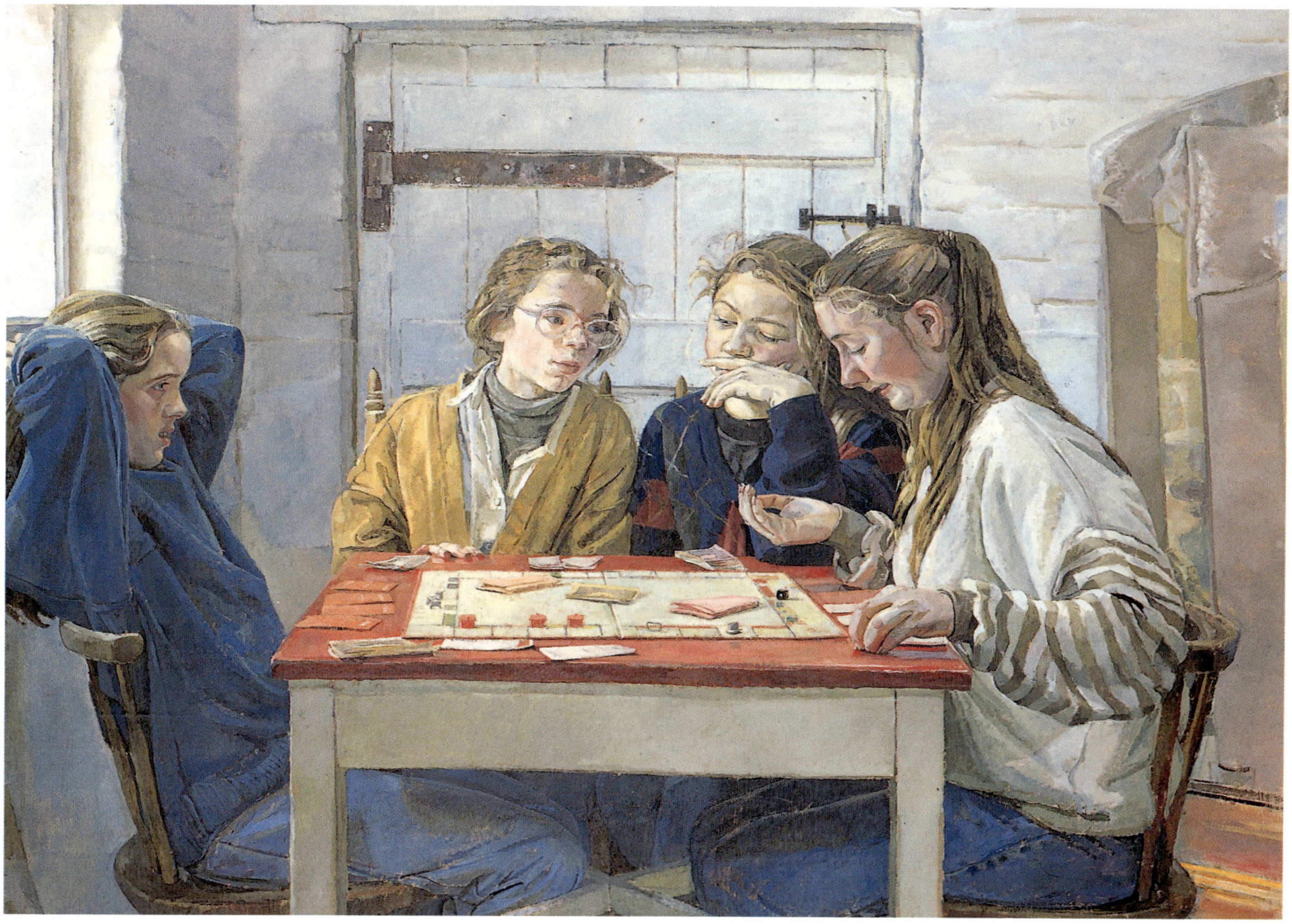

[136] *Monopoly,* 1990
88.9 x 121.9 cms 35 x 48 ins

SITTING FOR DAPHNE
by William Holland, Chief Executive, Universal Records, Classics and Jazz

Daphne arrived at my home for the first of what was to be ten sittings of around four hours each. I noticed that she was carrying a piece of board rather than a canvas. At around 2.5 ft x 2 ft, it was larger than I had envisaged, but then I had envisaged very little. Is there a protocol for portrait sitters? To me, the process was an adventure and I had no preconception of what to expect. Daphne seemed happy when I said that I was totally in her hands with regard to the location, composition and mood. My music room, crammed from ceiling to floor with CDs, scores and memorabilia appealed to her. The natural light was good and the background interesting without being distracting. I was excited when Daphne said that she would like to try something quite different creatively. I asked if she objected to my listening to music. She was agreeable (with some provisos) which I was later to discover were typical of her delightfully teasing and tongue-in-cheek sense of humour. As Daphne started painting I relaxed and got lost listening to my desert island discs. Every now and then my wife, Rosie, appeared with refreshments. I took the opportunity during these brief breaks to see how the picture was progressing. Daphne tended not to talk while she worked and if I did ask a question, such was her concentration, it could take some time for her to respond. Each night Daphne took the painting away with her as she liked to reflect on it overnight. Before she did so I photographed the picture and it was fascinating to monitor the progress of the work as it gradually took shape over the two weeks. After a couple of days the work took what was, to me, an unexpected turn. Instead of the one full face looking out, there was another. The other was semi-reclining in much the way I frequently do when immersed in my music. As it transpired there would eventually be four heads. As each appeared I was thrilled. In my view, each reflects totally different moods created by the eclectic range of music to which we listened. Quite incredibly, Daphne managed to capture the tear that appeared as I listened to Dido's lament. As the picture neared completion, Daphne had another surprise in store for me. She felt that as music was, and had been, such a dominant force in my life, both professionally and as a personal obsession, therefore the actual shape of the picture should reflect that fact. As a result the top right and bottom left of the picture subtly reflect the curve of both a compact disc and the treble clef. I am delighted with the result, although I suspect the framer may well have been less so when faced with such a daunting challenge.

I can imagine that each sitter has a very different and unique experience. You can feel vulnerable, almost as if you are baring your soul by osmosis. In my case, the whole experience was overwhelmingly positive, even life-enhancing, and resulting in an enduring special bond between sitter and a truly remarkable artist.

Bill Holland
29 June 2007

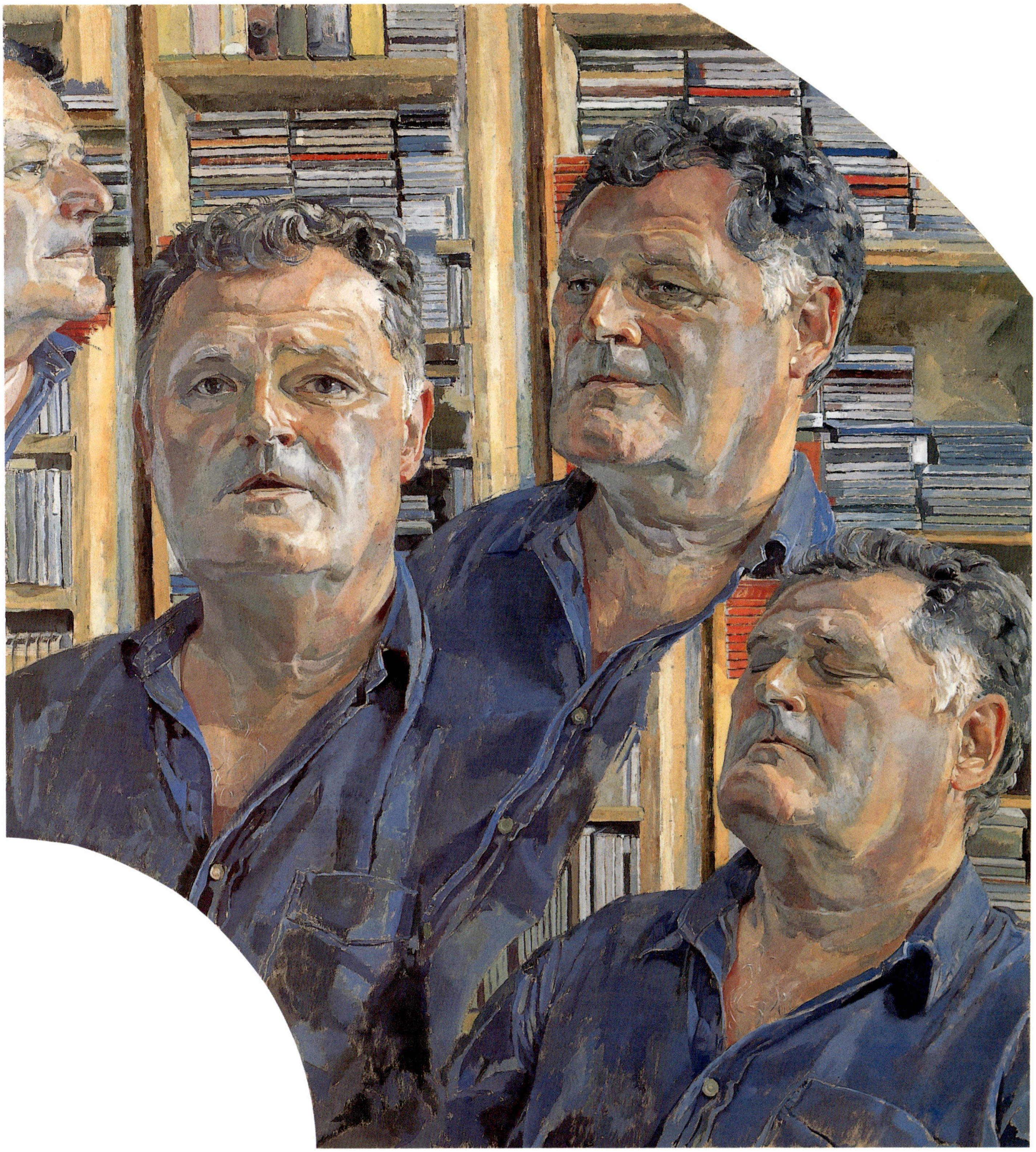

[137] *Bill Holland, Universal Records*, 2004
61 x 66 cms 24 x 26 ins

DAPHNE TODD
by Sir Christopher Ondaatje, OC, CBE, Trustee of the National Portrait Gallery

I first discovered Daphne Todd while rummaging through endless portraits done by members of the Royal Society of Portrait Painters in 1985. My old school, Blundell's, in the west country, had demanded that I commission a portrait of me to hang in the newly constructed Ondaatje Hall in the school. It was an endlessly difficult decision. However, one painting continued to haunt me in my search – a double portrait of a man and his noticeably unhappy wife. Almost ignoring the complacent character of the man I was consistently drawn to the almost tortured expression of the woman. How could an artist possibly have grasped the pained torment of an obviously unhappy relationship? My discovery presented a challenge and I invited the artist down to North Devon to tackle the project. What a discovery! Her painting of me, in my cricket blazer and flannels, still hangs in my study at Glenthorne. It is by far my favourite painting. I refused to part with it. Somehow Daphne Todd, without much conversation and with some magic, had plunged her hand into my body, grasped my soul and smeared it onto her canvas. Far from being pleased with the portrait at first I secretly refused to share what she had discovered with the hundreds of people who would see the painting in the busy school hall. Since then I have had four further portraits by Daphne Todd, one of which does indeed hang in Ondaatje Hall at Blundell's School, and one in the National Portrait Gallery in London. Each painting has drawn both criticism and acclaim but each in its own way displays a recognisable aspect of my character. Sitting for Daphne Todd has been quite an experience.

Daphne Todd is clearly a product of the Slade School of Art following in a long line of artists relying on sustained observation. She told me she was attracted to the school through its association with Victor Pasmore and was taught almost exclusively by Sir William Coldstream, Patrick George and Euan Uglow – all of whom espoused the quasi-scientific method of measuring the subject from the eye and working always with the subject before them. These now well-known and seemingly pioneering artists were keen both to build their images from provable 'facts' of projection and to preserve the integrity of the picture plane. They sternly did not allow themselves to be seduced by appearances. Much of Todd's student work also displayed their trademark dots and dashes. However, by the time I had met her, later development had led her to feel that a more naturally human response was required and made her work much more expressive. I know from experience that Todd preferred to give herself up to her subject, to accept what is there and work with it, rather than imposing her will on the subject as did her mentors. This was particularly true of Uglow whose working method Todd absorbed at first hand during long hours of posing for him. As she explained, and I was fascinated to learn, the ideas for Uglow's painting actually came before his models had even been found. Indeed on occasion several substitute models were used for the same figure in a painting. Uglow's paintings, unlike Todd's, were emphatically not 'about' the person posing.

Todd, however, as I observed, responds to the psychology and body language of the sitter and usually to their surroundings. She is unashamedly seduced by the play of light on surfaces and textures. Post-Slade, and not surprisingly, her work has sometimes been compared with that of Stanley Spencer who was himself a product of the Slade.

I have now had a long, intense, and involved relationship with Daphne Todd, including a very productive six years when she was President of the Royal Society of Portrait Painters. I can recognise her unique style anywhere and am not at all surprised to see that her portraits now hang in many of our finest institutions. I do feel however that there is yet another development still to come from this extraordinarily gifted artist. What's past is prologue.

Christopher Ondaatje
29 June 2007

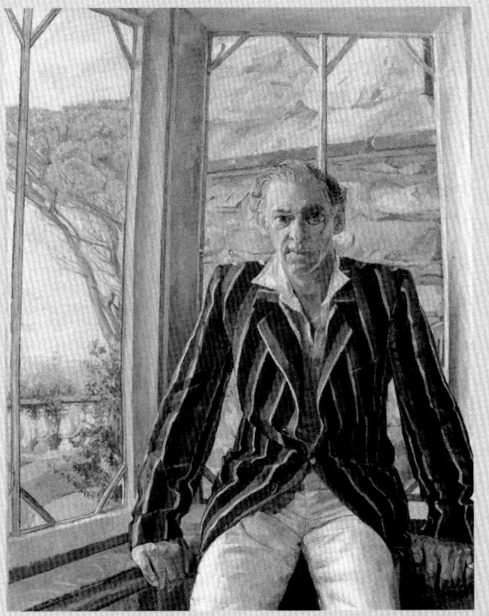

[138] *Sir Christopher Ondaatje,* 1985
124.5 x 94 cms 49 x 37 ins

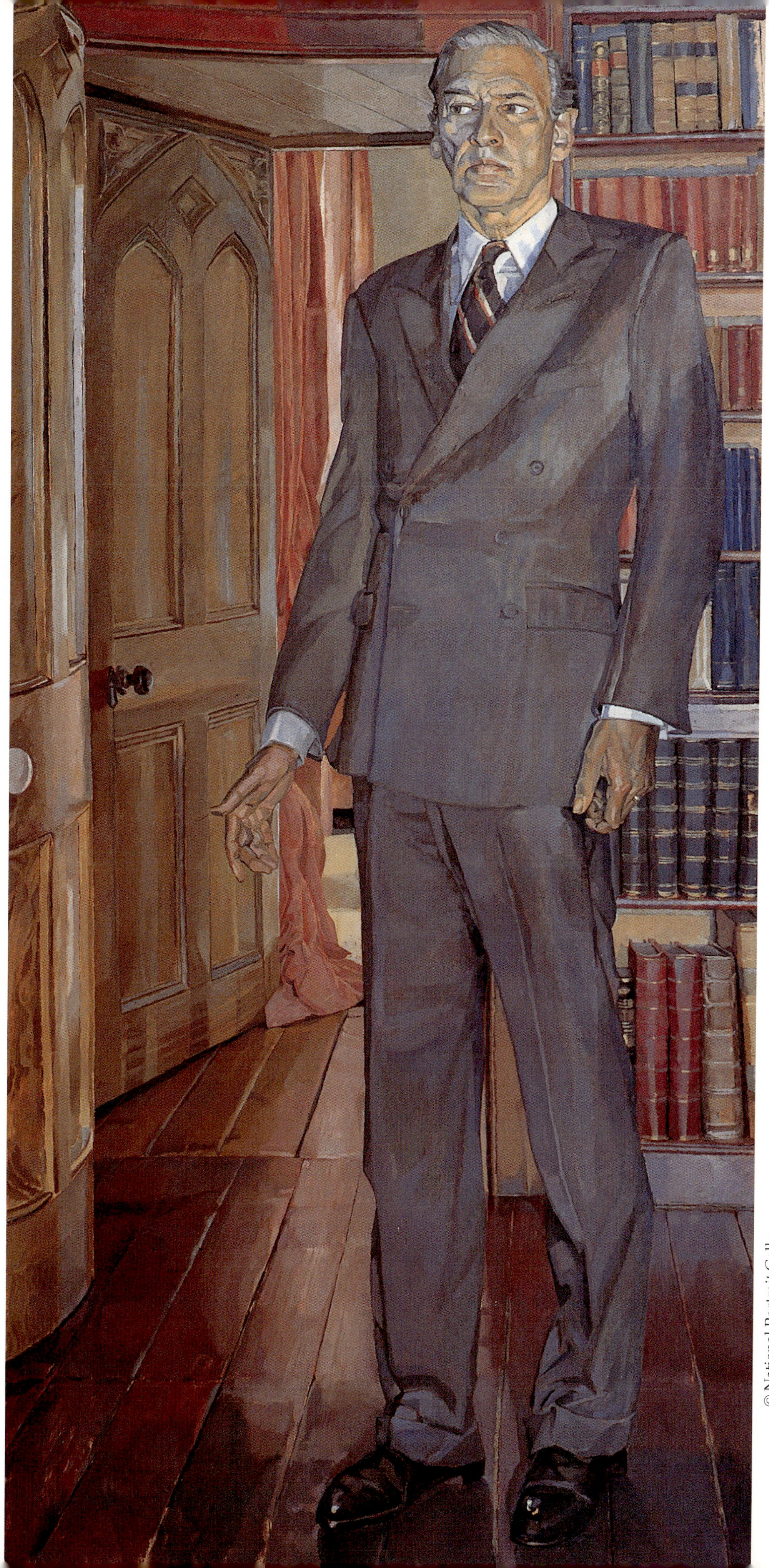

[139] *Sir Christopher Ondaatje,*
1995
152.4 x 73.7 cms 60 x 29 ins

DAPHNE TODD
by The Right Honourable the Lord Armstrong of Ilminster, GCB, CVO

I first came to know Daphne Todd when she was President of the Royal Society of Portrait Painters, and I was invited to join an advisory group formed in order to help the officers of the Society to work out how the role and activities of the Society could be adapted to meet contemporary needs and tastes, and how it could increase the resources available to it to do so.

As we came to know each other better, Daphne asked me if I should be prepared to sit for her. This project developed into a quadruple portrait, showing the sitter in four different moods and poses. That required four times the amount of sitting time needed for a single portrait. So over the period when the portrait was being painted I spent a good deal of time in Daphne's company.

Sitting to her, I was impressed above all by her uncompromising integrity in her work as an artist. The painter and the sitter had to be in exactly the same places at each of the many sittings: in the same north light, and in the same relationship to and the same distance from each other. The position of my chair was precisely defined by marks on the floor. The openings of the curtains had to be adjusted according to the brightness of the light coming in from the outside. Not for Daphne the use of photographs to supplement or abbreviate the sittings: there could be no short cuts or adventitious aids. Her purpose is to reproduce on canvas (or on the board which she often prefers to use) exactly what she sees of the appearance of the sitter and of his or her character and personality as they are reflected through that appearance.

In her sittings there are periods of concentration so intense that she seems almost to withdraw into a trance-like state in which nothing exists beyond her eye, her paintbrush and the picture. This requires of the sitter a concentration hardly less intense; but then the reward is Daphne's enchanting smile when the spell is finally broken and both parties can relax.

There comes a time when Daphne seems to feel that she has gone as far as she can go towards achieving the end at which she is aiming. She will hardly admit to being satisfied with the result: perhaps no artist of integrity is ever fully satisfied with his or her work. It is just that she has reached a point where she believes that further work on the picture will not improve it or get her nearer to the perfection of absolute satisfaction.

The sitter is probably the last person who is qualified to judge the success of a portrait. I can only say, with Daphne's portrait constantly before me, that I think that I am coming to understand what she has seen in me, and thus perhaps what others may also see if they are blessed with Daphne's gift of perceptiveness.

Robert Armstrong
30 June 2007

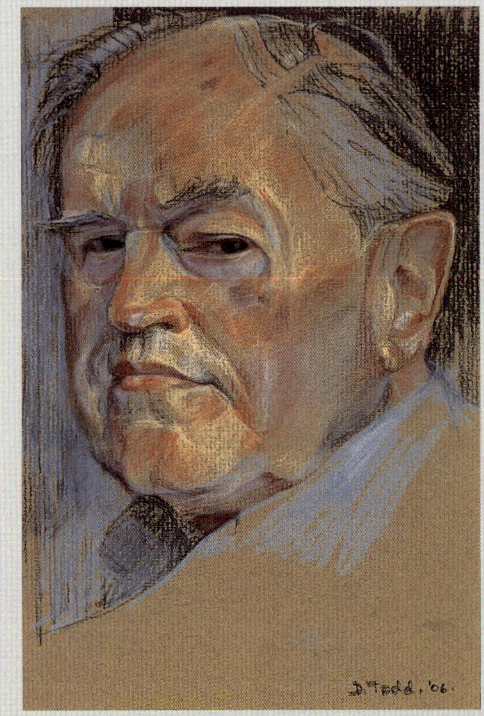

[140] *Lord Armstrong*, 2006
15.2 x 10.2 cms 6 x 4 ins

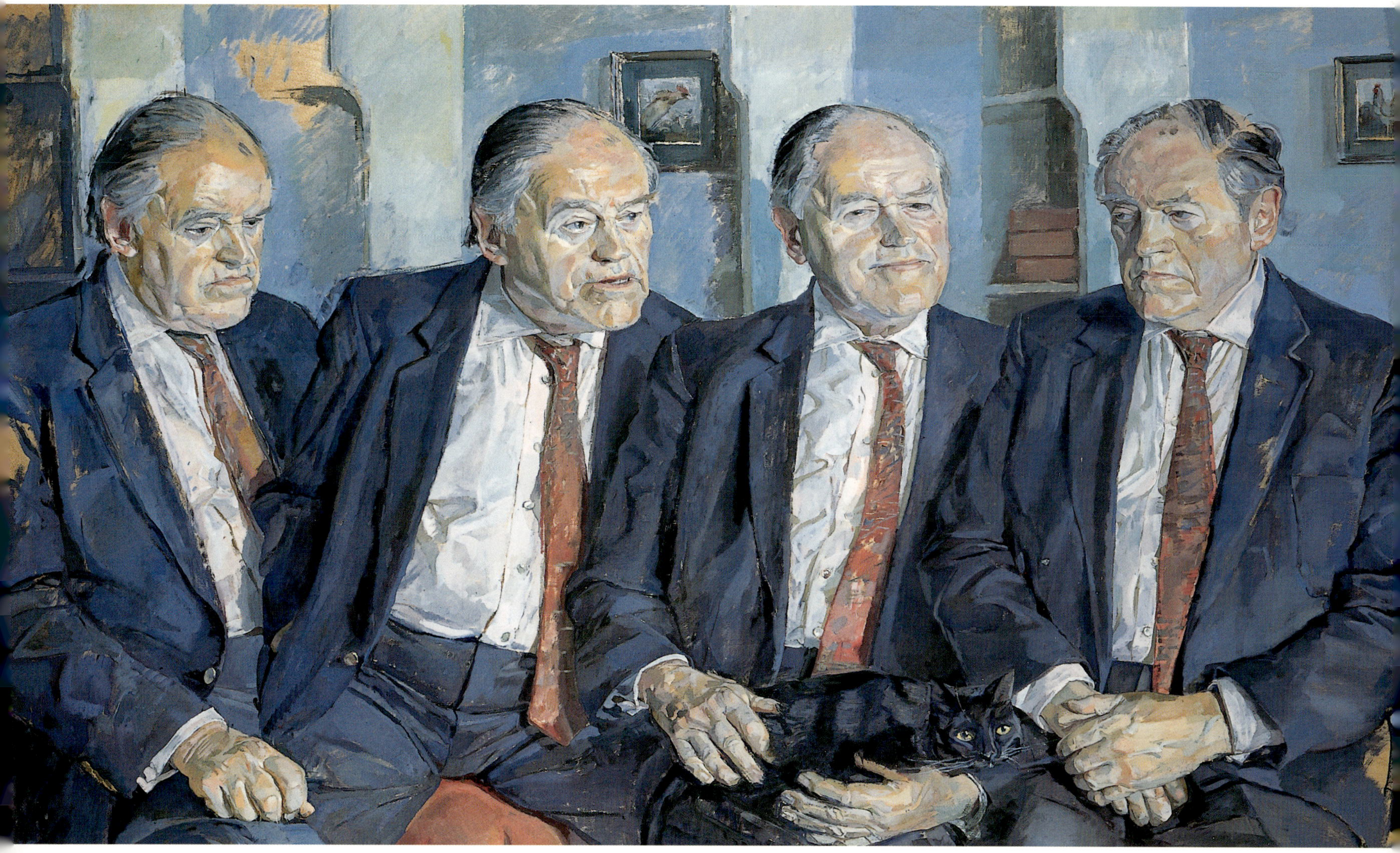

[141] *Lord Armstrong of Ilminster,* 2005
101.6 x 170.2 cms 40 x 67 ins

SITTING FOR DAPHNE
by William Packer, formerly Art Critic of the Financial Times

Quite why two beautiful and talented painters should lately have asked me to sit to them remains something of a puzzle – I dream on. But, puzzle or not, in both cases the experience proved as fascinating as it was memorable, and, for something apparently so passive, remarkably positive. Not that I came to it entirely unprepared. From my art-school days in the life-room on, to paint or draw from the live model has been a normal, if for periods intermittent, part of my working life. The only thing is that hitherto I had always been at the other end of the brush. And whether the model was a professional in the studio, a complaisant friend, a member of the family temporarily bribed or coerced, or simply, from time to time, myself in the mirror, I simply got on with it in my own way, taking it all rather for granted that this was the way it was always done since that was the way I did it. I may have played some music, chatted a bit, and made a cup of tea for us both in the rest, but really I had never thought of what it was like, not to paint, but to pose and be painted.

And what I found was that the practice was as various as the artists themselves, and that yet some things were so very much the same. I found, insofar as I was able to move my eyes, that I followed closely how each of them worked, fast or slow, with each her little tricks of technique – Jenny McRae darting about to and fro like a fencer; Daphne Todd as still as a monument; Jenny measuring and checking from now here, now there; Daphne measuring precisely always from the same spot; Jenny working piecemeal through from the drawing on the bare canvas; Daphne painting more broadly and at first more speculatively on her piece of board, to which she eventually tacked on an extension; Jenny with a palette pitched high and light in tone; Daphne's lower, cooler, more sombre. And so my image in both cases, for I was always allowed to look, grew before my eyes.

But then what was it like actually to sit? Ah, yes: that perhaps was most interesting of all. I went once or twice a week to Jenny's studio, at that time high up in a Bermondsey warehouse: Daphne likewise came to mine. In neither case was a principle involved, only mutual convenience. Jenny kept the wireless on, Radio 4, 'sotto voce', and made me tea. With Daphne it was music, my choice and timed more or less to last each session between the rests, and I made the tea since it was my house. I kept no count of the sittings, but my feeling is that there were about 10 or 12 in both cases, always mornings, Jenny's lasting roughly two hours, Daphne's between 2 and 3. It added up overall to quite some time.

To remain thus still over an extended period is a discipline and a test, yet oddly addictive and even refreshing, as zen-like one relaxes into it and the mind is set free to wander. With both Jenny and Daphne conversation was desultory, gossipy, at times intense, inconsequential, and ever liable to a sudden, arbitrary breaking-off as the painter's more particular concentration took over. But the odd thing was, and is – and in this I recognise my own experience as a painter too – that there was never any sense of frustration, let alone of resentment, at such breakings-off, but paradoxically of a heightened complicity in the exercise. And it is in this respect, I have come to think, in the pauses and silences of the sitting, that the curious intimacy that can grow up between artists and sitter truly lies. It may be born of a sympathy that already exists: it may grow out of the moment: it may of course be still-born if no such sympathy is there: it may last or fade. But it is a strange and rather lovely thing. And I'm extremely grateful to both Daphne and Jenny for the gift of it.

Bill Packer
August 2007

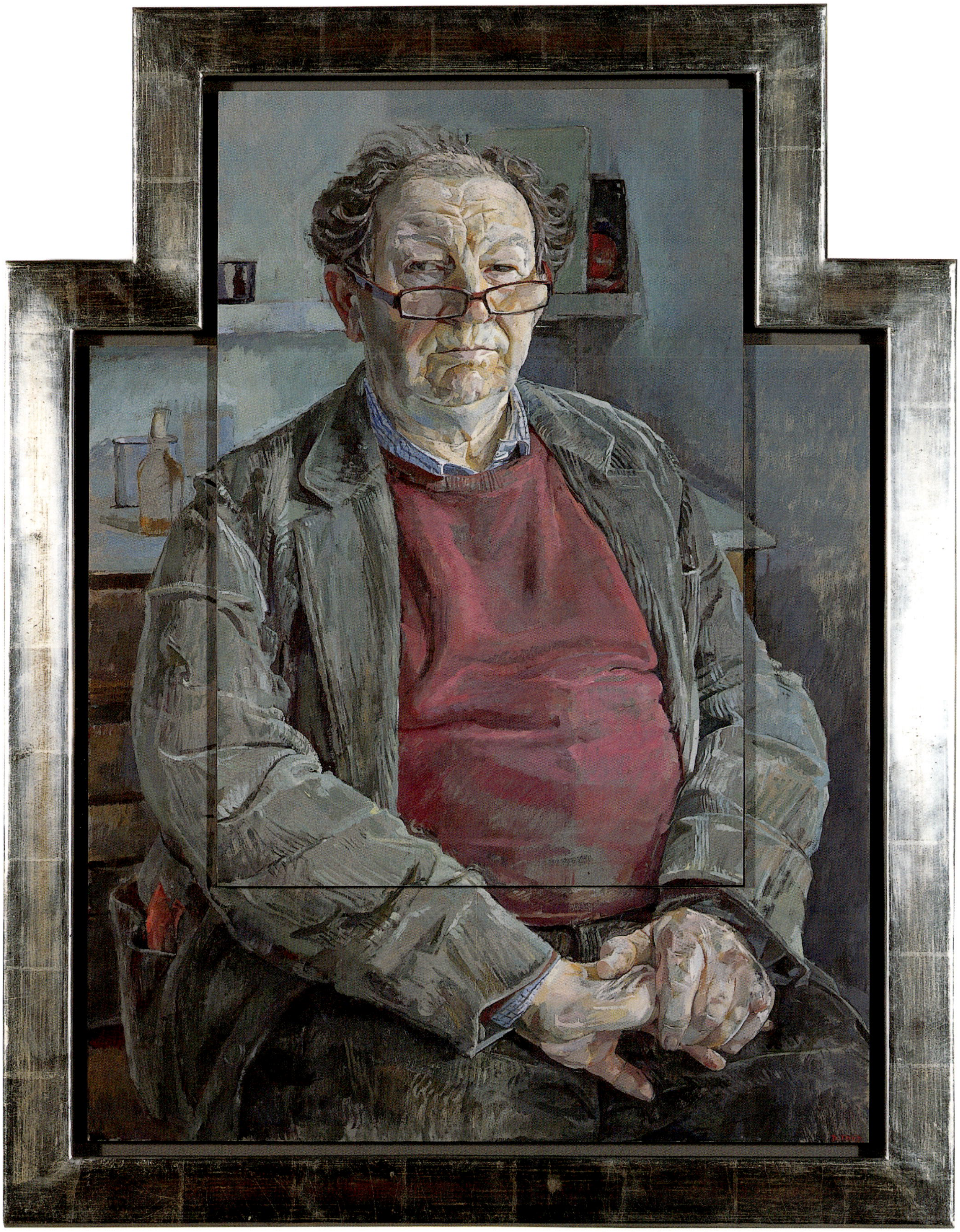

[142] *William Packer, Art Critic, Financial Times*, 2006
73.7 x 54.6 cms 29 x 21½ ins

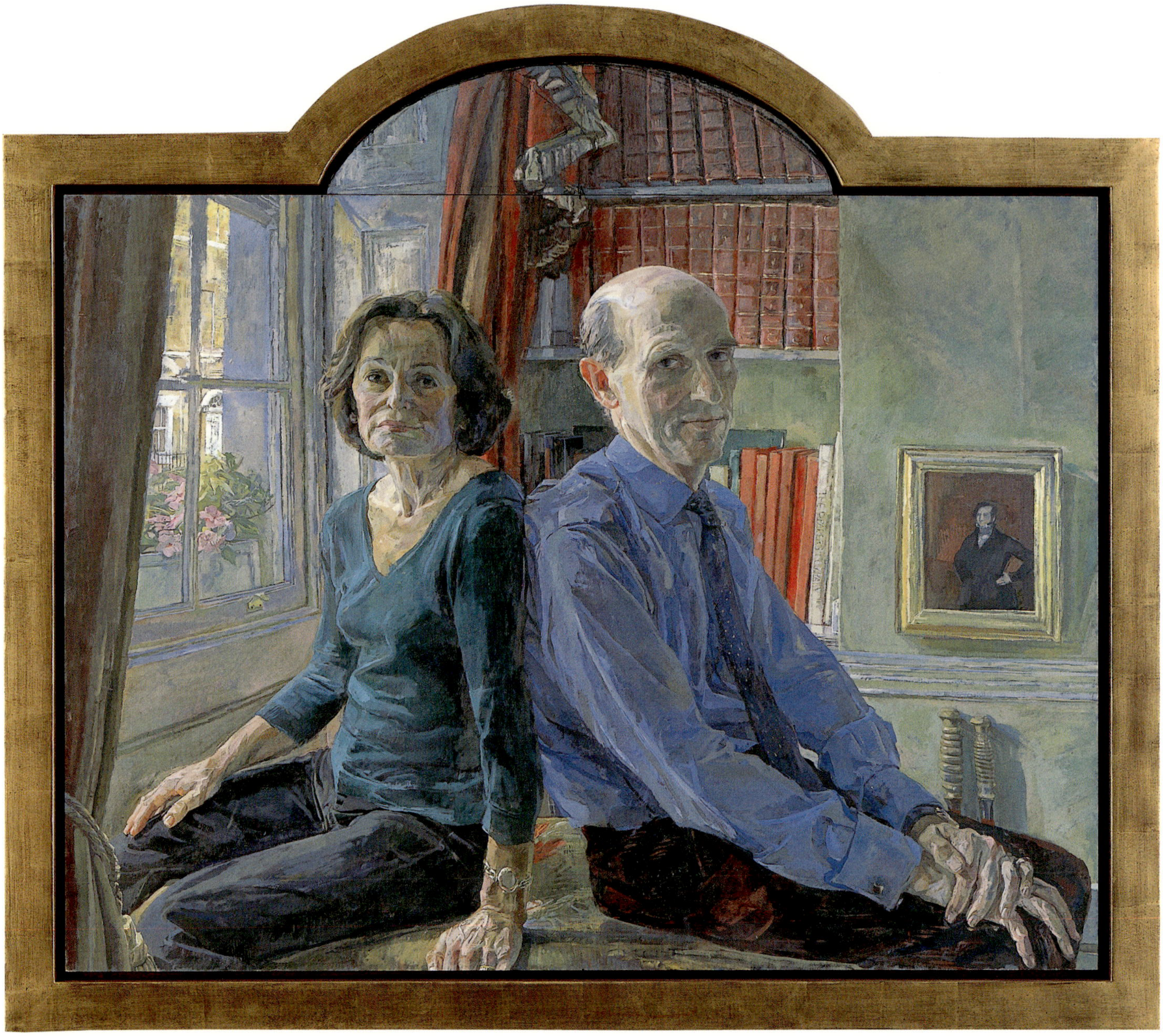

[143] *Mr and Mrs Richard Hunting,* 2007
116.8 x 76.2 cms 46 x 30 ins

List of Illustrations

All works not otherwise credited are in private collections.
Dimensions are given height x width.
All works oil on birch panel unless otherwise stated.

List of Illustrations

List of Illustrations

Sitters include:

Sir Edward Abraham
Lord Adrian
John Albery
Stuart Andrews
Mrs Stuart Andrews
Lord Armstrong
Stuart Arnold
Lord Ashburton

Nicholas Bagshawe
Daphne Bagshawe
Miss Alice Bagshawe & her niece Persephone
Dame Janet Baker
Mr & Mrs Roger Bance
Miss Fenella Barber
Tony Beadles
Professor Derek Beales
Miss Miranda Birch
Professor John Black
Viscount Bledisloe
Michael Bradley
Roderick Bowen

Tim Card
Hugh Carson
Mrs Hugh Carson
Margaret, Lady Carter
Mrs John Cavanagh
George Cawkwell
Mrs Joan Clanchy
Mr & Mrs Nicholas Clutton
Miss Laura Clutton
Sir William Coldstream
Mrs Crispian Collins
Miss Daisy Collins
Miss Harriet Collins
Dan Colman
Sir Neil Cossons
Mike Cottel
Miss Florence Crawford
Ted Crowe
The daughters of Giles Curtis

Colin Dare
Dame Ruth Deech
Conrad Dehn, QC
Mrs Conrad Dehn
Lord Deedes
Brigadier John Drake

John Eastaugh, Lord Bishop of Hereford
Christopher Everett
Oliver Everett

Miss Elizabeth Fahy
Lord Fellowes
Mrs Julian Fellowes
Dr Ian Field
Miss Sarah Flynn
Charles Foster

Sir Ian Gainsford
Reverend Peter Gant
Mrs Peter Gant
Colin Gilbraith
Miss Noreen Grant
Dr A.V. (Bill) Grimstone

His Honour Judge Hammerton
Elisabeth Hitchcock
Bill Holland
Mrs David Hughes
Mr & Mrs Richard Hunting
Gillian Hylson-Smith

Simon Jenkins

Sir Anthony Kenny
Mr & Mrs Larry Kirkwood
Miss Juliet Kirkwood
Miss Sara Kirkwood
Robert Kirkwood
Lord Kitchener of Khartoum & Broome
Baron Klingspor
The family of Udo Koch

Sir Kirby & Lady Laing
Nigel Lindsay-Fynn
Professor Kurt Lipstein, QC
Michael Lunt
H.R.H. the Grand Duke of Luxembourg

Miss Ann Mackay
Brigadier Peter Madson
Professor Tom Manley
Magnus Mansson
Mr & Mrs Oliver Mathews
Miss Lucy Mathews
Dr Polly Matzinger
Dr Christine McKie
Spike Milligan
The family of Maurice Minzly
Mr & Mrs Robert Monkton
Lord Morris of Castle Morris
Iris Morris
Dame Anne Mueller
Tom Muir

Miss Jemima Neal
Robert Neal
Eric Nevin
Freda Newcome
Mr & Mrs John Norman
Sir Christopher & Lady Ondaatje
Jonathan Ouvry

William Packer
Professor Ian Parrott
James Partridge
David Pattisson
John Pattisson
Diane Peacock
Dr Michael Peagram
Sir Austin Pearce
Lord Pennock
Mssrs Ron & Ray Pett
Sir Dennis Pettit

Maureen Rebbit
Dr Ken Riley
Ian Rosenberg
Albert Roux
Carol Rumens

Lord & Lady Sainsbury
Mr & Mrs Frank Sanders
Mark Sanders
Mike Scott
Peter Scott, QC
Lord Sharman
Mrs Selma Shrank
Sister Jean Sinclair
David Smith
Arnold Stevenson
Duncan Stewart
Sir Tom Stoppard
Professor Hartmut Pogge von Strandmann
Dame Marilyn Strathern
Sir Peter Strawson
Professor Barry Supple
Reverend Bill Sykes

Trevor Tasker
Lord & Lady Tebbit
Professor Allan Templeton
Gerry Tomkins
Lord Tugendhat

Professor John Uff
Miss Leonora Uff
Dr & Mrs Christopher Uff
Gosia Urbanowicz

John Walton
Roger Webb
Mrs Tom Wethered
Mrs Gill Wilson
Miss Georgina Wilson-Pemberton
Andrew Wilton

Chronology

1947	Born in York, 27 March
1958-65	Simon Langton Grammar School of Girls, Canterbury
1965-71	The Slade School of Art, London (undergraduate and post-graduate)
	Begins part-time teaching at Heatherley's and at the Byam Shaw School of Art during final year
1968	David Murray studentship for Landscape Painting
	Griffin Prize for Landscape Painting
	Spends 3 summer months in USA and Mexico including 7 weeks in the Hotel Chelsea, New York
1969	British Institute Award for Figurative Painting
	First painting exhibited at The Royal Academy
1970	Tonks Drawing Prize
1971-75	Visiting tutor, Byam Shaw School of Art. Lives in Clapham
1972	Critics' Choice Exhibition, Tooths Gallery
	Drives to Madrid during the summer to paint and to visit the Prado
1973	Returns to camp in the Guaderrama mountains for 3 months to complete landscape begun the previous summer
1974	Paints in Alcalã for 3 summer months, living in a mini-van
1975-77	Lives near Barcelona (with G.S.)
	Drives to London each spring with landscapes for the R.A.
1976	*Disused Cement Works* purchased "for the Nation" under the terms of the Chantrey Bequest
1977	Returns to London for birth of daughter
1979	Resumes part-time teaching. Moves to New Cross
1980-86	Director of Studies, Heatherley School of Fine Art
1980	Finalist, Hunting Group National Art Competition (2 works)
1982	Finalist, Hunting Group National Art Competition
1983	Second Prize, John Player Portrait Award, N.P.G.
	Commendation, Spirit of London Exhibition, Festival Hall
1984	First Prize: Oil Painting of the Year, Hunting Group National Art Competition
	Special Commendation, John Player Award, N.P.G.
	G.L.C. Prize, Spirit of London Exhibition, Royal Festival Hall
	Elected Member of the New English Art Club
	Marries Lt. Col. P.R.T. Driscoll. Moves to East Sussex
1985	Elected Member of the Royal Society of Portrait Painters
1986	Leaves teaching to paint full-time
	Trustee, Thomas Heatherley Educational Trust (to present day)
1989	Retrospective Exhibition, Morley Gallery
1989-91	Chairs Centenary Sub-Committee, Royal Society of Portrait Painters
1990-91	Honorary Secretary, Royal Society of Portrait Painters
1994-2000	President, Royal Society of Portrait Painters (first female President)
	Trustee, Federation of British Artists
1995	Honorary Member Society of Women Artists
1997	Freeman, City of London
1998	Hon. Doctorate of Arts, De Montfort University
2001	Solo Exhibition, Messum's, Cork Street, London
	Ondaatje Prize for Portraiture and Gold Medal
2001-2	'Mirror, Mirror: Self Portraits by Women Artists', N.P.G. and tour
2002	Awarded O.B.E. in New Year's Honours
2003	'The View: an exhibition about Richmond Hill'
2004	Honorary Liveryman, Worshipful Company of Painter-Stainers
	Solo Exhibition, Messum's, Cork Street, London
2005	Ambassador for East Sussex (to present day)
2007	Finalist, BP Portrait Award (newly open to the over 40s), N.P.G. and tour
2008	Treasurer, Friends of Argos Hill Windmill
	Solo Exhibition, Messum's, Cork Street, London

Bibliography

Mitchell Beazley, *The Complete Portrait Course*, 1990

John Cloake, *The View*, Petersham Trust, 2003

Celine George, *Inspired by Art*, Folens, 2004

The Heatherley's School of Fine Art 150th Anniversary, Heatherleys', 1996

James Horton, *How to Paint Skin Tones*, Quarto, 1995

Catherine Lampert, *Euan Uglow: The Complete Paintings*, New Haven and London: Yale University Press, 2007

Stanley Martin, *The Order of Merit*, IB Tauris & Co, 2007

Kenneth McConkey, *The New English*, London: Royal Academy, 2007

Messum's Fine Art, *Daphne Todd*, (exhibition catalogue) Studio Publications, 2001

Messum's Fine Art, *Daphne Todd*, (exhibition catalogue) Studio Publications, 2005

Brian Morris, *The Collected Poems of Brian Morris*, Rare Books & Berry, 2001

Sandy Nairne and Sarah Howgate, *The Portrait Now*, London: National Portrait Gallery, 2006

The Complete Illustrated National Portrait Gallery, London: National Portrait Gallery, 1994

Christopher Ondaatje, *The Power of Paper*, Harper Collins, 2006

William Packer, *The Hunting Art Prizes 1981-2005*, Hunting PLC, 2005

Liz Rideal, *Mirror Mirror*, National Portrait Gallery, 2002

The Royal Society of Portrait Painters Centenary, RP, 1991

Frances Spalding, *20th Century Painters and Sculptors*, Antique Collectors Club, 1990

Dame Marilyn Strathern, *Girton: Thirty Year*s, Third Millennium, 2005

Dame Marilyn Strathern, 'Getting In The Way', *Times Higher Educational Supplement*, 2001

Daphne Todd, 'The Portrait and Illusion', in *The Artist Magazine*, December 1983

Daphne Todd, 'Portraying the Unexpected', in *The Artist Magazine*, November 1989

Daphne Todd, 'Not-so-still Life' in *The Artist Magazine*, January 1991

Daphne Todd, 'Four Portrait Painters' in *The Artist Magazine*, October 1991

Daphne Todd, 'Four Studio Portrait Painters', in *The Artist Magazine*, November 1991

Daphne Todd, 'Something Off-Centre', *Times Higher Educational Supplement*, 2001

Lynne Truss, *BP Portrait Award*, London: National Portrait Gallery, 2007

David Twiston Davies (ed.), *The Daily Telegraph, Book of Letters*, 1998

Neville Weereratne, *Visions of an Island*, Harper Collins, 1999

Bruno Wollheim, 'In Your Face': Caluga Pictures: a series of short TV films on individual artists which has been repeated on several occasions since 2005

End Notes

1 Daphne Todd, recorded discussions between Daphne Todd and Jenny Pery, 2004 -2007.

2 Ibid.

3 Ibid.

4 Ibid.

5 Ibid.

6 Ibid.

7 Ibid.

8 Ibid.

9 Ibid.

10 Ibid.

11 Shepherd, Michael, The Daily Telegraph, 1972

12 Daphne Todd, recorded discussions between Daphne Todd and Jenny Pery, 2004-7

13 Ibid.

14 Ibid.

15 Ibid.

16 Ibid.

17 Ibid.

18 Ibid.

19 Ibid.

20 Ibid.

21 Daphne Todd, Letter to the Daily Telegraph, 18 October 1997, *The Daily Telegraph Book of Letters* edited by David Twiston Davies, 1998

22 Daphne Todd, Recorded Discussions between Daphne Todd and Jenny Pery, 2004-7

23 Ibid.

24 Strathern, Dame Marilyn, Girton College Annual Review, 2001

25 Dame Janet Baker, interviewed by Andrew Macpherson for *Faces* from the National Portrait Gallery, 1987

26 Daphne Todd, Recorded discussions between Daphne Todd and Jenny Pery, 2004-7

27 Sir Christopher Ondaatje, Catalogue of Daphne Todd exhibition at Messum's Fine Art, 2001

28 Lord Morris of Castle Morris, Letter to Daphne Todd, 23 October 2000

29 Daphne Todd, Recorded discussions between Daphne Todd and Jenny Pery, 2004-7

30 Ibid.

31 Packer, William, Hunting Art Prizes, 2005

32 Rideal, Liz, Catalogue for *Mirror Mirror*, 2001

33 Daphne Todd, Recorded discussions between Daphne Todd and Jenny Pery, 2004-7

34 Ibid.

Author's Acknowledgement

I would like to thank my 'portrait subject', Daphne Todd, for generously sharing her memories and ideas with me over many meetings, and for giving me a privileged insight into the workings of an extraordinarily incisive and pragmatic artistic mind. My thanks also go to David Messum and Carol Tee, whose advice and encouragement have been invaluable in the production of this book, which I hope will effectively bring the range and quality of Todd's work to the attention of a much wider public.

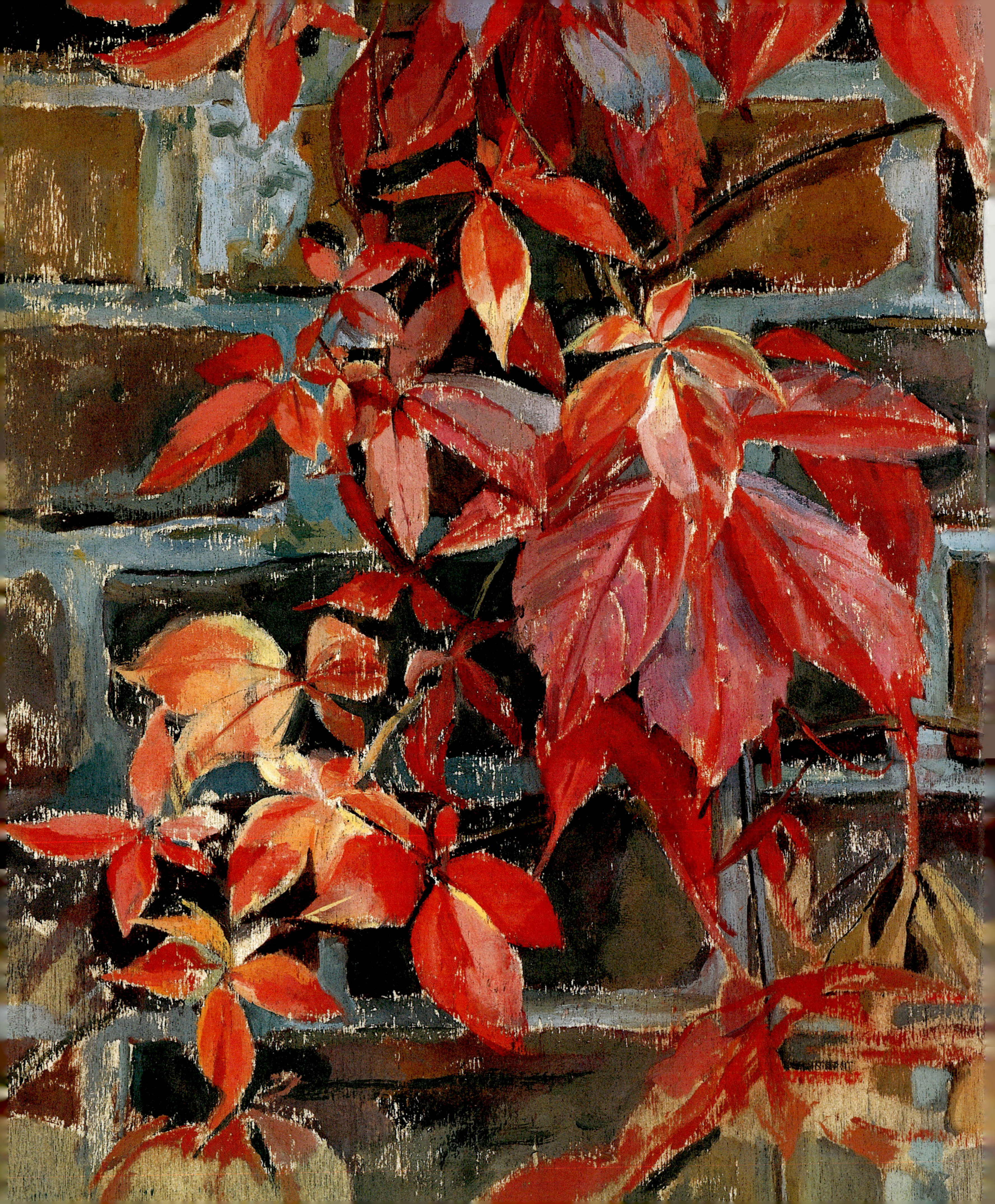